Time Out Guides Limited
Universal House
251 Tottenham Court Road
London W1T 7AB
Tel + 44 (0)20 7813 3000
Fax + 44 (0)20 7813 6001
Email guides@timeout.com
www.timeout.com

Editorial

Editor Lesley McCave
Deputy Editor Daniel Smith
Listings Editors Shane Armstrong, Jill Emeny, Cathy Limb,
  Kate Wiggans, Stefanie Eschenbacher, Patrick Welch
Proofreader Patrick Mulkern
Indexer Jackie Brind

Editorial/Managing Director Peter Fiennes
Series Editor Ruth Jarvis
Deputy Series Editor Lesley McCave
Business Manager Gareth Garner
Guides Co-ordinator Holly Pick
Accountant Kemi Olufuwa

Design

Art Director Scott Moore
Art Editor Tracey Ridgewell
Senior Designer Josephine Spencer
Digital Imaging Dan Conway
Ad Make-up Jenni Prichard

Picture Desk

Picture Editor Jael Marschner
Deputy Picture Editor Tracey Kerrigan
Picture Researcher Helen McFarland

Advertising

Sales Director Mark Phillips
Sales Manager Alison Wallen
Advertising Sales Executives Ben Holt, Ali Lowry,
  Jason Trotman
Advertising Assistant Kate Staddon

Marketing

Marketing Director Mandy Martinez
Marketing & Publicity Manager, US Rosella Albanese

Production

Production Director Mark Lamond
Production Controller Marie Howell

Time Out Group

Chairman Tony Elliott
Managing Director Mike Hardwick
Group Financial Director Richard Waterlow
Group Commercial Director Lesley Gill
Group General Manager Nichola Coulthard
Group Circulation Director Jim Heinemann
Group Art Director John Oakey
Online Managing Director David Pepper
Group Production Director Steve Proctor
Group IT Director Simon Chappell

Contributors

Introduction Lesley McCave. **History** *Jumping Jack slash, London's lost lingos* Paul Hines; *The nutty protestors* Joe Bindloss. **London Today** Michael Marshall (*The in and out club* Mark Pratt). **Architecture** Pamela Buxton. **A-Z Cheap London** adapted from *Time Out London* magazine. **Where to Stay** Lisa Ritchie. **Sights Introduction** Daniel Smith. **The South Bank & Bankside** Charlie Godfrey-Faussett (*Save our South Bank* Patrick Welch). **The City** Joe Bindloss (*Do the strand* Jan Fuscoe). **Holborn & Clerkenwell** Andrew Staffell. **Bloomsbury & Fitzrovia** Stefanie Eschenbacher. **Marylebone** Lisa Ritchie. **Mayfair & St James's** John Watson. **Soho** Stefanie Eschenbacher (*Walk on* Daniel Smith). **Covent Garden & St Giles's** Jill Emeny. **Westminster** Charlie Godfrey-Faussett (*Circling the square* Alex Coidan). **South Kensington & Knightsbridge** Ronnie Haydon. **Chelsea** Ronnie Haydon. **North London** John Watson. **East London** Andrew Staffell (*Walk on* Lesley McCave). **South-east London** Ronnie Haydon. **South-west London** Christi Daugherty. **West London** Edoardo Albert (*Walk on* Lesley McCave). **Restaurants** Alexia Loundras, Daniel Smith and contributors to *Time Out Eating & Drinking* (*Reinventing the meal, Stars and their pies* Guy Dimond). **Pubs & Bars** Sam Le Quesne and contributors to *Time Out Pubs & Bars*. **Shops & Services** Holly Furneaux and contributors to *Time Out Shopping* (*Chocs away!* Claire Fogg). **Festivals & Events** Kathryn Miller. **Children** Ronnie Haydon. **Comedy** Sharon Lougher. **Dance** Allen Robertson. **Film** Dave Calhoun. **Galleries** Helen Sumpter. **Gay & Lesbian** Paul Burston. **Music** Manish Agarwal (*Classical with a twist* Buffy Noble). **Nightlife** Simone Baird. **Sport & Fitness** Tom Davies (*Sporting giant* Andrew Staffell). **Theatre** Natalie Whittle. **Trips Out of Town** Stefanie Eschenbacher. **Getting Around** Cathy Limb. **Resources A-Z** Cathy Limb.

Maps JS Graphics (john@jsgraphics.co.uk).

Photography by Andrew Brackenbury (artwork on page 177 by John Hayward), except: page 10 V&A Images; pages 15, 17, 21 Corbis; page 19 Mary Evans; pages 22, 24 AP/Empics; page 22 Rex; pages 23, 26, 34, 204, 219, 229, 310 Rob Greig; pages 31, 33 Gordon Singer; page 37 Morley von Sternberg; pages 82, 87, 99, 101, 106, 119, 120, 144, 150, 154, 156, 157, 275 Jonathan Perugia; page 83 Aine Donavan; pages 102, 129, 166, 181, 200, 215 Héloïse Bergman; page 122 Time Life Pictures/Getty; pages 125, 349 Gordon Rainsford; page 135 Jay Jopling/White Cube; page 155 Jael Marschner; pages 161, 297, 300 Piers Allardyce; pages 163, 333 London2012; pages 170, 181 Matt Carr; pages 195, 199, 210, 223, 231, 249, 254, 260, 273, 325, 326 Alys Tomlinson; page 203 Paul Mattson; page 208 Michael Franke; pages 216, 251 Tricia de Courcy Ling; page 232 Thomas Skovsende; pages 241, 246, 253, 256, 301, 302 Britta Jaschinski; page 243 Nicki Willcock; page 259 Anthony Webb; page 271 Will Amlot; page 282 Richard Haughton; page 299 Mamad Mossadegh; page 308 Gideon Mendel; page 322 Muir Vidler; page 335 Lorenzo Agius; page 338 Manuel Harlan, page 342 Mockford & Bonetti; pages 343, 351, 356, 358 britainonview.com.
The following images were provided by the featured establishment/artist: pages 51, 65, 70, 107, 226, 239, 264, 266, 267, 268, 304, 352, 353, 356, 358.

The Editor would like to thank Gabriel Bailey, Amanda Brooks, Dermott Calpin, Inge Carrington, Hannah Collingbourne, Simon Coppock, Rebecca Davies, Lily Dunn, Ali Hislop, Julie Lee, Abigail Lelliott, Ben McKnight, Poppy Mcpherson, Hilary Merrett, James Mitchell, Nicholas Royle, Ros Sales, Albanne Spyrou, Gabriel Tate, Rebecca Taylor, Pete Watts and all contributors to previous editions of Time Out London, whose work forms the basis for parts of this book.

Contents

National Gallery. See p133.

Introduction

From Guy Fawkes in 1605 to suicide bombers in 2005, London has long had to cope with threats to its civic life. Guy Fawkes famously failed in his attempt – the 7/7 bombers didn't.

But London absorbed the damage and moved on. After a few tense weeks, during which nobody wanted to get on the tube or ride a bus – in many cases choosing to walk or cycle (both statistically far riskier) – the city returned to near normal. For those not directly affected by the attacks, the only difference was that people were a bit less reserved, a bit more ready to check out fellow commuters – and their bags. In a city where minding one's own business is almost an art form, Londoners began to take more notice. Not enough to change the habits of a lifetime, but enough to get us through the first month or so, until the sharp edge of outrage and fear dulled.

More lasting was the impact on tourism and retail spending, both of which declined as non-Londoners stayed away in the months that followed. In response, Mayor Ken Livingstone introduced the 'One London' campaign, determined to get the message across that the city is open for business.

There are those who would say that Ken's grip on London has become a stranglehold: in September 2005 he announced that the Congestion Charge zone would expand westwards in 2007. And let's not forget – how could we? – that he went back on his decision not to get rid of the Routemaster bus, that world-famous emblem of London (OK, not great for wheelchair users or people over six feet tall, we'll admit, but adored by the rest of the population).

But London still knows how to have a good time. For starters, from November 2005 clubs and bars can finally open later than the traditional 11pm closing time. Doomsayers warn that this will mean more binge drinking on the streets, leading to the end of civilisation as we know it, but it's more likely that people will be able to decide for themselves when they want to go home for the evening. And the city is firmly looking to the future. London is, after all, hosting the Olympics in 2012.

In the meantime, enjoy London for what it is. There's so much going on it's hard to know where to start, but here are a few ideas. Spend an afternoon wandering around Bloomsbury; take in a musical in Covent Garden; enjoy dim sum in Chinatown; stroll along the South Bank, stopping at the Tate Modern and dropping by the London Eye for a spin; shop in the West End (no, not Oxford Street, but Westbourne Grove and Notting Hill, or, if your budget won't stretch that far, Hoxton and Spitalfields); go for a lazy Sunday brunch then a walk through Hyde Park; visit Columbia Road market on a Sunday. That's the real London – some things will never change.

ABOUT TIME OUT CITY GUIDES

This is the 14th edition of *Time Out London*, one of an expanding series of Time Out guides produced by the people behind the successful listings magazines in London, New York and Chicago. Our guides are all written by resident experts who have striven to provide you with all the most up-to-date information you'll need to explore the city or read up on its background, whether you're a local or a first-time visitor.

THE LIE OF THE LAND

Thanks to the chaotic street plan – or, rather, the lack of one – London is one of the most complicated of all major world cities to find your way around. To make life a bit easier, we've included an area designation for every venue in this guide. Our area divisions are based on local usage and are clearly marked on the colour-coded map on pages 394-395. Most entries also have a grid reference that points to our street maps at the back of the book (starting on page 396).

ESSENTIAL INFORMATION

For all the practical information you might need for visiting the area – including visa and customs information, details of local transport, a listing of emergency numbers, information on local weather and a selection of useful websites – turn to the Directory at the back of this guide. It begins on page 360.

THE LOWDOWN ON THE LISTINGS

We have tried to make this book as easy to use as possible. Addresses, phone numbers, transport information, opening times and admission prices are included in the listings. However, businesses can change their

arrangements at any time. Before you go
out of your way, we strongly advise you to
phone ahead to check opening times and other
particulars. While every effort has been made to
ensure the accuracy of the information contained
in this guide, the publishers cannot accept
responsibility for any errors it may contain.

PRICES AND PAYMENT

We have noted where venues such as shops,
hotels, restaurants and theatres accept the
following credit cards: American Express
(AmEx), Diners Club (DC), MasterCard (MC)
and Visa (V). Some venues also accept other
cards, such as Delta, Switch or JCB, and some
also take euros (€) as payment. Some of the
major sights, designated 'LP', offer discounts
to London pass holders, and some to members
of English Heritage (EH) and the National
Trust. For details, see p76.

The prices in this guide should be treated as
guidelines, not gospel. If they vary wildly from
those we've quoted, ask if there's a good reason.
If not, go elsewhere. Then please let us know.
We aim to give the most up-to-date advice,
and want to know if you've been overcharged.

TELEPHONE NUMBERS

The area code for London is 020; regular
numbers have eight digits in two groups of
four. The 020 code is not used internally within
London and is not given in our listings. From
abroad, dial your country's exit code (01 in the
US) followed by 44 (the international code for
the UK), then 20 for London (thereby dropping
the first zero of the area code) and the eight-digit
number. Mobile phone numbers have a five-
digit code, usually starting 07, then a six-digit

number. Freephone numbers start 0800, national-
rate numbers 0870 and local-rate numbers 0845.
For more on telephones and codes, see p376.

MAPS

The map section at the back of this book
includes orientation and neighbourhood maps
of the London area, and street maps of central
London, with a comprehensive street index.
The street maps start on page 396, and now
pinpoint specific locations of hotels (**❶**),
restaurants (**❶**) and cafés and bars (**❶**)

LET US KNOW WHAT YOU THINK

We hope you enjoy *Time Out London*, and
we'd like to know what you think of it. We
welcome tips for places you consider we
should include in future editions and take
note of your criticism of our choices. You
can email us at guides@timeout.com.

Advertisers

We would like to stress that no
establishment has been included in this
guide because it has advertised in any
of our publications and no payment of
any kind has influenced any review. The
opinions given in this book are those of
Time Out writers and entirely independent.

There is an online version of this book,
along with guides to over 45 other
international cities, at **www.timeout.com**.

Conceived and designed by Marks Barfield Architects

Why not push the boat out?

London Eye flight and river cruise from £23

Why not see London by both air and water? Our River Cruise Experience includes a flight on the London Eye and a fantastic 40 minute cruise along the Thames taking in such sights as St. Paul's Cathedral and the Houses of Parliament. Perfect for exploring the best of London with friends and family. **Book online at ba-londoneye.com and save 10% or call 0870 5000 600.**

Make the most of your London Eye visit.

BRITISH AIRWAYS
London eye

TimeOut

London

timeout.com/london

Published by Time Out Guides Ltd, a wholly owned subsidiary of Time Out Group Ltd.
Time Out and the Time Out logo are trademarks of Time Out Group Ltd.

© Time Out Group Ltd 2006
Previous editions 1989, 1990, 1992, 1994, 1995, 1997, 1998, 1999, 2000, 2001, 2002, 2003, 2004, 2005.

10 9 8 7 6 5 4 3 2 1

This edition first published in Great Britain in 2006 by Ebury Publishing
Ebury Publishing is a division of The Random House Group Ltd,
20 Vauxhall Bridge Road, London SW1V 2SA

Random House Australia Pty Limited 20 Alfred Street, Milsons Point, Sydney, New South Wales 2061, Australia
Random House New Zealand Limited 18 Poland Road, Glenfield, Auckland 10, New Zealand
Random House South Africa (Pty) Limited Isle of Houghton, Corner Boundary Road & Carse O'Gowrie,
Houghton 2198, South Africa

Random House UK Limited Reg. No. 954009

Distributed in USA by Publishers Group West
1700 Fourth Street, Berkeley, California 94710

Distributed in Canada by Penguin Canada Ltd
10 Alcorn Avenue, Toronto, Ontario, Canada M4V 3B2

For further distribution details, see www.timeout.com

ISBN
To 31 December 2006: 1904978533
From 1 January 2007: 9781904978534

A CIP catalogue record for this book is available from the British Library

Colour reprographics by Icon, Crowne House, 56-58 Southwark Street, London SE1 1UN

Printed and bound in Germany by Appl

Papers used by Ebury Publishing are natural, recyclable products made from wood grown in sustainable forests

In Context

Westminster Abbey. *See p138.*

Old London Bridge from the West, Claude de Jongh (1632).

History

Londinium in the continuum.

Peter Ackroyd has said that London is like 'a labyrinth which is constantly expanding, reaching outwards towards infinity'. But while the capital's size and rapid expansion have long fascinated visitors, the city's origins are much less grand. Celtic tribes lived in scattered communities along the banks of the Thames before the Romans arrived in Britain, but no evidence suggests there was a settlement on the site of the future metropolis before the invasion of the Emperor Claudius in AD 43. During the Roman conquest of the country, they forded the Thames at its shallowest point (near today's London Bridge) and, later, built a timber bridge here. A settlement developed on the north side of this crossing over the following decade.

During the first two centuries AD, the Romans built roads, towns and forts in the area, and trade flourished. Progress was brought to a halt in AD 61 when Boudicca, the widow of an East Anglian chieftain, rebelled against the Imperial forces who had seized her land, flogged her and raped her daughters. She led the Iceni in a savage revolt, destroying the Roman colony at Colchester and then marching on London. The inhabitants were massacred and the settlement burned to the ground.

After order was restored, the town was rebuilt and, around AD 200, a two-mile long, 18-foot (six-metre) high wall constructed around it. Chunks of the wall survive today, and early names of the original gates – Ludgate, Newgate, Bishopsgate and Aldgate – are preserved on the map of the city. The street known as London Wall traces part of its original course.

By the fourth century, racked by barbarian invasions and internal strife, the Empire was in decline. In 410 the last troops were withdrawn and London became a ghost town. The Roman way of life vanished, their only enduring legacies being roads and early Christianity.

CHRISTIANITY ARRIVES IN LONDON

During the fifth and sixth centuries, history gives way to legend. The Saxons crossed the North Sea and settled in eastern and southern England. Apparently avoiding the ruins of London, they built outside the walls.

Pope Gregory sent Augustine to convert the English to Christianity in 596. Ethelbert, Saxon King of Kent, proved a willing convert, and consequently Augustine was appointed the first Archbishop of Canterbury. Since then, the Kentish city has remained the centre of the English Christian Church. London's first Bishop, though, was Mellitus: one of Augustine's missionaries, he converted the East Saxon King Sebert and, in 604, founded a wooden cathedral dedicated to St Paul inside the old city walls. On Sebert's death, his fickle followers gave up the faith and reverted to paganism, but later generations of Christians rebuilt what is now St Paul's Cathedral.

London, meanwhile, continued to expand. The Venerable Bede, writing in 731, described 'Lundenwic' as 'the mart of many nations resorting to it by land and sea'. This probably refers to a settlement west of the Roman city in the area of today's Aldwych (Old English for 'old settlement'). During the ninth century the city faced a new danger from across the North Sea: the Vikings. The city was sacked in 841 and, in 851, the Danish raiders returned with 350 ships, leaving London in ruins. It was not until 886 that King Alfred of Wessex – aka Alfred the Great – regained the city, soon re-establishing London as a major trading centre with a merchant navy and new wharfs at Billingsgate and Queenhithe.

Throughout the tenth century the Saxon city prospered. Churches were built, parishes established and markets set up. However, the 11th century brought more harassment from the warlike Vikings, and the English were even forced to accept a Danish king, Cnut (Canute, 1016-35), during whose reign London replaced Winchester as the capital of England.

In 1042 the throne reverted to an Englishman, Edward the Confessor, who devoted himself to building the grandest church in England two miles west of the City at Thorney ('the isle of brambles'). He replaced the timber church of St Peter's with a huge abbey, 'the West Minster' (Westminster Abbey; consecrated in December 1065), and moved his court to the new Palace of Westminster. A week after the consecration, Edward died and was buried in his new church. London now grew around two hubs: Westminster, as the centre for the royal court, government and law, and the City of London, as the commercial centre.

WILLIAM CONQUERS

On Edward's death, there was a succession dispute. William, Duke of Normandy, claimed that the Confessor, his cousin, had promised him the English Crown, but the English instead chose Edward's brother-in-law Harold. Piqued,

William gathered an army and invaded; on 14 October 1066 he defeated Harold at the Battle of Hastings in Sussex and marched on London. City elders had little option but to offer William the throne, and the conqueror was crowned in Westminster Abbey on Christmas Day 1066.

Recognising the need to win over the prosperous City merchants by negotiation rather than force, William granted the Bishop and burgesses of London a charter – still kept at Guildhall – that acknowledged their rights and independence in return for taxes. But, 'against the fickleness of the vast and fierce population', he also ordered strongholds to be built alongside the city wall, including the White Tower (the tallest building in the Tower of London) and the now-lost Baynard's Castle at Blackfriars. The earliest surviving written account of contemporary London was penned 40 years later by a monk, William Fitz Stephen, who conjured up the walled city and the pastures and woodland outside the perimeter.

THE MAYOR AND THE MAGNA CARTA

In the growing city of London, much of the politics of the Middle Ages – the late 12th to the late 15th centuries – revolved around a constant three-way struggle for power between the king and the aristocracy, the Church, and the Lord Mayor and city guilds.

The king and his court frequently travelled to other parts of the kingdom and abroad in the early Middle Ages. However, during the 14th and 15th centuries, the Palace of Westminster became the seat of law and government. The noblemen and bishops who attended court built themselves palatial houses along the Strand from the City to Westminster, with gardens stretching to the river.

The Model Parliament, which agreed the principles of government, was held in Westminster Hall in 1295, presided over by Edward I and attended by barons, clergy and representatives of knights and burgesses. The first step towards establishing personal rights and political liberty – not to mention curbing the power of the king – had already been taken in 1215 with the signing of the Magna Carta by King John. In the 14th century, subsequent assemblies gave rise to the House of Lords (which met at the Palace of Westminster) and the House of Commons (which met in the Chapter House at Westminster Abbey).

Relations between the monarch and the City were never easy. Londoners guarded their privileges with self-righteous intransigence, and resisted all attempts by successive kings to squeeze money out of them to finance wars and building projects. Subsequent kings were forced to turn to Jewish and Lombard moneylenders,

Step inside for an exciting journey into London's past.

ADMISSION FREE
Open daily
⊖ St Paul's, Barbican
⇌ Moorgate, City Thameslink
Bus: 4, 56. 100, 172

Museum of London
London Wall London EC2
0870 444 3851
www.museumoflondon.org.uk

MUSEUM OF LONDON

Explore the epic story of London's East End.

Kids go free
Open daily
⊖ Canary Wharf
⊖ West India Quay
Bus: 277, D3, D6, D7, D8, 115

Museum in Docklands
West India Quay London E14 4AL
0870 444 3856
www.museumindocklands.org.uk

 **MUSEUM IN DOCKLANDS**

Registered Charity Number 1060415

London's lost lingos

Everyone's heard of cockney rhyming slang – and if you watch an episode of *EastEnders* you'd be forgiven for thinking that Londoners still speak it on a regular basis – but what about the capital's other languages?

Those who follow such things may also be familiar with Polari. Often associated with the gay community, but not an exclusively gay slang, Polari (aka Palare, Palary and Palyaree) is a sociolect (a language spoken by a subculture) that seems to have originated to facilitate international business. An early form was used at the London docks in the 18th century, when traders and sailors of different nationalities needed a common language. Polari found its way into the East End via stevedores and the huge number of Italian street entertainers, such as Punch and Judy men and organ grinders, who were arriving in the capital. Once it hit the streets, Polari was enriched by those whose business pursuits and leisure interests welcomed a language that could be used as a code. That's why it has a far weightier claim than cockney to being the patois of London's underclasses. All 19th-century London sub-groups, from thieves and prostitutes to actors, would, when they were actually sober enough to speak, have been fluent.

Polari's grammar and syntax both follow English, but its vocabulary is derived from its extraordinarily rich origins: Italian gave the lingo its name, 'parlare' ('to speak'); Occitan (the Romance language spoken in southern France, Spain and Italy) provided, among many others, the best-known Polari word, 'bona', meaning 'good' or 'lovely', and it also contributed the much-used adjective of aesthetic approval, 'bijou'. Yiddish brought words such as 'meese' ('ugly' or 'horrible') while French lent 'savvy' (from 'savoir', 'to know'). Londoners' practice of pronouncing words as if their spelling were reversed – back-slang – brought more colour. Thus we have 'riah' for 'hair' and 'eek' (via 'ecaf') for 'face'. Rhyming slang supplied terms such as 'bexleys', meaning 'teeth' (from 'Bexley Heath'). Further codification took place, to the extent that even acronyms such as 'naff' ('not worth bothering with', from 'Not Available For Fucking') appeared.

Polari was adopted by gay men via the theatre. As street entertainers moved first into music halls and then West End theatres, they mixed with the many homosexuals who worked there. Until 1967 homosexuality was outlawed in Britain, so Polari's cryptic possibilities were again embraced. Although the Polari-gay conjunction proved to be mutually beneficial at first, it eventually put an end to the sociolect's main attraction – secrecy. It gained a wittily subversive edge that made it ideal material for comic characters such as Julian and Sandy in the 1960s BBC radio show *Round the Horne*. At first the laughter came from those in the know, but the show gradually familiarised the nation with Polari's language and its (often double, sometimes triple) meanings.

While Polari has effectively died out over the intervening decades, another well-known (and globally spoken) language is still going strong after more than a hundred years. Though Esperanto was founded in Warsaw in the late 19th century, it's still spoken and used in publication around the world. Indeed, the London Esperanto Club celebrated its centenary in 2003, and its 100 members meet regularly in Camden to discuss a range of topics with invited speakers (all in Esperanto, of course). For more information, check their website at www.phon.ucl.ac.uk/home/wells/lek/ – if you can make any sense out of it, that is.

but the City merchants were as intolerant of foreigners as of the royals. Rioting, persecution and the occasional lynching and pogrom were all commonplace in medieval London.

The privileges granted to the City merchants under Norman kings, allowing independence and self-regulation, were extended by the monarchs who followed, in return for financial favours. In 1191, during the reign of Richard I, the City of London was formally recognised as a commune – a self-governing community – and in 1197 it won control of the Thames, which included lucrative fishing rights that the City retained until 1857. In 1215 King John confirmed the city's right 'to elect every year a mayor', a position of great authority with power over the Sheriff and the Bishop of London. A month later the Mayor had joined the rebel barons in signing the Magna Carta.

Over the next two centuries, the power and influence of the trade and craft guilds (later known as the City Livery Companies) increased as trade with Europe grew, and the wharfs by London Bridge were crowded with imports such as fine cloth, furs, wine, spices and precious metals. Port dues and taxes were paid to Customs officials, including part-time poet Geoffrey Chaucer, whose *Canterbury Tales* were the first published work of English literature.

'In the streets around Smithfield, butchers dumped the entrails of slaughtered animals.'

The City's markets, already established, drew produce from miles around: livestock at Smithfield, fish at Billingsgate and poultry at Leadenhall. The street markets, or 'cheaps', around Westcheap (now Cheapside) and Eastcheap were crammed with a variety of goods. As commerce increased, foreign traders and craftsmen settled around the port; the population within the city wall grew from about 18,000 in 1100 to well over 50,000 in the 1340s.

THE PEASANTS ARE REVOLTING

Not surprisingly, lack of hygiene became a serious problem in the City. Water was provided in cisterns at Cheapside and elsewhere, but the supply, which came more or less direct from the Thames, was limited and polluted. The street called Houndsditch was so named because Londoners threw their dead animals into the furrow that formed the City's eastern boundary, and in the streets around Smithfield (the Shambles), butchers dumped the entrails of slaughtered beasts.

These appalling conditions provided the breeding ground for the greatest catastrophe of the Middle Ages: the Black Death of 1348 and 1349, which killed about 30 per cent of England's population. The plague came to London from Europe, carried by rats on ships. Although the epidemic abated, it recurred in London several times during the next three centuries, each time devastating the population.

The outbreaks of disease left the labour market short-handed, causing unrest among the overworked peasants. The imposition of a poll tax of a shilling a head proved the final straw, leading to the Peasants' Revolt of 1381. Thousands marched on London, led by Jack Straw from Essex and Wat Tyler from Kent. In the rioting and looting that followed, the Savoy Palace on the Strand was destroyed, the Archbishop of Canterbury was murdered and hundreds of prisoners were set free. When the 14-year-old Richard II rode out to Smithfield to face the rioters, Wat Tyler was fatally stabbed by Lord Mayor William Walworth. The other ringleaders were subsequently rounded up and hanged. But no more poll taxes were imposed.

ROSES, WIVES AND BLOODY MARY

Under the Tudor monarchs (1485 to 1603) and spurred by the discovery of America and the ocean routes to Africa and the Orient, London became one of Europe's largest cities. Henry VII ended the Wars of the Roses by defeating Richard III at the Battle of Bosworth and marrying Elizabeth of York. Henry VII's other achievements included building a merchant navy and the Henry VII Chapel in Westminster Abbey, his eventual resting place.

Henry VII was succeeded in 1509 by arch wife-collector (and dispatcher) Henry VIII. Henry's first marriage to Catherine of Aragon failed to produce an heir, so in 1527 the King determined the union should be annulled. When the Pope refused to co-operate, Henry defied the Catholic Church, demanding to be recognised as Supreme Head of the Church in England and ordering the execution of anyone who opposed the plan (including his chancellor Sir Thomas More). Thus it was that England began the transition to Protestantism. The subsequent dissolution of the monasteries transformed the face of the medieval city with the confiscation and redevelopment of all property owned by the Catholic Church.

On a more positive note, Henry found time to develop a professional navy, founding the Royal Dockyards at Woolwich in 1512 and at Deptford the following year. He also established palaces at Hampton Court and Whitehall, and built a residence at St James's Palace. Much of the land he annexed for hunting became the Royal Parks, including Greenwich, Hyde, Regent's and Richmond parks.

After Henry, there was a brief Catholic revival under Queen Mary (1553-8), though her marriage to Philip II of Spain met with much opposition in London. She had 300 Protestants burned at the stake at Smithfield, earning her the nickname 'Bloody Mary'.

RENAISSANCE REBIRTH

Elizabeth I's reign (1558-1603) saw a flowering of English commerce and arts. The founding of the Royal Exchange by Sir Thomas Gresham in 1566 gave London its first trading centre, allowing it to emerge as Europe's leading commercial centre. The merchant venturers and the first joint-stock companies (Russia Company and Levant Company) established new trading enterprises, and Francis Drake, Walter Raleigh and Richard Hawkins sailed to the New World and beyond. In 1580 Elizabeth knighted Drake on his return from a three-year circumnavigation; eight years later, Drake and Charles Howard defeated the Spanish Armada.

As trade grew, so did London. It was home to some 200,000 people in 1600, many living in dirty, overcrowded conditions; plague and fire

Robert Winter · Christopher Wright · John Wright · Thomas Percy · Guido Fawkes · Robert Catesby · Thomas Winter · Bates

Guy Fawkes and his not-so-merry men.

were constant, day-to-day hazards. The most complete picture of Tudor London is given in John Stow's *Survey of London* (1598), a fascinating first-hand account by a diligent Londoner whose monument stands in the City church of St Andrew Undershaft.

The glory of the Elizabethan era was the development of English drama, popular with all social classes but treated with disdain by the Corporation of London, which banned theatres from the City in 1575. Two theatres, the Rose (1587) and the Globe (1599, now restored), were erected on the south bank of the Thames at Bankside, and provided homes for the works of Christopher Marlowe and William Shakespeare. Bankside, deemed 'a naughty place' by royal proclamation, was the Soho of its time: home not just to the theatre, but to bear-baiting, cock-fighting, taverns and 'stews' (brothels).

The Tudor dynasty ended with Elizabeth's death in 1603. Her successor, the Stuart King James I, narrowly escaped assassination on 5 November 1605, when Guy Fawkes and his gunpowder were discovered underneath the Palace of Westminster. The Gunpowder Plot was hatched in protest at the failure to improve conditions for the persecuted Catholics, but only resulted in an intensification of anti-papist feelings in London. To this day, 5 November is commemorated with fireworks as Bonfire Night.

Aside from the Gunpowder Plot, James I deserves to be remembered for hiring Inigo Jones to design court masques (dramas with singing and dancing), and the first – beautiful and hugely influential – examples of classical Renaissance style in London, the Queen's House in Greenwich, south-east London (1616), and the Banqueting House in Westminster (1619).

ROYALISTS AND ROUNDHEADS

Charles I succeeded his father in 1625, but gradually fell out of favour with the City of London (from whose citizens he tried to extort taxes) and an increasingly independent-minded and antagonistic Parliament. The last straw came in 1642 when he intruded on the Houses of Parliament in an attempt to arrest five MPs. The country soon slid into a civil war (1642-9) between the supporters of Parliament (the Roundheads, led by Puritan Oliver Cromwell) and those of the King (the Royalists).

Both sides knew that control of the country's major city and port was vital for victory. London's sympathies were firmly with the Parliamentarians and, in 1642, 24,000 citizens assembled at Turnham Green, west of the City, to face Charles's army. Fatally, the King lost his nerve and withdrew. He was never seriously to threaten the capital again; eventually, the Royalists were defeated. Charles was tried for treason and, though he denied the legitimacy of the court, he was declared guilty. He was then taken to the Banqueting House in Whitehall on 30 January 1649 and, declaring himself to be a 'martyr of the people', beheaded.

For the next 11 years the country was ruled as a Commonwealth by Cromwell, and then for a brief period by his son Richard. The younger Cromwell's inability to continue his father's powerful rule, however, along with the closing of the theatres, the banning of Christmas (supposedly a Catholic superstition), and Puritan strictures on the wickedness of any sort of fun, meant that the restoration of the exiled Charles II in 1660 was greeted with relief and rejoicing by the populace. The Stuart king had Cromwell posthumously executed.

In Context

PLAGUE, FIRE AND REVOLUTION

However, two major catastrophes marred the first decade of Charles's reign in the capital. In 1665 the most serious outbreak of bubonic plague since the Black Death killed many of the capital's population. By the time the winter cold had put paid to the epidemic, nearly 100,000 Londoners had died. On 2 September 1666 a second disaster struck. The fire that spread from a carelessly tended oven in Farriner's baking shop on Pudding Lane was to rage for three days and consume four-fifths of the City, including 89 churches, 44 livery company halls and more than 13,000 houses.

The Great Fire at least allowed planners the chance to rebuild London as a rationally planned modern city. Many blueprints were considered, but, in the end, Londoners were so impatient to get on with business that the City was reconstructed largely on its medieval street plan, albeit in brick and stone rather than wood. The towering figure of the period turned out to be the prolific Sir Christopher Wren, who oversaw work on 51 of the 54 churches rebuilt. Among them was his masterpiece, the new St Paul's, completed in 1710 and, effectively, the world's first Protestant cathedral.

In the wake of the Great Fire, many well-to-do former City dwellers moved to new residential developments in the West End. In the City, the Royal Exchange was rebuilt, but merchants increasingly used the new coffee houses to exchange news. With the expansion of the joint-stock companies and the chance to invest capital, the City was emerging as a centre not of manufacturing, but of finance.

Anti-Catholic feeling still ran high. The accession of Catholic James II in 1685 aroused fears of a return to papistry, and resulted in a Dutch Protestant, William of Orange, being invited to take the throne with his wife, Mary Stuart (James's daughter). James fled to France in 1688 in what became known – by its beneficiaries – as the 'Glorious Revolution'. The Bank of England was founded during William III's reign, in 1694, initially to finance the King's wars with France.

CREATION OF THE PRIME MINISTER

After the death of Queen Anne, according to the Act of Settlement (1701), the throne passed to George, great-grandson of James I, who had been born and raised in Hanover, Germany. Thus, a German-speaking king – who never learned English – became the first of four long-reigning Georges in the Hanoverian line.

During his reign (1714-27), and for several years afterwards, Sir Robert Walpole's Whig party monopolised Parliament. Their opponents, the Tories, supported the Stuarts

Queen Victoria – not amused. *See p18.*

and had opposed the exclusion of the Catholic James II. On the King's behalf, Walpole chaired a group of ministers (the forerunner of today's Cabinet), becoming, in effect, Britain's first prime minister. Walpole was presented with 10 Downing Street (constructed by Sir George Downing) as a residence; it remains the official home of all serving prime ministers.

> ## 'Public executions at Tyburn were among the most popular events in the social calendar.'

During the 18th century London grew with astonishing speed, in terms of both population and construction. New squares and many streets of terraced houses spread across Soho, Bloomsbury, Mayfair and Marylebone, as wealthy landowners and speculative developers, who didn't mind taking a risk given the size of the potential rewards, cashed in on the demand for leasehold properties. South London, too, became more accessible with the opening of the first new bridges for centuries, Westminster Bridge (1750) and Blackfriars Bridge (1769). Until then, London Bridge had been the only bridge over the Thames. The old city gates, most of the Roman Wall and the remaining houses on Old London Bridge were demolished, allowing traffic access to the City.

GIN RUINS POOR, RICH MOCK MAD

In the older districts, however, people were still living in terrible squalor and poverty, far worse than the infamous conditions of Victorian times. Some of the most notorious slums were located around Fleet Street and St Giles's (north of Covent Garden), only a short distance from streets of fashionable residences maintained by large numbers of servants. To make matters worse, gin ('mother's ruin') was readily available at very low prices, and many poor Londoners drank excessive amounts in an attempt to escape the horrors of daily life. The well-off seemed complacent, amusing themselves at the popular Ranelagh and Vauxhall Pleasure Gardens or with organised trips to Bedlam to mock the mental patients. Similarly, public executions at Tyburn – near today's Marble Arch – were among the most popular events in the social calendar.

The outrageous imbalance in the distribution of wealth encouraged crime, and there were daring daytime robberies in the West End. Reformers were few, though there were exceptions. Henry Fielding, author of the picaresque novel *Tom Jones*, was also an enlightened magistrate at Bow Street Court. In 1751 he and his blind half-brother John set up a volunteer force of 'thief-takers' to back up the often ineffective efforts of the parish constables and watchmen who were the only law-keepers in the city. This crime-busting group of early cops, known as the Bow Street Runners, were the forerunners of today's Metropolitan Police (established in 1829).

Disaffection was also evident in the activities of the London mob during this period. Riots were a regular reaction to middlemen charging extortionate prices, or merchants adulterating their food. In June 1780 London was hit by the anti-Catholic Gordon Riots, named after ringleader Lord George Gordon; the worst in the city's violent history, they left 300 people dead.

Some attempts were made to alleviate the grosser ills of poverty with the founding of five major new hospitals by private philanthropists. St Thomas's and St Bartholomew's were long established as monastic institutions for the care of the sick, but Westminster (1720), Guy's (1725), St George's (1734), London (1740) and the Middlesex (1745) went on to become world-famous teaching hospitals. Thomas Coram's Foundling Hospital for abandoned children was another remarkable achievement of the time.

INDUSTRY AND CAPITAL-ISM

It wasn't just the indigenous population of London that was on the rise. Country people, whose common land had been replaced by sheep enclosures, were faced with starvation wages or unemployment, and drifted into the towns in large numbers. The East End became the focus for poor immigrant labourers with the building of the docks towards the end of the century. London's population had grown to almost a million by 1801, the largest of any city in Europe. And by 1837, when Queen Victoria came to the throne, five more bridges and the

capital's first passenger railway (from Greenwich to London Bridge) gave hints that a major expansion might be around the corner.

As well as being the administrative and financial capital of the British Empire, which by this time spanned a fifth of the globe, London was also its chief port and the world's largest manufacturing centre, with breweries, distilleries, tanneries, shipyards, engineering works and many other grim and grimy industries lining the south bank of the Thames. On the one hand, London boasted splendid buildings, fine shops, theatres and museums; on the other, it was a city of poverty, pollution, disease and prostitution. The residential areas were becoming polarised into districts with fine terraces maintained by squads of servants, and overcrowded, insanitary, disease-ridden slums.

The growth of the metropolis in the century before Victoria came to the throne had been spectacular, but during her reign (1837-1901), thousands more acres were covered with housing, roads and railway lines. If you visit a street within five miles of central London, its houses will be mostly Victorian. By the end of the 19th century, the city's population had swelled to more than six million – an incredible growth of five million in one hundred years.

Despite social problems – memorably depicted in the writings of Charles Dickens – major steps were being taken to improve conditions for the majority of Londoners by the turn of the century. The Metropolitan Board of Works installed an efficient sewerage system, street lighting and better roads. The worst slums were replaced by low-cost building schemes funded by philanthropists such as the American George Peabody, who established the Peabody Donation Fund, which continues to this day to provide subsidised housing to the working classes. The London County Council (created in 1888) also helped to house the poor.

The Victorian expansion would not have been possible without an efficient public transport network with which to speed workers into and out of the city from the new suburbs. The horse-drawn bus appeared on London's streets in 1829, but it was the opening of the first passenger railway seven years later that heralded the commuters of the future. The first underground line, which ran between Paddington and Farringdon Road, opened in 1863 and proved an instant success, attracting more than 30,000 travellers on the first day. Soon after, the world's first electric track in a deep tunnel – the 'tube' – opened in 1890 between the City and Stockwell, later becoming part of the Northern Line. The penny farthing bicycle was also refined in the 1870s.

Jumping Jack slash

It's fair to say that even in this day and age, the sight of someone leaping over a house would cause eyebrows to be raised. But if such a spectacle were to have been witnessed in the London of the late 1830s and '40s, it would have caused the alarm to be raised, for it could mean only one thing: London's Public Enemy Number One, Spring-Heeled Jack was out and about.

Spring-Heeled Jack held London in terror, and his grip on its popular imagination was tightened because he was believed to be a fiend of supernatural origin. His victims' descriptions of him suggest that he was over seven feet tall, with eyes that shone like fire, claws for hands, and the ability to spit fire and jump to astonishing altitudes. His uniform was classic fiend: black cloak, mask and a helmet that glowed in the dark.

If the above seems fanciful now, the nature of the attacks attributed to him ensured that he was taken seriously in his day. In September 1837, a barmaid, Polly Adams, was sexually assaulted in Clapham. Three weeks later, Mary Stevens was molested on Clapham Common, and left with lacerations on her breasts and stomach, wounds that the victim swore were left by a beast with claws. The day after the Stevens attack, a man in a cloak ran in front of a carriage, causing it to swerve and crash; witnesses claimed that he then jumped over a wall ten feet in height.

When London's Lord Mayor, Sir John Cowan, declared Jack to be a public menace, dozens of other victims came forward to report encounters with a creature matching Spring-Heeled Jack's description. Women and children were encouraged not to leave their homes after dark and gangs of vigilantes roamed London in search of the villain. Even the Duke of Wellington led a posse in an attempt to apprehend him. Jack's response was to intensify the frequency of his crimes.

In February 1838 a girl called Lucy Scales was molested in Green Dragon Alley in Limehouse. Afterwards, witnesses reported seeing a man leap from street level to the roof of a house. Two days later Jane Alsop was attacked in Bow. There is no record of his resorting to murder, but we cannot know what horrors Jack inflicted on members of London's underclass, who were perceived to lead gin-alley lives that precluded serious police interest in their deaths.

On the tombstone, with upraised arms and rage in every feature, towered the terrific form of Spring-Heeled Jack. Freezer and Links stood transfixed; their ghastly burden slipped slowly to the grass, but they remained gaping, terror-struck. Vengeance had fallen!

If you eliminate the possibility that he possessed a jet pack, Spring Heeled Jack was probably an urban legend constructed around the activities of at least one sex attacker stalking London. The contemporary view among the upper classes was that Jack was in fact the Marquis of Waterford, a theory built on the flimsy allegation that Waterford was a misogynist who liked to play practical jokes and the dubious testimony of a servant boy who claimed to have seen a golden 'W' embroidered on Jack's clothing. The Lord Mayor's revelation of Jack's crimes may well have spawned copycat attacks – after all, any suspect would only have to show that he had fingers instead of claws and was unable to leap 30 feet into the air to prove that he was not Spring-Heeled Jack. The legend was disseminated via the 'penny dreadfuls' and Jack became London's first celebrity criminal since Dick Turpin.

Though Jack was never caught, he remained in the public consciousness long after the attacks ceased: 50 years after he first struck, a ferocious serial killer who butchered East End prostitutes emerged, and may have decided to pay tribute to the mysterious masked bounder by choosing to name himself Jack the Ripper.

THE CRYSTAL PALACE

The Great Exhibition of 1851 captured the zeitgeist: confidence and pride, discovery and invention. Prince Albert, the Queen's Consort, helped organise this triumphant event, for which the Crystal Palace, a giant building of iron and glass – designed not by a professional architect but by the Duke of Devonshire's gardener, Joseph Paxton – was erected in Hyde Park. During the five months it was open, the Exhibition drew six million visitors from Great Britain and abroad, and the profits inspired the Prince Consort to establish a permanent centre for the study of the applied arts and sciences: the result is the South Kensington museums and Imperial College. After the Exhibition, the Palace was moved to Sydenham and used as an exhibition centre until it burned down in 1936.

When the Victorians were not colonising the world by force, they combined their conquests with scientific developments. The Royal Geographical Society sent navigators to chart unknown waters, botanists to bring back new species, and geologists to study the earth. Many of their specimens ended up at the Royal Botanic Gardens at Kew.

ZEPPELINS ATTACK FROM THE SKIES

During the brief reign of Edward VII (1901-10), London regained some of the gaiety and glamour it lacked in the dour last years of Victoria's reign. A touch of Parisian chic came to London with the opening of the Ritz Hotel in Piccadilly; the Café Royal hit the heights of its popularity as a meeting place for artists and writers; and 'luxury catering for the little man' was provided at the Lyons Teashops and new Lyons Corner Houses (the Coventry Street branch, which opened in 1907, could accommodate an incredible 4,500 people). Meanwhile, the first modern department store, Selfridges, opened on Oxford Street in 1909.

Road transport, too, was revolutionised. Motor cars put-putted around the city's streets, before the first motor bus was introduced in 1904. Double-decked electric trams had started running in 1901 (though not through the West End or the City), and continued doing so for 51 years. By 1911 the use of horse-drawn buses had been abandoned.

A few years later, London suffered its first devastating air raids in World War I. The first bomb over the city was dropped from a Zeppelin near Guildhall in September 1915, and was followed by many gruelling nightly raids on the capital; bomb attacks from German Gotha GV bombers began in July 1917. In all, around 650 people lost their lives as a result of Zeppelin raids, but the greater impact was the psychological fear of helplessness.

ROARING BETWEEN THE WARS

Political change happened quickly after World War I. David Lloyd George's government averted revolution in 1918-19 by promising (but not delivering) 'homes for heroes' – ie the embittered returning soldiers. But the Liberal Party's days in power were numbered, and in 1924 the Labour Party, led by Ramsay MacDonald, formed its first government.

After the trauma of World War I, a 'live for today' attitude prevailed in the Roaring '20s among the young upper classes, who flitted from parties in Mayfair to dances at the Ritz. But this meant little to the mass of Londoners, who were suffering greatly in the post-war slump. Civil disturbances, brought on by the high cost of living and rising unemployment, resulted in the nationwide General Strike of 1926, when the working classes downed tools in support of the striking miners. Prime Minister Baldwin encouraged volunteers to take over the public services and the streets teemed with army-escorted food convoys, aristocrats running soup kitchens and students driving buses. After nine days of chaos, the strike was called off by the Trades Union Congress (TUC).

The economic situation only worsened in the early 1930s following the New York Stock Exchange crash of 1929; by 1931 more than three million Britons were jobless. During these years, the London County Council began to have a greater impact on the city's life, undertaking programmes of slum clearance and new housing, creating more parks and taking under its wing education, transport, hospitals, libraries and the fire service.

London's population increased dramatically between the wars, too, peaking at nearly 8.7 million in 1939. To accommodate the influx, the suburbs expanded quickly, particularly to the north-west with the extension of the Metropolitan Line to an area that became known as Metroland. Identical, gabled, double-fronted houses sprang up in their hundreds of thousands, from Golders Green to Surbiton.

Londoners were entertained by the new media: film, radio and television. London's first radio broadcast was beamed from the roof of Marconi House in the Strand in 1922, and families were soon gathering around enormous Bakelite wireless sets to hear the British Broadcasting Company (the BBC; from 1927 called the British Broadcasting Corporation). TV broadcasts started on 26 August 1936, when the first telecast went out live from Alexandra Palace. Successful early broadcasts included King George VI's coronation procession on 12 May 1937, the first Wimbledon coverage (June 1937), and the first televised FA Cup Final (30 April 1938).

St Paul's Cathedral during the Blitz.

WORLD WAR II (1939-45)

During the 1930s Neville Chamberlain's policy of appeasement towards Hitler's increasingly aggressive Germany collapsed when the Germans invaded Poland, and on 3 September 1939 Britain declared war. The government implemented precautionary measures against the threat of air raids – including the evacuation of 600,000 children and pregnant mothers – but the expected bombing raids did not happen during the autumn and winter of 1939-40, a period that became known as the Phoney War. In July 1940, though, Germany began preparations for an invasion of Britain with three months of aerial attack that came to be known as the Battle of Britain.

For Londoners, the Phoney War came to an abrupt end in September 1940, when hundreds of German bombers dumped their loads of high explosives on east London and the docks, destroying entire streets. Despite precautions such as air raid shelters and sirens, the dead and injured numbered more than 2,000. The Blitz had begun. The raids on London continued for 57 consecutive nights, then intermittently for a further six months. Londoners reacted with tremendous bravery and stoicism, a period still nostalgically referred to as 'Britain's finest hour'. After a final massive raid on 10 May 1941, the Germans focused their attention elsewhere, but by the end of the war, a third of the City and the East End was in ruins.

From 1942 onwards, the tide of the war began to turn, but Londoners still had a new terror to face: the V1, or 'doodlebug'. Dozens of these deadly, explosives-packed, pilotless planes descended on the city in 1944, causing widespread destruction. Later in the year, the more powerful V2 rocket was launched and, over the winter, 500 of them dropped on London, mostly in the East End. The last fell on 27 March 1945 in Orpington, Kent, around six weeks before Victory in Europe (VE Day) was declared on 8 May 1945.

'YOU HAVE NEVER HAD IT SO GOOD'

World War II left Britain almost as shattered as Germany. Soon after VE Day, a general election was held and Churchill was heavily defeated by the Labour Party under Clement Attlee. The new government established the National Health Service in 1948, and began a massive nationalisation programme that included public transport, electricity, gas, postal and telephone services. For most people, however, life remained regimented and austere.

> **'The city basked in its new-found reputation as the music and fashion capital of the world.'**

In war-ravaged London, the most immediate problem faced by both residents and the local authorities was a critical shortage of housing. Prefabricated bungalows provided a temporary solution for some (though many of these buildings were still occupied 40 years later), but the huge new high-rise housing estates that the planners devised were often badly built and proved to be unpopular with their residents.

However, there were bright spots during this dreary time. London hosted the Olympics in 1948; three years later came the Festival of Britain (100 years after the Great Exhibition), a celebration of British technology and design.

The festival exhibitions that took over land on the south bank of the Thames provided the incentive to build the South Bank Centre.

As the 1950s progressed, life and prosperity gradually returned to London, leading Prime Minister Harold Macmillan in 1957 famously to proclaim that 'most of our people have never had it so good'. The coronation of Queen Elizabeth II in 1953 had been the biggest television broadcast in history, and there was the feeling of a new age dawning.

However, many Londoners were moving out of the city. The population dropped by half a million in the late 1950s, causing a labour shortage that prompted huge recruitment drives in Britain's former colonies. London Transport and the National Health Service were particularly active in encouraging West Indians to emigrate to Britain. Unfortunately, as the Notting Hill race riots of 1958 illustrated, the welcome these new immigrants received was rarely friendly. Yet there were several areas of tolerance: among them was Soho, which, during the 1950s, became famed for its smoky, seedy, bohemian pubs, clubs and jazz joints, such as the still-jumping Ronnie Scott's.

THE SWINGING '60S
By the mid '60s, London had started to swing. The innovative fashions of Mary Quant and others broke Paris's stranglehold on couture: boutiques blossomed along the King's Road, while Biba set the pace in Kensington. Carnaby Street became a byword for hipness as the city basked in its new-found reputation as the music and fashion capital of the world. The year of

The Beatles arrive at London Airport, 1964.

student unrest in Europe, 1968, saw the first issue of *Time Out* (a fold-up sheet for 5d) hit the streets in August. The decade ended with the Beatles naming their final album *Abbey Road* after their studios in London, NW8, and the Rolling Stones playing a free gig in Hyde Park that drew around 500,000 people.

The bubble, though, had to burst – and burst it did. Many Londoners remember the 1970s as a decade of economic strife: inflation, the oil crisis and international debt caused chaos, and the IRA began its bombing campaign on mainland Britain. The explosion of punk in the second half of the decade, sartorially inspired by the idiosyncratic genius of Vivienne Westwood, provided some nihilistic colour.

THE IRON FIST OF THE IRON LADY
Historians will regard the 1980s as the decade of Thatcherism. When the Conservatives won the general election in 1979 under Britain's first woman prime minister, Margaret Thatcher, their monetarist economic policy and cuts in public services widened the divide between rich and poor. In London, riots in Brixton (1981) and Tottenham (1985) were linked to unemployment and heavy-handed policing. The Greater London Council (GLC), led by Ken Livingstone, mounted spirited opposition to the government with a series of populist measures, the most famous being a fare-cutting policy on public transport. So effective was the GLC, in fact, that Thatcher decided to abolish it in 1986.

The replacement of Margaret Thatcher by John Major in October 1990 signalled a shortlived upsurge of hope among Londoners.

Free love – and music – **Hyde Park**, 1967.

The nutty protesters

Londoners have a deserved reputation for avoiding social interaction – just look at the way commuters avoid making eye contact on the tube. Not getting involved has been elevated to an art form and anyone saying hello to strangers can expect to be branded a lunatic immediately.

All the more reason to applaud those Londoners who do stand up and get noticed. Despite the twitchiness locals feel about drawing attention to themselves, many city dwellers will happily shout their causes from the rooftops if they feel their fundamental liberties are being eroded.

There are those who seem to have been around for so long that they're part of the furniture. These include Phil, aka 'the Sinners and Winners' man, who stands at Oxford Circus, preaching through his megaphone about how God can save us all, and Brian Haw (*pictured*), the anti-war protester who has been staked outside the Houses of Parliament since June 2001. In spring 2005 Haw was nominated as a candidate in the general election, and later narrowly escaped eviction. You can catch up with his news at www.parliament-square.org.uk.

Then there are those who go to even greater lengths, staging elaborate one-off events to get noticed. Frustrated father David Chick dressed up as Spider-Man and climbed a crane next to Tower Bridge in 2003. The enraged arachnid stayed up there for six days, causing traffic chaos throughout the City, before he was finally talked down by counsellors from the Metropolitan Police.

This was just the first of dozens of appearances by the organisation Fathers 4 Justice, who are campaigning for a reform of child custody laws. They staged another high-profile stunt in September 2004, when protesters dressed as Batman and Robin scaled the walls of Buckingham Palace. In January 2005, 'super dads' kitted out as Superman, Spider-Man and Batman blocked all the main roads into London, and in March 2005 fathers dressed as Benedictine monks scaled St Paul's Cathedral.

Other organisations have staged similarly wacky protests in the capital. In September 2004 a group of campaigners from the pro-hunting Countryside Alliance broke into the Houses of Parliament through the back door and charged around the debating chamber making animal noises. Six youths, including the son of Roxy Music frontman Bryan Ferry, were arrested for causing 'harassment, alarm or distress' inside the seat of government.

More witty than wacky, two Greenpeace activists ascended Big Ben in 2004 to unfurl a sign declaring 'Time for Truth' beneath the clock face. They were among the millions who questioned Bush and Blair's war on Iraq.

Sadly, the increased police presence on the streets in the aftermath of the 7 July bomb attacks seems, in the short term at least, to have deterred many would-be protesters. Here's hoping that this situation will change in future, and that London's wacky protests won't be a thing of the past. We'll see you at the next annual Naked Bike Ride through Hyde Park, a bare-faced – and bare everything else – challenge to the use of cars in the capital.

A riot in Trafalgar Square had helped to see off both Maggie and her inequitable Poll Tax. Yet the early 1990s were scarred by continuing recession and terrorist attacks by the Irish Republican Army (IRA), a separatist group, punctuated the decade. Homelessness in London became an increasing problem and the *Big Issue* was launched in 1991 to give a voice to this socially marginalised group.

THINGS CAN ONLY GET BETTER?

In May 1997 the British people ousted the tired Tories and Tony Blair's Labour Party swept to the first of three general election victories. However, initial enthusiasm from a public delighted to see fresh faces in office didn't last. The government hoped the Millennium Dome, built on a patch of Greenwich wasteland, would be a 21st-century rival to the 1851 Great

Exhibition. It wasn't. Badly mismanaged, the Dome ate nearly £1 billion of public money and became a national joke along the way. But now it's set to become a major sporting venue, hosting basketball and gymnastics competitions in the 2012 Olympics.

The government's plans for Iraq in 2003 generated the largest public demonstration in London's history: over one million participated – to no avail. This wasn't the first time the government had ignored the people's wishes. The new millennium saw Ken Livingstone, charismatic former leader of the GLC and general thorn in the Labour Party's flesh, become London's first directly elected mayor. Blair had imposed his own candidate on the party and Livingstone quit Labour in disgust. He ran in the election as an independent and won in a landslide to head the new Greater London Assembly (GLA). After a second victory in 2004 – having been welcomed back into Labour – it became clear that Ken's popularity was no flash in the pan. The legacies of his first term are now firmly established, if not always popular. The congestion charge, for one, which forces drivers to pay £8 to enter the city centre, has been controversial (how can people be expected to use the shambolic public transport system, some argue); if the figures are to be believed, though, it has been a success, helping cut down the city's traffic gridlock. Ken's Totally London Campaign, launched in 2003 to get visitors back into the city following the tourist slump of 2001-2002, also proved successful, with visitor numbers back to pre-9/11 levels.

For a few weeks in the summer of 2005, London was riding the crest of a wave. First came Live8, a star-filled rockfest in Hyde Park watched by nearly ten people in the UK, aiming to raise the awareness of global poverty (the event was deliberately held the weekend before the G8 summit in Edinburgh). On the following Wednesday, 6 July, came the announcement that London had trounced Paris in the bid to host the 2012 Olympics. But jubilation turned to horror just one day later, when bombs on tube trains and a bus killed 52 people and injured 700. These were followed two weeks later by similar, though unsuccessful, attacks. The change in atmosphere was palpable, with many Londoners avoiding public transport and instead walking, driving, or even cycling to work. The high state of alert was blamed for panicked police shooting dead an innocent Brazilian man, Jean Charles de Menezes. But, as always, Londoners were keen to carry on as normal, with the mayor firmly behind them, pushing his One London campaign for unity in the face of terrorism. The mood of the country

and the capital was given a major boost by the English cricket team's victory over Australia in September 2005, and their parade through Trafalgar Square saw tens of thousands of people turn out to heap adulation upon them. For now the bombings have been pushed to the back of people's minds – after all, the capital has bounced back from even graver disasters in the past – and, despite warnings as we went to press of the coldest winter for 40 years, the mood is definitely one of optimism.

Olympics jubilation...

... and post-bombings sadness.

Key events

AD 43	The Romans invade; a bridge is built on the Thames; Londinium is founded.
61	Boudicca burns Londinium; the city is rebuilt and made the provincial capital.
122	Emperor Hadrian visits Londinium.
200	A city wall is built; Londinium becomes capital of Britannia Superior.
410	Roman troops evacuate Britain.
c600	Saxon London is built to the west.
604	St Paul's is built by King Ethelbert.
841	The Norse raid for the first time.
c871	The Danes occupy London.
886	King Alfred of Wessex takes London.
1013	The Danes take London back.
1042	Edward the Confessor builds a palace and 'West Minster' upstream.
1066	William I is crowned in Westminster Abbey; London is granted a charter.
1067	The Tower of London begun.
1123	St Bartholomew's Hospital founded.
1197	Henry Fitzalwin is the first mayor.
1213	St Thomas's Hospital is founded.
1215	The Mayor signs the Magna Carta.
1240	First Parliament sits at Westminster.
1290	Jews are expelled from London.
1348-9	The Black Death.
1381	The Peasants' Revolt.
1388	Tyburn becomes place of execution.
1397	Richard Whittington is Lord Mayor.
1476	William Caxton sets up the first ever printing press at Westminster.
1512-3	Royal Dockyards at Woolwich and Deptford founded by Henry VIII.
1534	Henry VIII cuts off Catholic Church.
1555	Martyrs burned at Smithfield.
1566	Gresham opens the Royal Exchange.
1572	First known map of London printed.
1599	The Globe theatre opens.
1605	Guy Fawkes fails to blow up James I.
1642	The start of the Civil War.
1649	Charles I is executed; Cromwell establishes Commonwealth.
1664-5	The Great Plague.
1666	The Great Fire.
1675	Building starts on the new St Paul's.
1686	The first May Fair takes place.
1694	The Bank of England is established.
1710	St Paul's is completed.
1750	Westminster Bridge is built.
1766	The city wall is demolished.
1769	Blackfriars Bridge opens.
1773	The Stock Exchange is founded.
1780	The Gordon Riots take place.
1784	The first balloon flight over London

1803	The first horse-drawn railway opens.
1812	PM Spencer Perceval assassinated.
1820	Regent's Canal opens.
1824	The National Gallery is founded.
1827	Regent's Park Zoo opens.
1829	London's first horse-drawn bus runs; the Metropolitan Police Act is passed.
1833	The London Fire Brigade is set up.
1834	Parliament burns down.
1835	Madame Tussaud's opens.
1836	The first passenger railway opens.
1843	Trafalgar Square is laid out.
1848-9	Cholera epidemic sweeps London.
1851	The Great Exhibition takes place.
1853	Harrods opens its doors.
1858	The Great Stink: pollution in the Thames reaches hideous levels.
1863	The Metropolitan Line, the world's first underground railway, opens.
1866	London's last major cholera outbreak; the Sanitation Act is passed.
1868	The last public execution is held at Newgate prison.
1884	Greenwich Mean Time established.
1888	Jack the Ripper prowls the East End; London County Council is created.
1890	The Housing Act enables the LCC to clear the slums; the first electric underground railway opens.
1897	Motorised buses introduced.
1915-8	Zeppelins bomb London.
1940-1	The Blitz devastates much of the city.
1948	The Olympic Games are held.
1951	The Festival of Britain takes place.
1952	The last London 'pea-souper' smog.
1953	Queen Elizabeth II is crowned.
1966	England win World Cup at Wembley.
1975	Work begins on the Thames barrier.
1981	Riots in Brixton.
1982	The last of London's docks close.
1986	The GLC is abolished.
1990	Poll Tax protesters riot.
1992	Canary Wharf opens; an IRA bomb hits the Baltic Exchange in the City.
2000	Ken Livingstone is elected mayor; Tate Modern and the London Eye open.
2001	The Labour government re-elected.
2002	Queen Mother dies aged 101.
2003	London's biggest public demonstration ever against the war on Iraq.
2005	London wins bid to host the 2012 Olympics. Four suicide bombers kill 52 people. England cricket team wins the Ashes for the first time since 1987.

MINI CAR SERVICE

PRESS
THE
BELL

London Today

Best-selling novelist Michael Marshall reflects on
a strange year in the capital.

I'll tell you when I felt most like a Londoner. It was a week to the day after the 7 July bombings, and purely by coincidence I found myself down in Kentish Town tube station 15 minutes before the commemorative silence for those who'd died. There was, unsurprisingly, somewhat of an atmosphere. People stood on the platform as they would on any other day, as individuals or in motley clumps, waiting for the next southbound Northern Line train. There was an unusual openness in the way they regarded one another, however, and I suspect much of this came from us all going through an identical thought process: "Say these lunatics wanted to do that thing again. Where might they do it? And when might make a good day, a good time?" It would be right here and now.

You might expect this to have created something of a froideur, a pall of suspicion and fear. In fact it was exactly the opposite. To be fair, I look nothing like an Islamic extremist,

but I felt welcomed and validated by the gaze of my fellow city-dwellers in a way I'd never experienced before. Londoners looked each other up and down, determined that we looked OK. Instead of being merely another extra in the endless parade of background colour, on that day – and for the week before, and several weeks afterwards – being a Londoner was a positive quality. It was being part of something that suddenly remembered it was important.

The train eventually arrived. Another series of glances around the carriage followed, as the newcomers ran the same check on those already in position. The train travelled just one stop, and then it was time.

During the period of commemoration the train was stationary at Camden tube station, the doors open. All announcements ceased. An Italian woman sitting opposite continued chattering, evidently unaware of what was going on, and was firmly shushed.

Then there was a silence. It felt long.

Then the doors shut, and the train started to move into the next portion of tunnel, onwards into the heart of the city, weaving through dirt and old foundations and dust. People breathed out, started talking again, turned back to their books. By the time we re-emerged into the light at Tottenham Court Road the next chapter in London's story had begun. The noise, the smell of cabs and buses, the milling people, all said the same thing: That's that, then. Life goes on.

London basically took the bombings and shrugged, and as a result feels more grounded than in a very long time. It might have been different if the second attack had gone off properly, but our response still made us proud, in a vague way: and I say this as someone who has sneered cynically at talk of Blitz spirit. Nobody's perfect, and if Hurricane Katrina had hit London it would have proved we're no angels either.

'London interacts with a wider spread of nationalities than the Director General of the UN.'

But when they first saw the T-shirts with the words 'Not Afraid', everyone had to smile. It crystallised everything we'd felt in the days since the bombings – and which now seems to have revitalised London's sense of itself. A simple, bloody-minded determination that the river like flow of London's existence not be deflected from its course. An hour after the bombs went off, I had my hair cut. This had nothing to do with bravery and everything to do with pragmatism. I had an appointment. I thought I might as well keep it. The guy cutting my hair evidently felt the same. It was a terrible haircut, but then it always is. While it happened I watched the world through the shop window. People came and went, doing the usual stuff, keeping business as usual. The following night I spent the evening with friends in the Junction Tavern in Tufnell Park. The pub was full. People ate, drank, had a good time. There was no studied sombreness. Nobody was undergoing post-traumatic therapy or carving ice sculptures of members of the emergency services – grateful for their good offices though we all are. There was compassion for the victims and their families, and anger on their behalf, but everyone was just doing what they always did. The old song of London was being sung anew in every clatter of cutlery, in the sound of each glass being put back on the table: That's that, then. Life goes on.

In *London Fields* Martin Amis says: 'London is a pub.' It's a great line (obviously: he's Martin Amis) but it was written in 1989 and the pubs have changed since then – to the point where finding an old-school boozer can be a bit of an expedition. Anyway, I believe London's not a place but a person; not the bar itself but the person standing at it, unconsciously rapping a pound coin on the counter as he or she waits fairly patiently to get served. And today? Well… London still drinks a little more than you'd expect, knocking back the lagers and dry whites and vodka tonics any night of the week with a brio that visitors may find mildly disconcerting. London tried Atkins for a while but lost interest a little ahead of the rest of the world. It's got into the whole organic thing now, and would prefer its foodstuffs not to have been too badly duffed up throughout their lives. On the other hand, a kebab's a kebab. London's still smoking too, for the moment – Marlboro Lights, mainly – sort-of trying to give up, but making the most of it before Ken Livingstone and his familiars ban it from public places for the good of people we'd prefer not to share our public places with anyhow. London thinks Dublin is a wuss for bending over and taking it from the health Nazis. London thinks non-smokers should have their own cruelty-free pubs and leave everyone else the hell alone. London still kind of misses the old-fashioned pub vibe and those wooden bits above the bar that people used to pull glasses down from, but it's getting used to them being done out in mushroom and taupe and leather mirror frames – and happily admits the Pad Thai and slow-roast pork belly and little dishes of garlic-studded olives are a step up from pork scratchings and chicken in a basket.

London adapts, after all: it always has. Five years ago it could take or leave coffee, but now it's been swamped with Starbucks and Costa and Nero it has taken to the stuff with a will. London is a place that will take a gander at the new and weird and say 'Yeah, okay, we'll try some of that – with chips.' London can't really understand the flap the rest of the country gets into over asylum seekers: it's always thrown everyone together and seen what happens. Yes, there have been race riots in the past, and the city's Metropolitan Police has been accused of institutional racism, but in the course of an average day – between work, pub, corner store, bus, mini-mart – London interacts with a wider spread of nationalities than the Director General of the UN. You'd have to come from a funny old part of the world to look out of place on the Holloway Road, and you can always tell what bit of the planet is having an internecine rumble without even following the news: the destitute come over and start driving minicabs

The in and out club

Sport, nightlife and anti-social behaviour – the fun things in life. But what's hot, and what's not, at the moment?

The Olympics

Although overshadowed to a degree by the events of 7/7, London's successful bid will bring the Games back to the UK for the first time since 1948 – transforming the social, architectural and sporting landscape of the capital. Now all we need is a glittering collection of gold medals...

Cricket

The scale of England's cricket craze has perhaps been overemphasised, but the nation celebrated its Ashes success to full effect, with tens of thousands of people lining the streets to welcome the winners. Rarely have we had a team of such talent.

Cycling

Bike sales reportedly surged by a third following the 7/7 bombings, suggesting the Mayor's Transport Strategy has, although through unfortunate circumstance, gained an audience. That said, stats show that fewer than two per cent of journeys in London are currently made by bike.

Drinking

In summer 2005 many premises belatedly began applying to have their opening hours extended beyond 11pm (from 24 November 2005). While many people are glad that Tony Blair has finally updated England's archaic licensing laws, it remains to be seen whether this will reduce instances of binge drinking.

Football

Bookmaker Paddy Power has already paid out on Chelsea winning the Premiership in 2006 – a premature move, perhaps, and one that only goes to boost claims that the Premiership is boring, with saturated television coverage, rising prices and declining crowds.

Smoking

2005 became a bad year for smokers in the UK as the anti-smoking lobby gained strength; an overwhelming 83 per cent of people said they agreed with a smoking ban in restaurants and cafés. Plans are now in place for a ban in venues serving food, from summer 2007.

Congestion Charge

In September 2005 Ken Livingstone announced that from February 2007 the congestion charge zone is to be extended westwards. While the benefits that the £8 fee has brought to London's traffic are apparent, over 70 per cent of residents and firms are against the move.

ASBOs

The number of Anti-Social Behaviour Orders issued more than doubled in the last year. Bluewater Shopping Centre, just outside London, was so worried about it that it even imposed a dress code on shoppers, banning hooded tops ('hoodies'), saying they intimidated other people.

inaccurately around your part of town. Just as they're starting to get the hang of the local geography they're replaced by the next bunch, who are prepared to work even longer hours for even less pay. It makes getting around a somewhat unpredictable experience, but you hear some extraordinary stories.

And that's what London is today, more than anything else, a collection of extraordinary stories, intermingling and rubbing up against each other, abiding the present and awash with the past. London's been around for a while. It's seen the excellent and the dreadful. It's had triumphs and bad hair days. It's been the centre

of an empire the like of which the planet hasn't seen since, but has been stomped on and invaded by more people than most. The apparently unstoppable progress of English as the world's lingua franca owes more than a little to a richness and depth caused by the absorption of words from each bunch of warriors who came here and called themselves the victors for a while, before becoming assimilated and fighting off the next invasion.

And it's not just the winners, either. London's willingness to provide a home to the dispossessed and badly treated has contributed massively to the muscularity and range of the

Symbols of London, including the much-loved, sorely missed Routemaster buses.

city's cultural landscape: a tradition we should do everything in our power to maintain. The moment a city starts picking and choosing who gets to live in it is the moment it starts to die.

> **'London finds it impossible to understand why buses that *catch fire* are supposed to be an improvement on Routemasters.'**

It's not all roses, naturally. There are things that piss London off, make no mistake. It really does mind paying eight bleeding quid to drive into the centre of its own city, and finds it impossible to understand why generic, could-be-any-city bendy buses that clog the roads and *catch fire* are supposed to be an improvement on insouciant hop-on-hop-off Routemasters, or why we had to lose the conductors who personalised the public transport experience

(though, interestingly, complaints about buses and, in particular, bus drivers have tripled in the last three years). It is getting increasingly narked about being charged head-turning sums to park outside its own house, with the roving packs of meter men, and with roads bristling with speed and bus lane cameras. It feels, every now and then, as if it is being taxed – and taxed heavily – for living where it has to live. It considers itself too old and sorted and battle-scarred to be politicised or used for personal aggrandisement.

But ultimately it wouldn't want to be anywhere else, and so in the end it shrugs, and pays the fine, and gets on with life. Events shock and surprise, and a reaction follows, before the city absorbs the strange new input and moves on to the next distraction. It's always been the way. Today is short, but the future is long.

And life goes on.

Michael Marshall's latest novel, Blood of Angels, *is out now.*

Pillars of strength: how London could look in future.

Architecture

London's a building sight.

How does Sir Norman Foster do it? Not content with being the architect of London's latest icon the Swiss Re tower (aka **the Gherkin**) at 30 St Mary Axe in the City, his practice is also responsible for the new **Wembley Stadium** – whose soaring arch is sure to become another instantly recognisable symbol of the capital (*see p333* **Sporting giant**). Beset by delays and the financial difficulties of owner Multiplex, the eagerly awaited stadium is nonetheless sure to set new standards in sports design.

And that's a subject, following London's shock win of the bid to host the 2012 Olympic Games, that we'll be hearing an awful lot about over the next few years, as the hard work of transforming inhospitable brownfield sites in Stratford's Lea Valley into exemplary Games facilities gathers speed. Architecturally, London's strategy was very strong, with a £2billion buildings proposal including an aquatics centre by star architect Zaha Hadid. No doubt there will be many wrangles and

controversies along the way, but one thing's for sure: the Lower Lea Valley will never be the same again. For so long neglected, it finally has its chance for regeneration. *See also p163* **Eastern promise**.

TOWERING ABOVE

The future of the capital may be out in the east and beyond in the Thames Gateway but, for the moment, there is no shortage of new building activity in the City and especially in Docklands. As ever, this rivalry between old and new financial centres rumbles onwards – and upwards. **Canary Wharf**, now no longer a one-tower skyline, may soon swell even further in size with the addition of two huge towers by Richard Rogers Partnership, which have been given planning permission. The proposed redevelopment of nearby Wood Wharf would add even more momentum to the Isle of Dogs as a business rival to the City.

Back in the City, the **Gherkin** dominates elegantly. But this and the Docklands towers could soon be dwarfed. At 1,020 feet high, the proposed **Bishopsgate** tower designed by American practice KPF is the daddy of them all, just outstripping the **Shard**, a pointed tower at London Bridge proposed by Renzo Piano. However, a host of shorter (but still lofty) towers, all taller than the Gherkin, are more likely to win planning permission. These include another two towers at Bishopsgate, two in the Square Mile and a tower of flats down in Vauxhall, all over 600 feet. Undoubtedly, many of these won't get built, but there seems little doubt that the trend for ultra-high rise buildings seems here to stay.

High-rises don't have the monopoly on long-running planning sagas, though. There are some key sites in London that lurch from one proposed scheme to another with plenty of dithering and dispute but little hope of anything actually happening. **Battersea Power Station** is a prime example: it's nearly two decades now since Margaret Thatcher famously visited the 36-acre site and promoted John Broome's ill-fated scheme to turn it into a theme park. Current owner Victor Hwang's latest scheme is certainly exciting – a £1.5-billion redevelopment incorporating offices, hotels, art centres, apartments and showrooms led by leading architects and engineers Arup with star design contributors including Ron Arad, Nicholas Grimshaw and UN Studio. But as ever with this site, don't hold your breath.

On the South Bank there has also been some progress on the disputed transformation of **Jubilee Gardens** into a world-class park, with the appointment of a design team, West 8. But even before this materialises, there's plenty to enjoy on a riverside walk on the south side, from the **London Eye** past the revitalised **Royal Festival Hall** and splendid new **Hungerford Bridge**, along past the **Tate Modern** and its **Millennium Bridge** and past the curvy **GLA Building** to **Tower Bridge**. Away from the river, Southwark is seeing great change as well. The Tate Modern halo effect is continuing, with new offices springing up between Waterloo and London Bridge. There's also the prospect of a first UK building by Zaha Hadid, who is designing new premises for the Architecture Foundation on Southwark Street (*see p33* **Visionary positions**).

We can also look forward to a debut UK building from Foreign Office Architects, the glamorous London-based practice responsible for the amazing Yokohama Ferry Terminal in Japan. FOA is designing the new **Music Box** for the BBC at White City, which promises to be stunning when it finally goes ahead. However, the project, originally planned for completion by the end of 2006, is now on hold while the Corporation restructures. The aim is to house

concert, rehearsal and production space in the building, which is designed to broadcast music and visual works through the animated surface of the structure's external skin.

Importantly (and thankfully), not all of London's new architecture is of the mega-scheme variety. It's not just the buildings but the bits in between that count, as shown by the huge popularity of **Trafalgar Square**'s partial pedestrianisation a few years back. The GLA is proposing 100 new or revamped public spaces by 2009 across the capital, which do their bit for improving the urban landscape on a day-to-day basis, whether it's a revamped central square in Brixton or a new park alongside the GLA itself.

These little gems will eventually play a part in changing the character of this elderly city. Which is typical. Unlike many major cities, London has never been planned. It is a hotchpotch, a gradual accumulation of towns and villages, adapted, renewed and disfigured by the changing needs of its populace.

BURN, BABY, BURN

Any number of events have left their imprint on the buildings of the city, but the Great Fire of 1666 is a useful marker: it signals the end of medieval London and the start of the city we know today. The fire destroyed five-sixths of the city, burning 13,200 houses and 89 churches, and is commemorated by Sir Christopher Wren's 202-foot (62-metre) Monument. Much of what can now be seen is a testament to the talents of this man, the architect of the great remodelling, and his successors.

London was a densely populated place built of wood, where fire control was primitive. It was only after the three-day inferno that the authorities felt they could insist on a few basic building regulations. Brick and stone became the construction materials of choice, and key streets were widened to act as firebreaks.

In spite of grand proposals from architects hoping to reconfigure it along classical lines, London reshaped itself around its historic street pattern, with buildings that had survived the Fire standing as monuments to earlier ages. One of these was the 13th-century **St Ethelburga-the-Virgin** (68-70 Bishopsgate, The City, EC2), noteworthy as the city's smallest chapel. Sadly, the IRA destroyed two-thirds of this building in a 1993 bomb attack. The church has now been reconstructed as a peace and reconciliation centre.

The Norman **Tower of London**, begun soon after William's 1066 conquest and extended over the next 300 years, remains the country's most perfect example of a medieval fortress. The Navy cheated the advancing

Visionary positions

At last London has a place where visitors can go to discover more about the capital's new architecture. The **New London Architecture** (NLA; *pictured*) permanent exhibition opened in July 2005 with the aim of providing an overview of the key developments in London for the general visitor and design professional alike. The centre's impressive centrepiece is a 12-metre-long scale model of London, stretching from Battersea

Power Station in the south up to King's Cross and out to Docklands and Stratford in the east. It's a fascinating bird's-eye view of what the capital looks like now, and what it might soon become – existing buildings are in grey Perspex while new proposals (with planning permission but not yet built) are in white. Currently there are more than 150 unbuilt schemes on the model, including spectacular 1,000-foot proposals for the City and London Bridge. As jaw-dropping as these are, they represent just a fraction of the £100 billion worth of redevelopment projected for London over the next couple of decades. Especially interesting is the section of the model with the proposed Olympics 2012 facilities, which the bid team used as part of its campaign. Intended to help both Londoners and tourists alike orientate themselves, the NLA offers a great way to get an understanding of how different parts of the capital link up, and how big things are. The model is accompanied by a regularly changing exhibition on a specific aspect of the capital's built environments. Content of these displays is updated every three months and there are plans to make the model interactive.

The NLA will soon be joined by another new architecture centre: the **Architecture Foundation** is hoping to open a Zaha Hadid-designed building with exhibition and café space in 2007 in Bankside. Until June 2006 it has events and exhibitions at its temporary gallery, The Yard, which concentrates on aspirational and experimental architecture and its relationship with other disciplines such as film and fashion. Check the website for other events and venues.

For those interested in London's built environment, a third resource is the **Hackney Building Exploratory**, a hands-on interactive exhibition that understandably has a local bias, with exhibits showing how the area has changed over the past 2,000 years, and how it might look in future. But it's also of general interest to those wanting to learn about housing and construction methods. One of its most popular displays is the model of Cedar Court, a local tower block demolished in 2002; you can even hear model 'residents' discussing life on the 15th floor.

Architecture Foundation

Until June 2006 at The Yard, 49 Old Street, EC1V 9HX, Shoreditch (7253 3334/www. architecturefoundation.org.uk). Phone or check website for location after June 2006. Barbican, Old Street or Farringdon tube/rail. **Open** noon-6pm Tue-Sat. **Admission** free. **Map** p404 P4.

Hackney Building Exploratory

Professional Development Centre, Albion Drive, Hackney, E8 4ET (7275 8555/www. buildingexploratory.org.uk). Liverpool Street tube/rail then 149, 242 bus/Old Street tube/rail then 243 bus. **Open** 1-5.30pm Thur, Fri, occasional Sat. *Tours* phone for details. **Admission** free.

New London Architecture

Building Centre, 26 Store Street, Fitzrovia, WC1E 7BT (7692 4000/ www.newlondonarchitecture.org). Tottenham Court Road or Goodge Street tube. **Open** 9am-6pm Mon-Fri; 10am-4pm Sat. **Admission** free. **Map** p401 K5.

NatWest Media Centre. *See p36.*

flames of the Great Fire by blowing up the surrounding houses before the inferno could get to it. Then there is **Westminster Abbey**, begun in 1245 when the site lay far outside London's walls and completed in 1745 when the church architect Nicholas Hawksmoor added the west towers. Though the abbey is the most French of England's Gothic churches, deriving its geometry, flying buttresses and rose windows from across the Channel, the chapel, added by Henry VII and completed in 1512, is pure Tudor. Centuries later, Washington Irving gushed: 'Stone seems, by the winning labour of the chisel, to have been robbed of its weight and density, suspended aloft, as if by magic.'

The Renaissance came late to Britain, making its London debut with Inigo Jones's 1622 **Banqueting House**. The addition of a sumptuously decorated ceiling by Rubens in 1635 made the building a key piece of London's architecture. The following decade, King Charles I provided the public with an even greater spectacle as he was led from the building and beheaded on a stage outside. Tourists also have Jones to thank for their beloved **Covent Garden** and the **Queen's House** at Greenwich, but these are not his only legacies. By the 1600s Italian architecture was all the rage, so he mastered the art of piazzas, porticos and pilasters, changing British architecture forever. His work not only influenced the careers of succeeding generations of architects, but also introduced a habit of venerating the past that caught on in a big way, and would take 300 years to kick.

PHOENIX FROM THE FLAMES

Nothing cheers a builder like a natural disaster, and one can only guess at the relish with which Christopher Wren and co began rebuilding after the Fire. They brandished classicism like a new broom: the pointed arches of English Gothic were rounded off, Corinthian columns made an appearance and church spires became as multi-layered and complex as a baroque wedding cake. (Indeed, the spire of Wren's **St Bride**, Fleet Street, is said to have inspired the now-traditional form of the wedding cake.)

Wren blazed the trail with daring plans for **St Paul's Cathedral**, spending an enormous £500 on the oak model of his proposal. But the scheme, incorporating a Catholic dome rather than Protestant steeple, was too Roman for the reformist establishment and the design was rejected. Wren quickly produced a redesign and gained planning permission by incorporating the much-loved spire, only to set about a series of mischievous U-turns to give us the building – domed and heavily suggestive of an ancient temple – that has survived to this day.

Wren's architectural baton was picked up by Nicholas Hawksmoor and James Gibbs, who benefited from a 1711 decree that 50 extra churches should be built. Gibbs became busy in and around Trafalgar Square, building the steepled Roman temple of **St Martin-in-the-Fields**, the baroque **St Mary-le-Strand** (Strand, Covent Garden, WC2) and the tower of **St Clement Danes**. A £34 million programme will see St Martin-in-the-Fields restored to its original state by 2007, with upgraded grounds.

All in all, Gibbs's work was well received, but the more prolific and experimental Hawksmoor had a rougher ride. His imposing **St Anne** (Commercial Road, Limehouse, E14) proved so costly that the parish couldn't afford a vicar, and **St George** in Bloomsbury cost three times its £10,000 budget and took 15 years to build. St George – dismissed in 1876 as the 'most pretentious and ugliest edifice in the metropolis' – aims to evoke the spirit of the ancients. Rather than a spire, there is a pyramid topped by a statue of George I decked out in a toga, while the interior boasts all the Corinthian columns, round arches and gilding you'd expect from a man steeped in antiquity. Many of these features are repeated in Hawksmoor's rocket-like **Christ Church, Spitalfields**.

THE ADAM FAMILY VALUES

One of a large family of Scottish architects, Robert Adam found himself at the forefront of a movement that came to see Italian baroque as a corruption of the real thing. Architectural exuberance was eventually dropped in favour of a simpler interpretation of the ancient forms.

The best surviving work of Adam and his brothers James, John and William can be found in London's great suburban houses **Osterley Park**, **Syon House** and **Kenwood House**, but the project for which they are most famous no longer stands. In 1768 they embarked on the cripplingly expensive **Adelphi** housing estate off the Strand. Most of the complex was pulled down in the 1930s and replaced by an office block. Part of the original development survives in what is now the **Royal Society of Arts** (8 John Adam Street, Covent Garden, WC2).

Just as the first residents were moving into the Adelphi, a young unknown called John Soane was embarking on a tour of his own. In Rome, Soane met the wealthy Bishop of Derry who persuaded the 25-year-old to accompany him to Ireland in order to build a house. The project came to nothing, so Soane dealt with the setback by working hard and marrying into money. His loss was our gain, as he went on to build the **Bank of England** and **Dulwich Picture Gallery**, recently extended. Sadly, the Bank was demolished between the wars, leaving nothing but the perimeter walls and depriving London of Soane's masterpiece. A hint of what these bankers might have enjoyed can be gleaned from a visit to Soane's house, now the quirky **Sir John Soane Museum**, a collection of exquisite architectural experiments with mirrors, coloured glass and folding walls.

A near-contemporary of Soane's, John Nash was arguably a less talented architect, but his contributions to the fabric of London have proved comparable to those of Wren. Among his buildings are **Buckingham Palace**, the **Haymarket Theatre** (Haymarket, St James's, W1) and **Regent Street** (Mayfair/Soho, W1). The latter began as a proposal to link the West End to the planned park further north, as well as a device to separate the toffs of Mayfair from Soho riff-raff or, in Nash's words, a 'complete separation between the Streets occupied by the Nobility and Gentry, and the narrow Streets and meaner houses occupied by mechanics and the trading part of the community'.

'19th-century architecture would today be condemned as the Disneyfication of history.'

INVASION OF THE GOTHS

By the 1830s the classical form had been established for 200 years, and a handful of upstarts began pressing for change. In 1834 the **Houses of Parliament** burned down, leading to the construction of Sir Charles Barry's Gothic masterpiece. This was the beginning of the Gothic Revival, a move by the new romantics to replace what they considered to be foreign and pagan with a style that was native and Christian.

Barry sought out a designer whose name alone makes him worthy of mention: Augustus Welby Northmore Pugin. Pugin created a Victorian fantasy that, while a fine example of the perpendicular form, shows how the Middle Ages had become distorted in the minds of 19th-century architects. The riot of turrets, towers and winding staircases would today be condemned as the Disneyfication of history.

Architects would often decide that buildings weren't Gothic enough; as with the 15th-century **Guildhall**, which gained its corner turrets and central spire only in 1862. Bombed by the Luftwaffe, the Guildhall was rebuilt largely as the Victorians had left it, apart from the interior statues of Gog and Magog, the protagonists in a legendary battle between ancient Britain and Troy: these two creatures got even uglier.

The argument between classicists and goths erupted in 1857, when the government commissioned Sir George Gilbert Scott, a leading light of the Gothic movement, to design a new HQ for the Foreign Office. Scott's design incensed anti-goth Lord Palmerston, then prime minister, whose diktats prevailed. But Scott exacted his revenge by building an office in which everyone hated working, and by going on to construct Gothic edifices all over town, among them the **Albert Memorial** and **St Pancras Chambers**, the station frontage housing the Midland Grand Hotel.

St Pancras was completed in 1873, after the Midland Railway commissioned Scott to build a London terminus that would dwarf that of its rivals next door at King's Cross. Using the project as an opportunity to show his mastery of the Gothic form, Scott built an asymmetrical castle that obliterated views of the train shed behind, itself an engineering marvel completed earlier by William Barlow. This 'incongruous medievalism' did not go unnoticed by critics; one was prompted to comment, sniffily: 'Their porters might be dressed as javelin men, their guards as beefeaters.'

Still, the Gothic style was to dominate until the 20th century, leaving London littered with charming and imposing buildings such as the **Royal Courts of Justice**, the **Natural History Museum**, **Liberty** and **Tower Bridge**. World War I and the coming of modernism led to a spirit of tentative renewal. **Freemason's Hall** (Great Queen Street, Covent Garden, WC2) and the BBC's **Broadcasting House** (Portland Place, Marylebone, W1) are good examples of the pared-down style of the '20s and '30s. The latter is currently being extended and modernised by MacCormac Jamieson Prichard, with work expected to be completed in 2010.

CONCRETE ISLAND
Perhaps the finest example of between-the-wars modernism can be found at **London Zoo**. Built by Russian émigré Bertold Lubetkin and the Tecton group, the spiral ramps of the Penguin Pool (sadly no longer used by penguins) were a showcase for the possibilities of concrete. Also put to good use on the Underground, it enabled the quick, cheap building of large, cavernous spaces with sleek lines and curves. The Piccadilly Line was a particular beneficiary: its 1930s expansion yielded the likes of Charles Holden's **Arnos Grove** station, the first of many circular station buildings and the model for **Canada Water** station on the Jubilee Line.

'Refurbishment work has been restoring what little grandeur the builders managed to impart.'

There was nothing quick or cheap about the art deco **Daily Express** building (Fleet Street, The City, EC4). A black glass and chrome structure built in 1931, it is an early example of 'curtain wall' construction where the façade is literally hung on to an internal frame. The building has been recently refurbished, but the deco detailing of the original building – crazy flooring, snake handrails and funky lighting –

remains intact. Public access is not guaranteed, but it's worth sticking your head around the door of what the *Architects' Journal* has called a 'defining monument of 1930s London'.

TOWER BLOCK-HEADS
World War II left large areas of London ruined, providing another opportunity for builders to cash in. Lamentably, the city was little improved by the rebuild, and, in many cases, was worse off. The destruction left the capital with a dire housing shortage, so architects were given a chance to demonstrate the speed and efficiency with which they could house large numbers of families in tower blocks.

There were post-war successes, however, including the **Royal Festival Hall** on the South Bank. The sole survivor of the 1951 Festival of Britain, the RFH was built to celebrate the war's end and the centenary of the Great Exhibition. It can be a crowded and awkward space, but refurbishment work has been restoring what little grandeur the builders of post-war Britain managed to impart. The RFH is now a much-loved piece of London's fabric – unlike the neighbouring **Hayward Gallery** and **Queen Elizabeth Hall**, exemplars of the 1960s vogue for brutalist experimentation.

But brutalism couldn't last forever. The '70s and '80s offered up a pair of architectural replacements: post-modernism and high-tech. The former is represented by Cesar Pelli's **Canary Wharf** tower (Isle of Dogs, E14), an oversized obelisk that has become the archetypal expression of 1980s architecture and holds an ambiguous place in the city's affections. Richard Rogers's **Lloyd's Building** (Lime Street, The City, EC3) is London's best-known example of high-tech, in which commercial and industrial aesthetics cleverly combine to produce what is arguably one of the most significant British buildings since the war. Mocked upon completion in 1986, the building still manages to outclass newer projects, a fact not lost on Channel 4 when it commissioned Rogers to design its HQ in Horseferry Road, SW1, in the early 1990s.

Equally groundbreaking is Future Systems' **NatWest Media Centre** at Lord's Cricket Ground (St John's Wood Road, St John's Wood, NW8). Built from aluminium in a boatyard and perched high above the pitch, it's one of London's most daring constructions to date, especially given its traditional, old world setting. And Will Alsop's multicoloured **Peckham Library** (171 Peckham Hill Street, Peckham, SE15) redefined community architecture so comprehensively that it walked away with the £20,000 Stirling Prize in 2000.

Will Alsop's new medical school, part of **Queen Mary, University of London**.

OUTSIDE-IN

With the heritage lobby still strong, much new architecture is to found cunningly inserted into old buildings. The **National Portrait Gallery**, the **Royal Opera House** and, in particular, Herzog & de Meuron's fabulous transformation of a power station on Bankside into **Tate Modern** are good examples of architects adding modern signatures to old buildings, while the **British Museum**, the **National Maritime Museum** and the **Wallace Collection** have all gone one better. With the help of large lottery grants, these last three added to their facilities by invading external courtyards. Foster's exercise in complexity at the British Museum, where the £100 million Great Court created the most spectacular and largest covered square in Europe, is without doubt the most impressive – every one of its 3,300 triangular glass panels is unique.

The **National Gallery** is next in line for this treatment, with Dixon Jones, the architects responsible for redeveloping the National Portrait Gallery and the Royal Opera House, slotting new galleries and public spaces into neglected courtyards. Around the corner is the **Coliseum**, home of the English National Opera (St Martin's Lane, Covent Garden, WC2), which finally completed its long-awaited £40million revamp in 2004.

Some of the most exciting architecture is to be found underground – for example in the Jubilee Line Extension stations such as **Canary Wharf station**. Hop on to the DLR and head south to see the other great London building by Tate Modern architects Herzog & de Meuron, Deptford's iridescent **Laban** dance centre. The capital also has its first building by the acclaimed Daniel Libeskind, who has designed

a small graduate centre for the **London Metropolitan University** (Holloway Road, Holloway, N7). Interesting, but not a patch on what his Spiral gallery extension for the Victoria & Albert Museum would have been if it had ever gone ahead.

But overseas superstar architects aren't snaffling up all the major commissions. Two of the most exciting new buildings in London are by home-grown talent. Will Alsop, architect of the Peckham Library, has designed a stunning £45-million medical school building for **Queen Mary, University of London** (Mile End Road, E1). It's highly colourful with projected moving images on the outside and on the inside, the lively interior includes focal points such as Spikey and Cloud – two distinctive suspended 'pods' containing meeting rooms and seminar space. Nearby on Whitechapel Road, E1, David Adjaye has designed his second new-build **Idea Store** (www.ideastore.co.uk) to follow on from his acclaimed building in Poplar (Chrisp Street, E14). With its sleek and crisp aesthetic, it's a world away from the traditional Victorian library in design as well as name and function, and should confirm Adjaye as a major player on the architectural scene. Tellingly, both these new landmarks are in the east. As the capital's focus shifts firmly towards the Olympics-inspired regeneration of east London, they are surely just the fore-runners of a huge period of change that will have a lasting impact on the capital's built environment.

> ▶ Where no location is given in the text, buildings are listed elsewhere in this book; for details consult the index.

A-Z Cheap London

In this notoriously pricey city, we show you how to make the pennies go further.

It's official: London is bloody expensive. In a survey conducted by Mercer Human Resource Consulting in 2005, the capital was rated the third most expensive city in the world for living costs (below Tokyo and Osaka, and just ahead of Moscow). But it's not all bad news: follow our alphabetical guide to thriftiness, and you'll be able to enjoy yourself and still have enough money to get home at the end of the day.

A is for...

Accommodation For no-frills visitor rooms, try university halls of residence during holidays. A twin room at **International Students House** (229 Great Portland Street, Marylebone, 7631 8300, www.ish.org.uk; *see also p74*) is £25.50 a night per person, with no age limit; some of its dormitory rooms cost just £12 per person. The **University of London** accommodation website (www.studenthousing. lon.ac.uk) has links to hostels, halls of residence,

and a contact list for students seeking short-stay room hire with other students. An online halls booking service is planned for summer 2006. If only a proper hotel room will do, consider **easyHotel** (14 Lexham Gardens, W8, www.easyhotel.com; *see also p44*), where the rooms are as small as the price (from £20).

B is for...

Buskers Why buy an MP3 player when you can have tunes for free (or for only a small tip, depending on how generous/tight you are)? In total there are 25 Carling-associated licensed busking spots at the following tube stations in central London: Angel, Bank/Monument, Bond Street, Canary Wharf, Charing Cross, Euston, Green Park, King's Cross/St Pancras, Leicester Square, London Bridge, Oxford Circus, Piccadilly Circus, South Kensington, Tottenham Court Road, Victoria, Waterloo and Westminster.

C is for...

Comedy nights For chuckles on the cheap, try the **Comedy Café** in Shoreditch (66-68 Rivington Street, 7739 5706, www.comedycafe. co.uk; *see also p280*), which has free stand-up shows on a Wednesday night. At **Lee Hurst's Back Yard Comedy Club** (231 Cambridge Heath Road, Bethnal Green, 7739 3122, www. leehurst.com; *see also p281*), meanwhile, you have to pay £10-£15 to get in, but on a Thursday you get a curry thrown in for free. Can't say fairer than that.

D is for...

Dogs For a cheap night out that could end up paying for itself (and more), head to one of the four greyhound tracks around the capital. For an admission fee that's never more than £6, you can enjoy the art deco glories of **Walthamstow** (Chingford Road, 8531 4255, www.wsgreyhound.co.uk), the decent restaurants at **Wimbledon** (Plough Lane, 8946 8000, www.wimbledonstadium.co.uk), the chirpy charms of **Romford** (London Road, 01708 762345, www.trap6.com/romford) or the relaxed atmosphere at **Crayford** (Stadium Way, 01322 557836). Small stakes (we're talking coins rather than tenners) are accepted at most venues. Just one judicious punt could keep you in drinks all evening. For more information, visit www.thedogs.co.uk.

E is for...

Eating London can be a nightmare for dining on a budget, but there are plenty of places where you can chow down for next to nothing. Time Out's *Cheap Eats in London* guide (£6.99) has reviews of over 700 venues, in all types of cuisines. For something quick and cheap, though, you could do worse than **Benjys** (50 & 149 Oxford Street, 7287 1820; other locations around town). Its coffee is arguably better than Starbucks' and costs only 69p for a regular-sized cup, plus it offers a jacket spud with cheese or beans for just £1.79. Now all you need to do is overcome the shame factor... For a taste of history on the cheap, how about a pie and mash shop? A dying breed, they offer, well, a pie and a wodge of mash for less than a fiver. Our favourites include M Manze (87 Tower Bridge Road, 7407 2985) and F Cooke (9 Broadway Market, 7253 6458) in Hackney.

F is for...

Films One of our favourite low-cost cinemas, the Prince Charles (*see p289*), has offers throughout the week to those who fork out the £7.50 annual membership. While this makes the Leicester Square (alright, Leicester Place) people's picture palace a pretty good deal, its Monday Madness (when members are charged a mere £1 and non-members £1.50) crowns it the best-value cinema in town. Check out its wide selection of films on second run, plus (for a few dollars more) sing-a-long-a movies.

G is for...

Galleries (and museums) The capital's major sights, from the Wallace Collection to the Tate Modern to the British Museum, are free (though donations are appreciated at the latter). Even some guided tours, such as the **British Museum**'s 90-minute Eye openers, won't cost you a bean. In addition, there are loads of lesser-known free sights dotted around the capital. Among our favourites are **Hogarth's House** (Hogarth Lane, Great West Road, Chiswick, 8994 6757, www.hounslow.info/ hogarthshouse; *see also p192*); **Orleans House Gallery** (Riverside, Twickenham, Middx TW1 3DJ, 8831 6000, www.richmond.gov.uk/ orleans_house_gallery; *see also p183*); **Museum in Docklands** (No.1 Warehouse, West India Quay, Hertsmere Road, (0870 444 3856, www.museumindocklands.org.uk; *see also p167*; OK, it's a fiver to get in, but you get unlimited entrance for a year).

H is for...

Haircuts Big-name salons offer reductions on model nights, when supervised trainees get to practise techniques on the public. Top choice for colour is the salon of celebs' stylist **Andrew Jose** (1 Charlotte Street, Fitzrovia, 7323 4679, www.andrewjose.com), which offers 50 per cent off, making half a head of highlights an affordable £30. Alternatively, **Mr Topper's** (13A Great Russell Street, Bloomsbury, 7631 3233; other locations throughout town; *see also p256*) gives the boys a mean cut for a ridiculously cheap £6 (or ladies for £10). Proper training academies include **L'Oréal Technical Centre** (255 Hammersmith Road, W6 8AZ, 8762 4200, www.loreal.com; prices from £8 for a cut, or £15 with colour); **Toni & Guy Academy**

(71-75 New Oxford Street, WC1A 1DG, St Giles's, 7836 0606, www.toniandguy.co.uk; colour from £10) and **Vidal Sassoon's Advanced Academy** (19-20 Grosvenor Street, Mayfair, 7491 0030, www.vidalsassoon.co.uk; cuts £11, or £6.50 for students, sometimes with colouring).

I is for...

Internet The eBay revolution is as virulent in London as elsewhere, and thousands prefer to seek out bargains (and make some money) online rather than have to leave the house. **Gumtree** (www.gumtree.com), **MoveThat** (www.movethat.com), **London Lately** (www.londonlately.com) and other web-based community noticeboards can yield great deals on accommodation, and also offer 'swap shop' services. If you do want to head outdoors, Islington Council has installed a 'technology mile' of WiFi along Upper Street, N1, from Angel tube right up to Highbury & Islington, which is free for anyone who can connect.

J is for...

Justice During the week, members of the public can visit the most famous court in the land, the **Old Bailey** (officially known as the Central Criminal Court; Newgate Street & Old Bailey, The City, 7248 3277; *see also p94*). It's pretty unlikely you'll get to see a trial of the magnitude of those of Oscar Wilde (in 1895), the Krays (1969) or Ruth Ellis (1955), the last woman to be hanged in Britain, all of which were held here, but you never know.

K is for...

Kids' stuff Visiting the capital with wee ones in tow needn't cost you an arm and a leg. There are plenty of sights to visit for free (*see p38* **Galleries and museums** *and p41* **Parks**), as well as free or cheap activities such as art classes, activity mornings and play sessions. For plenty more ideas, *see pp272-272* or pick up Time Out's *London for Children* guide (£8.99).

L is for...

Libraries OK, so you have to be a London resident to join one, but if you are you can read to your heart's content for nowt. For a list of centrally located libraries, *see p371.*

M is for...

Music Classical music needn't be an expensive hobby. Lunchtime is a good time for free concerts, often by young artists or students: try **St Martin-in-the-Fields** in Trafalgar Square (*see p134 & p306*), **St Anne & St Agnes** on Gresham Street in the City (*see p307*) or **St James's Piccadilly** (*see p306*). London's greatest unsung secret, however, is the free music available at conservatories and colleges. Quite often the concerts are graced by conductors or soloists of international stature who are acting professors, and experts in their field. The **Royal College of Music**, **Trinity College of Music**, **Royal Academy of Music** and the Barbican's **Guildhall School of Music & Drama** all have several attractions a week open to the public, though you should call ahead to check whether tickets are needed. For more details, *see p307*.

Jazz fans on a budget are also catered for: you will hear high quality jazz for a very reasonable price at one of London's best-established jazz houses, the **606 Club** (90 Lots Road, Chelsea, 7352 5953; *see also p316*). From Monday to Thursday you pay £7 to hear the trumpet's wails bounce off the low basement ceiling. Prices are higher at weekends and booking is always advisable. For a full-on fest, there's the five-week **Ealing Jazz Festival** (Walpole Park, Matlock Lane, 8825 6640, www.ealing. gov.uk/ealingsummer; *see also p316*), which is the largest free jazz event in Europe.

N is for...

Nails Manicures are no longer the preserve of ladies with as much bling as time on their hands – **Nails Inc** does a speedy 'shape and paint' for a tenner (41 South Molton Street, Mayfair, 7499 8333, www.nailsinc.com). Just up the road, **NYNC** (17 South Molton Street, 7409 3332, www.newyorknailcompany.com) has far fewer outposts but is a better bet; you'll pay more for shape and paint (£14 for hands), but staff spend an extra ten minutes on the job.

O is for...

Open-air fun Rejoice for global warming! OK, not really, but do make the most of the sun on the rare occasions it graces us with its presence. London is home to an increasing number of free open-air events, from an annual jamboree in Trafalgar Square, **Summer in the Square** (*see also p271* **Air play**) to the multicultural **Diaspora Music Village Festival** (*see also p308* **The great outdoors**), held in Kew Gardens. The number of clubs with open-air spaces and terraces is growing too, as London takes its tips from Ibiza and Ayia Napa; for our pick of the best, *see p319*.

Keen gardeners, meanwhile, might be interested in the annual **Open Garden Squares Weekend** (http://myweb.tiscali. co.uk/london.gardens/squares/index.html; *see also p267*), which allows a sneaky peak at private gardens, courtyards and roof terraces that are normally off limits to the public. Tickets are just a fiver.

P is for...

Parks When you're crammed with culture, sick of the sights, or your spending is spent, relax and save money in one of London's lovely green spaces. There are parks all over London, of course, from the centrally located **Regent's Park** (*see p116*) and **St James's Park** (*see p118*) to the further-flung expanses of **Richmond Park** (*see p180*) and **Wimbledon Common** (*see p182*); to local gems like **Waterlow Park** in Highgate (*see p154*) and **Victoria Park** in Hackney, **Mile End Park** (for both, *see p162*) and **Dulwich Park** (College Road) in south-east London. If the weather's good, you can enjoy a bit of sunbathing or a picnic with friends, and if you need to work off the calories afterwards, you can have a kickabout. On more blustery days it's not unusual to see flocks of coloured kites flying high above the greener areas, especially on **Primrose Hill** (*see p151*). Lovely stuff.

Q is for...

Quid There used to be a time when you could do a whole week's shopping and still have change from a pound. We exaggerate a tad, perhaps, but what can you get now for a measly quid? Not a lot. But that's all you'll need in your pocket if you visit an imaginatively named pound shop. They're perhaps not the place to go for Christmas presents to impress, but, no-brand washing-up liquid, padded envelopes that come unstuck in seconds and gargantuan bars of obsolete chocolate aside, they're usually worth a browse. Camden High Street is home to a high number of pound shops, for some reason, which sometimes seem to have prices wars – 90p jewellery anyone?

How much?

How London compares with New York, Tokyo, Paris and Sydney.

Bus or subway ticket
London £1.50; New York £1; Tokyo £1.34; Paris £0.96; Sydney £0.99.

Fast food meal
London £4.39; New York £3.24; Tokyo £3.28; Paris £4.06; Sydney £2.65.

Cup of coffee
London £1.79; New York £1.86; Tokyo £2.09; Paris £1.51; Sydney £1.48.

CD
London £12.97; New York £11.23; Tokyo £12.54; Paris £16.16; Sydney £10.27.

Luxury two-bedroom apartment rental (per month)
London £1,700; New York £1,971; Tokyo £2,386; Paris £1,307; Sydney £823.
Statistics from www.finfacts.com

R is for...

Running If you're staying in a hotel, the concierge should be able to recommend a decent local running path (some even have a wee map you can follow, though chances are that if you're reading this you won't be staying in that kind of hotel). Otherwise, **Hyde Park**, **Kensington Gardens** (for both, *see p143*) and **Battersea Park** (*see p179*) all have good jogging trails.

S is for ...

Second-hand shops You can venture out to shop for clothes in London's most stylish areas with your featherweight wallet and no worries – as long as you stick to the charity shops, that is. You can get a lovely new outfit (bargain accessories are a particularly brilliant find) for a fraction of the price for a new garment, and it's all for a good cause as well. The Association of Charity Shops (7422 8620, www.charity shops.org.uk) has details of all outlets; alternatively, you can try individual chains like www.oxfam.org.uk or www.traid.org.uk. Check for outlets in Kensington, Chelsea and Notting

Hill, where cast-offs are of incredibly high standard. Just be prepared to rummage. If you'd prefer your clothes not to be 'previously cherished', the high street is home to several chains offering excellent catwalk copies for a fraction of the price: for ideas, including TK Maxx, Primark, *see p242*.

T is for...

Tickets Buy cut-price theatre tickets from the **tkts** booth on the south side of Leicester Square piazza or at Canary Wharf station (no phone, www.officiallondon theatre.co.uk; *see also p337*). Tickets (limited to two pairs per person) for some shows are half-price, though there's also a £2.50 service charge on each one. Other places worth trying include the **National Theatre** (South Bank, SE1 9PX, 7452 3000, www.nationaltheatre.org.uk; *see also p337*), where you can buy seats for £10 from 10am on the day of performance. Up-to-the-minute offers can also be found on www.whatsonstage.com and www.lastminute.com. For more on film, *see p38*; for comedy, *see p38*; for music, *see p40*.

U is for...

Underground Ensure you don't pay over the odds for your travel on the tube. The Oyster Pre Pay card probably offers the best value, and is now the only way you can buy a weekly travelcard. Using Oyster also ensures you will never pay more than the cost of a daily travelcard (paying with cash at the time of travel will always be more). Aside from Oyster, three-day travelcards are available for £15.40 for unlimited travel in zones 1 and 2, or £37.20 for zones 1-6. For more on fares, *see p361*.

V is for

Views For an eyeful of the city that will cost you precisely zero, set your sights high, namely **Primrose Hill** (*see p151*). If you suffer from vertigo, head instead to one of the bridges on the Thames, in particular Waterloo Bridge (*see p81*), with its picture-postcard views of sights both upstream and downstream. And if that brings out the romantic in you, and you don't mind shelling out a bit, you can't beat the city-sweeping vistas, day or night, from the **London Eye** (£12.50 for a regular adult ticket, but concessionary rates are available; *see also p79*). *See also p77* **The best sights**.

W is for...

Walking There are many benefits to taking Shanks's Pony (ie your own legs) to tramp the streets. First, it's free. Secondly, you're getting some exercise. Thirdly, you notice things you wouldn't normally notice (and we don't just mean litter and dog shit: we're talking places of interest and sales in the shops).

X is for...

XFM Ah, the letter designed to give A-Z compilers problems. Rather than recommend you get a free X-ray on the NHS, or hang about to see the giant tree in Trafalgar Square at Xmas, we're sure you'd prefer to catch XFM's free monthly live sessions, usually held at the Carling Academy Islington (*see p311*). Around 800 tickets every month are given away free to listeners of the capital's best rock radio station. You will need to listen and call in, or go to www.xfm.co.uk to win tickets. Previous acts include Bloc Party, Keane and the Streets. It's a good station too, so even the listening and waiting will be fun.

Y is for...

Yoga Stretch your body without stretching your budget. **Yogahome** (11 Allen Road, Stoke Newington, 7249 2425, wwww.yogahome.com) is one of the cheapest places we've found, with 90-minute classes from just £7. Not quite as cheap, but still a bargain, is **Yoga Junction** in Finsbury Park (Fonthill Road, 7263 3113, www.yogajunction.co.uk), where it's £8.50 per 75-minute session. For other venues, *see p332*.

Z is for...

Zoos London Zoo (*see p116*) costs £14 for an adult, and £10.75 for children up to 15 (it's free for under-3s). Not exactly bargain basement, agreed, but with a new squirrel monkey enclosure and the new African Bird Safari, plus more stuff planned, there's plenty to occupy a whole day. Outside of town, more animal antics can be had at **Chessington World of Adventures** in Surrey (*see p277*); it costs £28 for adults and children over 12, but for each of these a child aged 4-11 goes free. Discounts are also offered for online bookings.

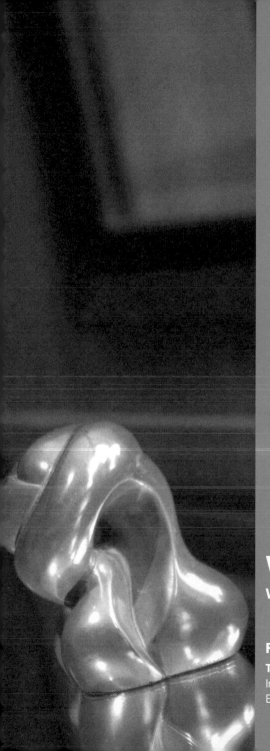

Where to Stay

Where to Stay

Go and sleep around.

Until recently, unless you were prepared to shell out the equivalent of a week's rent, you could be in for a rough night when it came to bedding down in the capital. Visitors complained of cramped quarters, dated decor and service straight out of *Fawlty Towers* – and that was before you even got to the rates. In the late 1990s the scene got a burst of energy with the arrival of a slew of sleek designer hotels – **St Martins Lane**, the **Metropolitan** et al – but they provided no relief to the long-suffering budget brigade.

It took a combination of forward-thinking hoteliers and a slump in tourism to set the wheels of change in motion. Clued-up entrepreneurs, such as the team behind the **Zetter**, spotted the gap in the market for affordably cool accommodation for the young loft-dwelling generation. And after 2003, when occupancy rates dropped to record lows, the luxury hotels started offering special deals, while budget chains and small guesthouses made an effort to smarten up. Following the bomb attacks of July 2005, this trend is set to continue. Many hoteliers reported only a temporary downturn in occupancy rates in the months following the attacks, but the long-term reality is that hotels can't afford to be complacent. The proliferation of discount hotel websites means it's a buyer's market, in all price categories.

Indeed, visitors on the tightest of budgets have never had it so good. As well as dramatic improvements in an increasing number of B&Bs, the big chains have upped their design cred and opened outposts in hotspots such as Covent Garden (**Travelodge**; www.travelodge. co.uk) and Camden (**Holiday Inn**; www. holiday-inn.com). Another newcomer, slated to open in 2006, first at Gatwick and Heathrow airports, then at a central London site, is **Yotel** (www.yotel.co.uk), from the people behind the conveyor belt sushi chain YO!, which crosses the Japanese capsule-hotel concept with a first-class aircraft cabin. Tiny but luxurious rooms with facilities such as flatscreen TVs will cost around £70 a night. Equally minuscule – but far more back-to-basics – are the rooms at **easyHotel**, though the cheapest (£20) rooms seem to get snapped up far in advance. *See also p38.*

At the other end of the scale, meanwhile, the ever-booming luxury market is showing no signs of slowing down: indeed, a total of 4,000 luxury rooms are slated to open in the capital in the next five years. Nick Jones, the hotelier behind Soho House in London and Babington House in Somerset, is opening not two hotels in the capital in the latter half of 2006: a hotel/club/spa/brasserie in Chiswick, followed by a hotel/cinema/brasserie in Shoreditch. For more information, contact Soho House (7734 5188).

For our pick of the city's best hotel bars, *see p226* **Rooms with a brew.**

The best Hotels

For being where the action is
The **Soho Hotel** (*see p59*) and the **Covent Garden Hotel** (*see p61*): need we say more?

For budget boutique style
The **Mayflower Hotel** (*see p73*) and **B&B Belgravia** (*see p63*) are cheap and chic.

For period drama
Hazlitt's (*see p59*) and the **Rookery** (*see p48*) evoke 18th-century London, while the **Gore** (*see p68*) is a tribute to the Victorian age.

For afternoon tea
The **Lanesborough** (*see p66*), **Claridge's** (*see p57*) and **The Dorchester** (*see p57*) all know how to put on an impressive spread.

For shoppers
Myhotel chelsea (*see p68*) and **Claridge's** (*see p57*) are perfectly placed for posh boutiques, while antiques hunters should check in to **Miller's Residence** (*see p71*).

For louche history
If walls could talk at the **Cadogan** (*see p66*) and the **Courthouse Kempinski** (*see p59*), the clamour would be deafening.

For modern British style
The classy update of **Brown's** (*see p55*) is worthy of its impressive pedigree.

For outings *en famille*
The **Swiss House Hotel** (*see p69*) caters to babes in arms, while the **New Linden** has a posh two-level family pad (*see p72*).

B&B Belgravia. *See p63.*

INFORMATION AND BOOKING

Many of London's swankier hotels are found in Mayfair (W1). Bloomsbury (WC1) is good for mid-priced hotels and B&Bs. For cheap hotels, areas to try include Ebury Street near Victoria (SW1), Gower Street in Bloomsbury, Earl's Court (SW5), Bayswater, Paddington (W2) and South Kensington (SW7).

It's always advisable to book ahead, but if you haven't, the obliging staff at **Visit London** (1 Lower Regent Street, Piccadilly Circus, 08701 566366, www.visitlondon.com; *see also p377*) will look for a place within your selected area and price range for free. You can also check availability and reserve rooms either on its website or by going in person to its office on Lower Regent Street in Piccadilly.

PRICES AND CLASSIFICATION

We don't list official star ratings, which tend to reflect facilities rather than quality; instead, we've classified hotels within each area heading according to the price of a double room per night, beginning with the most expensive.

Many high-end hotels sneakily quote room prices exclusive of VAT. Always check. We've included this 17.5 per cent tax in rates listed here; however, room rates change frequently, so do call and verify rates before you book. With the exception of most B&Bs, breakfast isn't included.

Hotels are constantly offering special deals, particularly for weekends; check websites or ask for a special rate when booking. Also check discount hotel websites – such as www.alpharooms.com or www.london-discount-hotel.com – for prices that can fall well below the rack rates listed here.

FACILITIES AND ACCESSIBILITY

In this chapter, we have listed the main services offered by each hotel; concierges can often arrange far more than are included here, including theatre tickets and meal reservations. We have also tried to note which hotels offer rooms adapted for disabled customers, but it's always best to ring ahead to confirm the precise facilities. **Holiday Care** (0845 124 9971, www.holidaycare.org.uk) has details of wheelchair accessible places. We've also stated which hotels offer parking facilities, but it's worth enquiring about the actual cost before pitching up in your car: rates can be pricey (though occasionally parking is free), and spaces sometimes limited.

---

❶ Green numbers given in this chapter correspond to the location of each hotel as marked on the street maps. *See pp396-409.*

The South Bank & Bankside

Moderate

Southwark Rose

43-47 Southwark Bridge Road, SE1 9HH (7015 1480/www.southwarkrosehotel.co.uk). London Bridge tube/rail. **Rates** £120 double; £165-£185 suite. **Credit** AmEx, MC, V. **Map** p406 P8 ❶
It may sound like a dodgy faux-Tudor guesthouse, but the Southwark Rose (handily placed for Tate Modern, Borough Market and Shakespeare's Globe) is the antithesis: a slick, purpose-built, budget-conscious property with the elements that have become shorthand for 'modern luxury hotel'. There's a minimalist lobby with leather armchairs and arty photos, the rooms are dressed in regulation sleek, dark wood and crisp white linen, as well as the obligatory mosaic-tiled bathrooms. Good-value suites are equipped with kitchenettes and an extra sofabed. It doesn't have a gym, but you can use the one at Novotel next door. There's even an exclusive red and black guests' bar that seems to have taken style cues from the Met Bar.
Bar. Disabled-adapted rooms. No-smoking rooms. Internet (high speed). Parking. Restaurant. TV (cable/satellite; pay movies).

Cheap

Mad Hatter

3-7 Stamford Street, SE1 9NY (7401 9222/www.fullershotels.com). Southwark tube/Waterloo tube/rail. **Rates** £85-£115 double. **Credit** AmEx, DC, MC, V. **Map** p406 N8 ❷
Owned by the Fuller's pub chain, the Mad Hatter has recently ditched the 'Ye Olde England' pastiche in its non-smoking rooms for contemporary colour schemes and modern wall-mounted headboards. They don't exactly ooze character, but they're large and well kept, and the attached Fuller's pub offers a decent selection of English ales. Tate Modern and the South Bank theatres are nearby.
Bar. Concierge. Disabled-adapted rooms. Internet (dataport). No-smoking rooms. Restaurant. TV.

Premier Travel Inn Metro London County Hall

County Hall, Belvedere Road, SE1 7PB (0870 238 3300/www.travelinn.co.uk). Waterloo tube/rail. **Rates** £84.95-£86.95 double. **Credit** AmEx, DC, MC, V. **Map** p403 M9 ❸
A room in a landmark building on the Thames, next to the London Eye, for less than £90? County Hall's former tenants, the Greater London Council, have been gone for over two decades, but the prices at this outpost of the Premier Travel Inn chain are more in line with the 1980s. Just don't expect the opulence of the exterior to carry on inside. Purple walls and modern prints in the lobby don't dispel the airport check-in feel, and the rooms, while modern and clean, have an institutional feel. Don't expect any Thames views

either, as they've all been snaffled by the Marriott that shares the vast building. There's an attempt at urban hip in the bar, useful for a swift nightcap as it's open until 1am.

Bar. Disabled-adapted rooms. Internet (dataport). No-smoking rooms. Restaurant. TV.
Other locations: throughout the city.

The City

Deluxe

Great Eastern Hotel
40 Liverpool Street, EC2M 7QN (7618 5000/www. great-eastern-hotel.co.uk). Liverpool Street tube/rail. **Rates** £265 single; £335-£394 double; £470-£675 suite. **Credit** AmEx, DC, MC, V. **Map** p407 R6 ④

Once a faded railway hotel, the Great Eastern was given a £70m overhaul by Sir Terence Conran in 2000. It's now a mammoth urban style mecca, though with a design sympathetic to the glorious Victorian building. The lobby is a showcase for modern art and there are regular exhibitions and cultural events (*see p67* **Inns and arts**). The six-storey atrium is a showstopper, while the gym occupies a mysterious room in the style of an Egyptian temple. Bedrooms wear the regulation style mag uniform: Eames chairs, chocolate shagpile rugs and white Frette linens. And, as you would expect from a Conran enterprise, you'll never go hungry or thirsty here. The hotel has seven restaurants and bars, including Terminus brasserie, Miyabi, the mandatory Japanese joint, the atmospheric George, a faux-Elizabethan pub, and the lovely modern European Aurora, with its elegant stained-glass dome and fantastic bar, complete with jazz pianists.
Bars (4). Business centre. Concierge. Disabled-adapted rooms. Gym. Internet (dataport, high-speed). No-smoking floors. Parking. Restaurants (5). Room service. TV (pay movies/music/DVD).

Expensive

Saint Gregory
100 Shoreditch High Street, E1 6JQ (7613 9800/ www.saintgregoryhotel.com). Shoreditch tube/Old Street or Liverpool Street tube/rail. **Rates** £168-£195 double. **Credit** AmEx, MC, V. **Map** p405 R4 ⑤

The Saint Gregory has got all the ingredients to be fashionable: trendy Shoreditch location, modern building, bold interior design. Yet for all that, it feels a bit like a Holiday Inn masquerading as a style hotel. But that's no bad thing. The rates, particularly special weekend deals, are reasonable. The staff are chipper. And the bedrooms – decorated in a game attempt at retro chic, right down to the brown and orange colour schemes – are spacious and comfortable with swanky Villeroy & Boch bathrooms. The airy Globe Restaurant on the seventh floor boasts mesmerising views of the City, while the ground-floor red-and-cream Saint's Bar oozes 1970s-style sex appeal.

Bars (2). Concierge. Disabled-adapted rooms. Gym. Internet (web TV). No-smoking rooms/floors. Parking. Restaurant. Room service. TV (pay movies/music).

Threadneedles
5 Threadneedle Street, EC2R 8AY (7657 8080/ www.theetoncollection.com). Bank tube/DLR. **Rates** £183-£288 double; £347-£476 suite. **Credit** AmEx, MC, V. **Map** p407 Q6 ⑥

Occupying the former HQ of the Midland Bank, Threadneedles successfully integrates modern design with a monumental space. In the lobby, modern walnut panels blend seamlessly with ornamental pillars, and contemporary leather chairs and suede pouffes are arranged below an exquisite stained-glass ceiling dome. Because of the constraints of developing a listed building, rooms aren't uniform shapes and most have original 19th-century windows. The decor is soothingly neutral, with Korres natural toiletries in the serene limestone bathrooms. Little stress-busting comforts reflect its business-friendly location: fleecy throws, a scented candle lit at turndown, a 'movie treats' menu of popcorn, ice-cream and Coke (albeit at a price that may raise your blood pressure), and there are weekend deals to tempt non-execs. The lively Bonds restaurant serves pan-European dishes. **Photo** *p49.*
Bar. Concierge. Disabled adapted rooms. No-smoking rooms. Internet (wireless). Restaurants. Room service. TV (satellite/music/DVD).

Holborn & Clerkenwell

Expensive

Rookery
12 Peter's Lane, Cowcross Street, EC1M 6DS (7336 0931/www.rookeryhotel.com). Farringdon tube/rail. **Rates** £235 single; £253 double; £465 suite. **Credit** AmEx, DC, MC, V. **Map** p404 O5 ⑦

Hidden down an alleyway in Clerkenwell, the Rookery is straight out of a Dickens novel. Part of the same group that owns Hazlitt's (*see p59*) and the Gore (*see p68*), the hotel has been converted from a row of 18th-century buildings. In keeping with the history, it's crammed full of glorious antiques: Gothic oak beds, plaster busts and clawfoot bathtubs. But it's equipped with modern creature comforts too: Egyptian cotton sheets and plush towels draped over heated towel racks; broadband internet and LCD TVs are imminent. Judging from the guest book, everyone who stays here falls in love with the place, from business travellers to tourists to honeymooners (the hotel also recently applied for a licence to hold civil ceremonies). Rooms vary in size, and all are characterful, though the star attraction is definitely the Rook's Nest, a huge split-level suite with views over the surrounding area, plus a working Edwardian bathing machine.
Bar. Concierge. Disabled-adapted rooms. Internet (dataport). No-smoking rooms/floors. Room service. TV.

Bank on brilliant attention to detail at **Threadneedles**. *See p48.*

Moderate

Malmaison

*Charterhouse Square, EC1M 6AH (7012 3700/
www.malmaison.com). Farringdon tube/rail.*
Rates £99-£217 double; £165-£250 superior
double. **Credit** AmEx, DC, MC, V. **Map** p404 O5 ❽
When the first Malmaison opened in Edinburgh
more than a decade ago, it seemed to be performing
a slick sleight of hand. Despite providing the kind
of facilities that the market craved – handsome,
thoughtfully specced rooms, non-institutional public areas and restaurants that weren't just for guests
who didn't have the initiative to go out – the 'Mal'
nevertheless charged rates well below anything
comparable in style and services. The London outpost brought the formula to Clerkenwell a couple of
years ago. In general, it works well: the decor in the
rooms is enjoyable and comfortable (appealing
colour schemes, tactile modern fabrics, lovely photos of London), and instead of ego-massaging luxuries to bump up the rates, you get stuff you need:
24-hour room service, CD players, free broadband
access, and bottles of French wine. But as with any
chain, you are aware it is a formula.
*Bar. Disabled-adapted rooms. Gym. Internet (free
broadband). No-smoking floors. Restaurant. Room
service. TV.*

Zetter Restaurant & Rooms

*86-88 Clerkenwell Road, EC1M 5RJ (7324 4444/
www.thezetter.com). Farringdon tube/rail.* **Rates**
£159-£230 double; £265-£329 suites. **Credit** AmEx,
MC, V. **Map** p404 O4 ❾
True to its trendy Clerkenwell location, the Zetter is
a bone fide loft hotel in a converted warehouse, with
a soaring atrium, exposed brick and funky 1970s
furniture. There's a refreshing lack of attitude – the
place is comfortable and fun. Instead of minibars,
vending machines in the corridors dispense everything from champagne to disposable cameras.
Rooms are bathed in natural light from the huge
industrial windows and cosied up with such homely comforts as hot-water bottles and old Penguin
books; the walk-in Raindance showers are stocked
with Elemis products. The rooftop suites have fantastic wooden decks (and, of course, the best views
in the house). Prices beat the West End hands down,
and while the buzzing Italian restaurant has
received mixed reviews, the area's main attraction
is its wealth of eating and drinking spots.
*Bar. Concierge. Disabled-adapted rooms. Internet
(dataport, high-speed, web TV, wireless). No-smoking
rooms/floors. Restaurant. Room service. TV (pay
movies/music/DVD).*

Bloomsbury & Fitzrovia

Deluxe

Sanderson

*50 Berners Street, W1T 3NG (7300 1400/
www.morganshotelgroup.com). Oxford Circus
tube.* **Rates** £310-£500 double; £658 loft studio.
Credit AmEx, DC, MC, V. **Map** p408 V1 ❿
Design hotels may be two a penny in London these
days, but this five-year-old Schrager and Starck creation is still a knock-out, partly perhaps because the
Sanderson – unusually – combines modern minimalism with a playful, theatrical style. The lobby
resembles a surreal film set, with its sheer flowing

Sanderson.

curtains, Salvador Dali red-lip sofa and an array of curiously shaped chairs. The ultra-hip drama continues upstairs in the bedrooms, with silver-leaf sleigh beds piled with pillows; super-modern, glass bathrooms (the toilet area is frosted, you will be relieved to hear) with toiletries from the hotel's sumptuous Agua spa; and dreamy, electronically operated white curtains. The pricey Long Bar and Spoon+ restaurant fill nightly with fashionable types; also downstairs is the quieter Purple Bar, open to guests only. The Sanderson's room prices are admittedly out of most people's league, but this is a slick, sexy operation in a great location – a rare combination. Photo p51.

Bars (2). Business services. Concierge. Disabled-adapted rooms. Gym. Internet (dataport, wireless). No-smoking rooms/floors. Restaurant. Room service. Spa. TV (DVD).

Expensive

Charlotte Street Hotel

15-17 Charlotte Street, W1T 1RJ (7806 2000/ www.firmdale.com). Goodge Street, Oxford Circus, Tottenham Court Road or Warren Street tube. **Rates** £230 single; £241-£335 double; £388-£935 suite. **Credit** AmEx, MC, V. **Map** p401 K5 ⓫
Another member of Kit and Tim Kemp's Firmdale hotel group, the Charlotte Street is one of the newer kids on the block, having opened in 2000. Yet it oozes tradition and class, with nods to the area's heritage (the drawing rooms are hung with works by Vanessa Bell, Roger Fry and Duncan Grant). All rooms have telltale Firmdale touches – pastel tones such as soft beiges and greys spiced up with brazen plaid-floral combinations (never twee or girlie); while the light, airy suites are among the nicest hotel rooms in London. In addition to must-have Miller Harris products, the marble bathrooms come with mini TVs, making it tempting to never leave your room. Assuming you do, though, you needn't go further than downstairs to the Oscar bar/restaurant, which serves decent Modern British food. Visit on a Sunday night and you can combine a three-course set meal with a screening of a classic film in the mini cinema for just £35 (booking advisable).
Bar. Concierge. Disabled-adapted room. Gym. Internet (high-speed, wireless). No-smoking rooms. Restaurant. Room service. TV (DVD).

Moderate

Academy Hotel

21 Gower Street, WC1E 6HG (7631 4115/www.the etoncollection.com). Goodge Street tube. **Rates** £141 single; £164 double; £217-£225 suite. **Credit** AmEx, DC, MC, V. **Map** p401 K5 ⓬
'Wonderful', 'very comfortable' and 'restful' are a few of the comments that crop up repeatedly in the Academy's guest book. Comprising five Georgian townhouses, the hotel has a tastefully restrained country-house style – most rooms are done up in

soft, summery florals and checks, although eight suites have recently been recast in more sophisticated solid colour schemes. Guests are effectively cocooned from busy Bloomsbury – both conservatory and library open on to fragrant walled gardens, where drinks and breakfast are served in summer, and windows are double-glazed to keep out the noise. Great location for the British Museum too.
Bar. Disabled-adapted rooms. Internet (dataport, wireless broadband). No-smoking rooms. Room service. TV.

Harlingford Hotel

61-63 Cartwright Gardens, WC1H 9EL (7387 1551/ www.harlingfordhotel.com). Russell Square tube/ Euston tube/rail. **Rates** £79 single; £99 double; £110 triple; £115 quad. **Credit** AmEx, MC, V. **Map** p401 L3 ⓭
On the corner of a Georgian crescent lined with cheap hotels, the Harlingford is a stylish trailblazer in this Bloomsbury B&B enclave. A couple of years ago the owner chucked out the chintz, slapped on the white paint, and gave the once-dowdy guesthouse the mother of all makeovers. The last Granny Smith-green mosaic tiled bathrooms (all rooms are now en suite) were just being installed at time of writing. The tasteful guests' lounge, scattered with current trendy light fittings and modern prints, almost makes you forget this is a budget hotel. But while staff are eager to please, don't expect a porter to carry your bags upstairs, and do turn a blind eye to the odd suitcase scuff on the paintwork (flock wallpaper has its advantages, after all). The adjacent garden and tennis court are available to guests. TV.

Jenkins Hotel

45 Cartwright Gardens, WC1H 9EH (7387 2067/ www.jenkinshotel.demon.co.uk). Russell Square tube/Euston tube/rail. **Rates** £72 single; £85 double; £105 triple. **Credit** MC, V. **Map** p401 L4 ⓮
In the centre of the same sweeping crescent as the Harlingford (see above), the Jenkins is more traditional – once inside, you could be in a Sussex village guesthouse. It has been a hotel since the 1920s, so it's fitting an episode of Agatha Christie's Poirot was filmed in room nine. But don't expect a period look – just tidy, freshly-painted en suite rooms furnished with pretty bedspreads, crisp, patterned curtains and, unusually, a small fridge. Guests have access to the garden and tennis court.
No smoking throughout. TV.

Morgan Hotel

24 Bloomsbury Street, WC1B 3QJ (7636 3735/ www.morganhotel.co.uk). Tottenham Court Road tube. **Rates** £75 single; £95 double; £120 triple. Flat £110 1 person; £130 2 people; £160 3 people. **Credit** MC, V. **Map** p401 K5 ⓯
Imagine EastEnders transplanted to Bloomsbury. The three Shoreditch-bred Ward siblings have been running this cheap and cheerful hotel since the 1970s, and they're satisfied the upkeep is done well, because they do it themselves. At time of writing, a

three-year renovation plan was being wrapped up. While the place doesn't aspire to boutique status, the air-conditioned rooms have extras beyond basic B&B standard: modern headboards with handy inbuilt reading lamps, smart brocade drapes, new bathrooms with granite sinks and – as in the top hotels – a phone by the loo. The cosy, panelled breakfast room, with its framed London memorabilia, is the perfect setting for a 'full English'. The hotel's annexe of spacious flats, equipped with stainless-steel kitchenettes, is one of London's best deals.
No-smoking rooms/floors. TV.

Cheap

Arosfa

83 Gower Street, WC1E 6HJ (tel/fax 7636 2115/ www.arosfalondon.com). Goodge Street tube. **Rates** £45 single; £66 double; £79 triple. **Credit** MC, V. **Map** p401 K4 ⓰
Arosfa means 'place to stay' in Welsh, but we reckon this townhouse B&B sells itself short. Yes, the accommodation is fairly spartan, but it's spotless, and all the rooms have en suite shower/WC (albeit tiny). It has a great location – in the heart of Bloomsbury, opposite a huge Waterstone's – and a pleasing walled garden. At press time, the hotel was up for sale. Let's hope the new owners don't change its best asset: the prices.
No smoking throughout. TV.

Ashlee House

261-265 Gray's Inn Road, WC1X 8QT (7833 9400/ www.ashleehouse.co.uk). King's Cross tube/rail. **Rates** (per person) £34-£36 single; £22-£24 twin; £20-£22 triple; £11-£20 dorm. **Credit** MC, V. **Map** p401 L3 ⓱
Ashlee House is a rare beast: a youth hostel with a bit of style – although maintaining it in the face of guests' habits is a challenge. The funky lobby is decorated with sheepskin-covered sofas and arty mesh wallpaper digitally printed with London scenes. It's got all the handy hostel stuff – internet stations, TV room, luggage storage, laundry and kitchen (£5 deposit gets you a crockery and cutlery set). There's no curfew and, unlike its rival, the Generator (*see below*), the partying doesn't seem quite so relentless.
No smoking throughout. TV.

Generator

37 Tavistock Place, WC1H 9SE (7388 7666/ www.generatorhostels.com). Russell Square tube. **Rates** (per person) £35 single; £20 twin; £17 multi; £10-£15 dormitory. **Credit** MC, V. **Map** p401 L4 ⓲
In the cafeteria of the Generator, there are posters advertising drinking contests, breakfast menus entitled 'the Big Hangover Cure' and, on the noticeboard, Polaroids of people mooning. Like a London version of a Club 18-30 holiday, this place is party central for the backpacker brigade. It's got an 'MTV industrial' look: steel, exposed pipes and neon signs. There's no curfew, and the massive bar hosts

Pull up a pew at the **Mandeville**. *See p55.*

karaoke nights and happy hours galore. There's also a games room and a movie lounge. When you've sobered up, there's practical stuff: a travel agent, a shop, an internet room and multilingual staff. Oh, we almost forgot: there are beds, too, 837 of them, should you ever want to get some sleep.
Bar. No smoking throughout. Restaurant.

St Margaret's Hotel

26 Bedford Place, WC1B 5JL (7636 4277/ www.stmargaretshotel.co.uk). Holborn or Russell Square tube. **Rates** £53.50-£55.50 single; £65.50-£99.50 double; £91.50-£123.50 triple. **Credit** MC, V. **Map** p401 L5 ⓳
This sprawling townhouse hotel has 64 rooms, but retains a homely ambience thanks to the Marazzi family, who have run it for 55 years. The rooms are simple, comfy and relatively spacious, and huge triples are especially good for families. Costs are kept down with shared, scrupulously clean bathrooms (only a dozen are en suite), and cooked breakfasts are served in an old-fashioned chandeliered dining room. Rear rooms have views of two gardens: the Duke of Bedford's formal affair and the hotel's own little green patch. Guess which one you can go in.
Disabled-adapted floors. No-smoking rooms/floors. TV.

Marylebone

Expensive

Cumberland

Great Cumberland Place, W1A 4RF (0870 333 9280/www.guoman.com). Marble Arch tube. **Rates** £140-£370 single; £160-£389 double; £340-£458 suite. **Credit** AmEx, DC, MC, V. **Map** p400 G6 ⑳

The sheer scale of this hotel takes your breath away. It has 900 rooms (plus another 119 in an annexe down the road) and the echoey lobby, with its arresting, large-scale artworks and wall and floor panels that change colour throughout the day, looks like a cross between an airport and a wing of Tate Modern (*see p67* **Inns and arts**). After buying the art deco behemoth from Meridien, Guoman Hotels embarked on a two-year, £95m reinvention. The results will elicit mixed reactions, but you have to admire its chutzpah. Rooms are fairly minimalist, with etched-glass headboards, designer bathrooms, huge plasma TVs and a cotton kimono in a mesh zip bag rather than a fluffy robe. Comfortable, yes, but lacking personality. The place seems to be doing a roaring trade, though, with guests ranging from business people (hardly surprising given its 26 meeting rooms) to Arab and American families. In summer 2005 the casual brasserie was taken over by celebrity chef Gary Rhodes and renamed Rhodes W1 (*see p201*), while the fine dining room next door was due to be given similar treatment as this guide went to press.

Mandeville

Mandeville Place, W1U 2BE (7935 5599/ www.mandeville.co.uk). Bond Street tube. **Rates** £130-£250 single; £150-£275 double; £275-£450 suite. **Credit** AmEx, DC, MC, V. **Map** p400 G6 ㉑

Increasingly chi-chi Marylebone has lacked a hotel to match its fashion status – until now. Spotting a gap in the market, the owners of the Mandeville commissioned interior designer Stephen Ryan to turn an unremarkable traditional hotel into a style statement. The hotel's dreary Boswells pub morphed into the DeVille restaurant, with neo-Victorian wallpaper, life-size mannequins in Venetian masks and a globe-spanning menu, while the DeVigne bar (presided over by an ex-Met Bar mixologist) sports an eye-popping combination of mink suede sofas, primary-coloured leather stools and Dutch Master paintings given a makeover with Day-Glo lippy and nail varnish. So far, so showy. Those expecting theatrics in the bedroom will be disappointed, however, as the stage-set decor doesn't extend past the ground floor. The rooms are perfectly nice, with faux leather headboards, Versace-esque classical-print curtains and Italian marble bathrooms, but we're not convinced they have the extras or the glam factor to justify their rack rates. **Photo** *p53*.
Bar. Concierge. Disabled adapted rooms. No-smoking rooms. Internet (wireless). Room service. Restaurant. TV (satellite).

Moderate

Sherlock Holmes Hotel

108 Baker Street, W1U 6LJ (7486 6161/www. sherlockholmeshotel.com). Baker Street tube. **Rates** (breakfast incl weekends) £151-£235 double; £475 suite. **Credit** AmEx, DC, MC, V. **Map** p400 G5 ㉒

How do you transform a dreary, chintz-filled Hilton into a hip boutique hotel? It's elementary: hype up the Baker Street address, banish the bland decor, and create a sleek lobby bar that gives the place a buzz. That's what the Park Plaza chain did when it snapped up the Sherlock Holmes a few years ago. Guests can mingle with local office workers in the casually chic bar or retreat to the residents-only lounge, which looks rather like a glossed-up gentlemen's club. The rooms, meanwhile, resemble hip bachelor pads: beige and brown colour scheme, leather headboards, pinstripe scatter cushions and spiffy bathrooms. Split-level 'loft' suites make innovative use of the first floor's double-height ceilings. There's a decent gym with sauna and steam rooms, and it's fun checking out the memorabilia, which ranges from expressionist paintings of Holmes and Watson in Sherlock's Grill (forgive the name) to framed Victorian magnifying glasses.
Bar. Business centre. Concierge. Disabled-adapted rooms. Gym. Internet (dataport). No-smoking rooms. Restaurant. Room service. Spa. TV (pay movies).

22 York Street

22-24 York Street, W1U 6PX (7224 2990/ www.22yorkstreet.co.uk). Baker Street tube. **Rates** £89 single; £120 double; £141 triple. **Credit** AmEx, MC, V. **Map** p400 G5 ㉓

There's no sign on the door; people usually discover Liz and Michael Callis's immaculately kept B&B by word of mouth. Unpretentious and comfortable, it's perfect for those who loathe hotels and are uncomfortable in designer interiors. The rooms in these two graceful neighbouring Georgian townhouses may not be *Wallpaper* material but they are subtly tasteful, with wooden floorboards, antique pieces and French quilts. Most are en suite; all have an exclusively allocated bathroom. Breakfast is an occasion, served at a huge, curving wooden table in the traditional kitchen, and there's a computer room in the basement with free internet access. The area has the best of everything: it's three minutes' walk to Regent's Park and the shops and restaurants of Marylebone. **Photo** *p63*.
Internet (wireless). TV.

Mayfair & St James's

Deluxe

Brown's

Albemarle Street, W1S 4BP (7493 6020/www. roccofortehotels.com). Green Park tube. **Rates** £323-£646 double; £1,000-£2,932 suite. **Credit** AmEx, DC, MC, V. **Map** p408 U8 ㉔

Brown's was the quintessential London hotel, opened in 1837 by Lord Byron's butler, James Brown. Its afternoon teas were legendary, but to the chagrin of scone-seeking tourists, it has been closed since Rocco Forte added it to his portfolio in 2003 and embarked on a top-to-toe refurbishment in a modern English style. We have to admit, we were worried. But after a hard-hat tour of the completed rooms, we were reassured – impressed even. Forte's sister, Olga Polizzi, was charged with the design and like her Hotel Tresanton in Cornwall, Brown's has captured the feel of a chic private home. The bedrooms have understated colour schemes and clean lines, softened by flannel headboards, suede seating and angora throws. In the beautiful silvery mosaic bathrooms, deluge shower heads bump up the luxury quotient. The revamped public spaces respect the Edwardian oak panelling and stained-glass windows. As for the dining options, former Savoy Grill chef Laurence Glayzer will preside over the new Grill, while afternoon tea will no doubt continue to lure the ladies who lunch (though we admit we'll miss the tearoom's fusty, mismatched settees). There are plans for a spa too.
Bar. Business centre. Concierge. Disabled adapted rooms. Gym. Internet (high speed, wireless). Restaurant. Room service. TV (music/pay movies/satellite).

Claridge's

55 Brook Street, W1A 2JQ (7629 8860/www. claridges.co.uk). Bond Street tube. **Rates** £257- £480 single; £339-£598 double; £480-£4,992 suite. **Credit** AmEx, DC, MC, V. **Map** p400 H6 ㉙
Claridge's is a byword for upper-class English lodgings, evoking elegance, discretion, top-drawer glamour and cucumber sandwiches by the trolleyful. It dates back in its present form to 1898 and a signature art deco redesign, but though it remains traditional it's neither stuffy nor backwards looking: its bar and restaurant (Gordon Ramsay; *see p205*) are both actively fashionable, the decor has distinctly stylish modern touches and guests include a sprinkling of younger hipsters. It is far from cheap, but not necessarily an awful lot more expensive than newer style hotels: even if this isn't in your natural price bracket you might consider it for a treat (while wincing at the extras). Occupying your own slice of deco original (or Victorian – the 200 rooms divide equally between the two) is a magical experience, and the public areas are gorgeous too.
Bar. Business services. Concierge. Gym. Internet (dataport, high-speed). No-smoking rooms. Restaurants (2). Room service. Spa. TV (pay movies).

The Dorchester

53 Park Lane, W1A 2HJ (7629 8888/www.the dorchester.com). Hyde Park Corner tube. **Rates** £411 single; £476-£582 double; £740-£1,763 suite. **Credit** AmEx, DC, MC, V. **Map** p402 G7 ㉖
One of the grandes dames of the London hotel scene, the Dorchester is a perennial favourite with celebs. Yet despite its opulence – it has the grandest hotel lobby in town, complete with Liberace's piano – staff

are refreshingly down to earth, and there's not a hint of fustiness. The hotel is continually upgrading the older rooms to the same high standard, with floral (but not chintzy) decor, antiques and lavish marble bathrooms; some boast views of Hyde Park. Similarly, it's all change on the food and drink front: within weeks of opening in September 2005, China Tang was the place to be seen, while the newly refurbed Grill Room (*see p204*) is bound to be as popular as its earlier incarnation. Afternoon tea remains deservedly popular, and the revamped spa is affordable even for non-guests.
Bar. Concierge. Disabled-adapted rooms. Gym. Internet (dataport, high-speed, web TV). No-smoking rooms/floors. Parking. Restaurants (3). Room service. Spa. TV (pay movies/music/DVD).

Metropolitan

19 Old Park Lane, W1K 1LB (7447 1000/www. metropolitan.co.uk). Green Park or Hyde Park Corner tube. **Rates** £250-£390 double; £528-£3,524 suite. **Credit** AmEx, DC, MC, V. **Map** p402 H8 ㉗
This modern upstart caused quite a stir when it joined the old guard on Park Lane in 1997. The minimalist rooms were an exciting antidote to ostentatious gilt and chintz, and everyone wanted to gain access to the guests- and members-only Met Bar, which heaved nightly with misbehaving celebs. However, now that modern corporate hotels have appropriated its style – blond wood headboards, creamy soft furnishings, suede scatter cushions, marble bathrooms – it doesn't seem so special. The standard doubles are actually quite small, although the hotel has an upgrade policy when larger ones are available. Still, the rooms have recently been refurbished, so everything is pristine, and you can't beat the views on the park side from the floor-to-ceiling windows. Upstairs, Nobu (*see p205*) is an unchallenged destination dining spot and, should you need some proper pampering, massages are available in the elaborately named COMO Shambhala Urban Escape (really just two nice treatment rooms). You can still recapture something of the hotel's heyday in the refurbished Met Bar. There have also been rumours that the A list are slinking back.
Bar. Business centre. Concierge. Disabled-adapted rooms. Gym. No-smoking rooms/floors. Parking. Restaurant. Room service. Spa. TV (cable/pay movies/DVD).

The Ritz

150 Piccadilly, W1J 9BR (7493 8181/www.theritz london.com). Green Park tube. **Rates** £388 single; £470-£588 double; £705-£1,058 suite. **Credit** AmEx, DC, MC, V. **Map** p402 J8 ㉓
The reputation of this lavish establishment precedes it. After all, it's the only London hotel whose name has – no kidding – spawned an adjective meaning 'ostentatiously luxurious and glamorous'. Founded by hotelier extraordinaire César Ritz, the hotel celebrates its centenary in 2006. The high-ceilinged, Louis XVI-style rooms have been painstakingly renovated to their former glory in a range of restrained

Hazlitt's – all about the history. *See p59.*

pastel colours. Less restrained are the swanky 24-carat gold leaf features and the magnificently heavy curtains. The real show-stopper is the ridiculously ornate, vaulted Long Gallery, an orgy of chandeliers, rococo mirrors and marble columns (jackets are compulsory for gentlemen, though this rule is lifted for breakfast). The overall atmosphere of the Ritz is one of old-world luxury, but mod cons have thankfully slipped through, including wireless internet, large TVs and a gym. In the likely event that you can't afford a stay at the Ritz, tours are available and a fine afternoon tea is served in the Palm Court.
Bar. Business centre. Concierge. Gym. Internet (dataport, high-speed, wireless). No-smoking rooms/floors. Restaurant. Room service. TV (DVD/VCR).

Expensive

No.5 Maddox Street

5 Maddox Street, W1S 2QD (7647 0200/www.living-rooms.co.uk). Oxford Circus tube. **Rates** £290-£420 double suite; £540 2-bedroom suite; £730 3-bedroom suite. **Credit** AmEx, DC, MC, V. **Map** p408 U3 ㉙
Blink and you'll miss the entrance of this discreet bolthole between Regent Street and Bond Street. Perfect for those who want to pretend they're Londoners, whether for two nights or two months, because it doesn't look like a hotel. Instead of rooms, accommodation is in chic flats, done up in the East-meets-West style that was all the rage when it opened in the late 1990s: bamboo floors and dark wood furniture mixed with fake sable throws and the obligatory crisp white sheets. There's no bar, but Soho is nearby. And the kitchens are stocked with saintly organic as well as naughty treats (room service will shop for you too), so you can whip up dinner and throw your own party.
Concierge. Internet (dataport, high-speed). No-smoking rooms. Room service. TV (DVD).

Soho & Chinatown

Expensive

Courthouse Kempinski

19-21 Great Marlborough Street, W1F 7HL (7297 5555/www.courthouse-hotel.com). Oxford Circus tube. **Rates** £290-£352 double; £587-£2,350 suite. **Credit** AmEx, DC, MC, V. **Map** p408 U2 ㉚
Many of the celebrities who have passed through these imposing double doors over the years wished they hadn't. In its previous life as the Marlborough Street Magistrates' Court, the building was the scene of such notorious scenes as Mick Jagger's drug trial and the Profumo scandal. The oak-panelled courtroom remains almost entirely intact, while the jail is now a slick bar – three of the old cells, complete with Victorian toilet and bunk, are private drinking nooks. The judges' robing rooms have been turned into ten stylish suites with high ceilings, original fireplaces, parquet flooring and sumptuous marble bathrooms,

while the glitzy Lalique Suite was the police commissioner's apartment. The new wing, however, is a bit disappointing. The bedrooms are comfortable, albeit in standard-issue contemporary-corporate style, though the bathrooms are marble. We found the Eastern-influenced lobby a touch gaudy, with its torch-style lamps and potted palms, and the bright yellow-and-red colour scheme of the street-facing Carnaby brasserie. Our verdict: the best thing about the Courthouse is its history. **Photo** *p61.*
Bar. Concierge. Disabled-adapted rooms. Gym. No-smoking rooms/floors. Internet (wireless, high speed). Pool (1 indoor). Restaurant (2). Room service. Spa. TV (pay movies/music).

Hazlitt's

6 Frith Street, W1D 3JA (7434 1771/www.hazlittshotel.com). Tottenham Court Road tube. **Rates** £205 single; £240 double; £350 suite. **Credit** AmEx, DC, MC, V. **Map** p408 W2 ㉛
Named after the 18th-century essayist William Hazlitt – just one of the eclectic cast of characters who have resided here – this idiosyncratic Georgian townhouse hotel has an impressive literary pedigree. Jonathan Swift once slept here (there's a room named after him), it was immortalised in Bill Bryson's *Notes from a Small Island* and the library contains signed first editions from such guests as Ted Hughes and JK Rowling. Rooms are as true to period as possible, with fireplaces, carefully researched colour schemes, massive carved wooden beds and clawfoot bathtubs. But don't worry, you don't have to sacrifice 21st-century comforts. You'll find air-conditioning, web TV hidden away in antique cupboards and triple-glazed windows to keep out the sounds of Soho. In 2006 the hotel celebrates its 25th anniversary, and plans are afoot to expand the property into nearby buildings. **Photo** *p58.*
Business services. Concierge. Internet (dataport, web TV). No-smoking floors. Room service. TV (pay movies/DVD).

Soho Hotel

4 Richmond Mews (off Dean Street), W1D 3DH (7559 3000/www.firmdale.com). Tottenham Court Road tube. **Rates** £276-£346 double; £411-£2,937 suite; £1,645-£6,991 apartment (weekly). **Credit** AmEx, MC, V. **Map** p408 W2 ㉜
For her sixth hotel, the queen of English interior design, Kit Kemp, gave her signature contemporary country-house style an urban edge, in keeping with its location. The new-build red-brick structure, tucked down a Soho alleyway, resembles a converted warehouse, while in the drawing room, shocking pink and lime green curtains offset a huge antique dresser. The individually designed bedrooms are classic Kemp – soft neutrals, bold pinstripes, modern florals – but the industrial-style windows and the odd splash of surprising colour keep the mood current. In the granite and oak bathrooms the lotions by Miller Harris are a real treat. In keeping with the Firmdale formula are the trademark facilities: extensive guest lounging areas with honesty bar,

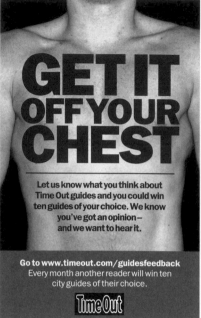
    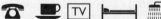
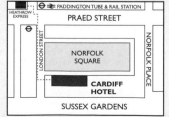

Courthouse Kempinski – don't worry, those aren't the bedrooms. *See p59.*

buzzy bar/restaurant Refuel, two luxurious screening rooms and gym and treatment rooms.
Bar. Business services. Concierge. Disabled-adapted rooms. Gym. Internet (high-speed, dataport). No-smoking rooms. Room service. TV (widescreen/DVD).

Cheap

Piccadilly Backpackers

12 Sherwood Street, W1F 7BR (7434 9009/www. piccadillybackpackers.com). Piccadilly Circus tube. **Rates** (per person) £37 single; £54 double; £17 multi; £12 dorms. **Credit** AmEx, MC, V. **Map** p408 V7 ⊕
Let's cut to the chase. Piccadilly Backpackers has two things going for it: rates (from £12 per night) and location. The accommodation is basic, although walls have been painted in colourful shades in an attempt to perk things up. Should you get bored of sightseeing, slob out in the common room, where you can surf 100 channels on the widescreen TV, or get online in the 24hr internet café. There are also handy facilities such as a travel shop and a backpackers' bar a few minutes' walk away (4 Golden Square, 7287 9241), where the drinks are cheaper than most of Soho's overpriced watering holes. And as the hostel has no curfew, you can make the most of a night on the town.
Disabled-adapted rooms. No smoking throughout.

Covent Garden & St Giles's

Deluxe

Covent Garden Hotel

10 Monmouth Street, WC2H 9LF (7806 1000/www. firmdale.com). Covent Garden or Leicester Square tube. **Rates** £247 single; £300-£358 double; £412-£1,052 suite. **Credit** AmEx, MC, V. **Map** p409 X2 ⊕
Smack bang in the heart of theatreland, Kit Kemp's second hotel has attracted starry custom since it opened in the mid 1990s. Film stars and Hollywood executives attend screenings in the luxurious basement cinema (which also shows classics for guests every Saturday night) and the ground-floor Brasserie Max, with its retro zinc bar, is a popular meeting spot – though you're more likely to rub shoulders with celebs in the panelled private library or drawing room. Kemp's distinctive modern English style mixes traditional touches – pinstriped wallpaper, pristine white quilts, floral upholstery – with bold, contemporary elements. Every comfortable bedroom is unique, but all have two Kemp trademarks: upholstered mannequins and shiny granite and oak bathrooms. One room boasts what must be London's biggest four-poster – the same size as the Great Bed of Ware in the British Museum.
Bar. Business centre. Concierge. Disabled-adapted rooms. Gym. Internet (dataport). No-smoking rooms. Parking. Restaurant. Room service. TV (DVD).

One Aldwych

1 Aldwych, WC2B 4RH (7300 1000/www.onealdwych. com). Covent Garden or Temple tube/Charing Cross tube/rail. **Rates** £253-£382 single; £335-£464 double; £429-£1,234 suite. **Credit** AmEx, DC, MC, V. **Map** p409 Z3 ⊕
One Aldwych is a modern classic. It's housed in a magnificent Edwardian newspaper HQ (designed, appropriately, by the architects who created the Ritz), but the contemporary rooms come equipped with up-to-date gadgetry and an ecologically sound water system. While it has the attentive service of a traditional grand hotel, the staff – dapper in lavender shirts by Richard James – are young and cosmopolitan. The dramatic Lobby Bar, with its huge, arched windows and striking sculpture, is as popular with Londoners as guests. In the bedrooms, minimalist lines are softened by tactile upholstery, silk

drapes and, in some rooms, original period features. The attention to detail is remarkable: fresh fruit and flowers are delivered daily to all rooms, there are original artworks in every room, and mini TVs and 100% natural toiletries in the terrazzo-stone bathrooms. The restaurants are suitably high-end (Axis, in particular, gets good reviews for its well-executed Modern European food) and there's also a private cinema with sumptuous Italian seats (dinner-and-a-movie packages are available). Aveda and Carita treatments are on offer in the refurbished spa and there's a spacious, well-equipped gym. But the pièce de résistance is undoubtedly the shimmering 18m swimming pool, complete with subtle lighting and relaxing music piped into the water.
Bars (3). Concierge. Disabled-adapted rooms. Gym. Internet (dataport, wireless). No-smoking floors. Parking. Pool (1 indoor). Restaurants (2). Room service (24hrs). Spa. TV (pay movies, DVD).

The Savoy

Strand, WC2R 0EU (7836 4343/www.fairmont.com). Covent Garden or Embankment tube/Charing Cross tube/rail. **Rates** £300-£500 double; £546-£1,821 suite. **Credit** AmEx, DC, MC, V. **Map** p409 Z4 ⓺
Built in 1889 to put up theatre-goers from Richard D'Oyly Carte's Gilbert & Sullivan shows next door, the Savoy is London's original grande dame. And what a legacy. Monet painted the views from the River Suites; Noel Coward played in the Thames Foyer; and Vivien Leigh met Laurence Olivier in the Savoy Grill. More importantly, a bartender introduced Londoners to the Martini at the (now tourist-clogged) American Bar. Less ostentatious than the Ritz, the Savoy mixes neo-classical, art deco and gentlemen's club aesthetics. Choose a traditional, modern English or art deco bedroom: all have watering-can showerheads and the latest technology such as internet access. The rooftop gym, with a small pool, is another asset. The hotel has undergone some changes in the past few years: the legendary Savoy Grill was revamped, and Banquette, a chi-chi homage to a 1950s American diner, was introduced. And since the property was bought by Fairmont Hotels in 2005, more changes are afoot, with a £30 million room restoration scheme set to start in 2006. Let's hope none of its character is lost in the process.
Bars (3). Business centre. Concierge. Disabled-adapted rooms. Gym. Internet (dataport, wireless). No-smoking floors. Pool (1 indoor). Restaurants (3). Spa. TV (pay movies, DVD).

St Martins Lane Hotel

45 St Martin's Lane, WC2N 4HX (7300 5500/ reservations 0800 634 5500/7300 5500/ www.morganshotelgroup.com). Covent Garden tube/Charing Cross tube/rail. **Rates** £230-£260 single; £252-£581 double; £1,410-£1,645 penthouse. **Credit** AmEx, DC, MC, V. **Map** p401 L7 ⓷⓻
Back when it opened in 2000 as a Schrager property, this was the toast of the town. The flamboyant lobby was always buzzing; the Light Bar was filled with celebrities, and guests giggled at Philippe

Starck's playful decor. The novelty may have worn off, but it remains a bolthole for high-profile guests seeking a refuge from hype, as well as tourists snapping up special offers. Although Starck objects – such as the gold tooth stools in the lobby – have become positively mainstream, and the space lacks the impact of its heyday, the all-white bedrooms have comfortable minimalism down to a T, with floor-to-ceiling windows, soft throws, gadgetry secreted in sculptural cabinets and modern free-standing tubs in the limestone bathrooms. Asia de Cuba (the only survivor of the hotel's three original eateries) remains a good restaurant, and the place still raises a smile.
Bar. Business services. Concierge. Disabled-adapted rooms. Gym. Internet (dataport, high-speed). No-smoking rooms. Parking. Restaurant. Room service. TV (pay-movies, DVD).

Westminster

Deluxe

Trafalgar

2 Spring Gardens, SW1A 2TS (7870 2900/www. hilton.co.uk/trafalgar). Charing Cross tube/rail. **Rates** £327-£386 double; £515 suite. **Credit** AmEx, DC, MC, V. **Map** p401 K7 ⓷⓼
Part of the Hilton group, the Trafalgar is its first 'concept' hotel – in other words, it's dropped the branding in favour of funky designer decor. Although it's housed in one of the imposing edifaces on the famous square (the former Cunard HQ, in fact, where the ill-fated *Titanic* was conceived), the mood inside is young and dynamic. The Rockwell Bar, which serves the largest selection of bourbon in London, has a varied programme of live music and DJs; it was recently refurbished in a somewhat incongruous style that melds modern chinoiserie with a dash of Edwardian fringing and a black and white colour scheme. The rooms have a masculine feel with minimalist walnut furniture and white or chocolate walls, and the bathtubs are made for sharing with the tap in the middle; full-size aromatherapy-based toiletries are a nice touch. The location is its biggest draw: corner rooms overlook the square and the small rooftop bar has panoramic views – though it's often closed for private parties. Surprisingly for a corporate chain hotel, the Trafalgar has hired a hip young creative director to devise a programme of arts events (*see p67* **Inns and arts**).
Bar (2). Concierge. Disabled-adapted rooms. Internet (dataport). No-smoking floors. Restaurant. Room service. TV (pay movies).

Expensive

City Inn Westminster

30 John Islip Street, SW1P 4DD (7630 1000/ www.cityinn.com). Pimlico tube. **Rates** £187-£234 double; £351-£1,116 suite. **Credit** AmEx, MC, V. **Map** p403 K10 ⓷⓽

22 York Street. *See p55.*

The City Inn opened to a great fanfare in 2003: it was London's largest new hotel in 40 years with 460 rooms, and its modern design has won several awards. But, apart from the blue, Lego-like exterior, don't expect anything flashy. The airy lobby has a clean, contemporary look, adorned with the odd piece of modern art. The bedrooms are modern and fairly minimal, but not stark. There's an emphasis on natural light, provided by floor-to-ceiling windows, and comfort (silk and suede scatter cushions, crisp white sheets). The Millbank Bar, with its 75-strong whisky 'library', is a great lounging spot for post-Tate tipples. The slick, spacious City Café, which has outside tables on the innovative 'Art Street' cut-through to the river (*see p67* **Inns and arts**) features a modern brasserie-style menu.
Bar. Business centre. Concierge. Disabled-adapted rooms. Gym. Internet (dataport, high-speed). No-smoking floors/rooms. Restaurant. Room service. TV (music/pay movies/DVD).

Dolphin Square

Dolphin Square, Chichester Street, SW1V 3LX (7798 8890/www.dolphinsquarehotel.co.uk). Pimlico tube.
Rates £175 studio; £195-£225 1-bedroom suite; £260-£330 2-bedroom suite; £450 3-bedroom suite.
Credit AmEx, DC, MC, V.
Dolphin Square is a London legend. This massive 1930s mansion block is built like a fortress and survived bombing during World War II. It's home to politicians, barristers and civil servants – even Princess Anne once had a pad here. And one wing of the building is devoted to an attractive hotel. The decor nods to its art deco past – the lobby, complete with an on-site travel agent, feels a bit like a cruise ship. All the rooms are suites, ranging in size from studio to three-bedrooms, equipped with kitchenettes. Choose from two styles of decor: we prefer

the 1930s-influenced contemporary to the somewhat characterless traditional English. Allium, the smart restaurant, run by former Savoy chef Anton Edelmann, is overlooked by a glam cocktail bar with original '30s chrome railings. There's also a more casual brasserie and bar looking on to the 18m indoor pool. Other highlights are the lush gardens, a full-size gym with squash courts and Decleor spa, and an old-fashioned shopping arcade housing everything from a greengrocer to a hairdresser. In 1935 AP Herbert remarked: 'A little drudgery is good for wives, perhaps the Dolphin lady may be spoiled.' Why not spoil yourself?
Bar. Business centre. Concierge. Disabled-adapted rooms. Gym. Internet (dataport). No-smoking rooms/floors. Pool (1, indoor). Restaurants (2). Room service. Spa. TV.

Moderate

B&B Belgravia

64-66 Ebury Street, SW1W 9QD (7823 4928/www. bb-belgravia.com). Victoria tube/rail. **Rates** £88 single; £94 double; £99 twin; £115-£160 family room. **Credit** AmEx, MC, V. **Map** p402 H10 ⑩
It wasn't long ago the terms 'bed and breakfast' and 'stylish' were as compatible as 'Elton John' and 'subtle'. But that's been gradually changing over the past few years and this one, which opened in September 2004, is one of the most attractive we've seen yet. The black and white lounge (leather sofa, arty felt cushions, modern fireplace) could be straight out of *Elle Decoration*. It may be pristine, but it's not precious. You'll find a laptop equipped with free internet connection and above it games and stuffed toys to keep the kids entertained, plus a collection of DVDs to watch on the flatscreen TV. There's also a

Halkin. *See p65.*

high-tech coffee machine, and guests can take their drinks out to tables in the large back garden. The bedrooms are simply chic and predominantly white, with flatscreen TVs, sleek bathrooms with power showers and cream IKEA chairs that could pass for Starck. You can spend the money you save on accommodation in the exclusive shops of nearby Elizabeth Street. **Photo** *p45.*
Disabled-adapted rooms. Internet (high speed). TV.

Windermere Hotel

142-144 Warwick Way, SW1V 4JE (7834 5163/ www.windermere-hotel.co.uk). Victoria tube/rail. **Rates** £64-£99 single; £89-£129 double; £139-£149 family. **Credit** AmEx, MC, V. **Map** p402 H11 ④
The Windermere has a proud legacy: London's first B&B opened on this site in 1881. Surprise, surprise, the rooms are done up in English chintz, but they're well kept and not too frilly. Superior rooms are decked out with more opulent fabrics and the odd coronet bed, as well as extras such as that cliché of business travel, the trouser press. What is unusual for a B&B is that all rooms have modem points, wireless internet and satellite TV. The bathrooms are clean and modern, with power showers. A further boon is the rustic Pimlico restaurant – another

rarity for a budget hotel – with its sophisticated, reasonably priced menu.
Bar. Business services. Internet (dataport). No-smoking rooms/floors. Restaurant. Room service. TV.

Cheap

Morgan House

120 Ebury Street, SW1W 9QQ (7730 2384/www. morganhouse.co.uk). Pimlico tube/Victoria tube/rail. **Rates** £46-£76 single; £66-£86 double; £86-£110 triple; £122 quad. **Credit** MC, V. **Map** p402 G10 ④
Just steps away from the exclusive boutiques of Elizabeth Street, the Morgan is a quintessential small English B&B. The passages are narrow and the rooms small. The decor is more serviceable than striking, with pastel walls, traditional iron or wooden beds and print curtains, although framed prints, fireplaces in most rooms and the odd chandelier lend a gracious air. The top-floor rooms are airy and contemporary, including a family room that sleeps four in bunk beds. Husband and wife owners Rachel Joplin and Ian Berry lend the place a friendly feel, from the cheery breakfast room to the patio garden, where guests can chill out on a summer's evening with a bottle of wine.
No smoking throughout. TV.

South Kensington & Knightsbridge

Deluxe

Baglioni

60 Hyde Park Gate, SW7 5BB (7368 5700/www. baglionihotellondon.com). High Street Kensington/ Gloucester Road tube. **Rates** £352-£458 single/ double; £587-£2,233 suite. **Credit** AmEx, MC, V. **Map** p398 C9 ⑭

For a taste of *la dolce vita* in London, the Baglioni is hard to beat for exciting designer style that doesn't dip into theatrical excess. Occupying a Victorian mansion opposite Kensington Palace, it has none of the sniffy formality of some of its deluxe English counterparts. The ground-floor Italian restaurant and bar are part baroque, part Donatella Versace: spidery black chandeliers, burnished gold ceilings, gigantic vases and a truly magnificent mirror from Venice. The chic bedrooms are more subdued: black floorboards, taupe and gold-leaf walls, dark wood furniture enlivened by jewel-coloured cushions and soft throws. No instant coffee here – rooms are equipped with gleaming espresso machines. Instead of the usual marble, the swanky black-panelled

bathrooms have hammered iron sinks imported from Morocco. The health spa's perfecting treatments, which range from a four-step anti-ageing itinerary to Botox, cater to the high-profile clientele. The Baglioni has brought a welcome touch of bling to the boutique scene – we predict the new guests- and members-only basement bar could prove to be the long-overdue successor to the Met Bar.

Bar. Business centre. Concierge. Disabled-adapted rooms. Gym. No-smoking rooms. Internet (dataport, high-speed, web TV, wireless). Parking. Restaurant. Room service. Spa. TV (pay movies/music).

Blakes

33 Roland Gardens, SW7 3PF (7370 6701/ www.blakeshotels.com). South Kensington tube. **Rates** £200-£234 single; £323-£405 double; £664-£1293 suite. **Credit** AmEx, DC, MC, V. **Map** p398 C11 ⑭

The original London boutique hotel doesn't get that much press any more – and that's exactly how its publicity-shy devotees like it. Opened by Anouska Hempel back in 1983, Blakes has a maximalist decor that has stood the test of time, becoming a sort of living casebook for interior design students. Each room is in a different style, with influences from Italy, India, Turkey and China. Exotic antiques picked up on the designer's travels – intricately carved beds, Chinese birdcages, ancient trunks – are complemented with sweeping drapery and piles of plump cushions. Downstairs is the eclectic, Eastern-influenced restaurant, once described as resembling 'an opium den run by Coco Chanel'. In a bid to stay current, Blakes has opened a gym and installed wireless internet. Unsurprisingly, given its discreet off-the-beaten-track location and romantic decor, the hotel is a popular honeymoon spot, and you can even get married on site.

Bar. Business services. Concierge. Gym. Internet (dataport, wireless). Parking. Restaurant. Room service. TV (pay movies/DVD).

Halkin

Halkin Street, SW1X 7DJ (7333 1000/www. halkin.como.bz). Hyde Park Corner tube. **Rates** £388-£482 double; £605-£1,410 suite. **Credit** AmEx, DC, MC, V. **Map** p402 G9 ⑮

Popular with affluent businessmen and publicity-shy Hollywood stars, the Halkin is a gracious, hype-free hideaway. You'd never guess the world's only Michelin-starred Thai restaurant, Nahm (*see p212*), is behind its discreet Georgian-style façade, tucked down a Belgravia back street. The first hotel of Singaporean fashion magnate Christina Ong (whose COMO group includes the Metropolitan (*see p57*), among others) was ahead of the East-meets-West trend when it opened in 1991. Its subtle design – a successful marriage of European luxury and oriental serenity – looks more current than hotels half its age. The 41 rooms, located off mysterious, curving black corridors, combine creamy classical sofas and Italian linen padded headboards with black lacquer tables and the odd South-east Asian artefact. Each floor is loosely themed by element, reflected in the colour of the carpets and the spacious marble bathrooms – a russet tone for Fire, for example. Guest comfort is paramount: a recent upgrade has introduced high-tech touch-screen bedside consoles so you can control everything from the lights to a 'do not disturb' sign while lolling on the Egyptian cotton sheets. Service, from Armani-suited staff, is faultless. A peaceful, unpretentious place to be cocooned in luxury and comfort. **Photo** *p64*.

Bar. Concierge. Disabled-adapted rooms. No-smoking rooms. Internet (high speed, wireless). Parking. Restaurant. Room service. TV (pay movies/DVD).

The Lanesborough

Lanesborough Place, Hyde Park Corner, SW1X 7TA (7259 5599/www.lanesborough.com). Hyde Park Corner tube. **Rates** £347-£417 single; £488-£582 double; £699-£5,875 suite. **Credit** AmEx, DC, MC, V. **Map** p402 G9 ④⑥

That the Lanesborough came late to the ranks of London's historic luxury hotels – in 1991 – has been no bar to its competing at the top level. In fact, its relatively recent re-purposing has been an advantage in terms of incorporating the infrastructure for the most modern of cons without interfering with the grace of the building, an ex-hospital designed in 1825 by National Gallery architect William Wilkins in classical and Greek Revival style. The rooms too are classically furnished, but not over-fussily, and they also contain some of the most impressive hotel technology we've seen, including US-style air-con and state-of-the-art entertainment systems that pick up pretty much every TV channel in the world. No extra charges are made for this, one of several well-considered touches that should be, but aren't, regulation at top-end hotels – business cards with your name on, a cordless phone that works in the whole hotel, nightlights, the option of coffee with your wake-up call. Obviously, you pay a seriously hefty price for all this, but, hey, personal butler service is thrown in for free. Of the common facilities, the suave Library Bar is the biggest asset.

Bar. Business centre. Concierge. Disabled-adapted rooms. Gym. Internet (dataport). No-smoking rooms. Parking. Restaurant. Room service. Spa. TV (DVD).

Milestone Hotel & Apartments

1 Kensington Court, W8 5DL (7917 1000/ www.milestonehotel.com). High Street Kensington tube. **Rates** £352-£405 double; £670-£952 suite; £3,578 apartment/wk. **Credit** AmEx, DC, MC, V. **Map** p396 C9 ④⑦

Who says traditional equals dull? Rooms in this wonderfully old-school luxury hotel overlooking Kensington Gardens certainly don't lack imagination – the inspired decor is the work of South African owner Beatrice Tillman. Choose from such sumptuous themes as the floral fecundity of English rose, the masculine clubbiness of Savile Row, or the Safari suite, with its tent-like draperies and leopard-print upholstery. The spectacular Tudor Suite has an elaborate inglenook fireplace, minstrels' gallery and

a pouffe concealing a pop-up TV. There's a distinctly British style of service that is rapidly vanishing: a tray of sherry in reception, butlers on call 24 hours to unpack your bag should you require it. No piddling plastic bottles of shampoo here – you get full-sized Penhaligon's toiletries. Take tea under the ancestral portraits in the panelled drawing room, or something stronger in the equestrian-themed Stables bar. The more modern black and white Conservatory, with ponyskin cushions and film-icon portraits, is pure panache. The gym has recently been upgraded with new equipment; there's also a small treatment pool and a treatment room.

Bar. Business services. Concierge. Disabled-adapted rooms. Gym. Internet (dataport, wireless). No-smoking rooms. Pool (1, indoor). Restaurant. Room service. TV (pay movies).

Expensive

Bentley Kempinksi

Harrington Gardens, SW7 4JX (7244 5555/www. thebentley-hotel.com). Gloucester Road tube. **Rates** £199-£326 double; £575-£4,000 suite. **Credit** AmEx, DC, MC, V. **Map** p398 C10 ④⑧

If you want to put on the glitz, you'll find plenty of chandeliers to swing from at this opulent boutique hotel – in the bedrooms as well as the lobby. Although it has just 64 rooms, its style is on a grand scale: Louis XV-style furniture, gilt mirrors, gleaming marble – 600 tons of it, imported from Greece and Italy – and a sweeping circular staircase perfect for making a grand entrance. The bedrooms are pure *Dynasty*: plush carpets, satin bedspreads and dark marble bathrooms with gold fittings and jacuzzi tubs. Next to the glitzy restaurant 1880, the Malachite Bar is a dimly lit, decadent hideaway in deep red, green and leopard-print. But the real showpiece is the classical spa (a welcome change from the ubiquitous Eastern style), with gold-laced mosaics and a full-size Turkish hammam.

Bar. Business centre. Concierge. Disabled-adapted rooms. Gym. No-smoking rooms/floors. Internet (dataport, high speed). Restaurants (2). Room service. Spa. TV (pay movies/music/DVD).

Cadogan

75 Sloane Street, SW1X 9SG (7235 7141/www. cadogan.com). Sloane Square tube. **Rates** £288-£323 double; £352-£646 suite. **Credit** AmEx, DC, MC, V. **Map** p399 F10 ④⑨

Louche secrets lurked behind the doors of this terribly British hotel, which opened to paying guests in 1988. Edward VII visited his mistress Lillie Langtry here when it was her private home, and poor old Oscar Wilde was arrested in room 118. It remained a stiff-backed bastion of tradition until 2003, when a bit of flamboyant style was let out of the closet. The reception's Edwardian tiles were restored to their original splendour and the stuffy drawing room, bar and restaurant were lightened up with contemporary colour schemes, but the service remains impeccably old school. The bedrooms are also being spruced up

Inns and arts

'Hotel lobby art' used to be shorthand for the worst kind of mainstream painting – insipid seaside watercolours, mediocre 'ancestral' portraits – you get the idea. No longer. An increasing number of London's hotels display interesting works in both public spaces and rooms. **One Aldwych** (see p61) boasts a cache of over 300 contemporary pieces, while on the walls of the **Charlotte Street Hotel**'s private guest drawing room hang paintings by Bloomsbury Group artists Roger Fry and Winifred Nicholson (see p52). The revamped **Cumberland** (see p55) takes the concept a step further; upon entering, you may think you've accidentally stumbled into a modern art gallery – the hotel spent over £100,000 on contemporary pieces for the lobby alone. The vast, echoey white space is dominated by *Man with Potential Selves*, three disturbingly realistic, larger-than-life-size painted bronze figures by London artist Sean Henry, while other, more subtle works such as Estelle Thompson's abstract oil on aluminium *Citrine* and Matthew Radford's *Newsreel 2002*, a set of six photo-etchings, are dotted around the room. In addition to the bone fide artworks, Real Studios, which designed the space, installed further interesting features, such as light columns and underfloor grids that change colour during the course of the day, video 'wallpaper' behind the reception desk and a futuristic, pod-shaped 'chair' that plays random noises. The **Great Eastern Hotel** (see p48) has long-standing relationships with the nearby Whitechapel Gallery and

the Photographers' Gallery – Franko B's neon sign *You Make My Heart Go Boom Boom* illuminates the check-in desk, while photography by such luminaries as Nan Goldin and Philip-Lorca diCorcia decorates a couple of the suites. But it's not just about buying artworks and slapping them on the walls. The hotel collaborates with local arts organisations and performance artists to create site-specific events. In summer 2005, Adrienne, the confessional alter ego of performance artist Adrian Howells, was literally on the menu. Guests could 'order' her from room service to come for a breakfast, lunch or dinner chat on any subject. Other exhibitions tie in with themes of travel or have a London slant (or both), such as a recent multi-faceted display commemorating the Routemaster bus.

But one of London's most innovative hotel artworks is probably one of the least appreciated – office workers must pass through it daily without taking much notice. Supported by Westminster council and Tate Britain, Side Street is billed as 'the capital's first ever street conceived as a work of art'. The 80-metre covered pedestrian cut-through from John Islip Street to Millbank alongside **City Inn Westminster** (see p62) features four five-metre-high slate engravings by Susanna Heron, from her *Elements* series of drawings. A mirrored *Reflecting Wall* and slatted ceiling create an ever-changing interplay of light and shadow in the cool grey and white space. Pull up a co-ordinating Ron Arad chair at one of City Café's outside tables for a front-row view.

Cumberland.

with leather headboards, rich, couture-inspired fabrics, and all mod cons, including wireless internet and DVD players. The signature suites are great fun for history buffs – the Oscar Wilde is dressed in crushed velvet and feather prints, the Lillie Langtry is a period cream and pink confection. Access to the secluded Cadogan Place gardens and tennis courts opposite is included, and the beyond-luxe shops of Sloane Street are literally on the doorstep.

Bar. Business centre. Concierge. Gym. No-smoking rooms/floors. Internet (high speed, wireless). Parking. Restaurant. Room service. TV (DVD/pay movies/satellite).

Gore

189 Queen's Gate, SW7 5EX (7584 6601/www. gorehotel.com). South Kensington tube. **Rates** £136 single; £168 double; £249 deluxe. **Credit** AmEx, DC, MC, V. **Map** p399 D9 ⑤⓪

Like its sister hotels Hazlitt's (*see p59*) and the Rookery (*see p48*), the Gore is a classy, creaky period piece, but while they have a Georgian feel, this is mostly a homage to the era of Victoria and Albert. Housed in a couple of very grand Victorian townhouses, it's crammed with old paintings – 5,000 of them – and antiques. The bedrooms have fantastic 19th-century carved oak beds (some so high they need library steps), sumptuous drapes and shelves of old books. But it's the suites that steal the show: the Tudor Room has a minstrels' gallery and a wooden Thomas Crapper; tragedy queens should plump for the Venus room for a chance to sleep in Judy Garland's old bed. The hotel was recently refurbished, without disturbing its eccentric style, and now has such 21st-century amenities as air-conditioning, wireless internet and high-tech TVs. The casually elegant Bistrot 190 gets good reviews, and the spacious, oak-panelled bar is prime celeb-spotting territory.

Bar. Business centre. Concierge. Internet (dataport). No-smoking rooms/floor. Restaurant. Room service. TV.

myhotel chelsea

35 Ixworth Place, SW3 3QX (7225 7500/www. myhotels.com). South Kensington tube. **Rates** £176-£242 single; £217-£230 double; £305-£423 suite. **Credit** AmEx, DC, MC, V. **Map** p399 E11 ⑤①

The South Kensington myhotel is a softer, feminine incarnation of its Bloomsbury sister. Pink walls, a floral sofa and a plate of scones in the lobby offer a posh English foil to feng shui touches such as an aquarium and carefully-placed candles. No doubt this is to appeal to a clientele lured by the proximity of prime shopping territory – Brompton Cross is just steps away, while Harrods is a short stroll. The feminine mood continues in the rooms with dusky pink wallpaper, white wicker headboards and velvet cushions, although it's all fresh and modern. Every room has a 21in TV and DVD player. Chill-out places include the white-panelled, Cape Cod-influenced bar and conservatory-style lounge, and pampering is available courtesy of Aveda in the treatment room. Rooms at Bloomsbury site (well located for the

British Museum) tend to be on the small side, but have recently been given a makeover in brighter colours such as green and fuchsia.

Bar. Business centre. Concierge. Gym. No-smoking rooms. Internet (dataport, wireless). Restaurant. Room service. Spa. TV (pay movies/DVD).
Other locations: myhotel bloomsbury, 11-13 Bayley Street, Bloomsbury, WC1B 3HD (7667 6000).

Number Sixteen

16 Sumner Place, SW7 3EG (7589 5232/www. firmdale.com). South Kensington tube. **Rates** £112 single; £200-£294 double. **Credit** AmEx, MC, V. **Map** p397 D11 ⑤②

Kit Kemp's most affordable hotel rubs shoulders with budget establishments in this row of white stucco townhouses. The lower room rates at this gorgeous B&B are presumably down to the lack of bar/restaurant or big hotel perks, which leaves Kemp to get on with what she does best: create beautiful rooms. The whole place has a garden-fresh appeal: the drawing room is decorated with bird-and butterfly-themed modern art and fresh flowers; the bedrooms have a summery look, with tasteful floral patterns and muted creams, greens and mauves. Breakfast is served in the conservatory or the lovely, large garden.

Bar. Business centre. Concierge. Internet (dataport, wireless). No-smoking rooms. Parking. Room service. TV.

Moderate

Aster House

3 Sumner Place, SW7 3EE (7581 5888/www.aster house.com). South Kensington tube. **Rates** £116 single; £150 double; £188 deluxe. **Credit** MC, V. **Map** p399 D11 ⑤③

This award-winning B&B bravely attempts to live up to its upmarket address. In reality, the lobby – with its pink faux-marble and gold chandeliers – is more kitsch than glam, but the effect is still charming. So is the lush garden, with its pond and wandering ducks. Even lovelier is the palm-filled conservatory, where guests eat breakfast. The bedrooms are comfortable, with traditional floral upholstery, air-conditioning and smart marble bathrooms (ask for one with a power shower). Business travellers take note: staff can lend guests mobile phones during their stay, and the rooms all have wireless internet connection. The museums and big-name shops are all close at hand. A good, affordable option.

Business services. Internet (dataport, wireless). No smoking throughout. TV.

Five Sumner Place

5 Sumner Place, SW7 3EE (7584 7586/www. sumnerplace.com). South Kensington tube. **Rates** £100 single; £153 double. **Credit** AmEx, MC, V. **Map** p399 D11 ⑤④

Housed in a row of white Victorian townhouses, Five Sumner Place is a smart address, and a convenient one too. The decor, the usual faux-period English, is

pleasant enough; and the rooms are clean and comfortable. They're also technologically advanced for the price category: all rooms have free broadband wireless access and voicemail. Breakfast is served in a conservatory, and is included in the price.
Internet (dataport, wireless). No-smoking rooms/floors. TV.

Hotel 167

167 Old Brompton Road, SW5 0AN (7373 0672/ www.hotel167.com). Gloucester Road or South Kensington tube. **Rates** £72-£79 single; £90-£99 double; £115 triple. **Credit** AmEx, DC, MC, V. **Map** p398 C11 ⓺

It may be located in a Victorian townhouse, but this funky little hotel is no period clone. The lobby makes a bold statement, with its original black and white tiled floor and striking abstract art. Upstairs, the bedrooms are an eclectic mix of traditional and arty: the odd antique piece, Victorian painting or contemporary print. Run by the affable Irish owner for 30 years, the slightly bohemian (yet well-kept) place has inspired artists: it has been the subject of a song (an unreleased track by the Manic Street Preachers) and a novel (*Hotel 167* by Jane Solomons).
Internet (dataport). No-smoking rooms. TV.

Swiss House Hotel

171 Old Brompton Road, SW5 0AN (7373 2769/ www.swiss-hh.demon.co.uk). Gloucester Road tube. **Rates** £58-£80 single; £95-£120 double; £135 triple; £145 quad. **Credit** AmEx, DC, MC, V. **Map** p398 C11 ⓺

Don't expect an Alpine-themed hotel: this Victorian townhouse used to be a private residence for SwissAir crews, hence the name. Still, the whole place has a fresh appeal, from the attractive pine furniture to the dark wooden beams in the breakfast room. The airy bedrooms have a crisp, clean aesthetic, with new laminate floors, taupe walls and blinds instead of frou-frou curtains. It's also very child friendly, with seven family rooms, highchairs, bottle warmers and babysitting services.
TV.

Cheap

Vicarage Hotel

10 Vicarage Gate, W8 4AG (7229 4030/www. londonvicaragehotel.com). High Street Kensington/ Notting Hill Gate tube. **Rates** £46-£75 single; £78-£102 double; £95-£130 triple; £102-£140 quad. **No credit cards. Map** p396 B8 ⓺

This Victorian townhouse hotel has a split personality: the lobby is glitzy, with red and gold wallpaper, ornate mirrors and a chandelier, while the rooms are more what you would expect from a traditional B&B, painted in pastels and furnished with faux antiques and floral fabrics. The airy TV lounge is actually very pleasant: you might even consider sitting in it and relaxing. Another bonus: nine of the 17 rooms now have bathrooms.
TV.

North London

Cheap

Hampstead Village Guesthouse

2 Kemplay Road, Hampstead, NW3 1SY (7435 8679/www.hampsteadguesthouse.com). Hampstead tube/Hampstead Heath rail. **Rates** £50-£70 single; £75-£90 double; £95-£170 studio. **Credit** AmEx, MC, V.

Popular with visiting academics and families, this comfy B&B is set in a characterful Victorian pile in picturesque Hampstead. This is the place to stay if you hate hotels – the nine guest rooms in hostess Annemarie van der Meer's sprawling home are furnished with an eclectic collection of furniture, paintings and books; it's more like staying in an intellectual relative's spare room. Space is used to maximum effect, with quirky devices – children love the wardrobe that conceals a fold-out bed. There's a fridge in each room and most are en suite (although some bathrooms are tiny); one room has an iron bath in the middle of the floor. Breakfast is served in the kitchen or the secluded garden; there's also a modern studio in a converted garage, which sleeps five.
No smoking throughout. TV.

South-west London

Moderate

Windmill on the Common

Windmill Drive, Clapham Common Southside, Clapham, SW4 9DE (8673 4578/www.windmill clapham.co.uk). Clapham Common or Clapham South tube. **Rates** £85-£99 single; £95-£115 double. **Credit** AmEx, DC, MC, V.

Perched on the edge of Clapham Common, the Windmill is a pleasant neighbourhood pub in a building dating from 1729. It also boasts one of London's most reasonably priced hotels. In terms of comfort and decor, the bedrooms – decorated in typical chain period finery – are superior to most B&Bs in this price bracket. Central London is a short tube journey away, and Clapham is packed with bars and restaurants.
Bar. Disabled-adapted room. Internet (dataport). No-smoking rooms. Parking. Restaurant. Room service. TV (movies).

Cheap

Riverside Hotel

23 Petersham Road, Richmond-upon-Thames, Surrey TW10 6UH (8940 1339/www.riversiderichmond. co.uk). Richmond tube/rail. **Rates** £60-£65 single; £80-£95 double; £115-£125 suite. **Credit** AmEx, DC, MC, V.

A little slice of the country, 20 minutes from Waterloo by train, Richmond is a welcome respite from urban grime. This hotel, right on the edge of the Thames, has its own waterfront garden and half of the trad-

Essential Kit

Firm fixtures on the London hotel scene, husband and wife team Tim and Kit Kemp have launched four hotels in as many years, and there's no sign of the golden couple of hospitality slowing down. Their seventh hotel, the Haymarket, is due to open in June 2006 and looks to be the most luxurious addition to their Firmdale group yet – the first to have a swimming pool and spa. As well as the hotels reviewed in this chapter – **Charlotte Street** (*see p52*), **Covent Garden** (*see p61*), **Number Sixteen** (*see p68*) and the **Soho** (*see p59; pictured*) – the stable also includes the cosy **Knightsbridge**, tucked away on a side street near Harrods (10 Beaufort Gardens, SW3 1PT, 7584 6300), and the **Pelham** in South Kensington (15 Cromwell Place, SW7 2LA, 7589 8288).

So what is the Kemps' winning formula? One USP is the combination of lively public spaces with exclusive private ones. With the exception of the less-expensive Number 16 and the Knightsbridge, all the hotels have vibrant restaurants and bars frequented by Londoners, offering opportunities to mix with the locals. Yet every property has a drawing room and library (with a well-stocked honesty bar), where residents can retire for a quiet drink or read – a godsend for paparazzi-hounded celebs working in capital, such as Scarlett Johansson (spotted at the Charlotte Street) and David Schwimmer (seen at the Soho). But Firmdale's continuing appeal is largely thanks to Kit Kemp's vision – as design director, she creates all the interiors herself, and every bedroom in every hotel is

unique. Just to prove it, many rooms have framed 'mood boards' on the wall outside the door, with swatches and sketches charting their inspiration. Another typical touch is the dressmaker's dummy in co-ordinating fabric that can be found standing guard in most of the rooms.

Like an enthusiastic little girl with a dolls' house collection, Kemp is constantly moving items from one hotel to another and updating rooms – a boon for regular guests as it keeps things fresh. Her signature style, contemporary yet quintessentially English, offers design-savvy visitors the best of both worlds: it avoids fusty period stereotypes

style rooms have views of the river. It's also near Richmond Park, Kew Gardens and stately homes such as Marble Hill House. The rooms are decorated in a traditional English style, but the hotel's best feature is its proximity to the tranquil Thames Footpath. *Internet (dataport, wireless). No-smoking rooms. Parking. Room service. TV.*

West London

Deluxe

Hempel
31-35 Craven Hill Gardens, Bayswater, W2 3EA (7298 9000/www.the-hempel.co.uk). Lancaster Gate or Queensway tube/Paddington tube/rail. **Rates** £288 single; £311 double; £517-£1,163 suite. **Credit** AmEx, DC, MC, V. **Map** p396 C6 ⑤⑧

While pure minimalism may well be consigned to interior design history, you can't deny the impact of Anouska Hempel's blinding white spaces. The hotel's pristine, Japanesey bedrooms (which look remarkably fresh after more than a decade) still embody feng shui at its finest, but they're not as clinical as you might imagine, with touches of oatmeal linen, tactile faux fur and suede. One of the dreamy suites has a bed that hangs from the ceiling. The Hempel was sold in spring 2005 and the new owners have plans, as yet undisclosed, to revamp the stark, white lobby and tart up the bar – although, diehard minimalists will be relieved to hear its unlikely to stray far from the original vision. *Bar. Business services. Concierge. Disabled-adapted rooms. Internet (dataport, high-speed, wireless). No-smoking rooms. Restaurant. Room service. TV (DVD, pay movies/music).*

while staying true to its roots. Fresh floral fabrics, traditional white quilts, old wood panelling and overstuffed chintz sofas are all in evidence, mixed up with contemporary flower arrangements and modern art. But it's not just a design formula: each hotel reflects its location. Charlotte Street is a homage to Bloomsbury, featuring original artworks and hand-made furniture by members of the group of Victorian intellectuals; Number 16 is a glossed-up version of the B&Bs that proliferate in its South Kensington locale, complete with a pretty, sprawling garden, while the Soho mimics an urban loft development.

Kemp stresses that her main focus is on comfort, and there is something homely about the unexpected juxtapositions of traditional and modern, simplicity and opulence, solidity and whimsy – massive antique dressers with primitive artefacts, for example, a rough-hewn timber stool with a structured armchair, or an abstract painting hung on a panelled wall. Such eclecticism creates the illusion of being in someone's (immaculate) home. While some of the more exuberant prints and bold colour schemes may not be to everyone's taste, the balance of comfort and interest is right for a hotel – even if you don't want to stay there, you have to admit it's a nice place to visit.

Expensive

Miller's Residence

111A Westbourne Grove, Notting Hill, W2 4UW (7243 1024/www.millersuk.com). Bayswater or Notting Hill Gate tube. **Rates** £176-£270 double/ suite. **Credit** AmEx, MC, V. **Map** p396 B6 ⑤⑨
Owned by antiques expert Martin Miller, who set up Millers Antiques Price Guides back in the 1960s, this is a one-off. Behind an unmarked door in an unprepossessing side street is this slightly decadent cross between a baronial family pile and a Portobello arcade. Rooms, named after 19th-century poets (Shelley, Wordsworth, Keats et al), are furnished with Miller's finds, some with dramatic four-posters, but are balanced out with 21st-century perks such as air-conditioning and DVD players. The drawing room is an Aladdin's cave of ornate candelabra, clocks and curios, plus the odd Eastern artefact. It's even more atmospheric in the evenings, when it is lit by candles, and is highly conducive to relaxing by the elaborately carved fireplace with a whisky from the free bar. There's no restaurant, but there's plenty of choice right on the doorstep.
Internet (wireless). TV.

Moderate

Colonnade Town House

2 Warrington Crescent, Little Venice, W9 1ER (7286 1052/www.theetoncollection.com). Warwick Avenue tube. **Rates** £134-£174 single; £140-£203 double; £210-£338 suite. **Credit** AmEx, DC, MC, V. **Map** p396 C4 ⑥⓪

Little Venice is one of London's prettiest neighbourhoods. It's off the beaten track, though, which is why this dignified townhouse hotel is cheaper than its luxury competitors. Still, it's handy for Paddington and the Heathrow Express. And the stately bedrooms are wonderfully plush: the old-fashioned beds are draped in Egyptian cotton sheets and velvet bedspreads. What's more, the hotel oozes history: the JFK suite has an enormous four-poster bed built for the president's 1962 state visit; Sigmund Freud, another former guest, has a suite named after him; and Alan Turing, who cracked the Enigma code, was born here. In contrast, the modish E Bar serves cocktails and tapas.

Bar. Concierge. Internet (dataport, wireless). No-smoking rooms. Parking. Restaurant. Room service. TV.

Guesthouse West

163-165 Westbourne Grove, Notting Hill, W11 2RS (7792 9800/www.guesthousewest.com). Notting Hill Gate tube. **Rates** £153-£182 double. **Credit** AmEx, MC, V. **Map** p396 B6 ⑥①

Guesthouse West aims to offer a stylish, affordable antidote to exorbitant hotels by cutting out expensive luxuries such as room service and offering a handy list of local businesses to use during your stay. And as it's located in the middle of one of London's chicest neighbourhoods, those local businesses are the cat's (designer) pyjamas. The look is pure Notting Hillbilly hip: the retro lobby bar features a changing art display and front terrace made for posing (although the latter is only licensed to serve until 8pm). Minimalist bedrooms have just enough extras to keep hip young things happy: wireless internet access, flat-screen TVs and toiletries from REN. The hotel's relaunch in March 2004 (it was formerly the pricier Westbourne) was funded in part by a ground-breaking buy-to-let scheme: all the rooms are now owned by investors who can use them for 52 nights of the year, and split the rental income with the hotel. There are occasional resales, so if you've always fantasised about living in a hotel, get your name on the waiting list.

Bar. Internet (high-speed, wireless). No-smoking rooms. Restaurant. TV (pay movies/music/DVD).

New Linden

59 Leinster Square, Bayswater, W2 4PS (7221 4321/www.mayflower-group.co.uk). Bayswater tube. **Rates** £50-£65 single; £59-£110 double; £80-£140 triple; £99-£200 quad. **Credit** AmEx, MC, V. **Map** p396 B6 ⑥②

The latest addition to the excellent group comprising the Mayflower (*see p73*) and Twenty Nevern Square (*see below*), the New Linden was in the final stages of renovation as we went to press. By publication, it should be as much of a budget showpiece as its sisters. The finished rooms we saw had white walls, wooden floors and a combination of streamlined modern and Eastern furnishings. As at the other properties, marble bathrooms (some with deluge shower heads), flatscreen TVs and CD players come as stan-

dard. Some of the suites have balconies and one split-level family room retains elaborate period pillars and cornicing. The location – between Notting Hill and Kensington Gardens – is another pull.
TV.

Pembridge Court

34 Pembridge Gardens, Notting Hill, W2 4DX (7229 9977/www.pemct.co.uk). Notting Hill Gate tube. **Rates** £125-£165 single; £160-£195 double. **Credit** AmEx, DC, MC, V. **Map** p396 A7 ⑥③

What do Iggy Pop and this chintz-furnished townhouse hotel have in common? Surprisingly, his band often puts up here, along with numerous other music-biz people. The Pembridge is a popular spot for interviews and TV filming too. So you'll find copies of *Billboard* magazine scattered in the homely sitting room, presided over by ginger cat Churchill. The bedrooms are fairly standard traditional English affairs, but the walls are jazzed up with extraordinary framed pieces from nearby Portobello market: Victorian fans, Edwardian christening robes, 1940s cigarette cases, old school blazers – even a beautiful beaded flapper dress in one room.

Bar. Business services. Internet (dataport). Parking. Room service. TV (VCR).

Portobello Hotel

22 Stanley Gardens, Notting Hill, W11 2NG (7727 2777/www.portobello-hotel.co.uk). Holland Park or Notting Hill Gate tube. **Rates** £130 single; £170-£285 double. **Credit** AmEx, MC, V. **Map** p396 A6 ⑥④

This decadent Notting Hill mansion is the stuff of rock-star fantasies. The spectacular beds range from a Balinese four-poster to a ship's bunk, while in many rooms the Victorian bathtubs take centre stage. It's been the setting for many a steamy night over the past three decades. Room 16, for instance, has a round bed and a Victorian clawfoot bath in the middle of the room – Johnny Depp allegedly filled it with champagne for Kate Moss. A bit more romantic than Alice Cooper, who used his tub to house his boa constrictor. Among the many other themed pleasure pads are the seductive Moroccan Room, strewn with carpets and cushions, and the serene Japanese Water Garden Room with an elaborate spa bath, Buddhas and its own private grotto.

Bar. Internet (dataport). Restaurant. Room service. TV.

Twenty Nevern Square

20 Nevern Square, Earl's Court, SW5 9PD (7565 9555/www.twentynevernsquare.co.uk). Earl's Court tube. **Rates** £70-£89 single; £85-£150 double; £159 suite. **Credit** AmEx, DC, MC, V. **Map** p398 A11 ⑥⑤

The words 'stylish' and 'Earl's Court' don't usually appear in the same sentence, but the less-than-posh location of this immaculate boutique hotel keeps the rates reasonable. Tucked away in a secluded garden square, it feels far away from its less-than-lovely locale. The modern-colonial style was created by its well-travelled owner, who sourced many of the

exotic furnishings as well as those in even cheaper sister hotel the Mayflower (*see below*). Rooms are clad in a mixture of Eastern and European antique furniture and sumptuous silk curtains; in the sleek marble bathrooms, toiletries are tidied away in decorative caskets. The beds are the real stars, though, from elaborately carved four-posters to Egyptian sleigh styles, all with luxurious handmade mattresses. The Far East feel extends to the lounge and the airy conservatory breakfast room, with its white walls, dark wicker furniture and greenery.
Bar. Internet (dataport). No-smoking rooms/floors. Parking. Room service. TV.

Vancouver Studios

30 Prince's Square, Bayswater, W2 4NJ (7243 1270/www.vancouverstudios.co.uk). Bayswater or Queensway tube. **Rates** £69 single; £85-£95 double; £120 triple. **Credit** AmEx, DC, MC, V. **Map** p396 B6 ⓾

Staying here feels more like renting a small flat than putting up in a hotel. The fresh, unfussy studios are equipped with kitchenettes, flatscreen TVs and DVD players. The sitting room, which guests share with resident cat Panther, is cosy and funky, with Mexican upholstery, cacti and an old-fashioned gramophone. It opens on to a lush, walled garden with a gurgling fountain. There are also handy onsite facilities such as a laundry room with coin-operated washer and drier, and free wireless internet access for guests who have their own laptops. All in all, a great deal.
Internet (dataport, shared terminal). TV.

Cheap

Garden Court Hotel

30-31 Kensington Gardens Square, Bayswater, W2 4BG (7229 2553/www.gardencourthotel.co.uk). Bayswater or Queensway tube. **Rates** £40-£63 single; £64-£92 double; £84-£114 triple; £135 family room. **Credit** MC, V. **Map** p396 B6 ⓾

Run by the same family for more than 50 years, this budget hotel has recently been brought bang up to date. It now has a lift and an airy lounge with wooden floors and brown leather sofas facing the fireplace. It also has a bit of character: a giant antique Beefeater statue stands guard in the lobby, and the cheery bedrooms have modish modern wallpaper. As the name suggests, the hotel has a small walled garden; guests have access to the private square too (a rare privilege in London).
Business services. No-smoking hotel. TV.

Mayflower Hotel

26-28 Trebovir Road, Earl's Court, SW5 9NJ (7370 0991/www.mayflowerhotel.co.uk). Earl's Court tube. **Rates** £59-£79 single; £69-£109 double; £99-£129 triple; £110-£150 quad. **Credit** AmEx, MC, V. **Map** p398 B11 ⓾

At the forefront of the budget-hotel style revolution, this hotel has given Earl's Court – once a far from glamorous B&B wasteland – a kick up the back-

side. Following a spectacular makeover a couple of years back, the Mayflower proves cheap really can be chic. The minimalist lobby is dominated by a stainless steel water feature and a gorgeous teak arch from Jaipur; there's a fashionably battered leather sofa and a couple of caged love birds in the juice bar-cum-lounge. The wooden-floored rooms are furnished in an Eastern style with hand-carved beds and sumptuous fabrics or sleek modern headboards and units. Ceiling fans add a tropical feel, which extends to the palm trees in the garden. Marble bathrooms, CD players and dataports are hitherto unheard-of luxuries for such low rates.
Bar. Business centre. Internet (dataport). No-smoking rooms. Parking. TV.

Pavilion

34-36 Sussex Gardens, Bayswater, W2 1UL (7262 0905/www.pavilionhoteluk.com). Edgware Road tube/Marylebone or Paddington tube/rail. **Rates** £60 single; £85-£100 double; £120 triple. **Credit** AmEx, DC, MC, V. **Map** p397 E5 ⓾

In a row of dowdy hotels, the Pavilion is a shining star. Or more like a disco ball. When it comes to decor, this hilariously kitsch B&B has tongue firmly planted in cheek. The themed rooms are a riot: the Highland Fling is a tartan theme park, with plaid bedspreads and stag antlers; Better Red Than Dead is a glam extravaganza of crimson, vermilion and burgundy. Rock stars love the place: a favourite shag pad is Honky Tonk Afro, with its mirror ball, fuzzy dice and heart-shaped mirrored headboards. OK, so the location's not exactly rocking and the bathrooms are small, but there's more personality in this humble budget hotel than in many of the capital's big-name boutiques.
Parking. Room service. TV.

Apartment rental

The companies we have listed below specialise in holiday lets, although some of them have minimum stay requirements (making this an affordable option only if you're planning a relatively protracted visit to the city). Typical daily rates on a reasonably central property are around £70-£90 for a studio or one-bed, up to £100 for a two-bed, though, as with any aspect of staying in London, the sky's the limit if you want to pay it. Respected all-rounders with properties around the city include **Astons Apartments** (7590 6000, www.astons-apartments.com), **Holiday Serviced Apartments** (0845 060 4477, www.holidayapartments.co.uk), **Palace Court Holiday Apartments** (7727 3467, www.palacecourt.co.uk) and **Perfect Places** (8748 6095, www.perfectplaceslondon.co.uk). **Accommodation Outlet** (7287 4244, www.outlet4holidays.com) is a recommended lesbian and gay agency that has some excellent properties in Soho, in particular.

Camping & caravanning

If the thought of putting yourself at the mercy of the English weather in some far-flung suburban field doesn't put you off, the transport links into central London just might. Still, you can't argue with the prices.

Crystal Palace Caravan Club *Crystal Palace Parade, SE19 1UF (8778 7155). Crystal Palace rail/3 bus.* **Open** *Mar-Oct* 8.30am-6pm Mon-Thur, Sat, Sun; 8.30am-8pm Fri. *Nov-Feb* 9am-6pm Mon-Thur, Sat, Sun; 9am-8pm Fri. *Rates* £4.50-£8 caravan pitch; £3.80-£5; £1.10-£1.80 concessions. **Credit** MC, V.

Lee Valley Campsite *Sewardstone Road, Chingford, E4 7RA (8529 5689/www.leevalley park.org.uk). Walthamstow Central tube/rail then 215 bus.* **Open** 8am-9pm daily. Closed Nov-Mar. **Rates** £6.15; £2.75 under-16s. **Credit** AmEx, MC, V.

Lee Valley Leisure Centre Camping & Caravan Park *Meridian Way, Edmonton, N9 0AS (8803 6900/www.leevalleypark.org.uk). Edmonton Green rail/W8 bus.* **Open** 8am-10pm daily. **Rates** £6; £2.60 concessions; free under-5s. **Credit** MC, V.

Staying with the locals

Several agencies can arrange for individuals and families to stay in Londoners' homes. Prices range from around £20 to £85 single and £45 to £105 double, including breakfast, depending on the location and degree of comfort. They include **At Home in London** (8748 1943, www.athomeinlondon.co.uk), **Bulldog Club** (02392 631714, www.bulldogclub.com), **Host & Guest Service** (7385 9922, www.host-guest.co.uk), **London Bed & Breakfast Agency** (7586 2768, www.londonbb.com) and **London Homestead Services** (7286 5115, www.lhslondon.com). There may be a minimum stay. Alternatively, check out noticeboard-style 'online community' websites such as **Gumtree** (www.gumtree.com) and **London Lately** (www.londonlately.com) for both short- and longer-term offers.

University residences

During university vacations much of London's dedicated student accommodation is open to visitors, providing basic but cheap digs.

Goldsmid House *36 North Row, Mayfair, W1K 6DN (7493 6097/uclgoldsmid@studygroup.com). Bond Street or Marble Arch tube.* **Rates** *July, Aug* from £30 single; £20 (per person) twin; *June, Sept* from £25 single; £15 (per person) twin. **Available** 12 June-15 Sept 2006. **Map** p400 G6 ⑩

International Students House *229 Great Portland Street, Marylebone, W1W 5PN (7631 8300/www.ish.org.uk). Great Portland Street tube.* **Rates** (per person) £12-£18.50 dormitory; £33.50 single; £25.50 twin. **Available** all year. **Map** p400 H4 ⑪

King's College Conference & Vacation Bureau *Strand Bridge House, 138-142 Strand, Covent Garden, WC2R 1HH (7848 1700/www. kcl.ac.uk/kcvb). Temple tube.* **Rates** £19-£39 single; £42-£49.50 twin. **Available** 30 June-14 Sept 2006. **Map** p409 Z3 ⑫

Walter Sickert Hall *29 Graham Street, Islington, N1 8LA (7040 8822/www.city.ac.uk/ems). Angel tube.* **Rates** £32-£40 single; £60 twin. **Available** 12 June-8 Sept 2006 (executive rooms available all year). **Map** p402 O3 ⑬

Youth hostels

Hostel beds are either in twin rooms or dorms. If you're not a member of the International Youth Hostel Federation (IYHF), you'll pay an extra £2 a night (after six nights you automatically become a member). Alternatively, join the IYHF for £13 (£6.50 for under-18s) at any hostel, or through www.yha.org.uk. Prices include breakfast.

City of London *36-38 Carter Lane, EC4V 5AB (7236 4965/www.yha.org.uk). St Paul's tube/Blackfriars tube/rail.* **Reception** open 7am-11pm daily; 24hr access. **Rates** £15-£30; £15-£24 under-18s. **Map** p406 O6 ⑭

Earl's Court *38 Bolton Gardens, SW5 0AQ (7373 7083/www.yha.org.uk). Earl's Court tube.* **Reception** open 7am-11pm daily; 24hr access. **Rates** £19.50-£26.80; £17.20 under-18s. **Map** 398 B11 ⑮

Holland House *Holland Walk, W8 7QU (7937 0748/www.yha.org.uk). High Street Kensington tube.* **Reception** open 7am-11pm daily; 24hr access. **Rates** £21.60; £19.30 under-18s. **Map** p396 A8 ⑯

Oxford Street *14 Noel Street, W1F 8GJ (7734 1618/www.yha.org.uk). Oxford Circus tube.* **Reception** open 7am-11pm daily; 24hr access. **Rates** £22.60-£24.60; £18.20 under-18s. **Map** p408 V2 ⑰

St Pancras *79-81 Euston Road, NW1 2QE (7388 9998/www.yha.org.uk). King's Cross tube/rail.* **Reception** open 7am-11pm daily; 24hr access. **Rates** £24.60; £20.50 under-18s. **Map** p401 K3 ⑱

YMCAs

You may need to book months ahead; this Christian organisation is mainly concerned with housing young homeless people. A few of the larger London hostels open to all are listed below (all are unisex), but you can get a full list from the **National Council for YMCAs** (8520 5599, www.ymca.org.uk). Prices are around £25-£30 per night for a single room, £40-£45 for a double.

Barbican YMCA *2 Fann Street, EC2Y 8BR (7628 0697/www.ymca.org.uk). Barbican tube/rail.* **Map** p404 P5 ⑲

London City YMCA *8 Errol Street, EC1Y 8SE (7628 8832/www.ymca.org.uk). Barbican or Old Street tube/rail.* **Map** p404 P4 ⑳

Kingston & Wimbledon YMCA *200 The Broadway, SW19 1RY (8542 9055/www.ymca. org.uk). South Wimbledon tube/Wimbledon tube/rail.*

Sightseeing

Features

British Airways London Eye. *See p79.*

Introduction

A few ideas on where to start.

London is undeniably a wonderful place to visit, but its sheer size can also make it overwhelming to the novice. With an understanding of its geography and transport, it's easy to navigate.

GETTING AROUND

The tube is the most straightforward way to get around, popping you up within ten minutes of your destination pretty much everywhere in the central area. Services are frequent and, outside rush hours, you'll usually get a seat. But mix your tube journeys with bus rides to get a handle on London's topography. Some good routes for stringing the sights together are the 7, 8, 11 and 12 (all double-decker) and the RV1, a single-decker plying the river circuit.

Two wonderful Routemasters may finally have gone (the last one, the 159, ran until December 2005), but they're set to continue in the form of two Heritage Routes (the 9 and 15), due to be up and running soon. Check http://www.routemaster.org.uk/ for details. It would also be clever to add river services to your transport portfolio (*see p363*), and walking is often a pleasant option. For more information on all methods of transport, *see pp360-365*.

A BRIEF TOUR

In the ever-fascinating **City** (*see pp91-102*), reminders of London's ancient and historic past jostle with today's financial industry. The areas north and east of here, the old industrial hinterlands of **Shoreditch** and **Hoxton** (for both, *see p160*), are known for their nightlife. Heading west, **Clerkenwell** (*see pp106-107*) used to do the dirty work for the medieval city, but now has some of London's best restaurants and gastropubs, while **Holborn** (*see pp103-106*) is the legal quarter. Where High Holborn crosses Tottenham Court Road/Charing Cross Road, it becomes Oxford Street, running east to west. Dominated by the Centrepoint skyscraper, this junction is a handy reference point. In the north-east quadrant is literary **Bloomsbury** (*see pp108-112*), home to the British Museum; boho **Fitzrovia** (*see pp112-113*) is across Tottenham Court Road to the north-west. South-east is **Covent Garden** (*see p128-131*), with its theatres and opera houses, diverting streets and touristy Piazza, then comes London's spiciest square mile, **Soho** (*see pp124-127*), to the south-west.

Further west, after the intersection with Regent Street at Oxford Circus, Oxford Street becomes the divider betwen affluent, appealing **Marylebone** (*see p114-116*) to the north and affluent, important **Mayfair** (*see pp117-121*) to the south. From Oxford Circus, Regent Street leads south to Piccadilly Circus and the start of more stately London: to the east, Piccadilly – which runs east to west south of Oxford Street – is the southern border of Mayfair, and the northern edge of **St James's** (*see pp121-123*) and royal London. Trafalgar Square is a short hop away from Piccadilly Circus. As well as being the home of the National and National Portrait Galleries and a worthy destination in its own right, it is the gateway (literally, via Admiralty Arch) to the politics and pomp of **Westminster** (*see pp133-140*).

To the west, Oxford Street and Piccadilly end at the easily identifiable landmarks of Marble Arch and Wellington Arch respectively, which are linked by Park Lane. To its west are Hyde Park and Kensington Gardens. After Wellington Arch, Piccadilly becomes **Knightsbridge** (home of designer shopping), south of which are **Chelsea** (*see p146-148*) and **South Kensington** (*see p141-143*), location of the great Victorian museums.

London's areas are clearly delineated on our colour-coded map, *see pp394-395*.

PRACTICALITIES

To avoid queues and overcrowding follow the tips given in the text, and try to avoid weekends. Many attractions are free to enter, so if you're on a budget you can tick off large numbers of places on your 'must see' list for the price of a bus pass. If you want to extend your options to more expensive places a **London Pass** (0870 242 9988, www.londonpass.com) gives you pre-paid access to more than 50 sights and attractions (from £27 daily per adult, or £32 with a Travelcard thrown in).

In our listings, the initials '**LP**' before the admission price means your London Pass will allow free admission, tours or free entry to exhibitions. '**EH** ' mean the sight is an **English Heritage** (7973 3000, www.english-heritage.co.uk) property, so members can get in free. '**NT**' means that **National Trust** (0870 458 4000, www.nationaltrust.org.uk) members can expect free admission. It's always best to pre-book tickets if you're seeking a group discount.

Sightseeing

We've always tried to give last entry times, but don't turn up just before a place closes if you want to appreciate it fully. Some sights close at Christmas and Easter – ring ahead to confirm openings if you're not sure.

See the sights

By boat

City Cruises (*7740 0400/www.citycruises.com*). City Cruises' Rail and River Rover (£9.50; £4.75 concessions) combines a cruise with unlimited travel on the Docklands Light Railway.

By bus

Big Bus Company *48 Buckingham Palace Road, Westminster, SW1W 0RN (7233 7797/www.big bustours.com).* **Open-top bus tours** 3 routes, 2hrs Red tour, 3hrs Blue tour and ½-hour Green British Museum link tour; commentary recorded on Blue route, live on Red and Green. Tickets include river cruise and walking tours. **Departures** every 10-15mins from Green Park, Victoria & Marble Arch. *Summer* 8.30am-6pm daily. *Winter* 8.30am-4.30pm daily. **Pick-up** Green Park (near the Ritz); Marble Arch (Speakers' Corner); Victoria (outside Thistle Victoria Hotel, 48 Buckingham Palace Road). **Fares** £20 (£18 if booked online); £8 concessions; free under-5s. Tickets valid for 24hrs, interchangeable between routes. **Credit** AmEx, DC, MC, V.

Original London Sightseeing Tour
(8877 1722/8877 2120/www.theoriginaltour.com. **Departures** *Summer* 9am-7pm daily.*Winter* 9am-5.30pm daily. **Pick-up** Grosvenor Gardens; Marble Arch (Speakers' Corner); Baker Street tube (forecourt); Coventry Street; Embankment station; Trafalgar Square. **Fares** £16; £10 concessions; free under-5s; £60 family (£1 discount on individual tickets, £10 on family if booked online or by phone). **Credit** MC, V.

By duck

London Duck Tours *55 York Road, Waterloo, SE1 7NJ (7928 3132/www.londonducktours.co.uk).* **Tours** *Feb-Dec* daily (ring for departure times). **Pick-up** Chicheley Street (behind the London Eye). **Fares** £17.50; £12-£14 concessions; £53 family. **Credit** MC, V.
City of Westminster tours in an amphibious vehicle. 75-minute road and river trip starting at the London Eye and going in the Thames at Vauxhall.

By pedal power

London Bicycle Tour Company *Gabriel's Wharf, 56 Upper Ground, Waterloo, SE1 9PP (7928 6838/www.londonbicycle.com).* **Open** 10am-6pm daily. **Tours** 2pm Sat, Sun; 3½ hours (including pub stop). **Fares** *Bike hire* £3 per hour; £15 per day; £7 subsequent days; £48 per week. *Bike tours* £16.95/person.

Metrobike *(08450801952/7978 6399/www.promobikes.co.uk).* **Fares** from £2-£5 for a short trip; £40/hr private hire. **No credit cards**.
These futuristic bike taxis can take two people. Based around Regent Street.

By taxi

Black Taxi Tours of London (*7935 9363/www.blacktaxitours.co.uk.*) **Cost** £80 for 2hr tour during day; £85 evening tours. **No credit cards**. A tailored two-hour tour for up to five people.

On foot

Arguably the best company organising walks around London is **Original London Walks** (7624 9255, www.walks.com), with sorties on everything from the shadowy London of Sherlock Holmes to picturesque riverside pubs, and plenty of Jack the Ripper.
Other walking companies worth noting include **Citisights** (8806 4325), **Pied Piper Walks** (7435 4782), along with **Performing London** (www.performinglondon.co.uk) and **Silvercane Tours** (www.silvercanetours.com, 07720 715295). Good self-guided walks are listed in *Time Out London Walks* volumes 1 and 2 (£9.99 and £11.99). For out of town walks, see *Time Out Country Walks* (£12.99).

With the specialists

Open House Architecture *See p269.*
Tour Guides *7495 5504/www.tourguides.co.uk.* Tailor-made tours with Blue Badge guides for individuals or groups, on foot, by car, coach or boat.
Premium Tours *7278 5300/ www.premiumtours.co.uk*
Private tours of specific sites and attractions in London and the south of England.

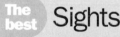

The best Sights

For bookish types

Dickens' House (*see p111*); **Dr Johnson's House** (*see p93*); **Keats House** (*see p153*).

For blood and gore

London Dungeon (*see p89*); the Chamber of Horrors in **Madame Tussaud's** (*see p116*); **Old Operating Theatre, Museum & Herb Garret** (*see p89*).

For drama queens

Shakespeare's Globe (*see p87*); **Theatre Museum** and **St Paul's Covent Garden** (for both, *see p129*).

For views of the city

Alexandra Park & Palace (*see p157*); **British Airways London Eye** (*see p79*); **Monument** (*see p100*); **Primrose Hill** (*see p151*); **Waterloo Bridge** (*see p82*).

Worth the suburban jaunt

Osterley House (*see p192*); **Syon House** (*see p192*); **Royal Air Force Museum Hendon** (*see p157*); **Royal Botanic Gardens** (*see p180*); **Eltham Palace** (*see p174*).

The South Bank & Bankside

This world-class riverside is looking better than ever.

The riverside promenade along the south bank of the River Thames now revels in the lion's share of London's most inspiring vistas. And not just from the top of the wheel. From the old stone lion and County Hall beside Westminster Bridge all the way to Shakespeare's Globe and Southwark Bridge, a 20-minute traffic-free wander along the Queen's Walk takes in many of the capital's most wonderful sights. Marketed as the Millennium Mile, the riverbank now easily rivals the city's more traditional tourist hotspots. The big wheel of the London Eye has become an internationally recognised landmark; the South Bank Centre is being refurbished; and Tate Modern has proved to be Europe's most popular gallery of modern art.

The transformation of this stretch of river over the last 50 years has been steady but laborious. The Festival of Britain in 1951 opened the way for the building of the blockish South Bank Centre, whose brutalist design is now considered one of the acmes of that movement's achievement. The biggest party, however, was the one to celebrate the turn of the century. Eight years earlier, Marks Barfield architects had taken part in a competition to come up with a structure to celebrate the new millennium. Their amazing big wheel, the London Eye, came second. No one can remember what won. The 'blade of light' shooting across the river to St Paul's Cathedral is the Millennium Bridge, and the equally lovely Golden Jubilee footbridges, linking the South Bank to Embankment, either side of Hungerford Bridge, are another reason to start a walking tour here.

The South Bank Marketing Group has an ordering line (7202 6900) for its free Walk This Way leaflets, but you can't really go wrong just wandering. Another way to explore is to hop on the eco-friendly RV1 bus, which links all the riverside attractions between Covent Garden and Tower Gateway.

The South Bank

Lambeth Bridge to Hungerford Bridge

Map p403 M8-10

Embankment or Westminster tube/Waterloo tube/rail.

Lambeth Bridge lands south of the river opposite the Tudor gatehouse of **Lambeth Palace**, official residence of the Archbishops of Canterbury since the 12th century. The palace and gardens open to the public on high days and holidays, notably during Open House London (*see p269*). The church next door,

St Mary-at-Lambeth, was deconsecrated then saved from demolition in 1977 by becoming the **Museum of Garden History** (*see p81*).

Heading north along Lambeth Palace Road, you come to the charming **Florence Nightingale Museum** (*see p81*), part of St Thomas's Hospital. From here, as you carry on north across Westminster Bridge, turn to catch a glance at the iconic Houses of Parliament and Big Ben over the river.

Now you're at the start of London's major riverside tourist zone. The **British Airways London Eye** (*see below*) packs in the crowds, while two attractions in the grand County Hall (once the residence of the London government) get them as they come off the wheel: the **London Aquarium** (*see p81*) bags the family market, while **Dalí Universe** (*see below*) attracts the art crowd. The **Saatchi Gallery**, which specialises in modern British and European art, was recently evicted from the building, but should open elsewhere in the near future.

British Airways London Eye

Riverside Building, next to County Hall, Westminster Bridge Road, SE1 7PB (0870 500 0600/customer services 0870 990 8883/www.ba-londoneye.com). Westminster tube/Waterloo/rail. **Open** *Oct-Apr* 9.30am-8pm daily. *May, June, Sept* 9.30am-9pm daily. *July, Aug* 9.30am-10pm daily. **Admission** £12.50; £6.50-£10 concessions (only applicable Mon-Fri Sept-June); free under-5s. **Credit** AmEx, MC, V. **Map** p403 M8.

It's hard to believe that this giant wheel was originally intended to turn majestically over the Thames for only five years after the turn of the new millennium. It's proved so popular that no one wants it to come down, and it's now scheduled to keep spinning for another 20 years (though intermittent rent hikes occasionally threaten its future, much to the horror of Londoners). The 450ft monster, whose 32 glass capsules each hold 25 people, commands superb views over the heart of London and beyond. A 'flight' (as a turn is called) takes half an hour, which gives you plenty of time to ogle the Queen's back garden and follow the silver snake of the Thames. You can buy a guide to the landmarks for £2. Some people book in advance (although they take a gamble with the weather), but it is possible to turn up and queue for a ticket on the day. Night flights offer a more twinkly experience, and you can even get married in a pod. There can be long lines in summer, and security is tight. **Photo** *below*.

Dalí Universe

County Hall Gallery, County Hall, Riverside Building, Queen's Walk, SE1 7PB (7620 2720/www.dali universe.com). Westminster tube/Waterloo tube/ rail. **Open** 10am-6.30pm daily (last entry 5.30pm). **Admission** *Oct-May* £8.75; £3.50-£7 concessions; £23 family. *June-Sept* £9.75; £4-£7.50 concessions; £29 family. **Credit** AmEx, DC, MC, V. **Map** p403 M9.

Get as close as you dare to the work of the Great Masturbator. Trademark attractions such as the *Mae West Lips* sofa and the *Spellbound* painting enhance the main exhibition, curated by long-term Dali friend Benjamin Levi. There are sculptures, watercolours (including his flamboyant tarot cards), rare etchings and lithographs, all exploring his favourite themes. Don't miss the hyper-surreal *Dreams and Fantasy*, the exotic and indulgent *Femininity and Sensuality*, and *Religion and Mythology*. Be sure to check out, too,

Sightseeing

British Airways London Eye.

the interesting series of Bible scenes by the Catholic-turned-atheist-turned-Catholic again. The gallery also shows works by new artists.

Florence Nightingale Museum
St Thomas's Hospital, 2 Lambeth Palace Road, SE1 7EW (7620 0374/www.florence-nightingale.co.uk). Westminster tube/Waterloo tube/rail. **Open** 10am-5pm Mon-Fri (last entry 4pm); 10am-4.30pm Sat, Sun (last entry 3.30pm). **Admission** £5.80; £4.20 concessions; £13 family; free under-5s. **Credit** AmEx, MC, V. **Map** p403 M9.

The nursing skills and campaigning zeal that made Florence Nightingale's Crimean War work the stuff of legend are honoured here with a chronological tour through her remarkable life. On returning from the battlefields of Scutari she opened the Nightingale Nursing School here in St Thomas's Hospital. Displays of period mementoes, clothing, furniture, books, letters and portraits include her stuffed pet owl, Athena. Free children's activities take place every other weekend. **Photo** *p82.*

London Aquarium
County Hall, Riverside Building, Westminster Bridge Road, SE1 7PB (7967 8000/tours 7967 8007/ www.londonaquarium.co.uk). Westminster tube/ Waterloo tube/rail. **Open** 10am-6pm daily (last entry 5pm) **Admission** (LP) £8.75; £5.25-£6.50 concessions; £25 family; free under-3s. (All prices £1 more during Mar-Sept and school hols; family £4 more). **Credit** AmEx, MC, V. **Map** p403 M8.

The aquarium, one of Europe's largest, displays its habitants according to geographical origin, so there are tanks of bright fish from the coral reefs and the Indian Ocean, temperate freshwater fish from the rivers of Europe and North America, and crustaceans and rockpool plants from shorelines. Rays glide swiftly around touch pools, coming up to the surface frequently. There are tanks devoted to jellyfish, octopuses, sharks and piranhas and even one containing robotic fish.

Museum of Garden History
Lambeth Palace Road, SE1 7LB (7401 8865/ www.museumgardenhistory.org). Waterloo tube/ rail. **Open** 10.30am-5pm daily. **Admission** free. *Suggested donation* £3; £2.50 concessions. **Credit** AmEx, MC, V. **Map** p403 L10.

Intrepid plant hunter and gardener to Charles I, John Tradescant, is buried here at the world's first museum of horticulture. In the graveyard a replica of a 17th-century knot garden has been created in his honour. Topiary and box hedging, old roses, herbaceous perennials and bulbs give all-year interest, and most of the plants are labelled with their country of origin and year of introduction to these islands. A magnificent Coade stone sarcophagus in the graveyard garden contains the remains of Captain Bligh. Inside are displays of ancient tools, exhibitions about horticulture through the ages, a collection of antique gnomes, a shop and a wholesome vegetarian café in the north transept. A little green-fingered marvel of a place.

HMS Belfast. *See p89.*

Hungerford Bridge to Blackfriars Bridge

Maps p403 M7-8 & p406 N7
Embankment or Temple tube/Blackfriars or Waterloo tube/rail.

When riverside warehouses were cleared to make way for the **South Bank Centre** in the 1960s, the big concrete complex containing the Royal Festival Hall, Purcell Room and Queen Elizabeth Hall was hailed as a daring statement of modern architecture. Together with the National Theatre and the Hayward Gallery, it comprises one of the largest and most popular arts centres in the world. The centrepiece, Sir Leslie Martin's **Royal Festival Hall** is currently being given a £90-million overhaul: the improvement of its river frontage has largely been completed, with the arrival of several retail outlets and cafés (Giraffe, Strada, Wagamama) on the ground floor. The main auditorium will have its acoustics enhanced, remaining closed until at least early 2007.

The **Hayward Gallery** (*see p82*) next door is a landmark of brutalist architecture. Its new pavilion was designed in collaboration with light artist Dan Graham. The gallery's trademark neon-lit tower, designed in 1970 by Phillip Vaughan and Roger Dainton, is a kinetic light sculpture of yellow, red, green and blue tubes controlled by the direction and speed of the wind. Another player, supposedly, in the proposed masterplan is the useful **National Film Theatre** (*see p289*), squatting underneath **Waterloo Bridge**. No one yet knows whether a proposed five-screen film centre will finally materialise, but we can all hope. The second-hand book stalls and semi-official skate park outside (*see p83* **Save our South Bank**) add to the atmosphere here. Next up is the **National Theatre** (*see p337*), which has free outdoor performances in summer.

The bridge itself famously provides some of the finest views of the City, especially at night, with great views opening up of Somerset House across the river and artful lighting in the trees tracing a path towards the octagonal viewing platform near Gabriel's Wharf, a fine place to enjoy a sandwich with spectacular views of St Paul's and the City.

Next stop, the deco tower of the **Oxo Tower Wharf** incorporates covert advertising for the stock cube company, which used to own the building. Earmarked for demolition in the 1970s, it was saved by the Coin Street

Community Builders, whose exhibition centre on the ground floor tells the full story and future plans of this welcoming stretch of the riverbank. It now also provides affordable housing, interesting designer shops and galleries, and a rooftop restaurant, bar and bistro with more wonderful views.

Hayward Gallery

Belvedere Road, SE1 8XX (information 7921 0813/ box office 0870 169 1000/www.hayward.org.uk). Embankment tube/Charing Cross or Waterloo tube/ rail. **Open** *During exhibitions* 10am-6pm Mon, Thur, Sat, Sun; 10am-8pm Tue, Wed; 10am-9pm Fri. **Admission** £9; £3-£6 concessions; free under-12s. Half-price to all Mon. **Credit** AmEx, MC, V. **Map** p403 M8.

In the Hayward's foyer extension and mirrored, elliptical glass, Waterloo Sunset Pavilion, casual visitors can watch cartoons on touch screens as they sip their Starbucks. Art lovers dismayed by the latter nonetheless enjoy the pavilion and the excellent exhibition programme. In 2006 this includes the first comprehensive exhibition of the work of American artist Dan Flavin, who pioneered sculptural paintings using fluorescent light in the 1960s. Also in 2006, look out for a major show called the 'The Enemy Within', celebrating the work of the proto-surrealist Georges Bataille and his influential magazine *Documents*. In autumn 'Intimate Relations: the Art of Sex' will explore representations in all media of copulation across the globe down the ages.

Around Waterloo

Map p406 N8-9

Waterloo tube/rail.

Redevelopment of the Belvedere Road area has improved access to **Waterloo Station**, where Nicholas Grimshaw's glass-roofed terminus for Eurostar trains provides an elegant departure point for travellers bound for Brussels and Paris. Outside, the stonking great £20-million **BFI IMAX** cinema (*see p289*) was plonked in the middle of the roundabout several years ago, displacing the area's notorious 'cardboard city'. The mural behind its glass facade is a massive blow-up of a Howard Hodgkin painting.

Another place of interest around the station is the street market on **Lower Marsh** (the name originates from the rural village known as Lambeth Marsh until the 18th century). On the corner of Waterloo Road and the street known as the Cut is the restored Victorian façade of the **Old Vic Theatre** (*see p337*). Known in Victorian times as the 'Bucket of Blood' for its penchant for melodrama, it is now in the hands of Hollywood actor Kevin Spacey. Further down the Cut is the new home of the **Young Vic** (*see p342*) that hotbed of theatrical talent, renovated, rebuilt and due to reopen in autumn 2006.

Florence Nightingale Museum. *See p81.*

Save our South Bank

The space underneath the Royal Festival Hall on the South Bank has long been the centre of the capital's skateboarding scene, much loved since the 1970s for its smooth concrete, steep banks and infamous seven steps. Yet throughout its slick grey caverns echo decades of moans from local skaters, lamenting the lack of actual obstacles available to skate.

'If you want something done properly, do it yourself' is an unlikely adage to be adopted by a group of youths you normally picture screeching about, doing flips and swapping slang, but that's exactly the kind of thing they've been saying since summer 2004, when a project called Moving Units was created by the Side Effects of Urethane, a creative union of skaters and artists involved in exhibitions that successfully blur the boundaries between art and skateboarding (urethane, incidentally, is what the wheels are made of). The group designed, built and paid for five skateable concrete structures that were deposited under the Royal Festival Hall with the consent of the South Bank Centre management.

Relations between the RFH and local skateboarders haven't always been so amicable, but according to Mike McCart of the South Bank Centre management this has changed fundamentally in recent years, due in no small part to the efforts of the local skateshop Cide (88 Lower Marsh, www.skatecide.com) to engage in communication and compromise on behalf of the South Bank's skaters. Nevertheless, as work has begun in earnest on the RFH's multi-million pound refurbishment, the days of watching the sunset over the river after a long afternoon of sweat, bruises and plain ol' hanging out, could be numbered. However, in an open letter to local skaters in September 2005, a spokesman for the Royal Festival Hall apologised for having reduced the area that could be skated and, furthermore, committed the South Bank Centre to working with the skaters to improve the undercroft zone. Not only that, it was promised that, 'if at all possible', an alternative provision for the local skaters would be found should the spot be re-developed further. Until then the local skaters wait with bated breath, hoping a compromise can be reached to prevent their beloved piece of London's street culture being replaced by yet more generic shops and cafés.

In the meantime the kids are also making the most of the city's other skateparks. Down south, Stockwell skatepark's facelift was recently completed, while summer 2006 sees the opening of the brand new, hugely expanded skatepark in Cantelowes Gardens (*see also p332*), courtesy of a rather gnarly Camden council. For further suggestions on where to skate, *see p332*.

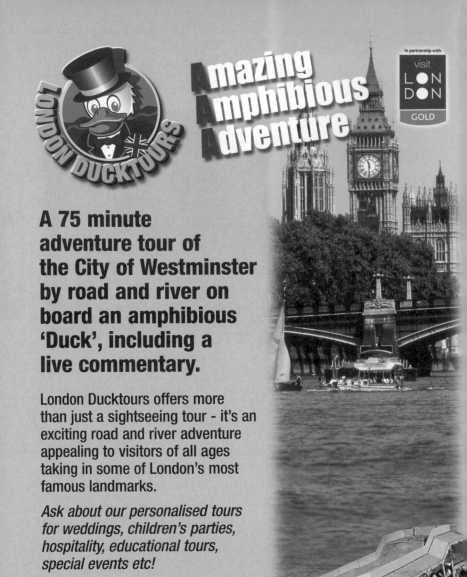

On the other side of the railway are the atmospheric terraces of early 19th-century artisans houses off Cornwall Road that make up part of the Lambeth Preservation Area, a popular period film location. Walking down Lower Marsh in the other direction takes you to Westminster Bridge Road, where at No.121 is what's left of the **London Necropolis Station**, founded in 1854 and used purely for train transport of the city's dead to an overflow cemetery in Surrey.

Bankside

Map p406 08-P8

Borough or Southwark tube/London Bridge tube/rail.
The area known as **Bankside**, south of the river between London Bridge and Blackfriars Bridge, was the epicentre of bawdy Southwark in Shakespeare's day. As well as playhouses such as the Globe and the Rose stirring up all sorts of trouble among the groundlings, there were the famous 'stewes' (brothels), seedy inns and other dens of iniquity. Presiding over all this depravity, the Bishops of Winchester made a tidy income from the fines they levied on prostitutes (or 'Winchester Geese' as they were known) and other lost souls. All that's left of the grand Palace of Winchester, home of successive bishops, is the rose window of the Great Hall on Clink Street, a short walk from the river, next to the site of the Clink prison (now the **Clink Prison Museum**; *see below*).

The parish church at this time was St Saviour's, formerly the monastic church of St Mary Overie and now (since 1905) the Anglican **Southwark Cathedral** (*see p87*). Shakespeare's brother Edmund was buried in the graveyard here and there's a monument to the playwright inside. You have to walk back down Clink Street, past **Vinopolis**, the wine attraction (*see p88*), to reach **Shakespeare's Globe** (*see p87*). Built on the site of the original, this reproduction in wattle and daub is separated from its neighbour, **Tate Modern** (*see p88*), by a wonky terrace of houses, where Sir Christopher Wren stayed while building St Paul's across the water. The Tate building was a power station designed by Sir Giles Gilbert Scott in a defining moment of utility architecture. The crowds that pass through its massive portals prove that it's culture vultures, rather than the clients of Winchester Geese, who seek their pleasures in Bankside now.

Bankside Gallery

48 Hopton Street, SE1 9JH (7928 7521/www. banksidegallery.com). Southwark tube/Blackfriars tube/rail. **Open** *During exhibitions* 11am-6pm daily. **Admission** free (optional donations). **Credit** DC, MC, V. **Map** p406 O7.

Crouching beside the Tate, this little gallery is the home of the Royal Watercolour Society and the Royal Society of Painter-Printmakers. Its changing exhibitions reflect established and experimental practices. Regular annual shows include the Royal Watercolour Society's in March and October, the Painter-Printmakers' in May, and the Society of Wood Engravers', generally every other August. Solo exhibitions planned for 2006 include works by Anita Klein (in April) and the contemporary Chinese woodblock prints of Chen Li (July). The shop has books and art materials, alongside prints and watercolours by members of both societies.

Bramah Museum of Tea & Coffee

40 Southwark Street, SE1 1UN (7403 5650/ www.bramahmuseum.co.uk). London Bridge tube/rail. **Open** 10am-6pm daily. **Admission** £4; £3.50 concessions; £10 family. **Credit** AmEx, DC, MC, V. **Map** p406 P8.

As a nation we get through 100,000 tons of teabags a year, a fact that no doubt appals tea purist Edward Bramah, a former tea taster who set up this museum in the early 1990s. Particularly popular are his regular tours, talks and teas. Bramah's collection displays pots, maps, caddies and ancient coffee makers. They work as visual aids to the history of the beverages and the role they have played in the history of different nations. The exhibition doesn't take long to work round, but it's tempting to linger in the (naturally) well-stocked café where a pianist usually tinkles away in the early afternoon.

Clink Prison Museum

1 Clink Street, SE1 9DG (7403 0900/www.clink. co.uk). London Bridge tube/rail. **Open** *June-Sept* 10am-9pm daily. *Oct-May* 10am-6pm Mon-Fri; 10am-7.30pm Sat, Sun. **Admission** £5; £3.50 concessions; £12 family. **Credit** MC, V. **Map** p406 P8.

This small, grisly exhibition looks behind the bars of the Clink, the hellish prison owned by the Bishops of Winchester from the 12th to the 18th centuries. Thieves, prostitutes and debtors served their sentences within its walls during an era when boiling in oil was legal. On display for the 'hands-on' experience are torture devices and the fetters whose clanking gave the prison its name. **Photo** *p87.*

Golden Hinde

St Mary Overie Dock, Cathedral Street, SE1 9DE (0870 011 8700/www.goldenhinde.co.uk). Monument tube/London Bridge tube/rail. **Open** daily; times vary. **Admission** £3.50; £2.50-£3 concessions; free under-4s; £10 family. **Credit** MC, V. **Map** p406 P8.

Weekends see this reconstruction of Sir Francis Drake's little 16th-century flagship swarming with children dressed up as pirates for birthday dos. When it hasn't been taken over by cutlass-wielding youths, the meticulously recreated ship is fascinating to explore. Thoroughly seaworthy, it has even reprised Drake's circumnavigatory voyage itself. 'Living History Experiences' (some overnight), in which participants dress in period clothes, eat Tudor

Sightseeing

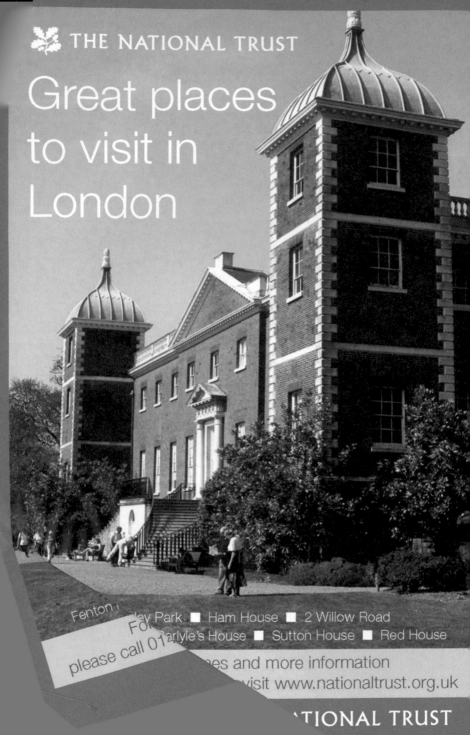

fare and learn the skills of the Elizabethan seafarer, are a huge hit with the young, as are the pirate parties (book well in advance) and the shop selling eye patches and cuddly parrots.

Rose Theatre

56 Park Street, SE1 9AR (7902 1500/www.rose theatre.org.uk). London Bridge tube/rail. **Open** by appointment only (*see below*). Closed Oct-Apr. **Credit** AmEx, MC, V. **Map** p406 P8.

Built by Philip Henslowe and operational from 1587 until 1606, the Rose was the first playhouse to be erected at Bankside. It's currently being looked after by the folks at Shakespeare's Globe (*see below*) while funds are sought for new excavation work in search of as-yet-uncovered portions of the old theatre, which could restore its original ground plan. In the meantime, the Rose is only accessible as part of the guided tour of Shakespeare's Globe.

Shakespeare's Globe

21 New Globe Walk, SE1 9DT (7902 1500/ www.shakespeares-globe.org). Mansion House or Southwark tube/London Bridge tube/rail. **Open** *Tours & exhibitions* Oct-Apr 10am-5pm daily. May-Sept 9am-noon daily. **Admission** (LP) £9; £6.50-£7.50 concessions. **Credit** AmEx, MC, V. **Map** p406 O7.

The original Globe theatre, where many of William Shakespeare's plays were first staged and which he co-owned, burned down in 1613 during a performance of Henry VIII. Nearly 400 years later, it was rebuilt not far from its original site under the auspices of actor Sam Wanamaker (who, sadly, didn't live to see it up and running), using construction methods and materials as close to the originals as possible. You can tour the theatre outside the May to September performance season, when historically authentic (and frequently very good) performances are staged (*see p339*). A fine exhibition based on the history of the reconstruction, Bankside and its Elizabethan theatres is open year round.

Southwark Cathedral

London Bridge, SE1 9DA (7367 6700/tours 7367 6734/www.dswark.org/cathedral). London Bridge tube/rail. **Open** 8am-6pm daily (closing times vary on religious holidays). *Services* 8am, 8.15am, 12.30pm, 12.45pm, 5.30pm Mon-Fri; 9am, 9.15am, 4pm Sat; 8.45am, 9am, 11am, 3pm, 6.30pm Sun. *Choral Evensong* 5.30pm Tue (boys & men), Fri (men only); 5.30pm Mon, Thur (girls). **Admission** (audio tour) £2.50. **Credit** AmEx, MC, V. **Map** p406 P8.

The oldest bits of this building, one of the few places south of the river that Dickens had a good word for, date back more than 800 years. The retro-choir was where the trials of several Protestant martyrs took place during the reign of Mary Tudor. After the Reformation, the church fell into disrepair and parts of it became a bakery and a pigsty; in 1905 it became a cathedral. An interactive museum called the Long View of London, a refectory and a lovely garden are some of the millennial improvements that make the building look so ship-shape these days. There are memorials to Shakespeare, John Harvard (benefactor of the US university), Sam Wanamaker (the force behind Shakespeare's Globe) and stained-glass windows with images of Chaucer, who set off on pilgrimage to Canterbury from a pub in Borough High Street, and John Bunyan, who preached locally.

Mind your manners at **Clink Prison Museum** – or you may never leave. *See p85.*

Strolling along the South Bank by the **Tate Modern**.

Tate Modern

Bankside, SE1 9TG (7401 5120/7887 8888/
www.tate.org.uk). Blackfriars tube/rail. **Open** 10am-
6pm Mon-Thur, Sun; 10am-10pm Fri, Sat. *Tours*
11am, noon, 2pm, 3pm daily. **Admission** free.
Temporary exhibitions prices vary. **Map** p406 O7.

A powerhouse of modern art, the Tate Modern's
imposing form is awe inspiring even before you
embark on a tour of the collection, moved here in
2000 from the original Tate (now called Tate Britain;
see p140). There's lots going on in 2006, not least the
complete re-hanging of the permanent collection
(due to be unveiled on 12 May). From 9 March to
4 June there's a comparison of the great Bauhaus
modernists Josef Albers and László Moholy-Nagy,
followed by an exhibition focussing on the first half
of the career of Kandinsky (9 June-24 Sept). The seventh in the Unilever Series of supersize works will
be displayed in the Turbine Hall from autumn
through spring 2007. From 25 October to 14 January
2007 the American abstract sculptor of plate metal,
machine parts and found objects David Smith gets
an airing, along with a retrospective exhibition
exploring the collaborative practice of contemporary
Swiss artists Peter Fischli and David Weiss.

If you don't know where to start in all the huge-
ness, take one of the guided tours (ask at the information desk). There are also various tour packages,
some combined with Shakespeare's Globe (*see p87*),
and others including lunch or dinner (the café on
Level 2 is highly recommended; *see p195*). Talks and
lectures complete the offerings.

The Tate-to-Tate boat service – decor courtesy of
Damien Hirst – links Tates Britain and Modern and
runs every 20 minutes, stopping along the way at the
London Eye and taking about 20 minutes. Tickets
are available from ticket desks at the Tates, on board
the boat, online or by phone (7887 8888). Prices are
£4 for an adult (£2.65 with a travelcard) or £7 (£4.65)
for a River Roamer day ticket. For under-16s, it costs
£2 for a single fare, £3.50 for a River Roamer (£2.35
with a travelcard); under-5s go free. **Photo** *above*.

Vinopolis, City of Wine

1 Bank End, SE1 9BU (0870 241 4040/www.
vinopolis.co.uk). London Bridge tube/rail. **Open**
Jan-Nov noon-9pm Mon, Fri, Sat; noon-6pm Tue-
Thur, Sun. *Dec* noon-6pm daily. Last entry 2hrs
before closing. **Admission** £13; £12 concessions;
free under-16s. **Credit** MC, V. **Map** p406 P8.

This wine visitor attraction is more for amateurs
than for oenophiles, but you do need to have some
interest to get a kick out of this glossy experience.
Participants are furnished with a wine glass and an
audio guide. Exhibits are set out by country, with
five opportunities to taste wine or champagne from
different regions. Gin crashes the party courtesy of
a Bombay Sapphire cocktail, and a whisky-tasting
area and a microbrewery were recently added.
Highlights include a virtual voyage through Chianti
on a Vespa and a virtual flight to the wine-produc-
ing regions of Australia. The wine shop has some
interesting offers for dedicated tipplers and there's
also a smart restaurant, Cantina Vinopolis. The complex also contains a tourist information centre.

Borough

Map p407 Q8-9

Borough or Southwark tube/London Bridge tube/rail.
Hard by Southwark Cathedral is **Borough
Market** (*see p259*), a busy food market dating
back to the 13th century. For years this
historic area has been under threat from the
Thameslink rail extension, but campaigners
now think that a large part of the market will
be safe for good. The area rings literary bells,
especially where Charles Dickens is concerned,

though few of the landmarks he wrote about survive today. Marshalsea Prison, where his father was imprisoned for debt, which once stood north of **St George-the-Martyr** church (on the corner of Borough High Street and Long Lane), is long gone, but one of his drinking haunts, the George pub (77 Borough High Street), remains – London's only surviving galleried inn.

The area around **Borough High Street** was lively, especially until 1750, because nearby London Bridge was the only dry crossing point on the river below Kingston Bridge. Nowadays bridges are plentiful on this stretch, but that hasn't stopped the powers that be from planning yet another, about two minutes away from London Bridge. If it goes ahead it will be the only covered bridge across the Thames.

To the north-west is the quirky **London Fire Brigade Museum** (94A Southwark Bridge Road, SE1 0EG (7587 2894, www. london-fire.gov.uk), which traces the history of firefighting in the capital from the Great Fire in 1666 to the present day. Entry to the museum is by guided tour only (10.30am, 2pm Mon-Fri, book in advance).

Around London Bridge Station tourist attractions clamour for attention. One of the grisliest, with its displays of body parts and surgical implements, is the **Old Operating Theatre, Museum & Herb Garret** (*see below*), while one of the scariest, and the one that draws the biggest queues at weekends, is the **London Dungeon** (*see below*). Blood-curdling shrieks emanate from the entrance, while next door the dulcet tones of Vera Lynn attempt to lure travellers to **Winston Churchill's Britain at War Experience** (*see p90*). Across Tooley Street from these pleasures stands a spookily empty mall called **Hay's Galleria**, once an enclosed dock, now dominated by a peculiar sculpture called *The Navigators* (by David Kemp). Here the twinkling Christmas Shop (7378 1998, www.thechristmasshop.co.uk) remains doggedly festive, and half-hearted craft stalls await custom. Exiting on the river side, past the great grey hulk of **HMS Belfast** (*see below*) – a sure-fire winner with children – you can walk east towards Tower Bridge and City Hall.

HMS Belfast

Morgan's Lane, Tooley Street, SE1 2JH (7940 6300/www.iwm.org.uk). London Bridge tube/rail. **Open** *Mar-Oct* 10am-6pm daily (last entry 5.15pm). *Nov-Feb* 10am-5pm daily (last entry 4.15pm). **Admission** £8; £1-£5 concessions; free under-16s (must be accompanied by an adult). **Credit** MC, V. **Map** p407 R8.

This 11,500-ton battlecruiser, the last surviving big gun World War II ship in Europe, is a floating branch of the Imperial War Museum. It makes an unlikely playground for children, who tear easily around its cramped complex of nine decks, boiler, engine rooms and gun turrets. *Belfast* was built in 1938, provided cover for convoys to Russia and was instrumental in the Normandy Landings. She also supported UN forces in Korea before being decommissioned in 1965; a special exhibition looks at that 'forgotten war'. Guided tours take in the living quarters, explaining what life was like on board. The Walrus Café is on the ship, the souvenir shop is on land. **Photo** *p81*.

London Dungeon

28-34 Tooley Street, SE1 2SZ (7403 7221/www.the dungeons.com). London Bridge tube/rail. **Open** *Sept-June* 10.30am-5.30pm daily. *July, Aug* 9.30am-7.30pm daily; longer in school hols. **Admission** £15.50; £10.95-£12.25 concessions. **Credit** AmEx, MC, V. **Map** p407 Q8.

Join the queue for this disturbing world of torture, death and disease under the Victorian railway arches of London Bridge, and you are led through a dry-ice fog past gravestones and hideously rotting corpses. Screeches and horror-movie soundtracks add to the experience. Don't inflict it on very young children or those liable to be offended by squeaking rats or spilled guts – there is plenty to offend.

White-faced visitors experience nasty symptoms from the Great Plague exhibition: an actor-led medley of corpses, boils, projectile vomiting, worm-filled skulls and scuttling rats. Other hysterical revisions of horrible London history include the Great Fire and the Judgement Day Barge, where visitors play the part of prisoners (death sentence guaranteed).

Old Operating Theatre, Museum & Herb Garret

9A St Thomas's Street, SE1 9RY (7188 2679/ www.thegarret.org.uk). London Bridge tube/rail. **Open** 10.30am-5pm daily (last entry 4.45pm). Closed mid Dec-early Jan. **Admission** £4.75; £2.75-£3.75 concessions; free under-6s; £12 family. **No credit cards. Map** p407 Q8.

The tower that houses this salutary revelation of antique surgical practice used to be part of the chapel of St Thomas's Hospital, founded on this site in the 12th century. When the hospital was moved to Lambeth in the 1860s most of the buildings were torn down to make way for London Bridge station and it was not until 1956 that the atmospheric old operating herb garret was discovered in the loft of the church. Visitors enter via a vertiginous wooden spiral staircase to view the medicinal herbs on display. Further in is the centrepiece: a Victorian operating theatre with tiered viewing seats for students. Just as disturbing are the displays of operating equipment that look like torture implements. Other cases hold strangulated hernias, leech jars and amputation knives. Check the website for events (such as Victorian surgery demonstrations) and lectures held on-site.

Winston Churchill's Britain at War Experience

*64-66 Tooley Street, SE1 2TF (7403 3171/www.
britainatwar.co.uk). London Bridge tube/rail.* **Open**
Apr-Sept 10am-6pm daily (last entry 5pm). *Oct-Mar*
10am-5pm daily (last entry 4pm). **Admission** £8.50;
£4.50-£5.50 concessions; £20 family; free under-5s.
Credit AmEx, MC, V. **Map** p407 Q8.

This old-fashioned exhibition recalls the privations
endured by the British during World War II. Visitors
descend from street level in an ancient elevator to a
reconstructed tube station shelter that doubles as
a movie theatre showing documentaries from the
period. The experience continues with displays about
London during the Blitz, including real bombs, rare
documents, photos and reconstructed shop fronts.
The displays on rationing, food production and Land
Girls are fascinating, and the set-piece walk-through
bombsite (you enter just after a bomb has dropped
on the street) is quite disturbing. It's a funny old
place, but it conjures up wartime austerity well.

Tower Bridge & Bermondsey

Map p407 R8-9

Bermondsey tube/London Bridge tube/rail.

Walking riverside from London Bridge to
Tower Bridge, you pass the pristine environs
(no skateboards, thank you!) of **City Hall**,
the home of the current London government.
Designed by Sir Norman Foster, the rotund glass
structure leans squiffily away from the river (to
prevent it casting shade on the walkers below).
It uses just a quarter of the energy of a normal
office building because of its simple water
cooling system (there's no air-conditioning).
The building has an exhibition blowing the
Mayor's trumpet on the ground floor, a café on
the lower ground floor and a pleasant outdoor
amphitheatre for lunch breaks and sunbathing.

Just near **Tower Bridge**, a noticeboard
announces when the bridge is next due to open
(which it does about 500 times a year for tall
ships to pass through). The bridge is one of
the lowest crossings over the Thames, which
is why the twin lifting sections (bascules)
were designed by architect Horace Jones and
engineer John Wolfe Barry. The original steam-
driven hydraulic machinery can still be seen at
the **Tower Bridge Exhibition** (*see p100*).

Further east, upmarket riverside dining is
mainly what **Butler's Wharf** is about, with its
series of Conran restaurants. Shad Thames is the
main thoroughfare behind the wharves, where in
days long gone dockworkers unloaded tea, coffee
and spices into huge warehouses (now pricey
apartments and offices, and the **Design
Museum**; *see below*). Shad Thames comes
from the area's original name St John at Thames,
as it was called under the Knights Templar.

Up past the Design Museum across Jamaica
Road and down Tanner Street is historic
Bermondsey Street, site of Zandra Rhodes'
the **Fashion & Textile Museum** (*see below*).
On the way, take a peek at **St Saviour's
Dock**, originally the mouth of the lost River
Neckinger, whose name comes from 'Devol's
Neckenger', a reference to this spot's popularity
as a place of execution for pirates. The
Neckinger was also responsible for the slime-
filled tidal ditches that surrounded a deeply
unwholesome part of Bermondsey once known
as Jacob's Island. Charles Dickens chose it as a
suitably pestilential place for Bill Sykes to meet
his end in *Oliver Twist*. Further south, around
Bermondsey Square, it's all Starbucks and delis,
new cobbles and hanging baskets. The Friday
antiques market (4am-2pm) here is lovely,
though it's well picked over by dealers by
the time most of us have had breakfast.

Design Museum

*28 Shad Thames, SE1 2YD (7403 6933/www.
designmuseum.org). Tower Hill tube/London Bridge
tube/rail.* **Open** 10am-5.45pm daily (last entry
5.15pm). *Apr-Sept* 10am-9pm Fri (last entry 8.30pm).
Admission £7; £4 concessions; free under-12s.
Credit AmEx, MC, V. **Map** p407 S9.

This white 1930s-style building was once a warehouse but is now a shrine to design. In 2006 the museum holds the annual Designer of the Year competition
from 4 March until 18 June and until 26 November
'Designing Modern Britain' looks at the radical
changes that homegrown design has undergone over
the last few decades. Petrolheads will be delighted by
'Formula One – The Great Design Race' (6 May to 3
September), which explores the fiercely competitive
world of racing car design. Other exhibitions include
a retrospective of the work of influential graphic
designer Jonathan Barnbrook (21 Oct-25 Feb 2007).
The Design Museum Tank is a little outdoor gallery
of constantly changing installations by leading contemporary designers, while the smart Blueprint Café
has a balcony overlooking the Thames.

Fashion & Textile Museum

*83 Bermondsey Street, SE1 3XF (7407 8664/
www.ftmlondon.org). London Bridge tube/rail.*
Open 10am-4pm Tue-Sat (last entry 3.30pm).
Admission £5; £3 concessions; £13 family;
free under-5s. **Credit** MC, V. **Map** p407 Q9.

Rather like the flamboyantly coiffed fashion designer who dreamed it up, this pink and orange museum stands out like a beacon among the grey streets
of south London. The grand pink foyer, with its
jewel-inlaid floor, leads to a long gallery and exhibition hall. The core collection comprises 3,000 garments donated by Zandra Rhodes, along with her
archive collection of paper designs and sketchbooks,
silk screens, finished textiles, completed garments
and show videos. At least two temporary exhibitions
are staged each year: check the website for details.

The City

Powerhouse of finance, repository of history.

In order to remain the economic heart of the capital for hundreds of years, London's Square Mile has had to survive many trials in its time: the Great Fire of 1666, the firestorms of the Blitz, the bombs of the IRA in the late 20th-century, and, most recently, the terrorist attacks of 7 July 2005. All have failed to leave a lasting dent in the City's confidence. After the July attacks, local workers were united in their resolve to get back to business as usual. The daily commute goes on undeterred, with some 300,000 suited businessmen and women moving purposefully through the streets like migrating wildebeest (albeit particularly well-dressed ones). Visit at the weekend and the contrast couldn't be more pronounced – buses are empty, shops and offices stay closed and only ambling tourists occupy the normally crowded thoroughfares.

The first Londoners were stone-wielding Neanderthals, but civilisation arrived with the Romans in around AD 43. The first Roman outpost was destroyed by Boudicca, but by AD 100 a permanent settlement known as Londinium had appeared on the north bank of the Thames. The Romans fortified the city with stone walls – still visible in places along London Wall – and constructed temples to Diana and Mithras as well as a 6,000-seat amphitheatre, now hidden in the basement of the Guildhall Art Gallery.

The modern City crudely follows the outline of the Roman walls, encompassing roughly 300 acres of some of the most expensive real estate in the world. The Romans pulled out of Britain in the fifth century and London faded from history for more than a century, before Anglo-Saxon settlers moved in and established a thriving trading community, just in time for the Vikings to sack it in the early ninth century.

London's development began in earnest after 1066, when the new Norman rulers of Britain built the first castle on the site of the Tower of London. In 1397 Dick Whittington was persuaded to become the Lord Mayor of London, though probably not by his cat nor the bells of the City's churches, as legend has it. The medieval period was marked by massive accumulation of wealth by London's traders and merchants and the foundation of many of the institutions that still control the City today, not least the London Guilds.

View from **London Bridge**.

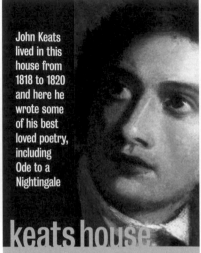

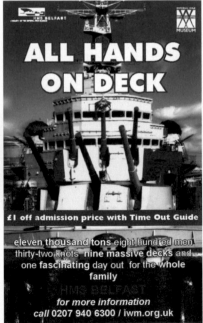

You might have thought the Great Plague of 1665 and the Great Fire of 1666 would stop London in its tracks, but the loss of nearly 80 per cent of the city's buildings only spurred London's architects on to new heights. Men like Sir Christopher Wren were drafted in to rebuild the City in brick and stone, and London emerged as the most modern capital in Europe, home to stately churches, proud banking houses and the mighty dome of St Paul's Cathedral.

As shipping on the Thames decreased, London shifted its attention from trade goods to the money markets that have formed the backbone of City business ever since. The dramatic growth of the British Empire in the 19th century created new avenues for trade and investment and the coffers of the Bank of England filled to overflowing.

It's tempting to think that London has declined since then, but the City's financial institutions still preside over the fourth largest economy in the world. The arcane and fiercely independent Corporation of London, the City's ruling body, is arguably the most powerful local council in the country, and certainly the richest.

Although money seems to be the driving forces behind the modern City, it hasn't quite forgotten its historical and spiritual roots. Street names hark back to vanished markets and monasteries, and 47 historic churches, many designed by Wren, are hidden away among the tower blocks and sandwich shops. If you start to feel like the crowds are closing in, do as the locals do and duck into a churchyard for a bit of quiet downtime (note that most churches are closed at weekends).

City Information Centre

St Paul's Churchyard, EC4M 8BX (7332 1456). St Paul's tube. **Open** *Apr-Sept* 9.30am-5pm daily. *Oct-Mar* 9.30am-5pm Mon-Fri; 9.30am-12.30pm Sat. **No credit cards. Map** p406 O6.
Come here for information and brochures on sights, events, walks and talks in the Square Mile, including a map of City churches.

Around Fleet Street

Map p406 N6

Chancery Lane tube/Blackfriars tube/rail.
Fleet Street takes its name from the largest of London's lost waterways, the river Fleet (*see p104* **Water lies beneath**). It was a major artery for trade and shipping into the capital, but silt closed the shipping channels in the 19th century and the river was covered over to provide land for construction of office buildings.

The history of journalism on Fleet Street dates back to 1702, when the first issue of the *Daily Courant* rolled off the presses, but the area has been a centre for printing since at least 1500,

when Wynkyn de Worde set up his printing press beside **St Bride's Church** (*see below*). Most of the newspapers moved away from Fleet Street during Rupert Murdoch's crackdown on the print unions in the 1980s. Murdoch returned in June 2005 to read the last rites over Fleet Street journalism in a bizarre ceremony at St Bride's when the last remaining news agency, Reuters, upped sticks to Canary Wharf.

These days, the *Beano* comic is the only periodical to be published on Fleet Street, but you can see some interesting relics from the media days, including the bingo hall-like **Daily Telegraph** building (No.135) and the sleek, black **Lubianka** (Nos.121-128), former home of the *Daily Express*. While you're here, stop for an ale at one of the pubs that once served liquid lunches to the rosy-faced hacks – El Vino (No.47) and the Punch Tavern (No.99), where *Punch* magazine was launched in 1841, are both decked out with Victorian finery.

Just off Fleet Street on Gough Square, you can visit the house of **Samuel Johnson** (*see below*), author of the first English dictionary. Johnson used to wet his whistle at the Ye Olde Cheshire Cheese pub, down the road at 145 Fleet Street (see p225). Nearby at No.66, the Tipperary is the oldest Irish pub outside Ireland – it opened in 1700 and sold the first pint of Guinness on the British mainland shortly after.

Dr Johnson's House

17 Gough Square, off Fleet Street, EC4A 3DE (7353 3745/www.drjohnsonshouse.org). Chancery Lane or Temple tube/Blackfriars tube/rail. **Open** *May-Sept* 11am-5.30pm Mon-Sat. *Oct-Apr* 11am-5pm Mon-Sat. *Tours* by arrangement; groups of 10 or more only. **Admission** £4.50; £1.50-£3.50 concessions; £10 family; free under-5s. *Tours* free. **No credit cards. Map** p406 N6.
Hidden away in a grand court of Georgian townhouses is the stately home of Dr Samuel Johnson (1709-84), author of the first *Dictionary of the English Language*, published in 1755. The museum is lent tremendous atmosphere by its creaky floorboards and Queen Anne furniture; you can almost feel the old wit's presence. Johnson, though, didn't always love his job: 'To make dictionaries is dull work,' he wrote in his definition of the word 'dull'.

St Bride's Church

Fleet Street, EC4Y 8AU (7427 0133/www.stbrides. com). Temple tube/Blackfriars tube/rail. **Open** 8am-6pm Mon-Fri; 11am-3pm Sat; 10am-1pm, 5-7.30pm Sun. **Admission** free. **Map** p406 N6.
The newspapers may have shifted to Wapping and Canary Wharf, but St Bride's is still known as 'the printers' and journalists' church'. Inside, you can see a glorious dark wood reredos (altarpiece) and choir topped by stern-looking statues of St Paul and St Bride. The Wren-designed staggered limestone spire is said to inspire the tiered wedding cake.

Map p406 O6

St Paul's tube.

The towering dome of **St Paul's Cathedral** (*see below*) is probably the definitive symbol of the City – an architectural two fingers up to the Great Fire and the German bombers that tried to bring London down. No other monument captures the resilience of Londoners so adroitly, and few buildings in the country can match St Paul's in terms of scale and grandeur.

There has been a cathedral dedicated to St Paul on this site since at least AD 604, but the first cathedral was destroyed by marauding Vikings and its Norman replacement burned to the ground in the Great Fire of London. The current incarnation was commissioned from Sir Christopher Wren in 1673 as London re-emerged, phoenix-like, from the ashes.

That we still have St Paul's today is largely due to the diligence of the St Paul's Fire Watch, who patrolled the roof of the cathedral through both World Wars, protecting it from incendiary bombs and flying cinders. They had their work cut out – most of the surrounding buildings were destroyed by the Blitz, and subsequently replaced with insipid modern office buildings.

Immediately north of the cathedral is the redeveloped **Paternoster Square**, a curiously sterile plaza full of rather pointless corporate art, as well as a Conran Restaurant. At the entrance to the square stands the oft-moved **Temple Bar**, the 1672 gateway to the City from the Strand, which was installed here in 2004. A rather more successful public space is the zigzag of steps down **Peter's Hill**, leading south to the Millennium Bridge. Halfway down is the 17th-century **College of Arms** (*see below*), the official seat of heraldry in Great Britain.

To the east is narrow **Bow Lane**, lined with quaint shops, bistros and champagne bars and bookended by **St Mary-le-Bow**, whose peals once defined a true Cockney, and **St Mary Aldermary**, with its pin-straight steeple, designed by Wren's office – though possibly not by Wren himself – as a tribute to the pre-Great Fire style.

South of St Paul's are five more Wren churches: St James Garlickhythe, St Mary Somerset, St Nicholas Cole Abbey, St Benet and the brilliantly-named St Andrew-by-the-Wardrobe, named for the king's official wardrobe, which stood here until the Great Fire. West of St Paul's, on Ludgate Hill, stands yet another Wren creation, **St Martin-within-Ludgate**, its lead spire still visible over the surrounding buildings as the architect intended. Around the corner is the most famous court in the land, the **Old Bailey** (*see below*).

Central Criminal Court (Old Bailey)

Corner of Newgate Street & Old Bailey, EC4M 7EH (7248 3277). St Paul's tube. **Open** *Public gallery* 10.30am-1pm, 2-4.30pm Mon-Fri. **Admission** free. No under-14s; 14-16s accompanied by adults only. **Map** p406 N6.

No name is more synonymous with crime in London than the Old Bailey, or Central Criminal Court. Founded in 1539 as a session house for Newgate Gaol, the court has hosted thousands of famous defendants, from American pioneer William Penn to Oscar Wilde (he gave his famous 'love that dare not speak its name' speech here in 1895) and East End gangsters the Kray brothers.

Members of the public are welcome to visit the courthouse – built by Edward Mountford in 1907 and topped by a famous gilded statue of Justice – and you can even watch British justice in action; a notice by the front door provides details of upcoming trials. It's really the wrong place to misbehave: note that bags, cameras, dictaphones, mobile phones and food are prohibited and there are no storage facilities provided.

College of Arms

130 Queen Victoria Street, EC4V 4BT (7248 2762/ www.college-of-arms.gov.uk). St Paul's tube/ Blackfriars tube/rail. **Open** 10am-4pm Mon-Fri. *Tours* by arrangement 6.30pm Mon-Fri; prices vary. **Admission** free. **No credit cards. Map** p406 O7.

The first coats of arms were created for medieval jousting tournaments, and heralds would use them in order to identify and organise competing knights. Heraldry soon became an integral part of family history for the British gentry. The arms of Britain's noble families are maintained by the heralds at the College of Arms and you can arrange tours to view the records or commission hand-drafted certificates of your family arms.

St Paul's Cathedral

Ludgate Hill, EC4M 8AD (7236 4128/www.stpauls. co.uk). St Paul's tube. **Open** 8.30am-4pm Mon-Sat. *Galleries, crypt & ambulatory* 9.30am-4pm Mon-Sat. Hours may change; special events may cause closure; check before visiting. *Tours of Cathedral & crypt* 11am, 11.30am, 1.30pm, 2pm Mon-Sat. **Admission** *Cathedral, crypt & gallery* £8; £3.50-£7 concessions; £19.50 family; free under-6s. *Tours* £3.50; £1-£3 concessions. **Credit** (shop) AmEx, MC, V. **Map** p406 O6.

London's – and arguably Britain's – most famous cathedral has been wrapped up in scaffolding for most of the last decade in preparation for its 300th anniversary in 2008, but now that the bulk of the work is finished, St Paul's positively glows. The Portland stone frontage has been returned to its original gleaming white, while the paintings held in the Whispering Gallery and the Byzantine-inspired mosaics below the dome are radiant. However, work is still ongoing to remove the soot from the north and south façades, deposited here by the coal-fired power station that now houses Tate Modern.

St Paul's Cathedral. *See p94.*

Do the strand

Paris has got one, why hasn't London? A beach, that is. For four years running, the Seine has unveiled a three-kilometre stretch of beach, complete with real sand, palm trees, deck chairs and a swimming pool.

It's not as if London hasn't had a beach before. Back in 1934 Tower Beach was created – over 1,500 tons of sand were heaped on to the mud flat between St Katharine's Steps and the Tower of London and between 1935 and 1939 over half a million people squeezed on to this popular little strip and imagined that they were by the sea for about five hours at low tide. The beach closed during World War II, but reopened later, only to finally close forever in 1971, owing to high levels of pollution.

Londoners have always been drawn to the river. The Romans were the first to settle along the banks of the Thames, building a fort near Cripplegate. The river provided a link to the sea and transport for boats carrying both goods and people; settlements grew steadily, and so did pollution. Open drains flowed into the river, and rubbish, along with offal and carcasses from the tanneries that lined the river, was tossed straight into the water. In the 17th century the south bank was a denizen of alehouses, theatres (including Shakespeare's Rose, Swan and Globe), bear-baiting and cock-fighting, as well as stewhouses (brothels).

With the advent of the Industrial Revolution the Thames was in serious trouble. Work connected with the laundries was more widespread than prostitution – and all the consequent toxic waste and water passed into the river. In spite of this, water was still being taken from the Thames for public consumption – cholera was rife and it wasn't until the third epidemic (1853-4) that a connection was made to the river (see p127), and the clean-up began. Not quickly enough, however. The 'Great Stink' of 1858 saw Members of Parliament hanging sheets soaked in chloride of lime from the House of Commons to combat the pong. By the middle of the 19th century pollution had killed off most of the fish.

Over time, laws were passed, sewers were built and eventually the river's quality began to improve. These days, salmon and trout are leaping up the Thames again, Bankside has become an area of culture and entertainment, with the city's first 'authentic urban beach' set for summer 2006; and even the neglected north bank is lined up for redevelopment, with plans for improved lighting, more greenery, restaurants and bars, and pedestrian access from London Bridge to the riverside path. The Riverside Walkway is due for completion in 2006. But still no official beach.

It could happen, though. A campaigning group named Reclaim the Beach is hopeful that once more the beach will be opened up and, as a way of promoting the idea, it holds regular beach parties. Around five times a year, once the tide goes out, crowds of like-minded folk head on to the foreshore in front of the Royal Festival Hall, bringing food, drink and music-making equipment (buckets and spades optional), then when the sun goes down a fire is built and some old-school partying begins (*sans* bears and stews, natch). Alternatively, of course, if global warming takes hold, rather than being able to sun ourselves on the beach year-round, the whole city will be underwater anyway...

Sir Christopher Wren had to fight to get his plans for this epic cathedral past the authorities – many thought it too large and expensive – and he changed his mind halfway through to create the massive dome for which St Paul's is now famous. At 108m, St Paul's is still one of the tallest monuments in the City, but a controversy is now raging about the legally protected view of St Paul's from Parliament Hill, which may soon be disturbed by the planned London Bridge Tower, aka the 'Shard' (*see p31*).

It's hard not to be spellbound by the main hall, with its soaring dome and monuments to empire, but be sure to take the 530 steps up to the open-air Golden Gallery for inspiring views over London. En route, you'll pass the outdoor Stone Gallery (378 steps to the top) and the Whispering Gallery (259 steps) inside the dome, designed to bounce even a whisper clearly to someone on the opposite side of the gallery. Look out for 18th-century graffiti as you clamber along the narrow stairwells.

Before leaving St Paul's, head down to the maze-like crypt, which contains memorials to the Duke of Wellington, Lord Nelson and Sir Henry Bartle Frere of Bombay, plus the graves of Wren, Reynolds, Turner, Sir Alexander Fleming, Henry Moore and Gilbert and Sullivan. Tours of the Triforium (pre-book on 7246 8357, £13 including admission) take place at 11.30am and 2.30pm Monday to Friday (advance booking essential). The bookshop in the crypt sells a useful guidebook for £4. **Photo** *p95*.

North to Smithfield

Maps p404 O5 & p406 O5

St Paul's tube/Barbican tube/rail.

From St Paul's, a short walk north across
Cheapside takes you to Foster Lane, and
another elegant Wren church, **St Vedast-
alias-Foster** (7606 3998, open 8am-6pm
Mon-Fri), built in 1673. Nearby, off Aldersgate
Street, is the delightful **Postman's Park**, with
its 'Heroes Wall', a display of Victorian ceramic
plaques commemorating fatal acts of bravery,
such as that of John Cranmer of Cambridge,
'a clerk in the London County Council who was
drowned near Ostend whilst saving the life of a
stranger and a foreigner (1901)'.

A few blocks west, St Bartholomew's
Hospital was founded in the 12th century by
the Augustinian prior Rahere, who now resides
in the crypt at the church of **St Bartholomew-
the-Great** (*see below*), the oldest parish church
in London. Nearby, on the wall of the hospital,
is a monument to the Scots hero William
Wallace, who was executed here in 1305;
it's still a place of pilgrimage for Scottish
nationalists. Today the hospital houses the
quaint St Bartholomew's Hospital Museum,
complete with a collection of sinister-looking
Victorian amputation tools. Every Friday at
2pm visitors can take a tour of the museum,
St Bartholomew-the-Great, Smithfield and the
little church of St Bartholomew-the-Less inside
the hospital compound (£5, 7837 0546 to book).

Behind St Bart's is the vast **Smithfield
Market**, built by Horace Jones in 1868. Until
World War II, this was the main food market
in the City, but it was torn apart in the Blitz
and today only the meat market survives. Early
risers (of the non-vegetarian sort) should visit
at first light, when the meat trucks start rolling
in and the corridors bustle with carcass-hauling
porters and jovial butchers. It's also an ideal
spot for a post-pub snack – the nocturnal
nature of the meat trade ensures that there
are plenty of all-night caffs.

However, things are changing at Smithfield.
The area is being gentrified and Clerkenwell-
style bars and brasseries are appearing on
every corner. One stalwart of the old Smithfield
is the Fox & Anchor pub at 115 Charterhouse
Street (7253 5075), which serves fried breakfasts
and pints from 7am.

St Bartholomew-the-Great

*West Smithfield, EC1A 7JQ (7606 5171/www.
greatstbarts.com). Barbican or Farringdon tube/rail.*
Open 8.30am-5pm Tue-Fri (till 4pm Nov-Feb);
10.30am-1.30pm Sat; 8.30am-1pm, 2.30-8pm Sun.
Services 9am, 11am & 6.30pm Sun; 12.30pm Tue;
8.30am Thur. **Admission** free; donations welcome.
Map p404 O5.

St Bartholomew's is probably the City's finest
medieval church. Parts of the building belong to the
12th-century hospital priory built by Rahere, a former courtier of Henry I, who founded St
Bartholomew's hospital after a vision on a pilgrimage to Jerusalem. The church was chopped about
during Henry VIII's reign and the interior is now
firmly Elizabethan. Appropriately, it was used as a
location for the movie *Shakespeare in Love*.
Benjamin Franklin trained here as a printer in 1724
before launching his political career in America.

Around Bank

Map p407 Q6

Mansion House tube/Bank tube/DLR.
Seven streets meet at Bank tube station, where
the Bank of England, the Royal Exchange and
Mansion House mark the symbolic heart of the
Square Mile. These towering Portland stone
monuments represent the wealth, status and
governance of the City of London and most of
the important decisions concerning the British
economy are made within this small precinct.

Easily the most dramatic building here is the
Bank of England, founded in 1694 to fund
William III's war against the French. Parts of
the fortress-like bank – which has no accessible
windows and just one public entrance – were
constructed by Sir John Soane in 1788, but most
of what you see today was built in the 1920s.
Access to the inner catacombs of the bank is
restricted, but members of the public can visit
the **Bank of England Museum** (*see p98*).

Next door is the neo-classical **Royal
Exchange**. The first exchange was founded
in 1565 by Sir Thomas Gresham, but the current
Parthenon-like building only dates from 1844.
In 1972, the London Stock Exchange shifted
to offices on Threadneedle Street, and later to
Paternoster Square. Today, the only money
changing hands is at the Gucci, Prada and de
Beers emporiums around the vast central court.

The third historic structure is the Lord
Mayor of London's official residence, **Mansion
House** (7626 2500, group visits by written
application to the Diary Office, Mansion House,
Walbrook, EC4N 8BH, two months in advance).
Designed by George Dance and completed in
1753, it's the only private residence in the UK
to have its own court of justice and prison cells.
Next door is arguably one of London's worst
architectural blunders, **Number 1 Poultry**;
the name fits – it's a total turkey, especially
as it replaced a beautiful structure, the
Mappin & Webb building.

Just south of Mansion House stands one
of the City's finest churches, **St Stephen
Walbrook** (7283 4444, open 9am-4pm Mon-
Fri). Topped by a coffered dome, the radiant

white interior has a wonderful sense of space and tranquillity. Unfortunately, the reredos was destroyed by bombing in World War II and replaced by an ugly round thing sculpted by Henry Moore. Further south on Cannon Street, you can observe the **London Stone**, thought to mark the centre point of London, although it's also said to signify a Roman temple, a druidic altar, or just a rock, depending on who you talk to.

On Lombard Street, you can see Hawksmoor's **St Mary Woolnoth** church, surrounded by 17th-century banking houses with gilded sign boards. Other significant churches in the area include Wren's **St Mary Abchurch**, off Abchurch Lane, and **St Clement**, on Clement's Lane, immortalised in the nursery rhyme *Oranges and Lemons*. Over on Cornhill are two more Wren churches, **St Peter upon Cornhill** and **St Michael Cornhill**, the latter containing a bizarre statue of a pelican feeding its young, sculpted by someone who had plainly never seen a pelican. There's another historic heap of stones on Queen Victoria Street at the **Temple of Mithras**, constructed by Roman soldiers in AD 240-250 in honour of the Persian god.

North-west of the Bank of England is the modern centre of London's civic life: the **Guildhall**. Here you'll find the headquarters of the Corporation of London, the **Great Hall** (*see below*), **Guildhall Library** (*see p99*) and **Clockmakers' Museum** (*see below*), the **Guildhall Art Gallery** (*see below*) and the church of **St Lawrence Jewry**, another restored Wren construction.

Heading east from Bank, past Gracechurch Street, **Leadenhall Market** comes as a pleasant surprise after all the franchise coffee houses and off-the-peg suit shops. This delightful covered arcade features a glorious vaulted ceiling by Horace Jones, who also constructed the market at Smithfield, restored to its original Victorian colour scheme of green, maroon and cream.

Behind the market is Sir Richard Rogers' high-tech **Lloyd's of London** building, with all its mechanical services (ducts, stairwells, lift shafts and even loos) on the outside. It looks like a disassembled washing machine but Londoners have come to love it. The original **Lloyd's Register of Shipping**, decorated with bas-reliefs of sea monsters and nautical scenes, is around the corner on Fenchurch Street. Further north, at 30 St Mary Axe, is the Sir Norman Foster-designed **Swiss Re Tower**, arguably London's finest modern building. It's known as the Gherkin for reasons that become immediately obvious once you see it, and dominates the skyline.

Bank of England Museum

Entrance on Bartholomew Lane, EC2R 8AH (7601 5491/www.bankofengland.co.uk/museum). Bank tube/DLR. **Open** *10am-5pm Mon-Fri. Tours by arrangement.* **Admission** *free. Tours free.* **Map** p407 Q6.

The bank originally built by Sir John Soane in 1788 has been extensively remodelled over the years, but the Stock Office has been restored to its original glory and today houses an amusing museum on the history of the national bank. You can see ancient coins and bills, original artwork for British bank-notes, minting machines and dioramas based on 18th-century political cartoons. The museum also provides a rare chance to lift a real gold bar – it's worth around £98,000 at current market rates and weighs more than two stone.

Clockmakers' Museum

Guildhall Library, Aldermanbury, EC2V 7HH (Guildhall Library 7332 1868/1870/www.clock makers.org). Mansion House or St Paul's tube/ Bank tube/DLR/Moorgate tube/rail. **Open** *9.30am-4.45pm Mon-Sat.* **Admission** *free.* **Map** p406 P6.

This well-presented horological exhibition at the Guildhall Library is filled with hundreds of ticking, chiming clocks that are produced by the London Clockmakers' Company. Among other venerable timepieces, you can see the marine chronometers that guided the ships of the British Empire and the watch Sir Edmund Hillary carried to the top of Everest in 1953. The museum also displays the world's oldest collection of mechanical pocket watches.

Guildhall

Gresham Street, EC2P 2EJ (7606 3030/tours ext 1463/www.corpoflondon.gov.uk). St Paul's tube/Bank tube/DLR. **Open** *May-Sept 10am-5pm daily. Oct-Apr 10am-5pm Mon-Sat. Last entry 4.30pm. Closes for functions, so phone ahead. Tours by arrangement; groups of 10 or more people only.* **Admission** *free.* **Map** p406 P6.

The cathedral-like Great Hall in the centre of the Guildhall compound has been the home of the Corporation of London for more than 800 years. Banners and shields of the 100 livery companies grace the walls, and every Lord Mayor since 1189 gets a namecheck on the windows. Around the walls you can see memorials to Pitt the Younger, Pitt the Elder, Nelson, Winston Churchill and the Duke of Wellington. These days the hall mainly serves as the setting for ceremonial events, including meetings of the Court of Common Council (the governing body for the Corporation of London).

Guildhall Art Gallery

Guildhall Yard, off Gresham Street, EC2P 2EJ (7332 3700/www.guildhall-art-gallery.org.uk). Mansion House or St Paul's tube/Bank tube/DLR/Moorgate tube/rail. **Open** *10am-5pm Mon-Sat (last entry 4.30pm); noon-4pm Sun (last entry 3.45pm).* **Admission** *£2.50; £1 concessions; free under-16s. Free to all after 3.30pm daily, all day Fri.* **Credit** *(over £5) MC, V.* **Map** p406 P6.

As you might expect, many of the paintings displayed at the Guildhall gallery are stuffy portraits of long-dead politicians, but there are a few surprises, including a delightful collection of pre-Raphaelite paintings with works by Rossetti and Millais. The centrepiece of the exhibition is the vast *Siege of Gibraltar* by John Copley – the largest painting in Britain – which spans two floors of the gallery. Elsewhere in the collection are grand paintings by Constable, Reynolds and others, covering such ground-breaking events as the freezing of the Thames in the Great Frost of 1739. Down in a sub-basement you can see the ruins of London's Roman amphitheatre, constructed in around AD 70.

Guildhall Library
Aldermanbury, EC2V 7HHJ (7332 1868/www.city oflondon.gov.uk). St Paul's tube/Bank tube/DLR. **Open** 9.30am-5pm Mon-Sat. **Admission** free. **Map** p406 P6.

The well-stocked library at the Guildhall has an extensive collection of books, manuscripts and prints relating to the history of London. Lithographs from the print collection are regularly displayed in the library exhibition space, along with a first edition of Samuel Johnson's dictionary.

Around the Tower of London

Map p407 R7/8
Tower Hill tube/Tower Gateway DLR.
Unlike certain other London attractions, the **Tower of London** (*see p100*) delivers plenty of entertainment for your money, but get here early to beat the crowds. It would be extremely bad form to leave London without seeing the Crown Jewels, the gleefully gruesome medieval weapons in the Royal Armoury and the Bloody Tower, where Sir Walter Raleigh was imprisoned and where the princes Edward V and Richard were brutally murdered, allegedly on the orders of Richard III.

Most people detour east to **Tower Bridge** (*see p100*) then move quickly on, but there's a fair bit to see in the area if you know where to look. Across the road from the Tower is one of the City's finest Edwardian buildings, the former **Port of London HQ** at 10 Trinity Square, with its towering neo-classical colonnade and gigantic statues of Commerce, Navigation, Export, Produce and Father Thames.

The surrounding streets and alleys have evocative names – Crutched Friars, Savage Gardens and Pepys Street, named for the famous diarist, Samuel Pepys, who lived and died close by in Seething Lane. In 1666 he oserved the Great Fire of London from **All Hallows by the Tower** (*see p100*). The diarist is buried in the church of **St Olave** on Hart Street, nicknamed 'St Ghastly Grim' by Dickens for the leering skulls at the entrance.

Swiss Re Tower. *See p98.*

On Lower Thames Street, between the tower and Monument, you can see several relics from the days when this part of the City was a busy port, including the old **Customs House** and **Billingsgate Market**, London's main fish market until 1982. The lanes behind the waterfront are packed with churches, including **St Magnus the Martyr** (*see p100*), St Mary-at-Hill, St Margaret Pattens and St Dunstan-in-the-East.

Still more historic churches can be seen between the tower and Liverpool Street Station, including **St Helen's Bishopsgate** (*see p100*) and **St Botolph's Aldgate** (*see p100*), and the tiny church of **St Katharine Cree** (7283 5733) on Leadenhall Street, one of only eight churches to survive the Great Fire. Inside is a memorial to Sir Nicholas Throckmorton, who was twice imprisoned in the Tower of London, despite – or perhaps because of – his close friendship with Queen Elizabeth I.

Nearby, in a courtyard off Bevis Marks, is the oldest synagogue in the country, the superbly preserved **Bevis Marks Synagogue** (7626 1274, closed Thur, Sat), built in 1701 by Sephardic Jews fleeing the Spanish Inquisition. Another haven in this area is the tiny 14th-century church of **St Ethelburga-the-Virgin** (*see below*), rebuilt after the IRA bomb of 1993.

All Hallows by the Tower

Byward Street, EC3R 5BJ (7481 2928/www. allhallowsbythetower.org.uk). Tower Hill tube. **Open** 9am-5.45pm Mon-Fri; 10am-5pm Sat, Sun. *Services* 11am Sun. **Admission** free; donations appreciated. **Map** p407 R7.

Often described as the oldest church in London, All Hallows is built on the foundations of a seventh-century Saxon church, but much of what you can see was reconstructed after World War II. The main hall contains a Saxon arch and a font cover carved by Grinling Gibbons in 1682. You can view Roman and Saxon relics and a Crusader altar in the undercroft.

The Monument

Monument Street, EC3R 8AH (7626 2717/www. towerbridge.org.uk). Monument tube. **Open** 9.30am-5pm daily. **Admission** £2; £1 concessions; free under-5s. **No credit cards. Map** p407 Q7.

The world's largest free-standing Doric column was constructed by Sir Christopher Wren in 1677 as a monument to the Great Fire of London. The 202 feet from the ground to the tip of the golden flame is the distance to Farriner's bakery in Pudding Lane, where the fire began. Inside, a 311-step spiral staircase winds up to a narrow gallery with giddying views over most of the landmarks in central London.

St Botolph's Aldgate

Aldgate High Street, EC3N 1AD (7283 1670/www. stbotolphs.org.uk). Aldgate tube. **Open** 10am-3pm Sun-Fri; Eucharist 1.05pm Mon, Thur. *Prayers* 9am Mon-Fri, 1.05pm Tue, Wed. **Admission** free; donations appreciated. **Map** p407 R6.

The oldest of three surviving churches of St Botolph, this red-brick church was built at the gates of Roman London as a homage to the patron saint of travellers. Reconstructed by George Dance in 1744, the church is noted for its beautiful ceiling decorated by John Francis Bentley. Daniel Defoe married here in 1683. A support service for the homeless is also based here.

St Ethelburga Centre for Reconciliation & Peace

78 Bishopsgate, EC2N 4AG (7496 1610/www. stethelburgas.org). Bank tube/DLR/Liverpool Street tube/rail. **Open** 11am-3pm Wed. **Admission** free; donations appreciated. **Map** p407 R6.

Built around 1390, the tiny church of St Ethelburga was almost obliterated by an IRA bomb in 1993. A decade later, it has risen from the ruins as a centre for peace and reconciliation. You can visit on Wednesdays to join the debate and observe the uses to which materials from the bombed building have been reused to fashion the new one.

St Helen's Bishopsgate

Great St Helen's, off Bishopsgate, EC3A 6AT (7283 2231/www.st-helens.org.uk). Bank tube/DLR/ Liverpool Street tube/rail. **Open** 9.30am-12.30pm Mon-Fri; also open some afternoons by appointment, call for details. *Services* 10.15am, 7pm Sun. **Admission** free. **Map** p407 R6.

Founded in 1210, St Helen's is actually two churches knocked into one, which explains its unusual shape. The church survived the Great Fire and the Blitz but was badly damaged by IRA bombs in 1992 and 1993. Repair work restored many of the church's original features. Inside you can see an impressive selection of 16th- and 17th-century memorials, including one to Sir William Pickering, Queen Elizabeth I's ambassador to Spain.

St Magnus the Martyr

Lower Thames Street, EC3R 6DN (7626 4481/www. stmagnusmartyr.org.uk). Monument tube. **Open** 10am-4pm Tue-Fri. *Mass* 11am Sun; 12.30pm Tue, Thur; 1.15pm Fri. **Admission** free; donations appreciated. **No credit cards. Map** p407 Q7.

Downhill from the Monument, this stately Wren church marks the entrance to the original London Bridge, which was lined with shops, monuments and fortifications. Sadly, town planners razed the buildings in 1758, but there's an impressive scale model of the old bridge inside the church. While you're here, check out the 18th-century wooden reredos and church organ, and the statue of axe-wielding St Magnus, the 12th-century Earl of Orkney.

Tower Bridge Exhibition

Tower Bridge, SE1 2UP (7403 3761/www.tower bridge.org.uk). Tower Hill tube. **Open** Apr-Sept 10am-5.30pm daily. Oct-Apr 9.30am-5pm daily. **Admission** £5.50; £3-£4.25 concessions; £14 family; free under-5s. **Credit** AmEx, MC, V. **Map** p407 R8.

The bridge that the Americans tried to buy and failed, Tower Bridge is an invaluable navigation point in the centre of the City. Even the German Luftwaffe relied on it to find their way around, saving the bridge from the bombs of the Blitz. In its day the drawbridge was a triumph of steam-powered Victorian technology, but these days few big ships venture this far upstream. Two towers and the west walkway have been converted into an exhibition on the history of the bridge – it's interesting stuff and the views from the top are stupendous.

Tower of London

Tower Hill, EC3N 4AB (0870 756 6060/www.hrp. org.uk). Tower Hill tube/Fenchurch Street rail. **Open** Mar-Oct 10am-6pm Mon, Sun; 9am-6pm Tue-Sat (last entry 5pm). Nov-Feb 10am-5pm Mon, Sun; 9am-5pm Tue-Sat (last entry 4pm). **Admission** £14.50; £9.50-£11 concessions; £42 family; free under-5s. **Credit** AmEx, MC, V. **Map** p407 R8.

One of the city's essential tourist attractions, the Tower of London is steeped in more than 900 years of history. Over the centuries, it has served as a fortress, a royal palace, a prison and an execution site

Fun and games (and executions): it's got to be the **Tower of London**. *See p100.*

for traitors to the state – this is where two of Henry VIII's wives were beheaded. Visitors mob the fortress daily, but there's so much to see that most people are happy to put up with the inconvenience. Getting into the Tower used to be a fairly convoluted process, but these days you just buy your ticket at the separate ticket office and enter through the Middle Tower. Before you come in, check out the interesting audio-visual display in the modernist Welcome Centre.

There are two ways to see the Tower: you can go it alone – with or without the audio tour – and stand some chance of having the displays to yourself, or join one of the free hour-long tours led by the Yeoman Warders (Beefeaters). Kids in particular will love the tours, with gruesome stories of treason, torture and execution delivered by cheery, red-coated former soldiers of the Crown.

The highlight is almost certainly the Crown Jewels, if only because they are so internationally renowned. Airport-style travelators glide past such treasures of state as Queen Victoria's Small Diamond Crown and the 2m-wide Grand Punch Bowl, which gives new meaning to the phrase 'family silver'. The other big drawcard is the armoury in the White Tower, with its execution axe and chopping block. Executions were actually carried out on the green in front of the Tower – a glass memorial by Brian Catling is scheduled to be in place on the site by early 2006.

Ongoing exhibitions for 2006 include 'Gunpowder Treason', celebrating the 400th anniversary of the Gunpowder Plot (set to run until June). New permanent additions include the torture exhibition in the Wakefield Tower and displays on famous prisoners

in the Bloody Tower and Beauchamp Tower – for example, consider the evidence for the murder of the 'Little Princes', then cast your vote. Don't forget to look out for the graffiti carved by former inmates.

You should book well ahead for the Christmas, half-term and summer events for families. Although disabled access has been improved, much remains inaccessible – call ahead if you require assistance. Combined tickets covering Hampton Court and Kensington Palaces are also available. **Photo** *above.*

North of London Wall

Map p404 P5

Barbican or Moorgate tube/rail.

You probably won't be surprised to learn that **London Wall** follows the approximate route of the old Roman walls of London. Although the area has been heavily developed since the end of World War II, often to the detriment of pedestrian access and aesthetics, patches of the Roman wall can still be seen poking up between today's modern glass-fronted office blocks. Fans of all things Roman can patrol the remaining stretches of the wall on a 1.75-mile interpretive walk, with panels (some of them barely legible) pointing out the highlights. The walk starts near the excellent **Museum of London** (*see p102*); the best-preserved sections are the bastions in the Barber-Surgeons Hall Gardens and the Salters' Garden in the atrium at the Salters' Hall on Fore Street.

Stained glass inside **Wesley's Chapel**.

The area north of London Wall was levelled during the Blitz and in 1958 the City of London and London County Council clubbed together to buy land for the construction of 'a genuine residential neighbourhood, with schools, shops, open spaces and amenities'. What Londoners got was the **Barbican**, a vast concrete estate of 2,000 flats that exudes little sense of warmth or community, despite having some of the highest property prices in London.

The Barbican feels more like an architect's giant model of how Londoners might live in the future than a place where 6,500 people go about their daily business. As wind moans through the empty concrete walkways and dust eddies skitter across the quadrangles, you may feel a sudden concern that there has been some terrible disaster, leaving you as the last human being on earth. However, the Barbican arts complex provides a measure of compensation, with a library, cinema, theatre and concert hall – reviewed in the appropriate chapters – plus an art gallery, housing a regularly changing collection of conceptual and esoteric art (box office 7638 8891). A recent improvement scheme has buffed up the foyer and entrances to good effect, and there's better signage.

Marooned amid the brick towers is the only pre-war building in the vicinity: the heavily restored 16th-century church of **St Giles Cripplegate** (7638 1997, closed Sat), where Oliver Cromwell was married and John Milton buried. Deeper inside the Barbican is the **Barbican Conservatory** (open noon-5pm Sun), a surprisingly pleasant greenhouse, full of exotic ferns and palms.

A short walk north-east, past the now-defunct Whitbread Brewery, takes you to **Bunhill Fields**. The site was an important burial ground for Nonconformists in the 19th century. Most of the graveyard is cordoned off, but you can stroll around the monuments to John Bunyan, Daniel Defoe and William Blake. Opposite Bunhill Fields on City Road is the **Museum of Methodism & John Wesley's House** (*see below*) where Margaret and Denis Thatcher married in 1951.

Museum of London

150 London Wall, EC2Y 5HN (0870 444 3851/2/ www.museumoflondon.org.uk). St Paul's tube/ Barbican tube/rail. **Open** 10am-5.50pm Mon-Sat; noon-5.50pm Sun. Last entry 5.30pm. **Admission** free; suggested donation £2. **Credit** (shop) AmEx, MC, V. **Map** p404 P5.

Reached through a brick bastion in the middle of a roundabout on London Wall, this well-thought-out museum traces the history of the capital from the earliest settlers to the outbreak of World War I. Galleries are laid out in chronological order and sound effects add character to the dioramas and displays of ancient artefacts from such surprising sites as the Saxon village under the Savoy Hotel on the Strand and Julius Caesar's camp at Heathrow.

Highlights include a model of the Great Fire, with a narrative from Pepys's diaries, an atmospheric walk-through Victorian street scene, an outrageous red-and-gold fairytale coach belonging to the Lord Mayor and an original hansom carriage, as patronised by London luminaries such as Sherlock Holmes and Jack the Ripper. The museum shop sells interesting London-related gifts and the central garden contains a curious botanical history of the City. As this guide went to press the museum's Medieval Gallery had just reopened, covering the period from the end of Roman rule in AD 410 to the accession of Elizabeth I in 1558.

Museum of Methodism & John Wesley's House

Wesley's Chapel, 49 City Road, EC1Y 1AU (7253 2262/www.wesleychapel.org.uk). Moorgate or Old Street tube/rail. **Open** 10am-4pm Mon-Sat; noon-2pm Sun. *Tours* arrangements on arrival; groups of 10 or more must phone ahead. **Admission** free; donations requested. **Credit** (shop) MC, V. **Map** p405 Q4.

This interesting museum is set in the former home and chapel of John Wesley (1703-91), the father of Methodism. The chapel crypt contains a quaint museum telling the story of the rise of Methodism, which contains a large collection of Wesleyan ceramics, and a pack of Methodist playing cards, among other objects. Next door is Wesley's house, displaying the minister's nightcap, preaching gown and personal experimental electric-shock machine. On the right side of the chapel are some of the finest public toilets in London – built in 1899 and with all their original fittings, including Victorian cisterns by Sir Thomas Crapper. **Photo** *above*.

Holborn & Clerkenwell

Lofty lawyers and loft conversions.

Holborn

Maps p401 & p409

Chancery Lane, Holborn or Temple tube (closed Sun).
The Saxon word 'Holburne' meant 'brook in
the hollow', but walking around the area just
west of the City today, you'd wonder what
inspired its quaint aquatic appellation. Look
harder, though, and you'll find many clues to
a watery geography, which, though mostly
obscured, endures underneath the streets
(*see p104* **Water lies beneath**). The gentle
slopes alongside the Farringdon Road down
to Holborn Viaduct are the banks of the buried
river Fleet, which runs in man-made pipes and
tunnels under the city, spilling out into the
Thames directly under Blackfriars Bridge.
Local street names also quietly echo this past,
including Fleet Street, now also being forgotten
after the newspapers moved out in the 1980s,
and Turnagain Lane, where carriages once had
to turn round and find their way back to the
bridge if they wanted to get across the Fleet.

Although modern shops and offices have
sprung up in recent decades along the main
routes, the area derives its essential character
from four medieval Inns of Court – tranquil,
leafy quadrangles that house the 'chambers'
(ie offices) of London's barristers.

Aldwych

Map p407

Temple tube (closed Sun).
Wandering away from the City along the
Strand takes you past some historic churches.
These include **St Clement Danes** (7242 8282),
on a traffic island just east of Aldwych. It's
believed that a church was first built here by
the Danish in the ninth century, but the
current building is mainly Sir Christopher
Wren's handiwork. Another church (**St
Clement Eastcheap**, 7623 5454) gave rise
to the nursery rhyme *Oranges and Lemons*;
the vicar of this church made a theme song of
it in 1920 and now the bells ring out the tune at
9am, noon, 3pm and 6pm (Monday to Saturday).
Nearby is **St Mary-le-Strand** (7836 3126,
open 11am-4pm Mon-Fri; music recitals 1.05pm
Wed, Fri), James Gibbs's first public building;
1714-17. The church was originally intended
to have a statue of Queen Anne on a column
aside it, but she died before it could be built
and the plan was scrapped. Before reaching
Waterloo Bridge you pass King's College, its
1960s buildings sitting uneasily with Robert
Smirke's 1829 originals, and the rather more
regal **Somerset House** (*see p105*). Just to
the north, on the Aldwych crescent, is a trio
of imperial buildings: India House, Australia
House and Bush House (home to the BBC's
World Service).

One of a handful of functioning cabmen's
shelters sits on **Temple Place** above the
Embankment. These green sheds, which
were not allowed to take up more space than
a horse and cab, are a legacy of the Cabmen's
Shelter Fund, set up in 1874 to give cabbies an
alternative to pubs. Nearby, on sinister **Strand
Lane**, is the so-called 'Roman' bath, reached via
Surrey Street, where Dickens took many a cold
plunge. Back near King's College, on the Strand
and on Surrey Street, are entrances to one
of London's ghost tube stations, Aldwych
(although the signs say 'Strand', the
station's earlier name).

Further north-west, opposite the **Royal
Courts of Justice** (*see p104*), are **Middle
Temple** (7427 4814, www.middletemple.
org.uk) and **Inner Temple** (7797 8183, www.
innertemple.org.uk). The name derives from
the Knights Templar, who owned the site for
150 years. Built around a maze of courtyards,
these Inns have a villagey feel and are especially
atmospheric when gas-lit after dark. If you book
in advance, tours of the Inner Temple can be
arranged at £10 per person (minimum ten
people, call 7797 8250). The **Middle Temple
Hall**, built in 1573, has a huge table made from
a single oak tree donated by Queen Elizabeth I,
and a smaller table made from the hatch of

Drake's ship the *Golden Hinde*. The Inner Temple has several fine buildings, and its lawns are a beautiful spot for picnics. Of particular note is **Temple Church** (King's Bench Walk, 7353 8559, www.templechurch.com); consecrated in 1185, it is London's only surviving round church. Part of Dan Brown's *The Da Vinci Code* is set here.

North of Middle Temple, on the Strand, is **Temple Bar**, which marks the historic boundary of the City of London with neighbouring Westminster. In the Middle Ages, it was a barrier to the City, past which the monarch could not stray without the approval of the Lord Mayor. Today the monument is a bronze griffin, but for many centuries it was a physical gate forming an entrance to the City. A magnificent stone archway designed by Sir Christopher Wren was Temple Bar for two centuries, but had to be dismantled 1878 when the Corporation of London decided to widen the road. Wren's Bar was then purchased by the brewer Sir Henry Meux who had it re-erected as an entrance to his country estate in Hertfordshire. From 1976 a charity, Temple Bar Trust, began pitching for its return to London; in 1984 they were able to buy it from the Meux estate for a mere £1. But it took around ten years (and many millions of pounds) before the resplendent arch was reconstructed and reopened at its new location in Paternoster Square, just north of **St Paul's Cathedral**'s impressive main entrance (*see p94*).

Three more historic churches are in close proximity along the Strand and Fleet Street. On the latter, heading back towards the City, by the junction with New Fetter Lane, is **St Dunstan in the West** (7405 1929, www.stdunstaninthewest.org), where the poet John Donne was rector from 1624 until his death in 1631. Incongruously, next door at 186 was where Sweeney Todd, the 'demon barber of Fleet Street', murdered his customers before selling their bodies to a local pie shop.

Royal Courts of Justice

Strand, WC2A 2LL (7947 6000/www.courtservice.gov.uk). Temple tube. **Open** 9am-5pm Mon-Fri. **Admission** free. **Map** p401 M6.

The magnificent Royal Courts preside over the most serious civil cases in British law. Members of the public are actually allowed to attend these trials (with exceptions made for sensitive cases), so if you want to see the British justice system in action, step inside. There are few trials in August and September. Note that cameras and children under 14 years of age are not permitted; it's probably not the best place to try breaking the rules.

Water lies beneath

In his 1885 novel *After London*, Richard Jefferies depicts a London that takes revenge on its inhabitants. After centuries of Londoners dumping their waste into the city's rivers, the rubbish builds up, causing rivers to overflow and sewage systems to explode. The morally unclean citizens are fittingly drowned in their own effluence.

The reality of London's numerous underground waterways is somewhat less extravagant, although no less fascinating to lovers of city secrets. The Fleet River, also known as the Fleet Ditch, is probably the best known of these. It begins at two separate sources at Hampstead and Highgate ponds, before converging just north of Camden Town. The current then wends its unseen way beneath King's Cross and Holborn, before emerging into the Thames besides Blackfriars Bridge.

The Anglo-Saxon word 'fleet' meant tidal inlet, and this was once an appropriate name for the lower reaches of the river: when the Romans arrived in Londinium the Fleet was significantly larger than it is now – some 600 feet wide at its mouth. The more northerly sections of the river were referred to as the River of Wells (near Clerkenwell) and Turnmill Brook (many mills lined its banks), and the Hole Bourne – 'the stream in the hollow' – named because of its positioning in a deep valley. This area, of course, is now known as Holborn, and the name Fleet is applied to the whole waterway.

Much of the Fleet's history is tied to filth and entrails. Newgate Street butchers were given permission to wash entrails behind the Fleet Prison in 1343. In the 17th century the Fleet was banked by squalid housing for the very poor; by the early 1700s it had simply become an open sewer. The problem was solved to some extent in 1733 when an arch was built over the river from Holborn Bridge to Fleet Bridge, a construction that eventually became Farringdon Road. And in 1766 the stretch of water from the Fleet Bridge down to the Thames was channelled underground, never to be seen again. Fittingly, the Fleet is now an official sewer. Perhaps London will get its revenge after all.

Somerset House

Strand, WC2R 1LA (7845 4600/www.somerset-house.org.uk). Temple tube (closed Sun). **Open** 10am-6pm daily (last entry 5.15pm); extended hours for courtyard & terrace. *Tours* phone for details. **Admission** *Courtyard & terrace* free. Exhibitions £5; £4 concessions. **Credit** (shop) MC, V. **Map** p403 M7.

The original Somerset House was a Tudor palace commissioned by the Duke of Somerset in 1547. It was extended and refurbished several times over two centuries, but it began to suffer from poor maintenance and in 1775 was demolished to make way for an entirely new building. The architect Sir William Chambers spent the last 20 years of his life working on the neo-classical mansion that now peers out over the Thames. It was built to accommodate learned societies including the Royal Academy; various governmental offices also took up residence, including the Inland Revenue. The taxmen are still here, but the rest of the building is open to the public, and houses three formidable art and museum collections (*see below*), the beautiful fountain court, which becomes an outdoor ice rink in winter (*see p271* **Air play**), a little café, a classy restaurant (the Admiralty; *see p209*) and a pleasant river terrace, with views of Westminster and St Paul's. **Photo** *p106*.

Somerset House museums

Strand, WC2R 0RN. Holborn or Temple tube (closed Sun). **Open** 10am-6pm daily (last entry 5.15pm). **Admission** *1 collection* £5; £4 concessions. *2 collections* £8; £7 concessions. *3 collections* £12; £11 concessions. Free students, under-18s; Courtauld Gallery free to all 10am-2pm Mon. *Tours* phone for details. **No credit cards. Map** p407 M7.

Courtauld Institute of Art Gallery

7848 2526/www.courtauld.ac.uk/gallery.

The Courtauld has one of Britain's most important collections of painting. The gallery is diverse and eclectic, yet on a more manageable scale than, say, the National. Old Masters, Impressionists and post-Impressionists are here alongside a range of prints, drawings, sculpture and other pieces. Famous works include Manet's *A Bar at the Folies L Bergère*, Van Gogh's *Self-Portrait with Bandaged Ear* and Degas' *Two Dancers on the Stage*. The collection of 20th-century works has also been expanded with pieces by Kandinsky, Matisse and Barbara Hepworth. The Gallery holds regular art-related talks and events.

Gilbert Collection

7420 9400/www.gilbert-collection.org.uk.

In 1949, British-born Sir Arthur Gilbert uprooted to California, where he subsequently made millions in real estate. He developed a predilection for all that glisters, collecting silver, gold and all sorts of gemmed, gilt and shiny objects. In 1996 Britain became the beneficiary of his opulence when he donated his entire collection, saying 'I felt it should return to the country of my birth' – and he even continued buying new pieces after the museum had been opened. The dazzling arsenal of objects is now proudly displayed at Somerset House. Two

Hunterian Museum. *See p106.*

floors are shamelessly bedecked with candelabras, mosaics, vases, urns, plates, mosaics, snuff boxes, and more. The museum also holds themed exhibitions throughout the year.

Hermitage Rooms

7845 4630/www.hermitagerooms.co.uk.

The Hermitage Rooms host rotating exhibitions of items belonging to the Winter Palace in St Petersburg; the rooms even recreate in miniature the decor of their Russian twin. New shows arrive twice a year and can include everything from paintings and drawings to decorative art and fine jewellery. For each ticket sold, £1 goes to the State Hermitage Museum in St Petersburg.

Lincoln's Inn & Gray's Inn

Map p401

Chancery Lane or Holborn tube.

Alighting at busy Holborn tube – a stone's throw from the West End – you'd never guess that just behind it lies the verdant tranquillity of **Lincoln's Inn Fields**, the largest public square in London. The Fields are flanked by a series of historic buildings. On the north side is **Sir John Soane's Museum** (*see p106*); south-west on Portsmouth Street is the **Old Curiosity Shop**, supposedly the oldest extant shop in London (now selling shoes); to the south is the Royal College of Surgeons, which houses the **Hunterian Museum** (*see below*), now open again to the public after an extensive £3 million renovation; and south-east is **Lincoln's Inn** (7405 1393, www.lincolnsinn.org.uk), the Inn of Court from which the fields take their name. The Inn's various buildings are a historical catalogue of architectures including Gothic, Tudor and Palladian; its Old Hall was built well over 500 years ago.

North of High Holborn, **Red Lion Square** is home to **Conway Hall**, the seat of the Ethical Society (7242 8037), which holds regular discussions and freethinking events. Heading east along either High Holborn or Theobald's Road brings you to **Gray's Inn** (7458 7800, www.graysinn.org.uk). Its gardens, known colloquially as the 'Walks', were laid out by Francis Bacon in 1606. They are open to the public on weekdays (10am-2.30pm Mon-Fri).

Opposite Chancery Lane tube is the half-timbered **Staple Inn**, one of the few buildings to have survived the Great Fire of London, and one of the only remaining Tudor structures in the capital. On Chancery Lane itself, visit the underground **London Silver Vaults** (7242 3844, www.thesilvervaults.com), where the goods of over 30 dealers constitute the world's largest 'collection' of antique silver. The vaults first opened in 1876, renting out strong rooms for the wealthy to protect their valuables.

Hunterian Museum

Royal College of Surgeons, 35-43 Lincoln's Inn Fields, WC2A 3PE (7869 6560/www.rcseng.ac.uk/museums). Holborn tube. **Open** 10am-5pm Tue-Sat. **Admission** free. **Map** p401 M6.

John Hunter (1728-1793) was a pioneering surgeon and anatomist, appointed surgeon to King George III and later Surgeon General to the British Army. Throughout his life he amassed a huge collection of many thousands of medical specimens. After he died, the collection was enhanced and expanded by other leading scientists; today it can be viewed in the recently refurbished Hunterian Museum at the Royal College of Surgeons. The bright, clean new space means there is nothing gory about the exhibits. That said, the place isn't without its challenges for the squeamish: the brain of 19th-century mathematician Charles Babbage and Winston Churchill's dentures are among the displays. There's also a collection of the (non-medical) paintings and artworks that Hunter amassed. **Photo** *p105*.

Sir John Soane's Museum

13 Lincoln's Inn Fields, WC2A 3BP (7405 2107/www.soane.org). Holborn tube. **Open** 10am-5pm Tue-Sat; 10am-5pm, 6-9pm 1st Tue of mth. *Tours* 2.30pm Sat. **Admission** free; donations appreciated. *Tours* £3; free concessions. **Map** p401 M5.

A leading architect in his day, Sir John Soane (1753-1837) obsessively collected art, furniture and other decorative objects – partly for enjoyment and

Somerset House...

partly for research. In the early 19th century, he turned his house into a museum so that 'amateurs and students' would be able to enjoy his collection. Much of the museum's appeal derives from its domestic atmosphere; it's the house of a rich art lover, where you're the lucky guest. Surfaces are covered with a pleasant chaos of sculptures, paintings, architectural models, antiquities, jewellery and other miscellaneous bits and pieces. The 3,300-year-old sarcophagus of an Egyptian pharaoh is a particular highlight, but many other pieces are just as striking.

Clerkenwell & Farringdon

Map p404

Farringdon tube/rail.

Clerkenwell means the clerks' well, another clue to the rivers that once flowed through the area, now erased from the landscape. The clerks' well drew water from the river Fleet, but it fell out of use and was covered over, probably because in its lower reaches the Fleet had become more of a sewer than a river. In 1924 builders carrying out work in Farringdon Lane chanced upon the old well, and it can now be seen through a window at 14-16 Farringdon Lane. The name Clerkenwell also contains another historical clue – its 'clerks' being indicative of the area's strong monastic links. A community flourished here as early as the 11th century, when the Order of St John of Jerusalem set up its priory near the current St John church. The visible reminder of the historic priory is **St John's Gate**, which dates from 1504. It contains the **Museum & Library of the Order of St John** (*see p107*), the Order which spawned today's St John's Ambulance service. The priory's Norman crypt also survives.

with its impressive piazza. *See p105.*

Clerkenwell Road cuts through the old priory's grounds. North of the modern road, more ecclesiastical history is visible. The current **St James Church** (Clerkenwell Close, 7251 1190, www.jc-church.org) stands on the former site of the nunnery of St Mary's Clerkenwell, just off the happy little village-like square of **Clerkenwell Green**, with its pubs and restaurants. Closer to the Barbican, south east of here, the Carthusian monastery of **Charterhouse** was established in 1370; its cloisters, 14th-century chapel and 17th-century library survive to this day. Back towards Holborn, **St Etheldreda** (*see below*) is Britain's oldest Catholic church.

During industrialisation, new trades took root on the fringes of the City, and many factories and workshops were constructed on the open spaces of Clerkenwell. Most of these trades have long since departed, though the area is still London's jewellery-making epicentre, with countless craftsmen and shops, especially in **Hatton Garden**, which runs parallel with Farringdon Road north of Holborn. The industrial legacy is mainly architectural, though. After a century of general disuse, in the 1980s and '90s the warehouses were eyed up by property developers and converted into modern flats and lofts. A forgotten and destitute district swiftly became a viable residence for City folk working just south, and restaurants, bars and nightclubs dutifully followed. The Eagle (159 Farringdon Road; *see p216* **Reinventing the meal**), which opened in 1991, is frequently touted as the very first gastropub and still knocks out first-rate fare; Fabric (77A Charterhouse Street; *see p320*) has become London's flagship superclub.

Museum & Library of the Order of St John

St John's Gate, St John's Lane, EC1M 4DA (7324 4000/www.sja.org.uk/history). Farringdon tube/rail. **Open** 10am-5pm Mon-Fri; 10am-4pm Sat. *Tours* 11am, 2.30pm Tue, Fri, Sat. **Admission** free. *Tours* free. Suggested donation £5; £4 concessions. **Credit** MC, V. **Map** p404 O4.

Today the Order of St John is best known in London for its provision of ambulance services, but it dates back to early Christian medical practice during the Crusades of the 11th-, 12th- and 13th-centuries. This museum charts the evolution of the medieval Order of Hospitaller Knights into its modern incarnation. There are fascinating collections of objects and artworks relating to this varied history, which visits Jerusalem, Malta and the Ottoman Empire. A separate collection relates specifically to the evolution of the modern ambulance service.

St Etheldreda

14 Ely Place, EC1N 6RY (7405 1061). Chancery Lane tube or Farringdon tube/rail. **Open** 8.30am-7pm daily. **Admission** free; donations appreciated. **Map** p404 N5.

St Etheldreda, which takes its name from an Anglo-Saxon saint, is Britain's oldest Catholic church and London's only surviving example of 13th-century Gothic architecture. Only saved from the Great Fire of London by a change in the wind, this is the last remaining building of the Bishop of Ely's palace. The crypt is dark and atmospheric, untouched by the noise of nearby traffic. The church's stained-glass windows (which, deceptively, are actually from the 1960s) are stunning. As an interesting piece of trivia, the strawberries once grown in the gardens of Ely Place were said to be the finest in the city, even receiving praise in Shakespeare's *Richard III*: 'My lord of Ely, when I was last in Holborn/I saw good strawberries in your garden there.'

Bloomsbury & Fitzrovia

Intellectual property.

Bloomsbury

Map p401

Chancery Lane, Holborn, Euston Square, Russell Square or Tottenham Court Road tube.
Though often associated with the group of writers and artists who once colonised its townhouses, and more recently with the many universities with centres in this area, Bloomsbury hasn't always been a refuge for the high-minded. Back in the 11th century, for instance, the neighbourhood was a breeding ground for pigs. What's more, its pretty floral name also has humdrum origins: it's taken from 'Blemondisberi', or 'the manor of William Blemond', who acquired the area in the early 13th century. It remained rural until the 1660s, when the fourth Earl of Southampton built Bloomsbury Square around his house, though none of the original architecture remains. The Southamptons intermarried with the Russells, the Dukes of Bedford, and both families developed the area as one of London's first planned suburbs. During the next couple of centuries, they built a series of grand squares and streets, laid out in the classic Georgian grid style: check out **Bedford Square** (1775-80), London's only complete Georgian square, and huge **Russell Square**, now an attractive public park. Gower Street also showcases an uninterrupted stream of classic Georgian terraced houses.

Things are not so posh now (witness the aforementioned students), but the shabby grandeur is undeniably charming. The area's main charm lies in the sum of its parts, in an afternoon spent meandering through open spaces, peering into museum display cabinets and losing yourself in the throngs of a student café. Keep an eye out for the blue plaques, which read like a 'who's who' of English literature: William Butler Yeats once lived at 5 Upper Woburn Place; Edgar Allan Poe lived at 83 Southampton Row; Mary Wollstonecraft lived on Store Street, the birthplace of Anthony Trollope (he was born at No.6). Then there's Charles **Dickens' House**, at 48 Doughty Street, now a museum (*see p111*). As for the famous Bloomsbury Group, its headquarters was at 50 Gordon Square, where EM Forster, Lytton Strachey, John Maynard Keynes, Clive and Vanessa Bell and Duncan Grant would discuss literature, art and politics. Virginia and Leonard Woolf lived at 52 Tavistock Square. **Gordon Square** also holds an allure for orientalists – the erudite **Percival David Foundation of Chinese Art** is at No.53 (7387 3909) – but the real academia is clustered around Bloomsbury's western borders. Here, Malet Street, Gordon Street and Gower Street are dominated by the **University of London**. The most notable building is **University College**, on Gower Street, founded in 1826 and built in the Greek Revival style by William Wilkins, the architect responsible for the National Gallery. Inside lies one of the strangest exhibits in London: the preserved remains of philosopher Jeremy Bentham, who introduced the world to utilitarianism. Nearby, is the iconic **BT Tower** (60 Cleveland Street), given Grade II-listed status in 2003.

The massive **Senate House**, over on Malet Street, holds the university's biggest library. It was a particular favourite of Hitler: had Germany won the war, he had planned to make his headquarters here. South of the university lies the renowned **British Museum** (*see p109*), with its collection of the world's riches, not the least of which are the marble friezes from the Parthenon in Athens.

Such grand institutions may have put Bloomsbury on the map, but aficionados claim that the real delights lie in hidden pockets. **Sicilian Avenue**, a pedestrianised stretch of colonnaded shops that links Bloomsbury Way with Southampton Row, is one such. On the former, **St George's Bloomsbury** (7405 3044, www.stgeorges bloomsbury.org.uk), a Hawksmoor church, is closed until spring/summer 2006 as it undergoes a £10 million restoration project.

North-east of here is **Lamb's Conduit Street**, a convivial area with a good selection of old-fashioned pubs and stylish restaurants. At the top of this street lies wonderful **Coram's Fields** (*see p276*), a children's park (adults are only admitted if accompanied by a child) built on the former grounds of Thomas Coram's Foundling Hospital, which provided for abandoned children. The legacy of the great Coram family is now commemorated in the beautiful **Foundling Museum** (*see p111*). Tucked away behind the student-land is **Mecklenburgh Square**, and to the north-west lies budget hotel-land and **Cartwright Garden**. **Woburn Walk** is a pleasant stretch of shops and cafés.

It's not all Georgian grandeur. Take the **Brunswick Centre**, just opposite Russell Square tube station. When it was built in 1973, Patrick Hodgkinson's concrete jungle was hailed as the future for community living: a complex of shopping centre, flats, a cinema and an underground car park. Thirty years on, modernism's young dream is Bloomsbury's worst eyesore. Still, film fans love the **Renoir Cinema** (*see p286*), and fossicking readers frequent Skoob Russell Square (No.10, 7278 8760) for second-hand books. For new ones,

there's the massive Waterstone's (*see p237*) on Gower Street; for alternative ones Gay's the Word (66 Marchmont Street, 7278 7654) and Bookmarks (1 Bloomsbury Street, 7637 1848) is all left-wing tomes. Comic buffs, take note: the **Cartoon Museum** (formerly the Cartoon Art Trust) left its Brunswick Centre home in late 2005 and was hoping to relocate to new premises at 35 Little Russell Street from February 2006 (check the website – www.cartoonmuseum. co.uk – for more up-to-date news).

British Museum

Great Russell Street, WC1B 3DG (7636 1555/ recorded information 7323 8783/www.thebritish museum.ac.uk). Russell Square or Tottenham Court Road tube. **Open** *Galleries* 10am-5.30pm Mon-Wed, Sat, Sun; 10am-8.30pm Thur, Fri. *Great Court* 9am-6pm Mon-Wed, Sun; 9am-11pm Thur-Sat. *Highlights tours (90mins)* 10.30am, 1pm, 3pm daily. *Eye opener tours (50mins)* phone for details. **Admission** free; donations appreciated. *Temporary exhibitions* prices vary. *Highlights tours* £8; £5 concessions. *Eye opener tours* free. **Credit** (shop) DC, MC, V. **Map** p401 K/L5. Officially London's most popular tourist attraction, the museum is a neo-classical marvel built in 1847 by Robert Smirke, one of the pioneers of the Greek Revival style. Also impressive is Sir Norman Foster's glass-roofed Great Court, the largest covered space in Europe, opened in 2000. This £100m

Capsule collection

A 30-minute dash round the British Museum.

Start: 0-2mins

Don running shoes and sports bra (optional). Take the main entrance at Great Russell Street. Jog through the iron gates, then up the steps and into Sir Norman Foster's impressive glass-roofed Great Court. Have a gawp by all means, but try not to tread on too many tourists.

Stage 2: 3-9 mins

Swerve left into Ancient Civilisations (Gallery 8) – via the Reading Room to soak up the calm – to check out the Rosetta Stone. Next: the Elgin Marbles (Gallery 18), still causing rows between the British and Greek governments. Take a moment to reflect upon our great nation's talent for plunder, then wipe away a tear and move on.

Stage 3: 10-20 mins

Bound up the West Stairs to the Egyptian Galleries. Note the stunning Turkish and North African mosaics on the way. Forge ahead to Gallery 62 for a gander at the

lavishly decorated coffins. Warning: you may need pointed elbows to fend off schoolkids – there's no time to stand politely aside while they get their mummy-fix.

Stage 4: 21-23 mins

Press ahead to Gallery 56. First a breather in front of the Queen of the Night, a detailed relief of a Mesopotamian goddess, then a sprint down the East Stairs, dominated by an 36-foot carved red cedar Canadian Totem.

Stage 5: 24-29 mins

Dash around the Enlightenment Gallery. If you've been keeping an eye on the clock, you should have enough time to visit the hands-on table to play with fossils, ancient pots or tiles. Try not to steal anything.

Finish: 30 mins

Don't forget to leave a donation in one of the boxes before you dash out the door. Much is needed since the admission charge was scrapped in 2001.

landmark surrounds the domed Reading Room, where Marx, Lenin, Thackeray, Dickens, Hardy and Yeats once worked. Star exhibits include Ancient Egyptian artefacts – the Rosetta Stone, statues of the pharaohs, mummies – and Greek antiquities, such as the marble freizes from the Parthenon. The Celts gallery has the Lindow Man, killed in 300 BC and preserved in peat. The Wellcome Gallery of Ethnography holds an Easter Island statue and regalia from Captain Cook's travels.

The King's Library, which opened in 2004, is the finest neo-classical space in London, and home to a permanent exhibition, Enlightenment: Discovering the World in the 18th Century, a 5,000-piece collection devoted to the formative period of the museum. Its remit covers physics, archaeology and the natural world, and it contains objects as diverse as 18th-century Indonesian puppets and a beautiful orrery.

You won't be able to see everything in one day, so buy a souvenir guide and pick out the showstoppers, or plan several visits. The Highlights tours focus on specific aspects of the collection; the Eye opener tours are introductions to world cultures, led by volunteers. Scheduled exhibitions for 2006 include 'Michelangelo Drawings: Closer to the Master' (23 Mar-25 June) and 'French Drawings from the British Museum: Clouet to Seurat' (26 June-26 Nov). **Photo** *right*.

Dickens' House
48 Doughty Street, WC1N 2LX (7405 2127/www. dickensmuseum.com). Chancery Lane or Russell Square tube. **Open** 10am-5pm Mon-Sat; 11am-5pm Sun. *Tours* by arrangement. **Admission** £5; £3-£4 concessions; £14 family. **Credit** (shop) AmEx, DC, MC, V. **Map** p401 M4.

London is scattered with plaques marking the many addresses where the peripatetic Charles Dickens lived but never quite settled, including Devonshire Terrace near Paddington and Camden's Bayham Street, but this is the only one of the author's many London homes that is still standing. Dickens lived here for three years between 1837 and 1840 while he wrote *Nicholas Nickleby* and *Oliver Twist*. Restored to its former condition, the house is packed with Dickens ephemera. There are personal letters, all sorts of manuscripts and his writing desk.

Foundling Museum
40 Brunswick Square, Bloomsbury, WC1N 1AZ (7841 3600/www.foundlingmuseum.org.uk). Russell Square tube. **Open** 10am-6pm Tue-Sat; noon-6pm Sun. **Admission** £5; £3 concessions; free under-16s. **Credit** MC, V. **Map** p401 L4.

This is a child-friendly place in every sense. Opened in 2004, the museum recalls the social history of the Foundling Hospital, set up by a compassionate shipwright and sailor, Captain Thomas Coram in 1739. Returning to England from America in 1720, he was appalled by the number of abandoned children on the streets, and securing royal patronage, he gained the artist William Hogarth and the composer GF Handel as governors. Hogarth decreed that the building should also be the first public art gallery,

The unrivalled **British Museum**. *See p109.*

and artists including Gainsborough, Reynolds and Wilson donated their work. The museum uses pictures, manuscripts and objects to recount the social change in the period, with interactive exhibits, and a case of mementos left by mothers for their babies.

Petrie Museum of Archaeology
University College London, Malet Place, WC1E 6BT (7679 2884/www.petrie.ucl.ac.uk). Euston Square, Goodge Street or Warren Street or tube. **Open** 1-5pm Tue-Fri; 10am-1pm Sat. **Admission** free; donations appreciated. **Map** p401 K4.

If you get lost while looking, don't give up, the Petrie is hard to find (the entrance is through the UCL Science Library), but it's worth it. The rather gloomy interior and 1950s wooden display cabinets give it all a kind of 'Indiana Jones on home leave' vibe, and some of the labelling is suitably professorial (read: dry). But there's fun to be had among the various girly bits: make-up pots, grooming accessories, jewellery, and a dress dating back to 2800 BC. Some things never change. Check out the coiffured head of a mummy with eyebrows and lashes intact.

St Pancras New Church
Euston Road (corner of Upper Woburn Place), NW1 2BA (7388 1461/www.stpancraschurch.org). Euston tube/rail. **Open** 12.45-2pm Wed; noon-2pm Thur; 9.15-11am, 3-5pm Sat; 7.45am-noon, 5.30-7.15pm Sun; occasional lunchtimes Tue, Fri. *Services* 8am, 10am, 6pm Sun; 1.15pm Wed. **Admission** free. **Map** p401 K3.

Built in 1822, this church is a spectacular example of the Greek Revivalist style. At the time of its construction, it was, at £89,296, the second most expensive church in London, after St Paul's. Inspired by the Erechtheion in Athens, its most notable feature is its Caryatid porches, entrances to the burial vaults. The interior is more restrained but has beautiful 19th-century stained-glass windows. Free lunchtime concerts (Thursdays, 1.15pm) soothe the jangled nerves of local workers with performances by violinists, pianists and sopranos. In July 2005 the church was in the public gaze when flowers were laid outside after the nearby bus bombing. **Photo** *p113*.

Somers Town & King's Cross

Map p401

Euston or King's Cross tube/rail.
Currently undergoing an extensive makeover as part of the Channel Tunnel Rail Link development (see www.ctrl.co.uk for the latest news), Somers Town, King's Cross and the surrounding area are set to see significant changes in the near future. The former, situated on the north side of Euston Road between St Pancras and Euston stations, is where Dickens located his darker characters, and where locals lived in fear of the 'Somers Town mob'. Even today the area exudes a gritty realism. **Euston Station** is a bleak 1960s building that tragically replaced Philip Hardwick's beautiful Victorian structure. **St Pancras Station**, by contrast, has a gorgeous Victorian glass and iron train shed fronted by Sir George Gilbert Scott's Gothic hotel, the Midland Grand. This building is now **St Pancras Chambers** and, at press time, was still open to the public for tours (7713 6514), pending redevelopment work.

To the east lies **King's Cross**, which is the kind of place your mother warned you about. Immortalised in Neil Jordan's *Mona Lisa* and various TV dramas, the area is notoriously seedy, and a favourite of prostitutes and junkies. It only gets worse, as north of here is pure industrial wasteland. But that's cool: there are now a few hip clubs in the area. And you can bet when the Eurostar terminal opens at St Pancras in 2007, grimy King's Cross will be gentrified beyond belief.

British Library

96 Euston Road, NW1 2DB (7412 7332/www.bl.uk).
Euston Square tube/Euston or King's Cross tube/rail.
Open 9.30am-6pm Mon, Wed-Fri; 9.30am-8pm Tue; 9.30am-5pm Sat; 11am-5pm Sun. **Admission** free; donations appreciated. **Map** p401 K/L3.
This is one of the greatest libraries in the world, with 150 million items. Each year, it receives a copy of every publication produced in the UK and Ireland. The judgement 'one of the ugliest buildings in the world', famously passed by a Parliamentary com-

mittee, has been just one of the controversies that have dogged the new British Library since it opened in 1997. The project went over budget by £350m and took 20 years to complete (and was 15 years behind schedule). When it finally opened, architecture critics ripped it to shreds.

But don't judge a book by its cover: the interior is spectacular, all white marble, glass and light. In the piazza sits Antony Gormley's sculpture *Planets*, a new addition in 2003. In the John Ritblat Gallery, the library's main treasures are displayed: the Magna Carta, the Lindisfarne Gospels and original manuscripts from Chaucer. There's fun stuff too: Beatles lyric sheets, first editions of *The Jungle Books* and archive recordings of everyone from James Joyce to Bob Geldof. The library is also famous for its 80,000-strong stamp collection. The focal point of the building is the astonishing King's Library, a six-storey glass-walled tower that houses George III's collection. If you're here for research purposes, you're in for a treat: facilities are superlative.

St Pancras Old Church & St Pancras Gardens

St Pancras Road, NW1 1UL (7387 4193).
Mornington Crescent tube/King's Cross tube/rail.
Open *Gardens* 7am-dusk daily. *Services* 9am Mon-Fri; 9.30am Sun; 7pm Tue. **Admission** free. **Map** p401 K2.
The Old Church, whose site may date back to the fourth century, has been ruined and rebuilt many times. The current structure is handsome, but it's the recently restored churchyard that delights. Among those buried here are writer William Godwin and his wife, Mary Wollstonecraft; over this grave, their daughter Mary Godwin (author of *Frankenstein*) declared her love for poet Percy Bysshe Shelley. The grave of Sir John Soane is one of only two Grade I-listed tombs (the other is Karl Marx's, in Highgate Cemetery; *see p155* **The Magnificent Seven**); its dome influenced Sir Giles Gilbert Scott's design of the classic British phone box.

Fitzrovia

Map pp400-401

Tottenham Court Road or Goodge Street tube.
Squeezed in between Gower Street, Oxford Street, Great Portland Street and Euston Road, Fitzrovia may not be as famous as Bloomsbury but its history is just as rich. It only became known as Fitzrovia during the 20th century. The origins of its name are hazy: some believe it comes from Fitzroy Square, which was named after Henry Fitzroy, the son of Charles II. Others insist that the neighbourhood was named after the famous Fitzroy Tavern (7580 3714) at 16 Charlotte Street, London bohemia's ground zero for much of the 20th century. Once a favourite with radicals and artists, regulars included Dylan Thomas, George Orwell, Aleister Crowley and Quentin Crisp.

St Pancras New Church – you'd still get change from £90,000. *See p111.*

The neighbourhood's radical roots go deep. In 1792 Thomas Paine lived at 154 New Cavendish Street – the same year he published *The Rights of Man* and incurred governmental wrath. His friend Edmund Burke lived at 18 Charlotte Street. During the early 19th century the district became a hotbed of Chartist activity and working men's clubs. Later, Karl Marx attended Communist meetings in Tottenham Street, Charlotte Street and Rathbone Place. He was also a regular on the Tottenham Court Road pub scene: his favourites included the Rising Sun (No.46); the Court (No.108); the Mortimer Arms (No.174); and the Jack Horner (then known as the Italian, No.236).

A century later, Fitzrovia played pop. In the 1960s the Stones played gigs at the 100 Club (100 Oxford Street). A young Bob Dylan made his British debut singing at the King & Queen Pub (1 Foley Street) in 1962. Concert scenes for the Beatles' *A Hard Day's Night* were filmed at the Scala Theatre, then at 21-25 Tottenham Street. Pink Floyd and Jimi Hendrix were regulars at the Speakeasy at 50 Margaret Street. As flower power declined, punk took over. Regular performers at the 100 Club included the Sex Pistols, Siouxsie and the Banshees, the Damned and the Clash. At this time, Fitzrovia was descended upon by squatters, among them Boy George. During the 1980s Fitzrovia's raffish image was transformed when the media moved in. ITN started broadcasting from 48 Wells Street, and Channel 4's first office was at 60

Charlotte Street in 1982. Meanwhile, the BBC's simple, pared-down Broadcasting House has been on the western fringe of the area – 2-8 Portland Place – since 1922.

All Saints

7 Margaret Street, W1W 8JG (7636 1788/www. allsaintsmargaretstreet.org.uk). Oxford Circus tube. **Open** 7am-7pm daily. *Services* 7.30am-8am, 1.10pm, 6pm, 6.30pm Mon-Fri; 7.30am, 8am, 6pm, 6.30pm Sat; 8am, 10.20am, 11am, 5.15pm, 6pm Sun. **Admission** free. **Map** p408 U1.

This 1850s church was designed by William Butterfield, one of the great Gothic Revivalists. It is squeezed into a tiny site, but its soaring architecture and lofty spire – the second-highest in London – disguise this fact. Its lavish interior is one of the city's most striking, with rich marble, flamboyant tile work, and glittering stones built into its pillars.

Pollock's Toy Museum

1 Scala Street (entrance on Whitfield Street), W1T 2HL (7636 3452/www.pollockstoymuseum.com). Goodge Street tube. **Open** 10am-5pm Mon-Sat. **Admission** £3; £1.50 concessions; free under-3s. **Credit** (shop) MC, V. **Map** p400 J5.

Housed in a wonderfully creaky Georgian townhouse, Pollock's is named after Benjamin Pollock, the last of the Victorian toy theatre printers. The nostalgia value of old board games, clockwork trains and Robertson's gollies can hardly be overestimated for adults. For young children, however, the displays can seem a bit static and irrelevant; what they seem to enjoy most are the shop and the regular free puppet shows (generally held on Saturdays).

Sightseeing

Marylebone

When it comes to shopping, who needs Knightsbridge?

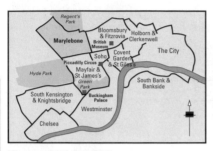

Maps p397 & p400

Baker Street, Bond Street, Edgware Road, Great Portland Street, Marble Arch, Oxford Circus or Regent's Park tube/Marylebone tube/rail.

Walk north of Oxford Street and the mood swiftly changes. Instead of jostling crowds and big department stores, there are quiet squares and a pretty high street that looks more like it belongs in an affluent provincial town. Over the past decade, the area that has been rebranded 'Marylebone Village' has become increasingly fashionable and desirable.

The area has not always been so genteel. It was once made up of two ancient manors, Lileston (Lisson) and Tyburn (named after a stream – or bourn – that flowed into the Thames). In the 14th century they were violent places. Tyburn was the site of a famous gallows until 1783, a spot marked by a plaque on the traffic island at Marble Arch (*see p116*).

After the original parish church was demolished in 1400, a new one was built near the top of what is now **Marylebone High Street**. It was called St Mary by the Bourne, a name that came to cover the entire village. This had been abbreviated to Marylebone by 1626.

Although nothing remains of the first two parish churches, the foundations of the third – damaged in the war, demolished in 1949 – were preserved as the Memorial Garden of Rest (due to building works at the neighbouring St Marylebone School, the garden is closed until late 2006). The fourth church, on Marylebone Road, was built to accommodate a rapidly growing population in 1817. It was here that Elizabeth Barrett of 50 Wimpole Street secretly married fellow poet Robert Browning in 1846. Charles Dickens, who lived next door at 1 Devonshire Terrace (demolished in 1959), had his son baptised in the church.

In the 16th century the northern half of Marylebone – now **Regent's Park** (*see p116*) – became a royal hunting ground, while the southern section was bought up by the Portman family. Two centuries later, the Portmans developed many of the elegant streets and squares that lend the locale its dignified air. Some, such as **Bryanston Square** and **Montagu Square**, have survived well; others, such as **Cavendish Square**, marred by an ugly brick wall and underground car park, are less attractive. One of the squares, laid out in 1761, still bears the Portman name; another, 1776's **Manchester Square**, is home to the **Wallace Collection** (*see p115*). **Harley Street** and **Wimpole Street** have been associated with highbrow healthcare since the 1800s.

Running parallel to both, **Portland Place** was the glory of 18th-century London. At **Langham Place**, where it links with John Nash's handsome **Regent Street**, Nash's only remaining church, **All Souls** (1822-4), daringly combines a Gothic spire and classical rotunda. Echoing the curve of its façade is the BBC's newly restored 1932 **Broadcasting House**, featuring external sculptures by Eric Gill; next door, a state-of-the-art broadcast centre (due for completion in 2007/8) will house the BBC's national and international news operations. Over the road is the **Langham Hotel**, which was the first of London's grand hotels (1865); further north is the **Royal Institute of British Architects (RIBA)**, before the street forks into Park Crescent, opposite Regent's Park. A few blocks west by York Gate, the **Royal Academy of Music** has a small museum (7873 7373; 12.30-6pm Mon-Fri; 2-5.30pm Sat, Sun).

North of Marylebone Road, the landscape gives way to 1950s and '60s housing at Lisson Grove. It's worth taking a detour to Bell Street for the cutting-edge **Lisson** gallery (*see p291*), as well as a couple of small second-hand bookshops. **Church Street** has a popular local food and general market that is rapidly gentrifying at its eastern end, home to **Alfie's Antiques Market** (*see p235*).

Opposite Marylebone railway station is the **Landmark Hotel**. Originally the Great Central, it was the last significant Victorian hotel to be built in the golden age of steam (1899). It was closed in 1939, used as offices, then redeveloped as a hotel in 1986.

Around Marylebone High Street

With its varied eating options and array of interesting independent shops (plus some tasteful chains), Marylebone Village lures Londoners and visitors alike. The past year has seen a slew of chic openings and a significant casualty – sadly, Marylebone's traditional fishmonger, Blagden, closed after 100 years of trading, blaming not chicification, but the Congestion Charge. On the whole, the more interesting shops are towards Marylebone Road, including beautiful Edwardian Daunt Books (Nos.83-84 Marylebone High Street; *see p237*) and eclectic clothes boutique Sixty 6 (No.66, 7224 6066), although a couple of notable newcomers have colonised Marylebone Lane – shoe designer Tracey Neuls (No.29; *see p250*) and womenswear label Saltwater (No.98, 7935 3336). This winding backstreet retains the neighbourhood's original character. In corner pub the Golden Eagle at No.59 (7935 3228) there are nostalgic singalongs around the piano, and 106-year-old lunchroom-deli Paul Rothe & Son (No.35, 7935 6783) is presided over by the original Rothe's grandson and great-grandson. Marylebone is a magnet for foodies with a clutch of gourmet shops – such as La Fromagerie (*see p203*) on **Moxon Street**, which leads to the site of the weekly farmers' market on Sundays (in the Cramer Street car park behind Waitrose, 10am-2pm). There are also some great restaurants, including the Providores & Tapa Room and FishWorks (for both, *see p203*).

Hemmed in between buildings behind Spanish Place, **St James's Roman Catholic Church** (22 George Street) has a surprisingly soaring Gothic interior (1890). The church stands opposite the site of a Spanish chapel around the corner from the former embassy and contains objects from the older building, including Alfonso XIII's personal standard. Its Lady Chapel was designed by JF Bentley, architect of Westminster Cathedral. Vivien Leigh wed barrister Leigh Holman here in 1932. But a more interesting example of ecclesiastical architecture lies to the west on Crawford Street. **St Mary's, Wyndham Place**, which was designed by British Museum architect Sir Robert Smirke and completed in 1824, is a dramatic example of the Greek Revival style, set in a stone courtyard (you'll probably only get to admire the exterior as it is usually kept closed).

Wallace Collection

Hertford House, Manchester Square, W1U 3BN (7935 0687/www.wallacecollection.org). Bond Street tube. **Open** 10am-5pm daily. **Admission** free. **Credit** (shop) AmEx, MC, V. **Map** p400 G5.

Presiding over leafy Manchester Square, this handsome late 18th-century house contains a collection of furniture, paintings, armour and objets d'art. It all belonged to Sir Richard Wallace, who, as the illegitimate offspring of the fourth Marquess of Hertford, inherited the treasures his father amassed in the last 30 years of his life. There's room after room of Louis XIV and XV furnishings and Sèvres porcelain, galleries of lush paintings by Titian, Velázquez, Boucher, Gainsborough and Reynolds; Franz Hals's *Laughing Cavalier* is one of the best-known masterpieces. There are also regular temporary exhibitions. The attractive Café Bagatelle, in the glass-roofed courtyard, ranks among the best London museum eateries (*see p201*).

A rolling refurbishment programme is restoring the state rooms to their original opulence – four have been completed and a further two will be unveiled in spring 2006.

Marylebone High Street.

Regent's Park

With its varied landscape, from formal flowerbeds to extensive playing fields, Regent's Park (open 5am-dusk daily) is one of London's most treasured green spaces. But it wasn't created for public pleasure; indeed, the masses weren't allowed in until 1845. Originally Henry VIII's 'chase', the park was designed in 1811 by John Nash as a private residential estate to raise royal revenue. The Regency terraces of the **Outer Circle**, the road running around the park, are still Crown property, but of the 56 villas planned, only eight were built. Development of the Royal Park, with its botanic and zoological gardens, took almost two more decades, but rehabilitation after wartime damage and neglect in the mid 20th century was not completed until the late 1970s. As well as the famous zoo (*see below*), it has a boating lake (home to wildfowl), tennis courts, cafés and a lovely open-air theatre (*see p337*). To the west of the park is the **London Central Mosque**.

Just south of the park on Marylebone Road is tourist attraction *extraordinaire* **Madame Tussauds** (*see below*). Nearby, **Baker Street**, which leads to Oxford Street, is forever associated with a certain fictional detective. The **Sherlock Holmes Museum** at No.221B (7935 8866, www.sherlock-holmes.co.uk) occupies the famous address and contains atmospheric room sets, and serious Sherlockians may want to check out the Sherlock Holmes Collection (books, photos and so on) at **Marylebone Library** (7641 1206, by appointment only).

London Zoo

Regent's Park, NW1 4RY (7722 3333/http:www.zsl. org/london-zoo). Baker Street or Camden Town tube then 274, C2 bus. **Open** *Late Oct-mid Mar* 10am-4pm daily. *Mid Mar-late Oct* 10am-5.30pm daily. **Admission** £14; £10.75-£12 concessions; £45 family; free under-3s. **Credit** AmEx, MC, V. **Map** p400 G2.

Opened in 1828, this was the world's first scientific zoo, and today umbrella charity ZSL stresses its commitment to worldwide conservation. The zoo's habitats keep pace with the times – the elephants have been given room to roam at sister site Whipsnade Wild Animal Park in Bedfordshire, and the penguins have been moved from Lubetkin's famous modernist pool to a more suitable space. The new 1,500sq m walk-through squirrel monkey enclosure allows you to get close to the animals in an open environment based on a Bolivian rainforest, while the African Bird Safari, another new walk-through habitat, has replaced three small, outdated bird enclosures. There are plans for a gorilla island in 2007. It's advisable to follow the recommended route to avoid missing anything in the 36-acre site; check the daily programme of events to get a good view at feeding times.

Madame Tussauds & London Planetarium

Marylebone Road, NW1 5LR (0870 400 3000/ www.madame-tussauds.com). Baker Street tube. **Open** 9am-6pm daily (last entry 5pm); times vary during holiday periods. **Admission** *9.30am-3pm* £24.99; £15.99-£20.99 concessions; £79.20 family (internet booking only). *3-5pm* £15.99; £9-£11 concessions; £12.99 concessions; £66 family. **Credit** MC, V. **Map** p400 G4.

As you enter the first room, 'Blush', you're dazzled by fake paparazzi flashbulbs, and starry-eyed kids can even take part in a 'Divas' routine with likenesses of Britney, Beyoncé and Kylie. A cunningly posed wax snapper provides a double-take moment. Surprisingly, visitors are encouraged to touch the figures; you can smack J-Lo's bottom or stroke Brad Pitt's soft face – he was the first of the new generation of silicone figures. Poor Robbie Williams was so ravaged by amorous attentions he needed extensive repairs; he was spruced up in spring 2005, complete with a hidden sensor activated by kisses to produce a 'twinkle' in his eye. Figures are constantly being added to keep up with new stars, movies and TV shows – the latest are *Little Britain*'s Matt Lucas and David Walliams, in character as wheelchair-bound Andy and his carer Lou. Other rooms contain public figures past and present, from Henry and six of his wives to Blair and Bush, by way of the Fab Four circa 1964. Below stairs, the Chamber of Horrors surrounds you with hanging corpses and eviscerated victims of torture. For an extra £2 over-12s can be terrorised by serial killers in the Chamber Live. Children love the kitsch 'Spirit of London Ride' – you climb aboard a moving black taxi pod for a whirlwind trundle through 400 years of the city's history. Dazed, you're ushered into the Planetarium for a ten-minute digital show, before exiting through the huge gift shop.

South to Oxford Street

Heading south, Marylebone High Street turns into Thayer Street, then Mandeville Place. Across Wigmore Street, famous for **Wigmore Hall** (*see p307*), narrow shop- and café-lined pedestrian alleyway **St Christopher's Place** widens to a fountain courtyard, which in summer is filled with tables from nearby cafés. Carrying on after it contracts to even narrower alley Gees Court will take you to pedestrian- and bus-choked **Oxford Street**, packed with big chains, department stores and tourist tat.

Marble Arch, another Nash creation, marks Oxford Street's western extent. This unremarkable monument was intended to be the entrance to Buckingham Palace but, deemed too puny, was moved to this site in 1851. Only members of the Royal Family and some military types are allowed by law to walk through the central portal.

Mayfair & St James's

A quiet air of refinement.

Sightseeing

Mayfair

Map p402 H7

Bond Street or Green Park tube.

The image of gaiety suggested by its name – deriving from the fair that used to take place here long ago each May (*see p117*) – is belied by the staid atmosphere of Mayfair. It's easy to feel like you don't belong in some of the deadly quiet residential streets that, over the centuries, attracted many of London's biggest wigs with their rarefied air. Even in the commercial parts, you can feel out of place without a platinum card (but if you do have one, there's no better place in the capital to burn it up on an armful of lovely designer shopping bags). Not for nothing is this the most expensive property on a Monopoly board.

It is generally agreed that Mayfair is the area between Oxford Street, Regent Street, Piccadilly and Park Lane. When it was all rolling green fields at the edge of London town, it belonged to the Grosvenor and Berkeley families, who bought the land in the mid 17th century. In the 1700s they developed the pastures into a posh new neighbourhood. In particular they built a series of squares surrounded by elegant houses – although the three biggest squares, Hanover, Berkeley and the immense Grosvenor, are ringed by offices and embassies these days. The most famous of these, Grosvenor (that's 'Grove-ner'), is where you'll find the drab US Embassy. Finished in 1960, it takes up one whole side of the square and its only decoration is a fierce-looking eagle, a lot of protective fencing and some heavily armed police. Out front, a big statue of President Dwight Eisenhower has pride of place, although there's also a grand statue of President Franklin D

Roosevelt standing nobly in the square nearby. When in London, Eisenhower stayed at the exclusive hotel **Claridge's** (*see p57*), a block away on Brook Street.

The toffs are still in residence elsewhere in Mayfair, and the tone of the area remains sky-high. It has always been smart: the Duke of Wellington is its most distinguished former resident – he briefly lived at 4 Hamilton Place, before moving to **Apsley House** (*see p118*) – but he has stiff competition from Admiral Lord Nelson (147 New Bond Street), Benjamin Disraeli (29 Park Lane), Florence Nightingale (10 South Street) and Sir Robert Peel (16 Upper Grosvenor Street). Brook Street has its musicians: GF Handel lived at No.25 and Jimi Hendrix briefly next door at No.23. These adjacent buildings have been combined into a museum dedicated to Handel's memory (*see p118*).

Crowded, noisy Oxford Street to the north is least typical of Mayfair's consumer facilities. Other than a handful of good department stores it's a chain-store rat race. More representative are **New Bond Street**, the designer drag, and **Cork Street**, gallery row. A couple of streets away is Albemarle Street, where you'll find the Royal Institution (No.21), home to the **Faraday Museum** (7409 2992, www.rigb.org), which is due to reopen in 2007 after refurbishment.

The most famous Mayfair shopping street is **Savile Row** (*see p250*), the land of made-to-measure suits of the highest quality. At No.15 is the estimable Henry Poole & Co, which over the years has cut suits for clients including Napoleon Bonaparte, Charles Dickens, Winston Churchill and Charles de Gaulle. No.3 was the home of Apple Records, the Beatles' recording studio. The fabulous four famously played their last gig here in February 1969, up on the roof.

Savile Row leads on to the equally salubrious **Conduit Street**, where fashion shocker Vivienne Westwood (No.44) faces the more staid Rigby and Peller (No.22A; *see also p247*), corsetières to the Queen. From here you can follow **St George Street** into **Hanover Square**. Here you'll find St George's Church, built in the 1720s and once everybody's favourite place to get married. Among the luminaries who said their vows at the altar were George Eliot and Teddy Roosevelt. Handel, who married nobody, attended services here.

While all of this is so very chi-chi, the area around **Shepherd Market** (named after a food market set up here by architect Edward Shepherd in the early 18th century) is perhaps the true heart of the neighbourhood. From 1686 this was where the raucous May Fair was held, until it was shut down for good in the late 18th century after city leaders complained of 'drunkenness, fornication, gaming and lewdness'. Today it seems a pleasant, upscale area with a couple of fine pubs (Ye Grapes at 16 Shepherd Market and the Shepherd's Tavern at 50 Hertford Street) and some of London's most agreeable pavement dining. But, in keeping with its background, you'll often also see prostitutes working from tatty apartment blocks. Their accommodation probably bears little resemblance to the clutch of sophisticated hotels – the Hilton, the Dorchester (*see p57*), the Metropolitan (*see p57*) and the Inter-Continental – moments away on Park Lane.

Handel House Museum

25 Brook Street (entrance at rear in Lancashire Court), W1K 4HB (7495 1685/www.handel house.org). Bond Street tube. **Open** 10am-6pm Tue, Wed, Fri, Sat; 10am-8pm Thur; noon-6pm Sun. **Admission** £5; £2-£4.50 concessions; free under-5s. **Credit** MC, V. **Map** p402 H6.

George Frideric Handel moved to Britain from his native Germany aged 25 and settled in this Mayfair house 12 years later, remaining here until his death in 1759. The house has been beautifully restored with original and recreated furnishings, paintings and a welter of the composer's scores (in the same room as photos of Jimi Hendrix, who lived here rather more recently). The programme of events here is surprisingly dynamic for a museum so small: there are activities tilted at kids at weekends, recitals every Thursday and most days there's somebody playing in the Rehearsal Room. And we won't be forgetting the Beer & Baroque evening in a hurry.

Piccadilly & Green Park

Map p402 H8

Green Park or Hyde Park Corner tube.
Grandiose **Piccadilly** links the traffic-strewn bear-pit of **Hyde Park Corner** with the pick-pocket heaven of **Piccadilly Circus** (*see p121*). Its undeniably charming name comes from the fancy suit collars ('picadils') favoured by the posh gentlemen who once paraded down its length. It's not really very high class any more, but you can still see remnants of its glossy past in the Regency shopping arcades, designed to protect shoppers from mud and horse manure and continuing to offer an exclusive service to toffs. One of the nicest is the skylit **Burlington Arcade**. According to archaic laws still on the books,

it is illegal to sing, whistle or hurry in the arcade, and there are top-hatted beadles on the job to catch anybody doing any of the above. Just next door to the arcade, the **Royal Academy of Arts** (*see p120*) lures with innovative arts exhibitions. Across Piccadilly from the Academy, it's virtually impossible to pass the wonderfully overwrought, mint green veneer of the department store **Fortnum & Mason** (*see p238*) without stepping in.

The simple-looking church at No.197 is **St James's** (*see p120*). This was the personal favourite of its architect Sir Christopher Wren, a fact that may come as a surprise to those who would expect him to have had a soft spot for glorious St Paul's. There's often a market out front, and a handy coffeeshop with outdoor seating is tucked into a corner by a quiet garden.

Head west down Piccadilly, and the old-fashioned uniforms sported by the doormen and the excellent 1950s-style lighted sign leave no doubt that you've reached the **Ritz** (*see p57*), one of the city's best-known hotels and the place to go for afternoon tea. The simple green expanse just beyond the Ritz is the aptly named **Green Park**. Once a plague pit, where the city's many epidemic victims were buried, it may not be able to match the grandeur of Regent's Park or the sheer scale of Hyde Park, but it has its charms, most evident in the spring, when its gentle slopes are covered in bright daffodils (there are no planted flowerbeds here, hence the name). Further along Piccadilly, work your way past the queue outside the Hard Rock Café to the Duke of Wellington's old homestead, Apsley House, opposite **Wellington Arch** (*see p120*), both at Hyde Park Corner.

The arch now marks the end of Constitution Hill, which separates Green Park from **Buckingham Palace** (*see p119*) and its extensive gardens, and ends at the Queen Victoria Memorial. She gazes down the Mall where, to the south, **St James's Park**, with its lovely views and exotic birdlife, does rather overshadow Green Park's bland greensward. Originally a royal deer park for St James's Palace, its pastoral landscape owes its influence to John Nash, who redesigned it in the early 19th century under the orders of George IV. The view of Buckingham Palace from the bridge over the lake is wonderful, especially at night when the palace is floodlit. The lake is now a sanctuary for wildfowl, among them pelicans (fed at 3pm daily) and Australian black swans.

Apsley House: The Wellington Museum

149 Piccadilly, W1J 7NT (7499 5676/www.english-heritage.org.uk). Hyde Park Corner tube. **Open** 10am-4pm Tue-Sun. *Tours* by arrangement. **Admission** £4.95; £2.50-£3.70 concessions.

St James's Park. *See p118.*

Tours phone in advance. *Joint ticket with Wellington Arch* £6.30; £3.20-£4.70 concessions; £15.80 family. **Credit** MC, V. **Map** p402 G8.

Called No.1 London because it was the first London building one encountered on the road from the village of Kensington, Apsley House was built by Robert Adam in the 1770s. The Duke of Wellington had it as his London residence for 35 years. Though his descendants still live here, some rooms are open to the public and contain interesting trinkets, including extravagant porcelain dinnerware and plates – the Portuguese Service is a 26ft-long silver fantasy. Ask someone to demonstrate the crafty mirrors in the scarlet and gilt picture gallery, where a fine Velázquez and Correggio hang near Goya's portrait of the Iron Duke after he defeated the French in 1812 (a last-minute edit, as X-rays revealed that Wellington's head had been brushed over that of Joseph Bonaparte, Napoleon's brother).

Buckingham Palace & Royal Mews

SW1A 1AA (7766 7300/Royal Mews 7766 7302/ www.royal.gov.uk/www.royalcollection.org.uk). Green Park or St James's Park tube/Victoria tube/rail. **Open** *State Rooms* early Aug, Sept 9.30am-5.30pm daily. Sept 5.30pm daily. Closed early Jan-early Feb. *Royal Mews* Oct-July 11am-4pm daily. Aug, Sept 10am-5pm daily. Last entry 45mins before closing. **Admission** *Palace* £13.50; £7-£11.50 concessions; £34 family; free under-5s. *Queen's Gallery* £7.50; £4-£6 concessions; £19 family; free under-5s. *Royal Mews* £5.50; £3.50-£4.50 concessions; £15.50 family; free under-5s. **Credit** AmEx, MC, V. **Map** p402 H9.

The world's most famous palace, built in 1703, started life as a grand house for the Duke of Buckingham, but George III liked it so much he bought it, in 1761, for his young bride Charlotte. It became known as the Queen's house and 14 of their 15 children were born there. His son, George IV, hired John Nash to convert it into a palace. Thus construction on the 600-room palace began in 1825. But the project was beset with disaster from the start. Nash was fired after George IV's death – he was too flighty, apparently – and the reliable but unimaginative Edward Blore was hired to finish the job. After critics saw the result, they dubbed him 'Blore the Bore'. What's more, Queen Victoria, who was the first royal to live here, hated the place, calling it 'a disgrace to the country'.

Judge for yourself. In August and September, while the Windsors are off on their holidays, the ostentatious State Apartments – used for banquets and investitures – are open to the public. After the initial thrill of being inside Buckingham Palace, it's not all that interesting unless the exhibition excites you.

The Queen's Gallery, which is open for most of the year (but best avoided around noon when the Changing of the Guard-watchers move in), contains highlights of Liz's decorative and fine art collection: Old Masters, Sèvres porcelain, ornately inlaid cabinets and the Diamond Diadem (familiar from millions of postage stamps) and other glittering baubles. Paintings of the Grand Canal are the centrepiece of 'Canaletto in Venice', which runs until 23 April 2006. Further along Buckingham Palace Road, the Royal Mews holds horses (when they're not out trooping the colour) and those royal carriages that are rolled out for the royals to wag their

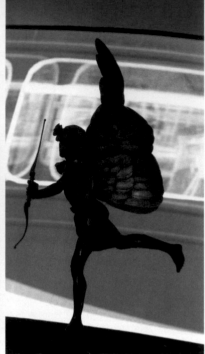

Piccadilly Circus. *See p121.*

hands from on very important occasions. Best of Show award must go to Her Majesty's State Coach, a breathtaking, double gilded affair built in 1761.

Royal Academy of Arts

Burlington House, Piccadilly, W1J 0BD (7300 8000/ www.royalacademy.org.uk). Green Park or Piccadilly Circus tube. **Open** 10am-6pm Mon-Thur, Sat, Sun; 10am-10pm Fri. **Admission** varies. **Credit** AmEx, DC, MC, V. **Map** p408 U4.

Britain's first art school was founded in 1768 and moved to the extravagantly Palladian Burlington House a century later. It's best known these days for its galleries, which stage a roster of populist temporary exhibitions. Those in the John Madejski Fine Rooms are drawn from the RA's holdings – ranging from Constable to Hockney – and are free (and provide a good excuse to peek at the ornate interiors). Major exhibitions scheduled for 2006 include Qing Dynasty artworks and artefacts until 17 April, landscapes by Jacob van Ruisdael (25 Feb-4 June), and Rodin sculptures, from 23 September until the new year. The Academy's biggest event is the Summer Exhibition, which for more than two centuries has drawn from works entered by the public. Some 12,000 pieces are submitted each year, with 10% making it past the judges.

St James's Church Piccadilly

197 Piccadilly, W1J 9LL (7734 4511/www.st-james-piccadilly.org). Piccadilly Circus tube. **Open** 8am-7pm daily. *Evening events* times vary. **Admission** free. **Map** p408 V4.

Consecrated in 1684, St James's is the only church Sir Christopher Wren built on an entirely new site. It's a calming building without architectural airs or graces but not lacking in charm. It was bombed to within an inch of its life in World War II, but later painstakingly reconstructed. Grinling Gibbons's delicate limewood garlanding around the sanctuary survived and is one of the few real frills. This is a busy church as, along with its inclusive ministry, it runs a counselling service, stages regular classical concerts, provides a home for the William Blake Society (the poet was baptised here) and hosts markets in its churchyard: antiques on Tuesday, arts and crafts from Wednesday to Saturday.

Wellington Arch

Hyde Park Corner, W1J 7JZ (7930 2726/www. english-heritage.org.uk). Hyde Park Corner tube. **Open** *Apr-Oct* 10am-5pm Wed-Sun; Wed-Sun. *Nov-Mar* 10am-4pm Wed-Sun. **Admission** £3; £1.50-£2.30 concessions; free under-5s. *Joint ticket with Apsley House* £6.30; £3.20-£4.70 concessions; £15.80 family. **Credit** MC, V. **Map** p402 G8.

Built in the late 1820s to mark Britain's triumph over Napoleonic France, Decimus Burton's Wellington Arch was shifted from its original location to accommodate traffic at Hyde Park Corner in 1882. It was initially topped by an out-of-proportion equestrian statue of Wellington, but since 1912 Captain Adrian Jones's 38-ton bronze *Peace Descending on the Quadriga of War* has finished it with a flourish. It was restored in 1999 by English Heritage, and has three floors of displays, covering the history of the arch and the Blue Plaques scheme. From the balcony, you can see the Houses of Parliament and Buckingham Palace, though trees obstruct much of the view in summer.

Piccadilly Circus & Regent Street

Map p408

Oxford Circus or Piccadilly Circus tube.
Undeniable landmark though it is, the **Piccadilly Circus** of today is an uneasy mix of the tawdry and the grandiose, and would certainly not correspond to what its architect John Nash had planned for it. His original 1820s design for the intersection of two of the West End's most elegant streets was a harmonious circle of curved frontages. But 60 years later, Shaftesbury Avenue muscled its way in, to create the present lopsided effect; in an attempt to compensate, a delicate aluminium statue in honour of child-labour abolitionist Earl Shaftesbury was erected. Its subject was the Angel of Christian Charity, but it looks like **Eros** and so now is thus known. His unseeing eyes have gazed on further indignities: the arrival of the billboards in 1910, the junkie culture of the 1980s and the invasion of tourist tack: overpriced pizza and boring arcades.

Connecting Piccadilly Circus to Oxford Circus to the north and Pall Mall to the south, **Regent Street** is a broad, curving boulevard designed by Nash in the early 1800s to separate the

wealthy of Mayfair from the working classes of Soho. The grandeur of the sweeping road is impressive – although much of Nash's architecture was destroyed in the early 20th century, some does survive (look up above the shopfronts). Home to famous children's emporium **Hamleys** (*see p261*) and the landmark **Liberty** store (*see p238*), it remains far classier than Oxford Street, despite the inevitable incursion of the chains, still attracting one-offs like the sleek Apple Store at No.235.

St James's

Maps p408 U-W5 & p402 J8

Green Park or Piccadilly Circus tube.
One of central London's quieter parts, St James's does not get many visitors – nor many Londoners, for that matter. Bordered by Piccadilly, Haymarket, the Mall and Green Park, it's even posher than Mayfair, its comrade-in-swank north of Piccadilly. This is a London that has remained unchanged for centuries: it's all very charming in its way, although it remains resolutely rich and gently conceited all the same.

The material needs of the venerable gents who habituate the private clubs of St James's are met by the anachronistic shops and restaurants of Jermyn Street and St James's Street, with the timewarp shopfronts, among them cigar retailer James J Fox (19 St James's

Nash's curving **Regent Street**.

A right royal quiz

Are you a monarchist or republican, or not sure where your allegiances lie? Take our quiz and find out.

1. How many countries has the Queen visited?

2. Buckingham Palace has more than 500 rooms. How many of those are bathrooms?

3. What is the name of the crown the Queen sports on a standard first-class stamp?

4. For her silver wedding anniversary, the Queen received a seven-year-old elephant. The president of which country gave it to her?

5. How many godchildren does Her Majesty have to remember to buy gifts for?

6. What was the first football match that Liz attended?

7. The Queen interrupted an overseas tour only once, in 1974. Why?

8. The Queen has four 'dorgis'. What are they?

9. The Queen failed to open Parliament in 1959 and 1963. Why?

10. Elizabeth II is the second-longest serving head of state. The king of which country is the only one to have been on the throne longer?

11. At age 76, the Queen was the oldest British monarch to celebrate a Golden Jubilee. Who was the youngest?

12. Over the years, the Queen has given out 75,000 of what to her staff?

13. The Queen has sat for 120 portraits throughout her reign. Who painted the most recent one?

14. During her reign, roughly how many pieces of correspondence have been addressed to the Queen?

15. What was Liz's childhood nickname?

16. The Queen has launched 18 ships. In what year did she crack the bubbly against the Royal Yacht *Britannia*?

17. When was the first televised Christmas Broadcast?

18. Which great-great-grandparent do the Duke of Edinburgh and his wife have in common?

---

1. 128.
2. 78.
3. The Diamond Diadem (see p119).
4. Cameroon.
5. 30.
6. The 1953 FA Cup Final.
7. A snap general election was called.
8. A dachshund-corgi cross.
9. She was pregnant with Andrew and Edward.
10. Thailand.
11. James I (James VI of Scotland), age 51.
12. Christmas puddings.
13. Rolf Harris, for her 80th birthday.
14. Three million.
15. Lilibet.
16. 1953.
17. 1957.
18. Queen Victoria.

How many did you get right?
11 or more You'd better nip round the palace for an extra three letters after your name.

3-10 Queen Vic – that's the name of a pub, isn't it? Well, never mind, at least you're still a staunch supporter of all things British.

2 You always get the sports questions right.... thank God there was a footie question thrown in for good measure.

1 A true republican – you could happily reel off a dozen of Prince Philip's most memorable (read: embarrassing) witticisms.

0 Shouldn't you stick to pulling pints in Earl's Court?

Street, 7930 3787) and upmarket cobbler John Lobb (No.9, 7930 3665). To stroll around the alleys is to step back in time, and up in class.

Around the corner from St James's Street is the Queen Mother's old residence, **Clarence House** (*see below*). Now the official London home of Prince Charles, his sons Harry and William and new wife Camilla, it is open to the public in summer. Adjacent to Clarence House, **St James's Palace** was originally built for Henry VIII in the 1530s. It has remained the official residence of the sovereign throughout the centuries, despite the fact that since 1837 the monarchs have all actually lived at nearby Buckingham Palace. It has great historic significance to the monarchy: Mary Tudor surrendered Calais here, Elizabeth I lived here during the campaign against the Spanish Armada, and Charles I was confined here before his execution in 1649.

Today St James's Palace is used by the Princess Royal and various minor royals, and it is, essentially, the address of the now largely defunct government of the monarch. Tradition still dictates that foreign ambassadors to the UK are officially known as 'Ambassadors to the Court of St James's'. Although the palace is closed to the public, you can attend Sunday services at the historic **Chapel Royal** (first Sun, Oct-Easter Sunday; 8.30am, 11.15am) within its confines.

Across Marlborough Road lies the **Queen's Chapel**, which was the first classical church to be built in England. Designed by the mighty and prolific Inigo Jones in the 1620s for Charles I's intended bride of the time, the Infanta of Castile, the chapel now stands in the grounds of **Marlborough House** and is only open to the public during Sunday services (Easter-July; 8.30am, 11.15am). The house itself was built by Sir Christopher Wren.

Two other notable St James's mansions stand nearby and overlook Green Park (they're visible from Queen's Walk). The neo-classical **Lancaster House** was rebuilt in the 1820s by Benjamin Dean Wyatt for Frederick, Duke of York, and impressed Queen Victoria with its splendour. Closed to the public, it's now used mainly for government receptions and conferences. A little further north, on St James's Place, is the beautiful, 18th-century **Spencer House** (*see below*), ancestral townhouse of the late Princess Diana's family and now infrequently open as a museum and art gallery.

Reached from the west via King Street or Pall Mall to the south, **St James's Square** was the most fashionable address in London for the 50 years after it was laid out in the 1670s: some seven dukes and seven earls were residents by the 1720s. Alas, no private houses survive

on the square today, though among the current occupants is the prestigious **London Library**. This private library was founded by Thomas Carlyle in 1841 in disgust at the inefficiency of the British Library. Eisenhower planned and launched Operation Overlord (the D-Day invasion) from **Norfolk House**, in the south-east corner of the square.

Further east, overlooking the Mall, is **Carlton House Terrace**, which was built by Nash in 1827-32 on the site of Carlton House. When the Prince Regent came to the throne as George IV, he decided his home was not ostentatious enough for his elevated station and levelled what Horace Walpole had once described as 'the most perfect palace' in Europe. Nos.8 and 9 Carlton House Terrace, currently occupied by the Royal Society, were converted into a single building as the German Embassy during the Nazi era; their interiors were renovated by Albert Speer, Hitler's architect.

Clarence House

SW1A 1AA (7766 7303/www.royal.gov.uk). Green Park tube. **Open** *Aug-mid Oct* 9.30am-6pm daily (last entry 5pm). **Admission** £6; £3.50 concessions; free under-5s. *Tours* All tickets must be pre-booked. **Credit** AmEx, MC, V. **Map** p402 J8.

Standing austerely beside St James's Palace, Clarence House was erected between 1825 and 1827, based on designs by John Nash. It was built for Prince William Henry, Duke of Clarence, who lived there as King William IV until 1837. During its history, the house has been much altered by its many royal inhabitants, the most recent of whom was the Queen Mother, who lived there until she died in 2002. Prince Charles and his two sons have since moved in, but parts of the house are open to the public in summer: five receiving rooms and the small but significant art collection, strong in 20th-century British art, accumulated by the Queen Mother. Among the art on display is a lovely 1945 portrait of her by Sir James Gunn. There are also works by John Piper, WS Sickert and Augustus John. Tickets are hard to come by and tend to sell out by the end of August.

Spencer House

27 St James's Place, SW1A 1NR (7499 8620/ www.spencerhouse.co.uk). Green Park tube. **Open** *House* Feb-July, Sept-Dec 10.30am-5.45pm Sun (last entry 4.45pm). *Restored gardens* spring, summer (phone to check). **Admission** *Tours* £9; £7 concessions. Under-10s not allowed. **No credit cards. Map** p402 J8.

Designed by John Vardy and built for John Spencer, who became Earl Spencer the year before his house was completed, this 1756-66 construction is one of the capital's finest examples of a Palladian mansion. The eponymous Spencers moved out just over a century ago and the lavishly restored building is now used chiefly as offices and for corporate entertaining, hence the limited access.

Sightseeing

Soho

Whatever turns you on – you'll find it here.

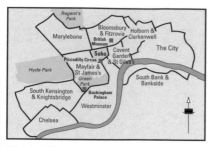

With its skinny avenues and buzzing street life, Soho is still just about London's spiciest square mile. It isn't dominated by any single coterie: businessmen, celebs, hookers, market traders, journalists, tourists and queers all cosy up in the area bounded by the four Circuses (Oxford, Piccadilly, Cambridge and St Giles's). Wealthy and poor, cultured and seedy – this area has had many different characters during its long and fruitful life: in the past, artists, immigrants, showgirls and prostitutes all left their marks.

Documented Soho really begins in the Middle Ages, when the area was a rural idyll used as a hunting ground by London's aristocracy. It was after the Great Fire of 1666 that Soho became residential, when thousands were forced to relocate. Around this time, Soho also got its first wave of immigrants: Greek Christians (hence Greek Street) fleeing Ottoman persecution, and French Protestants (Huguenots) forced out of France by Louis XIV. Soon, the only trace of the neighbourhood's pastoral roots was its name: the huntsmen who once rode the pastures here used to cry 'So-ho!' when they spotted their prey.

As the immigrants poured into Soho, wealthy residents moved out. The architect John Nash encouraged this social apartheid in 1813, when he designed Regent Street (which marks Soho's western boundary) to provide what he called 'a complete separation between the Streets occupied by the Nobility and Gentry [Mayfair], and the narrower Streets and meaner houses occupied by mechanics and the trading part of the community'. With Nash's kind of thinking ruling the day, Soho became one of Britain's worst slums during the 19th century.

Change came again soon enough, though. The early years of the 20th century saw showgirls, prostitutes and artists (of a variety

of stripes) define the area's character, with the 1950s prime time for the latter. Painter Francis Bacon and photographer John Deakin lunched and boozed their way around the area; Britain's earliest rock 'n' roll singers congregated at the long-since closed 2 i's Coffee Bar at 59 Old Compton Street. In 1962 Georgie Fame started his sweat-soaked residency at the Flamingo Club (33-37 Wardour Street); the nearby Marquee (then at 90 Wardour Street, now in Leicester Square; see p127) hosted early gigs by Jimi Hendrix and Pink Floyd.

The sex industry expanded to a phenomenal degree in the 1960s and '70s. At one point, there were well over 200 sex-related businesses here, many allowed to operate by a police force on the take from the owners. But soon after the corruption was uncovered, Westminster Council clamped down; in the mid 1980s the number of strip joints, porn cinemas and sex shops in the area fell by 80 per cent (although a hardy few continue to prosper). By and large, though, the gay community moved in to replace them: while pubs such as the Golden Lion on Dean Street had long been the haunt of gay servicemen (as well as writer Noël Coward), the '90s saw myriad gay bars, restaurants and shops set up on Old Compton Street and the nearby streets.

The future? As ever, it's impossible even to speculate what may become of this area. In many places, there are already the first telltale signs of homogenisation: an identikit bar here, a nationwide supermarket chain there. And with the sky-high rents showing no signs of dropping, it could very easily get worse. That said, though, it'd be a fool who'd bet on this most characterful and gutsy of neighbourhoods going the way of nearby Covent Garden. Soho has, and always has had, a resilient nature.

Old Compton Street & around

Map p408 W3 & p409 X2

Leicester Square or Tottenham Court Road tube.
All human life hangs on **Old Compton Street**, Soho's main artery, and your experience can range from shock (at the number of sex clubs), to hilarity (possibly also at the sex clubs). While Soho is well known as a very gay-friendly area, it's better to think of it as a friendly area in

PTONS *of Soho*

Old Compton Street.

general. While there are one or two bars whose bouncers may suggest the place isn't for you (if you're straight), the area throngs with all varieties of über-cool people in tight T-shirts who couldn't care less about your bedroom activities, thank you very much.

The place buzzes; if not quite 24/7, then certainly 17/ or 18/7. Also joining the fray are gaggles of girls out on the razzle, lairy stag parties down from the north, illegal minicab drivers touting for work (don't even think about it), elderly jazz buffs en route to the local jazz club, and confused tourists either heading to or leaving the immensely popular production of *Mary Poppins* at the Prince Edward Theatre (*see p.339*). At dawn, club-goers wander distractedly along the traffic-free street, the homeless finally settle down to sleep in doorways and the street cleaners move in to begin mopping up in preparation for the locals to do it all over again tonight.

A couple of stone's throws north of Old Compton Street, **Soho Square** forms the neighbourhood's northern gateway. This tree-lined quadrangle was initially called King Square, and a weather-beaten statue of Charles II stands in the centre. It's held up pretty well: not as grand as it once was (traffic cruises around it all day and night, waiting for one of the area's few parking bays to become available), but popular with local workers, who pack the grass in summer. Jackie Leven and Kirsty MacColl wrote songs about the square; the latter, who died in 2000, has a bench dedicated to her on the south side. Two churches provide spiritual nourishment, but the area is dominated by the advertising and film industries: both the British Board of Film Classification and 20th Century Fox have their offices here.

The two streets that link Old Compton with Soho Square are rich with history. Casanova and Thomas de Quincey once lodged on **Greek Street**, though the street is now notable mainly for the gloriously old-fashioned **Gay Hussar** restaurant (No.2, 7437 0973). Parallel **Frith Street**, once home to Constable, Mozart and William Hazlitt, is livelier, thanks to legendary jazz club **Ronnie Scott's** (*see p316*) and the similarly mythologised all-night café **Bar Italia**, at No.22 (*see p206*). The latter, above which John Logie Baird first demonstrated television in 1926, feels like the centre of the world on busy nights, the whole of London revolving around its overworked espresso machine.

Dean Street, just west of Frith Street, has an equally colourful history, mostly composed of the bohemian characters who got drunk in its pubs. Dylan Thomas held marathon drinking sessions at the York Minster (south of Old Compton Street at No.49), then nicknamed 'the French Pub' for its association with Charles de Gaulle and the Free French resistance movement. It's now called the **French House** (*see p228*), and still retains its louche charm. Also on Dean Street is the members-only **Groucho Club** (No.45), where London media types quench their thirst, and the **Sunset Strip** (No.30), the sole remaining legitimate strip club in Soho (in contrast to the unlicensed places further west, the prices are reasonable and the girls actually take their clothes off). Hard to believe that Karl Marx, who lived both at No.28 and No.44 for a time, would have approved. Further north is the **Soho Theatre** (*see p342*), which has fast cemented a reputation for its programme of new plays and comedy, and the **Crown & Two Chairmen** (No.31), arguably the best old-school pub in Soho.

Wardour Street, the next street along, is less interesting, its buildings predominantly providing homes to an assortment of film and TV production companies. On Wardour Street just to the south of Old Compton Street is the churchyard of **St Anne's**; bombed during the Blitz, only the 19th-century tower remains. Those with a keen eye and an expansive record collection will clock the next street along from the cover of the Oasis album (*What's the Story) Morning Glory?*, and **Berwick Street** (that's four streets west of Greek Street, for those not paying attention at the back) repays the favour. This road and those just off it are awash with independent record stores, selling everything from speciality dance 12-inches at premium prices to chart favourites at several pounds less than are offered at Oxford Street's chain stores.

The music retailers are joined on Berwick Street by two other cottage industries: the fruit and veg salesmen who make up the bulk of the

Sightseeing

Walk on Rock your world

Start: Oxford Street, W1.
Finish: Wardour Street, W1.
Length: A mile.

It may have been invaded by ten-a-penny coffee shops and chain stores, but Soho still retains a gritty feeling that stems from its rock 'n' roll heyday. Indeed, it's still the centre of the capital's media and music world, and some of the recording studios that turned suburban up-and-comers into household names are in existence even today.

Just by Oxford Circus, head south from Oxford Street down Argyll Street. At the **London Palladium** on the left (No.8), four Liverpool lads performed live for ITV's *Sunday Night at the London Palladium* on 13 October 1963, causing hysteria in their fans. Just down the road at **Sutherland House** (Nos.5-6), where Beatles manager Brian Epstein kept his offices, John Lennon famously claimed that his band were 'more popular than Jesus'.

Turn left into Great Marlborough Street, then cross over the road to Liberty, and head right into **Carnaby Street**, home of all things Swinging (or at least, that's the marketing image). This is where Mary Quant's miniskirt first went on sale, and not long after, the Kinks sang about 'the Carnabytion Army' in their pointed 'Dedicated Follower of Fashion'.

Walk south to the end of the street, then left into Beak Street. A right down Upper James Street takes you to Brewer Street via Lower James Street and Golden Square. Turn left and head east past Lexington Street. A young David Jones played a gig with the King Bees in 1964, at the Jack of Clubs (No.10, now **Madam Jo Jo's**; *see p321*). The band was paid £100, despite calling off the gig after only two songs. No one was interested. David later changed his surname to Bowie.

A quick right-left at the Wardour Street end of Brewer Street and you're in Old Compton Street. Immediately on the right, at No.59, the **2 i's Coffee Bar** (now Boulevard Bar & Dining Room) was where young hopefuls performed in the '50s. In 1958 Hank Marvin and Bruce Welch played here, and were invited to join Cliff Richard's backing band, the Drifters, who became the Shadows in 1959. Marc Bolan worked here as a barista in the 1960s.

Walk east to the corner of Old Compton and Frith Streets, where Mick Jones met Joe Strummer on the way to a Tom Waits gig, and persuaded him to join the Clash.

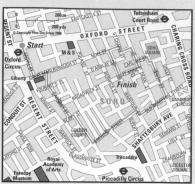

Turning left into Frith Street, you soon spy **Ronnie Scott's** on the left (No.47). While this classic venue is usually associated with the most evocative four-letter word (jazz), many rock 'n' rollers have plied their trade here too. The Who showcased their rock opera, *Tommy*, here in 1969, and Genesis were signed to Charisma Records in 1970. Jimi Hendrix visited on 16 September 1970, to see the Eric Burdon Band – whom he joined on stage for a jam. The next day, Hendrix was dead.

Following Frith Street north, you arrive at **Soho Square**, home of MPL Communications (No.1), Paul McCartney's publishing company. This is the historic place where Macca came up with the name for his new band, Wings.

Exit the square on Carlisle Street, then detour left down Dean Street and pop into St Anne's Court, home of **Trident Studios** (No.17). It was here that Bowie re-recorded *Space Oddity* in June 1969, a month before Neil Armstrong landed on the moon. The studio piano was used to record 'Hey Jude', in 1968, and 'Bohemian Rhapsody' (1975).

Returning to Dean Street, turn left to head north again, and then turn left into Fareham Street, right on to Great Chapel Street, left on to Hollen Street, then over Wardour Street to Noel Street. The cover photo of Oasis's *(What's the Story) Morning Glory?* was shot on the corner of Noel and Berwick streets.

Retrace your steps and walk back down Wardour Street. On the left, No.90 is now the site of swanky lofts, but on 16 October 1968 it was where Led Zeppelin played their first London gig. The Sex Pistols also played here, on 14 February 1976, after which Neil Spence of the *NME* coined the term 'punk rock'.

street market (see p259; come late in the afternoon for the bargains), and the prostitutes who conduct their trade at the top of a number of scruffy stairwells. At the southern end of Berwick Street, what remains of the Soho sex industry is at its most visible. Tiny **Walkers Court** (linking Berwick and Brewer Streets) and even smaller **Tisbury Court** (joining Wardour and Rupert Streets) are lined with insalubrious strip joints that lure punters with the promise of untold bodily riches and then send them away again a half-hour later with a bar bill running to several hundred pounds and nary a tit in sight. Nearby **Rupert Street** is home to several other establishments that perform similar cash-guzzling services.

Broadwick Street, just off Berwick Street, is famous for a couple of reasons: it was the birthplace of William Blake, and the epicentre of a severe cholera outbreak in 1854. Local doctor John Snow became convinced that the disease was transmitted by polluted water and had the street's water pump closed. Snow's hypothesis proved correct, leading to a vital breakthrough in epidemiology. The doctor is commemorated by a handle-less replica water pump and a red granite kerbstone outside the street's pub, which is named after him.

West Soho

Map p408 U2-W3
Piccadilly Circus tube.
West of Berwick Street, and just north of Shaftesbury Avenue, Soho grows noticeably quieter, which is bizarre when you consider the more central location. The roads that spout off Brewer Street don't offer a great deal of note, either, but **Great Windmill Street** does present a glimpse of Soho's seedy history. In 1932 the **Windmill Theatre** (Nos. 17-19) embarked on its now-legendary 'revuedeville' shows with erotic 'tableaux' of stationary naked girls, in order to comply with '30s laws. It's now a lap-dancing joint, the premises around it filled with unlicensed clip joints of the kind found in the vicinity of Walkers and Tisbury Courts.

North of Brewer Street, things grow calmer for a while, with **Golden Square** now home to some of the area's grandest residential buildings. Just north of here is **Carnaby Street**: four decades ago the epitome of swinging London and then a rather seamy commercial backwater, it's recently undergone a revival of sorts. On Carnaby Street and **Newburgh Street**, a mix of independent and familiar shops trade happily off the area's history. The sole reason to visit **Argyll Street**, which runs north to Oxford Street, is the grand old **London Palladium** theatre (see p126).

Chinatown & Leicester Square

Map p409 W-X3/4
Leicester Square tube.
Shaftesbury Avenue, which wends its way down from New Oxford Street to Piccadilly Circus, is the heart of Theatreland (see pp334-342). The Victorians built seven grand theatres here; six of them still stand. A profusion of Chinese restaurants and shops mark the northern edge of **Chinatown**, a district that extends to Leicester Square.

Soho has always attracted immigrants, but the Chinese were relative latecomers: most arrived in the 1950s from Hong Kong. Migrating west from their original location in Limehouse in Docklands, and attracted by the cheap rents along Gerrard and Lisle Streets, thousands of Chinese moved in, and soon the neighbourhood developed its distinctive personality. The ersatz oriental gates, stone lions and pagoda-topped phone boxes suggest a Chinese theme park, but this is a close-knit residential and working enclave. **Gerrard Street** is the glitziest spot, crammed with restaurants (see pp206-209) and twinkly lights. Currently, though, the area is under threat from development, with a property company planning to demolish old buildings around pedestrianised Newport Place (by the pagoda) for a shopping centre. For the latest news, and links to the Save Chinatown campaign, see www.minquan.co.uk/save-chinatown.

Just south of here is **Leicester Square**, which, in the 17th and 18th centuries, used to be one of London's most exclusive addresses. By the 19th century, as Soho became a ghetto, the aristos moved out, and they've never really returned. These days, despite a remodelling a while back, it's still no fun: most Londoners avoid the cheap fast fooderies, expensive cinemas and deafness-inducing buskers, and so should you. However, it's not all bad news. The south side of the square is where you'll find the **tkts** booth (see p337), operated by the Society of London Theatres and retailer of cut-price tickets to that day's theatre shows. (The other ticket shops in or near the square are unofficial and often rather more expensive.) And north in Leicester Place is the **Prince Charles Cinema** (see p289), which screens an eclectic mix of recent movies (and the occasional cult classic) at knockdown prices. Grown men dressed as nuns come here to watch sing-a-long-a-*Sound of Music*. Between the cinema and the square you'll see the French Catholic church of **Notre Dame de France**, which contains murals by Jean Cocteau.

Covent Garden & St Giles's

Theatrical playground, past and present.

Covent Garden

Map p409 Y/Z 2-4

Covent Garden or Leicester Square tube.
The area originally designated as the 'Convent of Saint Peter at Westminster' came to the hands of John Russell, first Earl of Bedford, shortly after the dissolution of the monasteries, although it wasn't until the fourth Earl Francis Russell inherited the land that it began its gradual development into the market we recognise today. Russell's aim was to transform the area into a trendy, upmarket residence 'fitt for the habitacions of Gentlemen and men of ability' and he employed the sought-after architect of the day Inigo Jones for the project. With Jones's appreciation of Italian architecture, an open square was constructed in the Palladian style, with St Paul's Church eventually forming the western boundary and the remaining three sides consisting of tall terraced houses opening on to a central courtyard. Over the following years, fashionable London flocked to the area and paid good money for the privilege of residency.

The first recorded market in Covent Garden appeared on the south side of the square in 1640, selling fruit and vegetables, although it was only later in 1670 that Charles II granted a royal charter to the fifth Earl to hold an official market, allowing him to charge tolls.

In time, coffee houses became commonplace, circulating the aroma of roasting java around the marketplace and becoming a trendy gathering point for the literary and theatrical folk of the day – the likes of Henry Fielding, James Boswell, Alexander Pope and David Garrick among them. Another attraction may well have been the numerous theatres, gambling dens and brothels that sprang up in the locality over the coming years.

During the next three centuries the market grew from strength to strength, gradually picking up business from its competitors until it became London's pre-eminent fruit and vegetable wholesaler, employing over 1,000 porters. During this transitional period, a flower market was added (where London's Transport Museum – closed for a major redevelopment until 2007 – now stands) and the market building itself was redesigned by the architect Charles Fowler. It then remained in the Bedfords' hands until 1918, by which time it had been upgraded with new buildings and market halls.

In 1974, when the restored market was moved south to Vauxhall, property developers loomed over the empty stalls and offices, and it was only through mass squats and demonstrations that the area was saved. Today there exists a thriving residential community alongside a mix of established shops and small enterprises, and a sprinkling of cultural venues carrying on the theatrical heritage. The chain stores may have moved in, but it's still a nice place to stroll.

Covent Garden Piazza

Much has changed since the original square was built by Jones, although much of Fowler's design (with the later addition of a glass roof) is still standing. The Piazza remains an attractive galleried space despite its years, with lots of outdoor restaurant seating in summer, cobbled stone pavement and no cars allowed. Tourists flock here for a combination of gentrified shopping, a variety of street artists and classical renditions in the lower courtyard. The majority of the street entertainment takes place under the portico of **St Paul's** church. It was here that Samuel Pepys observed what is thought to be Britain's first Punch

& Judy show, on 9 May 1662. Shoppers favour the old covered market (7836 9136, www.coventgardenmarket.co.uk), now a collection of small, sometimes quirky shops, many of them with a twee, touristy appeal, as well as upmarket chain stores such as Hobbs, Whistles and Crabtree & Evelyn. The **Apple Market**, in the North Hall, has arts and crafts stalls every Tuesday to Sunday, and antiques on Monday. Across the road, the cheaper, tackier **Jubilee Market** deals mostly in novelty T-shirts and unofficial calendars, although it, too, is filled with antiques every Monday and crafts on a weekend.

St Paul's, the Actors' Church (*see below*), launched its own Avenue of the Stars in September 2005, immortalising British- and Commonwealth- born entertainers. The list of people with their own silver star outside the church so far includes Sir Laurence Olivier, Charlie Chaplin and Sir Alec Guinness, plus comedy favourites the Two Ronnies. To represent today's talent are Ricky Gervais and even TV presenters Ant & Dec.

Royal Opera House

Bow Street, WC2E 9DD (7304 4000/www.royal operahouse.org). Covent Garden tube. **Open** 10am-3.30pm Mon-Sat. **Admission** free. *Stage tours* £9; £8 concessions. **Credit** AmEx, DC, MC, V. **Map** p409 Y3.

The Royal Opera House has witnessed no fewer than three fires in its lifetime. The current building is the third on the site, the second having been leased in 1855 to John Anderson, who had already seen two theatres burnt down and promptly added a third. But that's the least of the dramas associated with this stage. Handel premièred *Samson, Judas Maccabaeus* and *Solomon* here, among many other works. Frenzied opera lovers twice rioted against ticket price rises, for 61 nights in 1809, while the 1763 fracas came within an iron pillar of bringing down the galleries. When actors did manage to get in front of the lights, they then promptly collapsed, Peg Woffington and Edmund Kean doing so during *As You Like It* and *Othello* respectively. Productions for the 2006 season include *The Mikado, La Belle Hélène, Madam Butterfly, Ariodante* and *King Arthur*. **Photo** *p131*.

St Paul's Covent Garden

Bedford Street, WC2E 9ED (7836 5221/www.actors church.org). Covent Garden tube or Charing Cross tube/rail. **Open** 9am-4.30pm Mon-Fri; 9am-12.30pm Sun. *Services* 1.10pm Wed; 11am Sun. *Choral Evensong* 4pm 2nd Sun of mth. **Admission** free; donations appreciated. **Map** p409 Y3.

Known as the Actors' Church for its association with Covent Garden's theatreland, this plain Tuscan pastiche was designed by Inigo Jones in 1631. Actors commemorated on its walls range from those now confined to obscurity – AR Philpott, 'Pantopuck the Puppetman' – to those destined for ambrosial

Covent Garden Piazza. *See p128.*

immortality – Vivian Leigh, 'Now boast thee, death, in thy possession lies a lass unparallel'd'. George Bernard Shaw set the first scene of *Pygmalion* under the church's rear portico, and the first known victim of the plague, Margaret Ponteous, is buried in the pleasant churchyard, a calm place to ease one's feet. In front of the church is Britain's very own Avenue of the Stars.

Theatre Museum

Tavistock Street (entrance on Russell Street), WC2E 7PA (7943 4700/www.theatremuseum.org). Covent Garden tube. **Open** 10am-6pm Tue-Sun. *Last entry 5.30pm.* **Admission** free. **Credit** (shop) AmEx, MC, V. **Map** p409 Z3.

The various colourful threads of Covent Garden's theatrical history are spun into a vivid tapestry in this little museum. The permanent galleries form an intriguing window into the heroes of a bygone age – David Garrick, Edmund Kean, Eliza Vestris – as well as the plays that cast them into the public eye. There are daily make-up classes and costume workshops, while larger exhibitions include an interactive biography of the Redgrave family and a study of the cultural explosion in the UK from 1955 to 1964 called 'Unleashing the Nation'. A good museum for children too, with activities such as dressing up boxes and art projects along the route (have a go at creating characters for a miniature theatre play), plus daily workshops (children must be accompanied by an adult).

River Cruises

Discover The Heart of London

HOPPER PASS

UNLIMITED one-day travel between Embankment, Waterloo, Bankside, Tower of London and Greenwich.

CIRCULAR CRUISES

MULTI-LINGUAL COMMENTARY

A premier 50-minute, non-stop, multi-lingual circular cruise from Westminster Pier, taking in all of the river's key attractions.

CATAMARAN CRUISERS

T: **020 7987 1185** E: **info@bateauxlondon.com**
www.catamarancruisers.co.uk

Royal Opera House. *See p129.*

Elsewhere in Covent Garden

The area offers a mixed bag of entertainment, eateries and shops: from opposite ends of **St Martin's Lane** – and the social spectrum – Stringfellows, the well-known lap-dancing establishment (7240 5534) faces down the **Coliseum** (7836 0111; *see p307*), the home of the English National Opera. Meanwhile, neighbouring alleys in the shadow of the Wyndham and Albany theatres exude an overpowering old world charm; from the nook and cranny antiques stores of **Cecil Court** to the clockwork-operated gas lighting of **Goodwin's Court**, which nightly illuminates a row of bow-fronted 17th-century housing.

Further towards the Piazza, most of the older, more unusual shops have been superseded by a homogenous mass of cafés, and by the time you reach the far end of King Street, Covent Garden offers only token gestures towards its colourful history. High-profile fashion designers (and a few trendy up-and-comers supported by their celebrity parents) have all but domesticated **Floral Street**, **Long Acre** and, most noticeably, **Neal Street**, but more interesting shopping experiences wait on **Monmouth Street** and **Earlham Street**. The latter is lined with streetwear labels, as well as bookstores such as the Dover Bookshop (No.18, 7836 2111), which has a good range of industry publications, and Magma (No.8, 7240 8498), probably the best source of fashion, art, film and fashion literature in London. Dress Circle (57-59 Monmouth Street, 7240 2227) is a must for die-hard theatre fans seeking CDs, tapes and records of their favourite musicals, although more conventional tastes may prefer Fopp (1 Earlham Street; *see also p260*).

Where Monmouth, Mercer and Earlham streets meet Shorts Gardens, is the **Seven Dials** roundabout, which was named after both the number of sundials incorporated into the central monument (the seventh being formed by the pillar itself) and streets branching off it. The original pillar, a notorious criminal rendezvous, was removed in 1773. A stone's throw from Seven Dials, **Neal's Yard** is known for its co-operative cafés mingling cheerfully with herbalists and head shops.

Towards Holborn, Covent Garden becomes less distinguished. **Endell Street** is perhaps most noticeable for the queues leading to the ace chippie Rock & Sole Plaice (No.47; *see p209*). These days **Drury Lane** is largely ignored even by theatre-goers: the current Theatre Royal (the first was built there in 1663) opens on to Catherine Street, with its excess of restaurants vying for the attention of pre- and post-performance diners. Meanwhile, the historical depravity of the area is remembered at the **Bow Street Magistrates Court**, home to author and one-time magistrate Henry Fielding's Bow Street Runners (the original precursors to the Metropolitan Police), as well as the site of Oscar Wilde's notorious conviction, in 1895, for committing 'indecent acts'. Finally, the **Freemasons' Hall** – the impressive white building at the point where Long Acre becomes Great Queen Street (7831 9811; call for guided tours) – is worth a peek, if only for its solemn, symbolic architecture.

That this is a residential neighbourhood is evident in peaceful **Ching Court**, off Shelton Street, and the beautiful **Phoenix Garden** (21 Stacey Street, 7379 3187), *rus in urbs* writ large, where willow trees, fruit trees and honeysuckle attract many birds and lunchtime dreamers.

St Giles's

Map p409 X2

Tottenham Court Road tube.

The reality of St Giles's may never have lived up to the legend, but immortalised so unfavourably in Hogarth's *Gin Lane*, and described with such venom by neighbour Charles Dickens, this once-squalid area can nonetheless be considered to have improved significantly in recent years, despite being overshadowed by the much-reviled **Centrepoint** office tower. Indeed, the dozen or so acres of predominantly Irish slums, which struck such fear into the heart of central London, remained a threat until the Metropolitan Board of Works scattered their inhabitants to make way for New Oxford Street in 1847. After an alarmingly effective mopping-up operation, all that remains of those dangerous days is the original church of **St Giles-in-the-Fields** just behind Centrepoint on the High Street, which, in its current form dates back to the early 1700s, although there has been a house of prayer on this site for more than 900 years. Just along the road, a pub known to Elizabethans simply as the Bowl mercifully offered last pints to condemned men on their walk from Newgate to the gibbet at Tyburn. Don't be put off, however: the Angel (61 St Giles Street, 7240 2876), which now stands in its place, is a great little drinking hole.

Beyond this, St Giles's is probably best known for the musical heritage of **Denmark Street**, affectionately known as Tin Pan Alley, and once home to Regents Sound Studios, where the Stones recorded 'Not Fade Away' and the Kinks cut their first demo. The Small Faces were signed at the Giaconda Café, where Bowie also met his first band, and the Sex Pistols wrote 'Anarchy in the UK' in what is now a guitar shop at No.6. These days, instrument sales and repairs are what Denmark Street does best (expect to be serenaded by an army of bedroom guitar soloists 'testing' the latest Fenders), although the **12 Bar Club** (*see p315*) remains the city's most intimate songwriters' venue.

Charing Cross Road is very big on books. Remaining our favourite is the still-traditional if now more efficient Foyles (*see p237*). Still, the real gems are to be found in the smaller, specialised and second-hand stores including Henry Pordes Books (arts and humanities; No.58-60, 7836 9031) and Shipley (7836 4872), which has two stores on Charing Cross Road (Nos. 70 and 72), offering a diverse selection of new and out of print art titles. Cult crews can snap up comics and movie memorabilia at Comic Showcase (No.63, 7434 4349).

The Strand & Embankment

Map p409 Y/Z 4-5

Embankment tube/Charing Cross tube/rail.

In 1292 the body of Eleanor of Castile, consort to Edward I, completed its funerary procession from Lincoln to the Westminster end of the **Strand**, which was then marked by the last of 12 elaborate crosses, reconstructed in 1863 behind the railings of Charing Cross Station. Strange to think that back then this bustling street once ran directly beside the Thames.

The Strand has endured its fair share of slings and arrows throughout history. As far back as the 14th century, the street was lined with waterside homes and gardens for the well-educated and well-to-do, and was still a highly reputable part of London at the time when Inigo Jones was poring over plans for the main square. Just as his Piazza proved too small for the swelling market, so the Strand proved too thin for the wave of licentiousness rushing to fill the void left by the fleeing upper classes. It was a blackspot for poverty and prostitution until the late 1600s, when Sir Christopher Wren suggested the creation of a reclaimed embankment to ease congestion and house the main sewer.

By the time George Newnes's *Strand* magazine was introducing its readership to Sherlock Holmes (1891), things were starting to look up. While never quite regaining the composure of more central parts of Covent Garden (there's little among its collection of overbearing office blocks and underwhelming restaurants to really fire the imagination today), Richard D'Oyly Carte's **Savoy Theatre**, pre-dating the famous hotel (*see p62*) by eight years, gives some indication of how its fortunes began to change once again after the reinforced concrete Embankment was completed.

The **Embankment** itself can be approached down Villiers Street. Cut down Embankment Place to **Craven Street**, where, at No.36, Benjamin Franklin lived from 1762 to 1788. Restoration work on the house recently finished, and it is now open to the public (for details, see www.rsa.org.uk/franklin or call 7930 9121).

Back to the Embankment, from where a number of boat tours with on-board entertainment embark. On dry land, across from Embankment Gardens, a tranquil park with an annual programme of free summer music played out on its small public stage, stands **Cleopatra's Needle**. This stone obelisk was first erected in Egypt under Pharaoh Tothmes III c1500 BC, and underwent truly epic adventures (not least of which was its being abandoned and then rescued after a storm in the Bay of Biscay in 1877) before being repositioned on the Thames in 1878.

Westminster

London's centrepiece, home of the nation's masterpieces.

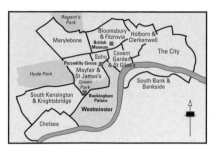

The heart of the beast and the seat of the powers that be, this is the London that England – let alone the folks back home – expects you to see: Trafalgar Square, the Houses of Parliament, Westminster Abbey, Big Ben. Stronger stuff may take some finding around these official enclaves. Westminster has been the centre of the Church and monarchy for almost 1,000 years, since Edward the Confessor built his 'West Minster' and palace on marshy Thorney Island in the 11th century. Politics came to the fore in the 14th century, when the first Parliament met in the abbey. Today the splendid Houses of Parliament provide an iconic backdrop for holiday photos: go on, put yourself in the picture beneath Big Ben.

Trafalgar Square

Map p409 X5

Leicester Square tube or Charing Cross tube/rail.
The centrepiece of London was conceived by the Prince Regent, later George IV, who was obsessed with building monuments to imperial Britain. He commissioned John Nash to create a grand square to pay homage to Britain's naval power. It wasn't fully laid out until 1840, after the king's death, but Nash certainly did as he was told. The focal point is **Nelson's Column**, a tribute to the heroic Horatio, who died during the Battle of Trafalgar in 1805. This Corinthian column, designed by William Railton, is topped by a statue of Nelson by neo-classical architect Charles Barry. The granite fountains were added in 1845 (then redesigned by Lutyens in 1939); and the bronze lions – the work of Sir Edwin Landseer – in 1867. Statues of George IV and a couple of Victorian military heroes anchor three of the square's corners; modern sculpture

takes up the fourth plinth (*see p136* **Circling the square**). A statue of Charles I, dating from the 1630s, and the first equestrian bronze in England, faces down Whitehall. Mayor Ken Livingstone is still fighting to place a nine-foot statue of Nelson Mandela on the square's north terrace; Westminster Council would prefer it to be situated in front of South Africa House.

Neo-classical buildings overlook the square: James Gibbs's **St Martin-in-the-Fields** (*see p134*), and one of the world's great art museums, the **National Gallery** (*see below*). Don't miss the smaller but equally exquisite **National Portrait Gallery** (*see p134*). Trafalgar Square has always been a natural meeting point, even more so since it was semi-pedestrianised in 2003. Protest marches finish here, and it's a boisterous spot on New Year's Eve and during summer (*see p271* **Air play**). Technically, this is the geographical centre of London: on a traffic island on the south side there's a plaque to prove it.

National Gallery

Trafalgar Square, WC2N 5DN (7747 2885/ www.nationalgallery.org.uk) Leicester Square tube/ Charing Cross tube/rail. **Open** (incl Sainsbury Wing) 10am-6pm Mon, Tue, Thur-Sun; 10am-9pm Wed. *Tours* 11.30am, 2.30pm daily; additionally 6pm 6.30pm Wed; 12.30pm, 3.30pm Sat. **Admission** free. *Special exhibitions* prices vary. **Credit** (shop) MC, V. **Map** p409 X5.

Founded in 1824, this is a national treasure. From a mere 38 paintings, the collection has grown into one of the greatest in the world, with more than 2,000 western European pieces. There are masterpieces from virtually every school of art, starting with 13th-century religious works and culminating in Van Gogh. You name it, they're here: da Vinci, Raphael, Rubens, Rembrandt, Van Dyck, Caravaggio, Turner, Constable, Gainsborough, Monet, Cézanne, Picasso… You can't see everything in one visit, but guided tours take in the major works and there are excellent free audio guides.

The Sainsbury Wing concentrates on the early Renaissance period, with an emphasis on Italian and Dutch painters. In the North Wing, look out for masterpieces by Rubens, Rembrandt and Vermeer. The East Wing has a strong collection of English paintings, include Constable's *The Hay Wain*, Turner's romantic watercolours and works by Gainsborough, Reynolds and Hogarth. The real big-ticket items, however, are the Impressionist paintings: Monet's *Water Lilies* series, Van Gogh's *Chair* and Seurat's *Bathers at Asnières* are the stars.

On 24 September 2005 the National Gallery's main portico was re-opened following extensive structural refurbishment to open up the lobby and reveal formerly whitewashed ceiling decoration by the 19th-century artist John Dibblee Crace. It represents the culmination of a £22.5 million re-development of the gallery designed to improve visitor access to the UK's most popular art gallery.

Major exhibitions in 2006 are 'Americans in Paris 1860-1900' (22 Feb-21 May); 'Rebels and Martyrs: The Artist in the Nineteenth Century' (28 June-10 Sept); and Velázquez (18 Oct-14 Jan 2007). Smaller free shows include Renaissance-reconstruction photographer Tom Hunter's 'Living in Hell and Other Stories' (until 12 Mar); Mary Cassatt: Prints (22 Feb-7 May); 'Bellini and the East' (12 Apr-25 June); The Mond Bequest (8 Sept-10 Dec); and 'Cézanne in British Collections' (4 Oct-7 Jan 2007). **Photo** *p135*.

National Portrait Gallery

2 St Martin's Place, WC2H 0HE (7306 0055/ www.npg.org.uk). Leicester Square tube/Charing Cross tube/rail. **Open** 10am-6pm Mon-Wed, Sat, Sun; 10am-9pm Thur, Fri. *Tours* throughout Aug, times vary. **Admission** free. *Special exhibitions* prices vary. **Credit** AmEx, MC, V. **Map** p409 X4.

Subjects of the portraits hanging here range from Tudor royalty to present-day celebrities, of interest for contributions not only to history but to culture, sport, science, business and government. Londoners drop in frequently, partly because it has a personal feel to it (a result of the subject matter, its manageable size and its attractive design) and partly because there's a lovely restaurant and bar on the top floor.

The portraits are organised chronologically from top to bottom: start on the second floor and work your way down. One of the gallery's most prized possessions is the only known contemporary portrait of William Shakespeare. The first painting in the collection, it will play a part in the gallery's 150th anniversary celebrations in 2006. The gallery also forms a fascinating 'who's who' of medieval monarchy: there's a room devoted to pictures of Mary, Queen of Scots, and a portrait of Henry VIII by Holbein. Dickens, Darwin and Disraeli (the latter painted by Millais) are among those on the first floor. Recent figures include union leader Arthur Scargill and his nemesis Margaret Thatcher, photographed by Helmut Newton. She didn't have much time for him, and it shows. New to the collection are footballer David Beckham, architect John Pawson, novelist Margaret Drabble, broadcaster Sue MacGregor and a squadron of Athens 2004 successes.

Exhibitions for 2006 include 'Searching for Shakespeare', celebrating the 150th anniversary of the gallery, including various other portraits of the bard (2 Mar-29 May); 'Icons and Idols: commissioning contemporary portraits' explores the process of the gallery's commissioning strategy over the past 25 years, with a selection of 130 portraits, from Bryan Organ's Prince Charles to Sam Taylor-Wood's video portrait of David Beckham snoozing

(2 Mar-18 June); a celebration of photographer Angus McBean's portraits (5 July-22 Oct), including black-and-white photos from the 1930s to the '60s of the likes of Vivien Leigh, Audrey Hepburn and Shirley Bassey; and an exhibition of David Hockney's portraits (12 Oct-21 Jan 2007), including new works specially created for the show.

St Martin-in-the-Fields

Trafalgar Square, WC2N 4JJ (7766 1100/Brass Rubbing Centre 7930 9306/box office evening concerts 7839 8362/www.stmartin-in-the-fields.org). Leicester Square tube/Charing Cross tube/rail. **Open** *Church* 8am-6pm daily. *Services* 8am, 5.30pm Mon-Fri; 1pm, 5pm, 6pm Wed; 9am Sat; 8am, 10am, noon, 2.15pm, 5pm, 6.30pm Sun. *Brass Rubbing Centre* 10am-6pm Mon-Sat; noon-6pm Sun. *Evening concerts* Thur-Sat & alternate Tue 7.30pm. **Admission** free. *Brass rubbing* £3-£15. *Evening concerts* prices vary. **Credit** MC, V. **Map** p409 X4.

A church has stood on this site since the 13th century, 'in the fields' between Westminster and the City; this one was built in 1726 by James Gibbs, who designed it in a curious combination of neo-classical and baroque styles. This is the parish church for Buckingham Palace (note the royal box to the left of the gallery), but it is perhaps best known for its classical music concerts (*see p306*). It also has a good café, a small gallery and the London Brass Rubbing Centre. The churchyard contains Reynolds's grave. The church is in the middle of a £34-million refurbishment project, due for completion around Easter 2007; improved underground spaces will be entered through a new glazed pavilion.

Around the Mall

Maps p402 J9 & p403 K8

Leicester Square tube or Charing Cross tube/rail.
From Trafalgar Square, the grand processional route of the Mall passes beneath Aston Webb's 1910 Admiralty Arch to the Victoria Memorial. The road was not designed as a triumphal approach to Buckingham Palace (*see p119*) at the other end, despite being tarmacked in pink to match the Queen's forecourt: Charles II had the street laid out before the palace was even a royal residence. He wanted a new pitch for 'pallemaille', a popular game that involved hitting a ball through a hoop at the end of a long alley. Nearby Pall Mall, his favourite pitch, had become too crowded for the sport.

As you walk along the Mall, look out on the right for **Carlton House Terrace**, the last project completed by John Nash before his death in 1835. It was built on the site of Carlton House, George IV's home until he decided it wasn't fit for a king and enlarged Buckingham House into a palace to replace it. Part of the terrace now houses the multidisciplinary **Institute of Contemporary Arts** (ICA; *see p135*) which runs a wide range of events.

The **National Gallery** – space for endless contemplation. *See p133.*

On the south side of St James's Park, the Wellington Barracks, home of the Foot Guards, contains the **Guards' Museum** (*see below*). At the park's southern end is Birdcage Walk, named after the aviary that James I built there.

Guards' Museum

Wellington Barracks, Birdcage Walk, SW1E 6HQ (7414 3428). St James's Park tube. **Open** 10am-4pm daily (last entry 3.30pm). **Admission** £2; £1 concessions; free under 16s. **Credit** (shop) AmEx, MC, V. **Map** p402 J9.

The Changing of the Guard is one of London's great spectacles. This small, immaculately maintained museum, founded in the 17th century under Charles II, records the history of the British Army's five Guards regiments. It contains mainly uniforms (many of them spectacular examples of ceremonial splendour), some important paintings, intriguing memorabilia and medals, including the first ever minted for the army, for their victory over the Scots at the Battle of Dunbar in the 17th century. The shop has a good selection of toy soldiers.

ICA Gallery

The Mall, SW1Y 5AH (box office 7930 3647/ www.ica.org.uk). Piccadilly Circus tube/Charing Cross tube/rail. **Open** *Galleries* noon-7.30pm daily. **Membership** *Daily* £1.50, £1 concessions Mon-Fri; £2.50, £1.50 concessions Sat, Sun; free under-14s. *Annual* £30; £20 concessions. **Credit** AmEx, DC, MC, V. **Map** p403 K8.

Founded in 1948 by the anarchist Herbert Read, the Institute of Contemporary Arts still revels in a remit that challenges traditional notions of art from its incongruously establishment-looking home. Scores of challengers have held their first exhibitions here: Henry Moore, Picasso, Max Ernst, Damien Hirst, Helen Chadwick and Gary Hume. Its cinema (*see p286*) shows London's artiest films, its theatre stages performance art and quality gigs and its art

exhibitions are always talking points. All this is achieved to the high presentation standards befitting a national institution. The annual Beck's Futures exhibition and art prize (mid Mar-mid May) features some of the best contemporary painting, sculpture, photography, installation and video.

Whitehall to Parliament Square

Map p403 L8-9

Westminster tube or Charing Cross tube/rail.

You're in civil servant territory now. Lined with government buildings, the long, gentle curve of **Whitehall** is named after Henry VIII's magnificent palace, which burned to the ground in 1698. The street is still home to the Ministry of Defence, the Foreign Office and the Treasury among others. They're closed to the public, but pop into the **Whitehall Theatre** (No.14) for a peek at its gorgeous art nouveau interior. Halfway down the street, the **Horse Guards** building faces the **Banqueting House** (*see p137*), London's first Italianate building.

Nearby is Sir Edwin Lutyens' plain memorial to the dead of both world wars, the **Cenotaph**, and, on **Downing Street** (closed off by iron security gates), the equally plain homes of the prime minister and chancellor, at Nos.10 and 11. At the end of King Charles Street, home of the Foreign Office, sit the **Cabinet War Rooms** (*see p137*), the operations centre used by Churchill during World War II air raids, along with the new **Churchill Museum**.

A few hundred feet from the Cenotaph stands the new memorial to the women of World War II. Unveiled by the Queen on 9 July 2005, as part of the commemorations marking

Circling the square

Nowhere in London gives a better sense of Britain's long-departed imperial greatness than Trafalgar Square. Surrounded by imposing 18th- and 19th-century neo-classical stone buildings, the square itself is dominated by the 185-foot column of Lord Nelson, commemorating his victory at the Battle of Trafalgar in 1805.

Nelson aside, there are four other major plinths. The first three feature military and crown, albeit not obvious heroes of Empire like Nelson. King George IV went up in 1830 on a supposedly temporary basis – by the century's end his name had to be added so people knew who he was. Another two were funded by public subscription, which tends to favour military heroes (head to Embankment, opposite the London Eye, for a modern example: the new Battle of Britain sculpture, featuring Churchill's line 'Never was so much owed by so many to so few'), and deemed the little-known General Charles Napier and Major General Sir Henry Havelock worthy of tribute. Napier added what is now Pakistan to the Empire in 1843, and Havelock delayed Indian independence by 90 years by putting down a 1857 uprising against British rule.

Which leaves the fourth plinth, on the north-west corner of Trafalgar Square, opposite the National Gallery's Sainsbury Wing. It was designed and built by Sir Charles Barry in 1841 to display a statue of a horse, but no one could find the money to complete the job, so it remained empty for over 150 years. After three pieces of modern art were displayed during 1998, its future was finally resolved – no horse, but an ongoing series of temporary works of art from leading national and international artists. The first of these is the ground-breaking *Alison Lapper Pregnant* by leading BritArt player Marc Quinn. The 12-foot statue, which took ten months to carve from white Carrara marble, is of artist Alison Lapper, who was born with no arms and shortened legs. She modelled for the statue

when eight months pregnant with her son, Parys, who was born in 2000. Lapper herself was seemingly daunted yet excited by the prospect of being portrayed in such a way, in such a prominent place, quipping 'I'm going to be up in Trafalgar Square. Little me.'

So far reactions to the sculpture have been mixed – some people love it, others hate it. Robert Simon, editor of the *British Art Journal*, labelled it 'horrible', not because of the subject matter but because of its 'shiny, slimy surface'. Quinn himself admits that he expected a huge diversity of opinion, but is pleased with the result, saying it makes people question what the rest of the square means, rather like in a dream, where you're confronted with 'a familiar square but an unfamiliar sight'. He puts forward the argument that the fourth plinth can become a symbol of London respecting its traditions, yet simultaneously moving forward into the future, challenging itself through constant reinterpretation.

Alison Lapper Pregnant will be displayed until April 2007, when it will be replaced by Thomas Schutte's *Hotel for the Birds*.

the 60th anniversary of the end of the war, the 22.5-foot bronze monument features 17 sets of work clothes hanging on pegs. It was designed by the sculptor John Mills, inspired by the advice given in 1945 to the seven million or so women who had contributed to the war effort 'to hang up your uniforms and overalls and go home – the job is done.'

At the end of Whitehall, **Parliament Square** has architecture on an appropriately grand scale. Constructed in 1868, it features the fantastical, neo-Gothic **Middlesex Guildhall** (1906-13) on the west side. Just behind that is **Westminster Central Hall**, with its great black dome, used for conferences (the first assembly of the United Nations was held here in 1946) and Methodist church services. The buildings overlook the shady square with its statues of British politicians, such as Disraeli and Churchill, and one outsider, Abraham Lincoln, who sits sombrely to one side.

Nearby, **Westminster Abbey** (*see p138*) is the most venerable ancient building in central London. Much smaller, **St Margaret's Church** (*see p138*) stands beside it: Pepys and Churchill were both married here and it's still a popular choice for society weddings.

If it is true, as some say, that few buildings in London really dazzle, the extravagant **Houses of Parliament** (*see below*) are an exception. Although formally still known as the Palace of Westminster, the only surviving part of the medieval royal palace is Westminster Hall (and the **Jewel Tower**, just south of Westminster Abbey; *see p138*). One note: the legendary **Big Ben** is actually the name of the bell, not the clock tower that houses it. In its shadow, at the end of Westminster Bridge, stands a statue of the warrior Boudicca and her daughters gesticulating toward Parliament.

Banqueting House

Whitehall, SW1A 2ER (7930 4179/www.hrp.org.uk). Westminster tube/Charing Cross tube/rail. **Open** 10am-5pm Mon-Sat. **Admission** £4; £2.60-£3 concessions; free under-5s. **Credit** MC, V. **Map** p403 L8.

Designed by the great neo-classicist Inigo Jones in 1622, this was one of the first Palladian buildings in London. The austere simplicity of the exterior belies the sumptuous ceiling in the beautifully proportioned first-floor hall, painted by Rubens no less. Charles I commissioned the Flemish artist to glorify his father James I, 'the wisest fool in Christendom', and celebrate the divine right of the Stuart kings. A bust over the entrance commemorates the fact that Charles was beheaded just outside in 1649. The event is marked annually on 31 January with a small ceremony. Call to check the hall is open before you visit: the building sometimes closes for corporate and government functions. Lunchtime concerts are held here on the first Monday of every month except August.

Cabinet War Rooms & Churchill Museum

Clive Steps, King Charles Street, SW1A 2AQ (7930 6961/www.iwm.org.uk). St James's Park or Westminster tube. **Open** 9.30am-6pm daily (last entry 5pm). **Admission** £10.50; £4.50-£8 concessions; free under-15s. **Credit** MC, V. **Map** p403 K9.

A serious and informative blast from the past, this small underground set of rooms was Churchill's bunker during World War II. Almost nothing has been changed since it was closed on 16 August 1945: every book, chart and pin in the map room remains in place, as does the BBC microphone he used when making his famous addresses. Churchill's bedroom,

the setting for his catnaps, displays a chamber pot and nightshirt; the Transatlantic Telephone Room had a hotline to the White House; and there's also a collection of Churchill's papers and speeches. The furnishings are spartan, vividly evoking the wartime atmosphere, and the audio guide's sound effects – wailing sirens, Churchill's wartime speeches – add to the nostalgia. Occupying an underground space adjoining the War Rooms is the new Churchill Museum, which opened in February 2005. It provides an in-depth look at the great man's life and times; central to the cunningly arranged displays, which include one of his red-velvet 'romper suits', Bowker hat, champagne and cigars, and plenty of hands-on exhibits, is the Lifeline, an illuminated interactive information table. Touch in a date and hope for a 'reward': 11 November 1918 covers the table with poppies; 6 August 1945 turns the table white. An entertaining way to learn those important dates.

Houses of Parliament

Parliament Square, SW1A 0AA (Commons information 7219 4272/Lords information 7219 3107/tours information 0870 906 3773/ www.parliament.uk). Westminster tube. **Open** *(when in session) House of Commons Visitors' Gallery* 2.30-10.30pm Mon, Tue 11.30am-7.30pm Wed; 11.30am-6.30pm Thur; 9.30am-3pm Fri. *House of Lords Visitors' Gallery* from 2.30pm Mon-Wed; from 11am Thur, occasional Fri. *Tours* summer recess only; phone for details. **Admission** *Visitors' Gallery* free. *Tours* £7; £5 concessions; free under-5s. **Credit** MC, V. **Map** p403 L9.

This neo-Gothic extravaganza is so spectacular it's almost enough to make you want to go into politics. The ornate architecture is the ultimate expression of Victorian self-confidence, even if its style was a throwback to the Middle Ages. Completed in 1860, it was the creation of architect Charles Barry, who won the architectural competition to replace the original Houses of Parliament, which were destroyed by fire in 1834. Barry was assisted on the interiors by Augustus Pugin. The original palace was home to the young Henry VIII, until he upped sticks to Whitehall in 1532. Although the first Parliament was held here in 1275, Westminster did not become its permanent home until Henry moved out. Parliament was originally housed in the choir stalls of St Stephen's Chapel, where members sat facing each other from opposite sides, and the tradition continues today. The only remaining parts of the original palace are the Jewel Tower and the almost mythically historic Westminster Hall, one of the finest medieval buildings in Europe.

In all, there are 1,000 rooms, 100 staircases, 11 courtyards, eight bars and six restaurants (plus a visitors' cafeteria). None of them is open to the public, but you can watch the Commons or Lords in session from the galleries. In truth, there's not much to see: most debates are sparsely attended and unenthusiastically conducted. Visitors queue at St Stephen's Entrance (it's well signposted) and, in high season, may wait a couple of hours. The best spectacle is Prime Minister's Question Time at noon on Wednesday, but you need to book advance tickets through your MP or embassy, who can also arrange tours. Parliament goes into recess in summer, at which times tours of the main ceremonial rooms, including Westminster Hall and the two houses, are available to the general public.

Jewel Tower

*Abingdon Street, SW1P 3JY (7222 2219/www.
english-heritage.org.uk). Westminster tube.* **Open**
Apr-Oct 10am-5pm daily. *Nov-Mar* 10am-4pm daily.
Admission (EH) £2.60; £1.30-£2 concessions; free
under-5s. **Credit** MC, V. **Map** p403 L9.
Emphatically not the home of the Crown Jewels, this old stone tower was built in 1365 to house Edward III's gold and silver plate. It's still worth a look, though, because, along with Westminster Hall (*see p137*), it is one of only two surviving parts of the medieval Palace of Westminster. From 1621 to 1864 the tower stored Parliamentary records, and it contains an exhibition on Parliaments past. On the ground floor, look out for the ninth-century Rhenish sword dug up in the gardens over the road in 1948.

St Margaret's Church

*Parliament Square, SW1P 3PL (7654 4840/www.
westminster-abbey.org/stmargarets). St James's Park
or Westminster tube.* **Open** 9.30am-3.45pm Mon-Fri;
9.30am-1.45pm Sat; 2-5pm Sun (times may change at short notice due to services). *Services* 11am Sun; phone to check for other days. **Admission** free. **Map** p403 L9.
Some of the most impressive pre-Reformation stained glass in London can be found here. The east window (1509) commemorates the marriage of Henry VIII and Catherine of Aragon. Later windows celebrate Britain's first printer, William Caxton, buried here in 1491, explorer Sir Walter Raleigh, executed in Old Palace Yard, and writer John Milton (1608-74), who married his second wife, Katherine Woodcock, here. Founded in the 12th century, this historic church was demolished in the reign of Edward III, but rebuilt from 1486 to 1523. Since then it has been restored many times. As it's the official church of the House of Commons since 1614, its bells are rung when a new Speaker is chosen. Above the doorway is a bust of Charles I, looking across the street at a statue of his old adversary, Cromwell.

Westminster Abbey

*20 Dean's Yard, SW1P 3PA (7222 5152/tours 7654
4900/www.westminster-abbey.org). St James's Park
or Westminster tube.* **Open** *Chapter House, Nave
& Royal Chapels* 9.30am-3.45pm Mon, Tue, Thur,
Fri; 9.30am-7pm Wed; 9.30am-1.45pm Sat. *Abbey
Museum* 10.30am-4pm Mon-Sat. *Cloisters* 8am-6pm
Mon-Sat. *Garden* Apr-Sept 10am-6pm Tue-Thur.
Oct-Mar 10am-4pm Tue-Thur. Last entry 1hr before closing. *Services* 7.30am, 8am, 12.30pm, 5pm Mon-Fri; 8am, 9am, 3pm Sat; 8am, 10am, 11.15am, 3pm, 5.45pm, 6.30pm Sun. **Admission** £8, £6 concessions; free under-11s with paying adult; £18 family. **Credit** MC, V. **Map** p403 K9.

Westminster Abbey has been synonymous with British royalty since 1066, when Edward the Confessor built a church on the site just in time for his own funeral (it was consecrated eight days before he died). Since then, a 'who's who' of monarchy has been buried here, and, with two exceptions (Edwards V and VIII), every ruler since William the Conqueror (1066) has been crowned in the abbey. Of the original abbey, only the Pyx Chamber (the one-time royal treasury) and the Norman undercroft remain; the Gothic nave and choir were rebuilt in the 13th century; the Henry VII Chapel, with its spectacular fan vaulting, was added in 1503-12; and, finally, Nicholas Hawksmoor's west towers completed the building in 1745.

The interior is cluttered with monuments to statesmen, scientists, musicians and poets. Poets' Corner contains the graves of Dryden, Samuel Johnson, Browning and Tennyson – although it has plaques for many more, most are buried elsewhere. The centrepiece of the octagonal Chapter House is its faded 13th-century tiled floor, while the Little Cloister, with its pretty garden, offers respite from the crowds, especially during free lunchtime concerts (call for details). Worth a look, too, are ten statues of 20th-century Christian martyrs in 15th-century niches over the west door. Come early, late, or on midweek afternoons to avoid the crowds. **Photo** *p139.*

Millbank

Map p403 L10-11

Pimlico or Westminster tube.
Millbank runs along the river from Parliament to Vauxhall Bridge. Just off here is **Smith Square**, home to **St John's, Smith Square**, an exuberant baroque fantasy built as a church in 1713-28, but which has now become a venue for classical music (*see p306*) with a basement bar-restaurant. Nearby, on Lord North Street – one of the most prestigious addresses in London – is a clutch of fine Georgian houses. By the river, the **Victoria Tower Gardens** contain a statue of suffragette leader Emmeline Pankhurst, a cast of Rodin's glum-looking *Burghers of Calais* and the Buxton Drinking Fountain, which commemorates the emancipation of slaves.

Further along the river, just north of Vauxhall Bridge, stands the **Tate Britain** gallery (*see p140*), with its excellent collection of British art. It occupies the former site of the Millbank Penitentiary, one of Britain's fouler Victorian prisons, which was eventually demolished in 1890. Overshadowing the Tate is the 387-foot **Millbank Tower**, erstwhile home to the Labour Party. Across the river, the curious cream and green-glass block is the rather conspicuous HQ of the Secret Intelligence Service (SIS), which people more commonly refer to as MI6.

Little Cloister's garden,
Westminster Abbey. *See p138.*

Tate Britain

Millbank, SW1P 4RG (7887 8000/www.tate.org.uk).
Pimlico tube. **Open** 10am-5.50pm daily. *Tours*
11am, noon, 2pm, 3pm Mon-Fri; noon, 3pm Sat,
Sun. **Admission** free. *Special exhibitions* prices
vary. **Credit** (shop) MC, V. **Map** p403 K11.

Tate Modern (*see p88*), its younger, sexier sibling,
seems to get all the attention, but don't forget the
Britain: it contains London's second great collection
of historical art, after the National Gallery. With the
opening of the Modern, oodles of space was freed up
to accommodate the collection of British art from the
16th century to the present day.

The collection more than fills the 'something for
everyone' remit that you'd hope from a gallery whose
exhibits span five centuries. It takes in works by
artists such as Hogarth, the Blakes (William and
Peter), Gainsborough, Constable (who gets three
rooms all to himself), Reynolds, Bacon and Moore.
Turner is particularly well represented, even more so
since 2003 when the gallery recovered two classics –
Shade and Darkness – The Evening of the Deluge and
Light and Colour (Goethe's Theory) – which had been
stolen in 1994.

Tate Modern doesn't have a monopoly on contemporary artists, either: there are works here by
Howard Hodgkin, Lucian Freud and David Hockney.
The shop is well stocked with posters and art books,
and the restaurant is highly regarded. You can also
have the best of both art worlds, thanks to the Tate-
to-Tate boat service (*see p88*).

Exhibitions that are planned for 2006 include
'Gothic Nightmares: Fuseli, Blake and the Romantic
Imagination' (15 Feb-1 May); 'Tate Triennial' (1 Mar-
14 May), the third of its kind, this year curated by
Beatrix Ruf, Director of the Kunsthalle, Zurich, looking at the contemporary art practice of re-loading;
'Constable' (1-28 June), celebrating his masterpieces;
a major retrospective of the work of Howard Hodgkin
(14 June-17 Sept) from the 1950s to the present day,
curated by Tate Director Sir Nicholas Serota; and
'Holbein in England' (28 Sept-7 Jan 2007), a rare
exhibition of works created over two periods, the
second as court painter to Henry VIII. The annual –
and always headline grabbing – Turner Prize exhibition for contemporary artists runs from 17 Oct to
7 Jan 2007, with the shortlist announced on 16 May.

Victoria & Pimlico

Map p402 J11

Pimlico tube or Victoria tube/rail.

Victoria Street, stretching from Parliament
Square to Victoria Station, links political
London with a rather more colourful and
chaotic backpackers' London. Victoria Coach
Station, one of the city's main arrival termini
for visitors from the rest of Europe, is a short
distance away in Buckingham Palace Road;
Belgrave Road provides an almost unbroken
line of cheap (and fairly grim) hotels.

Not to be confused with the Abbey in
Parliament Square, **Westminster Cathedral**
(*see below*) is part-hidden by office blocks, and
comes as a pleasant surprise. The striking, red-
brick Byzantine church was built between 1895
and 1903, although its interior decoration is
still unfinished. Continuing along Victoria
Street towards Parliament Square, you come
to **Christchurch Gardens**, burial site of
Thomas ('Colonel') Blood, the 17th-century
rogue who nearly got away with stealing the
Crown Jewels in 1671. A memorial is dedicated
to the suffragettes, who held meetings at
Caxton Hall, visible on the far side of the
gardens. **New Scotland Yard**, with its
famous revolving sign, is in Broadway,
but there's nothing much else to see there.
Strutton Ground, on the other side of Victoria
Street, has a small market. Sir Richard Rogers's
iconic **Channel Four Building** is on the
corner of Chadwick and Horseferry Roads.

At the other end of Victoria Station from
Victoria Street, smart **Pimlico** fills the
triangle of land formed by Chelsea Bridge,
Ebury Street, Vauxhall Bridge Road and the
Thames. Thomas Cubitt built the elegant
white stucco streets and squares in the 1830s.
Generally speaking, Pimlico is residential and
a bit dull for tourists.

Westminster Cathedral

Victoria Street, SW1P 1QW (7798 9055/www.
westminstercathedral.org.uk). Victoria tube/rail.
Open 7am-7pm Mon-Fri, Sun; 8am-7pm Sat.
Services 7am, 8am, 10.30am, 12.30pm, 1.05pm,
5.30pm Mon-Fri; 8am, 9am, 10.30am, 12.30pm,
6pm Sat; 8am, 9am, 10.30am, noon, 5.30pm, 7pm
Sun. **Admission** free; donations appreciated.
Campanile £3; £1.50 concessions. **No credit
cards. Map** p402 J10.

Westminster Abbey might be more famous, but
Westminster Cathedral is spectacular in its own
bizarre way. Part wedding cake, part sweet stick, this
neo-Byzantine confection is Britain's premier
Catholic cathedral, built between 1895 and 1903 by
John Francis Bentley, who was inspired by the Hagia
Sophia in Istanbul. The land on which it is built
had formerly been a bull-baiting ring and a pleasure
garden before being bought by the Catholic Church
in 1884. With such a festive exterior, you'd expect an
equally ornate interior. Not so: the inside has yet to
be finished. Even so, you can get a taste of what the
faithful will eventually achieve from the magnificent
columns and mosaics (made from more than 100
kinds of marble). Eric Gill's sculptures of the Stations
of the Cross (1914-18) are world renowned. Simple
and objective, they were controversial at the time of
installation, labelled Babylonian and crude by critics. The nave of Westminster Cathedral is the broad-
est in England, and dark wood floors and flickering
candles add to the drama. The view from the 273ft
bell tower is superb: best of all, it's got a lift.

South Kensington & Knightsbridge

Where London makes an exhibition of itself.

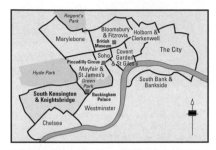

South Kensington

Map p399 D9-D10

Gloucester Road or South Kensington tube.
This is the land of plenty, as far as cultural and academic institutions are concerned. Three heavyweight museums, three lofty colleges and one ginormous concert hall dominate the area once known as Albertopolis, in honour of the prince who oversaw their inception. Today, £186,000 won't buy much, but back in the 1850s this sum, the profit of the 1851 Great Exhibition, bought the 87 acres of land for the building of institutions to 'extend the influence of Science and Art upon Productive Industry'. Prince Albert did not survive to see the resulting oasis of learning, which includes the **Natural History Museum** (*see below*), the **Science Museum** (*see p142*) and the **Victoria & Albert Museum** (*see p142*). Don't be tempted to try to see all three on the same day; each contains an encyclopedia's worth of content and rewards multiple visits. Adventurers are honoured at the **Royal Geographical Society** (1 Kensington Gore, 7591 3000), where statues of Ernest Shackleton and David Livingstone stand proud in alcoves in its walls, and a lively events programme inside. The three colleges in question are Imperial College, the Royal College of Art and the **Royal College of Music** (Prince Consort Road, 7589 3643; call for details of concerts and Wednesday openings of the musical instrument museum), which forms a unity with the **Royal Albert Hall** (*see p305*), the great, rotund performance space whose murky acoustics test conductors

and musicians during the world-famous summer Proms concerts (*see p309*). Looking out across Kensington Gore from the Hall gives a great view of the golden tribute to the royal benefactor, the **Albert Memorial** (*see below*).

South Kensington's Victorian flowering was residential as well as cultural. This was a prime area for planned estate development, resulting in an unusual degree of uniformity. Elegant terraces of family houses sprang up, in retrospective Georgian style. A number of these are now occupied by international institutes (French, German, Polish, Islamic).

Albert Memorial

Kensington Gardens (opposite Royal Albert Hall), SW7 (tours 7495 0916). South Kensington tube.
Tours 2pm, 3pm 1st Sun of mth. **Admission** free.
Tours £4.50; £4 concessions. **No credit cards.**
Map p397 D8.
'I would rather not be made the prominent feature of such a monument' was Prince Albert's reported response when the subject of commemoration came up. Quite what he would have made of this overblown memorial, unveiled 15 years after his death, is hard to imagine. It is, however, one of the great sculptural achievements of the Victorian period. Created by Sir George Gilbert Scott, it centres around a gilded Prince Albert holding a catalogue of the Great Exhibition of 1851. He's guarded on four outer corners by massive representations of the continents and sits enshrined in a white marble frieze depicting poets and painters; pillars are crowned with bronze statues representing the sciences, and the arts are shown in a series of intricate mosaics. Overhead, the dramatic 180ft spire is inlaid with semi-precious stones.

Natural History Museum

Cromwell Road, SW7 5BD (information 7942 5725/ switchboard 7942 5000/www.nhm.ac.uk). South Kensington tube. **Open** 10am-5.50pm Mon-Sat; 11am-5.50pm Sun. *Tours* every 30mins 11am-4pm daily (depending on guide availability). **Admission** free; charges apply for special exhibitions. *Tours* free. **Credit** (shop) MC, V. **Map** p399 D10.
This cathedral to the wonders of creation was deliberately designed by Alfred Waterhouse to inspire awe. Certainly, the elaborate Romanesque style is impressive, as is the giant cast of a Diplodocus skeleton in the main hall of the Life Galleries. If you've come with children, you may not see much more than

Take your time. The **Victoria & Albert Museum** isn't going anywhere…

the Dinosaur gallery, with its star turn, the animatronic Tyrannosaurus rex, roaring in its enclosure.

But there's much more to the museum than extinct reptiles – 70 million plants, animals, fossils, rocks and minerals, to be exact. Some of the galleries are pretty static and dry; others, like Creepy Crawlies, so beloved of children you can hardly get near the exhibits. The giant blue whale model in the Mammals gallery is impressive in size, and the Birds gallery is fascinating, especially the giant case of preserved songbirds and the stuffed dodo.

Entry to the Earth Galleries is portentous: you travel via an escalator, passing through a giant suspended globe and twinkling images of the star system. You go straight into a noisy gallery called Restless Surface, whose most famous exhibit is a mock-up of a Kobe supermarket, where the floor shakes to video coverage of the 1995 earthquake.

The Darwin Centre, whose first stage of development was completed in 2002, houses about 22 million specimens, with 450,000 stored in jars of alcohol. The second, final phase will store the insect and plant collections (due for completion in 2008). A daily programme called Darwin Centre Live (2.30pm Tuesday to Friday, noon and 2.30pm weekends) allows visitors to meet researchers and curators to find out about their work and view the museum's vast collections.

The Wildlife Photographer of the Year show runs from October each year. Outside, the Wildlife Garden (open Apr-Oct, £1.50) is the Natural History Museum's living exhibition, with a range of British lowland habitats.

A major temporary exhibition, looking at how and what dinosaurs ate, is scheduled to open in June 2006.

Science Museum

Exhibition Road, SW7 2DD (7942 4454/booking & information line 0870 870 4868/www.sciencemuseum. org.uk). South Kensington tube. **Open** 10am-5.45pm daily. **Admission** free; charges apply for special exhibitions. **Credit** AmEx, MC, V. **Map** p399 D9.

The Science Museum demonstrates with great aplomb how science filters down through myriad elements of daily life, with displays on engines, cars, planes, ships, the home, medicine and computers. From waterplay for tiny tots in the basement discovery area to adult events centred on contemporary science issues in the debate venue known as the Dana Centre, the vast collection is a crowd pleaser for all age groups. Landmark inventions such as Stephenson's Rocket, Whittle's turbojet engine, Arkwright's spinning machine and the Apollo 10 command module are celebrated in the Making the Modern World gallery. The Wellcome Wing consists of four storeys of discovery, from the IMAX cinema (*see p289*) on the ground, upstairs to the Who Am I? gallery, which explores human characteristics and discoveries in genetics, brain science and psychology, up to In Future, where visitors choose how much they'll allow science to affect their fates.

Forthcoming temporary exhibitions include 'Inside the Spitfire', which runs until spring 2007. The museum's ten-year-long project to revamp its galleries has resulted in a new-look Energy Hall on the ground floor, which now includes Energy: Fuelling the Future, a hands-on gallery all about power and energy-saving.

Victoria & Albert Museum

Cromwell Road, SW7 2RL (7942 2000/www.vam.ac. uk). South Kensington tube. **Open** 10am-5.45pm Mon, Tue, Thur-Sun; 10am-10pm Wed & last Fri of mth. *Tours* daily; phone for details. **Admission** free; charges apply for special exhibitions. **Credit** (shop) MC, V. **Map** p399 E10.

The 150-year old V&A dazzles: its grand galleries contain about four million pieces of furniture, textiles, ceramics, sculpture, paintings, posters, jewellery, glass and metalwork from cultures across the world. Items are grouped by theme, origin or age. The museum boasts the finest collection of

Italian Renaissance sculpture outside Italy. Home-grown treasures – including the Great Bed of Ware, Canova's *The Three Graces* and Henry VIII's writing desk – are housed in the British Galleries, where you'll find a range of interactive exhibits for children. Take time to admire the Fashion galleries, which run from 18th-century court dress right up to a summer chiffon number for 2005. The Architecture gallery and study centre has videos, models, plans and descriptions of various architectural styles, while the museum's famous Photography collection, started in 1852, holds over 500,000 images. The Ceramics collection holds ancient Egyptian artefacts to contemporary studio pottery ceramics. A fine area for contemplation is the John Madejski Garden, designed by Kim Wilkie, with its beds of lilies and lemon trees.

Exhibitions for 2006 include, until 23 July, 'Modernism: Designing a New World', 'Leonardo da Vinci: Experience, Experiment and Design' (14 Sept-7 Jan 2007) and 'Renaissance at Home' (Oct-Jan 2007). Futureplan is the museum's extensive ten-year refurbishment, which will result in the temporary closure or relocation of a number of galleries; see www.vam.ac.uk/futureplan for details. **Photo** *p142*.

Hyde Park & Kensington Gardens

Maps p396 & p397

Hyde Park Corner, Knightsbridge, Lancaster Gate or Queensway tube.

At 1.5 miles long and about a mile wide, **Hyde Park** (7298 2100, www.royalparks.gov.uk) is the largest of London's Royal Parks. The land was once part of a medieval manor, before being bequeathed to the monks of Westminster Abbey. In 1536 it was appropriated by Henry VIII for hunting deer. Despite opening to the public in the early 1600s, the parks were only frequented by the upper echelons of society. At the end of the 17th century, William III, averse to the dank air of Whitehall Palace, relocated to **Kensington Palace** (*see p144*). A corner of Hyde Park was sectioned off to make grounds for the palace, and although today the two merge, **Kensington Gardens** was closed to the public until King George II opened it on Sundays to those

Capsule collection

A 30-minute dash round the Victoria & Albert Museum.

Start: 0-1.5mins
Go in via the main Cromwell Road entrance. While they're checking your bag admire Dale Chihuly's great glass chandelier.

Stage 2: 1.6-5mins
Go down the stairs on the right. This room may be dimly lit but it's packed with treasures and rarely busy – great for escaping tourists and for pretending you've stumbled into a rich relative's attic. Look for a macabre armchair and matching mirror adorned with deer's antlers, and a winged dragon door knocker that looks like a prop from *Harry Potter*.

Stage 3: 6-8mins
Head to the China room to see the teeny shoes worn by women with bound feet. Onwards to Japan. See the collection of *netsuke* – small ornaments tied to belts. Great swords too.

Stage 4: 9-11mins
Leave Japan, turn left and go up the stairs to level three. No time to see the famed Great Bed of Ware (it's at the opposite side of the museum on a different level) or Tippoo's Tiger, so you'll have to make do with gates, coffers and candlesticks in Ironworks. Splendid.

Stage 5: 12-14 mins
You should now be looking down on the Cast Courts. Been to Rome? Then you'll recognise the life-size cast of Trajan's Column. Obviously the Roman one hasn't been chopped in half to fit under a roof.

Stage 6: 15-20mins
Zip through Textiles and into Silver. See that giant wine cooler? It's a Victorian copy of one commissioned by an 18th-century London banker and oenophile. He raffled the thing off to raise funds to build a new bridge over the Thames at Westminster. Now head downstairs.

Stage 7: 21-26mins
Into the Morris, Gamble and Poynter rooms. These stunningly decorated rooms were once the chosen hangouts of London's glam arty types. No time to linger, though...

Finish 8: 27-30mins
Take a left out of Morris, Gamble and Poynter, and look for the disabled toilet sign on a cream door in Room 16. This ornate tiled unisex toilet must rank as London's finest public convenience. Take your time, before leaving via the Exhibition Road entrance.

Princess Diana Memorial Fountain.

in formal dress only. Today, the best element of Kensington Gardens, if you're a child, is the **Diana, Princess of Wales Memorial Playground** (*see p276*). Adults may prefer the **Serpentine Gallery** (*see p145*). Across the road is the ring-shaped **Princess Diana Memorial Fountain**, created by US architect Kathryn Gustafson. Almost as soon as it had been unveiled by the Queen, in July 2004, the fountain (more of a babbling moat) was in the headlines for the wrong reasons: people slipping on the granite while paddling. The problems have now been resolved, though you'll probably want to restrict yourself to dipping a toe in.

Back across the road and further north, by the Long Water, is a bronze statue of Peter Pan, built by Sir George Frampton in 1912 to honour Peter's creator, JM Barrie. Other sculptures of note include GF Watts's violently animated *Physical Energy* and Jacob Epstein's *Rima, Spirit of Nature*.

Hyde Park has long been a focus for freedom of speech. It became a hotspot for mass demonstrations in the 19th century and remains so today – a march against war in Iraq in 2003 was the largest in its history, and the Live8 concert of July 2005 was attended by the lucky thousands who sent a text to Sir Bob Geldof. The legalisation of public assembly in the park led to the establishment of **Speakers' Corner** in 1872, where ranters both sane and bonkers have the floor. This isn't the place to come for balanced, political debate, but Marx, Engels, Lenin, Orwell and the Pankhursts all attended.

A rather more orderly entertainment takes place at at 10.30am every morning (9.30am on

Sundays), when you can watch the Household Cavalry emerge smartly from their barracks on South Carriage Drive. They ride across the park to Horse Guards Parade, prior to the Changing of the Guard (*see p264*). Year round the park's perimeter is popular with both inline- and roller-skaters, as well as with bike- and horse-riders (for the riding school; *see p331*). If you're exploring on foot and the vast expanses defeat you, look out for the Liberty Drives electric buggies (May to October). Driven by cheerful volunteers (there's no fare, but a donation is appreciated), these pick up and deposit groups of sightseers around the parks. Cyclists should stick to the designated tracks; only under-tens are allowed to ride on the footpaths.

At the western side of the park is the **Serpentine**, London's oldest boating lake, home to ducks, coots, swans and tufty-headed grebes. You can rent rowing boats and pedalos from March to October. The Serpentine also has its own swimming club (*see p329* **Taking the lidos**), whose keen members have been known to break the ice to indulge in their daily dip.

Kensington Palace

Kensington Gardens, W8 4PX (7937 9561/booking line 0870 751 5180/www.hrp.org.uk). Bayswater, High Street Kensington or Queensway tube. **Open** *Mar-Oct* 10am-6pm daily. *Nov-Feb* 10am-5pm daily. Last entry 1hr before closing. **Admission** (LP) £11; £7.20-£8.30 concessions; £32 family; free under-5s. **Credit** MC, V. **Map** p396 B8.

Sir Christopher Wren extended this Jacobean mansion to palatial proportions on the instructions of William III, who afterwards moved in with his wife Mary II. The asthmatic king considered the countryside location would be better for his health. The sections of the palace that the public are allowed to see give the impression of intimacy, although the King's Apartments, which you enter via Wren's lofty King's Staircase, are pretty grandiose. In the King's Gallery hang portraits of the first glamorous royals to live here. It appears from the Queen's Apartments, however, that William and Mary lived quite simply in these smaller rooms. The Royal Ceremonial Dress Collection is a fascinating display of the tailor's and dressmaker's art, with lavish ensembles worn for state occasions and a permanent collection of 14 dresses worn by Diana, Princess of Wales, the palace's most famous resident. Make time for tea in Queen Anne's Orangery (built 1704-5) and admire – through the hedge – the piece of horticultural perfection that is the Sunken Garden.

A photographic exhibition of Diana, Princess of Wales, by Mario Testino will run until spring 2007. The display will also feature dresses that were auctioned off as a charity event shortly after the famous photo shoot for *Vanity Fair* in 1997. Until 2 April 2006 you can also have a guided tour of Number 1A Kensington Palace, featuring a photographic exhibition about ordinary people who lived at the palace.

Serpentine Gallery

Kensington Gardens (nr Albert Memorial), W2 3XA (7402 6075/www.serpentinegallery.org). Lancaster Gate or South Kensington tube. **Open** 10am-6pm daily. **Admission** free; donations appreciated. **Credit** AmEx, MC, V. **Map** p397 D8.

Its secluded location, sitting pretty to the west of the Long Water, makes this light and airy gallery for contemporary art an attractive place for a spontaneous visit while walking in the park. A rolling two-monthly programme of often challenging exhibitions keeps the Serpentine in the arts news, as does the annual Serpentine Pavilion commission. Every spring an internationally renowned architect, who has never built in the UK before, is commissioned to design and build a new pavilion, which is open to visitors (and increasingly vociferous critics) from June until September (*see also p271* **Air play**). Exhibitions in 2006 include Ellsworth Kelly (Mar).

Knightsbridge

Map p399 F9

Knightsbridge or South Kensington tube.

Knightsbridge in the 11th century was a village celebrated for its taverns, its highwaymen, and the legend that two knights once fought to the death on the bridge that spanned the Westbourne river (later dammed up to form the Serpentine). Nowadays, urban princesses are too busy unsheathing their credit cards to look out for duelling knights. Modern Knightsbridge is a shopper's paradise, with the voguish **Harvey Nichols** (*see p238*) holding sway at the top of **Sloane Street**.

Sloane Street.

Expensive brands dominate this otherwise unremarkable road – Gucci, Prada, Chanel and Christian Dior announce that you're in a moneyed neighbourhood.

For tourists, Knightsbridge means one thing: **Harrods** (*see p238*). From its tan bricks to its olive green awning and green-coated doormen, it's an instantly recognisable retailing legend. Originally a family grocer's, it is now the world's most famous department store, employing about 5,000 people. Under owner Mohammed Al Fayed it is ageing gracefully, but Harrods wasn't without its misspent youth: its first aeroplane was sold in 1919, and in 1967 the Prince of Albania purchased a baby elephant from here for Ronald Reagan.

Brompton and **Belgravia** serve primarily as residential catchment areas for the wealthiest London residents, so it's perhaps not surprising to find a pillar of penitence like the **Oratory Catholic Church** (*see below*) amid the excess.

There's not much else in Brompton to fire the imagination, however, bar Arne Jacobsen's **Danish Embassy** building (55 Sloane Street) and the prospect of peering into residents' living rooms. Belgravia is better, because it has some great pubs tucked away behind its serious marble parades: the best ones are the delightfully nostalgic Nag's Head (52 Kinnerton Street; *see also p229*) and the shabbily grand Grenadier on Wilton Row (No.18, 7235 3074). **St Paul's Knightsbridge**, on Wilton Place, is an appealing Victorian church with scenes from the life of Jesus in ceramics tiling the nave, and a wonderful wood-beamed ceiling. Otherwise, the area is characterised by a cluster of foreign embassies around Belgrave Square.

Oratory Catholic Church (Brompton Oratory)

Thurloe Place, Brompton Road, SW7 2RP (7808 0900/www.bromptonoratory.com). South Kensington tube. **Services 7am, 10am,** 12.30pm, 6pm Mon-Fri; 7am, 8.30am, 10am, 6pm Sat; 7am; 8am, 9am, 10am, 11am, 12.30pm, 4.30pm, 7pm Sun. **Admission** free; donations appreciated. **Map** p399 E10.

The second-biggest Catholic church in the country (after Westminster Cathedral), the London Oratory of St Philip of Neri is awesome. Completed in 1884, it feels older – partly because of its Baroque Italianate style, but also because many of its marbles, mosaics and statuary pre-date the structure. Mazzuoli's late 17th-century apostle statues, for example, were once in Siena's cathedral. The vast main space culminates in a magnificent Italian altarpiece and a number of ornate confessionals stand in the several chapels flanking the nave. Confessions are heard on Sunday mornings and the 11am Solemn Mass sung in Latin is enchanting. During the Cold War, the church was used by the KGB as a dead letter box.

Sightseeing

Chelsea

The artists' quarter that grew fat on fashion.

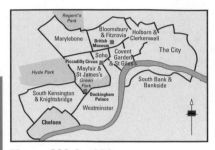

Maps p398 & p399

Sloane Square tube then various buses.

As early as the 15th century the picturesque fishing village of Chelsea was earning itself a fashionable reputation, with aristocrats building themselves country manors in the area. Chelsea's grandeur was further enhanced when Sir Thomas More, Lord Chancellor to Henry VIII, came to live here in 1520. Other bigwigs followed, including the King, whose lofty presence endowed Chelsea the title 'Village of Palaces'. Elizabeth I also lived in the area for a spell in the late 1540s, under the care of her father's surviving wife, Katherine Parr.

Chelsea's idyllic riverside location also attracted writers and intellectuals, although Thomas Carlyle was in two minds about moving there in 1834, because at that time the area was still separated from civilised Westminster by the type of marshy common land beloved of criminals. The surrounding countryside was built over during his lifetime, which disturbed him even more. His house is preserved at 24 Cheyne Row (*see below*).

Artists and sculptors were drawn by Chelsea's reputation for creativity and culture enhanced by the presence of the Chelsea Porcelain Works, which operated in Lawrence Street from 1745 to 1784, and the restorative **Chelsea Physic Garden** (*see p147*), established by the Apothecaries' Company in 1676.

Chelsea's bohemian reputation lasted well into the 20th century. Between the wars Dylan Thomas was the local celeb – he drank in the nearby pubs, and made derisory comments about the trendy set of **Cheyne Walk** (George Eliot, Dante Gabriel Rossetti, and later Henry James and TS Eliot, had all lived on this pleasant riverside road).

These days the artistic presence is reduced to a vast number of blue plaques (*see p148* **Plaque attack**), while Cheyne Walk, though still attractive, is marred by thundering embankment traffic. The western end of this famous street becomes Cremorne Road, whose well-kept riverside park, though a far cry from the rowdy pleasure gardens of its Victorian heyday, affords uplifting views east to Old Ferry Wharf and west to the exclusive **Chelsea Harbour**, which has been transformed from industrial wasteland into opulent offices, swish hotels, shops, restaurants and marina to make it a playground for the rich and famous.

The oldest street in Chelsea, **Old Church Street**, provides some relief from the traffic. The church in question (*see p147*) was founded in the 13th century but largely destroyed in World War II. Sir Thomas More sang in the choir here and there's a river-facing statue to his memory nearby. At No.143 the private **Chelsea Arts Club** is another relic of the area's artistic heritage. It was founded in 1891 on the suggestion of Whistler, and its members number hundreds of painters, sculptors, designers and writers. Art students, once associated with the swinging Chelsea of the 1960s, no longer brighten up the area, however. In 2005 the Chelsea School of Art & Design, which opened in 1895 on Manresa Road and Chelsea Square, moved to Millbank, next to Tate Britain (*see p293* **Bright young things**).

Carlyle's House

24 Cheyne Row, SW3 5HL (7352 7087/www. nationaltrust.org.uk). Sloane Square tube/11, 19, 22, 49, 211, 319 bus. **Open** 2-5pm Wed-Fri; 11am-5pm Sat, Sun. Closed Nov-Mar. **Admission** (NT) £4.20; £2.10 concessions. **Map** p399 E12.

Thomas Carlyle and his wife Jane, both towering intellects, moved to this four-storey, Queen Anne house in 1834. In 1896, 15 years after Carlyle's death, the house was preserved as a museum, offering an intriguing snapshot of Victorian life. From the stone-flagged basement kitchen, with its little bed for the maid, up several flights of stairs to Carlyle's attic office, the atmosphere is lent authenticity by the creaking floorboards. Evidence of the writer's desperate quest for peace and quiet strikes a chord today – there is much information on Carlyle's attempts to soundproof the attic; he was plagued by the sound of fireworks and revelry from nearby Cremorne Pleasure Gardens and the clucking of next door's poultry.

Sightseeing

Antiquarius, antidote to the run-of-the-mill shops on the King's Road.

Chelsea Old Church

*Cheyne Walk, Old Church Street, SW3 5DQ
(7352 5627/www.chelseaoldchurch.org.uk). Sloane
Square tube/11, 19, 22, 49, 319 bus.* **Open** 2-4pm
Tue, Thur. *Services* 8am, 10am, 11am. *Evensong*
6pm. **Admission** free; donations appreciated.
Most of the ancient church, which dates back to the
13th century, was destroyed by a bomb in 1941. The
Thomas More Chapel remains on the south side, and
legend has it that his headless body is buried somewhere under the walls (his head, after being spiked
on London Bridge was 'rescued' and buried in a family vault in St Dunstan's Church, Canterbury).

Chelsea Physic Garden

*66 Royal Hospital Road (entrance on Swan Walk),
SW3 4HS (7352 5646/www.chelseaphysicgarden.
co.uk). Sloane Square tube/11, 19, 239 bus.*
Open *Apr-Oct* noon-5pm Wed; 2-6pm Sun. *Tours*
times vary; call to check. **Admission** £6; £3.50
concessions; free under-5s. *Tours* free. **Credit**
(shop) AmEx, MC, V. **Map** p399 F12.
The garden was set up in 1673, but the key phase of
development was under Sir Hans Sloane in the
18th century. The 3.8-acre grounds are filled with
beds containing healing herbs and rare trees, dye
plants and medicinal vegetables. The world's first
rock garden was built here in 1772, using bits of old
stone from the Tower of London. The physic garden
opened to the public in 1893, but nowadays hours are
restricted. Free tours conducted by entertaining volunteers trace the history of the medicinal beds, where
herbs are grown for their efficacy in treating illness.

Sloane Square & the King's Road

Today Chelsea's most notable artistic venue
is the **Royal Court** theatre (*see p337*), which
looks out over Sloane Square and the
King's Road, Chelsea's high street. One of
the highlights of the street at the north-eastern
end, also directly on the square, is **Peter
Jones**, the polished department store with
fabulous views from the top-floor café. Nearby
is **Duke of York Square**, an upmarket
shopping development that includes a branch

of Pâtisserie Valerie (*see p206*), plus summer
fountains much loved by overheated children.
In fact, kids actually do better than adults for
King's Road shopping these days – unless the
adult happens to be a particular fan of (albeit
posh) chain stores. Gems include **Antiquarius**
(Nos.131-141; *see also p235*) for antiques,
and childrenswear shop **Daisy & Tom**
(Nos.181-183; *see also p245*). At the south-
western 'World's End' end of the road, Vivienne
Westwood's shop at No.430, with its backwards-
spinning clock, was a punk pilgrimage site in
the early '80s, when it was owned by Westwood
and Malcolm McLaren and called, simply, SEX.

It's the pretty streets that branch off the
King's Road that are the nicest. Sydney Street
takes you to **St Luke's Church**, a vast place
of worship where Charles Dickens was married
in 1836. Tucked-away crescents and streets to
the south are beautiful – **Glebe Place** has a
little children's nursery, while at Nos.49 and 50
is a mansion covered in statuary and climbers.

Royal Avenue, from the Sloane Square end of
King's Road, cuts through attractive terraces to
Royal Hospital Road. The grounds of the **Royal
Hospital Chelsea** (*see p148*) and Ranelegh
Gardens are best known these days as the site of
the **Chelsea Flower Show** (*see p266*), but for
most of the year the area is peaceful, as befits a
place of sanctuary for retired soldiers. Next door
is the **National Army Museum** (*see below*).

National Army Museum

*Royal Hospital Road, SW3 4HT (7730 0717/
www.national-army-museum.ac.uk). Sloane Square
tube/11, 137, 239 bus.* **Open** 10am-5.30pm daily.
Admission free. **Credit** (shop) AmEx, MC, V.
Map p399 F12.
Some eccentric exhibits and displays make this
museum dedicated to the history of the British Army
far more entertaining than the modern exterior might
suggest. The collection kicks off with Redcoats,
a gallery that starts at Agincourt in 1415 and ends
with the American War of Independence. Upstairs,
the Road to Waterloo marches through the 20-year
struggle against the French, featuring 70,000 model

Plaque attack

Chelsea wears its artistic history on its sleeve – or at least on the front of its houses. Blue plaques, distinctive discs 19 inches in diameter, have festooned buildings since 1867, when the Royal Society of Arts decided to mark the residences of the capital's famous and notorious. The earliest surviving plaques, from 1875, are in central London, one for 17th-century poet **John Dryden** at 43 Gerrard Street in Soho, and one to the lesser-known Napoleon (**Napoleon III**) at 1C King Street, St James's. The design format and blue colour were not standardised until 1921; many original manufacturers used brown, as it was less expensive. By the time the London County Council took over from the RSA in 1901, there were 36 brown plaques around town.

English Heritage inherited the plaque scheme when the LCC was abolished in the 1980s, and there are now more than 760 plaques in London. Anyone can propose a plaque, but English Heritage will only consider dedicating them to people who have been dead for 20 years and whose names are instantly recognisable. Around 20 new plaques are added each year.

Few streets can boast as many of these tablets as Chelsea's Cheyne Walk, which is peppered with plaques. Novelist **Elizabeth Gaskell** was born at No.93 in 1810. Near-neighbours while she was growing up were the Brunels, at No.98. **Marc Isambard Brunel** and his son, **Isambard Kingdom Brunel**, travelled downriver to begin work on their famous tunnel in Rotherhithe (*see p168*). **George Eliot** died at the Queen Anne house at No.4 in 1880, only three weeks after moving in. **Sylvia Pankhurst** campaigned for women's rights from No.120. Numerous visual artists also converged on the area in the 19th century. American painter **James Abbott McNeill Whistler** resided at No.96 in 1859. His painting of Old Battersea Bridge was completed during his stay, and it was from here that he suggested the creation of an artists' club (*see p146*), along with **Philip Wilson Steer**, who lived at No.109, and others. **Walter Greaves** lived at No.104 from childhood until 1897, while No.108 was home to the sculptor **John Tweed**. **Dante Gabriel Rossetti** and **Algernon Charles Swinburne** set up a poetic and painterly alliance at No.16.

DANTE
GABRIEL
ROSSETTI
1828 - 1882
AND
ALGERNON CHARLES
SWINBURNE
1837 - 1909
lived here
LONDON COUNTY COUNCIL

Once you've examined the ten plaques on Cheyne Walk, you can branch out into the rest of Chelsea for the 30 or more others. The most famous plaque-earner here is **Oscar Fingal O'Flahertie Wills Wilde**, who lived at 34 Tite Street. He couldn't persuade Whistler to decorate his house, but he loved the place, and wrote warmly about the street, saying that it could 'never be as other streets: it must always be full of wonderful possibilities.' Sadly, after Wilde had been arrested, his house and its valuable contents were sold to pay his court costs. When the LCC announced in 1950s that a plaque to Wilde was to be erected, there was uproar.

For more on the blue plaque scheme, log on to www.english-heritage.org.uk/blueplaques.

soldiers, bloodstained souvenirs of Waterloo. The experiences of the Victorian soldier, army life during the two world wars and a gallery devoted to National Service bring the soldier's life right up to date. On display upstairs is the kit of Olympic medal winner Kelly Holmes (an ex-army athlete), and Major Michael 'Bronco' Lane, conqueror of Mount Everest, has kindly donated his frostbitten fingertips.

Royal Hospital Chelsea

Royal Hospital Road, SW3 4SR (7881 5200/www. chelsea-pensioners.org.uk). Sloane Square tube/ 11, 19, 22, 137, 211, 239 bus. **Open** *Oct-Apr* 10am-noon, 2-4pm Mon-Sat. *May-Sept* 10am-noon, 2-4pm Mon-Sat; 2-4pm Sun. **Admission** free. **Map** p399 F12.

About 350 Chelsea Pensioners (retired soldiers) live here. Their quarters, the Royal Hospital, was founded in 1682 by Charles II, and the building was designed by Sir Christopher Wren, with later adjustments added by Robert Adam and Sir John Soane.

Retired soldiers are eligible to apply for a final posting here if they are over 65, in receipt of an Army or War Disability Pension for Army Service. The inpensioners (as opposed to the Chelsea Pensioners who live elsewhere) are organised into companies, along military lines, with a governor and other officers. They have their own club room, amenity centre, billiards room, library, bowling green and gardens. The museum (open at the same times as the Hospital) tells us more about their life.

North London

From the crush of Camden Market to the peace of cemeteries.

Camden

Camden Town or Chalk Farm tube.
You'd certainly not realise it while encountering the cacophony outside Camden Town tube station, but over the past few decades this has become one of London's most fashionable addresses. Like many newly desirable areas, Camden Town has had a long association with lowlife. Cheap lodging houses dominated the area around the time when the Regent's Canal was laid out in 1816, and it was rough in Victorian times, too, according to Charles Dickens, who grew up in Bayham Street. In the mid-1800s Irish and Greek immigrants laid down roots here, and by the 1960s this indisputably poor area had earned itself a raffish, bohemian reputation.

Around this time, arty types, among them writer Alan Bennett, saw the potential of the tall, spacious houses and elegant crescents, and moved into them. White-collar professionals followed, and today Camden has a middle-class flavour: residents now shun the markets and buy their provisions from Nicholas Grimshaw's high-tech Sainsbury's supermarket on Camden Road. Yet the area retains an edge: every night, Camden Town tube is garlanded with exotica, whether punks and goths in full regalia, vocal street preachers, or the less photogenic (but usually harmless) junkies.

Teenagers and students love the area for the various sites grouped together as **Camden Market** (*see below*), but this once-alternative hangout has become one of London's big tourist attractions, which means crowds can be unpleasant and real bargains are quite rare. Worthwhile stalls include collectibles in the Stables Market, and unusual homewares and crafts in the main hall of Camden Lock Market: to get to them you will have to persist through grime and masses of people trying too hard to have a good time. You'd do best to explore the rest of the neighbourhood out of market hours, or at least on weekdays, to avoid the rabble.

The **Roundhouse** on Chalk Farm Road opened as a steam-engine repair depot in 1846 before becoming a music venue in the 1960s, hosting gigs by the likes of Pink Floyd, Jimi Hendrix and the Doors. After extensive redevelopment, it is reopening as a major performance space and 'creative centre for young people' (7424 9991) in spring 2006. The lovely **Jewish Museum** (*see p151*), just off Parkway, is a gem, a reflection of the area's cultural diversity. But Camden is let down by its eating and drinking options; there are some grim bars and restaurants round here. Further to the suggestions in our Restaurants & Cafés chapter (*see pp194-221*), try a cheap cake or seafood pasta dish from one of the Portuguese cafés on Plender Street or excellent pub food at the Engineer (65 Gloucester Avenue, 7722 0950) in Primrose Hill, and then cool down with an ice-cream at Marine Ices (8 Haverstock Hill, opposite Chalk Farm tube), a local institution. Fresh & Wild (49 Parkway, 7428 7575) offers tasty organic snacks, or drink good coffee on comfy sofas in Bean 'n' Cup (104 Camden High Street, 7267 7340). Well worth a detour is Time Out's Best Burger award-winning burger joint Haché, at 24 Inverness Street (*see also p208* **The burger kings**).

Camden Market

Camden Market *Camden High Street, junction with Buck Street, NW1 (7278 4444).* **Open** 9.30am-5.30pm daily.
Camden Canal Market *off Chalk Farm Road, south of junction with Castlehaven Road, NW1 9XJ (7485 8355/www.camdenlock.net).* **Open** 9.30am-6.30pm Fri-Sun.
Camden Lock *Camden Lock Place, off Chalk Farm Road, NW1 8AF (7485 3459/www.camdenlock market.com).* **Open** 10am-6pm daily.
Electric Ballroom *184 Camden High Street, NW1 8QP (7485 9006/www.electric-ballroom.co.uk).* **Open** 10.30am-3.30pm Fri; 10.30am-6pm Sat; 9am-4pm Sun before bank hols; record & film fairs occasional Sats throughout the year.
Stables *off Chalk Farm Road, opposite junction with Hartland Road, NW1 8AH (7485 5511/www. camdenlock.net).* **Open** 10am-6pm daily (reduced stalls Mon-Fri).
All *Camden Town or Chalk Farm tube.*
If you value elbow space, you won't like Camden Market. It heaves with locust-plague numbers of people (mostly tourists), particularly at weekends when the greatest number of stalls are open. And as a market, it's far from inspiring. The section advertised as Camden Market (formerly Buck Street Market), just next to the tube station, flogs cheap sunglasses and cut-price interpretations of current fashions; the rest bears little resemblance to the cutting-edge place it was years ago. The Electric Ballroom sells second-hand clothes and young designers' wares, but it's neither cheap nor particu-

How to get an even better view from
Primrose Hill. *See p151.*

larly exciting. Camden Lock Market, set around a courtyard next to Regent's Canal, is nicer. Crafty shops and stalls sell funky lighting, contemporary fashion, ethnic homewares, arts, antiques and more. These days, the Stables Market is full of permanent clothes and food huts, rather like an alternative shopping mall, set to become more entrenched with the opening of the glass-wrapped Triangle's shops, restaurants and entertainment venues. In the railway arches, upmarket, permanent retro stalls and clubwear outlets have taken over – the freaky dayglo clubwear and cool T-shirts at Cyberdog are particularly worth a peek. Head to the further end, in and around the Horse Hospital (which once cared for horses injured while pulling canal barges), for outlets selling antiques and 20th-century design furniture. In the area across the road, beside the canal, is an avenue of yet more food stalls, with some interesting craft stalls selling bags and accessories.

Jewish Museum, Camden

Raymond Burton House, 129-131 Albert Street, NW1 7NB (7284 1997/www.jewishmuseum.org.uk). Camden Town tube. **Open** 10am-4pm Mon-Thur; 10am-5pm Sun. **Admission** £3.50; £1.50-£2.50 concessions; free under-5s. **Credit** MC, V.

One of a pair (its sister is in Finchley; *see p157*), Camden's Jewish Museum provides a fascinating insight into one of Britain's oldest immigrant communities. Jewish life over six centuries is illustrated through oil paintings, artefacts from a tailor's 'sweatshop', silver and chinaware, photographs and passports. The museum also has one of the world's finest collections of Jewish ceremonial art, including a collection of silver Hanukkah candlesticks, spice boxes and an amazing 17th-century Venetian synagogue ark, brought to Britain in the 1800s. Temporary exhibitions in 2006 include 'Passover: Journey to Freedom' (until May 14), an exhibition exploring contemporary British identity (June-Oct) and a retrospective on Janusz Korczak, the heroic Warsaw Ghetto paediatrician (Nov-early 2007).

Around Camden

Primrose Hill, to the west of Camden Town, with its gracious terraces, is as pretty as the actors, writers and pop stars who live there (look out for Noel Gallagher's home, Supernova Heights). Past the park and its namesake hill (with grand views over London), Regent's Park Road becomes a pleasant mix of independent cafés, quality gastropubs and restaurants, and smart shops. Up to the north, **Kentish Town**, with its profusion of bargain stores, looks fairly grubby by comparison.

The still-operative **Regent's Canal**, which cuts across Camden, fully opened in 1820 to provide a working waterway to link east and west London. This route was opened to the public as a scenic path in 1968, and the canal's industrial trappings have been transformed

London Canal Museum.

over the decades since. Any stretch of the canal is worth a stroll, but the most popular patch is from Camden Town to Little Venice, passing Regent's Park and **London Zoo** (*see p116*). Riverboat cruises travel the route in summer and on winter weekends (London Waterbus Company, 7482 2660; Jenny Wren, 7485 4433; Jason's Canal Boat Trip, 7286 3428). Follow the canal east and south of Camden Market to reach bucolic **Camley Street Natural Park** (*see p275*), the London Wildlife Trust's flagship reserve. Further along, the **London Canal Museum** (*see below*) tells the history of the vessels, along with a giant ice well.

London Canal Museum

12-13 New Wharf Road, King's Cross, N1 9RT (7713 0836/www.canalmuseum.org.uk). King's Cross tube/rail. **Open** 10am-4.30pm Tue-Sun (last entry 3.45pm). **Admission** (LP) £3; £1.50-£2 concessions; free under-8s. **Credit** MC, V. **Map** p401 M2.

The warehouse containing this small museum on the Regent's Canal's Battlebridge Basin was built in the 1850s by Carlo Gatti, an Italian immigrant who made a fortune importing ice from Norway's frozen lakes to the vast ice well that's open to view in the museum floor. Photos and videos tell the Gatti story, and exhibitions explore the role of horses and the hardships endured by the families working the canals. There are a few model boats and a barge cabin in which visitors can sit, as well as a 1924 silent film, *Barging Through London*.

Lord's.

St John's Wood

St John's Wood or Swiss Cottage tube.
Rural calm prevailed in St John's Wood until
well into the 19th century, when the only
developments around the wooded hills and
meadows were smart stucco villas. The pure
air attracted artists, scientists and writers:
George Eliot often held receptions at her house
(The Priory, North Bank). A blue plaque marks
the house at 44 Grove End Road once owned
by the artist Sir Lawrence Alma-Tadema but,
sadly, the interior is closed to the public.

In the 19th century the inexpensive but
pretty dwellings suited rich men, who used
them to house their mistresses. The building
work carried out by the Great Central Railway
in 1894 destroyed the rural calm, but sensitive
redevelopment during the 1950s has left the
area smart, desirable and fabulously expensive
– just take a look at the chic boutiques of the
exceedingly couth High Street. **Lord's**, the
world's most famous cricket ground (*see below*),
is the reason why most people visit. However,
Beatles fans have their own motives: Grove End
Road leads to **Abbey Road**, made famous by
the Fab Four when its recording facility was
still called EMI Studios (No.3), and the site of
London's most photographed zebra crossing.

Up the Finchley Road from St John's Wood,
you'll find that a Swiss Cottage actually exists
on the site of a Swiss-style tavern at the former
Junction Road Toll Gate. The excitement stops
at the entrance so, instead, sample the cakes at
nearby Louis Hungarian Pâtisserie (12 Harben
Parade, 7722 8100).

Lord's Tour & MCC Museum

*Marylebone Cricket Club, Lord's, St John's Wood
Road, NW8 8QN (7616 8595/www.lords.org). St
John's Wood tube.* **Tours** *Oct-Mar* noon, 2pm daily.
Apr-Sept 10am, noon, 2pm daily. **Admission** £8; £5-
£6 concessions; £22 family; free under-5s. **Credit**
MC, V.
The wearers of the famous egg-and-bacon striped
tie have come to love the NatWest Media Centre, the
stunning raised pod that dominates the self-pro-
claimed home of cricket. The centre joins the por-
trait-bedecked Long Room on the guided tour (you'll
need to book), along with the expected collection of
battered bats, photos and blazers. There's plenty of
WG Grace ephemera and, of course, the Ashes. After
years of Australian domination cricket's holy grail
is now back in our hands thanks to England's astonishing performance in the 2005 series. **Photo** *left.*

Hampstead

*Golders Green or Hampstead tube/Gospel Oak or
Hampstead Heath rail.*
Exclusive Hampstead was a popular retreat in
times of plague and remains a delightful place
to wander in relative calm. It has long been the
favoured roosting place for literary and artistic
bigwigs; Keats and Constable called it home in
the 19th century, while modernist and surrealist
artists Barbara Hepworth and Henry Moore
lived the London village idyll here in the 1930s.

Hampstead tube station stands at the top of
the steep High Street. The higgledy-piggledy
Georgian terraces that make up Church Row,
one of Hampstead's most beautiful streets, lead
down to **St John at Hampstead** (7794 5808),
whose cemetery is less ostentatious than its
near-neighbour Highgate, but just as restful
and bucolic. Among those of note buried here
are Constable and the comedian Peter Cook.

On Holly Mount, is Hampstead's antique
Holly Bush pub, which was painter George
Romney's stable block (his house still stands
on Holly Bush Hill). A minute's climb will bring
you to **Fenton House** (*see p153*), while the
celestially inclined should potter up
to the **Hampstead Scientific Society
Observatory** (Hampstead Grove, 8346 1056).

East of Heath Street, a maze of attractive
streets shelters **Burgh House** on New End
Square (7431 0144), a Queen Anne house that
contains a small local history museum and
gallery space, and **2 Willow Road** (*see p154*),
the residence that émigré Hungarian architect
Ernö Goldfinger built in the 1930s. Nearby,
off Keats Grove, is **Keats House** (*see p153*),
where the poet did most of his best work. The
bullet-marked Magdala pub on South Hill Park
(No.2A, 7435 2503) is where Ruth Ellis shot her
former boyfriend in 1955, and so became the
last woman to be hanged in Britain.

Hampstead Heath, the inspiration for CS Lewis's Narnia, is the city's countryside. Its charming contours and woodlands conspire to make it feel far larger and more rural than it is (something over a mile in each direction). The views of London from the top of **Parliament Hill** are stunning and on hot days the murky bathing ponds (men's, women's and mixed, open daily all year) are a godsend (swimmers have recently won the right to bathe even when lifeguards are off-duty). There's also a great lido at Gospel Oak (7485 5757). Pick up a map from one of the information points on the heath, which can also advise you of concerts held at the heath's two bandstands on summer Sundays. At the north end of the park is **Kenwood House** (*see below*).

Tucked in among the handsome residential streets in south-west Hampstead is the former home (and now museum) of Sigmund Freud. Nearby, the innovative **Camden Arts Centre** (Arkwright Road, corner of Finchley Road, 7472 5500) has been spruced up with new galleries and studios, a café and landscaped gardens.

Fenton House

3 Hampstead Grove, NW3 6RT (7435 3471/ information 01494 755563/www.nationaltrust. org.uk). Hampstead tube. **Open** *early Mar* 2-5pm Sat, Sun. *Apr-Oct* 2-5pm Wed-Fri; 11am-5pm Sat, Sun. *Tours* phone for details. Closed Nov-early Mar. **Admission** (NT) *House & gardens* £4.90; £2.45 concessions; free under 5s. *Joint ticket with 2 Willow Road* £6.70. *Gardens only* £2; £1 concessions. **No credit cards.**
Devotees of early music will be impressed by the collection of harpsichords, clavichords, virginals and spinets in this late 17th-century house. The bequest was made on condition that qualified musicians be allowed to play them, so you might be lucky enough to hear them in action (or phone for details of the lunchtime and evening concerts held here in summer, roughly fortnightly). The porcelain collection won't appeal to everyone – the 'curious grotesque teapot' certainly lives up to its billing – but for fans, there's work by Meissen and Rockingham. The maze-like series of sunken gardens are a delight, with the small orchard coming into its own for October's Apple Day celebration. Out of season, you can only see the exterior or join one of the 'Heights of Hampstead' walking tours, which take in grand houses of various periods and end up here (£6; 01494 755572). Easter egg trails for children will take place 14 to 17 April (£1.50 per child).

Freud Museum

20 Maresfield Gardens, NW3 5SX (7435 2002/www. freud.org.uk). Finchley Road tube. **Open** noon-5pm Wed-Sun. **Admission** £5; £3 concessions; free under-12s. **Credit** AmEx, MC, V.
After Anna Freud's death in 1982, the house she and her father Sigmund shared for the last year of his

life became a museum. The analyst's couch sits in the study, round glasses and unsmoked cigars setting the scene, and the copious library is impressive, but more intellectual or biographical context would be appreciated by the uninitiated. Upstairs is Anna's room – with another couch – and a gallery. This is one of the few buildings in London to have two blue plaques: commemorating both father and daughter (she was a pioneer in child psychiatry), they were unveiled by comedian John Cleese in 2002.

Keats House

Keats Grove, NW3 2RR (7435 2062). Hampstead Heath rail/Hampstead tube/24, 46, 168 bus. **Open** *Apr-Oct* 1-5pm Tue-Sun. *Nov-Mar* 1-5pm Tue-Sun. *Tours* 3pm Sat, Sun. **Admission** £3.50; £1.75 concessions; free under-16s. **Credit** MC, V.
The Romantic poet made his home here from 1818 to 1820, when he left for Rome (where he died of tuberculosis the following year, aged 25). Today it attracts an obscene number of visitors every year. As well as mooching through the rooms, you can attend events and talks in the poetry reading room and see a display on Keats's sweetheart, Fanny Brawne, who lived next door. The industrial carpets ruin the overall ambience – something which may be corrected if their grant for renovations goes ahead (you're advised to ring for news of any closures). The garden in which he wrote 'Ode to a Nightingale' is a pleasant place to wander in romantic reverie.

Kenwood House/Iveagh Bequest

Hampstead Lane, NW3 7JR (8348 1286/www. english-heritage.org.uk). Hampstead tube/Golders Green tube then 210 bus. **Open** *Apr-Sept* 11am-5pm daily. *Nov-Mar* 11am-4pm daily. *Tours* by appointment only. **Admission** free; donations appreciated. *Tours* £3.50; £1.50-£2.50 concessions. **Credit** MC, V.
Built in 1616, Kenwood House was remodelled by Robert Adam from 1764 to 1779 for William Murray the first Earl of Mansfield (whose decision as Chief Justice in a test case in 1772 made it illegal to own slaves in England). Brewing magnate Edward Guinness bought it in 1925, filling it with his art collection. Now English Heritage is in charge, endorsing Guinness's wish 'that the atmosphere of a gentleman's private park should be preserved'. Art includes Vermeer's *The Guitar Player*, a Rembrandt self-portrait, works by Hals and Van Dyck and Gainsborough's *Countess Howe*. Outside, Humphrey Repton's landscape remains mostly unchanged from its creation in 1793. An ivy tunnel leads from the flower garden to a raised terrace with lovely views over the lakes – one of Repton's famous 'surprises'. Part of Kenwood's grounds is now listed as a Site of Special Scientific Interest, for its four species of bat and nine Nationally Scarce invertebrates. People are scarce, too, on what feel like country lanes winding through the middle of the woods, whereas seats are the rarity at the café adjacent to Kenwood House, which does a terrific breakfast. In July and August there are concerts by the lake.

Houseboats on the **Regent's Canal**: water way to live! *See p151.*

2 Willow Road

*2 Willow Road, NW3 1TH (7435 6166/www.
nationaltrust.org.uk). Hampstead tube/Hampstead
Heath rail.* **Open** *Mar, Nov* noon-5pm Sat. *Apr-Oct*
noon-5pm Thur-Sat (last entry 4.30pm); 5-9pm 1st
Thur of mth. *Tours* phone for details. **Admission**
£4.70; £2.35 concessions; £11.75 family; free under-
5s. *Joint ticket with Fenton House* £6.70. **No credit
cards.**

This strange and atmospheric 1939 building is the
National Trust's only example of international modernism. James Bond author Ian Fleming was so
annoyed by its Austro-Hungarian architect, Ernö
Goldfinger, that he named one of his villains after
him. The light pouring through the windows is a feature in itself, and the perfect functionalism of original fixtures and fittings is a revelation, and it also
contains works by Max Ernst and Henry Moore.

Highgate

Archway or Highgate tube.
Highgate's name comes from a tollgate that
once stood on the site of the Gate House pub
on the High Street. Legend has it that Dick
Whittington,walking away from the city at the
foot of Highgate Hill, heard the Bow bells peal
out 'Turn again Whittington, thrice Mayor of
London.' The event is commemorated on the
Whittington Stone, near the hospital. The
area is today best known for the burial
grounds of **Highgate Cemetery** (*see p155*
The Magnificent Seven), which house Karl
Marx's grave. Adjoining it is the beautiful
Waterlow Park, donated to Londoners by
low-cost housing pioneer Sir Sydney Waterlow
in 1889, which has terrific views, ponds, a mini
aviary, tennis courts and, in 16th-century
Lauderdale House, a garden café. Swains
Lane leads down to **Hampstead Heath** (*see
p153*): pass the mock-Tudor flats built to house
single women in the 1920s, peep through the
Gothic entrance to **Holly Village**, a private

village built in 1865 by heiress Angela Burdett
Coutts, or grab a pavement table at the lovely
gastro café Kalendar (No.15A, 8348 8300).

Hornsey Lane, on the other side of Highgate
Hill, leads you to **Archway**, a Victorian
viaduct offering vertiginous views of the City
and the East End. The famous **Archway
Bridge** has long been popularly known as
Suicide Bridge – the first recorded jumper took
the plunge in 1908 – but the addition of fencing
has made this cast-iron Victorian arch rather
less conducive to leaping. Hurry away east
down Hornsey Lane to comfortable, middle-
class **Crouch End** (or detour along the two-
mile Parkland Walk, a nature trail along an old
railway bed). Here, the 1895 clock tower and the
Hornsey Town Hall preside over a pleasant
community. The High Street houses an eclectic
mix of boutiques and decent restaurants.

North of Highgate tube, shady **Highgate
Woods** were mentioned (under another name)
in the Domesday Book. Nowadays, this is a
conservation area with a nature trail, children's
playground and space for ball games.

Islington

Map p404

Angel tube/Highbury & Islington tube/rail.
Henry VIII owned houses for hunting in this
once-idyllic village, but by the 19th century it
was already known for its shops, theatres and
music halls. From 1820, the **Regent's Canal**
brought industrial slums along with it, and
Islington declined into one of London's poorest
boroughs. However, its Georgian squares and
Victorian terraces have been gentrified in recent
decades. These days, despite stubborn pockets
of poverty, this is a wealthy middle-class area;
emerge from Angel tube and walk along Upper
Street, past the glass façade of the Business
Design Centre (and, opposite, hoary old Camden

The Magnificent Seven

By the early 19th century, churchyards in London were in a parlous state. The living population had nearly doubled in just a few decades, and room had to be found for the corresponding legions of dead. Shortage of space led to unscrupulous (and often illegal) practices like exhuming long-dormant corpses to make way for fresh ones, and burying bodies on top of others. Because these shallow graves were less than the requisite six feet under, the risk of disease was increased and cemeteries were rightly considered unwholesome places to be avoided. Something needed to be done.

In 1830 Scottish landscape gardener John Claudius London proposed a series of attractive cemeteries surrounding the capital, a campaign taken up in the next decade by barrister George Frederick Carden. The General Cemetery Company laid out Kensal Green Cemetery (*see p186*) in 1833, and the commercial success of this venture spurred the formation of further companies – and burial grounds. West Norwood and Highgate cemeteries were begun in 1836. By 1841 Brompton, Abney Park, Nunhead and Tower Hamlets cemeteries had joined them. These were the 'Magnificent Seven'.

Suddenly cemeteries were fashionable places to visit, whether or not you had loved ones interred there. The natural beauty of the parklands was accentuated as tombs and monuments began to be seen as status symbols, their location, size and decoration attesting to the wealth and influence of the deceased or their family.

Unfortunately, as the cemeteries began to reach capacity in the mid to late 1900s, the income for maintaining them declined and they became decrepit. But for visitors of today this has turned out to be a blessing, essentially creating nature reserves with a romantic atmosphere of ivy-covered neglect.

The most famous of these is **Highgate Cemetery** (Swains Lane, N6, 8340 1834, www.highgate-cemetery.org), marked by its dramatic tombs of towering angels, shrouded urns and broken columns. The original West Cemetery (guided tours only, no under-8s; prior booking advisable) is a breathtaking place: long pathways wind through tall tombs, gloomy catacombs and the graves of poet Christina Rossetti and chemist Michael Faraday. Prize sites included the tombs lining

Egyptian Avenue (Pharonic styling being all the rage in the 1830s), and the ring of neo-classical tombs known as the Lebanon Circle. On the hill above, Julius Beer, a poor German Jew who made it big in the City but was snubbed by society, built the grandest tomb, finally getting his revenge by obstructing the views from the church balcony where society ladies promenaded.

Highgate's success as a commercial venture resulted in addition of the East Cemetery just 15 years later. Although not quite as atmospheric, it allows you to wander freely and seek out the memorials to Karl Marx (*pictured*) and George Eliot. The cemetery closes during burials, so call ahead.

In contrast to the other six, **Abney Park Cemetery** (Stoke Newington High Street, N16, 7275 7557, www.abney-park.org.uk) was originally planned as a Nonconformist burial ground, essentially taking over the role of Bunhill Fields in the City (*see p102*). A rambling old boneyard centred on a derelict Gothic revival chapel, it's also a nature reserve with rare butterflies, woodpeckers and bats. It was originally planned to be a tourist attraction, not just a place to rest forever after. As an arboretum, it rivalled Kew Gardens in its heyday, with more than 2,000 trees and shrubs, and at one point had over 1,000 different types of roses.

Passage antiques market; *see p235*), along the side of the triangular Green and up towards **Highbury**. En route, you'll take in countless boutiques, the excellently named **Screen on the Green** cinema (*see p288*), the **Almeida Theatre** (*see p341*) and the Union Chapel.

Taking this route you'll graze the south entrance of the N1 Centre shopping mall, near the Angel, which includes a music venue (the **Carling Academy Islington**; *see p311*), a big and loud Vue cineplex and lots of mainstream chain stores. This behemoth is a symptom of the increasing influx of high-street names into the area, turning a unique locale into something more standard-issue. But for every Starbucks, newcomers such as the yummy minimalist Ottolenghi café (287 Upper Street; *see p213*) and cosy Keston Lodge bar (Nos.287 & 131; *see p230*) offer some compensation.

You might spy more cabbies than usual around here too: Penton Street, at the end of Chapel Market, is where all cab drivers once chewed down a pencil taking 'the Knowledge', a detailed exam based on London streets and buildings that all London cabbies must pass.

On the way along Upper Street, take a detour to **Canonbury Square**, a Regency square once home to George Orwell (No.27) and Evelyn Waugh (No.17A). The **Estorick Collection of Modern Italian Art** (*see below*) is worth a look, while to the east is the tranquil New River, beside the less-than-tranquil Marquess Estate.

Just beyond the end of Upper Street is **Highbury Fields**, where 200,000 Londoners fled to escape the Great Fire of 1666. Smart Highbury is best known as home to its beloved Arsenal football club, who move from their small but perfectly formed art deco Highbury Stadium to the new 60,000-capacity Emirates Stadium down the road in time for the 2006 season opener. Occasional 90-minute guided tours, which end at the museum, will continue at the new ground (call 7704 4504 to book).

Estorick Collection of Modern Italian Art

39A Canonbury Square, N1 2AN (7704 9522/ www.estorickcollection.com). Highbury & Islington tube/rail/271 bus. **Open** 11am-6pm Wed-Sat; noon-5pm Sun. **Admission** £3.50; £2.50 concessions; free under-16s, students. **Credit** AmEx, MC, V.
Eric Estorick was a US political scientist, writer and art collector whose collection includes work by some fine Italian Futurists, such as Balla's *Hand of the Violinist* and Boccioni's *Modern Idol*, as well as pieces by Carra, Russolo and Severini. The museum has a library with over 2,000 modern Italian art books , a shop and a café. Temporary exhibitions in 2006 include 'Responding to Rome 1995-2005' (until 26 Mar) and 'Morandi's Legacy: Influences on British Art' (5 Apr-18 June).

Clissold Park.

Dalston & Stoke Newington

Dalston: Dalston Kingsland rail/30, 38, 56, 67, 149, 242, 243, 277 bus. Stoke Newington: Stoke Newington rail/73 bus.
Bishopsgate starts in the City, passes through Shoreditch, becomes Kingsland Road and runs north to Dalston and Stoke Newington, and past the Hassidic enclave of Stamford Hill. Though scruffy and, at times, intimidating, **Dalston** is a vibrant place, with shops, Ridley Road's market stalls, cafés, all-night restaurants and clubs. It's also home to the Dalston Jazz Bar (4 Bradbury Street, 7254 9728), which is good for late drinks, plus live jazz on a Wednesday; around the corner on the newly created Gillett Square is the relocated Vortex Jazz Club (*see p316*), part of the Dalston Culture House. By summer 2006 the building will also contain a café, gallery and artists' studio, and have an outdoor space for performance.

Stoke Newington has been labelled the place people move to when they can't afford Islington. Stoke Newington Church Street has a number of good restaurants: Rasa (No.55, 7249 1340) is famed for its meat-free Keralan cooking. There are second-hand bookshops, one-off boutiques selling new and vintage clothes, and the colourful Route 73 Kids toy store (No.92, 7923 7873). The street's bookended by two lovely green spaces: **Clissold Park** (7923 3660) has a small zoo, tennis courts, a lake and a tearoom; rather more other-worldly is the wildlife-filled **Abney Park Cemetery** (*see p155* **The Magnificent Seven**).

Further north

Dalston's immigrant communities are chiefly Afro-Caribbean and Turkish, and their influence can be seen in the cafés and clubs. The tidy suburban streets at north London's perimeter are also enlivened by the immigrant communities that have made them their home. Golders Green, Hendon and **Finchley** have large Jewish communities, the last of these the location of north London's second **Jewish Museum** (80 East End Road, 8349 1143; *see also p151*), where there's an exhibition tracing the life of Leon Greenman, a British Jew who survived Auschwitz. He's in his 90s now but still comes in on Sundays to chat to visitors about his experiences. **Golders Green** is the focus of a growing population of both Chinese and Japanese City workers, with the Oriental City shopping mall (399 Edgware Road, 8200 0009) supplying their needs. There's been a Jewish cemetery on Hoop Lane since 1895; cellist Jacqueline du Pré is buried here. TS Eliot, Marc Bolan and Anna Pavlova ended up at **Golders Green Crematorium** (8455 2374).

The neighbourhoods of **Tottenham** and **Haringey** have sizeable Greek Cypriot, Turkish Cypriot and Kurdish communities. Aside from occasional clashes, the groups live side by side in **Green Lanes**, where food-related business success is evident in the thriving kebab shops, supermarkets and bakeries. Finally, **Alexandra Palace** (*see below*) is as good a reason as any to visit the more northwesterly Muswell Hill.

Alexandra Park & Palace

Alexandra Palace Way, N22 7AY (park 8444 7696/ information 8365 2121/boating 8889 9089/www. alexandrapalace.com). Wood Green tube/Alexandra Palace rail/W3, W7, 84A, 144, 144A bus. **Open** *Park 24hrs daily. Palace times vary.*

'The People's Palace', when it opened in 1873, was supposed to provide affordable entertainment for all. It burned to the ground just 16 days later. Rebuilt, it became the site of the first TV broadcasts by the BBC in 1936, but in 1980 was destroyed by fire once more. The born-yet-again palace has remained upright for the past 25 years and yields panoramic views of London. Its grounds provide ice skating, boating, pitch-and-putt, while its entertainment and exhibition centre hosts fairs, concerts and events.

Royal Air Force Museum Hendon

Grahame Park Way, NW9 5LL (8205 2266/www.rafmuseum.org). Colindale tube/Mill Hill Broadway rail/32, 226, 292, 303 bus. **Open** 10am-6pm daily. *Tours times vary.* **Admission** free. **Credit** AmEx, MC, V.

Claiming to be the birthplace of aviation in Britain, Hendon Aerodrome currently houses more than 80 aircraft – among them World War I Fokkers, World War II Spitfires and a state-of-the-art Eurofighter Typhoon, together with all manner of aviation memorabilia – in World War I hangars and a listed aircraft factory building. A new structure, part of an £11-million redevelopment, houses the Milestones of Flight exhibition, which traces a century of aviation history. Other attractions include an interactive Battle of Britain show (a Red Arrows flight simulator), and a 'touch and try' Jet Provost cockpit. The museum also offers specialist tours for groups; phone for details.

East London

Buoyed up by new investment and now the successful Olympic bid, the multicultural East is primed to emerge as a vital new epicentre.

Whitechapel & Spitalfields

Maps p405 & p407

Aldgate, Aldgate East, Shoreditch or Whitechapel tube.
Lying right on the City's doorstep, the enclaves of Whitechapel and Spitalfields were some of its earliest suburbs, springing up naturally around the main road that joined London to Colchester (and which has now become the A11). Their story is one of relentless change, seasoned by high drama: Jack the Ripper earned the area notoriety in the late 19th century with a brutal spree of prostitute murders; in 1911 a huge gun battle between police and an anarchist gang took place in Sidney Street; and a few decades later the area became one of the main casualties of the Blitz.

Today over half of the population of the borough (Tower Hamlets) is from non-white ethnic groups, and this fact reflects a long history of immigration into the area. French Huguenots, Germans, Irish, Jews and, latterly, Bangladeshis, have all flocked here. Thoroughly multicultural, the area is also traditionally working class: from late medieval times it became an industrial hub housing factories, foundries, tanneries and breweries. These have departed, and although a working class contingent remains, the area is gradually going upmarket. Old factories have become trendy bars, cafés and restaurants, particularly around the Brick Lane area and Spitalfields Market. The gentrification looks set to continue when the East London Line extension (from Dalston in the north to West Croydon in the south) and Crossrail (a new, high-speed east to west transit) are completed some time over the next decade (*see p163* **Eastern promise**).

Whitechapel

The eponymous alba capella was part of the church of St Mary Matfelon, which stood at the foot of the Whitechapel Road. The original white stone chapel disappeared centuries ago, but a church remained here until it was bombed in 1940 and finally demolished a decade later. Today a small park, recently renamed the Altab Ali Park in memory of a local Bangladeshi murdered by racists in 1978, stands on the site.

The Blitz wreaked widespread destruction, but a number of historic buildings survive. A little further up the Whitechapel Road is the **Whitechapel Bell Foundry** (No.80-82, 7247 2599, www.whitechapelbellfoundry.co.uk), which has been knocking out bells since 1570, including Big Ben. You can visit the museum 9am-4.15pm Mon-Fri, but to see the actual foundry you'll need to reserve a place on one of the scheduled Saturday tours. Further on still, the **Bombay Saree House** (Nos.265-267) is where Joseph Merrick – the Elephant Man – was exhibited as a sideshow freak, before being rescued by surgeon Sir Frederick Treves. This information can be found in the **Royal London Hospital Archives & Museum** just round the corner in the former crypt of St Augustine with St Philip's Church (Newark Street, 7377 7608, open 10am-4.30pm Mon-Fri). Another historic relic is the deserted **Tower House** on Fieldgate Street, an enormous former doss house with 700 rooms. Jack London and Joseph Stalin are former tenants.

At daily markets along the Whitechapel Road and in nearby Wentworth Street you can stock up on standard market miscellanea (clothes, household goods, fruit and veg, and so on). The famous, salt-of-the-earth **Petticoat Lane Market** on Sundays takes over most of the streets around Middlesex Street (the modern name for the Lane), with more than 1,000 stalls. If the markets don't take your fancy, visit the somewhat incongruous **Whitechapel Art Gallery**, just next to Aldgate East tube (*see below*), or the **Women's Library** (Old Castle Street, 7320 2222, www.thewomenslibrary. ac.uk), which hosts exhibitions devoted to women's history and suffrage.

Whitechapel Art Gallery

80-2 Whitechapel High Street, E1 7QX (7522 7888/ www.whitechapel.org). Aldgate East tube. **Open** 11am-6pm Tue, Wed, Fri-Sun; 11am-9pm Thur. *Tours* 2.30pm occasional Sun. **Admission** free; 1 paying exhibition/yr, phone for details. **Map** p407 S6.
An unexpected cultural treat among the market streets and general bustle of Whitechapel, this gallery is an East London institution, having presented contemporary, forward-thinking exhibitions for over a century. Shows rotate regularly, and there are also poetry, music and film events. Check the website for details of forthcoming shows.

Spitalfields

For most Londoners, Spitalfields is synonymous with the historic covered **(Old) Spitalfields Market** (*see p258*) on Commercial Street. When the original fruit and vegetable market moved to a new venue in Leyton in 1991, Old Spitalfields was threatened with demolition; but impassioned campaigns by locals helped save it. The shops are open seven days a week, and the market every day except Saturday, but the best (and busiest) day to visit is Sunday, when a quality mixture of food, fashion, furniture, music and more is up for grabs. See www.visitspitalfields.com for more information. Within the market building is the Spitz (No.109; *see also p314*), a combined art gallery, music venue and bistro. A brand-new development next to the market, with shops and cafés such as Giraffe and Benefit (cosmetics), meanwhile, may be too harsh for some tastes. Directly opposite is **Christ Church Spitalfields** (*see below*), one of baroque architect Nicholas Hawksmoor's masterpieces.

Lesser-known attractions are peppered around the surrounding streets. Turn into Fournier Street from the church, and walk past the tall, shuttered Huguenot houses of Wilkes Street to **19 Princelet Street**. This unrestored 18th-century house was built by French silk merchants; later it was occupied by Polish Jews, who built a synagogue in the garden. The house is in such a fragile state that it's only open on a handful of days throughout the year (see www.19princeletstreet.org.uk). There are plans to turn the house into a permanent museum of cultural diversity – if enough money can be raised. On the other side of Commercial Road, in Folgate Street, is **Dennis Severs' House** (*see below*), another Huguenot house in much better health.

Christ Church Spitalfields

Commercial Street, E1 6QF (7247 7202/www.christchurchspitalfields.org). Liverpool Street tube/rail. **Open** 11am-4pm Tue; 1-4pm Sun. **Admission** free. **Map** p403 S5.

Built in 1729 by Nicholas Hawksmoor, Christ Church Spitalfields is now restored to its original state after being tastelessly altered in the mid 19th century. The revived interior is one of Hawksmoor's most detailed and impressive, and includes a formidable organ – almost as old as the church itself – designed by another British stalwart, Richard Bridge. There are plans to extend the church's opening times to the rest of the week; phone for details.

Dennis Severs' House

18 Folgate Street, E1 6BX (7247 4013/www.dennissevershouse.co.uk). Liverpool Street tube/rail. **Open** 2-5pm 1st & 3rd Sun of mth; noon-2pm Mon following 1st & 3rd Sun of mth; Mon eves (times vary). **Admission** £8 Sun; £5 noon-2pm Mon; £12 Mon eves. **Credit** MC, V. **Map** p405 R5.

Geffrye Museum. *See p160.*

The ten rooms of this original Huguenot house have been decked out to recreate, down to the smallest detail, snapshots of life in Spitalfields between 1724 and 1914. A tour through this compelling 'still-life drama', as creator Dennis Severs branded it, takes you through the cellar, kitchen, dining room, smoking room and upstairs to the bedrooms. With hearth and candles burning, smells lingering, and objects scattered haphazardly, it is as if the inhabitants only deserted the rooms just moments before.

Brick Lane

The building that houses the **Jamme Masjid Mosque**, at the south end of Brick Lane, symbolises the street's multiculturalism: it began life as a Huguenot chapel and was later used as a synagogue before being converted, in 1976, into a mosque. A lasting trace of the Jewish heritage is the unmissable 24-hour Beigel Bake further north at No.159, whose cheap but monstrous salt beef bagels are legendary across town. However, it's the Bangladeshi influence that's ubiquitous –the innumerable curry restaurants here have helped to earn this enclave the title of Banglatown. Still, quantity and quality are not the same thing, and there are much better places to eat curry in the capital (for our choice of restaurants and cafés in London, *see pp194-221*).

Brick Lane earned its name from the brick factories that once operated here alongside clothesmakers and the **Old Truman Brewery**, which is now an artistic and creative hub. North of the brewery, quirky cafés and clothes shops are dotted along the road. Brick Lane has now become a bustling, trendy nightspot, and many old factories also house spacious bars such as Vibe (Nos.91-95; *see p326*) and 93 Feet East (No.150; *see p322*). In spring 2006 the new **Rich Mix** building (39-47 Bethnal Green Road, www. richmix.org.uk) opens near the top end of Brick Lane. The multi-million pound cultural centre will have a cinema, café, bar and workspace for artists and designers.

Shoreditch & Hoxton

Map p405

Shoreditch tube or Old Street tube/rail.
Originally two distinct but neighbouring hamlets: **Shoreditch** at the junction of the Roman roads Old Street and Kingsland Road, and **Hoxton** just north of Old Street. Nowadays both names are buzzwords for the trendy, bohemian district that has risen from the ashes of an area left virtually derelict after the war. First adopted as a cheap hangout by a new generation of British artists (such as Tracey Emin and Damien Hirst) in the mid 1990s, it is now one of London's most vibrant and dynamic social centres. Rent prices have consequently skyrocketed, driving the artists out towards Hackney and Bethnal Green, but evidence of an enduring creative energy is visible at the **White Cube Gallery** (*see p295*).

DJ bars and clubs dominate Shoreditch High Street, Curtain Road, Old Street and Hoxton Square – formerly Hoxton Fields, where playwright Ben Jonson killed Gabriel Spencer in a duel in 1598. This is not the area's only theatrical connection: Shoreditch was home to London's first playhouse, built in 1576 at the corner of Great Eastern Street and New Inn Yard. In Victorian times, Shoreditch gained a mixed reputation for its boisterous music halls; the Queen of the Halls herself, Marie Lloyd, was born in Hoxton in 1870.

At the foot of Shoreditch High Street the boarded-up Bishopsgate Goods Yard has been in disrepair for decades. Over the next five years the new Shoreditch High Street station will be built on the site, as part of the East London Line extension. The new Hoxton station, a little way up the Kingsland Road, will drop visitors right next to the **Geffrye Museum** (*see below*), which, for now, is a short bus ride from the nearest tube stations.

Geffrye Museum

Kingsland Road, E2 8EA (7739 9893/recorded information 7739 8543/www.geffrye-museum. org.uk). Liverpool Street tube/rail then 149, 242 bus/Old Street tube/rail then 243 bus. **Open** *Museum* 10am-5pm Tue-Sat; noon-5pm Sun. *Almshouse tours* 10.30am, 11.15am, 12.15pm, 2pm, 3pm, 4pm of 1st Sat of mth & 1st & 3rd Wed of mth. **Admission** *Museum* free; donations appreciated. *Almshouse tours* £2; free under-16s. **Credit** *Shop* MC, V. **Map** p405 R3.

The Geffrye Museum is a marvellous physical history of the English interior, housed in a set of converted almshouses. It recreates quintessential English living rooms from the 17th century to the present day, and the museum also has a series of gardens designed on similar chronological lines. There's an airy restaurant and special exhibitions are mounted throughout the year. Due to refurbishment, the 19th-century period rooms will be closed from June to October 2006, and the 17th- and 18th-century rooms from January to October 2006. **Photo** *p159*.

Bethnal Green & Hackney

Bethnal Green tube/rail/Cambridge Heath, London Fields or Hackney Central rail.
Bethnal Green was once a suburb of spacious townhouses and gardens, but by the mid 1900s it was fast becoming one of the poorest slums in town, with multiple families crammed into rickety old buildings and the newer terraces. Things got worse, and in the 1960s much of the old housing was razed and replaced with new public housing blocks, though this scarcely improved overall quality of life. Now, at last, it's shaking off its run-down image and estate agents are even describing the pretty Victorian terraces as desirable. There are some obvious advantages: it's just minutes from the bustle of Shoreditch and in easy reach of the City for young professionals. Lovely **Victoria Park** (*see p162*) is a short stroll east; another attraction is the **Museum of Childhood** (*see p162*), closed for refurbishment until October 2006. Every Sunday, **Columbia Road**, a few minutes away towards Old Street, erupts into a riot of colour for the Sunday flower market (*see p258*). North of Bethnal Green, Mare Street leads into central Hackney. On the way, a short westerly detour brings you across tranquil London Fields to **Broadway Market**, until recently a shady and neglected market street, now a vital artery.

Although it contains the fabled 'murder mile' (aka Upper Clapton Road), **Hackney** is very much a part of the renaissance sweeping through the East End; the fully refurbished 1901 **Hackney Empire** (291 Mare Street, 8985 2424, www.hackneyempire.co.uk) is a symbol of this ascendance. Next door are the art deco

Columbia Road, in full bloom on a Sunday. *See p160.*

town hall and the **Hackney Museum** (1 Reading Lane, 8356 3500, www.hackney. gov.uk/museum), which celebrates the cultural diversity of the borough. Hackney remains largely residential, but there are a few sights. In Homerton, just to the east, is **Sutton House**, the oldest house in the East End (*see below*).

Bethnal Green Museum of Childhood

Cambridge Heath Road, E2 9PA (8983 5200/ recorded information 8980 2415/www.museum ofchildhood.org.uk). Bethnal Green tube/rail/ Cambridge Heath rail. **Open** 10am-5.50pm Mon-Thur, Sat, Sun. Closed until autumn 2006. **Admission** free; donations appreciated. **Credit** MC, V.

Officially part of the Victoria and Albert museum, the Museum of Childhood has amassed a huge collection of children's toys, games and costumes since it opened in 1872. There are plenty of hands-on activities for kids, including dressing-up boxes, giant drafts, a zoetrope and regular free workshops. Adults will enjoy the old board games and quirky toys, such as the special Hong Kong reunification issue Barbie doll. Upstairs, there's an astounding collection of dolls houses, dating from 1673 all the way up to 2001. As part of a refurbishment programme, designed to improve access and revamp the mezzanine galleries, the museum is closed until autumn 2006.

Sutton House

2 & 4 Homerton High Street, E9 6JQ (8986 2264/ www.nationaltrust.org.uk). Bethnal Green tube then 254, 106, D6 bus/Hackney Central rail. **Open** *Early Feb-late Dec* Historic rooms 12.30pm-4.30pm Thur-Sun. Café, gallery, shop noon-4.30pm Thur-Sun. Closed Jan. *Tours* phone for details. **Admission** £2.50; 50p 5-16s; free under-5s; £5.50 family. *Tours* free on admission. **Credit** MC, V.

Built in 1535 for Henry VIII's first secretary of state, Sir Ralph Sadleir, this red-brick tudor mansion is East London's oldest home. Miraculously, it has survived waves of development, and is now beautifully restored in authentic original decor, with a real Tudor kitchen to boot. Special events and activities are often held (check the website); there's also an art gallery exhibiting contemporary work by local artists.

Mile End & Bow

Bow Road or Mile End tube/Bow Church DLR.
Travellers on their way out of the City of London towards Colchester would have passed the first milestone somewhere around Stepney Green station, but it's the area a bit further east, just past the Regent's Canal, that takes its name from the vanished landmark – **Mile End**. Just beyond the canal you pass under the 'Green Bridge' of **Mile End Park**, a long, thin strip of green that stretches out on both sides of the main road. This grass-covered 'living bridge'

joins the north and south sections of the park, redeveloped a few years back with £25 million of lottery money and now including a terraced garden, ecology park and children's play area.

The northern tip of Mile End Park backs on to the resplendent **Victoria Park** at the confluence of the Regent's and Hertford Union canals. Just over the other side of Victoria Park, where Lauriston Road meets Victoria Park Road, is a bijou cluster of curiosity shops, gastropubs and cafés. At the other end of Mile End Park, a kilometre south, is the fascinating **Ragged School Museum** (*see below*).

Heading east, Mile End turns into **Bow**. This part of E3 managed to escape the heavy bombing that decimated the surroundings, so a good portion of marvellous Georgian and Victorian terraces remain. In general, there's not much to see except housing – nevertheless, the former Bryant & May match factory off Fairfield Road (now converted into homes) is an impressive Victorian building, and quite lovely in itself.

Further east the Bow Road crosses the River Lea, forming a series of small 'islands', among them **Three Mills Island** (*see below*). Northeast lies **Stratford**, an area that's set to be transformed into the jewel of the east as part of regeneration for the 2012 Olympics (*see p163* **Eastern promise**).

Ragged School Museum

46-50 Copperfield Road, E3 4RR (8980 6405/www. raggedschoolmuseum.org.uk). Mile End tube. **Open** 10am-5pm Wed, Thur; 2-5pm 1st Sun of mth. *Tours* by arrangement; phone for details. **Admission** free; donations appreciated.

Ragged schools were an early experiment in public education: they provided tuition as well as food and clothing for destitute children. The Copperfield Road Ragged School was the largest in London, and it was here that the famous Dr Barnardo taught. It's now a fascinating museum, and contains a complete mock-up of a typical ragged classroom, where historical re-enactments are staged for school children. There are also displays on local history and industry.

Three Mills Island

Three Mill Lane, E3 3DU (8980 4626/www. housemill.org.uk/). Bromley-by-Bow tube. **Tours** *May-Oct* 1-4pm Sun; also 1st Sun of mth *May-Dec.* Closed Jan-Feb. **Admission** £3; £1.50 concessions; free under-16s. **No credit cards**.

This large island in the River Lea takes its name from the three mills that used to grind flour and gunpowder here until the 18th century. Today the site is home to a media village housing TV studios. The House Mill, built in 1776, is the oldest and largest tidal mill in Britain, and though out of service, is occasionally opened to the public. The island offers pleasant walks, there's a small café, and a crafts market on the first Sunday of the month.

Eastern promise

It was inevitable that London's industry would flourish in the east. For one thing, the politicians and noblemen had already built their court and palaces west of the City in the 11th century. But it is meteorology that is the surprise protagonist of this chapter of London's evolution. Foul-smelling dye works, tanneries and factories prone to fires had to be built downwind – that is, in the east – to minimise risk (and unpleasantness) for the City's existing businesses and residents. And as empire grew and shipping became big business, the deeper reaches of the Thames proved more favourable to cargo ships, so the new docks naturally took their place alongside the existing industries. Working communities sprang up everywhere, and so the east became the notorious hub of London's working class; a status it retains to this day, as popular mythology (including the indefatigable soap opera *EastEnders*) testifies.

The myth endures, but the reality is more volatile. Industry has moved on, both technologically and geographically. The older factories departed long ago, but the seismic event was the development of a new system of cargo in the 1950s, which spelt doom for the Docklands: by 1980 they had all closed. However, it was only a matter of time before burgeoning new business seized upon the deserted land, and since the 1980s the Docklands have been comprehensively transformed by investment and construction. For years the growth was confined to riverside areas; at long last, the prosperity is beginning to nudge its way into other historically poor boroughs. The whole of the east is on the eve of an economic and cultural renaissance.

The successful 2012 Olympic bid has effectively guaranteed the gentrification of the east. Stratford, its nucleus, will be renovated beyond recognition during the next five years. Even before the Olympics were won, the new Channel Tunnel Rail Link was due to have a terminus at Stratford. The tunnels have been dug, the stations are under construction, and the first train will depart Stratford for Paris in 2007. And as soon as Stratford International has opened, the spoil from the new rail tunnels will be used to raise the disused land around the station by eight metres, providing a foundation for the new Stratford City complex – the largest planning

application ever approved in London. The ambitious project will contain 4,500 new homes, 6.5 million square feet of space including shopping and leisure facilities, hotels, and a new school, and promises to create some 30,000 new jobs.

The rest of the run-down east is already showing the signs of growth. House prices in Hackney and Bethnal Green are creeping up; the refurbished Hackney Empire symbolises a new injection of cultural energy for the area; and Dalston is losing its dangerous image. A new cultural centre and the reopened Vortex Jazz Club in Gillett Street (*see p316*) are a portent of things to come. Furthermore, in Walthamstow, an extensive strategy for regeneration won the Mayor's Award for Planning Excellence in 2004. And linking all of these places together will be a busy new set of transport links. The East London Line will run up through Hoxton and Haggerston to Dalston Junction. The Crossrail scheme, if it is ever approved, will provide frequent high speed trains linking West London with Whitechapel, Stratford, the Docklands and beyond and, in its second phase, will link Dalston with Clapham Junction.

And although the Olympics are still several years off, the huge catalogue of residential and commercial developments, both proposed and already underway (*see also p33* **Visionary positions**), shows that investors are happily feeding their money into the impoverished boroughs of Newham, Hackney, Tower Hamlets, Barking, through to Dagenham and beyond. The race is on to be ready for 2012. By then, the east might finally be shaking off its proletarian connotations – and the Queen Vic in *EastEnders* will probably be a gastropub.

Walthamstow

Walthamstow Central tube/rail.
Apart from the famous greyhound track,
Walthamstow Stadium (*see p39*),
Walthamstow's best asset is its quaint little
village, just a few minutes' walk from the tube.
Traditionally working class, the area is now
attracting waves of middle-class homebuyers
priced out of the central London housing market.

At the top of Orford Road is an ancient timber-
framed cottage, a relic of a settlement that stood
here long before the Victorian terraces sprung
up in their droves. Just opposite is **St Mary's
Church**, parts of which date back to the 16th
century, although a church has stood here since
the 1100s. The pretty cemetery doubles as a
nature reserve, and a few paces away is the
Vestry House Museum (*see below*), which has
an impressive collection of items of local history.

Back in the town centre, the daily market,
which spans the length of Walthamstow High
Street, is the longest in Europe, but is decidedly
unremarkable: cheap clothes, household goods
and fruit and veg create a monotonous pattern
all the way along. There are plans to improve
the market as part of a large regeneration
programme, which has already started with
the shiny new bus garage at the east end of
the high street. If you do take a walk along the
market, stop off at **L Manze** (No.76, 8520 2855)
for a taste of the historic East End. This pie and
mash eaterie opened in 1929; its original decor
is tastefully conserved – as are the recipes.

North of the town centre, the **Higham Hill**
area boasts some of the prettiest Victorian
terraces in Walthamstow. Young professionals
and new families are increasingly choosing to
settle here. A particular attraction is the peaceful
Lloyd Park, near the junction of Hoe Street and
Forest Road. It has excellent amenities – tennis
courts, a skate park, café, duck ponds, an aviary
and gardens. The grand Georgian house at the
entrance is home to the **William Morris
Gallery** (*see below*) – the Arts and Crafts
pioneer was a Walthamstow boy.

The magnificent, art deco town hall is just
east of Lloyd Park along Forest Road, which
leads into **Epping Forest**. We can thank the
Victorians for saving this peaceful green
lung: in 1878, Parliament granted the City of
London the power to buy land within 25 miles
(40 kilometres) of the city centre to be used for
the recreation of city dwellers. Queen Elizabeth I
maintained a hunting lodge in Epping Forest
that has now been converted into a free museum
(8529 6681, open 1-4pm Wed-Sun). The forest is
a wonderful space for walking, jogging, cycling,
riding and picnicking; stop in at the visitors'
centre (8508 0028) for information and maps.

Vestry House Museum

*Vestry Road, E17 9NH (8509 1917/www.lbwf.gov.
uk/index/leisure/museums-galleries/vestry-house-
museum.htm). Walthamstow Central tube/rail.*
Open 10am-1pm, 2-5.30pm Mon-Fri; 10am-1pm,
2-5pm Sat. **Admission** free.
The Vestry House has been a museum since 1930,
collecting artefacts and documents relating to the
history of Walthamstow and its borough, Waltham
Forest. The extensive collection now contains sections on domestic life, toys and games, photography,
policing and more. There's also a well-stocked shop.

William Morris Gallery

*Lloyd Park, Forest Road, E17 4PP (8527 3782/
www.lbwf.gov.uk/wmg). Walthamstow Central
tube/rail/34, 97 bus.* **Open** 10am-1pm, 2-5pm
Tue-Sat, 1st Sun of mth. *Tours* phone for details.
Admission free; donations appreciated.
Credit *Shop* MC, V.
Artist, socialist and wallpaper mogul William Morris
lived here between 1848 and 1856. You don't have to
be an Arts and Crafts buff to appreciate the wonderful wallpaper, fabric, stained glass and ceramics he
and his colleagues produced. Notable pieces include
a medieval-style helmet and sword made as props for
murals he painted, and Morris's personal coffee cup.

Leyton

Only football (two lower-league teams and a
prodigious top-flight player) has given Leyton
any kind of name outside the East End. The
footballer in question is David Beckham, of
course, who was born in Leytonstone, just east of
Leyton proper. **Lea Valley Park**, on either side
of Lea Bridge Road, has a number of attractions:
an ice rink, stables, good space for walking, plus
the WaterWorks Nature Reserve (Lammas Road,
8988 7566, open 8am-dusk daily). The water-
filter beds were built in 1849 to purify water
during a cholera epidemic but now house 322
species of plant, 25 species of breeding birds –
and scores of pitch and putt golfers.

Docklands

*Shadwell or Wapping tube/Various stops on the
Docklands Light Railway (DLR).*
London's docks were fundamental to the long
prosperity of Empire. Between 1802 and 1921,
ten separate docks were built between Tower
Bridge in the west and Woolwich in the east;
and thousands of people were employed by a
burgeoning import and export industry. Yet by
the 1960s, though the docks had briefly regained
momentum after sustaining massive damage in
the war, the shipping industry was changing
irrevocably. The new, more efficient 'container'
system of cargo demanded larger, deep-
draught ships, which London's docks could
not accommodate. By 1980 they had all closed.

Walk on The esoteric East

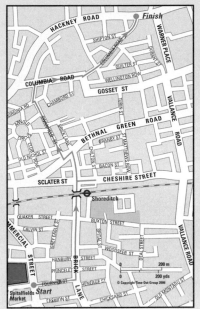

Sightseeing

Start: Old Spitalfields Market, E1.
Finish: Columbia Road, E2.
Length: A mile and a bit.
Brick Lane may be best known for its curry restaurants (quality: average at best), but the streets around it are crammed full of quirky, individual and independent shops – with new ones opening all the time. It's best to come on a Sunday morning, when the **Columbia Road** flower market and **Spitalfields Market**, on Commercial Street (*see p258*) are in full swing.

After visiting the market, head along Fournier Street, then turn left, walking north up Brick Lane. As you make your way up, the **Old Truman Brewery** (whose main entrance is at No.91) is on the left. Just before you get here, take a detour down Dray Walk. If you're already hungry, the first stop should be the **Story Deli** (No.3), selling yummy edibles such as organic pizzas (*see p214*). Trainer aficionados will love **Gloria's** (No.6, 7700 6024) for funky, limited-edition sneakers and retro toys. Fashion-wise, **Butcher of Distinction** (No.11, 7770 6111) is the

best bet, with smart casual- and footwear. The quirky interior, loosely based on a butcher's shop, is another reason to pop in.

Back on Brick Lane, second-hand clothing emporium **Rokit** (Nos.101 and 107, 7247 3777) is always worth a rummage. Opposite is cutting-edge jewellery in the **@work** gallery (No.156, 7377 0597) and, right next door, **Coffee@Brick Lane** (No.154, 7247 6735), selling delicious organic coffees and snacks in an ultra-chilled environment.

Next on the right, you hit the unmissable treasure trove that is Cheshire Street. First stop should be **The Shop** (No.3, 7739 5631), which is brilliant for high-quality vintage wear and handbags from the 1950s to the '70s. Up on the right at No.18, **Labour & Wait** (7729 6253) manages to combine cool with homespun, selling household accessories such as old-fashioned brooms and picnic hampers, while, next door, **Mar Mar Co** (No.16, 7729 1494) adds Scandinavian homewares to the mix. **Shelf** (No.40, 7739 9444) is the first place to go for individual gifts; sharing the same street number, but actually the next shop along, is **Mimi** (No.40, 7729 6699), where handcrafted leather bags are excellent value.

From here it's only a short skip up to the microcosmic retail community at **Columbia Road** (and nearby Ezra Street), which comes to life on Sunday mornings to coincide with the famous flower market (*see p258*).

Treacle (No.160, 7729 5657) is *the* place for groovy pieces of crockery and dinky cup cakes (tip: try to get there early, as they can sell out). Perfumer **Angela Flanders** (No.96, 7739 7555) has a lovely shop here, too, selling her sought-after perfumes and home fragrances and candles. Even if you don't have kids, don't miss **Bob & Blossom** (7739 4737) at No.140, which sells beautiful wooden toys and trademark tiny T-shirts emblazoned with cheeky mottos. A couple of doors down is **Marcos & Trump** at No.146 (07956 465126), a treasure trove of vintage gear.

After all that retail therapy, you'll have worked up an appetite. The area is littered with places to eat and drink. On Brick Lane itself, grab a bite at the legendary **Beigel Bake** (No.159, 7729 0616). Columbia Road provides tapas at **Laxeiro** (No.93, 7729 1147), and British cooking with a twist at **Perennial** (Nos.110-112, 7739 4556).

View over **Docklands**. *See p164.*

This abrupt change left a huge swathe of land virtually derelict, although some resilient neighbourhoods clung on to the old community spirit – which had once been so strong that in 1920 a group of Isle of Dogs dockers blocked the roads and declared independence. But in spite of their resilience, redevelopment was inevitable. As a financial hub, Docklands is now at least as important as the City itself. It's estimated that, by 2006, the number of workers commuting to Canary Wharf each day will be over 90,000 – an increase of some 40,000 in only a few years. Thames Clippers (0870 781 5049, www.thamesclippers.com) provides daily ferry connections between various jetties in Docklands and central London.

St Katharine's & Wapping

St Katharine's was one of the first London docks to be formally closed. In 1969 it was sold to the Greater London Council, which demolished the warehouses and drew up plans for the modern development, which now includes a yacht marina, luxury apartments, offices, restaurants, shops and other facilities.

The Saxon settlement of **Wapping**, a little further east, held maritime associations for centuries. In 1598 John Stowe described Wapping High Street as a 'continual street, or a filthy strait passage, with alleys of small tenements or cottages, built, inhabited by sailors'

victuallers'. A surprising number of these historic pubs survive, including the 1545 **Town of Ramsgate** (No.62), where 'hanging judge' George Jeffreys was captured in 1688 while trying to escape to Europe disguised as a woman. Other notable patrons included Captain Bligh and Fletcher Christian of HMS *Bounty* fame, and 'Colonel' Blood, who attempted to steal the Crown Jewels in 1671. At No.108, the **Captain Kidd** pub recalls the execution of privateer William Kidd in 1701 at Execution Dock, a gruesome spot near Wapping New Stairs where pirates were publicly hanged at low tide. Further east on Wapping Wall, the **Prospect of Whitby** (No.37) dates from 1520 and has counted Pepys, Dickens and Turner among its regulars.

Wapping's maritime associations were gradually lost and the new docks permanently changed the face of the area. After they closed, further drama was in store: in 1986 Wapping became the unlikely symbol of a journalistic revolution when Rupert Murdoch moved *The Times* and News Group newspapers here from Fleet Street, the first of a long line of news companies to move to more sophisticated premises. 'Fortress Wapping' sits ominously along Pennington Way. Opposite the Prospect of Whitby pub, the old London Hydraulic Power Company building has been converted to the **Wapping Project**, an impressive restaurant and art space (*see p295*).

Limehouse

Like its westerly neighbour Wapping, compact Limehouse held maritime associations for hundreds of years. Britain's first wave of Chinese immigrants, mostly seafarers, settled here in the 19th century, giving the area a reputation for gambling and opium dens. Oscar Wilde's Dorian Gray bought opium here and it was a hideout for Sax Rohmer's Fu Manchu. Charles Dickens also based his Six Jolly Fellowship Porters Tavern (in *Our Mutual Friend*) on the riverside Grapes pub (76 Narrow Street; *see p231*).

Away from the river, **St Anne's Church** (7515 0977) is another magnificent Nicholas Hawksmoor construction. It was gutted by fire in 1850 but restored, first by Philip Hardwick and again, in the mid 1990s, by Julian Harrap. The clock on the spire is the highest in London, enabling it to be seen from the river.

Isle of Dogs

The exact origin of the name 'Isle of Dogs' remains uncertain; the first known use of the name is on a 1588 map, and the popular theory is that Henry VIII kept his hunting dogs here. It is not strictly an island, but rather a peninsula that extends to create a prominent loop in the river, now immortalised in the title sequence of *EastEnders*. Originally Stepney Marsh, it was first drained in medieval times; then in the 19th century a huge system of docks completely reshaped the area. The building of the West India Docks, which bisected the Isle from west to east with gates into the Thames on both sides, finally created an island of sorts.

The natural isolation of the area and the formerly thriving docklands industry conspired to create a strong, compact community. In the 20th century this community took a heavy beating – first during the war, when the Isle of Dogs was one of the hardest hit areas. At the height of the Blitz, the docks were bombarded on 57 consecutive nights; this story is told powerfully at the **Museum in Docklands** (*see below*). But the final blow was to come when London's shipping trade was rerouted through downstream Tilbury in Essex. After a period of decline, new business moved in, salvaged the old warehouses and much of the housing, and staked out its territorial claim with its triumphal totem, **One Canada Square**.

Relatively little remains of the past, and the Isle is now a futuristic metropolis, the nearest London gets to Manhattan. The glittering skyscrapers come complete with Japanese-style gardens, luxury apartments, shopping malls housing high-street staples and top-end fashion

(visit www.mycanarywharf.com) and the raised Docklands Light Railway (DLR) snaking through the towers. Cesar Pelli's One Canada Square has been Britain's tallest habitable building since 1991; the HSBC and Citygroup towers recently now joined it into second and third place, and clones are springing up thick and fast.

Stroll south to **Island Gardens** for a great view across the river to Greenwich, allegedly Sir Christopher Wren's favourite vista during his construction of the Old Royal Naval College. You can cross the river through the Victorian tunnel (lift service 7am-7pm Mon-Sat, 10am-5.30pm Sun) that surfaces beside the *Cutty Sark*.

Museum in Docklands

No.1 Warehouse, West India Quay, Hertsmere Road, E14 4AL (recorded information 0870 444 3856/box office 0870 444 3857/www.museumindocklands. org.uk). West India Quay DLR/Canary Wharf tube. **Open** 10am-6pm daily. Last entry 5.30pm. **Admission** (unlimited entrance for 1yr) £5; £3 concessions; free under-16s. **Credit** MC, V.
This huge museum explores the long and diverse history of London's docklands over two millennia, from their use in Roman times, through their imperial heyday, up to the present. Many exhibits are narrated by people who saw the changes for themselves; the Docklands at War section is particularly harrowing. A ticket is valid for up to a year, which is useful considering how much there is to see, and how many one-off events they run.

Further east

The blighted **Millennium Dome** remains a major landmark of the Docklands area, although it is closed except for special events. It will gain a new lease of life (albeit briefly) when it hosts the gymnastics, trampolining and basketball events at the 2012 Olympics. Before that, though, there are plans to turn the space into an entertainment and sports venue, due for completion in spring 2007.

Further east still, the old Royal Victoria Dock is now home to the mammoth **ExCeL** exhibition and conference centre (7069 5000, www.excel-london.co.uk) which opened in 2000 and holds varied events throughout the year. Custom House and Royal Victoria are the nearest DLR stops; you can also alight here to visit the **Thames Barrier Park** (www.thamesbarrierpark.org.uk) on North Woolwich Road. Opened in 2001, this was London's first new park in half a century, and the lush sunken garden offers grand views over the Thames Barrier (*see pp171 & p172*). Further east, near City Airport, is the jolly little **North Woolwich Old Station Museum** (Pier Road, 7474 7244, open 1-5pm Sat, Sun, closed December).

South-east London

Indulge in a spot of naval gazing.

Rotherhithe

Rotherhithe tube.
Nestling in the loop of the river Thames on the north-eastern edge of the London Borough of Southwark, Redriffe, as Rotherhithe used to be known, was a shipbuilding village, with the mariners' church of **St Mary** (*see below*) at its heart. The Pilgrim ship, the *Mayflower*, sailed from here in 1620. Rotherhithe's docks have become smart homes, but an atmospheric slice of old Redriffe remains in the conservation area and its rickety old waterside pubs such as the Mayflower, St Mary's Rotherhithe, and the fascinating **Brunel Engine House & Tunnel Exhibition** (*see below*).

The **Norwegian Church & Seaman's Mission** lie at the mouth of Rotherhithe's road tunnel, completed in 1908, many years after Brunel's successful excavations. There are several Scandinavian churches around here, a relic of Rotherhithe's historical links with Nordic sailors, which date right back to the vikings. Across Jamaica Road, **Southwark Park**, London's oldest municipal park, has a community art gallery (open Wed-Sun), an old bandstand, landscaped lake and playgrounds.

Brunel Engine House & Tunnel Exhibition

Brunel Engine House, Railway Avenue, SE16 4LF (7231 3840/www.brunelenginehouse.org.uk). Rotherhithe tube. **Open** 11am-6pm Tue-Sun. *Tours* by appointment only. **Admission** £2; £1 concessions; £5 family; free under-5s. **No credit cards.**
The exhibition, which tells the story of the joint venture between Marc Isambard Brunel and his more famous son, Isambard Kingdom (*see p172* **Iron man**) to build the first ever tunnel under a river, is in the original engine house. A recent refurbishment funded by London Renaissance, which makes displays less text-heavy and more universally interesting, means the museum is all set up for Isambard Kingdom Brunel's bicentenary year, 2006. The award-winning sculpture garden by the river, scene of the popular annual summer playscheme, is just a few hundred yards from Millwall, the launch site of Brunel's last project, the monster ship *Great Eastern*.

St Mary's Rotherhithe

St Marychurch Street, SE16 4JE (7231 2465). Rotherhithe tube. **Open** 7am-6pm Mon-Thur; 8am-6pm Sat, Sun. **Admission** free.

Unless you're attending a service, all St Mary's treasures have to be viewed through the glass door. This beloved community church, completed in 1715, was built by the sailors and watermen of the parish. The style of the church, with wooden frame and barrel roof, suggests it was built by a shipwright, and all over are reminders of the area's links with the sea. *Mayflower* captain Christopher Jones was buried here in 1622. Grinling Gibbons contributed work to the beautifully carved reredos in the sanctuary, while the communion table in the Lady Chapel is made from timber salvaged from the warship *Fighting Temeraire*, the painting of which, by Turner, hangs in the National Gallery (*see p133*).

Deptford & Greenwich

Cutty Sark DLR for Maritime Greenwich or Deptford Bridge DLR/Greenwich DLR/rail/Deptford or Maze Hill rail.
The muddy creeks and abandoned wharves of riverside **Deptford** are being redeveloped faster than you can say 'riverside loft living'. **Convoys Wharf**, founded by Henry VIII in 1513, and now owned by News International, will soon be transformed into a mini village with its own exhibition centre. Inland, however, Deptford High Street remains gritty, although it recently earned a plaudit in a diversity survey. The handsomely refurbished **St Paul's Church** (Mary Ann Gardens, 8692 0989), built in Roman baroque style by Thomas Archer around 1712-1730, looms over the area.

Sailors in the 17th century worshipped at **St Nicholas's Church**, on Deptford Green (8692 8848). The crumbly skull-and-crossbone carvings on its gate piers lend a forbidding air. Christopher Marlowe, killed in a brawl in a Deptford tavern, is rumoured to be buried here.

Taking the DLR east affords a good view of one of the most striking symbols of Deptford's regeneration, **Laban Centre**, though maritime Greenwich downriver remains more visitor-friendly. The view downhill from the Wolfe Monument at the top of Greenwich Park is one of the best in London, taking in Greenwich treasures **Queen's House** (*see p171*), the **National Maritime Museum** (*see p170*) and the Old Royal Naval College.

Greenwich earned its reputation when it was a playground for Tudor royalty. Henry VIII and his daughters Mary I and Elizabeth I were all born here – Greenwich Palace was Henry's favourite residence. The palace fell into disrepair under Cromwell, and during the reign of William and Mary, who preferred Hampton Court and Kensington, it was designated as the Royal Naval Hospital. The hospital is now the **Old Royal Naval College** (*see p170*).

If you take a riverboat to **Greenwich Pier** (for information, *see p364*), you disembark in the shadow of the **Cutty Sark** (*see p170*). The Greenwich Foot Tunnel, which takes you under the Thames to Island Gardens and Docklands, is also here. **Greenwich Tourist Information Centre** (0870 608 2000) is based in Pepys House and is a useful first point of call.

Walk past the Old Royal Naval College with the river on your left, and you'll reach the Trafalgar Tavern – a favourite haunt of Thackeray, Dickens and Wilkie Collins – and also the Cutty Sark Tavern, which dates to 1695.

Back in town, the busy **Greenwich Market** (*see p258*) pulls in tourists at weekends, but the area's loveliest bits are away from the centre,

either along the riverside walk or around the prettiest of the Royal Parks, **Greenwich Park**, with the Wren-designed **Royal Observatory** (*see p171*). The park has formal gardens, deer enclosures, historic trees, and the **Ranger's House** (*see p171*). Nearby is one of the area's most idiosyncratic draws, the **Fan Museum** (*see p170*), one of only two in the world.

To the north sits the empty **Millennium Dome**, destined to become a sport and leisure complex and a major venue for the 2012 Olympics. To the south lie **Blackheath**'s grassy expanses. Some of Britain's earliest sports clubs started here: the Royal Blackheath Golf Club (1745), the Blackheath Hockey Club (1861) and the Blackheath Football Club (which actually plays rugby; 1862). Smart Georgian homes surround the heath, but the 18th-century **Paragon** is of particular note. This beautiful crescent of colonnaded houses was bombed in World War II, but has since been restored to become the area's most desirable address.

Sightseeing

Cutty Sark.
See p170.

National Maritime Museum.

Cutty Sark

King William Walk, SE10 9HT (8858 3445/
www.cuttysark.org.uk). Cutty Sark DLR/Greenwich
DLR/rail. **Open** 10am-5pm daily (last entry
4.30pm). *Tours* Mon-Fri, depending on availability.
Admission (LP) £5; £3.70-£3.90 concessions;
free under-5s; £12.50 family. *Tours* free.
Credit MC, V.
Launched in 1869 from Dumbarton on the Clyde, the
Cutty Sark took tea to China, and later, wool to
Australia. Now a museum, the lower hold contains
the largest collection of merchant figureheads in the
country. The old ship is in a poor condition after
standing in dry dock as a tourist attraction for so
many years; it's calculated that it will cost £25m to
save her. In early 2005 the Heritage Lottery Fund
granted £11.75m towards the project, with fundraising activities set to continue until October 2006,
when restoration work begins. Until then, people are
encouraged to phone first or look at the website to
check that the ship is still open for visitors, as it may
be out of action for a while beforehand. A learning
centre and catering facilities will be built after the
essential repairs are completed. **Photo** *p169.*

Fan Museum

12 Crooms Hill, SE10 8ER (8305 1441/www.fan-
museum.org). Cutty Sark DLR/Greenwich DLR/
rail. **Open** 11am-5pm Tue-Sat; noon-5pm Sun.
Admission £3.50; £2.50 concessions; free
under-7s, OAPs, disabled 2-5pm Tue. **Credit** MC, V.
A most unusual museum, and a rather restful place
to wander even if you're not a fan of fans. Housed in
a pair of restored Georgian townhouses, the Fan
Museum holds more than 3,000 hand-held folding
fans from every period since the 11th century. Only
a fraction of the collection is on display at any
one time, though, as antique fans are retired peri-
odically to give them a rest. The Orangery is a beautiful room with murals and exquisite furnishings.

National Maritime Museum

Romney Road, SE10 9NF (8858 4422/information
8312 6565/tours 8312 6608/www.nmm.ac.uk). Cutty
Sark DLR/Greenwich DLR/rail. **Open** *July, Aug*
10am-6pm daily. *Sept-June* 10am-5pm daily. *Tours*
phone for details. **Admission** free; donations
appreciated. **Credit** (shop) MC, V.
Devoted to an island nation's seafaring history, this
museum charts its specialist subject in great depth,
with two million items in its collections. Of the permanent galleries, 'Explorers' is devoted to pioneers
of sea travel and includes a chilling *Titanic* display,
where grainy launch footage is juxtaposed with
ghostly wreck images; while 'Passengers' is a history of the cruise holiday, with a cabin mock-up and
hilarious old footage of luxury ocean travel. 'Art of
the Sea' is the world's largest maritime art collection. Upstairs, the All Hands gallery provides fun
interactive learning for children. **Photo** *above.*

Old Royal Naval College

Greenwich, SE10 (8269 4747/tours 8269 4791/
www.greenwichfoundation.org.uk). Cutty Sark DLR/
Greenwich DLR/rail. **Open** 10am-5pm daily
(last entry 4.15pm). *Tours* by arrangement.
Admission free. **Credit** (shop) MC, V.
Sir Christopher Wren's 1696 neoclassical buildings
were originally a hospital, then a naval college and
are now part of the University of Greenwich and
Trinity College of Music. The public are allowed into
the rococo chapel and Painted Hall – a tribute to
William and Mary that took beleaguered artist Sir
James Thornhill 19 years to complete. In 1806 the
body of Lord Nelson lay in state here while thousands
came to pay their respects. The chapel has free organ
recitals on the first Sunday of each month. Greenwich
Gateway Visitor Centre, has an exhibition on
Greenwich history and the story of the Royal Hospital
for Seamen. The college runs events and re-enactments, and there's an ice rink outside in winter.

Queen's House

*Romney Road, SE10 9NF (8312 6565/www.nmm.
ac.uk). Cutty Sark DLR/Greenwich DLR/rail.* **Open**
10am-5pm daily (last entry 4.30pm). *Tours* noon,
2.30pm. **Admission** free; occasional charge for
temporary exhibitions. *Tours* free. **Credit** (over £5)
MC, V.

This handsome Palladian abode, intended for James
I's wife and passed on, unfinished, to Charles I's
queen, Henrietta Maria, was a labour of love for
Inigo Jones. It was finally completed in 1640, 24
years after the original commission. The beautiful,
square entrance hall, with its gallery, elaborate
painted ceiling and panels, and the elegant, spiral
Tulip Staircase, segue into the Orangery, which
affords sweeping views over undulating Greenwich
Park. The house is a perfect setting for the National
Maritime Museum's art collection, including paintings by Reynolds, Hogarth and Gainsborough. A
fascinating exhibition on the ground floor charts the
house's former life as a boarding school for the sons
of sailors. Today the Queen's House forms the central portion of the National Maritime Museum (*see
p170*), and a delightful colonnade connects them.

Ranger's House

*Chesterfield Walk, SE10 8QX (8853 0035/www.
english-heritage.org.uk). Blackheath rail or Cutty Sark
DLR/53 bus.* **Open** *Mar-late Sept* 10am-5pm Wed-
Sun. *Oct-Dec* group bookings only. Closed Jan, Feb.
Admission (EH) £5.30; £2.70-£4 concessions; free
under-5s. **Credit** MC, V.

This grand, early 18th-century house, once occupied by the Earl of Chesterfield, became the official
residence of the Greenwich Park Ranger in 1815.
After spending much of the last century in local
council hands it was acquired by English Heritage
and opened in 2002 to display the treasures of one
Julius Wernher, who was born in Germany and
amassed a considerable fortune in South Africa.
Twelve rooms filled with Wernher's striking collection include sculpture, tapestries, paintings and
Renaissance jewellery.

Royal Observatory & Planetarium

*Greenwich Park, SE10 9NF (8312 6565/www.rog.
nmm.ac.uk). Cutty Sark DLR/Greenwich DLR/rail.*
Open 10am-5pm daily (last entry 4.30pm). *Tours*
phone for details. **Admission** free. *Tours* free.
Credit MC, V.

This Observatory – built by Wren for Charles II in
1675 – is the place to straddle the Prime Meridian
Line, with one foot in each hemisphere. The exhibition in this historic building is an absorbing history
of celestial study, where you can wonder at the great
brains of Copernicus, the persecuted Galileo, and
John Flamsteed, the first Astronomer Royal.
Elsewhere, there are cases of clocks and watches,
from hourglasses to atomic clocks. The dome houses the largest refracting telescope in the country. A
high-tech planetarium, teaching areas with links to
the National Schools Observatory and a new horol-
ogy centre are planned for spring 2007.

Charlton & Woolwich

*Charlton, Woolwich Arsenal or Woolwich Dockyard
rail.*

Until 1872 **Charlton** was famous for the rowdy
Charlton Horn Fair – a gift to the people from
King John as recompense for seducing a local
miller's wife. Today, Horn Fair Park boasts
one of the few 50-metre open-air swimming
pools in London (Charlton Lido; *see p329* **Take
the lidos**) and the historic manor **Charlton
House** (*see below*). Further north, Maryon Park
takes you up towards Woolwich and the life-
saving **Thames Barrier** (*see p172*).

Woolwich's former role was anchorage for
the hellish Victorian prison ships (described by
Charles Dickens in *Great Expectations*).Vessels
to take note of nowadays are the free Woolwich
ferries (8921 5786). They transport pedestrians
and cars every ten minutes, daily. If you take
the ferry to the north shore, you disembark
right by the **North Woolwich Old Station
Museum** (*see p167*) and **Royal Victoria
Gardens**. Britain's first McDonald's opened
on Woolwich high street in 1974.

Established in Tudor times as the country's
main source of munitions, by World War I the
Woolwich Arsenal stretched 32 miles along
the river, had its own internal railway system
and employed 72,000 people. Much of the land
was sold off during the 1960s, but thankfully
the main section, with its beautiful cluster of
Georgian buildings, has been preserved and is
now open to the public, as is **Firepower**, the
artillery museum (*see below*). For more on the
arsenal, visit the **Greenwich Heritage
Centre** (Artillery Square, Royal Arsenal,
SE18 4DX, 8854 2452; closed Mon, Sun).

Charlton House

*Charlton Road, SE7 8RE (8856 3951/www.
greenwich.gov.uk). Charlton rail/53, 54, 380, 422
bus.* **Open** *Library* 2-7pm Mon, Thur; 10am-12.30pm,
1.30-5.30pm Tue, Fri; 10am-12.30pm, 1.30-5pm Sat.
Toy library 10.30am-12.30pm, 1.30-3.30pm Mon, Tue,
Fri. **Admission** free.

From the outside, this Jacobean manor house looks
like the grandest of stately homes – which it once
was. Built in 1612, it housed the tutor of Henry,
eldest son of James I. These days it's a library and
community centre (concerts are held every Friday 1-
3pm), but glimpses of its glorious past can be seen
in the creaky oak staircase, marble fireplaces and its
mulberry tree, which dates back to 1608.

Firepower

*Royal Arsenal, SE18 6ST (8855 7755/www.fire
power.org.uk). Woolwich Arsenal rail.* **Open** *Nov-
Mar* 10.30am-5pm Fri-Sun (last entry 3.30pm). *Apr-
Oct* 10.30am-5pm Wed-Sun (last entry 3.30pm).
Admission (LP) £5; £2.50-£4.50 concessions; free
under-5s; £12 family. **Credit** MC, V.

The Royal Artillery Museum traces the evolution of artillery from primitive catapults to nuclear war-heads. By way of introduction to the Gunners and their history, visitors are treated to a seven-minute film in the Breech Cinema, before being bombarded by the sounds, smoke and searchlights of a multi-media presentation called 'Fields of Fire'. In the Gunnery Hall, you can get up close to all sorts of artillery, including anti-aircraft, anti-tank, and coastal defence, self-propelled guns and missile launchers. The Real Weapons gallery, meanwhile, has an interactive exhibition on how guns work, which uses ammo such as table tennis balls. Kids love the first-floor Command Post, with its climbing wall, air-raid shelters and paintball gallery. Special events take place throughout the year (check the website for details). There are various armoury dis-plays and demonstrations, gun salutes for royal occasions, musical nights and, from 20 October to 31 December 2006, a fireworks exhibition (including a grand display on Bonfire Night).

Thames Barrier Information & Learning Centre

1 Unity Way, SE18 5NJ (8305 4188/www. environment-agency.gov.uk). North Greenwich tube/ Charlton rail, 180 bus. **Open** *Apr-Sept* 10.30am-4.30pm daily. *Oct-Mar* 11am-3.30pm daily. Closed 2wks Easter. **Admission** *Exhibition* £1.50; 75p-£1 concessions; free under-5s. **Credit** MC, V.

The key player in London's flood defence system looks like a row of giant metallic shark's fins span-ning the 1,700ft Woolwich Reach. The barrier is the world's largest adjustable dam and was built in 1982 at a cost of £535m; since then it has saved London from flooding nearly 70 times. The small Learning Centre shows which parts of London would be sub-merged if it stopped working. Time your visit to see the barrier in action: every September there's a full-scale testing, with a partial test closure once a month (ring for dates). The best way to see the barrier is by boat: Campion Cruises (8305 0300/8858 3996) runs trips from Greenwich (Mar-Oct only).

Sightseeing

Iron man

Isambard Kingdom Brunel, who came second (after Winston Churchill) in a recent BBC poll of the Greatest Britons ever, was born in 1806, and events are taking place all over England in 2006 to mark his bicentenary. Over in west London, one of his original cast-iron bridges (the name 'Isambard' actually means 'man of iron') spanning the Grand Union Canal, dismantled and put into storage by English Heritage as part of the huge Paddington Bridge Project, should be reconstructed and in place in time for the actual anniversary on 9 April 2006.

But few places will have as much going on as the **Brunel Engine House & Tunnel Exhibition** (*see p168*), the museum dedicated to Brunel's first job – which almost killed him. He was working with his father, Marc Brunel, on the first ever tunnel to go under a river. Father and son pioneered a method of tunnelling used in every tube system since, internationally. The tunnel shield, a giant iron box, was pushed forward through the river mud, while diggers worked from cells inside the box, scooping out the soil that they accessed via removable wooden planks. While the shield was pushed forward, workers behind lined the tunnel walls with brick. The job was fraught with difficulties, both in terms of budget and public confidence. To allay doubts after the tunnel flooded in May 1827, the flamboyant Isambard organised a banquet under the

river for 50 guests. Eleven weeks later, however, the Thames broke into the tunnel again; young Brunel almost drowned, and the whole project was abandoned.

The Thames Tunnel from Rotherhithe to Wapping was eventually completed in 1843, thanks to powerful lobbying for a government loan from the Tunnel Club, which met at a nearby pub (now the Mayflower) to drink Marc Brunel's health on his birthday. The Thames Tunnel, originally a spacious walkway, shopping arcade and the 'Eighth Wonder of the World', is now the oldest tunnel in the oldest underground system in the world. Guided tours through it, by tube, are arranged by Robert Hulse, curator at the Brunel Engine House museum, as part of an inspired annual programme of events for 2006. On 25 March there's a tour to mark the tunnel opening; April sees a Brunel birthday party organised with the Design Museum (*see p91*); a garden party in May coincides with the anniversary of the great flood. Most ambitiously, a winter charity dinner is planned to commemorate that foolhardy underwater banquet in 1827. Meanwhile, keep your eyes peeled for the giant model of Isambard during July at the Rotherhithe Festival and Bermondsey carnivals (check the website for dates) and also during the Thames Festival in September (*see p269*). He's about 15 feet tall and wears an unfeasibly large stovepipe hat with steam coming out of it – you can't miss him.

Kennington & the Elephant

Kennington tube/Elephant & Castle tube/rail.
Once owned by the Duchy of Cornwall, Kennington Common (now **Kennington Park**) was the main place of execution for the county of Surrey. During the 17th and 18th centuries, preachers, notably John Wesley, addressed large audiences here. By the 19th century the common had been 'poisoned by the stench of vitriol works and by black open sluggish ditches', according to poet Thomas Miller. It's improved a bit since then. The laying out of the present park put an end to local cricket matches, which led to the founding of the Oval Cricket Club, still the home base of Surrey County Cricket. It's now called the **Brit Oval** (*see p328*), and is fast becoming a shrine to the 2005 Ashes victory over Australia.

Just across from Kennington tube station is the **Black Cultural Archives** (Othello Close, 7582 8516), which charts the history of black people in London and holds interesting historic exhibitions and art displays. A short walk north takes you to the **Imperial War Museum** (*see below*), beyond which lies the shambolic **Elephant & Castle**. The Elephant and Castle Regeneration scheme has earmarked £1.5 billion to transform this area into a smart new town centre by 2014, though some campaigners fear that the current diverse range of market traders and stallholders will be lost to a 'clone town' of chain stores and cafés.

Imperial War Museum

Lambeth Road, SE1 6HZ (7416 5000/www.iwm. org.uk). Lambeth North tube/Elephant & Castle tube/rail. **Open** 10am-6pm daily. **Admission** free. **Credit** MC, V. **Map** p406 N10.
In 1936 the central wing of the old Bethlehem Royal Hospital (Bedlam) became the Imperial War Museum. Its collection covers conflicts, especially those involving Britain and the Commonwealth, from World War I to the present day. The exhibits range from tanks, aircraft and big guns to photographs and personal letters. There are also film and sound recordings, and some of the 20th century's best-known paintings, among them John Singer Sargent's *Gassed*.

The lower-ground floor has both the smelly 'World War I Trench Experience' and the teeth-chattering 'Blitz Experience'. The 'Holocaust Exhibition', on the third floor, traces the history of anti-Semitism and the rise of Hitler. A vast collection of salvaged shoes, clothes, spectacles and testimonials from survivors break the heart. On the fourth floor, 'Crimes Against Humanity' (over-16s only), covering genocide and ethnic violence in our time, leaves you in no doubt about the pointlessness of war. Among the temporary exhibitions is 'Lawrence of Arabia', marking the 70th anniversary of the death of TE Lawrence, which runs until 17 April 2006.

Camberwell & Peckham

Denmark Hill or Peckham Rye rail.
Camberwell Green, not as cute as it sounds, is in fact rather a frantic crossroads from which, travelling west, you reach Kennington and the Oval (*see p328*). Choose east and you pass **St Giles's Church**, an imposing early Victorian structure by Sir George Gilbert Scott of St Pancras Station fame. Further towards Peckham lies **Camberwell College of Arts** (Peckham Road, 7514 6300), London's oldest art college, and the **South London Gallery** (*see p296*), two reasons why estate agents try to compare arty Camberwell with trendy Hoxton.

Linking Camberwell to Peckham, **Burgess Park** was created by filling in the Grand Surrey Canal and razing rows of houses. The nicest bit of the park is **Chumleigh Gardens**, where there are picturesque almshouses, gardens and a pleasant park café (7525 1070). Walking through it to **Peckham** takes you to a canal-path cycle route that runs past the increasingly tatty-looking, but much lauded **Peckham Library** (122 Peckham Hill Street), designed by Will Alsop. Follow chaotic Rye Lane south to the recently smartened **Peckham Rye Common**, an airy stretch with ornamental gardens. At the top, Honor Oak and Forest Hill look down over suburban south-east London and Kent. The **Horniman Museum** (*see below*) is the best reason for taking to these hills.

Horniman Museum

100 London Road, SE23 3PQ (8699 1872/www. horniman.ac.uk). Forest Hill rail/363, 122, 176, 185, 312, 356, P4, P13 bus. **Open** 10.30am-5.30pm daily. **Admission** free; donations appreciated. **Credit** MC, V.
Tea trader Frederick J Horniman assembled a great number of curiosities in this jolly art nouveau museum, which was left to the people of London in 1901. In the Natural History gallery, skeletons, pickled animals, stuffed birds and insect models in old-fashioned glass cases are all presided over by a plump stuffed walrus on a centre plinth. The African Worlds gallery has Egyptian mummies, ceremonial masks and a huge Ijele masquerade costume. Be sure to visit the fabulous Apostle clock on the gallery above the Natural History collection; when it chimes four o'clock, 11 apostles come out and bow to the central Jesus, while the 12th, Judas, turns away. Outside, there is a spacious café and lovely gardens with an animal enclosure. Due for completion in spring 2006, a £1.5m basement aquarium will display more than 250 different species of animals and plants in seven distinctive zones. Running until 31 October 2006 'Amazon to Caribbean: Early Peoples of the Rainforest', reveals the cultural links between early Amazonian cultures and the flourishing of Caribbean art and identity. **Photo** *p175*.

Sightseeing

Crystal Palace, East Dulwich, Herne Hill, North Dulwich or West Dulwich rail.

Comfortable **Dulwich Village**, with its pretty park (once a favourite duelling spot), is home to a historic boys' public school, founded by the actor Edward Alleyn in 1616, and the **Dulwich Picture Gallery** (*see below*). West of it, Herne Hill is like a halfway point between posh, white Dulwich and multicultural **Brixton** (*see p176*).

The **Crystal Palace**, built by Joseph Paxton for the Great Exhibition in Hyde Park in 1851, was subsequently moved here, and made Sydenham a tourist attraction, until the glittering structure burned down in 1936. The original terrace arches and the sphinx from the exhibition's Egyptian-themed area can still be seen. From here you look down on to our troubled **National Sports Centre**, whose lease the London Development Agency (LDA) will take over in February 2006. The centre sits in 200 acres of parkland, which is also soon to be in the hands of the LDA. When **Crystal Palace Park** was originally laid out in the 1860s, part of it was given over to the world's first **Dinosaur Park**, created by Benjamin Waterhouse-Hawkins and depicting a journey through prehistory via life-size dinosaur statues.

Since being refurbished and restored in 2003, these prehistoric beasts now pose menacingly around a freshly landscaped tidal lake, not far from the replanted **Hornbeam maze**. The **Crystal Palace Museum** (Anerley Hill, SE19 2BA, 8676 0700, open Sun) is volunteer-run and has a display on the 1851 Great Exhibition. A small John Logie Baird display marks its status as the birthplace of television. Its display on the great Exhibtion includes Victorian artefacts from the original Hyde Park production, as well as video and audio presentations about the great glass building and the Baird Television Company, which had studios at Crystal Palace.

Dulwich Picture Gallery

Gallery Road, SE21 7AD (8693 5254/www. dulwichpicturegallery.org.uk). North Dulwich or West Dulwich rail. **Open** 10am-5pm Tue-Fri; 11am-5pm Sat, Sun. **Admission** £4; £3 concessions; free under-16s, students, unemployed, disabled. **Credit** MC, V.

Sir John Soane's neo-classical building, which inspired the National Gallery's Sainsbury Wing and the Getty Museum in Los Angeles, was England's first public art gallery (1814). Inside is like a roll-call of the greats: Rubens, Van Dyck, Cuyp, Poussin, Rembrandt, Gainsborough, Raphael and Reynolds. Exhibitions for 2006 include a solo show of Winslow Homer (22 Feb-21 May); 'Rembrandt & Co – The Art of Business in the Ulyenburgh Workshop' (7 June-3 Sept) and Adam Elsheimer (20 Sept-3 Dec).

Watling Street, the old pilgrims' way out of London en route to Canterbury, is now the A207 and the villages it once passed through are London suburbs, such as **Bexleyheath**. This was where William Morris chose to settle in the **Red House** (*see p175*), the home designed for him by young architect Philip Webb. A short walk from the Red House, in gracious Danson Park, lies **Danson Mansion**, an 18th-century Palladian villa, restored by the **Bexley Heritage Trust** (01322 526574) and open to visitors at certain times. More award-winning gardens, this time containing a Tudor mansion, are at **Hall Place**, just up the road (Bourne Road, Bexley, Kent DA5 1PQ, 01322 526574, www.hallplaceandgardens.com).

South of the pilgrims' way, **Eltham** was well known to Londoners, particularly to Geoffrey Chaucer, who served as the clerk of works during improvements to **Eltham Palace** (*see below*) in the reign of Richard II. The poor clerk was mugged on his way to work there.

Paths around the area link up with the **Green Chain Walk** (8921 5028, www.greenchain.com), a 40-mile network starting near the **Thames Barrier** (*see p172*) and ending at **Crystal Palace** (*see above*), taking in ancient woodland along the way. Heading further south into Kent, the village of **Chislehurst** has Druids' caves (8467 3264, www.chislehurstcaves.co.uk) to tempt day-trippers underground.

Eltham Palace

Court Yard, SE9 5QE (8294 2548/www.english-heritage.org.uk). Eltham rail. **Open** *Apr-Oct* 10am-5pm Wed-Fri, Sun. *Nov-Dec* 10am-4pm Wed-Fri, Sun. *Feb-Mar* 10am-4pm. Closed last wk of Jan. **Admission** (EH) *House & grounds* (incl audio tour) £7.30; £3.70-£5.50 concessions; free under-5s; £18.30 family. *Grounds only* £4.60; £2.30-£3.50 concessions; free under-5s. **Credit** MC, V.

A magnificent royal residence from the 13th century through to Henry VIII's heyday, Eltham Palace fell out of favour in the latter part of Henry's reign, and its Great Hall was used as a barn for many years. In 1931 Eltham Palace came back into fashion, thanks to arts patrons Stephen and Virginia Courtauld. They commissioned a thoroughly modern house, among the relics of the old palace, and the luxurious art deco interior has been preserved and furnished by English Heritage. The Great Hall, with its stained-glass and intricate hammer beam roof, plus a 15th-century stone bridge over the moat and various medieval ruins, are all that's left of the royal original. The interior is all polished veneer and chunky marble. The extensive grounds are beautifully restored and the traditional tea room and shop have a 1930s flavour.

Red House

13 Red House Lane, Bexleyheath, Kent DA6 8JF
(01494 755588/www.nationaltrust.org.uk).
Bexleyheath rail then 15min walk or taxi from station.
Open (pre-booked guided tour only) *Oct-Feb* 11am-
3.30pm Wed-Sun. *Mar-Sept* 11am-4.15pm Wed-Sun.
Admission (NT) £6; £3 concessions; £15 family.
This handsome redbrick house was purchased by
the National Trust in 2003. It was built for William
Morris, whose Society for the Protection of Ancient
Buildings in 1877 eventually gave rise to the Trust
itself. In furnishing Red House, Morris sought to
combine his taste for Gothic romanticism with the
need for practical domesticity. Beautifully detailed
stained glass, tiling, paintings and items of furniture
remain in the house, but there is plenty being uncovered in the continuing restoration work. Fundraising
is an ongoing concern if Red House is to become one
more 'the beautifullest place on earth', as Sir Edward
Burne-Jones so eloquently put it.

The Natural History gallery and gardens of the **Horniman Museum**. *See p173.*

South-west London

From Brixton's raw urban edge to Kew's cultivated gardens.

Vauxhall, Stockwell & Brixton

Brixton or Vauxhall tube/rail/Stockwell tube.
You wouldn't know it to walk there today, but in the 18th century Vauxhall was London's playground. In *Vanity Fair*, William Thackeray describes the infamous Vauxhall Pleasure Gardens as a titillating place, where the wealthy mingled (briefly) with the not-so-wealthy, drinking themselves into oblivion while wandering past its exotic pavilions, listening to its orchestras, and getting themselves into all kinds of trouble on its so-dark-anything-could-happen 'lovers' walks'. Samuel Pepys summed it all up, in his usual laconic way, as 'mighty divertising'.

After the gardens closed in 1859, **Vauxhall** became a rather ordinary, middle-class neighbourhood of reasonable respectability, and not much has changed since then. It's somewhat telling that its grande dame is the crumbling **Royal Vauxhall Tavern** (*see p299* for Duckie club), behind which is a drab park called **Spring Garden** – it's all that remains of the Pleasure Gardens. For a glimpse of old Vauxhall, move on to lovely, leafy Bonnington Square, a bohemian enclave with a chilled café and lavender garden. That's more like it.

Down on the river, MI6's benign-looking cream and emerald headquarters dominates the waterfront in Vauxhall, as do the green apartment towers at the adjacent **St George's Wharf** – a glitzy apartment complex justifiably nicknamed the 'five ugly sisters'.

Heading south from Vauxhall, **Stockwell** is prime commuter territory, and there's not much to lure a visitor to its busy main streets, which hold an unappealing stretch of housing estates. If you persevere, though, you'll find that its backstreets are less grim, and some are even Victorian gems: **Albert Square**, **Durand Gardens** and **Stockwell Park Crescent** are all charming. In fact, Stockwell was good enough for Vincent Van Gogh, who lived briefly at 87 Hackford Road in the 1870s. Another of the area's attractions is South Lambeth Road's **Little Portugal**, where Portuguese cafés, shops and tapas bars cluster.

South of Stockwell, you can sense **Brixton** before you reach it: the boom-boom-boom of the music, the funky street vibrations – this is as cool as south London gets. It's an interesting, unpredictable area, with a vast street market, late-night clubs such as **The Fridge** (*see p321*) and live music venues like the **Carling Academy Brixton** (*see p311*), plus a vibrant Afro-Caribbean community.

The main streets are modern and filled with chain stores, but attractive architecture is dotted here and there – check out the splendid 1911 **Ritzy Cinema** (*see p288*). Brixton's best-known street, **Electric Avenue**, was immortalised during the 1980s by Eddy Grant's eponymous song – it got its name when it became one of the first shopping streets to have electricity; its lights were turned on in 1880.

Other well-known songs provide potted histories about Brixton: both the Clash's *Guns of Brixton* and the Specials' *Ghost Town* reference the rage that swept through the area in the 1980s, 30 years after a wave of immigrants arrived from the West Indies to find their opportunities limited and their faces often unwelcome. The riots of 1981 and 1985 around **Railton Road** and **Coldharbour Lane** left the area scarred for years.

Start your Brixton wandering near the chaotic mess of Brixton station, at the **Brixton Art Gallery** (35 Brixton Station Road, 7733 6957), which has an excellent and constantly changing collection of contemporary art, in particular ethnic works. Turn a corner from the station and you're in the noisy craze of the long, colourful **Brixton Market** (*see also p258*), which sells everything from kebabs to jewellery and bright African garb.

Watch your handbag as you stroll – purse snatchers and pickpockets are a problem here – and always take a cab at night. Gentrification is underway, and the fringes of Brixton hold some pricey real estate, but that hasn't pushed out the anarchists, criminals and artists that give this place both its buzz and its danger.

Battersea

Battersea Park or Clapham Junction rail.
Battersea's origins are humble: 1,000 years ago it was a small Saxon farming settlement ('Batrices Ege', or Badric's Island), and, until the 19th century, its chief occupation was market gardening. But times change, and now it's home to much of the city's yuppie population.

Age of treason

In America his name is synonymous with treason – someone who betrays you is 'a Benedict Arnold'. In Britain he's largely forgotten, but he's a fascinatingly conflicted historical figure – a man capable of winning wars, but destroyed by his own arrogance.

Born in 1741 to a well-off family in Connecticut, and educated in Canterbury, Arnold had connections on both sides of the Atlantic, but when the War for Independence broke out in 1775, he joined up with famed rebels Ethan Allen and the Green Mountain Boys, fighting the British at Fort Ticonderoga.

Arnold was wounded a few months later in a vicious battle against British forces in Quebec, and again a few months after that. But he fought on, becoming one of the top-ranking officers in the fledgling American forces. Viewed as the country's most daring, imaginative field officer, Arnold became famous in the embattled colonies. Success led to jealousy, however, and lesser officers conspired against him. In the middle of the battle at Saratoga in 1777, General Horatio Gates relieved Arnold of his command, ostensibly for insubordination, but really because he considered him 'a pompous little fellow'.

Still Congress promoted him to commandant after the battle, and his career continued. But Arnold was an arrogant man, and the humiliation at Saratoga rankled. He was angry at his treatment and irritated that he had not been promoted more quickly. At the same time, an active social life left him deeply in debt, and he engaged in shady business deals to make up the shortfalls. When those were investigated a few months later, he was court-martialled.

Facing financial ruin, and bitter over the collapse of his reputation, Arnold began writing to Sir Henry Clinton, the British commander. The two corresponded secretly in notes carried back and forth by the British Major John Andre, as Arnold offered to deliver to the British the American garrison at West Point, complete with its 3,000 soldiers, in return for £20,000. He hoped this move would cause the American side to collapse.

In 1780, as Arnold was putting his plan into action, Andre was arrested carrying Arnold's letters, concealed in his stockings. Andre was executed, while Arnold was spirited out of the country to England.

From then on Arnold fought against America, for Britain, with the same bravery and innovation he'd shown for the other side – looting provisions, burning towns, destroying ships. After the war, however, he was abandoned by the British government. While Arnold was not seen as a traitor in Britain, he was viewed as untrustworthy. Ultimately his business efforts collapsed, and when he died in 1801 he was forgotten, and virtually penniless. He's buried in the crypt of **St Mary's Battersea** (*see p179*), where few come to pay their respects.

(*see p179*)

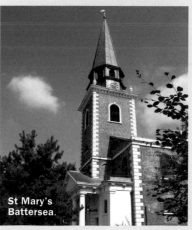

St Mary's Battersea.

Sightseeing

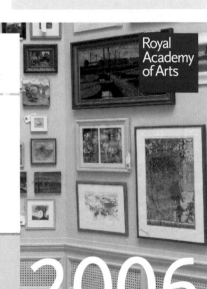

Its single most distinctive piece of architecture remains the gorgeous hulking ruin of **Battersea Power Station**. Designed by Sir Giles Gilbert Scott in 1933, the unmissible empty shell of a power generator has four brick towers with white caps, and stands just east of Chelsea Bridge – it can be seen from all trains leaving Victoria Station. It closed in 1983, but was too attractive to be destroyed. Still, until recently, no use had been found for it – now it's slated to be restored as a business and entertainment complex, and there's even talk of a hotel.

Near to the power station, the beautifully landscaped **Battersea Park** is filled with fountains, ponds and boating lakes. In 2004 it was relandscaped based on its original 19th-century plan, so what you see today is largely what the Victorians witnessed as they promenaded on sunny days. There are a few modern additions, of course: a **Peace Pagoda** (built by Japanese monks and nuns in 1985 to commemorate Hiroshima Day), and a small zoo (closed winter, 7924 5826; *see also p276*), and, just because it's Battersea, a tiny art gallery (the Pumphouse, 7350 0523). The park stretches all the way to the Thames, which has a wide riverside walk from which you can see both the elaborate **Albert Bridge** and the simpler, but lovely, **Battersea Bridge**, rebuilt in 1886-90 to Joseph Bazalgette's designs.

Further along the river is the wedge-shaped glass tower **Montevetro**. These high-tech luxury flats, designed by Richard Rogers, have been dubbed 'Monster Vetro' by some locals. By contrast, the adjacent **St Mary's Battersea** oozes historical grace: it was here that William Blake was married, American traitor Benedict Arnold was buried (*see p177* **Age of treason**), and JMW Turner came to paint the river.

Clapham & Wandsworth

Clapham Common tube/Wandsworth Common or Wandsworth Town rail.
Clapham first came of age in the 17th century, when plague racked the city and fire destroyed it, and Londoners fled in droves. Many people, including Samuel Pepys, settled here until things calmed down. In the 19th century the area was known for its 'Clapham Sect', a group of wealthy Anglicans who practised a muscular form of Christianity. By the 20th century Clapham was in decline, but an explosive burst of gentrification during the 1990s redeemed it as one of south London's most desirable addresses.

The heart of the neighbourhood is the green and pleasant **Clapham Common**, an oasis of peace surrounded by the roar of traffic. At its edge lies the **Holy Trinity Church**, where the Clapham Sect once worshipped enthusiastically. On sunny days the common is packed with joggers, footballers and sunbathers. However, a spate of violent homophobic attacks on the Common in 2005, including a murder, darkened the atmosphere somewhat.

From Clapham Common station, turn north into the street called The Pavement – it leads to the pubs and shops of Clapham Old Town. Alternatively, head south to Abbeville Road, the centre of **Abbeville Village**, with its endless array of smart shops and cafés.

The area to the west of the common is known (derisively by those who don't live there, ironically by those who do) as 'Nappy Valley', because of the many young middle-class families who reside there. They're out in force at weekends, pushing their prams. If you can fight your way between the baby carriages, head for **Northcote Road**, which has a good mix of shops, bars and restaurants. Try the superb Gourmet Burger Kitchen (No.44; *see also p208* **The burger kings**).

It's a short stroll from Northcote Road to **Wandsworth Common**, arguably prettier than Clapham's: the north-west side is dominated by a big old Victorian heap, the Gothic Royal Victoria Patriotic Building. It was originally an asylum for orphans of the Crimean War; during World War II it became a POW camp.

Putney & Barnes

East Putney or Putney Bridge tube/Putney or Barnes rail.
Peaceful, riverside **Putney** was chic in Tudor times, when it was home to Thomas Cromwell. The river has good, landscaped paths in either direction; heading west along the south side of the riverfront will take you past the **WWT Wetland Centre** (*see below*), which lies alongside **Barnes Common**. The main road across the expanse, **Queen's Ride**, humpbacks over the railway line below. It was here, on 16 September 1977, that singer Gloria Jones drove her Mini off the road, killing her passenger (and boyfriend), T-Rex singer Marc Bolan. The slim trunk of the sycamore tree hit by the car is covered with notes, poems and declarations of love; steps lead to a bronze bust of the curly-haired rockstar.

WWT Wetland Centre

Queen Elizabeth's Walk, SW13 9WT (8409 4400/ www.wwt.org.uk). Hammersmith tube then 283 bus/Barnes rail/33, 72 bus. **Open** *Mar-Oct* 9.30am-6pm daily (last entry 5pm). *Nov-Feb* 9.30am-5pm daily (last entry 4pm). **Admission** £6.75; £4-£5.50 concessions; £17.50 family; free under-4s. **Credit** MC, V.

A mere four miles from central London, the WWT Wetland Centre feels worlds away. Quiet ponds, rushes, rustling reeds and wildflower gardens teem with bird life – 150 species at last count. Botanists ponder its 27,000 trees and 300,000 aquatic plants; naturalists swoon at the 300 varieties of butterfly, 20 types of dragonfly, four species of bat and water vole. It wasn't always this pretty. Until 1989 the site consisted of four huge concrete reservoirs owned by the local water company. Then the naturalist Sir Peter Scott transformed the marshy space into a unique wildlife habitat. There are weekly activities here virtually year-round, and the attractive visitors' centre has a decent café with an outdoor terrace.

Kew & Richmond

Kew Gardens or Richmond tube/rail/Kew Bridge rail.
The leafy streets and rarefied air of **Kew** are almost as much of an attraction as its famed botanic gardens. It's a quaint world of teashops, florists, tiny bookstores and gift shops, and a lovely place to browse and wander past the expensive houses to the vast acreage of glorious **Kew Gardens** (*see below*).

The peace at Kew is only disturbed by the noise of 747s descending, one after another, en route to Heathrow Airport. The same planes destroy the carefully orchestrated local pretense that wealthy **Richmond**, about 15 minutes' walk west, down Kew Road, is a rural village. Otherwise, with its twisting narrow lanes, sweet village green, ancient pubs, and pleasant Thameside pathways, you might well be fooled.

Originally known as the Shene, the area has been linked with royalty for centuries: Edward III had a riverside palace here in the mid 1300s, and Henry VII loved it so much he built a palace here in 1501, naming it Richmond after his favourite earldom. Elizabeth I spent her last summers there, dying in 1603. Ultimately the whole neighbourhood took the palace's name, although the building itself is long gone – all that's left is a gateway on **Richmond Green**.

Once the site of royal jousting tournaments, the green is less noble now, but it's still a remarkably beautiful place, surrounded by gorgeous pre-Victorian architecture. On its east side narrow, medieval alleyways (such as Brewer's Lane) with ancient pubs tucked into every corner lead to the high street. Also of interest is the **Church of St Mary Magdalene**, on Paradise Road, with its curious blend of architectural styles ranging from 1507 to 1904. A short walk away in Richmond's Old Town Hall, the small **Museum of Richmond** (Whittaker Avenue, 8332 1141, www.museum ofrichmond.com, closed Mon, Sun) panders to a niche audience, with exhibits charting the town's development.

Nearby, the riverside promenade is eminently strollable and dotted with pubs, including the White Cross (8940 6844) with its special 'entrance at high tide' – the river floods regularly. This pub has watched the waters run by since 1835. **Richmond Bridge**, which, dating from 1774, is the oldest surviving crossing on the Thames, is surrounded by cafés and has magnificent, sweeping river views.

Richmond's biggest attraction is arguably the rugged **Richmond Park**. The largest park in the city, it's one of the last vestiges of the magnificent oak woodland that once dominated the countryside. Wonderfully uncultivated, it's suited to riding, rambling and off-road cycling. The park also forms a natural habitat for free-roaming herds of red and fallow deer. Amid its wilderness is **Pembroke Lodge**, the childhood home of philosopher Bertrand Russell (and now a café), and the Palladian splendour of **White Lodge**. Isabella Plantation offers a winding walk through landscaped gardens.

Royal Botanic Gardens (Kew Gardens)

Kew, Richmond, Surrey TW9 3AB (8332 5655/ information 8940 1171/www.kew.org). Kew Gardens tube/rail/Kew Bridge rail/riverboat to Kew Pier. **Open** *Late Mar-Aug* 9.30am-6.30pm Mon-Fri; 9.30am-7.30pm Sat, Sun. *Sept, Oct* 9.30am-6pm daily. *Late Oct-early Feb* 9.30am-4.15pm daily. *Early Feb-late Mar* 9.30am-5.30pm daily. **Admission** (LP) £10; £7 concessions; free under-16s. **Credit** AmEx, MC, V.
Kew's lush, landscaped beauty represents the pinnacle of the English gardening obsession. From the early 1700s until 1840, when the gardens were given to the nation, these were the grounds for two royal residences – the White House and Richmond Lodge. 18th-century residents Henry II and Queen Caroline were enthusiastic gardeners; Caroline was particularly fond of exotic plants brought back by voyaging botanists, and had a series of temples built around the grounds. In the mid 1700s, Lancelot 'Capability' Brown began designing an organised layout for the property, using the plants she had collected. Thus began the extraordinary collection that today attracts hundreds of thousands of visitors every year.

At 300 acres, Kew is enormous, so pick up a map at the ticket office, and follow the handy signs. The tourist train from Victoria Gate provides a 35-minute tour of the gardens' highlights (£3.50; £1 concessions). Any visit to Kew should take in the two huge 19th-century greenhouses filled to the roof with plants – some of which have been here as long as the fanciful glass structures. The sultry Palm House holds tropical plants – palms, bamboo, tamarind, mango and fig trees, not to mention fragrant hibiscus and frangipani. The Temperate House features the pendiculata sanderina, the Holy Grail for orchid hunters, with petals that are three feet long. Also of note is the Princess of Wales Conservatory, which houses ten climate zones under one roof.

Hampton Court Palace. *See p183*.

For an interesting perspective on 17th-century life, head to Kew Palace – the smallest royal palace in Britain. Once little more than an addition on the now-gone White House, it's a lovely structure that was due to reopen in early/mid 2006 after years of renovation. Queen Charlotte's Cottage, with its dazzling springtime bluebell garden, repays returning to year after year. Outside, the Rose Garden and Woodland Garden has a treetop walkway 33 feet high. All this walking may make you hungry: luckily, there are tearooms scattered throughout, including the impressive Orangery restaurant.

Wimbledon

Wimbledon tube/rail.
Once the annual tennis tournament (*see p330*) is over, wealthy suburban **Wimbledon** reverts to leafy, sleepy type. Running up the steep hill from the station to Wimbledon High Street, there is a picturesque road dotted with posh shops, pubs and restaurants.

Wimbledon Common, a huge, wild, partly wooded park, is criss-crossed by paths and horse tracks. In an eccentric touch, the common has a windmill housing a tearoom and hands-on milling museum (Windmill Road, 8947 2825). For something stronger, a couple of pubs provide refreshment: the Fox & Grapes (Camp Road, 8946 5599) and Hand in Hand (6 Crooked Billet, 8946 5720) are both excellent choices. East of the common is **Wimbledon Park**, with its boating lake and the **All England Lawn Tennis Club** and **Wimbledon Lawn Tennis Museum** (*see below*).

Tooting, an up-and-coming area east of Wimbledon, has been optimistically billed 'the New Clapham' by estate agents. But it's certainly true that **Tooting Common**, with its retro lido (*see p329* **Taking the lidos**), rivals its more famous neighbour. And though the area has a way to go in terms of trendy bars and eateries, it is renowned for its Indian restaurants. Two of the best are Radha Krishna Bhavan (86 Tooting High Street, 8767 3462) and Kastoori (188 Upper Tooting Road, 8767 7027).

Design historians should make a pilgrimage to **Colliers Wood**: bizarrely, this bland suburb was once the Arts and Crafts capital of the world. In 1881 William Morris opened his textiles workshops here, taking advantage of the rushing River Wandle for power. When Morris died, another textiles legend moved in: Arthur Liberty (of Regent Street fame). To see his old workshops, follow the river path down to **Merton Abbey Mills**, a quaint enclave famous for its weekend market. The William Morris pub (8540 0216) sits prettily on the river by the waterwheel.

Wimbledon Lawn Tennis Museum

Centre Court, All England Lawn Tennis Club, Church Road, SW19 5AE (8946 6131/www. wimbledon.org/museum). Southfields tube/39, 93, 200, 493 bus. **Open** 10.30am-5pm daily; ticket holders only during championships. Closed until spring 2006. **Admission** (LP) incl tours £14.50; £11-£13 concessions; free under-5s. **Credit** AmEx, MC, V.
From the starchy, serious-looking Victorian players to the foul-mouthed celebrities of today, this popular museum traces the history of tennis. Items on show include dresses worn by the Williams sisters and Boris Becker's shoes. A theatre replays classic matches and a gallery showcases tennis-related art from across the generations. Note that, aside from a display of trophies, the museum is closed until spring 2006, but in the meantime the guided tours (£6.50; £3.75-£5.50 concessions) will continue, from a temporary visitors' centre on site.

Further south-west

If the water table allows, follow the river from Richmond on a pastoral walk west to **Petersham**, home to the glorious **Petersham Nurseries** (8940 5230), with its lovely café (*see p220*), and **Ham**, or take in one of the grand country mansions, among them **Ham House** (*see below*) and **Marble Hill House** (*see p183*), in Marble Hill Park. Next to the park stands **Orleans House Gallery** (*see p183*).

Further along, the river meanders around **Twickenham** (home to Twickenham Stadium and its **Rugby Museum**; *see p183*) to the evocatively named **Strawberry Hill** (8240 4114), a Gothic Revival building that was once the home of Horace Walpole, author of *The Castle of Otranto*. Several miles further along, after a leisurely trip through suburban **Kingston**, the river arrives at the glorious **Hampton Court Palace** (*see p183*) – but if you want to go, take the train.

Ham House

Ham, Richmond, Surrey TW10 7RS (8940 1950/ www.nationaltrust.org.uk/hamhouse). Richmond tube/rail then 371 bus. **Open** *Gardens* 11am-6pm or dusk if earlier Mon-Wed, Sat, Sun. *House* 1-5pm Mon-Wed, Sat, Sun. Closed Nov-Mar. **Admission** *House & Gardens* £8; £4 concessions; £19 family; free under-5s. *Gardens only* £4; £2 concessions; £9 family; free under-5s. **Credit** MC, V.
Built in 1610 for one of James I's courtiers, this lavish red-brick mansion is an outstanding Stuart property, filled with period furnishings, rococo mirrors and ornate tapestries. Detailing is exquisite, down to a table in the dairy with sculpted cows' legs. The formal grounds attract the most attention: there's a trellised Cherry Garden dominated by a statue of Bacchus. The tearoom in the old orangery turns out historic dishes (lavender syllabub, for instance) using ingredients from the Kitchen Gardens.

Hampton Court Palace

East Molesey, Surrey KT8 9AU (0870 751 5175/ 24hr information 0870 752 7777/advance tickets 0870 753 7777/www.hrp.org.uk). Hampton Court rail/riverboat from Westminster or Richmond to Hampton Court Pier (Apr-Oct). **Open** *Palace* Apr-Oct 10am-6pm daily. Nov-Mar 10am-4.30pm daily (last entry 1hr before closing). *Park* dawn-dusk daily. **Admission** (LP) *Palace, courtyard, cloister & maze* £12; £9 concessions; £7.80 concessions; £35 family; free under-5s. *Maze only* £3.50; £2.50 concessions. *Gardens only* £4; £2.50-£3 concessions. **Credit** AmEx, MC, V.

Primarily remembered for chopping off Anne Boleyn's head, having six wives and bringing about the Reformation, Henry VIII is one of history's best-known monarchs. This Tudor palace is a suitably spectacular monument to him. It was built in 1514 by Cardinal Wolsey, Henry's high-flying lord chancellor, but Henry liked it so much he seized it for himself in 1528. For the next 200 years it was a focal point in English history: Elizabeth I was imprisoned in a tower here by her jealous and fanatical elder sister Mary I; Shakespeare gave his debut performance to James I here in 1604; and after the Civil War, Lord Protector Oliver Cromwell was so besotted by the building that he ditched his puritanical principles and moved in.

Centuries later, the rosy walls of the palace still dazzle. Its vast size can be daunting, so why not take advantage of the costumed guided tours? If you do decide to go it alone, it's probably best to start with King Henry VIII's State Apartments, which include the Great Hall, noted for its splendid hammerbeam roof, beautiful stained-glass windows and elaborate religious tapestries; in the Haunted Gallery, the ghost of Catherine Howard – Henry's fifth wife, executed for adultery in 1542 – can reputedly be heard shrieking and forever trying to flee.

The King's Apartments, added in 1689 by Sir Christopher Wren, are notable for a splendid mural of Alexander the Great, painted by Antonio Verrio. The Queen's Apartments and Georgian Rooms feature similarly elaborate paintings, chandeliers and tapestries. The Tudor Kitchens are great fun, with their giant cauldrons, fake pies and blood-spattered walls (no vegetarians in those days).

More spectacular sights await outside, where the exquisitely landscaped gardens include perfectly sculpted trees, peaceful Thames views, and the famous Hampton Court maze (in which, incidentally, it's virtually impossible to get lost). Just outside its borders, visitors can hire a horse and carriage for a ride through Hampton Court Park. **Photo** *p181.*

Marble Hill House

Richmond Road, Twickenham, Middx TW1 2NL (8892 5115/www.english heritage.org.uk). Richmond tube/rail/St Margaret's rail/33, 90, 490, H22, R70 bus. **Open** *Apr-Sept* 10am-2pm Sat; 10am-5pm Sun; group visits Mon-Fri by request. *Oct* 10am-4pm daily. *Nov-Mar* by request. **Admission** £4; £2-£3 concessions; free under-5s. **Credit** MC, V.

Ah, royal love. King George II spared no expense to please his mistress, Henrietta Howard. Not only did he build this perfect Palladian house (1724) for his lover, he almost dragged Britain into a war while doing so: by using Honduran mahogany to construct the grand staircase, he sparked a diplomatic row with Spain. In retrospect, it was worth it. Over the centuries, this stately mansion has welcomed the great and the good: luminaries such as Alexander Pope, Jonathan Swift and Horace Walpole were all entertained in the opulent Great Room. Pope and Swift are said to have drunk the cellar dry. Picnic parties are welcome; so are athletes (there are tennis, putting and cricket facilities). A programme of concerts and events keeps things humming in the summer. Ferries regularly cross the river to neighbouring Ham House (*see p182*).

Orleans House Gallery

Riverside, Twickenham, Middx TW1 3DJ (8831 6000/www.richmond.gov.uk/orleans_house_gallery). Richmond tube then 33, 490, H22, R68, R70 bus/ St Margaret's or Twickenham rail. **Open** *Apr-Sept* 1-5.30pm Tue-Sat; 2-5.30pm Sun. *Oct-Mar* 1-4.30pm Tue-Sat; 2-4.30pm Sun. **Admission** free. **Credit** MC, V.

Secluded in six acres of gardens, this lovely Grade I-listed riverside house was constructed in 1710. It was built for James Johnson, the then-secretary of state for Scotland, and was named after the Duke of Orleans, Louis-Philippe, who lived here between 1800 and 1817 in exile from Napoleonic France (he later returned and claimed the throne). Although it was partially demolished in 1926, the building retains James Gibbs's neoclassical Octagon Room, housing the impressive Richmond-upon-Thames art collection, a soothing pictorial record of the surrounding countryside from the early 1700s to the present. Pre-book a workshop and do some painting of your own, if you wish.

Rugby Museum/ Twickenham Stadium

Twickenham Rugby Stadium, Rugby Road, Twickenham, Middx TW1 1DZ (8892 8877/ www.rfu.com). Hounslow East tube then 281 bus/Twickenham rail. **Open** *Museum* 10am-5pm Tue-Sat; 11am-5pm Sun (last entry 4.30pm). *Tours* 10.30am, noon, 1.30pm, 3pm Tue-Sat; 1pm, 3pm Sun. **Admission** £9; £6 concessions; £30 family. **Credit** AmEx, MC, V.

The impressive Twickenham Stadium is the home of English rugby union. Tickets for international matches are extremely hard to come by, but this little museum offers some compensation. Tours take in the England dressing room, the players' tunnel and the Royal Box. A permanent collection of memorabilia, chosen from among the museum's 10,000-piece collection, charts the game's development from the late 19th century. It includes the oldest surviving international rugby jersey, and the Calcutta Cup, awarded annually to the winners of the Scotland-England match. Video snippets recall classic matches; a simulated scrum machine tests your strength.

Sightseeing

West London

With everything from Holland Park highlife to Chiswick's riverside tranquillity, it's the not-so-wild west.

'The west is the best.' That's what Jim Morrison claimed. Admittedly, later in the song he wants to kill his father and do something even more unnatural to his mother, so perhaps he cannot be regarded as authoritative. But the Lizard King was not the first to advocate the path of the setting sun: that road was taken by the sainted king, Edward the Confessor, who built the first Palace of Westminster upstream and upwind of the City. Ever since then London has moved steadily westwards along the banks of the Thames, spreading away from the water as alternative modes of transport developed. Now the city stretches amoeba-like along the major trunk routes to the west, a vast sprawl of suburban homes and industry. But there are sights, smells and sounds to be appreciated by the more intrepid or energetic visitor.

Paddington & Bayswater

Maps p396 & p397
*Bayswater, Lancaster Gate or Queensway tube/
Paddington tube/rail.*
The fact that a certain small, ursine Peruvian (*see p189* **Please look after this bear**) who immortalised **Paddington** was an émigré is appropriate, given that the area has long served as a home to refugees and immigrants. But the district owes its name to an Anglo-Saxon chieftain named Padda. He founded a settlement near the junction of the (originally Roman) Edgware and Bayswater roads. The legions had long since left, but the roads remained as paths through the renewed forest and from them farmers and axemen dug and cut the new settlement. Paddington stayed a country village until the 19th century; there are records dating from 1168 which record the farmers 'de Padintune' who rented the land from Westminster Abbey. The Crown seized the area after the Reformation and in 1550 Edward VI granted it to the Bishop of London, although over following centuries much of it came under the control of the Frederick family.

Paddington, now a very mixed borough, had its first brush with multiculturalism when it accommodated refugees from England's oldest enemy: France. Huguenots arrived in the 18th century. Not surprisingly, immigrants tend to settle around transport hubs, and Paddington has many. First came the Grand Junction Canal in 1801, linking London to the Midlands. Then, in 1838, that symbol of Victorian innovation, the railway. Indeed, Paddington was the terminus of Queen Victoria's first train trip, but it was Prince Albert who was not amused. 'Not so fast next time, Mr Conductor,' he requested. The current station was built in 1851 to the specifications of the great Isambard Kingdom Brunel (*see p172* **Iron man**), with wonderful ironwork decorations created by MD Wyatt. The triple roof of iron and glass is a particularly fine example of Victorian engineering.

Good infrastructure, including the later unlovely Westway, meant Paddington played host to further waves of immigrants: Greeks and Jews in the 19th century, followed by West Indians, Asians and Arabs in the 20th. In the 1950s there was poverty and overcrowding, but the area's proximity to central London meant property developers recognised its potential and the builders duly moved in. The slick **Paddington Central** development is a case in point: with its one million square feet of office space, canalside apartments and health club, it's a typical upmarket urban complex.

West of Paddington is **Bayswater**, an area of grand Victorian housing, much of which has been converted into flats and hotels. **Queensway**, the vertical spine of the area, was originally called Black Lion Lane but was later renamed in honour of Queen Victoria. At the southern end, the ice rink (17 Queensway, 7229 0172, www.queensiceandbowl.co.uk) is where many a London child first slip-slides away, while, near the top end of the street, the bustling Whiteleys shopping centre (7229 8844, www.whiteleys.com) was once a grand department store whose founder, William Whiteley, rather grandly used to call himself 'the Universal Provider'. Heading north over the junction with Bishops Bridge Road is the **Porchester Spa** (7792 3980; *see also p255*), one of the few surviving examples of the Victorian Turkish baths that once proliferated in Britain. For a more cultural experience head down Moscow Road to the Greek Orthodox cathedral of **St Sophia** (7729 7260, www.stsophia.org.uk, open 11am-2pm Mon, Wed-Fri, and for services) where Byzantine icons and golden mosaics glow in the candlelight.

Paddington Central. *See p184.*

A left at the top of Queensway takes you to **Westbourne Grove**, which has some fine restaurants and, at its posher western end, a good selection of small boutiques and galleries exuding the whiff of money. As this guide went to press, a new addition to the area was about to open: the **Museum of Brands, Packaging & Advertising** (Colville Mews, W11, www. museumofbrands.com), which aims to show how people's lives have changed over the past 200 years through the evolution of consumer brands. For a guided stroll of the area, *see p190* **Walk on**.

Alexander Fleming Laboratory Museum

St Mary's Hospital, Praed Street, W2 1NY (7886 6528/www.st-marys.nhs.uk/about/fleming_museum. htm). Paddington tube/rail. **Open** 10am-1pm Mon-Thur; by appointment 2-5pm Mon-Thur; 10am-5pm Fri. **Admission** £2; £1 concessions; free under-5s. **No credit cards. Map** p397 D5.

When Sir Alexander Fleming noticed the death of staphylococcus bacteria on a discarded petri dish, humanity was handed a powerful weapon against such enemies as pneumonia and tuberculosis. This room, where the groundbreaking 1928 discovery took place, preserves many artefacts from Fleming's day.

Maida Vale & Kilburn

Kilburn, Kilburn Park, Maida Vale or Warwick Avenue tube/Kilburn High Road or Brondesbury rail.
Running north-west from Marble Arch, the undeviating progress of **Edgware Road** gives a clue to its provenance: yes, the Romans laid it. It soon changes its name, first to Maida Vale and then Kilburn High Road. **Maida Vale** commemorates an 1806 victory over the French at Maida in southern Italy. The most rewarding area for exploration lies down Maida Avenue, alongside Regent's Canal. With the proximity of housing and water, this affluent area is known as **Little Venice**; the towpath is a relaxing route to Regent's Park, although you'll have to negotiate a tunnel under Maida Vale and St John's Wood which has no towpath.

North of Elgin Avenue the streets are lined with red-brick Edwardian apartment blocks, while **Paddington Recreation Ground** can claim a slice of athletics history: this is where medical student Roger Bannister trained before breaking the four-minute mile on 6 May 1954. Walking north along Kilburn Park Road brings you to **Kilburn High Road** and its pubs. This area was synonymous with the Irish in London in the 1960s and '70s, but more recently new waves of immigrants from Eastern Europe and North Africa have arrived. It's still a good place for a St Patrick's Day pub crawl, though, while the **Tricycle** theatre excels at most things cultural (*see p342*).

Notting Hill

Map p396

Notting Hill Gate, Ladbroke Grove or Westbourne Park tube.
There's a bit of an incline along Ladbroke Grove and Campden Hill Road, but Notting Hill isn't exactly hilly; knobbly is more like it. The mystery is partially resolved on learning that the area's original name, recorded in 1356, was *Knottynghull* – unfortunately, no one today knows what that means. Its modern cognate is clear, though: outrageously expensive housing exploiting the lingering street cred of the rapidly disappearing working-class residents. Still, there's much to appreciate in an area where many people look and act like they're permanently auditioning for *Notting Hill 2*.

The view from Notting Hill Gate is none too promising, but turn right up Pembridge Road, then left into Portobello Road and it becomes more interesting. The name honours the capture of Porto Bello from the Spaniards in 1739. No.22 has a blue plaque commemorating the residency of George Orwell, but the main reason to visit the winding Portobello Road is simply to shop.

Around the junction with Westbourne Grove are antiques stores, while fruit and veg stalls take over near Talbot Road. Heading further north and beneath the Westway for clothes stalls and (on Fridays and Saturdays) a flea market (*see p258*). It's also home to Lisboa Pâtisserie, one of the best Portuguese delis in London (57 Golborne Road, 8968 5242).

Trellick Tower, the concrete tower block at the north-eastern end of Golborne Road, divides opinion, but, love it or hate it, it's a significant piece of Brutalist architecture. Its designer, Ernö Goldfinger, not content with inflicting modernism on hapless council tenants, also demolished some fine Victorian properties to make way for his own home at Willow Road, Hampstead (*see p186*). A disgusted neighbour sought revenge by using Goldfinger's name as the villain in his latest book. The neighbour was Ian Fleming. When Ernö threatened to sue, the author enquired whether he would prefer James Bond's nemesis to be called 'Goldprick'. They settled out of court and the architect was immortalised as the man who 'loves only gold'.

Anyone hoping to bump into Hugh Grant or Julia Roberts while browsing through old copies of *Arabian Sands* should turn off Portobello Road and into Blenheim Crescent. At Nos.13-15 is the Travel Bookshop (7229 5260), the store that inspired *Notting Hill*'s bibliotech.

Towards the end of August, the famous **Notting Hill Carnival** (*see p269*) is an open invitation to drink beer and jubilate alongside its pulsating sound systems. Introduced in 1959 as a celebration of the West Indian immigrants who first moved to the area in the 1950s, the carnival continues despite many of those immigrants having long been priced out of the area. At the top end of Ladbroke Grove, meanwhile, is the famously spooky **Kensal Green Cemetery** (*see below*).

Kensal Green Cemetery

Harrow Road, Kensal Green, W10 4RA (8969 0152/www.kensalgreen.co.uk). Kensal Green tube. **Open** *Apr-Sept* 9am-6pm Mon-Sat; 10am-6pm Sun. *Oct-Mar* 9am-5pm Mon-Sat; 10am-5pm Sun. *Tours* 2pm Sun; tours incl catacombs 2pm 1st & 3rd Sun of mth. **Admission** free. *Tours* £5 donation; £4 concessions. **No credit cards.**
Behind the neo-classical gate is a green oasis of the dead. The resting place of both the Duke of Sussex, sixth son of King George III, and his sister, HRH Princess Sophia, was the place to be buried in the 19th century. Wilkie Collins, Anthony Trollope and William Makepeace Thackeray all lie here, but it is the mausoleums of lesser folk that make the most-eyecatching graves (bring a torch with you). If you're a big fan of graveyard architecture, *see also p155* **The Magnificent Seven**.

Portobello Market – blindingly good stuff. *See p186.*

Kensington & Holland Park

Maps pp396-398

High Street Kensington or Holland Park tube.
Across the road from Notting Hill Gate, a ten-minute walk down Kensington Church Street brings you to the old money. Recorded as Chenesit in the Domesday survey of 1086, it was a site of market gardens until the 19th century. For the rich and the noble, **Kensington** also allowed the building of country estates without the tiresome need for days spent travelling to get to or from London. Holland House was constructed in about 1606, while in 1689 William III commissioned Sir Christopher Wren to turn his newly purchased Nottingham House into the more appropriately regal Kensington Palace. Despite these aristocratic residences the area remained largely rural until the early 1800s, with a population of less than 10,000. By 1901 this had grown to 176,628.

Today **Kensington High Street** is lined by upmarket chains; just off it are roads and squares of beautiful 19th-century houses. **Kensington Church Street** is peppered with shops selling antique furniture. **St Mary Abbots**, at the bottom of the street, is a superb Victorian neo-Gothic church. Built by Sir George Gilbert Scott in 1869-72 on the site of the original 12th-century church, it has beautiful stained-glass windows that include the 'Healing' window funded by the Royal College of Surgeons.

Best of all, though, is **Kensington Square**, just behind the art deco Barkers department store, with its high density of blue plaques. Before his final home in Kensal Green Cemetery, Thackeray lived at No.16. The painter Edward Burne-Jones resided at No.41 and at No.18 John Stuart Mill's maid accidentally burnt the only copy of Thomas Carlyle's manuscript *The French Revolution*. Mrs Patrick Campbell, the actress and famous beauty, lived at No.33.

A little to the west is one of London's finest green spaces, **Holland Park**. At its heart is Holland House, which was originally built in 1606. After visiting in 1612, King James I complained that his sleep was disturbed by the wind blowing through the walls, while many years later the house was further ventilated by World War II bomb damage. Left derelict, it was bought by the London County Council in 1952. Only the ground floor, arcades, east wing and gateway survived. The east wing now houses the most exclusively sited youth hostel in town. In summer open-air theatre and opera are performed on the house's front terrace, while the garden ballroom is a Marco Pierre White restaurant, the Belvedere (off Abbotsbury Road, 7602 1238).

Three beautiful formal gardens are located close to the house; a bit further away is the Japanese-style Kyoto Garden, with huge koi carp and a charming bridge at the foot of a waterfall. Elsewhere rabbits hop freely (dogs must be kept on a lead) and peacocks strut about. There is a special playground for under-5s and an adventure playground for older kids. Disappear down one of the greenly lit paths further afield and it's like exploring ancient wildwood. Close by are two historic houses worth visiting, **Leighton House** and **Linley Sambourne House** (for both, *see below*).

Leighton House

12 Holland Park Road, W14 8LZ (7602 3316/www.rbkc.gov.uk/leightonhousemuseum). High Street Kensington tube. **Open** 11am-5.30pm Mon, Wed-Sun. *Tours* 2.30pm Wed, Thur; also by appointment (min group of 12). **Admission** £3; £1 concessions. **Credit** MC, V. **Map** p398 A9.
An under-appreciated gem, Leighton House was the home and studio of the artist Frederic, Lord Leighton (1830-96). He designed the place, which rather suggests that his tastes were influenced by Moroccan bordellos, but it certainly makes a change from Victorian chintz. A classicist, Leighton drew up to 50 preparatory sketches that honed his vision before reaching for the oils. Alongside his works are those by contemporaries John Everett Millais and Edward Burne-Jones. The garden is a serene spot to rest your weary feet.

Ten minutes' walk away is Linley Sambourne House (18 Stafford Terrace), the home of cartoonist Edward Linley Sambourne. The house was built in the 1870s and has almost all of its original fittings and furniture. Tours must be booked in advance (through the Leighton House switchboard).

Earl's Court & Fulham

Map p398

Earl's Court or Fulham Broadway tube/West Brompton tube/rail.
Earl's Court sells itself short, grammatically speaking. It should be Earls' Court, since it was once the site of the courthouse of both the Earl of Warwick and the Earl of Holland. But, let's face it, what's a misplaced apostrophe next to deportation and decapitation?

The 1860s saw Earl's Court move from rural hamlet to investment opportunity as the Metropolitan Railway was built. Twenty years later it was much as we see today, except for the kebab shops and fast food joints. In 1937 the **Earl's Court Exhibition Centre** was constructed, at that time the largest reinforced concrete building in Europe – a phrase that hardly makes one's heart sing. It hosts a year-round calendar of events, from trade shows, pop concerts (Pink Floyd built up and then tore

Please look after this bear

King's Cross Station may have platform 9¾, but Paddington has a bear. Paddington Bear, from Darkest Peru. However, unlike in the story, Michael Bond first met Paddington in Selfridges. It was Christmas Eve, 1957, and he was looking for a present for his wife, Brenda, when he chanced upon 'a small bear, looking, I thought, very sorry for himself as he was the only one who hadn't been sold'. Bond took the bear home and, some months later, sitting in front of his typewriter, he wrote: 'Mr and Mrs Brown first met Paddington on a railway platform. In fact, that was how he came to have such an unusual name for a bear, for Paddington was the name of the station.'

Bond had served in the army during World War II. He still had vivid memories of columns of refugees trudging along dusty roads, leaving behind everything they had once known, and evacuated children with labels tied around their necks and all their possessions in tiny suitcases. The small bear, sitting outside the Lost Property Office at Paddington Station, was just like that (apart from the fact that he was a bear, that is).

Although Paddington was in many ways a furry wartime refugee, the world in which Bond placed him was more reminiscent of England between the wars. When Mr and Mrs Brown took Paddington home to No.32 Windsor Gardens (Lansdowne Crescent in Bond's mind), he found the sort of middle-class household that no longer seems to exist. The children, Judy and Jonathan, both boarded at public schools, while Mrs Bird, the housekeeper, was based on a familiar pre-war figure: a widow to the Great War, reduced to making ends meet by housekeeping for distant relatives.

In fact, the terrible conflicts of the 20th century cast their long shadows on the books. Wanting a character who could understand something of what it was like for Paddington to find himself a stranger in a strange land, Bond introduced the bear to Mr Gruber, the Hungarian keeper of an antiques shop on the Portobello Road. Michael Bond had met many Hungarians during his time working for the BBC Monitoring Service, and had been impressed with their kindness and philosophical approach to life's hardships. Paddington and Mr Gruber, like so many exiles, would sit and talk for hours of their lost homes, although they tended to prefer cocoa and buns to the more usual cigarettes and coffee.

But despite the loss that's hinted at in the books, Paddington remains a kind and thoughtful bear throughout, a reminder of a now-distant England, where people raised their hats before saying 'Good afternoon,' and always said 'After you.' But lest politeness be mistaken for weakness, beware Paddington's hard stare, calculated to produce an uncomfortable blush in even the most supercilious of officials.

Walk on into the Grove

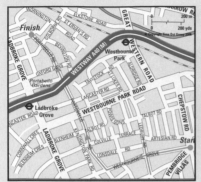

Start: Chepstow Corner, W2.
Finish: Portobello Road, W11.
Length: A mile and a quarter.
Not so long ago, shoppers ventured to Westbourne Grove in search of antique tables instead of designer labels. Blame it on the hype generated by *Notting Hill*, but these days you can hardly move for posh boutiques in the area. But the good news is that it's more fun shopping here than Knightsbridge or Bond Street; there's an interesting mix of quirky independents and upmarket chains. The bad news: you may need to clear purchases with your bank manager.

If you're heading towards Notting Hill along Westbourne Grove, things start to get interesting at Chepstow Corner (the corner of Chepstow Road and Westbourne Grove). Here you'll find a huge branch of cult toiletries store **Space NK** (complete with spa; *see also p255*); **Bill Amberg**'s gorgeous leather accessories and bags (21-22 Chepstow Corner, 7727 3560), and **Sweaty Betty** (2A Chepstow Road, 7727 8646), home of hip sportswear and yoga gear.

Heading westwards, take a short detour north to British perfumer **Miller Harris** at 14 Needham Road (7221 1545). More luxury scents and candles are to be had back on the Grove at **Diptyque** (No.195, 7727 8673), while across the street is jet-set holiday boutique **Heidi Klein** (No. 174, 7243 5665). Next door, at No.176, **Feathers** (7243 8800) is just one of the numerous designer outposts in the vicinity – if it's luxe labels you're after, also check out **Question Air** at No.229 (7221 8163);

Ledbury Road's **Matches** empire (Nos.60-64, 83 & 85, 7221 0255) and **JW Beeton** (Nos.48-50, 7229 8874).

Ledbury Road is a shopping trip in itself. Heading south, you come to the brilliantly named **VPL** (No.61A, 7221 6644), home of pretty camisoles and flirty knickers; over the road is **J&M Davidson** (No.42, 7313 9532), selling beautifully crafted, retro-inspired bags, clothes and homewares; **Aimé** at No.32 (7221 7070), a repository of slightly boho French chic for you and your home; and **Bodas** (No.38B, 7229 4464), which stocks undies.

Back on Westbourne Grove, heading up on the left side of the street before it forks, is the first stand-alone UK branch of funky San Francisco-born cosmetic company **Benefit** (No.227, 7243 7800); two doors along is **Themes & Variations** (No.231, 7727 5531), showcasing post-war and contemporary furniture and decorative art. If you choose the right-hand side of the road you'll come to **Dinny Hall** (No.200, 7792 3913), **Jigsaw** (Nos.190-192, 7727 0322), and, across from the **Wild at Heart** flower stall on the traffic island – **Joseph** (No.236, 7243 9920).

If you're up for a longer walk, there are further gems in every direction; our pick of the bunch is girlie boutique **Coco Ribbon** (21 Kensington Park Road, 7229 4904). At the weekend, root out vintage finds and items by up-and-coming designers at Portobello Green Market under the Westway flyover; the famous Saturday antiques market (*see p258*) is more southerly. Even further north on Portobello, past Golborne Road, are a couple of hip shops worth the walk – indie shoe queens **Olivia Morris** (No.335, 8962 0353) and Lagos-born designer Duro Olowu's cool studio/boutique, **OG2** (No.367, open by appointment only, so call first, on 8960 7570).

One thing's for sure – you won't be short of places to eat and drink round here. Tip-top delis are the mainstay: on Westbourne Grove there's **Tavola**, owned by restaurateur Alastair Little (No.155, 7229 0571) and **Tom's** (No.226, 7221 8818), frequented by celebs, while Ledbury Road has achingly cool deli/café **Ottolenghi** (No.63, 7727 1121; *see also p213*). **The Grocer on Elgin** (6 Elgin Crescent, 7221 3844) is popular for its seasonal, handmade ready meals, while **Hummingbird Bakery** (133 Portobello Road, 7229 6446) does brilliant cup cakes.

down *The Wall* here) to the Ideal Home Show. The area's large period houses are now mostly bedsits and cheap hotels, many inhabited by young Australians, the returning descendants of those once sentenced to deportation.

In contrast to Earl's Court, nearby **Parsons Green** airbrushes the apostrophe from its history entirely. The 'Green' of its name once supported a parson, but it later became known as the aristocratic end of Fulham. **Fulham** itself derives its name from Fulla's settlement and was a 'great fruit and kitchen garden', interspersed with the fine homes of rich Londoners seeking clean air away from the city's reek.

Fulham Palace

Bishop's Avenue, off Fulham Palace Road, SW6 6EA (7736 3233). Putney Bridge tube. **Open** *2-4pm Sat; phone to check. Tours 2pm 2nd & 4th Sun of mth.* **Admission** *free; under-16s must be accompanied by adult. Tours £3; free under-16s.* **No credit cards**.
The foundations of Fulham Palace can be traced back to 704, when the property was granted to Bishop Wealdheri. Tours of the palace as it stands now – a hotchpotch of architectural styles, having been the home of successive Bishops of London for around 700 years – are only available on certain Sundays. For the rest of the time, a small museum housing a number of artefacts goes a little way towards satiating curiosity.

Shepherd's Bush & Hammersmith

Goldhawk Road, Hammersmith, Shepherd's Bush or White City tube.
Frankly, it's hardly worth bothering with **Shepherd's Bush**. There's the triangular green, an eight-acre patch of grass hemmed in by traffic, the Bush Theatre (*see p341*), the Shepherd's Bush Empire (*see p312*) and that's about it. North of Shepherd's Bush is **White City**, home of BBC Television Centre. To date, none of the Corporation's many mediacracies has ended up in the other famous institution in the area, Wormwood Scrubs prison.

Walk south down Shepherd's Bush Road and you'll see Hammersmith's dominating architectural feature: the grey concrete flyover. The A4, or Great West Road, is one of the main trunk routes into London, with thousands of cars and lorries thundering along it each day. In the flyover's shadow, **Hammersmith Broadway** was once a bus garage but after a multi-million pound redevelopment now includes offices and a shopping mall. Cross the road – carefully – for the Carling Apollo (*see p311*), Lyric Hammersmith (*see p342*) and Riverside Studios (*see p289*), between them meeting your musical, theatrical and

cinematic needs, respectively. Meanwhile, **Hammersmith Bridge**, the city's oldest suspension bridge, is a green and gold hymn to Victorian ironwork, and a good place to access the riverside path to Chiswick.

BBC Television Centre Tours

Wood Lane, W12 7RJ (0870 603 0304/www.bbc. co.uk/tours). White City tube. **Tours** *by appointment only Mon-Sat.* **Admission** *£8.95; £6.50-£7.95 concessions; £25 family. Under-9s not allowed.* **Credit** *MC, V.*
Tours of the BBC include visits to the news desk, the TV studios and the Weather Centre, though you must book ahead to secure a place. To be part of a TV audience, log on to www.bbc.co.uk/whatson/ tickets, where you can apply for free tickets.

Chiswick

Turnham Green tube/Chiswick or Kew Bridge rail.
Walking the riverside path from Hammersmith to Chiswick is a lesson in transport history. To your left is the Thames, now quiet apart from the occasional rowing eight. To your right is the Great West Road and its constant traffic stream. Above, the main flight path into Heathrow Airport. Should the walk produce a thirst, never fear. As Benjamin Franklin said, 'Beer is proof that God loves us and wants us to be happy' – just off Chiswick Mall on Chiswick Lane South is **Fuller's Griffin Brewery**. There's been a brewery here since Elizabethan times, so the brewers have had the chance to get it right: we recommend a pint of London Pride.

Cross (under) the A4 to **Hogarth's House** (*see p192*) and the rather grander **Chiswick House** (*see below*). A bus is the easiest way to reach **Kew Bridge Steam Museum** (*see p192*), although it is possible to rejoin the river path after visiting Chiswick House, walking via the mini village of **Strand on the Green**, where willows line the river. Further upstream, overlooking **Kew Gardens** from the opposite side of the river, is **Syon House** (*see p192*).

Chiswick House

Burlington Lane, W4 2RP (8995 0508/www.english-heritage.org.uk). Turnham Green tube, then E3 bus to Edensor Road/Hammersmith tube/rail then 190 bus/Chiswick rail. **Open** *10am-5pm Wed-Fri, Sun; 10am-2pm Sat. Closed Nov-Mar.* **Admission** *(EH) £4; £2-£3 concessions; free under-5s.* **Credit** *MC, V.*
Richard Boyle, third Earl of Burlington, designed this lovely Palladian villa in 1725 as a place to entertain artists and writers. Sculptures by Rysbrack of Burlington's heroes, Inigo Jones and Palladio, stand in front of the house. William Kent was responsible for much of the interior. The gorgeous reception rooms interconnect with a magnificent central saloon. The grounds are a triumph of early 18th-century garden design, with many stately cedars.

Hogarth's House

Hogarth Lane, Great West Road, W4 2QN (8994 6757/www.hounslow.info/hogarthshouse). Turnham Green tube/Chiswick rail. **Open** *Apr-Oct* 1-5pm Tue-Sun. *Nov, Dec, Feb, Mar* 1-4pm Tue-Fri; 1-5pm Sat, Sun. Closed Jan **Admission** free; donations appreciated. **No credit cards.**

Despite the proximity of the A4, Hogarth's House has a garden tranquil enough for you to appreciate that this was the country retreat of 18th-century painter, engraver and social commentator, William Hogarth. On display are most of his engravings, including *Gin Lane, Marriage à la Mode* and a copy of *Rake's Progress.* Hogarth's grave lies just a few minutes' walk away at St. Nicholas's Church, while his mulberry tree, now almost 300 years old, still survives in the garden.

Kew Bridge Steam Museum

Green Dragon Lane, Brentford, Middx TW8 0EN (8568 4757/www.kbsm.org). Gunnersbury tube/rail/Kew Bridge rail/65, 237, 267, 391 bus. **Open** 11am-5pm daily. **Admission** *Mon-Fri* £4.25; £3.25 concessions; free under-16s. *Sat, Sun* £5.75; £4.75 concessions; free under-16s. **Credit** MC, V.

Housed in a Victorian pumping station, this museum explores the city's use of water, and exhibits a huge and fascinating range of the steam engines used to transport water round the city. One highlight is a walk through a section of the London ring main waterpipe, another is when the engines are in steam (weekends, 11am-5pm). Special events frequently include access to their 196ft- (60m-)high tower; booking is essential and children are not allowed to ascend the 261 steps to the top.

Syon House

Syon Park, Brentford, Middx TW8 8JF (8560 0883/www.syonpark.co.uk). Gunnersbury tube/rail then 237, 267 bus. **Open** *House* late Mar-Oct 11am-5pm Wed, Thur, Sun. *Gardens* year-round 10.30am-dusk daily. *Tours* by arrangement. **Admission** *House & gardens* £7.50; £6.50 concessions; £17 family. *Gardens only* £3.75; £2.50 concessions; £9 family. *Tours* free. **Credit** MC, V.

The Percys, Dukes of Northumberland, sure know a film tie-in when they see one. Their Northumbrian home, Alnwick Castle, stood in for Hogwarts in *Harry Potter and the Philosopher's Stone*, while Syon House took a starring role in *Gosford Park*. The house stands on the site of a Bridgettine monastery, which was suppressed by Henry VIII in 1534. The nun's father confessor, Richard Reynolds, refused to accept the King as head of the church and was executed. The building was turned into a house in 1547 for the Duke of Northumberland, and its neo-classical interior was created by Robert Adam in 1761. The gardens were designed by Lancelot 'Capability' Brown. Paintings by Van Dyck, Gainsborough and Reynolds hang inside. Other attractions include the London Butterfly House (8560 7272), the Tropical Experience (8847 4730), an indoor adventure playground and a trout fishery.

Further west

Ealing Studios put the westerly suburb of **Ealing** on the map. A team of filmmakers and developers owns the old site, where classic comedies *Kind Hearts and Coronets, The Ladykillers* and *Passport to Pimlico* were produced, and has converted the historic buildings into offices and production units. Movies aside, Ealing offers **Pitzhanger Manor (PM) Gallery & House** (*see below*). Further west still, in the middle of **Osterley Park**, is **Osterley House** (*see below*), another Robert Adam undertaking.

Just north of here, **Southall** is home to many Indian immigrants. The **Gurdwara Sri Guru Singh Sabha Southall** is the largest Sikh place of worship outside India. Don a headscarf – which is provided if you don't have one to hand – and remove your shoes to enter. Free vegetarian food is available to all visitors in the langar, the communal kitchen.

Neasden is famous for the multi-billion-rupee **Shri Swaminarayan Mandir Hindu** temple. It required 5,000 tons of marble and limestone and the work of around 1,500 craftsmen. Modest attire is strongly advised. For details, check www.mandir.org. To the west lies **Wembley Stadium** (*see p327*).

Osterley House

Osterley Park, off Jersey Road, Isleworth, Hounslow, Middx TW7 4RB (8232 5050/www.nationaltrust.org.uk/osterley). Osterley tube. **Open** *Park* year-round 9am-7.30pm (dusk if earlier) daily. *House* Mar 1-4.30pm Sat, Sun. Apr-Oct 1-4.30pm Wed-Sun. **Admission** (NT) *House* £4.90; £2.40 concessions; £12.20 family. *Park* free.

In 1761 Scottish architect Robert Adam was commissioned to transform Osterley from a crumbling Tudor mansion into a swish neo-classical villa. He did so in spectacular style, creating friezes, pilasters and ornate ceilings over the course of 19 years. For details of events run by the National Trust, call or check the website. The Jersey Galleries have contemporary art exhibitions from March to October.

PM Gallery & House

Walpole Park, Mattock Lane, Ealing, W5 5EQ (8567 1227/www.ealing.gov.uk/pmgallery&house). Ealing Broadway tube/rail. **Open** *May-Sept* 1-5pm Tue-Fri; Sun; 11am-5pm Sat. *Oct-Apr* 1-5pm Tue-Fri; 11am-5pm Sat. *Tours* by arrangement. **Admission** free.

Aside from one early wing (the west one) designed by George Dance, Pitzhanger House is the work of Sir John Soane, who bought the building as his weekend retreat in 1800 and then rebuilt it. The daughters of Britain's only assassinated Prime Minister, Spencer Perceval, moved into Pitzhanger House in 1843. Now it houses contemporary art exhibitions, and the largest collection of Martinware pottery in the country – 264 unique items (about 100 on show).

Eat, Drink, Shop

Restaurants & Cafés

It's official: London has the best food in the world.

It was quite a coup when, in 2005, *Gourmet*, the world's leading food magazine, named London the best place to eat in the world. We couldn't agree more: the number of outstanding restaurants in this city keeps on growing each year, and in all areas of town. The roll call for the past year includes **The Ledbury**, **Santa María del Buen Ayre** and **Princess**, none of which are in the West End, but all of which have proved a hit with diners. Likewise, Borough Market's culinary dominance continues apace, with the opening of **Tapas Brindisa**, and, as this guide went to press, **Roast** (Floral Hall, Stoney Street, 7940 1300), serving British fare.

Neither do celebrity chefs seem in danger of shrinking from the scene. On the contrary: London recently witnessed the opening of Gary Rhodes' **Rhodes W1**, and **Maze**, yet another Gordon Ramsay venture, cheffed by Jason Atherton (*see also p219* **Stars and their pies**). Likewise, London will always have its celebrity magnets – sister restaurants **The Ivy**, **The Wolseley** and **J Sheekey**, as well as **Locanda Locatelli**, **Nobu** and Gordon Ramsay's eponymous outposts – but even these are restaurants of substance. Quite simply, there has never been a better time to eat in this town.

DOS AND DON'TS

It's always best to book in advance where possible. Some establishments are entirely non-smoking and others allow smoking anywhere (though this will change in summer 2007, when smoking will be banned in places serving food); some set aside sections for smokers. Tipping is standard practice; ten to 15 per cent is usual. Some restaurants add service to the bill, so double-check or you may accidentally tip twice.

We've listed a range of meal prices for each place. However, restaurants often change their menus, so these prices are only guidelines. Many restaurants also have set meals: we have only listed these when more conventional à la carte menus are not offered.

For the best places to eat with kids, *see p274*; for more on eating out in London, buy the annual *Time Out Eating & Drinking Guide* (£10.99) and *Time Out Cheap Eats in London* (£6.99). For more gastropubs, *see pp222-234*.

The best Restaurants

For a taste of old England
St John (*see p197*); Sweetings (*see p197*).

For eating on a tight budget
Haché (*see p208*); Mandalay (*see p220*); Sea Cow (*see p217*); Sông Quê (*see p217*); Story Deli (*see p214*); Sardo (*see p201*).

For gourmet vegetarian food
Gordon Ramsay at Claridge's (*see p205*); Morgan M (*see p213*); Salt Yard (*see p201*).

For a pre-/post-dinner bite
Anchor & Hope (*see p216*); Christopher's (*see p210*); Livebait (*see p195*); Noura Central (*see p205*); J Sheekey (*see p209*).

For West End shopping & lunching
Busaba Eathai (Bird Street branch; *see p201*); Food for Thought (*see p210*); Salt Yard (*see p201*).

For a lazy weekend brunch
Flâneur Food Hall (*see p197*); Frizzante@ City Farm (*see p214*); Smiths of Smithfield (*see p200*); Story Deli (*see p214*).

The South Bank & Bankside

Cafés & brasseries

Konditor & Cook
10 Stoney Street, SE1 9AD (7407 5100/www.konditorandcook.com). London Bridge tube/rail. **Open** 7.30am-6pm Mon-Fri; 8.30am-4pm Sat. **Main courses** £2.10-£4.75. **Credit** AmEx, MC, V. **Map** p406 P8 ❶
Famed for excellent cakes, this delightful mini chain is a one-stop spot for indulgence of both the sweet and savoury kind (pastas, soups, pizza squares). Great for takeaway lunches and hampers.
Other locations: throughout the city.

❶ Purple numbers given in this chapter correspond to the location of each restaurant and café as marked on the street maps. *See pp396-409.*

Tate Modern Café: Level 2

*2nd Floor, Tate Modern, Sumner Street, SE1
9TG (7401 5014/www.tate.org.uk). Southwark
tube/London Bridge tube/rail.* **Open** 10am-5.30pm
Mon-Thur, Sun; 10am-9.30pm Fri, Sat. **Main
courses** £6.50-£9.50. **Credit** AmEx, DC, MC, V.
Map p406 O8 **②**
With three separate daytime menus (breakfast,
lunch and tea) – as well as tapas when the museum
is open late on Fridays and Saturdays – this café
offers plenty of choice from its modern British menu
(poached salmon, corn-fed chicken, fish and chips).

Fish

Livebait

*43 The Cut, SE1 8LF (7928 7211/www.sante
online.co.uk/livebait). Southwark tube/Waterloo tube/
rail.* **Open** noon-11pm Mon-Sat; 12.30-9pm Sun.
Main courses £9.75-£29. **Credit** AmEx, DC,
MC, V. **Map** p406 N8 **③**
Livebait dishes up simple shellfish platters and more
elaborate fish dishes in café environs. This branch's
great location, coupled with good-value set menus,
make it a handy pre- or post-event stop-off.
Other locations: throughout the city.

Gastropubs

Anchor & Hope

See p216 **Reinventing the meal.**

Global

Baltic

*74 Blackfriars Road, SE1 8HA (7928 1111/
www.balticrestaurant.co.uk). Southwark tube.
Restaurant* **Open** noon-3pm, 6-11.15pm Mon-Sat;
noon-10.30pm Sun. **Main courses** £9.50-£15.
Credit AmEx, MC, V. **Map** p406 N8 **④**
Baltic's spacious interior, complete with a 'wall of
amber' bar, makes a terrific setting for its varied,
modern menu and efficient waiting staff. The food is
a rare combination for an eastern European restaurant: both adventurous and authentic.

Glas

*3 Park Street, SE1 9AB (7357 6060/www.glas
restaurant.com). Borough tube/London Bridge
tube/rail.* **Open** noon-2.30pm, 6.30-10pm Tue-Fri;
1-10pm Sat. **Main courses** £3.95-£8.95. **Credit**
MC, V. **Map** p406 P8 **⑤**
Glas is, as expected, undeniably Swedish. The
smörgåsbord-style menu offers an enticing range of
tapas-like dishes of distinctly Scandinavian flavour
but with a modern twist.

Spanish

Tapas Brindisa

*18-20 Southwark Street, SE1 1TJ (7357 8880/
www.brindisa.com). London Bridge tube/rail.*

Baltic.

Open 11am-11pm Mon-Thur; 9am-11pm Fri,
Sat. **Tapas** £3-£6.75. **Credit** MC, V. **Map** p406
P8 **⑥**
This top-rate tapas bar perched on the edge of
Borough Market sets the benchmark for others of
its kind. Showcasing produce on sale at Brindisa's
stall in Borough Market and shop in Clerkenwell (32
Exmouth Market, EC1), it conjures quintessentially
Spanish fare with gusto and flair.

The City

Cafés & brasseries

De Gustibus

*53-55 Carter Lane, EC4V 5AE (7236 0056/www.
degustibus.co.uk). St Paul's tube/Blackfriars tube/
rail.* **Open** 7am-5pm Mon-Fri. **Main courses**
£4.95-£7.25. **Credit** MC, V. **Map** p406 O6 **⑦**
This award-winning baker supplies upmarket
restaurants with a mouthwatering range of artisan
breads, which also make up deep filled sandwiches
and accompany own-made soups. De Gustibus also
boasts a great salad bar, and serves up hearty full
English breakfasts too.
Other locations: 53 Blandford Street, Marylebone,
W1U 7HL (7486 6608); 4 Southwark Street, Borough,
SE1 1TQ (7407 3625).

Fish

Fishmarket

*Great Eastern Hotel, Bishopsgate, EC2M 7QN (7618
7200/www.fish-market.co.uk). Liverpool Street
tube/rail.* **Open** noon-2.30pm, 6-10.30pm Mon-Fri.
Main courses £11.50-£28. **Credit** AmEx, DC, MC,
V. **Map** p407 R6 **⑧**

delicious noodles

fabulou rice dishes

wines, sake, japanese beers

fast, fresh & friendly

clean, healthy & non smoking

bloomsbury WC1A
4 streatham st
tube ı tottenham court road

soho W1
10 lexington st
tube ı oxford st
piccadilly circus

west end W1
101 wigmore st
tube ı bond st

camden NW1
11 jamestown rd
tube ı camden town

kensington W8
26 high st kensington
tube ı high st kensington

knightsbridge SW1
harvey nichols
tube ı knightsbridge

covent garden WC2E
1 tavistock st
tube ı covent garden
/ charing cross

leicester square WC2H
14a irving st
tube ı leicester square

haymarket SW1
8 norris st
tube ı piccadilly circus

moorgate EC2
ropemaker st
tube ı moorgate
open: mon-fri

fleet street EC4
109 fleet st
tube ı st pauls
open: mon-fri

liverpool st EC2
old broad st (by tower 42)
tube ı liverpool st / bank
open: mon-fri

islington N1 0PS
N1 centre parkfield st
tube ı angel

canary wharf E14
jubilee place
tube ı canary wharf

tower hill
tower place (off lower thames st)
tube ı tower hill

mansion house EC4
4 great st thomas apostle
(off queen st & garlick hill)
open: mon-fri
tube ı mansion house

brent cross
shopping centre NW4
tube ı brent cross

putney SW15
50-54 high street
putney mainline station

richmond TW9 1SX
3 hill st
tube ı richmond tube

wimbledon SW19
wimbledon high rd
tube ı wimbledon tube

southbank SE1
royal festival hall
tube ı embankment /
waterloo

borough SE1
clink st (opposite vinopoli
tube ı london bridge

victoria SW1
cardinal walk
cardinal place
tube ı victoria

www.wagamama.c

One of the most pleasurable restaurants in the Conran empire, this sleek eaterie serves everything from oysters to lobsters. Enjoy the top-quality ocean-fodder at the dramatic, marble-topped counter in the airy bar or the smart, calming dining room.

Sweetings

39 Queen Victoria Street, EC4N 4SA (7248 3062). Mansion House tube. **Open** 11.30am-3pm Mon-Fri. **Main courses** £10.50-£24.50. **Credit** AmEx, MC, V. **Map** p406 P6 **9**
Comfortably old school, Sweetings' dishes comprise good – sometimes excellent – unfussy, fishy fare, accompanied by buttered sliced bread and washed down with silver tankards of British ales.

French

Le Coq d'Argent

1 Poultry, EC2R 8EJ (7395 5000/www.conran.com). Bank tube/DLR. **Open** *Bar & grill* 11.30am-3pm Mon-Fri. *Restaurant* 7.30-10am, 11.30am-3pm, 6-10pm Mon-Fri; 6.30-10pm Sat; noon-3pm Sun. **Main courses** *Bar & grill* £12-£16. *Restaurant* £15-£23. **Credit** AmEx, DC, MC, V. **Map** p406 P6 **10**
The regional French cooking here is as much a magnet as the luxuriant setting and spectacular roof-top location. Popular with business types during the day and well-heeled diners after office hours.

Mediterranean

Bar & Grill

2-3 West Smithfield, EC1A 9JX (0870 442 2541/ www.barandgrill.co.uk). Farringdon tube/rail. **Open** noon-midnight Mon-Thur; noon-1am Fri; 5pm-1am Sat. **Main courses** £6.75-£45. **Credit** AmEx, MC, V. **Map** p404 O5 **11**
This striking newcomer is a meat-eaters' delight. Pick from an exotic choice of steaks – including ostrich and Kobe – then choose your own rub and sauce. Pizzas, fish dishes and burgers are served alongside the expensive fleshy delights.

Eyre Brothers

70 Leonard Street, EC2A 4QX (7613 5346/www. eyrebrothers.co.uk). Old Street tube/rail. **Open** noon-3pm, 6.30-11pm Mon-Fri; 6.30-11pm Sat. **Main courses** £13-£25. **Credit** AmEx, DC, MC, V. **Map** p405 Q4 **12**
This joint's subtle, retro style combined with the Eyre brothers' fondness for Spanish flavours and Portuguese regional cooking make this a top-notch and unapologetically hearty dining experience.

Oriental

City Miyama

17 Godliman Street, EC4V 5BD (7489 1937). St Paul's tube/Blackfriars tube/rail. **Open** noon-2pm, 6-9.30pm Mon-Fri; 6-9.30pm Sat. **Main courses** £9-£25. **Credit** AmEx, DC, MC, V. **Map** p406 O6 **13**

Excellent (if expensive) sushi and nigiri are served on silver-brushed lacquerware, with menu choices including grilled black cod in miso sauce. **Other locations**: 38 Clarges Street, Mayfair, W1Y 7EN (7499 2443).

K-10

20 Copthall Avenue, EC2R 7DN (7562 8510/ www.k10.net). Moorgate tube/rail. Restaurant **Open** 11.30am-3pm Mon-Fri. **Main courses** £1.25-£5. **Credit** AmEx, MC, V. **Map** p407 Q6 **14**
A cut above most other kaiten contenders, this tiny, ground-floor takeaway gives no clue to the hi-tech kaiten-zushi bar that occupies the busy basement below. Watch as dishes fly past on the conveyor belt. **Other locations**: Northern Line Arcade, Moorgate Underground Station, EC2M 6TX (7614 9910).

Holborn & Clerkenwell

British

Medcalf

40 Exmouth Market, EC1R 4QE (7833 3533). Angel tube/Farringdon tube/rail. **Open** noon-11pm Mon-Thur, Sat; noon-12.30am Fri; noon-5pm Sun. **Main courses** £8.50-£12. **Credit** MC, V. **Map** p404 N4 **15**
This great local also attracts diners and drinkers from further afield. Set in a former butcher's shop, Medcalf is a fine purveyor of top-quality British food and a louche vibe that effortlessly masquerades as a drinking den after ten, once the kitchen shuts.

St John

26 St John Street, EC1M 4AY (7251 0848/4998/ www.stjohnrestaurant.com). Farringdon tube/rail. **Open** noon-3pm, 6-11pm Mon-Fri; 6-11pm Sat. **Main courses** £13-£21. **Credit** AmEx, MC, V. **Map** p404 O5 **16**
St John prides itself on winkling out forgotten regional dishes (gizzards, chitterlings) and creating riffs on well-worn classics (gooseberry fool with toasted brioche). Both here and at sister site, ingredients are seasonal, with cakes and breads for sale at the latter. **Other locations**: St John Bread & Wine, 94-96 Commercial Street, Spitalfields, E1 6LZ (7247 8724).

Cafés & brasseries

Flâneur Food Hall

41 Farringdon Road, EC1M 3JB (7404 4422). Farringdon tube/rail. **Open** noon-3pm, 6-10pm Mon-Fri; 6-10pm Sat. *Brunch served* 9am-4pm Sat, Sun. **Main courses** £8.50-£15.50. **Credit** AmEx, DC, MC, V. **Map** p404 N5 **17**
Lined with tall shelves packed full of well-sourced gourmet products, this gorgeous food hall-cum-restaurant is a foodies' treat. Also offered are fine wines, baked goods, cheeses, charcuterie and deli dishes to take away or eat in at the stylish tables.

Ultimate Burger

See p208 **The burger kings.**

Eat, Drink, Shop

Fish & chips

Fish Central

*149-151 Central Street, EC1V 8AP (7253 4970).
Old Street tube/rail.* **Open** 11am-2.30pm, 4.45-
10.30pm Mon-Sat. **Main courses** £4.95-£10.90.
Credit AmEx. MC, V. **Map** p404 P3 ⑬
As its fresh, modern-looking decor suggests, Fish
Central is more than a local chippie. This Hellenic-
run business also does rather fine steaks, sausages
and seared tuna. But despite the calibre of the extras,
the fresh fish and chips reign supreme.

French

Club Gascon

*57 West Smithfield, EC1A 9DS (7796 0600).
Barbican tube/Farringdon tube/rail.* **Open** noon-
2pm, 7-10pm Mon-Thur; noon-2pm, 7-10.30pm Fri;
7-10.30pm Sat. **Main courses** £8.30-£20. **Tapas**
£6-£16.50. **Credit** AmEx, MC, V. **Map** p404 O5 ⑭
Pascal Aussignac's accomplished eaterie is plush
and clubby, fitting for a foie gras specialist. The
restaurant serves imaginative concoctions with
witty presentation. Tasting courses start at £38.

Gastropubs

Coach & Horses

*26-28 Ray Street, EC1R 3DJ (7278 8990/www.
thecoachandhorses.com). Farringdon tube/rail.*
Open 11am-11pm Mon-Fri; 6-11pm Sat; noon-
3pm Sun. **Main courses** £10.50-£14. **Credit**
AmEx, MC, V. **Map** p402 N4 ⑳
Expect reliably delicious, unfussy dishes at this
charmingly updated (as opposed to refurbished) and
award-winning gastropub. The ingredients are lov-
ingly selected, and the interesting wine list shows
that real effort has been made with the drinks too.

Eagle

*159 Farringdon Road, EC1R 3AL (7837 1353).
Farringdon tube/rail.* **Open** noon-11pm Mon-Sat;
noon-5pm Sun. **Main courses** £5-£15. **Credit**
MC, V. **Map** p404 N4 ㉑
The flavours are big and brash, and the cooking
style mixes simple Mediterranean fare with hearty
British staples. But with its dedication to offering
decently priced seasonal food, this slightly raffish
local is not only London's first gastropub (*see p216*
Reinventing the meal), it continues to be one of
the city's best.

Easton

*22 Easton Street, WC1X 0DS (7278 7608/www.
theeaston.co.uk). Farringdon tube/rail.* **Open** noon-
11pm Mon Thur; 12.30pm-1am Fri; 5.30pm-1am Sat;
noon-10.30pm Sun. **Main courses** £5.95-£12.95.
Credit MC, V. **Map** p404 N4 ㉒
With its lovely retro wallpaper, pub-style tables and
a menu scrawled on a blackboard, this buzzy local
looks a top gastropub; majoring in interesting,

Princess.

generously portioned dishes packed with flavour, it
tastes like one too. Staff are young and seem infinitely
good-natured. A companionly vibe usually builds up
over the course of an evening.

Peasant

*240 St John Street, EC1V 4PH (7336 7726/
www.thepeasant.co.uk). Angel tube/Farringdon
tube/rail.* **Open** noon-11pm daily. **Main courses**
£9-£15. **Credit** AmEx, DC, MC, V. **Map** p404 O4 ㉓
The Peasant's cosy downstairs, with its battered
sofas and welcoming fireplace, is the perfect place
to share sumptuous bar snacks. Upstairs there's a
posher dining space, which makes a lovely setting
for sampling the diverse, uniformly top-notch menu.
The only difficulty is choosing which you'd prefer.

Princess

*76 Paul Street, EC2A 4NE (7729 9270). Old
Street tube/rail.* **Open** noon-11pm Mon-Fri; 5.30-
11pm Sat; noon-5.30pm Sun. **Credit** AmEx, MC,
V. **Map** p405 Q4 ㉔
You can feast like royalty in this appropriately
named gastropub. The smart upholstered chairs,
florid wallpaper and a fireplace create a comfortable
dining area in which to enjoy Italian starters, mains
from the Mediterranean and excellent international
wines. **Photo** *above.*

Sardo. *See p201.*

Modern European

Smiths of Smithfield

67-77 Charterhouse Street, EC1M 6HJ (7251 7950/
www.smithsofsmithfield.co.uk). Farringdon tube/rail.
Open *Ground-floor bar/café* 7am-5pm Mon-Fri;
10am-5pm Sat; 9.30am-5pm Sun. *Dining room* noon-
3pm, 6-11pm Mon-Fri; 6-10.45pm Sat. **Main courses**
Ground-floor bar/café £3.50-£6. *Dining room* £9.50-
£11.50. **Credit** AmEx, DC, MC, V. **Map** p404 O5
This warehouse-like eaterie, opposite the famous
market, caters for every mood. The ground-floor bar
serves brunch and snacks and there's a swish cocktail bar upstairs. For something more substantial
head upstairs to the lively brasserie or the top-floor
fine-dining restaurant.

Oriental

Matsuri

71 High Holborn, WC1V 6EA (7430 1970/www.
matsuri-restaurant.com). Chancery Lane or Holborn
tube. **Open** noon-2.30pm, 6-10pm Mon-Sat. **Main**
courses £8.50-£15 lunch, £13-£28 dinner. **Credit**
AmEx, DC, MC, V. **Map** p401 M5 ㉖
Decked out with sleek polished surfaces, white
walls, wooden screens and lots of glass, Matsuri St
James's style-conscious younger sister is a champion

all rounder. The cooking and ingredients are nothing
short of superb. Expensive, but worth it.
Other locations: 15 Bury Street, St James's,
SW1Y 6AL (7839 1101).

Spanish

Moro

34-36 Exmouth Market, EC1R 4QE (7833 8336/
www.moro.co.uk). Farringdon tube/rail. **Open** 12.30-
10.30pm Mon-Sat. **Main courses** £13.50-£17.50.
Tapas £2.50-£9. **Credit** AmEx, DC, MC, V.
Map p404 N4 ㉗
This bustling mainstay continues to set the standard
for Spanish and North African fare, nearly a decade
after it opened. Either pop in for a snack (tapas are
available all day, and tasting menus at Saturday
lunchtime) or settle down for a full meal.

Bloomsbury & Fitzrovia

Italian

Carluccio's Caffè

8 Market Place, W1W 8AG (7636 2228/www.
carluccios.com). Oxford Circus tube. **Open** 7.30am-
11pm Mon-Fri; 10am-11pm Sat; 10am-10pm Sun.
Main courses £5.95-£10.95. **Credit** AmEx, MC,
V. **Map** p408 U1 ㉘

With nearly 15 branches around London, Carluccio's may feel a bit chain-like, yet it continues to push the right buttons, blending classic and innovative regional Italian dishes with flair. Desserts are a high point, and include own-made ice-creams and sorbets. Staff are friendly and welcoming too.
Other locations: throughout the city.

Sardo
45 Grafton Way, W1T 5DQ (7387 2521/www.sardo-restaurant.com). Warren Street tube. **Open** noon-3pm, 6-11pm Mon-Fri; 6-11pm Sat. **Main courses** £8.90-£18. **Credit** AmEx, DC, MC, V. **Map** p400 J4 ㉙
This welcoming and unpretentious trattoria has acquired a reputation for being the place food critics go to spend their own money. Its speciality is seafood, but Sardo excels in applying a modern, imaginative twist to Italian dishes. It's good value too. **Photo** *p200*.
Other locations: Sardo Canale, 42 Gloucester Avenue, Primrose Hill, NW1 8JD (7722 2800).

Oriental

Busaba Eathai
22 Store Street, WC1E 7DS (7299 7900). Goodge Street or Tottenham Court Road tube. **Open** noon-11pm Mon-Thur; noon-11.30pm Fri, Sat; noon-10pm Sun. **Main courses** £5.10-£9. **Credit** AmEx, MC, V. **Map** p401 K5 ㉚
This is another brainchild of Wagamama creator Alan Yau, but here the no-smoking communal tables and no reservations template is more impressively executed, with surprisingly intimate design and excellent Thai-inspired dishes. **Photo** *p203*.
Other locations: 8-13 Bird Street, Marylebone, W1U 1BU (7518 8080); 106-110 Wardour Street, Soho, W1F 0TR (7255 8686).

Hakkasan
8 Hanway Place, W1T 1HD (7907 1888). Tottenham Court Road tube. **Open** noon-2.45pm, 6-11.30pm Mon, Tue; noon-2.45pm, 6pm-12.30am Wed-Fri; noon-4.30pm, 6pm-12.30am Sat; noon-4.30pm Sun. **Main courses** £11.50-£68. **Dim sum** £3.50-£6.15. **Credit** AmEx, MC, V. **Map** p408 W1 ㉛
There's no questioning the buzz about Alan Yau's flagship. Its slinky and effortlessly stylish basement interior – black lattice screens and spotlit tables – is matched by its innovative Chinese cuisine. The lunchtime dim sum is excellent. Pricey, though.

Roka
37 Charlotte Street, W1T 1RR (7580 6464/ www.rokarestaurant.com). Goodge Street or Tottenham Court Road tube. **Open** noon-midnight daily. **Main courses** £3.60-£21. **Credit** AmEx, DC, MC, V. **Map** p400 J5 ㉜
Conceived as a 'restaurant without walls', the gorgeously designed Roka (younger sister to Zuma in Knightsbridge; *see p212*) prides itself in appearances – and the food here is as beautifully turned out. A trip to the Shochu Lounge, the lovely basement bar, is also highly recommended (*see p227*).

Villandry
170 Great Portland Street, W1W 5QB (7631 3131/ www.villandry.com). Great Portland Street tube. **Open** 8am-11pm Mon-Fri; 9am-9pm Sat. **Main courses** £10.50-£22. **Credit** AmEx, MC, V. **Map** p400 H5 ㉝
Villandry's troika of mouth-watering deli, slick modern restaurant and bar continues to keep it at the head of the pack of central London's quality foodie destinations. Expect superb salads, hearty mains and cheese plates *par excellence*. A class act.

Spanish

Fino
33 Charlotte Street, entrance on Rathbone Street, W1T 1RR (7813 8010/www.finorestaurant.com). Goodge Street or Tottenham Court Road tube. **Open** noon-2.30pm, 6-10.30pm Mon-Fri; 12.30-2.30pm, 6-10.30pm Sat. **Tapas** £4-£15.50. **Credit** AmEx, MC, V. **Map** p400 J5 ㉞
Fino is invitingly bright despite its basement setting. Appearance is a priority that equally applies to its tantalisingly presented, uncontrived and directly flavoured tapas dishes. The desserts and wine list (plenty of sherries, natch) are further draws.

Salt Yard
54 Goodge Street, W1T 4NA (7637 0657/www.salt yard.co.uk). Goodge Street tube. **Open** noon-11pm Mon-Fri; 5-11pm Sat. **Tapas** £2.75-£7. **Credit** MC, V. **Map** p400 J5 ㉟
Stylishly pared down and dotted with elegant design features, Salt Yard is unusually restrained for a tapas bar/restaurant. Yet it delivers dishes with a twist – adding Italian touches into the usual Spanish fare. Excellent for vegetarians too.

Marylebone

British

Rhodes W1
The Cumberland, Great Cumberland Place, W1A 4RF (7479 3838). Marble Arch tube. **Open** 11am-11pm Mon-Sat; 11am-10.30pm Sun. **Main courses** £9.75-£38.50. **Credit** AmEx, MC, V. **Map** p400 G6 ㊱
Gary Rhodes' signature Modern British approach is writ large at this huge hotel restaurant. Oxtail is a favourite ingredient of the celebrity chef, but there are plenty of other British classics to salivate over.
Other locations: Rhodes Twenty Four, 24th Floor, Tower 42, Old Broad Street, The City, EC2N 1HQ (7877 7703).

Cafés & brasseries

Café Bagatelle
Wallace Collection, Manchester Square, W1U 3BN (7563 9505). Bond Street tube. **Open** 10am-4.30pm daily. **Main courses** £9-£15.50. **Set menu** Mon-Fri £15 2 courses; £20 3 courses. **Credit** AmEx, MC, V. **Map** p400 G5 ㊲

Eat, Drink, Shop

Busaba Eathai. *See p201.*

Located in a spacious, glass-roofed courtyard, Café Bagatelle is one of London's most charming museum restaurants. The menu is short, but ambitious, taking in Asian influences, alongside more standard Modern European fare. Utterly delightful.

La Fromagerie

2-4 Moxon Street, W1U 4EW (7935 0341/www. lafromagerie.co.uk). Baker Street or Bond Street tube. **Open** 10.30am-7.30pm Mon; 8am-7.30pm Tue-Fri; 9am-7pm Sat; 10am-6pm Sun. **Main courses** £6.50-£13.50. **Credit** AmEx, MC, V. **Map** p400 G5 🕉

This cheese and deli shop has done well from its rustic-styled café, which heaves at lunchtime. And rightly so. Cooking is of a consistently high standard: earthy soups, exquisite cheese platters and salad dishes. Note the Highbury branch has no café. **Other locations**: 30 Highbury Park, Highbury, N5 2AA (7359 7440).

Fish

FishWorks

89 Marylebone High Street, W1U 4QW (7935 9796/ www.fishworks.co.uk). Baker Street, Bond Street or Regent's Park tube. **Open** noon-2.30pm, 6-10.30pm Tue-Fri; noon-10.30pm Sat, Sun. **Main courses** £10.90-£19. **Credit** AmEx, MC, V. **Map** p400 G5 🕉

The formula is simple: a fishmonger at the front, and a light, bright eating area behind. Muse over the long menu or pick your own fish from the counter. The emphasis is on super-fresh ingredients, with no fuss. **Other locations**: 134 Upper Street, Islington, N1 1QP (7354 1279); 6 Turnham Green Terrace, Chiswick, W4 1QP (8994 0086).

Global

Providores & Tapa Room

109 Marylebone High Street, W1U 4RX (7935 6175/ www.theprovidores.co.uk). Baker Street or Bond Street tube. **Open** *The Providores* noon-2.45pm,

6-10.45pm Mon-Sat; noon-2.45pm, 6-10pm Sun. *Tapa Room* 9-11.30am, noon-10.30pm Mon-Fri; 10am-3pm, 4-10.30pm Sat; 10am-3pm, 4-10pm Sun. **Main courses** £15-£22. **Tapas** £1.50-£13. **Credit** AmEx, MC, V. **Map** p400 G5 🕘

The buzzy street-level Tapa Room is frequently packed by crowds seeking the exquisite global tapas and breakfasts. Upstairs, the restaurant itself is small and refined, producing a rarefied fusion of mainly Asian and Middle Eastern ingredients to produce very good dishes.

Italian

Locanda Locatelli

8 Seymour Street, W1H 7JZ (7935 9088/www. locandalocatelli.com). Marble Arch tube. **Open** noon-3pm, 7-11pm Mon-Thur; noon-3pm, 7-11.30pm Fri; noon-3.30pm, 7-11.30pm Sat; noon-3.30pm, 6.45-10pm Sun. **Main courses** £16-£30. **Credit** AmEx, MC, V. **Map** p400 G6 🕙

A meal at Locanda Locatelli seems indulgent, from the prices to the exclusive nightclub feel within. Many dishes put a contemporary spin on the Italian classics, and the ravioli served here are among the very best in the country.

Modern European

Orrery

55 Marylebone High Street, W1U 5RB (7616 8000/ www.orrery.co.uk). Baker Street or Regent's Park tube. **Open** noon-3pm, 7-11pm Mon-Sat; noon-3pm, 7-10.30pm Sun. **Main courses** £16.50-£30. **Credit** AmEx, DC, MC, V. **Map** p400 G4 🕘

From the vast *digestif* trolley to the army of flunkies committed to the opening of doors, the folding of napkins and so forth, there are very few haute cuisine clichés left undisturbed at Orrery. Still, André Garrett's deft Modern European cooking almost always passes muster.

Keep an eye on the kitchen action at **Maze**. *See p205.*

North African

Original Tagines
7A Dorset Street, W1H 3SE (7935 1545/www.
originaltagines.com). Baker Street tube. **Open**
noon-3pm, 6-11pm daily. **Main courses** £9.50-
£11.95. **Credit** MC, V. **Map** p400 G5 **43**
A great little neighbourhood restaurant, Original
Tagines is blessedly free of ethnic knick-knacks.
The standard double act of couscous and tagines
(several varieties of each) is lent support by an
atypically good selection of starters, although
portions aren't huge.

Mayfair & St James's

British

Dorchester Grill Room
The Dorchester, 53 Park Lane, W1A 2HJ (7317
6336/www.dorchesterhotel.com). Hyde Park Corner
tube. **Open** 7-11am, 12.30-2.30pm, 6-11pm Mon-Sat;
7.30-11am, 12.30-2.30pm, 7-10.30pm Sun. **Main**
courses £16-£30. **Credit** AmEx, DC, MC, V.
Map p402 G7 **44**
This renowned hotel eaterie had just undergone a
revamp as this guide went to press, with a spruced-
up interior by Thierry Despont, but you can still
expect the usual high standards. Service is impeccable without being snooty, and the cuisine offers a
wonderfully sybaritic mix of British steaks and
roasts and classic French-style cooking.

Inn The Park
St James's Park, SW1A 2BJ (7451 9999/www.
innthepark.co.uk). St James's Park tube. **Open**
8am-11am, noon-3pm, 6-10.30pm Mon-Fri;

9-11am, noon-4pm, 6-10.30pm Sat, Sun. **Main**
courses £4.50-£18.50. **Credit** AmEx, MC, V.
Map p403 K8 **45**
Nudging the lakefront and surrounded by leafy
greens, Inn The Park is an oasis for weary tourists.
Simple yet striking menus complement the relaxed
atmosphere: as well as full-on lunch and dinner
menus, there are informal teas and breakfasts.

Fish

Green's
36 Duke Street, SW1Y 6DF (7930 4566/www.
greens.org.uk). Green Park or Piccadilly Circus
tube. **Open** *Sept-Apr* 11.30am-3pm, 6-11pm Mon-
Sat; noon-3pm, 6-9pm Sun. *May-Aug* 11.30am-3pm,
6-11pm Mon-Sat. **Main courses** £11-£40. **Credit**
AmEx, DC, MC, V. **Map** p408 V5 **46**
With its clubby atmosphere, mahogany panelling,
leather banquettes and marble oyster bar, Green's
looks as if it has been around since the 1880s. Its
raison d'être is fish, although there is also plenty
available for committed carnivores.

French

Patterson's
4 Mill Street, W1S 2AX (7499 1308/www.
pattersonsrestaurant.co.uk). Oxford Circus or
Bond Street tube. **Open** noon-3pm Mon-Fri; 6-11pm
Mon-Sat. **Main courses** £13-£17. **Credit** AmEx,
MC, V. **Map** p408 U3 **47**
This Mayfair restaurant is low-key, but offers
unmistakable class and accomplishment. With an
attractive setting, excellent service and two courses
of delicious, expertly cooked food for £15 (lunchtime
only), it's also a corking bargain.

Indian

Tamarind

20 Queen Street, W1J 5PR (7629 3561/www. tamarindrestaurant.com). Green Park tube. **Open** noon-3pm Mon-Fri; 6-11.30pm Mon-Sat; noon-2.30pm, 6-10.30pm Sun. **Main courses** £14.50-£22. **Credit** AmEx, DC, MC, V. **Map** p402 H7 **48**

This classy, sumptuous, subterranean restaurant specialises in Mogul tandoori cuisine from the north-west of India. It is also currently the only Indian restaurant in the United Kingdom to hold a Michelin star. The cooking here is cautious rather than flamboyant, leaving the theatrics to kebab chefs in the open-view kitchen.

Middle Eastern

Noura Central

22 Lower Regent Street, SW1Y 4UJ (7839 2020/ www.noura.co.uk). Piccadilly Circus tube. **Open** noon-midnight Mon-Thur, Sun; noon-1am Fri, Sat. **Main courses** £9.75-£18.50. **Credit** AmEx, DC, MC, V. **Map** p408 W7 **49**

This new branch of the Parisian chain is a glam, air-conditioned sanctuary, offering numerous tasty Leventine mezes and main courses for both vegetarians and omnivores. To make the most of it, pick several dishes, dive in and share.

Modern European

Gordon Ramsay at Claridge's

Claridge's Hotel, 55 Brook Street, W1A 2JQ (7499 0099/www.gordonramsay.com). Bond Street tube. **Open** noon-2.45pm, 5.45-11pm Mon-Fri; noon-3pm, 5.45-11pm Sat; noon-3pm, 6-11pm Sun. **Set lunch** £30 3 courses. **Set dinner** £60 3 courses, £70 6 courses. **Credit** AmEx, MC, V. **Map** p400 H6 **50**

Slick presentation adds yet another layer of glamour to the vintage sparkle of this beautifully restored art deco hotel. It's nigh on impossible to get a table, but worth persevering, though we've had at least one curiously lacklustre meal here.

Maze

Marriott Grosvenor Square, 10-13 Grosvenor Square, W1K 6JP (7107 0000/www.gordonramsay.com). Bond Street tube. **Open** noon-3pm, 6-11pm daily. **Tapas** £5-£8.50. **Main courses** £13.50-£16.50. **Credit** AmEx, MC, V. **Map** p402 G6 **51**

Ignore the fact it's in a hotel: Gordon Ramsay's protégé Jason Atherton is the reason people visit Maze. Judging from the dining room's laughter and chatter, his tapas-sized dishes are going down a storm (there's a more conventional menu too). Attentive, friendly staff put diners at ease. **Photo** *p204.*

Sketch

9 Conduit Street, W1S 2XZ (0870 777 4488/ www.sketch.uk.com). Oxford Circus tube. **Open** *The Glade* noon-3pm Mon-Sat. *Gallery* 7-10.30pm Mon-Sat. *The Lecture Room* noon-2.30pm, 7-10.30pm Tue-Fri; 7-10.30pm Sat. **Main courses** *The Glade* £5-£14. *Gallery* £18-£33. *The Lecture Room* £45-£59. **Credit** AmEx, DC, MC, V. **Map** p408 U3 **52**

These trendy Mayfair premises are home to several dining options. On the lower level are the cheaper – relatively – Gallery (Modern Euro food; largely style over substance) and a new addition, Glade (French-inspired dishes that sound pretentious on paper but work well in practice). The first-floor Lecture Room delivers dramatic food at dramatic prices.

The Wolseley

160 Piccadilly, W1J 9EB (7499 6996/www. thewolseley.com). Green Park tube. **Open** 7am-midnight Mon-Fri; 9am-midnight Sat; 9am-11pm Sun. **Main courses** £8.75-£26. **Credit** AmEx, DC, MC, V. **Map** p408 U5 **53**

This handsome building was built in 1921 as a car showroom, and its huge windows and high vaulted ceilings doubtless befitted the role. But its current incarnation as a European-style grand café is surely the one it was born for. The Wolseley may be big, but with quality French and European fare, as well as a stunner of an afternoon tea, it's easy to see why it's always full to the rafters.

Oriental

Chisou

4 Princes Street, W1B 2LE (7629 3931). Oxford Circus tube. **Open** noon-2.30pm, 6-10.15pm Mon-Sat. **Main courses** £3.50 £22. **Credit** AmEx, DC, MC, V. **Map** p408 U2 **54**

London now has a large number of inexpensive, good-value Japanese restaurants. Chisou isn't one of them. This is a place where the quality of ingredients – from sushi and sashimi to select sakés and fundamentals like dashi – matters. They say you get what you pay for; Chisou proves the point.

Kai Mayfair

65 South Audley Street, W1K 2QU (7493 8988/ www.kaimayfair.com). Bond Street or Marble Arch tube. **Open** noon-2.30pm, 6.30-11pm Mon-Fri; 12.30-3pm, 6.30-11pm Sat; 12.30-3pm, 6.30-10.30pm Sun. **Main courses** £13-£39. **Credit** AmEx, DC, MC, V. **Map** p402 G7 **55**

Everything about Kai Mayfair whispers 'wealth'. You can order a £108 bowl of soup, but if your budget doesn't stretch that far there are plenty of less extravagant choices. Whatever you go for, the standard will be excellent and service welcoming.

Nobu

Metropolitan Hotel, 19 Old Park Lane, W1K 1LB (7447 4747/www.noburestaurants.com). Hyde Park Corner tube. **Open** noon-2.15pm, 6-10.15pm Mon-Thur; noon-2.15pm, 6-11pm Fri; 12.30-3pm, 6-11pm Sat; 12.30-3pm, 6-9.30pm Sun. **Main courses** £5-£27.50. **Credit** AmEx, DC, MC, V. **Map** p402 H8 **56**

It's still the most famous Japanese restaurant in town, yet Nobu is no longer the most fashionable or even the most expensive (judicious selection of

Eat, Drink, Shop

dishes can yield a filling meal at under £90 for two). The trim, efficient staff seem less bossy now, but are quick to clear plates – no lingering over the views. Nobu Berkeley has an annoying no-booking policy. **Other locations**: Ubon, 34 Westferry Circus, Docklands, E14 8RR (7719 7800); Nobu Berkeley, 15 Berkeley Street, Mayfair, W1J 8DY (7290 9222).

Soho & Chinatown

British

Lindsay House

21 Romilly Street, W1V 5AF (7439 0450/www. lindsayhouse.co.uk). Leicester Square tube. **Open** noon-2.30pm Mon-Fri; 6-11pm Mon-Sat. **Main courses** (lunch) £18-£22. **Set meal** (noon-2.30pm Mon-Fri, 6-6.45pm Mon-Sat) £25 3 courses. **Set dinner** £48 3 courses. **Credit** AmEx, DC, MC, V. **Map** p408 W3 ⑤⑦

The dining area of Soho's most elegant townhouse restaurant is a pleasant mix of modern minimalism and discreet period detail. Richard Corrigan's spectacular cooking is robust and colourful, drawing on a larder of top-notch European ingredients. Great wine list and charming staff add to the appeal.

Cafés & brasseries

Amato

14 Old Compton Street, W1D 4TH (7734 5733/ www.amato.co.uk). Leicester Square or Tottenham Court Road tube. **Open** 8am-10pm Mon-Sat; 10am-8pm Sun. **Main courses** £3.95-£8.25. **Credit** AmEx, DC, MC, V. **Map** p409 X2 ⑤⑧

Amato's art deco posters and dark wood furnishings are an impressive backdrop to its lush pastry and cake display, heaving with calorific treats. There's also a good choice of pasta dishes, soups and salads.

Bar Italia

22 Frith Street, W1V 5PS (7437 4520/www. baritaliasoho.co.uk). Leicester Square, Piccadilly Circus or Tottenham Court Road tube. **Open** 24hrs Mon-Sat; 7am-4am Sun. **Main courses** £3.20-£8. **Credit** (noon-3am only) AmEx, DC, MC, V. **Map** p408 W2 ⑤⑨

Now into its sixth decade, this Soho landmark coasts on much as it always has, with red leatherette stools, Formica surfaces, and the famous Rocky Marciano poster. Like the coffee the food isn't too bad, but it's really all about the atmosphere.

Maison Bertaux

28 Greek Street, W1V 5LL (7437 6007). Leicester Square, Piccadilly Circus or Tottenham Court Road tube. **Open** 8.30am-11pm daily. **Main courses** £1.50-£4.50. **No credit cards. Map** p409 X3 ⑥⓪

A true Soho landmark, Bertaux has wobbly tables, mismatched chairs and quirky artefacts, making it more like a theatre set than a French café. Ask for a menu and you'll draw a blank: the specials are whatever's come out of the oven. Service is charming.

Pâtisserie Valerie

44 Old Compton Street, W1D 4TY (7437 3466/www. patisserie-valerie.co.uk). Leicester Square, Piccadilly Circus or Tottenham Court Road tube. **Open** 7.30am-8.30pm Mon, Tue; 7.30am-9pm Wed-Fri; 8am-9pm Sat; 9.30am-7pm Sun. **Main courses** £3.75-£8.25. **Credit** (over £5) AmEx, DC, MC, V. **Map** p408 W3 ⑥①

Step back in time to the 1950s: Formica tables, an old-fashioned pastry counter and, more to the point, a selection of classic French pâtisserie. Grab a window table upstairs, a cheerier, lighter and airier space than the hemmed-in café downstairs. **Other locations**: throughout the city.

Indian

Masala Zone

9 Marshall Street, W1F 7ER (7287 9966/www. realindianfood.com). Oxford Circus tube. **Open** noon-3pm, 5.30-11pm Mon-Fri; 12.30-11pm Sat; 12.30-3.30pm, 6-10.30pm Sun. **Main courses** £5.50-£7.45. **Credit** MC, V. **Map** p408 V2 ⑥②

A stamping ground for young office types who are on a limited budget, this is a café that does chic on the cheap. The affable staff deliver meals in a jiffy. Starters tend to be more memorable than mains, but prices are hard to beat.

Other locations: 80 Upper Street, Islington, N1 0NP (7359 3399); 147 Earl's Court Road, Earl's Court, SW5 9RQ (7373 0220).

Red Fort

77 Dean Street, W1D 3SH (7437 2115/www.red fort.co.uk). Leicester Square or Tottenham Court Road tube. **Open** noon-2.15pm Mon-Fri, 5.45-11pm Mon-Sat. **Main courses** £12.50-£20. **Credit** AmEx, MC, V. **Map** p408 W2 ⑥③

Red Fort's beautiful, Jaipuri red sandstone walls with Mogul alcoves are supposedly modelled on Lal Quila, the Red Fort in Delhi. Food is convincing on the whole: spicing is subtle and flavours rich.

Modern European

Alastair Little

49 Frith Street, W1D 4SG (7734 5183). Leicester Square or Tottenham Court Road tube. **Open** noon-3pm, 6-11.30pm Mon-Fri; 6-11.30pm Sat. **Main courses** £24.50. **Credit** AmEx, MC, V. **Map** p408 W2 ⑥④

Alastair Little's short menu draws on quality ingredients and influences, but the beautiful food is never pretentious. Some find the decor a little plain, but we like the cosy, unshowy look, as well as the restaurant's unpretentious attitude and charming service.

North American

Bodean's

10 Poland Street, W1F 8PZ (7287 7575/www. bodeansbbq.com). Oxford Circus or Piccadilly Circus tube. **Open** *Deli* noon-11pm Mon-Sat; noon-10.30pm

Winner dinners

Every year *Time Out* recognises the best of London's eating and drinking establishments with a series of awards. The combination of our experience – we anonymously review 2,000 of the capital's restaurants each year – and the votes of *Time Out* readers results in a unique list that rewards the excellent but unfêted alongside the celebrated and well-known. Below we have listed the winners in each category of the 2005 awards.

Best alfresco dining
Petersham Nurseries Café. *See p219.*

Best bar
Shochu Lounge. *See p227.*

Best burger bar
Haché. *See p208* **The burger kings**.

Best cheap eats
Fish Club. *See p218.*

Best design
Inn The Park. *See p204.*

Best family restaurant
Gracelands. *See p213.*

Best gastropub
Gun. *See p216* **Reinventing the meal**.

Best local restaurant
Chez Kristof. *See p220.*

Best new restaurant
Maze. *See p205.*

Best vegetarian meal
Noura Central. *See p205.*

Sun. *Restaurant* noon-3pm, 6-11pm Mon-Fri; noon-11pm Sat; noon-10.30pm Sun. **Main courses** £6-£14. **Credit** AmEx, MC, V. **Map** p408 V2 **65**
This is what they'd call 'good eatin'' if you were somewhere down South. The atmosphere is laid-back but quite classy, with leather banquettes and wood-panelled walls. Service is professional and the meat is sublimely cooked (head straight for the ribs). Not somewhere for vegetarians.
Other locations: 169 Clapham High Street, Clapham, SW4 7SS (7622 4248).

Oriental

ECapital
8 Gerrard Street, W1D 5PJ (7434 3838). Leicester Square or Piccadilly Circus tube. **Open** noon-midnight Mon-Thur; noon-midnight Fri, Sat; noon-10.30pm Sun. **Main courses** £6.50-£19.80. **Credit** AmEx, DC, MC, V. **Map** p409 X3 **66**
These days you need to work a little harder to extract ECapital's speciality eastern Chinese dishes from a run-of-the-mill list of Chinatown favourites, but it's worth it. Pink, bright purple and off-white in colour, the smart dining room is fairly spacious by Chinatown standards.

Fook Sing
25-26 Newport Court, WC2H 7JS (7287 0188). Leicester Square or Piccadilly Circus tube. **Open** 11am-10.30pm daily. **Main courses** £3.90-£4.30. **No credit cards. Map** p409 X3 **67**
Yes, it's a basic caff with Formica tables and a rudimentary WC, but flick to the end of the lengthy menu and you'll find rare treasures from Fujian province. Portions are huge, prices are low and friendly service adds to the appeal.

Imperial China
White Bear Yard, 25A Lisle Street, WC2H 7BA (7734 3388/www.imperial-china.co.uk). Leicester Square or Piccadilly Circus tube. **Open** noon-11.30pm Mon-Sat; 11.30am-10.30pm Sun. **Main courses** £6-£24. **Minimum** £10. **Credit** AmEx, MC, V. **Map** p409 X3 **68**
Through the tiny alleyway and over the bridge, you're transported away from crowded Lisle Street to Imperial China. There's not much choice with the dim sum, but it's prepared with great skill; the full menu has lots of abalone and lobster dishes.

Mr Kong
21 Lisle Street, WC2H 7BA (7437 7341/9679). Leicester Square or Piccadilly Circus tube. **Open** noon-2.45am Mon-Sat; noon-1.45am Sun. **Main courses** £5.90-£26. **Credit** AmEx, DC, MC, V. **Map** p409 X3 **69**
Kong's menu has several enticing, unusual dishes, and this is surely the draw for the many Chinese who eat here. The list of 'special vegetarian dishes' lives up to the billing, especially the mock abalone. The food and the service are generally both up to scratch, although the seating would be improved by the addition of some breathing space.

New Mayflower
68-70 Shaftesbury Avenue, W1B 6LY (7734 9207). Leicester Square or Piccadilly Circus tube. **Open** 5pm-4am daily. **Main courses** £6.50-£45 (minimum £8). **Credit** AmEx, MC, V. **Map** p408 W3 **70**
This is a genuine Cantonese restaurant of the first order. Service was willing, spirited and efficient, and the people around us – almost all of them Chinese – were much too busy enjoying the delicious food to worry about their rather cramped surroundings.

Eat, Drink, Shop

The burger kings

In 2005 the winner of *Time Out*'s Best Burger Bar award (part of our annual series of eating and drinking awards) was **Haché** (*pictured*). Its burgers are made with the French *steak haché* in mind: high-quality Aberdeen Angus and an emphasis on flavour prevail over gimmicky toppings. Presentation is prioritised and staff are friendly. Plenty of joints call their burgers gourmet; Haché has earned that distinction.

Gourmet Burger Kitchen's imaginative selection of blimp-sized burgers is superb. It has dominated the high-quality fast food market for the past few years, garnering positive reviews and foodie awards aplenty, and remains a great favourite.

Hamburger Union seems to be doing very well for itself, and deservedly so. Its burgers aren't the best in London, but they are probably the cheapest at the top end of the market. Side dishes also go down well, though you have to tell staff how you want your burger cooked (they don't ask).

Ultimate Burger is another likeable, easy-going joint. Burgers are slightly smaller and more expensive than at other patty shacks, though the menu includes some interesting rarities. Not the ultimate burger experience, but a welcome contender nonetheless.

The **Fine Burger Company** does a lot right. The milkshakes are fantastic, the chips are even better, and the decor is well pitched. But we've had bad experiences: 'original' burgers sometimes arrive as a rubbery patty, barely better than the supermarket equivalent.

Fine Burger Company

330 Upper Street, Islington, N1 2XQ (7359 3026/www.fineburger.co.uk). Angel tube. **Open** noon-11pm Mon-Sat; noon-10pm Sun. **Main courses** £4.95-£8.95. **Credit** MC, V. **Map** p404 O1 (123)

Other locations: 50 James Street, Marylebone, W1U 1HB (7224 1890); 256 Muswell Hill Broadway, N10 3SH (8815 9292); 37 Bedford Hill, Balham, SW12 9EY (8772 0266).

Gourmet Burger Kitchen

44 Northcote Road, Battersea, SW11 1NZ (7228 3309/www.gbkinfo.co.uk). Clapham Junction rail. **Open** noon-11pm Mon-Fri; 11am-11pm Sat; 11am-10pm Sun. **Main courses** £4.95-£7.25. **Credit** MC, V.

Other locations: throughout the city.

Haché

24 Inverness Street, NW1 7HJ (7485 9100/ www.hacheburgers.com). Camden Town tube. **Open** noon-10.30pm Mon-Sat; noon-10pm Sun. **Main courses** £4.95-£9.95. **Credit** AmEx, DC, MC, V.

Hamburger Union

4-6 Garrick Street, Covent Garden, WC2E 9BH (7379 0412/www.hamburgerunion.com). Covent Garden tube. **Open** 11.30am-9.30pm Mon, Sun; 11.30am-10.30pm Tue-Sat. **Main courses** £3.95-£9.95. **Credit** MC, V. **Map** p409 Y3 (124)

Other locations: 22-25 Dean Street, Soho, W1D 3RY (7437 6004); 341 Upper Street, Islington, N1 0PB (7359 4436).

Ultimate Burger

334 New Oxford Street, Holborn, WC1A 1AP (7436 6641/www.ultimateburger.co.uk). Holborn tube. **Open** 10am-11.30pm daily. **Main courses** £5.45-£6.95. **Credit** MC, V. **Map** p409 Y1 (125)

Other locations: 98 Tottenham Court Road, Fitzrovia, W1T 4TR (7436 5355); 82 Fortis Green Road, Muswell Hill, N10 3HN (8883 6198).

Eat, Drink, Shop

New World
1 Gerrard Place, W1D 5PA (7734 0396). Leicester Square or Piccadilly Circus tube. **Open** 11am-11.45pm Mon-Sat; 11am-11pm Sun. **Main courses** £4.90-£10.50. **Credit** AmEx, DC, MC, V. **Map** p408 W3 🕖
The dim sum trolley system at this multi-floored behemoth takes the guesswork out of ordering. The lengthy full menu is also worth a look; either way, for a uniquely Chinese dining experience, you should lunch here at least once.

Yauatcha
15 Broadwick Street, W1F 0DE (7494 8888). Oxford Circus tube. **Open** noon-11pm Mon-Fri; 11am-11pm Sat; 11am-10pm Sun. **Main courses** £3.50-£12. **Credit** AmEx, MC, V. **Map** p408 V2 🕖
This Michelin-starred restaurant occupies two floors of Sir Richard Rogers's Ingeni building. Dim sum are the highlight of the menu – unusually, dim sum is served all day – but service can verge on amateur. The tea menu is wonderful, as are the cakes from the pâtisserie counter.

Yming
35-36 Greek Street, W1D 5DL (7734 2721/ www.yming.com). Leicester Square, Piccadilly Circus or Tottenham Court Road tube. **Open** noon-11.45pm Mon-Sat. **Main courses** £5-£10. **Credit** AmEx, DC, MC, V. **Map** p409 X3 🕖
Yming looks and feels like a European restaurant. Nevertheless, the regional net is thrown much further than the usual Cantonese classics, with impressive flavours and precision of cooking.

Spanish

Meza
100 Wardour Street, W1F 0TN (7314 4002/ www.conran.com). Tottenham Court Road or Leicester Square tube. **Open** noon 2.30pm, 5pm-2am Mon-Thur; noon-2.30pm, 5pm-3am Fri, Sat. **Tapas** £1.50-£12.50. **Credit** AmEx, MC, V. **Map** p408 W2 🕖
In overhauling the site of his old restaurant Mezzo, Terence Conran has created something of a Latin Quarter in the heart of Soho (for Cuban-themed Floridita, which is downstairs, *see p227*). The atmosphere is spirited and loud, but the food vies for centre stage – expect classic tapas, presented with splendid simplicity.

Covent Garden & St Giles's

Cafés & brasseries

Hamburger Union
See p208 **The burger kings**.

Paul
29 Bedford Street, WC2E 9ED (7836 3304/ www.paul.fr). Covent Garden tube. **Open** 7.30am-9pm Mon-Fri; 9am-9pm Sat, Sun. **Main courses** £3.50-£10.50. **Credit** MC, V. **Map** p409 Y4 🕖

With its elegant cake counter, dark wood panelling and black-and-white prints on the walls, Paul is the embodiment of an old-fashioned Parisian tea room. Our gold star goes to the buttery croissants and crusty walnut bread, though the salads, omelettes and sarnies are contenders too.
Other locations: throughout the city.

Fish/Fish & chips

Rock & Sole Plaice
47 Endell Street, WC2H 9AJ (7836 3785). Covent Garden tube. **Open** 11.30am-11pm Mon-Sat; noon-10pm Sun. **Main courses** £8-£14. **Credit** MC, V. **Map** p409 Y2 🕖
The Rock & Sole Plaice is London's oldest surviving fish and chip shop, and it's been through a few fish fingers since 1871. As long as you avoid Sundays and bank holidays, the fish will be fresh, well prepared and succulent.

J Sheekey
28-32 St Martin's Court, WC2N 4AL (7240 2565/ www.caprice-holdings.co.uk). Leicester Square tube. **Open** noon-3pm, 5.30pm-midnight Mon-Sat; noon-3.30pm, 6pm-midnight Sun. **Main courses** £10.75-£29.75. **Credit** AmEx, DC, MC, V. **Map** p409 X4 🕖
Sister establishment to the Wolseley (*see p205*), the Ivy (*see p210*) and Le Caprice in Mayfair (Arlington House, Arlington Street, 7629 2239), Sheekey's is worth a splurge. From the restrained elegance of the decor to the perfectly executed cooking (including the famous fish pie), it's hard to fault.

French

Admiralty
Somerset House, Strand, WC2R 1LA (7845 4646/ www.somerset-house.org.uk). Embankment or Temple tube/Charing Cross tube/rail. **Open** noon-2.30pm daily; 6-10.30pm Mon-Sat. **Main courses** £17.50-£23.50. **Credit** AmEx, DC, MC, V. **Map** p403 M7 🕖
The Admiralty is in a great location, set in a corner of Somerset House. The decor is playful and fun, with light streaming in through high windows, making for a warm atmosphere. Elegant presentation adds to the food's appeal – and the dishes taste every bit as good as they look.

Indian

Moti Mahal
45 Great Queen Street, WC2B 5AA (7240 9329/ www.motimahal-uk.com). Covent Garden tube. **Open** noon-3pm, 6pm-midnight daily. **Main courses** £14-£18. **Credit** AmEx, MC, V. **Map** p409 Z2 🕖
If you like proper, traditional Indian cooking, this place really does the job. The London branch of the Delhi landmark stays true to its northern roots, with delectable kebabs and succulent tandoori morsels.

Eat, Drink, Shop

Abeno Too.

Its discreet exterior makes it easy to miss, but this modest offspring of Abeno in Bloomsbury is always packed with hungry local workers and Japanese regulars. The furnishings are simple, the staff are polite and efficient, and the food is heartily delicious. **Photo** *left*.
Other locations: 47 Museum Street, Bloomsbury, WC1A 1LY (7405 3211).

Vegetarian & organic

Food for Thought
31 Neal Street, WC2H 9PR (7836 9072). Covent Garden tube. **Open** 9.30-11.30am, noon-5pm, 5-8.30pm Mon-Sat; noon-5pm Sun. **Main courses** £3-£6.50. **No credit cards. Map** p409 Y2 🚳
Food for Thought's dining room is in a tiny basement, the queues are always huge, and the food isn't wildy adventurous. So why is it so popular? Because the prices are low, portions enormous and service friendly. Don't miss the strawberry and banana scrunch – it's a legend in its own lunchtime.

Westminster

Indian

The Cinnamon Club
The Old Westminster Library, Great Smith Street, SW1P 3BU (7222 2555/www.cinnamonclub.com). St James's Park or Westminster tube. **Open** 7.30-9.30am, noon-2.30pm, 6-10.45pm Mon-Fri; 6-10.45pm Sat. **Main courses** £11-£26. **Credit** AmEx, DC, MC, V. **Map** p403 K9 🚳
Housed inside a converted 19th-century library, this elegant and spacious restaurant has the feel of an exclusive gentlemen's club. Chef Vivek Singh's regularly changing menu is a show-stopper from beginning to end; be sure to save room for dessert.

Italian

Quirinale
North Court, 1 Great Peter Street, SW1P 3LL (7222 7080). St James's Park or Westminster tube. **Open** noon-2.30pm, 6-10.30pm Mon-Fri. **Main courses** £12.50-£16. **Credit** AmEx, DC, MC, V. **Map** p403 L10 🚳
This creamy-coloured basement restaurant makes clever use of pale stone and wood, and a sneaky little skylight. Dishes are tremendous: duck with pistachio nuts, sea bream in salt crust, to name but two. The cheese list in itself makes a visit worthwhile.

Modern American/European

Christopher's
18 Wellington Street, WC2E 7DD (7240 4222/ www.christophersgrill.com). Covent Garden tube. **Open** noon-3pm, 5-11pm Mon-Fri; 11.30am-3pm, 5-11pm Sat; 11.30am-3pm Sun. **Main courses** £12-£28. **Credit** AmEx, DC, MC, V. **Map** p409 Z3 🚳
This casual-elegant eaterie's dining room is spacious, with huge windows, a creamy colour scheme, and polite, friendly staff. In recent years the modern American menu has veered from banal to elaborate; at the moment it's the best it's been in a long while.

The Ivy
1 West Street, WC2H 9NQ (7836 4751/www.caprice-holdings.co.uk). Leicester Square tube. **Open** noon-3pm, 5.30pm-midnight Mon-Sat; noon-3.30pm, 5.30pm-midnight Sun. **Main courses** £9.75-£38.50. **Credit** AmEx, DC, MC, V. **Map** p409 X3 🚳
It's still possible to go to the Ivy and feel pretty damn good about the world. Station yourself at a table by the bar near the entrance if you want to observe the flow of celebs. The food's just what it should be – mainly British classics (shepherd's pie, mixed grill, sticky toffee pudding) – done well.

Oriental

Abeno Too
17-18 Great Newport Street, WC2H 7JE (7379 1160). Leicester Square tube. **Open** noon-11pm Mon-Sat; noon-10.30pm Sun. **Main courses** £6.50-£7.80. **Credit** AmEx, DC, MC, V. **Map** p409 X3 🚳

Oriental

Hunan
51 Pimlico Road, SW1W 8NE (7730 5712). Sloane Square tube. **Open** 12.30-2.30pm, 6-11pm Mon-Sat. **Set meal** £32-£150 per person (minimum 2). **Credit** AmEx, DC, MC, V. **Map** p402 G11 🚳

This eccentric establishment remains one of the most delightful Chinese restaurants in London. Let staff decide what to feed you, then wait for a long procession of small and delicious dishes to arrive. The standard of cooking is astonishingly high.

Knightsbridge & South Kensington

French

Racine

239 Brompton Road, SW3 2EP (7584 4477). Knightsbridge or South Kensington tube. **Open** noon-3pm, 6-10.30pm Mon-Fri; noon-3.30pm, 6-10.30pm Sat; noon-3.30pm, 6-10pm Sun. **Main courses** £12.50-£25.50. **Credit** AmEx, MC, V. **Map** p399 E10 ⑰

Racine brings a slice of chic, Parisian style to stuffy old Knightsbridge. Push past the heavy curtain into a dark room – sleek dark leather, smoked mirrors, immaculate white tablecloths – and settle in for an indulgent array of French bourgeois classics.

Global

Lundum's

117-119 Old Brompton Road, SW7 3RN (7373 7774/www.lundums.com). Gloucester Road or South Kensington tube. **Open** 9am-4pm, 6-11pm Mon-Sat; noon-1.30pm Sun. **Main courses** £11.75-£24.25. **Credit** AmEx, DC, MC, V. **Map** p399 D11 ⑱

North European cuisine may be undergoing something of a renaissance. If so, long-established Lundum's demonstrates what we've been missing. The cooking and flavour combinations are tasteful, with fish a particular speciality.

Indian

Amaya

Halkin Arcade, SW1X 8JT (7823 1166/www. realindianfood.com). Knightsbridge tube. **Open** 12.30-2.15pm, 6.30-11.15pm Mon-Fri; 12.30-2.30pm, 6.30-11.15pm Sat; 12.45-2.45pm, 6.30-10.15pm Sun. **Main courses** £8.50-£25. **Credit** AmEx, DC, MC, V. **Map** p402 G9 ⑲

There's no doubt that Amaya is doing for Indian food what Nobu did for Japanese – namely making it cool, even fashionable. It's the acclaimed – and highly swish – newish venture from the Panjabi sisters (of Chutney Mary fame – *see p212* – among other restaurants), and specialises in kebabs.

Italian

Daphne's

112 Draycott Avenue, SW3 3AE (7589 4257/ www.daphnes-restaurant.co.uk). South Kensington tube. **Open** noon-3pm, 5.30-11.30pm Mon-Fri; noon-3.30pm Sat; 12.30-4pm, 5.30-10.30pm Sun. **Main courses** £12.25-£24.75. **Credit** AmEx, MC, V. **Map** p399 E10 ⑳

With its terracotta-coloured walls and olive bushes, Daphne's interior is happily evocative of a villa in Tuscany. The menu's dedication to seasonal produce also pays off, with comforting Italian classics such as gnocchi and polenta.

Modern European

Bibendum

Michelin House, 81 Fulham Road, SW3 6RD (7581 5817/www.bibendum.co.uk). South Kensington tube. **Open** noon-2.30pm, 7-11.30pm Mon-Fri; 12.30-3pm, 7-11.30pm Sat; 12.30-3pm, 7-10.30pm Sun. **Main courses** £19-£42. **Credit** AmEx, DC, MC, V. **Map** p399 E10 ㉛

If you go for Bibendum's three-course prix-fixe menu at £28.50, you'll feel decidedly pleased at what good value it is. Meals here – one of Conran's finest establishments – are often faultless, and you get to eat in a glorious room.

Boxwood Café

The Berkeley, Wilton Place, SW1X 7RL (7235 1010/ www.gordonramsay.com). Hyde Park Corner or Knightsbridge tube. **Open** noon-3pm, 6-11pm Mon-Fri; noon-4pm, 6-11pm Sat, Sun. **Main courses** £13.50-£25. **Credit** AmEx, MC, V. **Map** p402 G8 ㉜

Although Boxwood shares the same address as the Berkeley hotel, it feels a long way removed from any hallowed and gilded establishment. Staff are easy-going, the dining room is comfortable, and the menu is stuffed with naughtily indulgent foods.

The Fifth Floor

Harvey Nichols, Knightsbridge, SW1X 7RJ (7235 5250/www.harveynichols.com). Knightsbridge tube. **Open** *Café* 10am-10.30pm Mon-Sat; 11am-5pm Sun. *Restaurant* noon-3pm Mon-Fri; 11.30am-3.30pm Sat, Sun, 6-11pm Mon-Sat. **Main courses** *Café* £9.50-£15. *Restaurant* £15-£24. **Credit** AmEx, DC, MC, V. **Map** p397 F9 ㉝

The Fifth Floor recently had a revamp that brought in a new chef – both have proved to be successful changes. From the pale blue, rounded space to the staff's professionalism, everything now seems right. Main-course portions are small, but the density of flavours more than compensates.

Oriental

Mr Chow

151 Knightsbridge, SW1X 7PA (7589 7347/www. mrchow.com). Knightsbridge tube. **Open** 12.30-3pm, 7pm-midnight daily. **Main courses** £12.50-£25. **Credit** AmEx, DC, MC, V **Map** p397 F9 ㉞

Mr Chow is the Ivy of Chinese restaurants: long-established, much loved and fabulously glamorous in a lived-in way. The food is surprisingly good and authentic, given that most customers are non-Chinese and the ambience decidedly Western.

Nahm – not your average hotel food.

Nahm

The Halkin, Halkin Street, SW1X 7DJ (7333 1234/ www.nahm.como.bz). Hyde Park Corner tube. **Open** noon-2.30pm, 7-11pm Mon-Fri; 7-11pm Sat; 7-10pm Sun. **Main courses** £11-£16.50. **Credit** AmEx, DC, MC, V. **Map** p402 G9 **⑮**

Kitchen maestro David Thompson serves inspired modern Thai cooking at this ultra-stylish restaurant, situated in the exclusive Halkin hotel. When the thought-provoking menu works – royal Thai classics made with first-rate ingredients – it's simply spectacular. **Photo** *above*.

Zuma

5 Raphael Street, SW7 1DL (7584 1010/www. zumarestaurant.com). Knightsbridge tube. **Open** noon-2pm, 6-10.45pm Mon-Fri; 12.30-3pm, 6-10.45pm Sat; 12.30-3pm, 6-10pm Sun. **Main courses** £3.80-£54.80. **Credit** AmEx, DC, MC, V. **Map** p399 F9 **⑯**

Many diners seem to be here for the scene, which shows how silly they are, because the Japanese food is seriously good. If you come for the food, do lunch, as the loud bar scene at night can get tiresome.

Spanish

Cambio de Tercio

163 Old Brompton Road, SW5 0LJ (7244 8970/ www.cambiodetercio.com). Gloucester Road or South Kensington tube. **Open** 12.30-2.30pm, 7-11.30pm Mon-Fri; 12.30-3pm, 7-11.30pm Sat; 12.30-3pm, 7-11pm Sun. **Main courses** £13.50-£16.75. **Credit** AmEx, DC, MC, V. **Map** p399 C11 **⑰**

Though Cambio's decor might be looking a bit tired, the Spanish cooking is as good as ever. Foodie trends make occasional appearances – doses of fashionable foam, for example – but the essential, enjoyable virtues of each dish are never lost.

Chelsea

Gastropubs

Lots Road Pub & Dining Room

114 Lots Road, SW10 0RJ (7352 6645). Fulham Broadway tube then 11 bus/Sloane Square tube then 11, 19, 22 bus. **Open** noon-10pm Mon-Thur, Sun; noon-10.30pm Fri, Sat. **Main courses** £8-£13. **Credit** MC, V. **Map** p39 C13 **⑱**

This Chelsea staple is a bit off the beaten track unless you're en route to the harbour. The menu is stocked with standards, but it's the more adventurous options that really hit the spot. The Sunday deal (a main and dessert for £12.50 from 6pm) is good value.

Indian

Chutney Mary

535 King's Road, SW10 0SZ (7351 3113/ www.realindianfood.com). Fulham Broadway tube/11, 22 bus. **Open** 6.30-11pm Mon-Fri; 12.30-2.30pm, 6.30-11pm Sat; 12.30-3pm, 6.30-10.30pm Sun. **Main courses** £13.50-£25.50. **Credit** AmEx, DC, MC, V. **Map** p398 C13 **⑲**

Run by the Panjabi sisters – of Amaya (*see p211*) and Masala Zone (*see p206*) fame – this fine-dining restaurant boasts an airy conservatory, decorated in colonial style, contrasting with a more formal dining area. Spicing is well balanced and the wine list strong.

Modern European

Gordon Ramsay

68-69 Royal Hospital Road, SW3 4HP (7352 4441/ 3334/www.gordonramsay.com). Sloane Square tube. **Open** noon-2pm, 6.30-11pm Mon-Fri. **Set lunch** £35 3 courses. **Set meal** £65 3 courses, £80 7 courses. **Credit** AmEx, DC, MC, V. **Map** p399 F12 ⓬

Winning the lottery is easier than getting a table here, but if you manage it, you'll be bowled over by the experience. A perky three-course set lunch menu now makes this place a viable option for those of us who aren't millionaires, and dishes are generous, faultlessly prepared and rewarding.

North London

African/Caribbean

Cottons

55 Chalk Farm Road, Chalk Farm, NW1 8AN (7485 8388/www.cottons-restaurant.co.uk). Chalk Farm tube. **Open** 6pm-midnight Mon-Thur; 6pm-1am Fri, Sat; noon-4pm Sat; noon-midnight Sun. **Main courses** £10.25-£14.50. **Credit** AmEx, MC, V.

Even midweek there's a lively scene at Cottons. Ample seating is dispersed over three dining rooms, and friendly staff are happy to advise on the menu, a medley of Caribbean classics, cooked with aplomb.

Lalibela

137 Fortess Road, Kentish Town, NW5 2HR (7284 0600). Tufnell Park tube. **Open** 6pm-midnight daily. **Main courses** £7.50-£8.95. **Credit** AmEx, DC, MC, V.

Eating at Lalibela is always a treat, whether you sit on the ground floor in the art gallery area, or upstairs at the low stools by the window. Food is best ordered in combinations (platters of enjera bread, which you use to scoop up the separate dishes such as stew).

Queen of Sheba

12 Fortess Road, Kentish Town, NW5 2EU (7284 3947). Kentish Town tube/rail. **Open** 1-11.30pm Mon-Sat; 1-10.30pm Sun. **Main courses** £5-£10.50. **Credit** MC, V.

This laid-back restaurant is certainly a queen in north London's Ethiopian dining scene. There are some interesting dishes on an otherwise standard menu, and the kitchen doesn't hold back on flavour.

Tobia

First Floor, Ethiopian Community Centre, 2A Lithos Road, West Hampstead, NW3 6EF (7431 4213/ www.tobiarestaurant.co.uk). Finchley Road tube. **Open** noon-midnight Tue-Sun. **Main courses** £5-£10.50. **Credit** AmEx, DC, MC, V.

Tobia has garnered rave reviews and a consistent media presence; fortunately, the food matches the hype. Among the standard Ethiopian dishes you'll also find ancient family recipes. Wednesdays and Fridays are meat- and dairy-free.

Cafés & brasseries

Fine Burger Company

See p208 **The burger kings**.

Gracelands

118 College Road, Kensal Green, NW10 5HD (8964 9161). Kensal Green tube. **Open** 8am-5pm Mon-Fri; 9am-3pm Sat; 10am-2pm Sun. **Main courses** £2.50-£5. **Credit** MC, V.

Relaxed and friendly, Gracelands is big enough to satisfy Kensal Green's organically fed toddlers and their parents, as well as lunchers who can't resist the quiches. Entertainment options for the little 'uns are confined to a play area, but it is well equipped.

Haché

See p208 **The burger kings**.

French

Morgan M

489 Liverpool Road, Islington, N7 8NS (7609 3560/www.morganm.com). Highbury & Islington tube/rail. **Open** 7-10.30pm Tue; noon-2.30pm, 7-10.30pm Wed-Fri; 7-10.30pm Sat; noon-2.30pm Sun. **Set lunch** £19.50 2 courses, £25.50 3 courses. **Set dinner** £32 3 courses. **Tasting menus** £36 (vegetarian), £39 (non-vegetarian) tasting menu. **Credit** DC, MC, V.

Morgan M's airy dining room is a hushed haven in which to sample some of the best French cooking in London. The set menus may seem uncompromising to some (a minimum of three courses), but the food won't disappoint. A restaurant that makes it worth venturing into the Holloway hinterland.

International

Ottolenghi

287 Upper Street, Islington, N1 2TZ (7288 1454). Angel tube/Highbury & Islington tube/rail. **Open** 8am-11pm Mon-Sat; 9am-10pm Sun. **Meze** (dinner) £4.50-£8. **Set meze** (lunch) £10.50 3 meze, £11.50 4 meze. **Credit** MC, V. **Map** p404 O1 ⓫

Both branches of Ottolenghi are sleek, minimalist affairs, and, provided you don't mind communal tables, you'll feel spoilt rotten when you visit either of them. There's just such a good range of choices when it comes to the food – the soups, salad dishes, meats, artisanal breads, cakes and pastries are all equally irresistible. **Photo** *p215*.

Other locations: 63 Ledbury Road, Notting Hill, W11 2AD (7727 1121).

Oriental

Café Japan

626 Finchley Road, Golders Green, NW11 7RR (8455 6854). Golders Green tube/13, 82 bus. **Open** 6-10pm Wed-Fri; noon-2pm, 6-10pm Sat; noon-2pm, 6-9.30pm Sun. **Main courses** £12-£17. **Credit** MC, V.

This long, narrow café gets packed out quickly, so book or get there early. Sushi is superb – Café Japan must do the biggest nigiri toppings in London – but other dishes, such as miso-marinated black cod, should not be missed.

China Red

O₂ Centre, 255 Finchley Road, Swiss Cottage, NW3 6LU (7435 6888/www.chinaredrestaurant.com). Finchley Road tube. **Open** noon-11pm daily. **Main courses** £8.50-£13.50. **Credit** AmEx, MC, V.

The setting may lack appeal, but China Red deserves attention. Both its exciting dim sum and its full menus are geared as much to local Chinese as weary shoppers, and execution is of a high order.

Isarn

119 Upper Street, Islington, N1 1QP (7424 5153/ www.isarn.co.uk). Angel tube/Highbury & Islington tube/rail. **Open** noon-3pm, 6-11pm Mon-Fri; noon-11pm Sat; noon-10.30pm Sun. **Credit** AmEx, MC, V. **Map** p404 O1 **⑩**

This sexily designed new restaurant is owned by Alan Yau's sister – he's the man behind Hakkasan *(see p201)*, Yauatcha *(see p209)* and Busaba Eathai *(see p201)*. However, every last detail is very much its own. Expect good versions of the usual curries and authentic spicing.

Lemongrass

243 Royal College Street, Camden, NW1 9LT (7284 1116). Camden Town tube/Camden Road rail. **Open** 5.30-11pm daily. **Main courses** £5.50-£8.60. **Credit** MC, V.

For a fine taste of Cambodian cuisine, head to this small, homely restaurant. The chef is the star of the show, working busily at his woks, sending out one freshly cooked dish after another. Recommended.

Wagamama

11 Jamestown Road, Camden, NW1 7BW (7428 0800/www.wagamama.com). Camden Town tube. **Open** noon-11pm Mon-Sat; noon-10pm Sun. **Main courses** £5.50-£9.25. **Credit** AmEx, MC, V.

This no-frills eating formula has been repeated often enough, but its progenitor is seldom bettered. Long communal tables and shared benches may not be everyone's cup of green tea, but Wagamama is the place to go for those looking for quick, cheap and wholesome oriental food.

Other locations: throughout the city.

Turkish

İznik

19 Highbury Park, Highbury, N5 1QJ (7354 5697). Highbury & Islington tube/rail. **Open** 10am-4pm Mon-Fri; 6.30pm-midnight daily. **Main courses** £7.50-£9.50. **Credit** MC, V.

Much of Turkish cuisine is not grill-based; the excellent İznik offers a wide choice of the alternatives. Carved wooden screens divide up the large interior. The warm ambience helps, but it's the food that keeps the punters coming in.

Vegetarian & organic

Manna

4 Erskine Road, Chalk Farm, NW3 3AJ (7722 8028). Chalk Farm tube. **Open** 6.30-11pm daily; 12.30-3pm Sun. **Main courses** £8.95-£12.75. **Credit** MC, V.

Manna is the capital's oldest vegetarian restaurant, approaching its 40th birthday with self-assurance. It looks like a smart café, and the food's flavours are sophisticated, imaginative and harmonious.

East London

Cafés & brasseries

Frizzante@City Farm

Hackney City Farm, 1A Goldsmith's Row, Hackney, E2 8QA (7739 2266/www.frizzanteltd. co.uk). Liverpool Street tube/rail then 26, 48 bus/ Old Street tube/rail then 55 bus. **Open** 10am-4.30pm Tue-Sun. **Main courses** £5-£7. **Credit** MC, V. **Map** p405 S2 **⑩**

Breakfast fry-ups with free-range eggs are an obvious star turn at this award-winning café. The daily changing specials boards are less predictable, but cater creatively for vegetarians.

Other locations: Frizzante@ Unicorn Theatre, St Mark's Studios, Chillingworth Road, Holloway, N7 8QJ (7739 2266).

E Pellicci

332 Bethnal Green Road, Bethnal Green, E2 0AG (7739 4873). Bethnal Green tube/rail. **Open** 6.30am-5pm Mon-Sat. **Main courses** £4.20-£7.40. **No credit cards**.

This 105-year-old East End masterpiece now has Grade II-listed status. Maria Pellicci's range of own-cooked Italian specials, such as liver and bacon butties and steak pie, is unrivalled.

Story Deli

3 Dray Walk, The Old Truman Brewery, 91 Brick Lane, Spitalfields, E1 6QL (7247 3137). Liverpool Street tube/rail. **Open** noon-7pm daily. **Main courses** £5-£7.50. **Credit** AmEx, MC, V. **Map** p405 S5 **⑩**

This child-friendly place in the ex-Truman Brewery just off Brick Lane is a pleasant spot in which to while away a lazy Saturday morning or a casual weekday afternoon. Service can be slow, but the food (breakfasts, pizzas, cakes) makes it worthwhile.

French

Plateau

Canada Place, Canada Square, Docklands, E14 5ER (7715 7100/www.conran.com). Canary Wharf tube/DLR. **Open** *Bar & Grill* noon-11pm Mon-Sat; noon-4pm Sun. *Restaurant* noon-3pm, 6-10.30pm Mon-Fri; 6-10.30pm Sat; noon-3pm Sun. **Main courses** *Bar & Grill* £9.50-£33. **Main courses** *Restaurant* £14.50-£27. **Credit** AmEx, DC, MC, V.

Ottolenghi. *See p213*

RASPBERRY,

CHOCOLATE & UCARTON
BANANA DANISH
TARTS £1.80
£2.20

Reinventing the meal

Things have moved on a bit since pub food meant a ploughman's lunch. The gastropub revolution has swept London in the last 15 years – you're now more likely to find osso bucco on a pub menu than pickled eggs. The reason? Pub companies have been selling or sub-letting their less profitable boozers to a new generation of chef-proprietors who want to serve up proper food but can't afford to open a full-on restaurant.

There have always been pubs serving good food, but the seminal 'gastropub' in London was **The Eagle** in Clerkenwell (*see p199*). It (re)opened in 1991 as a pub serving great food and unwittingly became the template for venues city-wide: bare floorboards, a chalked-up blackboard menu, an open kitchen, and proper but simple cooking in a casual setting.

Some pubs have subsequently reclaimed the pub for proper British food. Among London's best gastropubs today is the **Anchor & Hope** in Waterloo (*pictured*), which is everything a good gastropub should be. First of all, it's a proper pub, serving decent beers (and wines), and you can feel comfortable just popping in for a drink. Secondly, there is no booking for tables: you show up and put your name down on the list. Thirdly, Jonathan Jones's take on British cooking is exemplary. Unusual combinations such as preserved rabbit, snail and watercress salad are surprisingly delicious (Jones learned his trade at places like St John; *see p197*). Rice pudding and rhubarb pot is a typical finale.

Another pub well worth a detour is the **Gun** in Docklands. Built in 1802, this used to be a waterside drinking den for seafarers and dockers from the adjacent West India Docks, but it has been resurrected with a restored original oak bar, reclaimed oak timber flooring, and Georgian-style fireplaces. There's a fine-dining modern British menu,

but also an option of earthier pub choices. Don't be dissuaded by the posh tablecloths – no one minds if you just order a plate of chips with the kitchen's fabulous own-made ketchup. Dishes might include Barnsley lamb chop – succulently pink and devastatingly tender at the bone, with the rich drizzle of meaty jus skirting a mound of garlicky mashed potato. And best of all, it's as welcoming to regulars out for a pint of Young's, Adnams or Flowers, as it is to champagne-quaffing, oyster-scoffing Canary Wharf suits.

Anchor & Hope

36 The Cut, Waterloo, SE1 8LP (7928 9898). Southwark tube/Waterloo tube/rail. **Open** *5-11pm Mon; 11am-11pm Tue-Sat.* **Main courses** £10.80-£14. **Credit** MC, V. **Map** p406 N8 ⓬

Gun

27 Coldharbour, Isle of Dogs, E14 9NS (7515 5222/www.thegundocklands.com). Canary Wharf tube/DLR/South Quay DLR. **Open** *Food served noon-3pm, Mon-Fri; 6-10.30pm Mon-Sat; noon-4.30pm Sat, Sun; noon-10pm Sun.* **Main courses** £10-£17. **Credit** AmEx, MC, V.

Plateau's space-age look is exactly right for Canary Wharf, with walls of glass, great views and groovy designer furniture (it's a Conran joint) that makes everyone look good. Good food; high prices.

Rosemary Lane

61 Royal Mint Street, Tower Hill, E1 8LG (7481 2602/www.rosemarylane.btinternet.co.uk). Tower Hill tube/Fenchurch Street rail/Tower Gateway DLR. **Open** *noon-2.30pm, 5.30-10pm Mon-Fri; 5.30-10pm Sat.* **Main courses** £13-£18. **Credit** AmEx, MC, V. **Map** p407 S7 ⓭

Judging by the number of suits at lunch, Rosemary Lane is no longer one of the best-kept secrets in the City. Its reputation is built on exceptional food, offering a modern take on French cuisine. Go now, before anyone else gets in on the act.

Les Trois Garçons

1 Club Row, Shoreditch, E1 6JX (7613 1924/www. lestroisgarcons.com). Liverpool Street tube/rail. **Open** *7-10.30pm Mon-Thur; 6.45-11pm Fri, Sat.* **Main courses** £18-£32. **Credit** AmEx, DC, MC, V. **Map** p405 S4 ⓮

Les Trois Garçons is a splendid place for a big night out. It's a handsomely converted former pub, run with warmth, verve and – despite its 'Edwardian camp' appearance – absolute seriousness in the kitchen. Expect adventurous pairings alongside tried-and-tested dishes, served among stuffed animals, under chandeliers and beside a display of jewelled evening bags. A true one-off.

Gastropubs

Gun
See p216 **Reinventing the meal.**

Global

Arkansas Café
Unit 12, Old Spitalfields Market, Spitalfields, E1 6AA (7377 6999). Liverpool Street tube/rail. **Open** noon-2.30pm Mon-Fri; noon-4pm Sun. Dinner served by arrangement. **Main courses** £7-£16. **Credit** MC, V. **Map** p405 R5 **107**
The most authentic barbecue restaurant in town, the Arkansas Café boasts a 'redneck chic' atmosphere, but the food is the thing. Meat (ribs, burgers, steaks) are fall-off-the-bone tender; sides (beans, 'slaw) are worthy accompaniments; desserts are heavy.

Italian

Fifteen
15 Westland Place, Hoxton, N1 7LP (0871 330 1515/ www.fifteenrestaurant.com). Old Street tube/rail. **Open** noon-2.30pm, 6.30-9.30pm Mon-Sat. **Main courses** £25-£29. **Credit** AmEx, MC, V. **Map** p405 Q3 **108**
The aim of Jamie Oliver's Fifteen Foundation is to change the lives of 30 youngsters each year by training them to become 'the next generation of star chefs'. In our experience, the food ranges from good to excellent, though wines start at a hefty £20 a bottle.

Latin American

Santa María del Buen Ayre
50 Broadway Market, Hackney, E8 4QJ (7275 9900/ www.buenayre.co.uk). Liverpool Street tube/rail then 48, 55 bus/26, 106, 277, 394 bus. **Open** 6-10.30pm Tue-Fri; noon-10.30pm Sat; 1-10.30pm Sun. **Main courses** £6.50-£14. **Credit** MC, V.
Atkins dieters, shoremen, Desperate Dan, prick up your ears: this place you must try. All kinds of juicy meat are sizzled to slow perfection on a grill; while own-made desserts make good use of *dulce de leche*, South America's ubiquitous milk fudge.

Oriental

Great Eastern Dining Room
54-56 Great Eastern Street, Shoreditch, EC2A 3QR (7613 4545/www.greateasterndining.co.uk). Old Street tube/rail. **Open** *Below 54 bar* 7.30pm-1am Fri, Sat. *Ground-floor bar* noon-midnight Mon-Fri. *Restaurant* 12.30-3pm Mon-Fri; 6.30-10.45pm Mon-Sat. **Main courses** *Below 54 Bar & Ground-floor bar* £4.50-£10.50. *Restaurant* £9-£14.50. **Credit** AmEx, DC, MC, V. **Map** p405 R4 **109**
The Great Eastern Dining Room is a stylish and spacious venue, with dark wood floors and striking contemporary chandeliers. The menu lists a modish range of pan-Asian dishes, so you'll find sushi sitting alongside curries, spicy soups, salads and noodle dishes. The puddings are almost too pretty to eat – but we're sure you'll find a way.

Sông Quê
134 Kingsland Road, Hackney, E2 8DY (7613 3222). Old Street tube/rail. **Open** noon-3pm, 5.30-11pm Mon-Sat; noon-11pm Sun. **Main courses** £4.40-£5.60. **Credit** AmEx, MC, V. **Map** p405 R3 **110**
With fake ivy and plastic lobsters on the walls, Sông Quê might not look a likely venue for exquisite food (appropriately enough, the name means 'rustic river'). Like a culinary excursion through Vietnam, though, the assortment of dishes covers specialities from all regions – and the results are delicious.

South-east London

Fish & chips

Sea Cow
37 Lordship Lane, East Dulwich, SE22 8EW (8693 3111). East Dulwich rail. **Open** 5-11pm Mon; noon-11pm Tue-Fri, Sun; noon-9pm Sat. **Main courses** £7-£9. **Credit** DC, MC, V.
Boasting a clean-lined modern style and an iced wet-fish counter, Sea Cow is a gem of a chippie. The menu is compact, offering the usual deep-fried cod, plaice and haddock, with the option of swordfish, red snapper and a daily special –all fresh and zingy. **Other locations**: 57 Clapham High Street, Clapham, SW4 7TG (7622 1537).

Modern European

Inside
19 Greenwich South Street, Greenwich, SE10 8NW (8265 5060/www.insiderestaurant.co.uk). Greenwich rail/DLR. **Open** 6.30-11pm Tue; noon-2.30pm, 6.30-11pm Wed-Fri; 11am-2.30pm, 6.30-11pm Sat; noon-3pm Sun. **Main courses** £10.95-£16. **Credit** MC, V.
What makes Inside special is the thought that goes into the whole dining experience. The menu has a Franco-Italian bent and offers some rich specialities: perhaps seared scallops with black pudding and pea and mint velouté. Quietly treasured by locals.

South-west London

Cafés & brasseries

Gourmet Burger Kitchen
See p208 **The burger kings.**

Crumpet

66 Northcote Road, Battersea, SW11 6QL (7924 1117). Clapham Junction rail. **Open** 9am-6pm Mon-Sat; 10am-6pm Sun. **Main courses** £3.95-£14.95. **Credit** AmEx, MC, V.

When it comes to child-friendliness, Crumpet takes the biscuit. The menu offers wholesome lunches (sandwiches, quiches) and proper teas (22 varieties). Cakes made by local mummies are typically yummy.

Fish & chips

Fish Club

189 St John's Hill, Battersea, SW11 1TH (7978 7115/www.thefishclub.com). Clapham Junction rail. **Open** noon-10pm Tue-Sat; noon-9pm Sun. **Main courses** £7.50-£12. **Credit** MC, V.

This modern chippie is a winner. Make your choice from the wet fish counter, then just tell the obliging staff how you'd like it cooked. Accompaniments are interesting too, among them double-fried chips made from sweet potatoes, and starters include such delights as own-made potted shrimps.

French

Le Bouchon Bordelais

5-9 Battersea Rise, Battersea, SW11 1HG (7738 0307/www.lebouchon.co.uk). Clapham Junction rail. **Bar Open** *Food* 10am-10pm daily. *Restaurant* noon-11pm Mon-Sat; noon-10.30pm Sun. **Main courses** £6.95-£25. **Credit** AmEx, MC, V.

Thanks to Michel Roux's involvement, Le Bouchon Bordelais has transformed into the very essence of a French brasserie. Eric Landeau's menu is carnivore heaven; beef and lamb are the specialities. **Other locations:** Le Bouchon Lyonnais, 36-40 Queenstown Road, Battersea, SW8 3RY (7622 2618).

Chez Bruce

2 Bellevue Road, Wandsworth, SW17 7EG (8672 0114/www.chezbruce.co.uk). Wandsworth Common rail. **Open** noon-2pm, 6.30-10.30pm Mon-Fri; 12.30-2.30pm, 6.30-10.30pm Sat; noon-3pm, 7-10pm Sun. **Set lunch** £23.50 3 courses (Mon-Fri), £25 3 courses (Sat), £29.50 3 courses (Sun). **Set dinner** £32.50 3 courses. **Credit** AmEx, DC, MC, V.

Bruce Poole's dining spot celebrated its tenth birthday in 2005, and the reasons for its success are clear: friendly, knowledgeable service, an unfussy, timeless space, and classy classic and regional French cuisine.

The Food Room

123 Queenstown Road, Battersea, SW8 3RH (7622 0555/www.thefoodroom.com). Battersea Park or Queenstown Road rail. **Open** noon-2.30pm, 7-10.30pm Tue-Fri; 7-10.30pm Sat. **Set lunch** £19.50 2 courses, £24.50 3 courses. **Credit** MC, V.

The low-key premises on Queenstown Road belie the quality of the modern French food served within. While the variations-on-beige interior creates a calm and pleasant backdrop, the food is the star.

Modern European

Glasshouse

14 Station Parade, Kew, Surrey TW9 3PZ (8940 6777). Kew Gardens tube/rail. **Open** noon-2.30pm, 7-10.30pm Mon-Thur; noon-2.30pm, 6.30-10.30pm Fri, Sat; 12.30-2.45pm, 7.30-10pm Sun. **Set lunch** (Mon-Sat) £23.50 3 courses; (Sun) £27.50 3 courses. **Set dinner** £35 3 courses, £45 7 courses. **Credit** AmEx, MC, V.

Forget the hot, hissing sprays in the leaf-filled Palm House at nearby Kew Gardens: this glasshouse is more like a conservatory extension from a local mansion. The cooking is excellent, combining classical French training with Mediterranean ingredients.

Lamberts

2 Station Parade, Balham High Road, Balham, SW12 9AZ (8675 2233/www.lambertsrestaurant.com). Balham tube/rail. **Open** 7-10.30pm Tue-Fri; 11am-3pm, 7-10.30pm Sat; 11am-9pm Sun. **Main courses** £12-£17. **Credit** MC, V.

The menu at this well-turned-out Balham local takes the provenance of its ingredients seriously, name-checking producers on the menu. There's plenty to entice, and the young, professional staff provide spot-on service.

Oriental

Chosan

292 Upper Richmond Road, Putney, SW15 6TH (8788 9626). East Putney tube. **Open** 6.30-10.30pm Tue-Fri; noon-2.30pm, 6.30-10.30pm Sat; noon-2.30pm, 6.30-10pm Sun. **Main courses** £3.30-£19.90. **Credit** MC, V.

Forget the Zen-style minimalism and reverential silence of many Japanese restaurants – Chosan is filled with knick-knacks, and the Japanese soundtrack can be less than calming. Yet it's one those places that every lover of Japanese cuisine cherishes simply because the food is so good.

Tsunami

5-7 Voltaire Road, Clapham, SW4 6DQ (7978 1610). Clapham North tube. **Open** 6-11pm Mon-Thur; 6-11.30pm Fri; noon-11.30pm Sat. **Main courses** £6.95-£16.50. **Credit** AmEx, MC, V.

With its smooth flooring and airy design, Tsunami attracts a lively following. The modern Japanese cooking includes the likes of yellowtail jalapeño sashimi and snow crab shumai dumplings.

West London

African/Caribbean

Tyme

133 Uxbridge Road, Ealing, W13 9AU (8840 7222/www.tyme.co.uk). Ealing Broadway tube/rail/West Ealing rail. **Open** 6-11pm Tue-Thur; noon-3pm Fri; 6pm-midnight Fri, Sat; 6-10pm Sun. **Main courses** £13.75. **Credit** AmEx, DC, MC, V.

Stars and their pies

We used to think Fanny Cradock was the ultimate celebrity chef – then Gordon Ramsay came along. Ramsay's a rough diamond, the loveable rogue that the British adore – a foul-mouthed ex-footballer with a quick wit and the best put-downs in the business. He's the perfect source of provocative quotes and tabloid stories, and has produced a string of popular TV series, from *Ramsay's Kitchen Nightmares* to *The F Word* (not to mention two US versions of his TV series *Hell's Kitchen*). But behind the media phenomenon is a well-orchestrated publicity machine (he employs several PR people to keep him, his chefs and his restaurants in the public eye), and then behind that, a staff of several hundred working in his several London restaurants. Despite the obvious hype, Gordon Ramsay Holdings restaurants (**Maze**, *see p205*; **Gordon Ramsay at Claridge's**, *see p205*; **Boxwood Café**, *see p211*; **Gordon Ramsay**, *see p213*) are actually really good: his pursuit of fame and fortune has not, so far, seen standards slip. His plan is to expand beyond London into a global brand: as well as restaurants already up and running in Tokyo and Dubai, he's planning one for New York in 2006.

So who the hell is Gordon Ramsay? He's a blindingly good haute cuisine chef, who trained with the best – then went one better. He is also a perfectionist and a control freak. He is also a scary big bloke who is superfit and has a famously short temper, so the sooner we stop dissing him, the better.

But what about Ramsay's rivals? The only TV chef coming close to Ramsay's ubiquity and fame is Jamie Oliver. A proper geezer

and man of the people, he's the one you'll find rescuing down-and-outs, reforming the nation's eating habits, helping old ladies cross the road and rescuing drowning puppies from wells, all while the cameras are rolling. His restaurant, **Fifteen** (*see p217*), is decent enough, but prices aren't exactly low – not that we can really complain, as all the money goes to charity.

Last, but by no means least, London has Gary Rhodes (*pictured*). Compared to the other two, he is like the Marx Brother who plays the straight rules. He is the chef who is genuinely respected by other chefs: the chef's chef, if you like. We think Gary's a top bloke, even more so now he has grown out of the silly haircuts. And we like his restaurants too: **Rhodes W1** and **Rhodes Twenty Four** (*see p201*).

It's great to be in a city with so many fabulous home-grown celebrity chefs, but, truth be told, we still miss Fanny.

From the welcoming atmosphere to its inventive menu (with Jamaican, Grenadian and European influences), Tyme is an all-round winner. Begin with a light starter, but plenty of room for mains.

Cafés & brasseries

Bush Garden Café
59 Goldhawk Road, Shepherd's Bush, W12 8EG (8743 6372). Goldhawk Road tube. **Open** 8am-5pm Mon-Sat. **Main courses** £4-£5. **Credit** (over £10) AmEx, MC, V.
The health-conscious of Shepherd's Bush have taken to this higgledy-piggledy café/food shop. It's popular for lunch: local yummies like it because their kids can play in the garden while they linger over the £7 quiche and salad deal (glass of wine included).

Notting Hill Brasserie
92 Kensington Park Road, Notting Hill, W11 2PN (7229 4481). Notting Hill Gate tube. **Open** noon-3pm, 7-11pm Mon-Sat; noon-3pm Sun. **Main courses** £18.50-£23.50. **Credit** AmEx, MC, V. Map p396 A6 ⓫
Probably one of the best – and certainly one of the smartest – restaurants in Notting Hill, this seafood-oriented brasserie is a big draw for the local bourgeoisie. The classical decor is restrained; the service assertive but warm; the house wines excellent.

Petersham Nurseries Café
Off Petersham Road, Petersham, nr Richmond, Surrey TW10 7AG (8605 3627/www.petersham nurseries.com). Richmond tube/rail then 30min walk or 65 bus. **Open** noon-3pm Thur-Sun. **Main courses** £11-£22. **Credit** MC, V.

Eat, Drink, Shop

Petersham Nurseries sits alongside the Thames, surrounded by meadows and paddocks. The food, overseen by ex-Sugar Club chef Skye Gyngell, is delivered with panache using quality produce, lots of it grown on site. The downside? Short opening hours.

Fish

Fish Hoek

8 Elliott Road, Chiswick, W4 1PE (8742 0766). Turnham Green tube. **Open** noon-2.30pm, 6-10.30pm Tue-Sat; noon-2.30pm Sun. **Main courses** £10-£30. **Credit** MC, V.
This small and bright South African fish specialist is a real one-off. The lengthy menu lists plenty of marine life you won't have come across elsewhere – stumpnose, kabeljou and butterfish, for example.

French

Chez Kristof

111 Hammersmith Grove, Hammersmith, W6 0NQ (8741 1177). Goldhawk Road or Hammersmith tube. **Open** 12.30-3pm; 6-11.15pm Mon-Fri; noon-11.15pm Sat; noon-10.30pm Sun. **Main courses** £9-£18. **Credit** AmEx, MC, V.
Chez Kristof is an all-round gem. The dining room is elegant and low-key, while the regional French cooking is tip-top. The deli next door serves café fare.

The Ledbury

127 Ledbury Road, Notting Hill, W11 2AQ (7792 9090/www.theledbury.com). Westbourne Park tube. **Open** noon-2.30pm, 6.30-11pm Mon-Sat; noon-2.30pm, 6.30-10pm Sun. **Set lunch** (Mon-Fri) £19.50 2 courses, £24.50 3 courses; (Sat, Sun) £24.50 2 courses, £29.50 3 courses. **Credit** AmEx, MC, V. **Map** p396 A5/6 **112**
The Ledbury represents a culinary step up for Notting Hill. The talented chef is Australian Brett Graham, and, small niggles aside, his handsome restaurant deserves to be around for a while.

Gastropubs

Cow Dining Room

89 Westbourne Park Road, Westbourne Park, W2 5QH (7221 0021). Royal Oak or Westbourne Park tube. Bar **Open Open** 7-11pm Mon-Sat; noon-3pm, 7-10.30 Sun. **Main courses** £14-£18. **Credit** MC, V. **Map** p396 A5 **113**
It may be just a small 1950s-styled room over a pub, but the Cow is surely one of the best restaurants in Notting Hill. The mix of classical and inventive on the short menu is admirable, and service is relaxed.

Global

Mandalay

444 Edgware Road, Paddington, W2 1EG (7258 3696). Edgware Road tube. **Open** noon-2.30pm, 6-10.30pm Mon-Sat. **Main courses** £3.90-£6.90. **Credit** AmEx, DC, MC, V. **Map** p397 D4 **114**

The road to Mandalay – aka the Edgware Road – is unpretty. It's a good job, then, that this restaurant itself is so welcoming and friendly. Ensure that your meal takes in all the sharp, hot, salty and sweet flavours that make up Burmese food.

Indian

Sagar

157 King Street, Hammersmith, W6 9JT (8741 8563). Hammersmith tube. **Open** noon-2.45pm, 5.30-10.45pm Mon-Thur; noon-2.45pm, 5.30-11.30pm Fri; noon-11.30pm Sat; noon-10.45pm Sun. **Main courses** £5-£11.45. **Credit** AmEx, DC, MC, V.
Sagar is one of the best places to sample vegetarian food from India's southern states. Modern furnishings, a glass-paned entrance and elegant Indian artefacts lend an airy and upmarket feel, while the 'mum's own' traditional cooking style provides an earthy contrast. Masala dosais are the biggest hits.

Zaika

1 Kensington High Street, Kensington, W8 5NP (7795 6533/www.zaika-restaurant.co.uk). High Street Kensington tube. **Open** noon-2.45pm, 6.30-10.45pm Mon-Fri; 6.30-10.45pm Sat; noon-2.45pm, 6.30-9.45pm Sun. **Main courses** £12.50-£19.50. **Credit** AmEx, DC, MC, V. **Map** p396 C8 **115**
The high-ceilinged dining room of this converted bank – decorated in warm jewel colours – is alive with the buzz of contented diners. The new menu is ambitious, with some unusual but seamless combinations of flavours.

Italian

The Ark

122 Palace Gardens Terrace, Notting Hill, W8 4RT (7229 4024/www.thearkrestaurant.co.uk). Notting Hill Gate tube. **Open** 6.30-11pm Mon; noon-3pm, 6.30-11pm Tue-Sat. **Main courses** £10-£18. **Set truffle tasting menu** (winter only) £55 5 courses. **Credit** AmEx, MC, V. **Map** p396 B7 **116**
Slinky tones and textures make the Ark feel like a place to go in two by two. Everything is impressive, from the superlative seafood via an informative wine list to desserts that are well worth breaking your diet for. The kitchen happily ventures beyond classic Italian dishes to offer some suprising combinations.

Assaggi

1st Floor, 39 Chepstow Place, Notting Hill, W2 4TS (7792 5501). Bayswater, Queensway or Notting Hill Gate tube. **Open** 12.30-2.30pm, 7.30-11pm Mon-Fri; 1-2.30pm, 7.30-11pm Sat. **Main courses** £16.95-£19.95. **Credit** DC, MC, V. **Map** p396 B6 **117**
A simple colourful room set above a pub, Assaggi is refreshingly free of trendy decoration, yet still manages to be fashionable. The menu relies on a succession of self-styled classics, many of which have a distinct Sardinian accent. The wine list is mercifully brief, and not too expensive, though there's plenty of scope for splurging too.

River Café

Thames Wharf, Rainville Road, Hammersmith,
W6 9HA (7386 4200/www.rivercafe.co.uk).
Hammersmith tube. **Open** 12.30-3pm, 7-9.30pm
Mon-Sat; 12.30-3pm Sun. **Main courses** £23-£32.
Credit AmEx, DC, MC, V.
While it's all too easy to be disenchanted by the
restaurants of celebrity chefs (in this case Rose Gray
and Ruth Roger), the River Café rarely disappoints.
This operation, which opened in 1987, seems only to
improve with age, continuing to rely on using top-
notch ingredients, simply cooked, to produce excellent meals time after time. The wine list is low on
detail, but broad in price range. Staff are friendly
and easy-going.

Timo

343 Kensington High Street, Kensington, W8 6NW
(7603 3888). High Street Kensington tube. **Open**
noon-2.30pm, 7-11pm Mon-Sat; noon-3pm, 7-10.30pm
Sun. **Main courses** £11.50-£18.50. **Credit** AmEx,
MC, V. **Map** p398 A9 ⓲
Timo feels like a destination restaurant, even if the
destination's more Olympia than Kensington. It's a
lovely serene space, with a fresh mood and an
enchanting walled garden. Dishes are a judicious
mix of the innovative and the familiar; service –
albeit a little stiff – is pleasant.

Middle Eastern

Alounak

10 Russell Gardens, Olympia, W14 8EZ (7603
7645). Kensington (Olympia) tube/rail. **Open**
noon-midnight daily. **Main courses** £5.60-£11.10.
Credit MC, V.
Of London's Iranian restaurants, Alounak remains
our favourite. It scores highly for its family-friendly
air and consistency of cooking: the rice is always
fluffy, the meat always tender and flavourful.

Al Waha

75 Westbourne Grove, Bayswater, W2 4UL (7229
0806/www.waha-uk.com). Bayswater or Queensway
tube. **Open** noon-midnight daily. **Main courses**
£9-£18. **Credit** MC, V. **Map** p396 B6 ⓾
With consistently excellent food, Al Waha is probably the most reliable Lebanese restaurant in town,
with meze running to over 50 good-tasting and good-
looking choices. The place itself is inviting, all done
out in warm yellow.

Maroush Gardens

1-3 Connaught Street, Marble Arch, W2 2DH (7262
0222/www.maroush.com). Marble Arch tube. **Open**
noon-midnight daily. **Main courses** £12-£22.
Credit AmEx, DC, MC, V. **Map** p397 F6 ⓬
There are now eight Maroush outlets in London,
plus four Ranoushes and one Beirut Express, all part
of the same chain. We prefer this one for its big, airy
main dining room – plus the fact that it does some
of the most refined Lebanese cooking in London.
Other locations: throughout the city.

Modern European

Clarke's

124 Kensington Church Street, Kensington, W8 4BH
(7221 9225/www.sallyclarke.com). Notting Hill Gate
tube. **Open** 12.30-2pm Mon; 12.30-2pm, 7-10pm Tue-
Fri; 11am-2pm, 7-10pm Sat. **Main courses** (lunch)
£14-£16. **Credit** AmEx, DC, MC, V. **Map** p396 B7 ⓺
For more than 20 years Sally Clarke's restaurant has
retained consistently high standards, producing simple cooking based on fresh, seasonal and meticulously sourced ingredients. Influences range from the
Med to California. For the deli next door, *see p251*.

Oriental

E&O

14 Blenheim Crescent, Ladbroke Grove,
W11 1NN (7229 5454/www.eando.nu). Ladbroke
Grove or Notting Hill Gate tube. **Open** noon-3pm,
6-10.30pm Mon-Sat; 1-3pm, 6-10pm Sun. **Main
courses** £6-£21.50. **Dim sum** £3-£6.50. **Credit**
AmEx, DC, MC, V.
This hip New York-style venue pulls in Prada-clad
A-listers by the limo-load. The design is suffused
with understated cool and staff are welcoming and
efficient. The chilli-salt squid is a must-try.

Wizzy

616 Fulham Road, Parsons Green, SW6 5PR
(7736 9171). Parsons Green tube. **Open** noon-3pm,
6-11.30pm daily. **Main courses** £8.50-£15. **Credit**
AmEx, MC, V.
The first 'modern Korean' restaurant in London is
the brainchild of chef Hwi Shim, aka Wizzy. Great
attention is paid to presentation, with good, interesting food artfully arranged on striking tableware.

Spanish

Café García

246 Portobello Road, Ladbroke Grove, W11 1LL
(7221 6119). Ladbroke Grove tube. **Open** 8am-7pm
Mon-Thur; 8am-11pm Fri, Sat; 10am-7pm Sun.
Tapas £1.50-£5. **Credit** AmEx, MC, V.
R Garcia & Sons, one of London's most respected
Spanish food importers, recently opened this café
and tapas bar next door. Everything we've sampled
has been superb, from paella to tortillas to salads.

Vegetarian & organic

The Gate

51 Queen Caroline Street, Hammersmith, W6 9QL
(8748 6932/www.gateveg.co.uk). Hammersmith tube.
Open noon-2.45pm, 6-10.45pm Mon-Fri; 6-10.45pm Sat.
Main courses £8.50-£13.50. **Credit** AmEx, MC, V.
Popular with people who holiday in Tuscany rather
than stereotypical hardcore veggies, this leading
vegetarian restaurant draws on its proprietors' Indo-
Iraqi-Jewish heritage to create eclectic dishes where
vegetables are truly allowed to shine. A lovely place.

Eat, Drink, Shop

Pubs & Bars

Get your drinking cap on.

Profit is the mother of reinvention: a slice of proverbial wisdom that London's new generation of entrepreneurial bar owner has taken very much to heart. Across town, abandoned institutions and neglected or ailing pubs are being given the Eliza Doolittle treatment, to the extent that, where once was a bank, a slaughterhouse or a prosaic little factory, now stands a spanking new gastropub, its open kitchen hissing and spluttering life, its clientele spilling merrily out into the freshly landscaped beer garden.

But despite the continuing restlessness of a drinking scene that has been thriving and shape-shifting for many centuries, there remains a solid anchor of tradition. Around every corner, squirrelled away down the most unlikely little mews, you can still find the London Pub of traditional lore, with its low beams and wonky floors and its thick-glassed little windows overlooking some forgotten alleyway.

The aforementioned gastropub phenomenon is a reflection of the 1990s surge of interest in what goes on in the kitchen: now, any pub or bar worth its salt and pepper has a daily changing blackboard menu. Drinks are catching up too. Heavily advertised lagers still dominate bar counters, but there's evidence that we no longer swallow the ad men's pitches: independent and specialist beers are a big growth area. It's also easier to get properly made, innovative cocktails.

But the best advice we can give is to start the night with a tube ticket: the days of the West End being home to the best bars are over. Try Hoxton and Shoreditch in the east, Notting Hill and Ladbroke Grove in the west and Brixton in the south and you'll not only find some excellent bars, but you'll also see London at its most cosmopolitan.

Should you find your drinking rudely interrupted by a ringing bell and the cry 'Time, please!', we apologise. There isn't an adult in London who has not been frustrated by the arcane law that means, without a special licence, pubs may only be open between the hours of 11am and 11pm (noon to 10.30pm on Sunday). But things may be about to change. As this guide went to press, many pubs, bars and clubs had applied for a late licence – due to

The best Drinking holes

For superior bar snacks
Shochu Lounge (see p227); **Milk & Honey** (see p228); **Match EC1** (see p225); **Tom & Dick's** (see p234).

For a bit of local atmosphere
Bull (see p230); **Ashburnham Arms** (see p232); **White Horse** (see p234).

For gazing over London
Vertigo 42 (see p224).

For impressing a date
Crazy Bear (see p225); **Loungelover** (see p231); **Salt Whisky Bar** (see p227); **Pengelley's** (see p229).

For time travel
Jerusalem Tavern (see p225); **Seven Stars** (see p225); **Guinea** (see p227); **Pride of Spitalfields** (see p232); **Elgin** (see p234).

For wines by the glass
Bleeding Heart (see p225); **Gordon's** (see p228); **Red Lion** (see p227); **Crazy Bear** (see p225).

For tip-top gastro fare
Seven Stars (see p225); **Bull** (see p230); **Hill** (see p230); **White Horse** (see p234).

For getting into the spirits
Boisdale (see p228); **Salt Whisky Bar** (see p227).

For a touch of the exotic
Floridita (see p227); **Opium** (see p228).

For cocktails to kill for
Apartment 195 (see p230); **Milk & Honey** (see p228); **Pengelley's** (see p229); **Loungelover** (see p231); **Napoleon Bar** (see p232); **Sosho** (see p232); **Trailer Happiness** (see p234).

Vertigo 42. *See p224.*

come into force on 24 November 2005 – and were waiting to see if they had been approved. But before you rejoice (or weep) at the prospect of 24-hour drinking, take note: most venues only applied for an extra hour's opening at most, and those in some saturated areas, such as Shoreditch, Camden and parts of Westminster, will be subject to a limitation in the number of licences that can be granted in that particular zone. Therefore, we suggest that, to be sure of a venue's opening times, you should call ahead.

Further possible changes are also on the cards, in the form of a ban on smoking in public places, though a final parliamentary debate on this had yet to happen at the time of writing. It's likely that any bans will be decided on a borough-by-borough basis.

For more gastropubs and restaurants with bars, including **Hakkasan** and **Baltic**, see our Restaurants & Cafés chapter (pp194-221). For a full survey of London drinking options we suggest you pick up a copy of the annual *Time Out Bars, Pubs & Clubs* guide (£8.99).

The South Bank & Bankside

Archduke

Concert Hall Approach, SE1 8XU (7928 9370). Waterloo tube/rail. **Open** 8.30am-11pm Mon-Fri; 11am-11pm Sat. **Credit** AmEx, DC, MC, V. **Map** p403 M8 ❶
The South Bank's culture vultures are attracted to this glass-fronted, split-level bar by the allure of decent modern European cooking and an affordable, varied wine list (everything from New Zealand sauvignon blanc, say, to southern Italian red).

Market Porter

9 Stoney Street, SE1 9AA (7407 2495). London Bridge tube/rail. **Open** 6am-8.30am, 11am-11pm Mon-Fri; noon-11pm Sat; noon-10.30pm Sun. **Credit** AmEx, MC, V. **Map** p406 P8 ❷
Wedged beneath the railway arches next to London's main foodie market, this atmospheric Borough pub has standing room only on most nights. If you're a fan of real ale, you'll know why: there are up to eight different, strangely named brews on tap at any given time (Slater's Top Totty being a typically silly example). One of London's finest real ale pubs.

Royal Oak

44 Tabard Street, SE1 4JU (7357 7173). Borough tube/London Bridge tube/rail. **Open** 11.30am-11pm Mon-Fri; 6-11pm Sat; noon-6pm Sun. **Credit** MC, V. **Map** p406 P9 ❸

---

❶ Pink numbers given in this chapter correspond to the location of each pub and bar as marked on the street maps. *See pp396-409.*

Still championing 'proper' beer (supplied by excellent Lewes brewer Harveys), the Oak remains one of the most characterful pubs in London. There might also be a lager on offer, but sadly the sign that read 'Lager drinkers will be served only if accompanied by a responsible adult' is gone.

White Hart

29 Cornwall Road, SE1 8TJ (7401 7151). Waterloo tube/rail. **Open** noon-11pm Mon-Sat; noon-10.30pm Sun. **Credit** AmEx, MC, V **Map** p406 N8 ❹
Beaded curtains, boutiquey brews and a brasserie atmosphere help this former backstreet boozer make the cut when it comes to after-work refreshment. Food ranges from light bites and sandwiches to main courses such as smoked haddock fishcakes and Aberdeen Angus burgers.

The City

Black Friar

174 Queen Victoria Street, EC4V 4EG (7236 5474). Blackfriars tube/rail. **Open** 11.30am-11pm Mon-Sat; noon-9.30pm Sun. **Credit** AmEx, MC, V. **Map** p406 O6 ❺
It's not often that the word 'beautiful' is used to describe a pub, but no adjective better fits this extraordinary little gem, with its original 1905 decor. It's a haven of stained glass, wooden floors, elaborate carvings and mosaics amid noisy traffic and modern office buildings. The selection of ales always includes a few guest brews, and the bar food (pies are a speciality) is excellent too.

Jamaica Wine House

St Michael's Alley, EC3V 9DS (7929 6972/ www.massivepub.com). Monument tube/Bank tube/ DLR. **Open** 11am-11pm Mon-Fri. **Credit** AmEx, MC, V. **Map** p407 Q6 ❻
Once the site of London's first coffee house, this pub has a colourful history. After being razed in the Great Fire, then rebuilt, it became a meeting place for slave traders and Jamaican plantation owners (hence the name). These days (after further alterations in 2002), its beautiful dark-wood interior is divided into intimate spaces lined with banquettes, and there's a restaurant upstairs. Wines and draught ales are tailored to the suited custom.

Vertigo 42

Tower 42, 25 Old Broad Street, EC2N 1HQ (7877 7842/www.vertigo42.co.uk). Bank tube/DLR/ Liverpool Street tube/rail. **Open** noon-3pm, 5-11pm Mon-Fri (reservations essential). **Credit** AmEx, DC, MC, V. **Map** p407 Q6 ❼
Champers and charming staff aside, there's only one thing that really counts at Vertigo 42: the view. Situated on the 42nd floor of the tallest building in the City, the bar enjoys a truly stunning panorama, and everyone who comes here reacts in the same way: 'Wow!' Eat before you come, though, unless you want (and can afford) a supper of caviar and pricey desserts from the short bar menu. **Photo** *p223.*

Ye Olde Cheshire Cheese

*145 Fleet Street, EC4A 2BU (7353 6170/www.
yeoldecheshirecheese.com). Blackfriars tube/rail.*
Open 11am-11pm Mon-Sat; noon-2.30pm Sun.
Credit AmEx, DC, MC, V. **Map** p404 N6 ❽
This marvellous labyrinth of a pub (hidden behind a
dark, unwelcoming entrance) has ten rooms of varying size and personality – from the comfortable wood-
panelled parlour closest to the entrance (with a fire
blazing in the hearth in winter) to the perilously low
beams of the cellar bar. Dickens, Doctor Johnson and
their posses were all regulars in their day.

Holborn & Clerkenwell

Bleeding Heart Tavern

*Bleeding Heart Yard, 19 Greville Street, EC1N 8SJ
(7242 2056/www.bleedingheart.co.uk). Farringdon
tube/rail.* **Open** 11am-11pm Mon-Fri. **Credit** AmEx,
DC, MC, V. **Map** p402 N5 ❾
In Dickens's day, tales of bloody murder were still
haunting this site; now, though, it specialises in
claret of a different kind. The superb wine list runs
to 450 varieties (there are some fine ales too); the food
is modern, French and tasty.

Café Kick

*43 Exmouth Market, EC1R 4QL (7837 8077/
www.cafekick.co.uk). Farringdon tube/rail.* **Open**
noon-11pm Mon-Sat; 1-10.30pm Sun. **Credit** MC, V.
Map p404 N4 ❿
Three René Pierre babyfoot tables are what give this
narrow, boisterous, loveable shack of a bar its name.
But really it's the excellent tapas and the fine Euro
beers (Sagres, Duval) that steal the show.
Other locations: Bar Kick, 127 Shoreditch High
Street, Shoreditch, E1 6JE (7739 8700).

Jerusalem Tavern

*55 Britton Street, EC1M 5NA (7490 4281).
Farringdon tube/rail.* **Open** 11am-11pm Mon-Fri.
Credit AmEx, MC, V. **Map** p404 O4 ⓫
The Jerusalem is the solitary London representative
of the St Peter's Brewery, whose eccentric beers
encompass lemon and ginger, cinnamon and apple
or, in the case of King Cnut Ale, a re-creation of a
typical beer of the first millennium using barley, net-
tles and juniper. The pub itself is a suitably kooky
tangle of niches, nooks and crannies.

Match EC1

*45-47 Clerkenwell Road, EC1M 5RS (7250 4002/
www.matchbar.com). Farringdon tube/rail.* **Open**
11am-midnight Mon-Fri; 5pm-midnight Sat. **Credit**
AmEx, DC, MC, V. **Map** p404 O4 ⓬
Lord knows it has had its imitators but none of them
can lure punters away from Match. Why? An unsur-
passed cocktail list: its Martinis are still the best in
town, while the choice of other mixological master
pieces is none too shabby either. There's a modest
sunken 'pit' area for serious upright drinking and
ringside seating for cocktails or snacky dining.
Other locations: Match Bar, 37-38 Margaret Street,
Fitzrovia, W1G 0JF (7499 3443).

Seven Stars

*53-54 Carey Street, WC2A 2JB (7242 8521).
Chancery Lane, Holborn or Temple tube.* **Open**
11am-11pm Mon-Fri; noon-11pm Sat; noon-10.30pm
Sun. **Credit** AmEx, MC, V. **Map** p401 M6 ⓭
Imagination runs riot in this fabulous little place. It
was built as a pub in 1602, hence the wooden front
and wonky beamed interior. The blackboard of gastropub grub proffers exquisite lunches to lawyers
from the nearby Royal Courts of Justice. Green-
and-white checked tableclothed dining areas at
either end of the narrow bar provide a rustic, French
appeal. The eccentricity, though, and more importantly, the beers, remain resolutely British.

Smiths of Smithfield

*67-77 Charterhouse Street, EC1M 6HJ (7251 7950/
www.smithsofsmithfield.co.uk). Farringdon tube/rail.*
Open 7am-11pm Mon-Thur; 7am-midnight Fri;
10.30am-midnight Sat; 9.30am-10.30pm Sun.
Credit AmEx, DC, MC, V. **Map** p404 O5 ⓮
A massive complex of bar, cocktail bar, brasserie
and restaurant, SOS (as the logoed T-shirts have it)
occupies four floors of a listed building facing
Smithfield market. The serious drinking part of the
operation is on the ground floor, a vast former warehouse with defiantly blokeish bare concrete, steel
columns, huge ducts and industrial light fittings.
The space is abuzz all day long, serving a café menu
and breakfast until 5pm. Post-work it gets very
boozy indeed. *See also p200.*

Bloomsbury & Fitzrovia

Bradley's Spanish Bar

*42-44 Hanway Street, W1T 1UT (7636 0359).
Tottenham Court Road tube.* **Open** noon-11pm
Mon-Sat; noon-10.30pm Sun. **Credit** MC, V.
Map p409 W1 ⓯
Ever popular, this poky bar tucked among the vinyl
junkie-yards is manned by a constant turnover of
Spanish and Portuguese alternative types… a
youngish post-work crowd drinks it dry nightly.
The draught beer is good, if pricey; the jukebox
sounds aren't as kitsch as they used to be; never-
theless, it carries on packing 'em in every night of
the week. There's not much by way of food, though.

Crazy Bear

*26-28 Whitfield Street, W1T 7DS (7631 0088/
www.crazybeargroup.co.uk). Goodge Street or
Tottenham Court Road tube.* **Open** noon-11pm
Mon-Fri; 6-11pm Sat. **Credit** AmEx, MC, V.
Map p401 K5 ⓰
There's a decent restaurant upstairs but you'll find
Crazy Bear's bar at the bottom of an ornate staircase. A hospitable hostess leads you to your spot –
on a swivelling cowhide bar stool, a red padded
alcove, or low leather armchair – in an art deco, mirrored wonderland. Drinks include impeccable long,
'short and muddled', champagne and Martini cocktails. Six quality wines of each colour are available
by the glass; there's a wider range by the bottle.

Eat, Drink, Shop

Rooms with a brew

Until a few years ago, the phrase 'hotel bar' was enough to conjure up images of stale nuts and warm lager. How times have changed. Recently the capital has become home to a handful of hotel bars that aren't just frequented by the hotel's guests, but are destinations in their own right.

Take the **American Bar** at the Savoy, just off the Strand (*see p62*), for example. This place has history – the White Lady cocktail was invented here – and in deference you should dress smartly. Equally sophisticated is the bar at **Claridge's** (*see p57*). This stylish den of Mayfair decadence draws in the wealthy hotel guests – so, again, make sure you don your Sunday best. Tip: we recommend the bourbon-laced Kentucky Highroller. At the **Berkeley's** Blue Bar (Wilton Place, Knightsbridge, SW1X 7RL, 7235 6000), grace and style define the clientele, and Sir Edwin Lutyens's original panelling adds the right touch of class. Nibbles are tip top, as are the cocktails.

Over in the City is the **Aurora Bar** in the Great Eastern Hotel (*see p48*). Complete with award-winning mixologists and live jazz pianists, it harks back to the classic hotel bars of the 1920s. Newer to the scene but just as highly recommended is **Bonds**, in Threadneedles hotel, also in the City (*see p48*). Here, cocktails come first; alongside

the classics, there are original concoctions and a magnificent wine list. Another favourite is the **Lobby Bar** in One Aldwych in Covent Garden (*see p61*). It's a beautiful, high-ceilinged room with vast windows and original sculptures. Martinis come in every flavour imaginable and there are 22 varieties of vodka on offer. Sheer luxury.

In addition to its historic hotel bars, London also has some quirkier offerings. Those who prefer something more flashy than classy might like the **Long Bar** at the Sanderson in Fitzrovia (*see p51*), whose famous 80-foot bar is undeniably ostentatious (with prices to match), or the **DeVigne** bar at Marylebone's Mandeville hotel (*see p55*), with its gloriously OTT mix of brightly coloured furniture and Old Master paintings. Top marks for best use of location, meanwhile, go to the bar in the **Courthouse Kempinski** (*see p59*) in Soho. It's situated on the site of the old Great Marlborough Street Magistrates' Court, the setting for several historic brushes with the law, including Oscar Wilde's 'Queensberry' case and various drugs-related Rolling Stones run-ins. There are private tables inside the original prison cells – complete with ice buckets tastefully situated in the urinals. Just make sure you sup up sharpish when last orders are called.

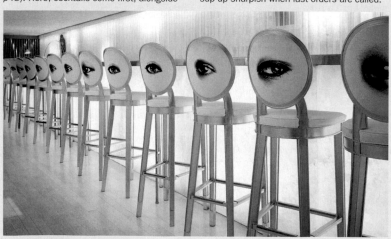

The **Long Bar** at the **Sanderson**.

Lamb

94 Lamb's Conduit Street, WC1N 3LZ (7405 0713).
Holborn or Russell Square tube. **Open** 11am-11pm
Mon-Sat; noon-4pm, 7-10.30pm Sun. **Credit** AmEx,
MC, V. **Map** p401 M4 **⑰**
Thanks to a sympathetic restoration in the 1960s,
the Lamb's ornate Victorian interior has been left
largely intact. The complete range of Young's beers
is on tap, including seasonal ales. Drinkers are a mix
of local office bods, students and academics from the
nearby halls of the University of London.

Nordic

25 Newman Street, W1T 1PN (7631 3174/
www.nordicbar.com). Tottenham Court Road tube.
Open noon-11pm Mon-Fri; 6-11pm Sat. **Credit**
AmEx, MC, V. **Map** p400 J5 **⑱**
This Scandinavian theme bar has changed little in
four years. The ice-cool selection of beers, spirits,
shots, cocktails and food has now been embellished
by outlandish arrivals such as canned Mac Arctic
beer from the world's northernmost brewery. A
mural of Max von Sydow still greets you on arrival.

Shochu Lounge

Basement, Roka, 37 Charlotte Street, W1T 1RR
(7580 6464/www.rokarestaurant.com). Goodge
Street or Tottenham Court Road tube. **Open**
5pm-midnight daily. **Credit** AmEx, DC, MC, V.
Map p400 J5 **⑲**
Winner of the 2005 *Time Out* Eating & Drinking
Best Bar award, this swanky venue sits in the basement of Japanese restaurant Roka. Cocktails, some
containing shochu, a vodka-like spirit made of buck-
wheat, barley, sweet potato or rice, are suitably stylish. Beers and other tipples are also available, while
the bar snacks and mains (brought down from the
restaurant) are superb.

Marylebone

Prince Regent

71 Marylebone High Street, W1U 5JN (7467 3811)
Baker Street or Regent's Park tube. **Open** noon-
11pm Mon-Sat; noon-10.30pm Sun. **Credit** AmEx,
MC, V. **Map** p400 G4 **⑳**
Savvy owners have chosen to celebrate this grand
old boozer's Victoriana with a sensitive refit. Ace
draught beers include Küppers Kölsch and Früli,
though the menu (sausage and mash, cold roast beef
sandwiches) waves the Union Jack.

Salt Whisky Bar

82 Seymour Street, W2 2JB (7402 1155). Marble
Arch tube. **Open** noon-1am Mon-Sat; noon-midnight
Sun. **Credit** AmEx, MC, V. **Map** p397 F6 **㉑**
Fashionably dark – barely illuminated by pretty tea-
lights and an underlit perspex bar counter – Salt is
a fabulous whisky (and whiskey) bar, attached to a
more ordinary restaurant. Islay malts, American
rye and even Japanese whiskies all feature. It's a
favourite haunt of staff from Broadcasting House,
though the vibe is more Radio 4 than Radio 1.

Mayfair & St James's

Guinea

30 Bruton Place, W1J 6NL (7499 1210/www.
theguinea.co.uk). Bond Street or Green Park tube.
Open 11am-11pm Mon-Fri; 6.30-11pm Sat. **Credit**
AmEx, DC, MC, V. **Map** p402 H7 **㉒**
This is Mortdecai's Mayfair: a creaking, dark-wood
pub tucked away in a mews, where expensively
dressed gents (the kind who would sport a rose in
their buttonholes on St George's Day) loosen their
silk ties and enjoy discreet conversation. Young's
beers and award-winning pies provide sustenance.

Red Lion

1 Waverton Street, W1J 5QN (7499 1307). Green
Park tube. **Open** 11.30am-11pm Mon-Fri; 6-11pm
Sat; 6-10.30pm Sun. **Credit** AmEx, MC, V.
Map p402 H7 **㉓**
The fire doesn't quite roar, and the bar is tended by
a handful of youngsters. Otherwise, though, this
delightful pub is the closest Mayfair gets to a village
local. The six or so beers include the likes of Young's
and Spitfire; there are also 14 wines by the glass and
a board proudly detailing the sausage of the day.

Soho & Leicester Square

Ain't Nothin' But... The Blues Bar

20 Kingly Street, W1B 5PZ (7287 0514). Oxford
Circus or Piccadilly Circus tube. **Open** 6pm-1am Mon-
Wed; 6pm-2am Thur; noon-2.30am Fri, Sat; 7.30pm-
midnight Sun. **Credit** MC, V. **Map** p408 U3 **㉔**
This rather splendid music enthusiasts' bar and
modest live venue recently celebrated '10 Rockin'
Years', and well it might. 12-bar sheet music, pho-
tos and concert bills constitute the main bar's decor;
a wall of fame covers the tiny staircase and cellar.
You'll find bands playing each night.

Cork & Bottle

44-46 Cranbourn Street, WC2H 7AN (7734 7807/
www.donhewitson.com). Leicester Square tube.
Open 11am-midnight Mon-Sat; noon-10.30pm Sun.
Credit AmEx, DC, MC, V. **Map** p409 X4 **㉕**
This old-fashioned wine bar is a world away from its
neighbours – sex and kebab shops. A narrow spiral
staircase winds down into two small, wonderfully
atmospheric rooms. Owner Don Hewitson loves his
wine, and has compiled a list that covers top choices
from the Rhône, California and New Zealand.

Floridita

100 Wardour Street, W1F 0TN (7314 4000).
Leicester Square, Piccadilly Circus or Tottenham
Court Road tube. **Open** 5.30pm-2.30am Mon-Sat.
Credit AmEx, DC, MC, V. **Map** p408 W2 **㉖**
Terence Conran teamed up with Cuba's renowned
(if tourist-pitched) Floridita bar to open this outpost.
Glitzy couples gaze at the film-set scene of hot wait-
resses swaying past with trays of exotic drinks, to
the rhythms of the house band. It's all a little forced,
but the quality of the cocktails cannot be gainsaid.

Eat, Drink, Shop

French House

49 Dean Street, W1D 5BG (7437 2799). Leicester Square or Piccadilly Circus tube. **Open** noon-11pm Mon-Sat; noon-10.30pm Sun. **Credit** AmEx, DC, MC, V. **Map** p408 W3 **27**

It's more arty and minimal these days, with John Claridge's black-and-white shots of Tommy Cooper and other luminaries on the walls – but the French House was built on legends larger than these (it was a London base for De Gaulle and his Resistance cohorts). A boho vibe lingers, although today's punters are more likely to be sipping house wine, Kronenbourg or bottles of Theakston than Ricard.

Milk & Honey

61 Poland Street, W1F 7NU (7292 9949/0700 065 5469/www.mlkhny.com). Oxford Circus tube. **Open** 6-11pm Mon-Fri; 7-11pm Sat (reservations only). **Credit** AmEx, DC, MC, V. **Map** p408 V2 **28**

Milk & Honey oozes exclusivity, with the unmarked door and ring-for-entry arrangement redolent of a Prohibition-era speakeasy. The interior is fantastic: a jazz-age affair of dimly lit booths, a low ceiling covered in diner-style aluminium and a business-like corner bar area lit like a Hopper painting. Cocktails are sublime, while the bar snacks barely add up to half a dozen choices (but they are fantastic). Anyone can visit, but ring ahead to book a two-hour slot.

Opium

1A Dean Street, W1D 3RB (7287 9608/www.opium-bar-restaurant.com). Tottenham Court Road tube. **Open** 5pm-3am Mon-Fri; 7.30pm-3am Sat. **Credit** AmEx, MC, V. **Map** p408 W2 **29**

This sumptuous French-Vietnamese bar-restaurant has gone from strength to strength since opening in 2003. The luxurious sunken interior and alluring, delicately carved alcoves complement imaginative, original cocktails of fine quality and oriental influence. Bar food is of the highest quality; the early evening 'Unbelievable Upgrade' lets you splurge on a budget.

Covent Garden & St Giles's

Albannach

66 Trafalgar Square, WC2N 5DS (7930 0066/www.albannach.co.uk). Charing Cross tube/rail. **Open** noon-1am Mon-Sat; noon-midnight Sun. **Credit** AmEx, MC, V. **Map** p409 X5 **30**

With an unrivalled location overlooking Nelson's column, striking design, postmodern Scottish theme and fare, Caledonian-inspired cocktails from Tony Conigliaro, this lavish, newish venue also has a decent snack menu and an encyclopedic whisky list, including a £12,000 bottle of 1937 Glenfiddich. There's even an illuminated stag in the basement bar.

Gordon's

47 Villiers Street, WC2N 6NE (7930 1408/www.gordonswinebar.com). Embankment tube/Charing Cross tube/rail. **Open** 11am-11pm Mon-Sat; noon-10pm Sun. **Credit** AmEx, DC, MC, V. **Map** p409 Y5 **31**

Unchanged since the era of *Brief Encounter* (you almost feel like paying in old money), this crumbling, candlelit wine bar was practically invented for affairs. Madeira is served from the wood in dock glasses, Graham's LBV comes by the schooner, beaker or bottle, and doorsteps of cheddar form the backbone of the ploughman's lunch.

Lamb & Flag

33 Rose Street, WC2E 9EB (7497 9504). Covent Garden tube. **Open** 11am-11pm Mon-Sat; noon-10.30pm Sun. **Credit** MC, V. **Map** p409 Y3 **32**

Accounts mounted beneath the original wooden frames and low ceilings of this indubitably ancient inn recall the 'Bucket of Blood' and bare-knuckle fighting days. Today's punters are treated to Young's and a changing line-up of guest ales; ploughman's lunches and doorstep sandwiches are downstairs, full pub grub is in the Dryden room upstairs.

Lowlander

36 Drury Lane, WC2B 5RR (7379 7446/www.lowlander.com). Covent Garden or Holborn tube. **Open** noon-11pm daily. **Credit** AmEx, MC, V. **Map** p409 Y2 **33**

The words in the window – 'London's premier Dutch and Belgian beer café' – are right for once: this is a superior gastrobar featuring the best of Benelux. Fourteen draught beers are served, plus 40 bottled varieties (split into Trappist & Abbey, Pilsner, Wheat and other categories). Both the all-day deli selections and the mains are worth sampling.

Westminster

Boisdale

13 Eccleston Street, SW1W 9LX (7730 6922/www.boisdale.co.uk). Victoria tube/rail. **Open** noon-1am Mon-Fri; 7pm-1am Sat. **Admission** £10 after 10pm Mon-Sat; £3.95 if already on premises. **Credit** AmEx, DC, MC, V. **Map** p402 H10 **34**

Before the arrival of the Albannach on Trafalgar Square (*see above*), this was the thane of Scottish bars, and is still a top-notch place. You can't argue with 147 malt whiskies – and nor should you want to. It's a superbly run operation (albeit a little pompous, in decor and clientele), with an outstanding range of wines and an excellent kitchen too.

Other locations: Boisdale Bishopsgate, Swedeland Court, The City, EC2M 4NR (7283 1763).

Red Lion

48 Parliament Street, SW1A 2NH (7930 5826/www.thespiritgroup.com). Westminster tube. **Open** 11am-11pm Mon-Fri; 11am-9pm Sat; noon-8pm Sun. **Credit** MC, V. **Map** p403 L9 **35**

No (public) bar sums up Westminster as well as this famous boozer, just yards from the Houses of Parliament. Upstairs is a grill room, and the cellar (not always open) holds a nice bar; but the handsome, skinny ground floor, complete with division bell, TV screening BBC Parliament and walls lined with memorabilia, is where the action is.

Smile for the CAMRA

It was recently calculated that 412 British brewers were producing some 2,342 different real ales. Sad, then, that four out of five pints of all beer sold in London are brewed by just four companies. These conglomerates spend millions promoting a handful of premium lagers and nitro-keg bitters – and practically nothing on real ale. Owing to the extra profitability of lager, there's nothing the big brewers would like more than to see real ale disappear altogether. In fact, they've spent most of their efforts and promotional budgets over the last 50 years trying to achieve just that.

But what exactly is this dangerous and subversive drink? The Chamber Concise Dictionary defines real ale as 'beer which continues to ferment and mature in the cask after brewing'. All lagers and bitters start out in much the same way – only the quality of the ingredients varies – but the unreal stuff is 'pasteurised', filtered and effectively killed before leaving the brewery. Such keg and nitro-keg beers then have to be 're-activated' by forcing CO_2 into them at the pump. Pasteurisation kills flavour while the artificial carbonation leaves beer gassy and flabby.

Real ale is a natural product. Retaining its own yeast, it should be flavoursome but not fizzy and never served warm. It does require a little extra work in the cellar – which can be comprehensibly taught in a couple of hours – but the results are worth it. Cask-conditioned

and bottle-conditioned (look out for sediment in the bottom of the bottle) ales are the premier cru of the beer world. Think the difference between farmhouse Stilton and Kraft cheese slices, between crusty organic baguettes and white sliced supermarket loaves. Thanks largely to the efforts of CAMRA (the Campaign For Real Ale), London's real ale presence is at an all-time high, with virtually every pub selling at least one.

The problem is that few of them sell well-kept real ale. As a general rule, it pays to avoid managed pubs owned by big pub-owning companies, where minimum wage staff don't know their ASB from their Elgood's. After strenuous and extensive research – well, someone's got to do it – we've concluded that, generally speaking, the most reliable place to sample a brewery's real ale is in a pub owned and run by that brewery. Young's beers taste better in Young's pubs, and so on. For some reason, the nearer the brewery, the sweeter the beer.

But if all that sounds too complicated, take note: there's a growing market in bottled real ale, as consumers of regular canned lager are turning to the proper stuff, and as an increasing number of pushed-for-time real ale lovers buy their booze from supermarkets and off-licences. If you're a complete rookie, here's a tip: just like their casked counterparts (make mine a pint of Slater's Top Totty), bottled real ales are recognisable by their silly names. Waggle Dance, anyone?

South Kensington & Knightsbridge

Nag's Head

53 Kinnerton Street, SW1X 8ED (7235 1135). Hyde Park Corner or Knightsbridge tube. **Open** 11am-11pm Mon-Sat; noon-10.30pm Sun. **No credit cards. Map** p402 G8 ❸❻
The idiosyncratic layout of this charming, cheerful and often-crowded little boozer lends itself nicely to

the rather eccentric decor. Bitter, Broadside and Old Ale from Adnams, and Bitburger on draught, are complemented by various bottles rare enough to drag discerning hopheads to this quiet strip on the Knightsbridge-Belgravia border.

Pengelley's

164 Sloane Street, SW1X 9QB (7750 5000/www. pengelleys.com). Knightsbridge tube. **Open** noon-1am daily. **Food served** noon-11pm daily. **Credit** AmEx, MC, V. **Map** p399 F9 ❸❼

An adjunct to the glamorous new Asian restaurant of the same name, this cocktail bar is a suitably slick operation. Abundances of time and money have clearly been spent on the look, which touts a kind of 1960s futurism, and lighting is intricately designed. The cocktail menu is compact but excellent; bar food comprises a delicious selection of dim sum.

Star Tavern

6 Belgrave Mews West, SW1X 8HT (7235 3019/ www.fullers.co.uk). Hyde Park Corner or Knightsbridge tube. **Open** 11am-11pm Mon-Sat; noon-10.30pm Sun. **Credit** AmEx, MC, V. **Map** p402 G9 **❸**
Behind the heavily fortified German Embassy, down a private cobbled lane past the Austrian Embassy, the Star was once a honeypot for London's gangsters, film stars and notorious characters of every stripe, who would frequent the tiny bar area, expansive lounge and first-floor room. These days Fuller's ales, respectful service and two welcoming fires draw a mix of locals and a smart after-work crowd.

Townhouse

31 Beauchamp Place, SW3 1NU (7589 5080/ www.lab-townhouse.com). Knightsbridge tube. **Open** 4-11.30pm Mon-Fri, Sun; noon-midnight Sat. **Credit** AmEx, MC, V. **Map** p399 F10 **❸**
From the street, Townhouse is little more than a discreet sign and a doorway – and even that is hidden behind a meaty bouncer. Get past him and you'll find a sleek, narrow bar, and a tiny seating area at the back. The cocktail list is as big as a phonebook, the crowd is a Chanel ad come to life. Next time we go we'll take our sunglasses.

Chelsea

Apartment 195

195 King's Road, SW3 5ED (7351 5195/www. apartment195.co.uk). Sloane Square tube/11, 22 bus. **Open** *Summer* 4-11pm Mon-Sat. *Winter* 4-11pm Mon-Sat; 4-10.30pm Sun. **Credit** AmEx, MC, V. **Map** p399 E12 **❹**
Apartment 195 arrived in a blaze of glory a couple of years ago and it remains a lovely (if less talked-about) space, its wood-panelling and battered leather seats sexed up with bright pop art and uptempo sounds. Saucily clad female mixologists serve stunning cocktails, while the decent bar menu is tailored to deep pockets. Beers are limited, presumably because beer just isn't a turn-on.

North London

Bull

13 North Hill, Highgate, N6 4AB (0845 456 5033/ www.inthebull.biz). Highgate tube. **Open** 11am-11pm Mon-Sat; 11am-10.30pm Sun. **Credit** MC, V.
A very popular haunt of sophisticated Highgate locals, this mid-priced gastropub offers dishes created by their Michelin star-winning chef Jeremy Hollingsworth. The drinks list includes chilled reds, lagers from the tap and cask ales.

Bullet

147 Kentish Town Road, NW1 8PB (7485 6040/ www.bulletbar.co.uk). Camden Town or Kentish Town tube. **Open** 5.30pm-midnight Mon-Wed, Sun; 5.30pm-1am Thur; 5.30pm-2am Fri, Sat. **Credit** MC, V.
A revamp has transformed a grungy rockin' dive into Bullet, a swanky cocktail hangout – and there aren't many of those between Camden and Kentish Town. The stylistic details are all too familiar (retro leather sofas, bare bricks, table football) but an easy-going vibe, fine cocktails and tapas bar snacks make up for any lack in originality.

Embassy Bar

119 Essex Road, Islington, N1 2SN (7226 7901/ www.embassybar.com). Angel tube. **Open** 4.30pm-midnight Mon-Thur, Sun; 4.30pm-2am Fri, Sat. **Admission** £3 after 9pm Fri; £4 after 9pm Sat. **Credit** MC, V. **Map** p404 P1 **❹**
For our money, the Embassy has a strong claim to the title of coolest bar in Islington. It's louche, loungey and lovable all at once, from the leather swivel high chairs and softly glowing red wall-lights to the unapologetic flock wallpaper and impeccable soundtrack. Downstairs, well-chosen DJs do their thing for a tightly packed but ample dancefloor.

Hill

94 Haverstock Hill, Belsize Park, NW3 2BD (7267 0033/www.geronimo-inns.co.uk). Belsize Park or Chalk Farm tube. **Open** noon-11pm Mon-Sat; noon-10.30pm Sun. **Credit** MC, V.
Between Camden and Hampstead, the Hill is a gastrobar that takes its food and drink seriously. In spacious, dainty surroundings, you can sup a pint of König Ludwig wheat beer, Fuller's Honey Dew or Aspall Suffolk cider. Alternatively, dine on the likes of braised New Zealand lamb shank while sampling the wine list, categorised to accompany food.

Keston Lodge

131 Upper Street, Islington, N1 1QP (7354 9535/ www.kestonlodge.com). Angel tube. **Open** noon-11.30pm Mon-Thur, Sun; noon-2am Fri, Sat. **Credit** MC, V. **Map** p404 O1 **❹**
The pegboard walls, metal piping handrails and plethora of crosshead screws at the dark and cosy Keston Lodge provide a welcome change in decor for these parts. City types and a contingent of older locals come for their fix of berry Martinis, inexpensive food and muted soundtrack.

Lock Tavern

35 Chalk Farm Road, Camden, NW1 8AJ (7482 7163/www.locktavern.co.uk). Camden Town tube. **Open** noon-11pm Mon-Sat; noon-10.30pm Sun. **Credit** MC, V.
Advertising itself as 'a tarted-up boozer on Chalk Farm Road', this geezerish pub is the ideal spot to nurse a hangover, thanks to its comfy armchairs, chilled music and pies from the Square Pie Company (in addition to a surprisingly refined menu). The roof terrace is the most popular spot.

Sosho – more than just so-so. *See p232*.

Florist

255 Globe Road, Bethnal Green, E2 0JD (8981 1100). Bethnal Green tube/rail/8 bus. **Open** 3-11pm Mon-Fri; noon-11pm Sat; noon-10.30pm Sun. **Credit** MC, V.
After a sensitive conversion a few years back, the Florist has bags of down-at-heel pubby charm (think burgundy walls, battered sofas and etched glass). Beers are limited to a handful on tap and a couple more by the bottle, but the cocktails are top-notch, and the tapas are some of the best going.

Grapes

76 Narrow Street, Limehouse, E14 8BP (7987 4396). Westferry DLR. **Open** noon-3pm, 5.30-11pm Mon-Fri; noon-11pm Sat; noon-10.30pm Sun. **Credit** AmEx, DC, MC, V.
There's been a pub here since 1583, while the current building dates back to 1720. It looks old too: it's a wonderfully cramped place, its floorboards slightly off-kilter, and the staircase a precariously creaking affair. A clutch of decent real ales supplement the standard taps, while glorious fish and chips are truly habit-forming. More serious food is served upstairs. If it was your local, you'd never leave Limehouse.

Home

100-106 Leonard Street, Shoreditch, EC2A 4RH (7684 8618/www.homebar.co.uk). Old Street or Liverpool Street tube/rail. **Open** 5.30pm-2am Mon-Sat. **Credit** AmEx, MC, V. **Map** p405 Q4 ④③
Home remains a popular destination for those who are intimidated by some of Hoxton's more cutting-edge options but are looking for a rough approximation of cocktail glamour. The low-ceilinged bar offers little in the way of good beer, food or cocktails, but it makes up for it in sheer numbers (of frisky after-work drinkers, that is). Grolsch, Grolsch, Grosch, say a trio of taps at the bar.

Loungelover

1 Whitby Street, Shoreditch, E2 7DP (7012 1234/ www.loungelover.co.uk). Liverpool Street tube/rail. **Open** 6pm-midnight Mon-Thur; 6pm-1am Fri; 7pm-1am Sat. **Credit** AmEx, MC, V. **Map** p405 S4 ④④
Gloriously camp, Loungelover is an eye-popping riot of colour and gaudy styling – stuffed hippo's head, grandfather clock, Victorian gas lamps, coloured perspex lights… the list goes on. The cocktails are divine, but be warned: those who don't bag a seat in any of the nooks (booking needed at weekends) are corralled into a tiny space by the bar.

Mother Bar

333 Old Street, Hoxton, EC1V 9LE (7739 5949/ www.333mother.com). Old Street tube/rail/55 bus. **Open** 8pm-3am Mon-Wed; 8pm-4am Thur-Sun. **Credit** MC, V. **Map** p405 R4 ④⑤
The mothership of Shoreditch's downbeat style retains every bit of its glamorous-seedy appeal. Stumble up the wanly lit stairs, and you'll find a large anteroom (complete with chaises longues) with a bohemian ballroom beyond. Excellent DJs and mediocre beers complete the picture.

Eat, Drink, Shop

Trailer Happiness – come for the rum. *See p234.*

Napoleon Bar

Bistrotheque, 23-27 Wadeson Street, Bethnal Green, E2 9DR (8983 7900/www.bistrotheque.com). Bethnal Green tube/Cambridge Heath rail/26, 48, 55 bus. **Open** 5.30pm-midnight Mon-Sat; 5.30-10.30pm Sun. **Credit** AmEx, MC, V.

Bistrotheque's bar (situated beneath a good French restaurant) is small, with bare brick walls, twinkling chandeliers and glass wall sconces; service is very friendly and efficient; and booze can be anything from pints of Kronenbourg to bottles of wine to tip-top cocktails, which are the real forte.

Pride of Spitalfields

3 Heneage Street, Spitalfields, E1 5LJ (7247 8933). Aldgate East or Whitechapel tube. **Open** 11am-11pm Mon-Sat; noon-10.30pm Sun. **Credit** MC, V. **Map** p405 S5 🟦

Outside, the Pride looks like somebody's house – a pot plant sits beside the suburban front door – but within is a friendly, smoky, unpretentious old boozer. Fuller's Pride and ESB are on draught.

Smersh

5 Ravey Street, Shoreditch, EC2A 4QW (7739 0092/www.smershbar.co.uk). Liverpool Street or Old Street tube/rail. **Open** 5pm-midnight Mon-Fri; 7pm-midnight Sat. **Credit** (over £10) AmEx, MC, V. **Map** p405 Q/R4 🟦

This tiny, red-painted basement makes the most of its KGB theming with Cold War newspaper cuttings in the loos and eastern European booze behind the bar. Staff are friendly and happy to suggest spirits to the uninitiated. Full marks to the eclectic DJ line-up.

Sosho

2 Tabernacle Street, Shoreditch, EC2A 4LU (7920 0701/www.sosho3am.com). Moorgate or Old Street tube/rail. **Open** noon-10pm Mon; noon-midnight Tue; noon-1am Wed; noon-2am Thur; noon-3am Fri; 7pm-3am Sat; 9pm-3am Sun. **Admission** £3-£5 after 9pm Thur-Sat. **Credit** AmEx, DC, MC, V. **Map** p405 Q4 🟦

Walk past the pop art Magnificent Seven prints on the wall, and you get to this award-winning space of industrial brickwork and leather settees, where the bar benevolently looms. Despite the quality of the bottled beers and wines, they take back seat to Dale DeGroff's peerless cocktails. **Photo** *p231.*

The Warwick

45 Essex Road, Islington, N1 2SF (7688 2882/www.thewarwickbar.com). Angel tube. **Open** 5pm-midnight Mon-Thur; 5pm-1am Fri; 2pm-1am Sat; 2pm-midnight Sun. **Credit** AmEx, MC, V. **Map** p404 O2 🟦

A homely and inviting bar that stands proudly apart from many of its east London counterparts' pretentiousness, the Warwick has a few ordinary beers on tap, eight or so wines, and three cocktails.

South-east London

Ashburnham Arms

25 Ashburnham Grove, Greenwich, SE10 8UH (8692 2007). Greenwich rail/DLR. **Open** noon-11pm Mon-Sat; noon-10.30pm Sun. **Credit** MC, V.

The classic, community-oriented Ashburnham Arms is the paradigm of what a local pub should be: it's a friendly focus of the neighbourhood, serves excellent ales (Porter and Spitfire among them) and the first-rate food. A patio garden completes the picture.

Liquorish

123 Lordship Lane, East Dulwich, SE22 8HU (8693 7744/www.liquorish.com). East Dulwich rail/P13 bus. **Open** 11am-midnight Mon-Thur; 11am-1am Fri, Sat; 11am-11.30pm Sun. **Credit** MC, V.

From the moment Liquorish wriggled into its tunnel-like premises on Lordship Lane, the place has been regularly packed to the rafters. The formula is simple: one part sleek cocktail bar, one part simple diner, with some decks for after-dark vibe control. Both the cocktail and wine lists are outstanding.

Trafalgar Tavern

Park Row, Greenwich, SE10 9NW (8858 2909/
www.trafalgartavern.co.uk). Cutty Sark Gardens
DLR/Maze Hill rail. **Open** noon-11pm Mon-Thur;
noon-1am Fri, Sat; noon-10.30pm Sun. **Credit** MC, V.
Stately in appearance, the landmark Trafalgar's four
ground-floor rooms increase in grandeur from high-
ceilinged bar rooms to the old-fashioned, upholstered wine lounge and fully fledged restaurant at
the back. Draught Boddington's, Flowers, Slater's
and Nelson's Blood are served, while the outdoor
riverside tables are the best spots for tucking into
superior pub lunches.

South-west London

Bread & Roses

68 Clapham Manor Street, Clapham, SW4 6DZ
(7498 1779/www.breadandrosespub.com). Clapham
Common or Clapham North tube. **Open** noon-11pm
Mon-Sat; noon-10.30pm Sun. **Credit** MC, V.
Gone are the days where debates on the socialist
state would be aired here (the pub is owned by trade
union fundraiser the Workers Beer Company), but
you'll still find good food, a fine outdoor area and a
decent set of beers.

Dogstar

389 Coldharbour Lane, Brixton, SW9 8LQ (7733
7515/www.thedogstar.com). Brixton tube/rail. **Open**
4pm-2am Mon-Thur; noon-4am Fri, Sat; noon-2am
Sun. **Admission** £3 10-11pm, £5 after 11pm Fri, Sat.
Credit AmEx, MC, V.
After years of blazing the bar-club trail, this Brixton
pioneer is still popular, and it continues to pull in a
loyal crowd for nightly doses of retro pop, hip hop
and drum 'n' bass. But there's nothing extraordinary
to be found behind the bar unless, that is, you're
impressed by alcopops.

Drawing Room & Sofa Bar

103 Lavender Hill, Battersea, SW11 5QL (7350
2564/www.galleryrestaurant.co.uk). Clapham
Junction rail/77, 77A, 345 bus. **Open** noon-11pm
Mon-Sat; noon-10.30pm Sun. **Credit** MC, V.
The walls of this quirky bar are lined with battered
star-shaped timepieces and fish-eye mirrors; the rest
of the decor is a style face-off somewhere between
Mad Hatter and Louis XIV. There are no beers on tap,
but there's a great choice of aperitifs and single malts.

Duke's Head

8 Lower Richmond Road, Putney, SW15 1JN (8788
2552). Putney Bridge tube/265 bus. **Open** 11am-
11pm Mon-Sat; noon-10.30pm Sun. **Credit** AmEx,
DC, MC, V.
This beautiful Victorian pile on the bank of the
Thames is partitioned into a public bar, a larger
saloon and a dining room where you can gaze
through picture windows at the river. There are also
a few tables outside (ringside seats for the Varsity
boat race). Grizzled regulars tuck into roasts, bangers
'n' mash and suchlike.

Fire Stables

27-29 Church Road, Wimbledon, SW19 5DQ (8946
3197). Wimbledon tube/rail then 93, 200, 493 bus.
Open 11am-11pm Mon-Sat; 11.30am-10.30pm Sun.
Credit MC, V.
The Fire Stables is one of Wimbledon's classiest
haunts. The stylish contemporary look ticks all the
right boxes: the requisite brown leather sofas, two
open fires and a garden area at the back. Admirable
wine and food lists too.

Harlem

469 Brixton Road (entrance in Coldharbour Lane
opposite Ritzy), Brixton, SW9 8HH (7326 4455/
www.harllemsoulfood.com). Brixton tube/rail. **Open**
11-2am Mon-Fri; 10-2am Sat; 10am-midnight Sun.
Credit AmEx, MC, V.
Friendly service, good atmosphere and interesting
sounds are the reasons to visit this second, sarf
London branch of the Notting Hill DJ bar and restaurant of the same name.
Other locations: 78 Westbourne Grove, Bayswater,
W2 5RT (7985 0900).

Sand

156 Clapham Park Road, Clapham, SW4 7DE
(7622 3022/www.sandbarrestaurant.co.uk).
Clapham Common tube/35, 37 bus. **Open** 6pm-
2am Mon-Sat; 6pm-1am Sun. **Admission** £5 after
9.30pm Fri, Sat; £8 after 11pm Sat. **Credit** MC, V.
Well established on this grimy stretch of Clapham
Park Road, this desert-themed bar caused quite a
storm when it opened a few years back. It remains
popular for its seductive and accessible vibe, well-
judged mixture of great cocktails and shorts, and
above-par food. Tiny TVs are mounted in the walls.

Ship

41 Jew's Row, Wandsworth, SW18 1TB (8870
9667/www.theship.co.uk). Wandsworth Town rail.
Open 11am-11pm Mon-Sat; noon-10.30pm Sun.
Credit AmEx, MC, V.
A lovely pub in unlovely surroundings (right by
an urban wasteland near the river), the Ship shines
like a beacon. The interior, revamped a few years
ago, runs to stripped and sanded wood, vintage jukebox and the like, while a split-level riverside beer
garden is the scene of some serious summer barbe-
cues. Young's ales are the beers of choice.

Sultan

78 Norman Road, Wimbledon, SW19 1BT (8542
4532). Colliers Wood or South Wimbledon tube.
Open noon-11pm Mon-Sat; noon-10.30pm Sun.
Credit MC, V.
The Sultan is a magnet for ale lovers: it is the
only London pub owned by Salisbury's Hopback
Brewery, and it serves that establishment's wonderful GFB, Summer Lightning and Entire Stout.
You can even take a polypin or minipin of draught
ale home with you. New pine tables and bar stools
furnish the interior, with unobtrusive piped radio
providing the backing track. There's also an appealing beer garden.

Eat, Drink, Shop

Tongue & Groove

50 Atlantic Road, Brixton, SW9 8JN (7274 8600).
Brixton tube/rail. **Open** 9pm-2am Wed, Sun; 9pm-
3am Thur-Sat. **Admission** £3 after 11pm Fri, Sat.
Credit AmEx, DC, MC, V.

T&G opens just three nights a week – but at least it
doesn't close till late. Its lustrous decor and wall-hug-
ging sofas foster a slick, classy aura with a relaxed
vibe. Around midnight, DJs up the tempo and drown
out the conversation with a pleasing mix of global
music (anything from Afro to house to kitsch).

West London

City Barge

*27 Strand-on-the-Green, Chiswick, W4 3PH (8994
2148). Gunnersbury tube/rail/Kew Bridge rail.*
Open 11am-11pm Mon-Sat; noon-10.30pm Sun.
Credit AmEx, DC, MC, V.

The Barge was already in operation when Agincourt
was a recent memory. One of a handful of decent
riverside pit stops that make up the Strand-on-the-
Green pub-hub, it's a cracker in its own right. Fuller's
supplies the ales, and there's a wholesome if old-
school menu of generously served pies and burgers.

Dove

*19 Upper Mall, Hammersmith, W6 9TA (8748 5405/
www.fullers.co.uk). Hammersmith or Ravenscourt
Park tube.* **Open** 11am-11pm Mon-Sat; noon-10.30pm
Sun. **Credit** AmEx, MC, V.

If you're looking for a landmark London boozer, you
couldn't pick a better one than this 400-year-old
beauty. It ticks all the boxes: dangerously low-
beamed ceiling, dark panelled walls, rickety furniture, terrace overlooking Father Thames and history
oozing from every pore. This is a Fuller's pub, and
dispenses London Pride and ESP.

Elgin

96 Ladbroke Grove, W11 1PY (7229 5663).
Ladbroke Grove tube. **Open** 11am-11pm Mon-Sat;
noon-10.30pm Sun. **Meals served** noon-10pm daily.
Credit AmEx, MC, V.

Built in 1853, Elgin's history can be discerned in the
treasure-trove of spectacular stained-glass screens,
lavish decorative wall tiles and delicious carved
mahogany. More recent additions to admire at this
three-bar, high-ceilinged boozer include three rotating real ales, boutique brews such as Wieckse Witte
and a decent supply of Belgian bottled beers.

Grand Union

*45 Woodfield Road, Westbourne Park, W9 2BA
(7286 1886). Westbourne Park tube.* **Open** noon-
11pm Mon-Sat; noon-10.30pm Sun. **Credit** AmEx,
MC, V.

The interior of this appealing little boozer by the
canalside displays little of the wearisome artiness
that one has come to expect from the gastro-centric
watering holes in this neck of the woods. The exterior boasts a pretty terrace. Beers and food are similarly unpretentious and well above par.

Graze

*215 Sutherland Avenue, Maida Vale, W9 1RU
(7266 3131/www.graze.co.uk). Maida Vale tube.*
Open 6pm-1am Tue-Sun. **Credit** AmEx, DC, MC, V.

Graze brings a touch of style to Maida Vale and is
becoming an increasingly buzzy space. The main
base on the shortish cocktails list is Wyborowa
vodka, though fruit Martinis are another speciality.

Lonsdale

*44-48 Lonsdale Road, Notting Hill, W11 2DE
(7228 1517/www.thelonsdale.co.uk). Notting Hill
Gate/Ladbroke Grove tube.* **Open** 6pm-midnight
daily. **Credit** AmEx, MC, V. **Map** p396 A6 🗓

This sassy little joint pulls off a genuinely exciting
formula of post-space-age chic (glinting bronze hemi-
spheres protrude from metallic walls) and a lengthy,
imaginative cocktail list.

Tom & Dick's

*30 Alexander Street, Bayswater, W2 5NU (7229
7711/www.tomanddicks.com). Royal Oak tube.* **Open**
6-11pm Mon-Thur; 6pm-midnight Fri, Sat; 6-10pm
Sun. **Credit** AmEx, MC, V. **Map** p396 B5 🗓

Auction-house furniture, hand-painted antique silk
wallpaper and assorted curios add to an atmosphere
that's two parts camp to one part calculated cool at
this great little haunt. A fruity cocktail menu and
excellent snacks add to the charm.

Trailer Happiness

*177 Portobello Road, Ladbroke Grove, W11 2DY
(7727 2700/www.trailerhappiness.com). Ladbroke
Grove/Notting Hill Gate tube.* **Open** 5-11pm Tue-
Fri; 6-11pm Sat. **Credit** AmEx, MC, V.

Beyond the sliver of an entrance, Trailer H has an
equally forgettable interior (brown, brown and more
brown). Your attention falls on the spotlit bar, which
is stocked with 37 largely Caribbean rums and produces some absolutely killer cocktails. **Photo** *p232.*

White Horse

*1-3 Parsons Green, SW6 4UL (7736 2115/www.
whitehorsesw6.com). Parsons Green tube.* **Open**
11am-11pm Mon-Sat; 11am-10.30pm Sun. **Credit**
AmEx, MC, V.

At the apex of the Green, this lovely old Victorian
pub, the boozer of choice for posh locals, has earned
the nickname Sloaney Pony. Don't be put off. A fine
gastro menu suggests both wine and beer to accompany each dish, and the taps dispense real ales such
as Harveys and Adnams Broadside.

White Swan

*Riverside, Twickenham, Middx, TW1 3DN (8892
2166/www.massivepub.com). Twickenham/
St Margaret's rail.* **Open** 11am-11pm Mon-Sat;
noon-10.30pm Sun. **Credit** MC, V.

Nestling on the north bank of the Thames, the White
Swan is found down a maze of narrow old streets that
seem impossibly idyllic – when they're not crawling
with people. The pub overlooks that final refuge for
keepers of the countercultural flame, Eel Pie Island.
On tap is a fine selection of ales and bitters.

Shops & Services

Credit cards at the ready.

London is, quite simply, one of the best places to shop on the planet. This chapter cannot claim to be comprehensive in such a big city, but it does include what we think are the capital's unmissable stores. But with so much to see, where to start?

Everyone knows that **Oxford Street** is the place to find most chain stores and department stores, but it can be an unpleasant experience. It's also increasingly full of tat, especially at the eastern end. Head to the quirkier parts of town – there are plenty of interesting boutiques selling designer 'street' fashion around **Hoxton** and **Spitalfields** to the east and **Westbourne Grove** in the west.

Marylebone High Street is finally coming into its own as a bona fide 'village', and now boasts a great mix of homewares, independent food shops and salons. Head for **Covent Garden** or **Knightsbridge** for expensive designer fashion, **Soho** for music and funkier clothes, **Charing Cross Road** for bookstores (new and antiquarian) and the **King's Road** for (expensive) homewares and kids' stuff. **Carnaby Street** is no longer the centre of cool fashion, but these days has some good mainline sports shops, plus the odd interesting boutique. Your adolescent children may want to skulk around **Camden**, but most adult Londoners avoid it.

THE BASICS

Central London shops are open late one night a week, usually till 7pm or 8pm. Those in the West End (Oxford Street to Covent Garden) are open until late on Thursdays, while Wednesday is late opening in Chelsea and Knightsbridge.

For more listings, reviews and a run-down of London's best annual shopping events, buy the extensive *Time Out Shopping Guide* (£9.99), updated every year. For suggested walks in east and west London, which take in some great shops, *see p165 and p190* **Walk on**.

Antiques

Islington, Kensington and Chelsea are the three antiques centres in London. *Antiques Trade Gazette* (www.antiquestradegazette.com), the *Collector* (www.artefact.co.uk) and *Antique Collecting* (www.antique-acc.com) have listings on dealers, plus details of auctions. **Greenwich Market** has a sizeable antiques section, as does **Portobello Road** (for both, *see p258*).

Alfie's Antique Market

13-25 Church Street, Marylebone, NW8 8DT (7723 6066/www.alfiesantiques.com). Edgware Road tube/Marylebone tube/rail. **Open** 10am-6pm Tue-Sat. **Credit** varies. **Map** p397 E4.
The bigger spaces at Alfie's tend to belong to 20th-century decorative arts, antiques and vintage clothing. Vincenzo Caffarella has some stunning pieces, particularly lighting; Ian Broughton has '30s to '50s kitsch. You can also find advertising posters, telephones, china and jewellery. The top floor is the best, and is home to Dodo Posters, Liz Farrow's huge collection of ads from the 1920s and '30s.

Antiquarius

131-141 King's Road, Chelsea, SW3 5EB (7351 5353/www.antiquarius.co.uk). Sloane Square tube then 11, 19, 22 bus. **Open** 10am-6pm Mon-Sat. **Credit** varies. **Map** p399 E12.
With its well-kept shops, this is a more pleasant venue than the often shabby arcades. It's a good source of Arts and Crafts and Aesthetic Movement objects, stunning antique Baccarat glass, jewellery, clocks and watches. The French-owned Art Deco Pavilion has stylish furniture, lamps, photo frames and cigarette accessories. All prices are negotiable.

Camden Passage

Camden Passage, off Upper Street, Islington, N1 5ED (7359 0190/www.antiquesnews.co.uk/camdenpassage). Angel tube. **Open** *General market* 7am-4pm Wed; 7am-5pm Sat. *Book market* 8.30am-6pm Thur. **Credit** varies. **Map** p404 O2.
Held in this pedestrianised backstreet near Angel, this market majors in costume jewellery, silver plate and downright junk – but that doesn't mean you can't find rare items at good prices. More interesting are the dealers in the surrounding arcades, who open to coincide with the market.

Grays Antique Market & Grays in the Mews

58 Davies Street, W1K 5LP, & 1-7 Davies Mews, Mayfair, W1K 5AB (76297034/www.graysantiques.com). Bond Street tube. **Open** 10am-6pm Mon-Fri. **Credit** varies. **Map** p400 H6.
Grays is just moments away from the chain-store anywheresville of Oxford Street, yet decades apart. A liveried doorman greets you as you enter from South Molton Street. Here are small shops selling jewellery; further back there are silver, glass and other antiques. The more varied dealers in the Mews building make hunting for affordable gifts rewarding. The long-established doll dealer Sandra Fellner is also here – look out for wax-faced war dolls and itsy-bitsy dolls' furniture.

Books

General

Blackwell's

*100 Charing Cross Road, St Giles's, WC2H 0JG
(7292 5100/www.blackwell.co.uk). Tottenham Court
Road tube.* **Open** 9.30am-8pm Mon-Sat; noon-6pm
Sun. **Credit** AmEx, MC, V. **Map** p409 X2.
One of London's best academic booksellers, covering
a broad spectrum of disciplines. This branch is strong
on history, philosophy, medical sciences and IT.
Other locations: throughout the city.

Books etc

*421 Oxford Street, Oxford Circus, W1C 2PQ
(7495 5850/www.booksetc.co.uk). Bond Street tube.*
Open 9.30am-8pm Mon-Wed, Sat; 9.30am-8.30pm
Thur, Fri; 11.30am-6pm Sun. **Credit** AmEx, DC,
MC, V. **Map** p400 G6.
Run by the US Borders Group – which also owns the
UK based Borders Superstores – Books etc is a
pared-down version of its larger sibling. Stores carry
a healthy selection of general interest material and
run offers on the current mainstream bestsellers.
Other locations: throughout the city.

Borders Books & Music

*203 Oxford Street, Oxford Circus, W1D 2LE
(7292 1600/www.borders.co.uk). Oxford Circus
tube.* **Open** 8am-11pm Mon-Sat; noon-6pm Sun.
Credit AmEx, MC, V. **Map** p408 U2.
This US import offers an extensive selection of
general interest and specialist titles spread over
five floors, plus a decent CD/video/DVD section and
a commendable stationery and magazine area at
ground level. There's also a coffee shop.
Other locations: throughout the city.

Daunt Books

*83-84 Marylebone High Street, Marylebone, W1U
4QW (7224 2295/www.dauntbooks.co.uk). Baker
Street tube.* **Open** 9am-7.30pm Mon-Sat; 11am-6pm
Sun. **Credit** MC, V. **Map** p400 G5.
A visit to this superb store is worthwhile just to marvel at the Edwardian interior, with its oak galleries
and central skylight running the length of the shop.
The books are arranged by country, over three levels, with stock boasting a comprehensive selection
of specialist travel guides (some second hand), plus
literature and maps. There's also a commendable
choice of general stock, including the latest quality
hardbacks, political biographies and children's
books, plus large sections devoted to gardening,
cookery and interior design.
Other locations: 51 South End Road, Hampstead,
NW3 2QB (7794 8206); 193 Haverstock Hill, Belsize
Park, NW3 4QL (7794 4006).

Foyles

*113-119 Charing Cross Road, Soho, WC2H 0EB
(7437 5660/www.foyles.co.uk). Tottenham Court
Road tube.* **Open** 9.30am-9pm Mon-Sat; noon-6pm
Sun. **Credit** AmEx, DC, MC, V. **Map** p409 X2.

Since the transformation of this famous, independent store and the opening of a smaller branch at the
Royal Festival Hall (the first new outlet for over 70
years), the team here has been feeling more pur-
poseful than ever. The café area surpasses those of
rivals, with organic food and music events organised by Ray's Jazz (incorporated into the store as part
of the refurbishment, along with Silver Moon
women's bookshop). Author book signings and talks
take place throughout the year. There's also a good
audio choice, and plans for a second-hand section.

London Review of Books

*14 Bury Place, Bloomsbury, WC1A 2JL (7269 9030/
www.lrb.co.uk/lrbshop). Tottenham Court Road
tube.* **Open** 10am-6.30pm Mon-Sat; noon-6pm Sun.
Credit AmEx, MC, V. **Map** p401 L5.
This modern, well-run shop is owned by the eponymous literary-political journal, is all polished wood,
quiet conversations and passionate staff. The range
of books is extraordinary, from Alan Bennett's latest offerings and the most recent academic, political
and biographical tomes, to up-to-date copies of the
New Yorker, *Art Review* and *Smoke*, plus a good
choice of the best poetry, cookery and gardening
titles. Regular readings and talks.

Waterstone's

*311 Oxford Street, Oxford Circus, W1C 2HP (7499
6100/www.amazon.co.uk). Oxford Circus tube.* **Open**
9am-8pm Mon-Wed, Fri, Sat; 9am-9pm Thur; noon-
6pm Sun. **Credit** AmEx, DC, MC, V. **Map** p400 H6.
The latest major branch from Britain's best-known
bookselling giant is a celebration of the capital. A
London section – on the right as you enter – contains
guides, recommended books, A-Zs and maps. Bays
highlighting London titles can be found throughout
three floors of well-stocked departments.
Other locations: throughout the city.

Used & antiquarian

The **Riverside Walk Market** (10am-5pm Sat,
Sun and irregular weekdays) on the South Bank
under Waterloo Bridge, sells cheap paperbacks.

Any Amount of Books

*56 Charing Cross Road, Leicester Square, WC2H
0QA (7836 3697/www.anyamountofbooks.com).
Leicester Square tube.* **Open** 10.30am-9.30pm Mon-
Sat; 11.30am-7.30pm Sun. **Credit** AmEx, MC, V.
Map p409 X3.
Any Amount of Books is a treasure trove. All subjects are covered, with large sections on literary criticism, biography, art, architecture, gender, history,
medicine and religion. A few first editions feature too.

Ulysses

*40 Museum Street, Bloomsbury, WC1A 1LU (7831
1600). Holborn tube.* **Open** 11am-6pm Mon-Sat.
Credit AmEx, MC, V. **Map** p401 L5.
One of the premier bookshops for affordable modern first editions. The space has a smart, homely feel
with plenty of scope for browsing.

Department stores

Fortnum & Mason

181 Piccadilly, St James's, W1A 1ER (7734 8040/ www.fortnumandmason.co.uk). Green Park or Piccadilly Circus tube. **Open** 10am-6.30pm Mon-Sat. *Restaurant & food hall only* noon-6pm Sun. **Credit** AmEx, MC, V. **Map** p408 V4.

F&M's famous ground-floor food hall is wonderfully over-the-top, with marbled pillars and chandeliers, while the elegant upper levels are blissfully quiet and make for very pleasant shopping. The women's clothing department closed in summer 2005, but there are up-to-date accessories by Lulu Guinness, Philip Treacy and Georgina von Etzdorf, plus an excellent perfumery, home to the Clive Christian range (exclusive in London). Formal lunch or tea at the St James's Restaurant and light meals at the Fountain and Patio restaurants don't come cheap, but they're a real slice of London.

Harrods

87-135 Brompton Road, Knightsbridge, SW1X 7XL (7730 1234/www.harrods.com). Knightsbridge tube. **Open** 10am-7pm daily. **Credit** AmEx, DC, MC, V. **Map** p399 F9.

The mother of all upscale department stores, with floor after floor of expensive designer clothing overseen by surprisingly friendly staff who know you can't afford to buy but don't mind you looking. And looking is fab – it costs nothing to soak up the ambience in the ground-floor Room of Luxury with accessories by the likes of Gucci, Dior and Hermès. Those who go beyond browsing can avail themselves of the new free personal shopping service based on the first floor. The legendary food halls are the biggest attractions (chocs, teas and coffees, deli counters and a Krispy Kreme outlet are just some of the highlights). For the Urban Retreat spa, *see p256*.

Harvey Nichols

109-125 Knightsbridge, SW1X 7RJ (7235 5000/ www.harveynichols.com). Knightsbridge tube. **Open** *Shop* 10am-8pm Mon-Fri; 10am-7pm Sat; noon-6pm Sun. *Café* 10am-10pm Mon-Sat; 10am-6pm Sun. *Restaurant* 10am-11pm Mon-Sat; 10am-6pm Sun. **Credit** AmEx, DC, MC, V. **Map** p399 F9.

Harvey Nicks is an elegant and urban one-stop shop for front-line fashion. New collections from the likes of Giambattista Valli, Luella and Kris van Assche maintain the store's reputation for eclectic ready-to-wear pieces for both sexes. The ground floor is a cosmetics junkie's paradise, and also houses Pout and Bliss concessions, as well as the holistic Beyond Beauty area. For refreshment there are the light-suffused fifth-floor bar, café and restaurant (*see p211*).

John Lewis

278-306 Oxford Street, Oxford Circus, W1A 1EX (7629 7711/www.johnlewis.co.uk). Bond Street or Oxford Circus tube. **Open** 9.30am-7pm Mon-Wed, Fri, Sat; 9.30am-8pm Thur; noon-6pm Sun. **Credit** MC, V. **Map** p400 H6.

Knocking on for 150 years of trade, John Lewis represents the best of British middle-class consumer values with its 'never knowingly undersold' prices. Nothing's super-stylish, but it's no longer embarrassingly outdated either, and the staff know what they're talking about. All departments – and there are plenty of them – are well stocked; haberdashery and kitchenware are positively legendary.

Liberty

210-220 Regent Street, Oxford Circus, W1B 5AH (7734 1234/www.liberty.co.uk). Oxford Circus tube. **Open** 10am-7pm Mon-Wed, Fri, Sat; 10am-8pm Thur; noon-6pm Sun. **Credit** AmEx, DC, MC, V. **Map** p408 U2.

Liberty's famous prints are coveted the world over, but tourists may not be aware of the other riches behind its façade. Menswear, women's shoes and lingerie are in the Regent House on Regent Street, as is the cosmetics department. But for body and bath products, as well as the celebrated scarf hall, you need to hop over to the lovely 1920s Tudor House on Great Marlborough Street. The fourth floor now houses a furniture department mixing vintage one-offs with 20th-century design classics, Arts and Crafts and modern pieces.

Marks & Spencer

458 Oxford Street, Oxford Circus, W1C 1AP (7935 7954/www.marksandspencer.co.uk). Marble Arch tube. **Open** 9am-9pm Mon-Fri; 9am-8pm Sat; noon-6pm Sun. **Credit** AmEx, DC, MC, V. **Map** p400 G6.

In spite of its rollercoasting fortunes (currently heading in the right direction), M&S is making admirable efforts to improve and update its stock. Womenswear has started to have a more boutiquey feel and menswear has been beefed up with a new Autograph range, featuring collections by Timothy Everest and Nigel Hall. The basics for which M&S is famous are still reliable – cotton Ts, everyday undies. This branch also has a well-stocked homewares section, a third-floor café, a bureau de change and instant cash VAT refunds for those eligible. **Other locations**: throughout the city.

Selfridges

400 Oxford Street, Oxford Circus, W1A 1AB (0870 837 7377/www.selfridges.com). Bond Street or Marble Arch tube. **Open** 10am-8pm Mon-Fri; 9.30am-8pm Sat; noon-6pm Sun. **Credit** AmEx, DC, MC, V. **Map** p400 G6.

You could blow your budget within seconds of stepping through Selfridges' door – that is, if you enter via the luxury fashion accessories department and fall under the spell of Miu Miu, Mulberry, Prada, Burberry... At the centre of the ground floor is a heaving cosmetics and fragrance marketplace, with Stila, MAC, Nars, Aveda and more, plus two brow bars and a mini Groom (*see p253* **Getting the right treatments**). The Superbrands section is dedicated to eight well-known designers (including Balenciaga and Marni). The layout doesn't always seem logical, but it's all here. Cafés, restaurants and a Moët champagne bar offer plenty of refuelling options.

The empires' new clothes

Never considered popping into Daks when you were looking for a cool cropped jacket? You thought Austin Reed was a stuffy old place full of boring grey suits? And that Burberry was only really for Japanese tourists? Think again, for the times they are a-changing. Granted, only a few years ago the thought of being able to buy a truly fashionable designer outfit in one of the capital's long-established fashion houses was quite ludicrous. Sure, you could find a fantastic rain mac, argyle knit or

cashmere twin set. But a natty Empire-line dress or sumptuous leather it-bag? Forget it. Fast forward to 2005/6 and suddenly those same labels have serious appeal for the most stylish urbanites, thanks to a new breed of talented designers enlisted to bring the labels into the 21st century.

The new stars? Stuart Vevers, enlisted as creative director of **Mulberry** (41-42 New Bond Street, 7491 3900, www.mulberry.com), who has been injecting a little rock 'n' roll cool into the traditional leather bag line, which is already giving Hermès and Gucci a run for their money. Then there's the eminently talented Christopher Bailey at **Burberry** (21-23 New Bond Street, 7839 5222, www.burberry.com), who has been recreating classics like the pea coat, trench and cashmere knits in vibrant

new colour combinations and modern shapes to international acclaim.

Over at **Aquascutum** (100 Regent Street, 7675 8200, www.aquascutum.co.uk), Michael Herz and Graeme Fidler have enlivened the 155-year-old brand with new takes on old classics like the 'Imperium' trench coat (luscious bottle-green corduroy), knits in acid colours and classic check over-dyed in Prussian blue. **Pringle of Scotland** (112 New Bond Street, 7297 4580, www.pringle scotland.co.uk), currently celebrating its 190th birthday, has enlisted new talent in the form of Royal College of Art graduate Claire Waight Keller, formerly of Calvin Klein and Ralph Lauren, to breath new life into the fashion side of things, while Simona Ciacchi, formerly of Gucci, will be taking care of accessories.

As for **Daks** (10 Old Bond Street, 7409 4040, www.daks.com; *pictured*), Anthony Cuthbertson and Bruce Montgomery play on the upper-crust British heritage while adding modern style. Even **Austin Reed** is a credible place to hang out now thanks to Equilibrium, a groovy art deco grooming salon on its lower ground floor (103 Regent Street, 7534 7719, www.re-aqua.co.uk); luxurious changing rooms; and affordable but slick ready-to-wear suits. So, forget Paris. Who needs Milan? These are exciting and progressive times in London.

Eat, Drink, Shop

Electronics

Tottenham Court Road, W1, has the city's main concentration of electronics and computer shops, but for good prices and expert advice on a smaller range, try **John Lewis** (*see p238*).

Computers

CeX
32 Rathbone Place, Fitzrovia, W1T 1JJ (0845 345 1664/www.cex.co.uk). Tottenham Court Road tube. **Open** 10am-7.30pm Mon-Wed, Sat; 10am-8pm Thur, Fri; 11am-7pm Sun. **Credit** MC, V. **Map** p401 K5.

A budget-conscious retro-gamer's paradise, CeX (or Computer Exchange) is the second-hand emporium par excellence, where you can pick up everything from the original Nintendo LCD Game & Watch hand-helds (around £30) to recent titles for Xbox, GameCube and PlayStation 2, including imports. CeX will also buy your old games.
Other locations: throughout the city.

Gultronics
264-267 Tottenham Court Road, Fitzrovia, W1T 7RH (7436 4120/www.gultronics.co.uk). Goodge Street or Tottenham Court Road tube. **Open** 10am-7pm Mon-Sat; 11am-5pm Sun. **Credit** AmEx, MC, V. **Map** p401 K5.

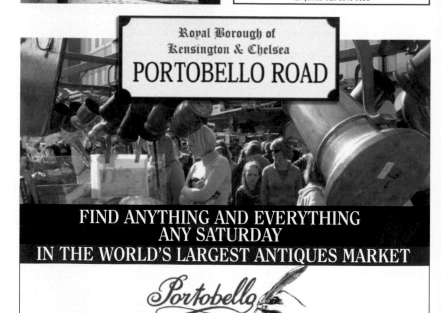

It sells most categories of consumer electronics, but it's the range of Toshiba and Sony laptops that makes Gultronics worth a visit. Prices are competitive and the shop stocks a good range of accessories, including printers and scanners.

Other locations: 91 Oxford Street, Oxford Circus, W1D 2HA (7439 2020); 52 Tottenham Court Road, Fitzrovia, W1P 9RE (7373 9188).

Micro Anvika

245 Tottenham Court Road, Fitzrovia, W1T 7QT (7467 6000/www.microanvika.co.uk). Goodge Street or Tottenham Court Road tube. **Open** 9.30am-6pm Mon-Wed, Fri, Sat; 9.30am-6.30pm Thur; 11am-5pm Sun. **Credit** AmEx, MC, V. **Map** p401 K5.

Micro Anvika has good selection of Macs and PCs. Laptops from Sony, Toshiba, IBM and others are supplemented by accessories, gadgets and software. There's also an outlet in Selfridges.

Other locations: 31 Alfred Place, Fitzrovia, WC1E 7DP (7467 6000); 13 Chenies Street, Fitzrovia, WC1E 7EY (7567 6000); 53-54 Tottenham Court Road, Fitzrovia, W1T 2EJ (7467 6000).

General & audio-visual

Ask Electronics

248 Tottenham Court Road, Fitzrovia, W1T 7QZ (7637 0353/www.askdirect.co.uk). Tottenham Court Road tube. **Open** 10am-7pm Mon-Wed, Fri, Sat; 10am-8pm Thur; noon-6pm Sun. **Credit** AmEx, DC, MC, V. **Map** p401 K5.

Boasting 'more than 10,000 product lines from over 400 suppliers', Ask offers an excellent range of quality computers, cameras, hi-fis, gadgets and accessories from leading brands. Merchandise is well displayed over four floors, prices are competitive and staff knowledgeable.

Photography

Chains all around town can do one-hour delivery; our favourite is **Snappy Snaps** (www.snappy snaps.co.uk). **Boots** (*see p255*) has a reliable provision at most branches, including digital.

Jacobs Photo, Video & Digital

74 New Oxford Street, St Giles's, WC1A 1EU (7436 5544/www.jacobsdigital.co.uk). Tottenham Court Road tube. **Open** 9am-6pm Mon-Wed, Fri, Sat; 9am-8pm Thur. **Credit** AmEx, MC, V. **Map** p409 X1.

Though part of a nationwide chain, Jacobs feels friendly and the staff are well informed. It has an excellent range of compact, digital and SLR cameras and accessories, and one of the best tripod selections in town. Prices are competitive, with frequent special deals to be had. The second-hand department is also worth a look. Next-day colour film processing is £4.99, while the one-hour service is £7.49.

Fashion

Boutiques

Austique

330 King's Road, Chelsea, SW3 5UR (7376 3663/ www.austique.co.uk). Bus 11, 19, 49. **Open** 10.30am-6.30pm Mon-Sat; noon-5pm Sun. **Credit** AmEx, MC, V. **Map** p399 D12.

Start. *See p242.*

Glamour kittens are scampering to this eclectic white-painted boudoir filled with iridescence and clothes by exclusive designers from Australia, New Zealand and New York, and S.P.A.N.K. and Julianne French lingerie. The shop is also a great source of jeans from not-yet-ubiquitous US labels such as Salt Works, Grass and 575 Denim.

Browns

23-27 South Molton Street, Mayfair, W1K 5RD (7514 0000/www.brownsfashion.com). Bond Street tube. **Open** 10am-6.30pm Mon-Wed, Fri, Sat; 10am-7pm Thur. **Credit** AmEx, DC, MC, V. **Map** p400 H6.

Joan Burstein's venerable store has reigned supreme over London's boutiques for more than 35 years. Around 100 top designers jostle for attention in its five interconnecting shops: Marc Jacobs, Chloé and Sophia Kokosalaki, plus an entire floor of Jil Sander. Those *sans* sugar daddy can peruse the almost-affordable diffusion and emergent-designer ranges, which are on offer at the adjacent Browns Focus, or Browns Labels for Less (No.50).
Other locations: 6C Sloane Street, Knightsbridge, SW1X 9LE (7514 0000).

The Cross

141 Portland Road, Holland Park, W11 4LR (7727 6760). Holland Park tube. **Open** 11am-5.30pm Mon-Sat. **Credit** AmEx, MC, V.

One of London's most successful boutiques. The eclectic compilation of designers takes in Easton Pearson, Betty Jackson, Gharani Strok and Clements Ribeiro. New for 2005/6 is eveningwear by British designers Jenny Dyer and Alice Lee. There's also casualwear from Ella Moss, Juicy Couture and Splendid, and the shop's own luscious cashmere.

Koh Samui

65-67 Monmouth Street, Covent Garden, WC2H 9DG (7240 4280/www.kohsamui.co.uk). Covent Garden tube. **Open** 10am-6.30pm Mon, Sat; 10.30am-6.30pm Tue, Wed, Fri; 10.30am-7pm Thur. **Credit** AmEx, DC, MC, V. **Map** p409 X3.

One of the capital's premier cutting-edge clothes emporiums. The collection is as strong as ever, with old favourites Chloé, Marc Jacobs, Balenciaga and Missoni much in evidence, plus a smattering of rising stars like Victim and Misconception. Balenciaga and Marc by Marc Jacobs bags, jeans by Chloé, James and Seven For All Mankind are other draws.

Labour of Love

193 Upper Street, Islington, N1 1RQ (7354 9333/ www.labour-of-love.co.uk). Highbury & Islington tube/rail. **Open** 10.30am-6.30pm Mon-Wed, Fri, Sat; 10.30am-7pm Thur; 12.30-5.30pm Sun. **Credit** MC, V. **Map** p404 O1.

Designer Francesca Forcolini's stylishly quirky boutique sells the wares of small, independent designers who are passionate about their craft. Expect the likes of Peter Jensen, Karen Walker and Laura Lees Label, plus fab accessories such as Porselli ballet shoes, Miss Budd's screen-printed metallic leather bags and jewellery by KT.

Start

42-44 Rivington Street, Shoreditch, EC2A 3BN (7729 3334/www.start-london.com). Old Street tube/rail. **Open** 10.30am-6.30pm Mon-Fri; 11am-6pm Sat; 1-5pm Sun. **Credit** AmEx, DC, MC, V. **Map** p405 R4.

This spacious boutique has a slick New York feel. Across the road from the original premises, which now house menswear, the two-level double shop is like a mini department store. A Becca cosmetics counter (offering free makeovers) complements carefully selected pieces by Cacharel, Alberta Ferretti and Miu Miu. The daywear collection boasts an excellent range of premium jeans – Superfine, Earnest Sewn and Radcliffe – while the striking accessories include Scott Stephen's jewellery. **Photo** *p241*.

Budget/mid-range chains

Chains worth checking out include **Miss Selfridge** (36-38 Great Castle Street, entrance on Oxford Street, Oxford Circus, 7927 0218, www.missselfridge.co.uk), which has tapped into the recent retro obsession via its Miss Vintage line; **Dorothy Perkins** (189 Oxford Street, Oxford Circus, 7494 3769, www.dorothyperkins.co.uk), a more conservative, highly affordable bet for well-detailed wardrobe staples; and **Monsoon** (5-6 James Street, Covent Garden, 7379 3623, www.monsoon.co.uk), which continues to successfully blend the boho look with more current styles.

These stores are constantly being challenged by the likes of **Primark** in Hammersmith (Kings Mall, King Street, 8748 7119, www.primark.co.uk), where you can find seasonal trends reproduced at cheaper-than-charity-shop prices. While you're in the area, it's worth checking out the local branch of **TK Maxx** (57 King Street, 8563 9200, www.tkmaxx.co.uk), which offers branded merchandise at up to 60 per cent off the recommended retail price. An Oxford Street outlet is planned for 2006. If you fancy a road trip, some large suburban branches of **Tesco** (0800 505 555, www.tesco.com) sell the cheap 'n' chic catwalk-copycat Florence+Fred line, while **Asda** fashion range George has a stand-alone store in Croydon (42-46 North End, 8603 0000, www.asda.co.uk).

French Connection

396 Oxford Street, Oxford Circus, W1C 7JX (7629 7766/www.frenchconnection.com). Bond Street tube. **Open** 10am-8pm Mon-Wed, Fri; 10am-9pm Thur; 10am-7pm Sat; noon-6pm Sun. **Credit** AmEx, MC, V. **Map** p400 G6.

Forget the cheeky double-take slogan T-shirts (of the 'FCUK it' variety): French Connection still produces some irresistibly elegant clothes. This good-quality label is back on form, with flattering women's pieces and young, predominantly casual menswear.
Other locations: throughout the city.

H&M

*261-271 Regent Street, Oxford Circus, W1B 2ES
(7493 4004/www.hm.com). Oxford Circus tube.* **Open**
10am-8pm Mon-Wed, Fri, Sat; 10am-9pm Thur; noon-
6pm Sun. **Credit** AmEx, MC, V. **Map** p408 U2.
The Swedish stalwart's fashion cachet has been
boosted in the past few years. In 2004 Karl Lagerfeld
designed a capsule collection for the store, while
Stella McCartney's eagerly awaited range was due
to hit the rails just as this guide went to press. Also
new is a jeans line, &denim. The main collection
offers some remarkably cheap directional items.
Other locations: throughout the city.

Mango

*233 Oxford Street, Oxford Circus, W1D 2LP (7534
3505/www.mango.com). Oxford Circus tube.* **Open**
10am-8.30pm Mon-Wed, Fri; 10am-9pm Thur; 11am-
6pm Sun. **Credit** AmEx, MC, V. **Map** p400 H6.
This sassy Spanish label combines signature jeans
and strappy tops with on-the-button catwalk-
inspired pieces. Its 2005/6 collection was slavered
over – and we can understand why.
Other locations: throughout the city.

New Look

*500-502 Oxford Street, Marble Arch, W1C 7HL
(7290 7860/www.newlook.co.uk). Bond Street or
Marble Arch tube.* **Open** 10am-9pm Mon-Sat;
noon-6pm Sun. **Credit** MC, V. **Map** p400 G6.
Once the prepubescent's favourite fashion store, New
Look reinvented itself a few years back. Clothes can
be bit hit-or-miss (polyester trousers, for instance),
but there are still many goodies to be had, with

fitted velvet jackets for a mere £25, and Ossie Clark-
esque print dresses for £30. The huge selection of
shoes also offers up some bargains. **Photo** *below.*
Other locations: throughout the city.

Oasis

*12-14 Argyll Street, Oxford Circus, W1F 7NT
(7434 1799/www.oasis-stores.com). Oxford Circus
tube.* **Open** 10am-7pm Mon-Wed, Fri, Sat; 10am-
8pm Thur; noon-6pm Sun. **Credit** AmEx, MC, V.
Map p408 U2.
The prevailing style here is quite ladylike compared
to some of the racier high-street brands, though
stock quality varies. The Love Rosa collection, featuring designer Anne-Louise Roswald's distinctive
prints, pretty Odille lingerie and the New Vintage
collection, which reproduces flapper dresses and
Victorian jackets, are among the highlights.
Other locations: throughout the city.

Reiss

*51 South Molton Street, Mayfair, W1K 5SD (7491
2208/www.reiss.co.uk). Oxford Circus tube.* **Open**
10am-7pm Mon-Wed, Fri, Sat; 10am-8pm Thur; noon-
6pm Sun. **Credit** AmEx, DC, MC, V. **Map** p400 H6.
The popularity of Reiss's female offshoot has been
cemented by the launch of this stand-alone womenswear store. The clothes have a designer feel: skirts
with unusual stitching details, or abstract 'patterns'
in the weave, cotton tops in contemporary blouson
shapes, modern tailoring, and understated draped,
ruched or wrapped dresses. It looks expensive, and
it's not cheap, but it's well worth it. **Photo** *p246.*
Other locations: throughout the city.

New Look.

Topshop

*36-38 Great Castle Street, Oxford Circus, W1W
8LG (7636 7700/www.topshop.co.uk). Oxford Circus
tube.* **Open** 9am-8pm Mon-Wed, Fri, Sat; 9am-9pm
Thur; noon-6pm Sun. **Credit** AmEx, DC, MC, V.
Map p408 U2.

The high-street darling of the fashion pack has
recently expanded its trend-led maternity range and
added a hat line to the vast, up-to-the-minute acces-
sory range. Known for nurturing young talent,
Topshop continues to feature ranges by recent graduates alongside established names in its Boutique
on level -1. The vintage section is still going strong.
Other locations: throughout the city.

Zara

*79-81 Brompton Road, Knightsbridge, SW3 1DB
(7590 6990/www.zara.com). Knightsbridge tube.*
Open 10am-7pm Mon-Sat; noon-6pm Sun. **Credit**
AmEx, MC, V. **Map** p399 F9.

For convincing catwalk copies, it's hard to beat this
Spanish success story. If you don't mind the odd
loose thread, the styles and fabrics are spot on, and
the choice is staggering. There's a dizzying stock
turnover, so it pays to visit frequently.
Other locations: throughout the city.

Children

Amaia

*14 Cale Street, Chelsea, SW3 3QU (7590 0999).
Sloane Square or South Kensington tube.* **Open**
10am-6pm Mon-Sat. **Credit** MC, V. **Map** p399 E11.

Friendly Amaia and her partner Sergolene aim to
dress children to look their age, rather than in mini
versions of adult street fashions. So there are no
combats or fake-fur gilets for pint-sized posers, just
rather beautifully made smart casuals for babies and
children. Prices are reasonable.

Caramel Baby & Child

*291 Brompton Road, South Kensington, SW3 2DY
(7589 7001). South Kensington tube.* **Open** 10am-
6.30pm Mon-Sat; noon-5pm Sun. **Credit** AmEx, MC,
V. **Map** p399 E9.

Ring the bell to enter this chicer-than-chic designer
shop. The deliciously cuddly, cashmere pullover for
six month olds and teeny Prada trainers are for seriously label-led mummies. There are rompers, skirts
and trousers for children up to ten, plus accessories.
Other locations: Also Caramel, 259 Pavilion Road,
Knightsbridge, SW1X 0BP (7730 2564).

Daisy & Tom

*181-183 King's Road, Chelsea, SW3 5EB (7352
5000/www.daisyandtom.com). Sloane Square tube
then 11, 319, 22 bus.* **Open** 9.30am-6pm Mon, Tue,
Thur, Fri; 10am-7pm Wed, Sat; 11am-5pm Sun.
Credit AmEx, MC, V. **Map** p399 E12.

A fun-packed emporium of quality kids' clothes,
nursery equipment and toys, with lots of play opportunities and demos. Junior shoppers are entertained
by the in-house puppet shows (every 30 minutes)
and the traditional ground-floor carousel.

Igloo

*300 Upper Street, Islington, N1 2TU (7354 7300/
www.iglookids.co.uk). Angel tube/Highbury &
Islington tube/rail.* **Open** 10am-6.30pm Mon-Wed;
9.30am-7pm Thur-Sat. **Credit** MC, V. **Map** p404 O1.

This lovely fashion and toy stop for babies and
under-eights has serious feel-good factor. To wear,
there are classics by Petit Bateau, Triple Star and
cheeky shirts by Bob & Blossom, plus separates by
Miniature and macs and gumboots by Blue Fish. At
the back of the shop is a Start-rite shoe outlet, complete with fitting gear and a range of cute little shoes.

Jakes

*79 Berwick Street, Soho, W1F 8TL (7734 0812/
www.jakesofsoho.com). Tottenham Court Road tube.*
Open 11am-7pm Mon-Sat. **Credit** AmEx, MC, V.
Map p408 V2.

Buy your child a hand-printed T-shirt and help make
a little lad's prospects brighter. Jake is a boy with
cerebral palsy, and a percentage of the profits made
on the clothing range (for adults and children up
to age eight) goes towards his future. The T-shirts
with logos are popular; other items include jumpers,
sweatshirts, combat trousers and baseball caps.

Sasti

*8 Portobello Green Arcade, Ladbroke Grove, 281
Portobello Road, W10 5TZ (8960 1125/www.sasti.
co.uk). Ladbroke Grove tube.* **Open** 10am-6pm Mon-
Sat. **Credit** AmEx, MC, V.

Sasti is very much the affordable end of individual,
British-made, designer clothes for children. Little girls
love the frill and flounce skirts in unusual fabrics and
prints, babies look sweet in the bright-red fleece
dinosaur suit, and the Pow! or Zap! tops are popular
with the boys. Staff here are cool but endearing.

Street

Adidas Originals Store

*9 Earlham Street, Covent Garden, WC2H 9LL
(7379 4042/www.adidas.co.uk). Covent Garden
tube.* **Open** 10.30am-7pm Mon-Sat; noon-6pm Sun.
Credit AmEx, MC, V. **Map** p409 X2.

The Adidas Originals Store aims to capitalise on the
enormous retrospective value of the Adidas brand.
Here you'll find remakes of classic footwear, T-
shirts, zip-ups and accessories. The 1980s are as productive an influence as ever, inspiring branded hip
hop jackets and zip-ups in retro colourways.

Antipodium

*5A Carlisle Street, Soho, W1D 3BH (7287 3841/
www.antipodium.com). Oxford Circus or Tottenham
Court Road tube.* **Open** 10am-7pm Mon-Fri; 10am-
6pm Sat. **Credit** AmEx, MC, V. **Map** p408 W2.

Antipodium sells exclusive Australasian imports for
both sexes from new and established designers. The
smart, compact store has offerings from Akira Red,
Gail Sorronda, Mjolk and others. Colourful, funky
Elke jewellery, and LIFEwithBIRD urban bags for
men are among the classy accessories.

Reiss. *See p243.*

Bread & Honey

205 Whitecross Street, The City, EC1Y 8QP (7253 4455/www.breadnhoney.com). Barbican tube or Old Street tube/rail. **Open** 10am-6.30pm Mon-Wed, Fri; 10am-7pm Thur; 11am-5pm Sat. **Credit** AmEx, MC, V. **Map** p404 P4.

An eclectic collection of funky, upscale streetwear mixing familiar labels like Stüssy with younger contenders such as MHI and Misericordia. Recent additions include menswear brands Umbro by Kim Jones, Carhartt, Merlin and Duffer and, for women, Religion, Sessùn and Blood & Glitter jeans. There are also bags by Ollie & Nic, shoes from Swear, Block headwear, plus extras like toys.

Maharishi

19A Floral Street, Covent Garden, WC2E 9HL (7836 3860/www.emaharishi.com). Covent Garden tube. **Open** 10am-7pm Mon-Sat; noon-5pm Sun. **Credit** AmEx, MC, V. **Map** p409 Y3.

In 1994 Hardy Blechman began Maharishi with the intention of reintroducing hemp into clothing on the grounds that it's more durable and environmentally friendly than cotton. By the late '90s the patterned combat trousers had become an essential. The clothes, especially the jackets, are based on simple military shapes, with subtly tweaked camouflage patterns and embroidery.

Urban Outfitters

200-201 Oxford Street, Oxford Circus, W1D 1NU (7907 0800/www.urbanoutfitters.com). Oxford Circus tube. **Open** 10am-8pm Mon-Wed, Fri, Sat; 10am-9pm Thur; noon-6pm Sun. **Credit** AmEx, MC, V. **Map** p408 U2.

At this aptly named American emporium, you can kit out your wardrobe and flat, then add to your record collection. Men's clothing comes courtesy of Full Count, Gravis, Smedley and others. For women there's a similarly wide selection of household names and more esoteric designers. Prices often stretch the budget, but there are some superb one-off finds. **Other locations**: 42-56 Earlham Street, Covent Garden, WC2H 9LA (7759 6390); 36-38 Kensington High Street, Kensington, W8 4PF (7761 1001).

Underwear

Agent Provocateur

6 Broadwick Street, Soho, W1V 1FH (7439 0229/www.agentprovocateur.com). Oxford Circus tube. **Open** 11am-7pm Mon-Wed, Fri, Sat; 11am-8pm Thur. **Credit** AmEx, DC, MC, V. **Map** p408 V2.

Agent Provocateur serves up decadent sauciness without descending into sleaze. Celebs and city boys alike flock here to be served by nubile staff wearing undersized pink nurses' uniforms and killer heels. Prices are ambitious but the quality is high. **Other locations**: 16 Pont Street, Belgravia, SW1X 9EN (7235 0229); 5 Royal Exchange, Threadneedle Street, The City, EC3V 3LL (7623 0229); 305 Westbourne Grove, Notting Hill, W11 2QA (7243 1292).

Aware

25 Old Compton Street, Soho, W1D 5JN (7287 3789/www.awareunderwear.com). Leicester Square tube. **Open** 11am-8pm Mon-Sat; noon-7pm Sun. **Credit** AmEx, MC, V. **Map** p408 W3.

This diminutive shop sells a comprehensive collection of men's designer labels. Expect to find boxers and briefs by Puma, Dolce & Gabbana, Hom and Calvin Klein. Swimwear, close-fitting T-shirts and beachwear are also available.

Coco de Mer

23 Monmouth Street, Covent Garden, WC2H 9DD (7836 8882/www.coco-de-mer.co.uk). Covent Garden tube. **Open** 11am-7pm Mon-Wed, Fri, Sat; 11am-8pm Thur. **Credit** AmEx, MC, V. **Map** p409 Y2.

Coco de Mer does sex in a risqué, vaguely Vicotian and rather intellectual way, with erotic literature among the ticklers, spankers and other assorted boudoir tools. The lingerie collection is small but well edited, with the sort of flirty items that manage to leave something to the imagination without sacrificing any eroticism.

Miss Lala's Boudoir

144 Gloucester Avenue, Primrose Hill, NW1 8JA (7483 1888). Chalk Farm tube. **Open** 10.30am-6.30pm Mon-Wed, Fri, Sat; 10.30am-6.30pm Thur; 1-5pm Sun. **Credit** DC, MC, V.

Fine Rees's pretty little boutique bills itself as a 'dressing-up shop for grown-up girls', and cheeky lingerie labels are its stock in trade. Less extravagant beribboned undies and broderie anglaise boy shorts are offset by showstoppers such as the Burlesque Collection by Buttress & Snatch. Campy Miss Lala T-shirts and tutu skirts round things off.

Rigby & Peller

22A Conduit Street, Mayfair, W1S 2XT (7491 2200/www.rigbyandpeller.com). Oxford Circus tube. **Open** 9.30am-6pm Mon-Wed, Fri, Sat; 9.30am 7pm Thur. **Credit** AmEx, MC, V. **Map** p402 H7.

Her Majesty's corsetière has been measuring busts since 1939. The company prides itself on its free expert fitting service – highly trained staff can often accurately guess your size by sight. They offer bras ready made and made to measure. Styles tend to be ultra-feminine, and prices match the standards. **Other locations**: 2 Hans Road, Knightsbridge, SW3 1RX (7225 4765).

Vintage

Bertie Wooster

284 Fulham Road, Fulham, SW10 9DW (7352 5662/www.bertie-wooster.co.uk). Earl's Court or Fulham Broadway tube. **Open** 10am-6pm Mon-Fri; 10am-5pm Sat. **Credit** MC, V. **Map** p398 C12.

Any man looking for sharp tailoring on a budget will be pleased to hear about this well-kept secret, a hit with dapper City boys. Bertie Wooster specialises in top-quality second-hand suits, handmade leather shoes and hats. Beautiful suits start at £165.

Eat, Drink, Shop

Butler & Wilson

*189 Fulham Road, Chelsea, SW3 6JN (7352 8255/
www.butlerandwilson.co.uk). South Kensington
tube.* **Open** 10am-6pm Mon, Tue, Thur-Sat; 10am-
7pm Wed; noon-6pm Sun. **Credit** AmEx, MC, V.
Map p399 E11.

Fans of costume jewellery have been snapping up
Simon Wilson's flamboyant baubles for 25 years;
less well known is that Butler & Wilson's Fulham
Road shop has a treasure trove of vintage clothes
upstairs. The stock includes Victorian crocheted
tops and shawls, sequinned 1920s dresses and '60s
mini dresses, plus beautiful antique jewellery.
Other locations: 20 South Molton Street, Mayfair,
W1K 5QY (7409 2955).

The Girl Can't Help It/
Cad Van Swankster

*G100, Alfie's Antique Market, 13-25 Church Street,
Marylebone, NW8 8DT (7724 8984/www.thegirl
canthelpit.com). Edgware Road tube/Marylebone
tube/rail.* **Open** 10am-6pm Tue-Sat. **Credit** AmEx,
MC, V. **Map** p397 E4.

Chi-chi owner Sparkle Moore goes to New York regularly to stock up on fantastical American lingerie,
Joan Crawford-esque garb and eye-catching accessories. The adjoining stall is owned by Cad Van
Swankster, who has a selection of suave 1940s and
'50s Hollywood-style menswear, plus bar accessories.

Shikasuki

*67 Gloucester Avenue, Primrose Hill, NW1 8LD
(7722 4442/www.shikasuki.com). Camden Town
or Chalk Farm tube.* **Open** 11am-7pm Mon-Sat;
noon-6pm Sun. **Credit** AmEx, MC, V.

Shikasuki is a delightful dressing-up box of a shop,
brimming with vintage gems for both sexes.
Downstairs are separate men's and women's boutiques, encompassing everything from shoes, wedding and party dresses, to kilts, shirts and suits.

Fashion accessories &
services

General

Accessorize

*22 The Market, Covent Garden, WC2H 8HB (7240
2107/www.accessorize.co.uk). Covent Garden tube.*
Open 9am-8pm Mon-Fri; 10am-8pm Sat; 11am-7pm
Sun. **Credit** AmEx, DC, MC, V. **Map** p409 Y3.

This high-street staple keeps quality high and prices
low. Accessories are regularly updated: woolly hats,
striped scarves, bags and jewellery crop up each winter; flip flops and beach hats are added in summer.
Other locations: throughout the city.

Doors by Jas MB

*8 Ganton Street, Soho, W1F 7PQ (7494 2288/
www.doorsbyjasmb.com). Oxford Circus tube.*
Open 11am-7pm Mon-Sat; 1-5pm Sun. **Credit**
MC, V. **Map** p408 V3.

An intoxicating smell of leather greets visitors to
this small boutique, which caters for men and
women. As well as leather goods, the shop sells
designer clothing and streetwise accessories by the
likes of Martin Margiela, Carpe Diem and Rust.

Orla Kiely

*31 Monmouth Street, Covent Garden, WC2H 9DD
(7240 022/www.orlakiely.com). Covent Garden tube.*
Open 10.30am-7pm Mon-Sat; noon-5pm Sun.
Credit MC, V. **Map** p409 X3.

This new flagship brings the designer's full collection of clothing and accessories under one roof.
Delectable bags come in a wide range of materials,
from her famous graphic prints to richly hued
leather and ponyskin. You can also pick up scarves,
hats, wellies, luggage, cushions and blankets.

Dry cleaning & laundry

Blossom & Browne's Sycamore

*73A Clarendon Road, Notting Hill, W11 4JF (7727
2635/www.blossomandbrowne.co.uk). Holland Park
tube.* **Open** 8.30am-5.30pm Mon-Wed, Fri; 8.30am-
4.30pm Thur; 8.30am-3pm Sat. **Credit** MC, V.

This venerable launderer and dry-cleaner caters to
Her Maj. A suit costs from £12, an evening dress
from £40. Alterations and repairs are undertaken,
and delivery is free.
Other locations: 160 Regent's Park Road, Primrose
Hill, NW1 8XN (7722 1713).

Danish Express

*16 Hinde Street, Marylebone, W1U 2BB (7935
6306). Bond Street tube.* **Open** 8am-7pm Mon-Fri;
9am-3pm Sat. **Credit** AmEx, MC, V. **Map** p400 G5.

This long-standing fixture offers everything from
sheets to shirts (£2.45, or less in bulk). The 'bag
wash' service costs around £7.50 per six kilos.

Jeeves of Belgravia

*8-10 Pont Street, Belgravia, SW1X 9EL (7235 1101/
collection & delivery service 8809 3232/www.jeeves
ofbelgravia.co.uk). Knightsbridge or Sloane Square
tube.* **Open** 8.30am-7pm Mon-Fri; 8.30am-6pm Sat.
Credit AmEx, MC, V. **Map** p399 F10.

Jeeves' new free delivery service is worth a try –
just phone to arrange van collection. An environmentally friendly non-toxic cleaning process is used,
and results are impressive. Skirts or trousers are
cleaned from £11.50; shirts are laundered for £4.90.
Other locations: throughout the city.

Jewellery

Angela Hale

*5 Royal Arcade, 28 Old Bond Street, Mayfair, W1S
4SE (7495 1920/www.angela-hale.co.uk). Green Park
tube.* **Open** 10am-6pm Mon-Sat. **Credit** AmEx, MC,
V. **Map** p408 U4.

This little boutique, which showcases the romantic,
whimsical aesthetics of Angela Hale's designs, will
make any girl swoon. The handmade creations are

based on hypo-allergenic bronze and set with beautiful Swarovski crystals. All manner of accessories are also available to jazz up a feminine outfit.

Asprey
167 New Bond Street, Mayfair, W1S 4AR (7493 6767/www.asprey.com). Bond Street or Green Park tube. **Open** 10am-6pm Mon-Sat. **Credit** AmEx, DC, MC, V. **Map** p400 H6.
This imposingly grand flagship has cabinets filled with all the aristocratic-chic jewellery you would expect from this long-standing brand. The white-gold, diamond-heavy Swirl necklace goes for a gasp-worthy £39,000, but there are also modern-looking pieces with smaller price-tags.

Aurum
8 Avery Row, Mayfair, W1K 4AL (7586 8656/ www.aurumgallery.com). Bond Street tube. **Open** 10.30am-6pm Tue-Sat. **Credit** AmEx, MC, V. **Map** p402 H6.
Aurum showcases designs by some 50 designers, including Scott Wilson, Tina Engell and Shaun Leane (whose celeb fans include David Bowie and Liv Tyler; his distinctive designs can be yours from £100). A bespoke service is also available.
Other locations: 12 England's Lane, Belsize Park, NW3 4TG (7586 8656).

Garrard
24 Albemarle Street, Mayfair, W1Y 4HT (7758 8520/www.garrard.com). Bond Street or Green Park tube. **Open** 10am-6pm Mon-Fri; 10am-5pm Sat. **Credit** AmEx, DC, MC, V. **Map** p408 U5.
Jade Jagger's input as creative director at the crown jewellers continues to rejuvenate the prestigious company. If you'd like to treat yourself to a bit of sparkle, the My First Diamond line begins at £220.

Lesley Craze Gallery
33-35A Clerkenwell Green, Clerkenwell, EC1R 0DU (7608 0393/www.lesleycrazegallery.co.uk). Farringdon tube/rail. **Open** 10am-5.30pm Tue-Sat. **Credit** AmEx, DC, MC, V. **Map** p404 N4.
Diamonds aren't the focus here, but the jewellery is certainly cutting edge. Over 100 designers are showcased, from as far afield as Australia and Japan, working with precious metals and imaginative mixed media. Many pieces are positively avant garde. Prices run from affordable to unthinkable.

Tiffany & Co
25 Old Bond Street, Mayfair, W1S 4QB (7409 2790/www.tiffany.com/uk). Green Park tube. **Open** 10am-6pm Mon-Fri; 10am-5.30pm Sat. **Credit** AmEx, MC, V. **Map** p408 U5.
An aura of Audrey Hepburn glamour will always linger around the legendary Tiffany's. You can even get a droll silver ring proclaiming 'Please return to Tiffany & Co'. At £105 it's one of the cheaper items; the diamond engagement rings are to sigh for.
Other locations: The Courtyard, Royal Exchange, Threadneedle Street, The City, EC3V 3LQ (7495 3511); 145 Sloane Street, Knightsbridge, SW1X 9AY (7499 4577).

Wright & Teague
1A Grafton Street, Mayfair, W1S 4EB (7629 2777/ www.wrightandteague.com). Green Park tube. **Open** 10am-6pm Mon-Wed, Fri; 10am-7pm Thur; 10am-5pm Sat. **Credit** AmEx, MC, V. **Map** p402 H7.
Husband and wife Gary Wright and Sheila Teague have been creating enchanting jewellery together for 25 years, and their lovely Mayfair store makes a fitting showcase. Most ranges come in a choice of silver, 18ct gold or platinum, and designs are a mix of classic and modern, some with a lovely folksy feel.

Shoes

The number of London shops given over mainly or entirely to trainers continues to grow. Those immersed in sneaker culture shouldn't miss the **Onitsuka Tiger UK** flagship (15 Newburgh Street, Soho, 7287 7480, www. onitsukatiger.co.uk), where (remade) classics are served alongside new designs. Independent boutiques such as **Gloria's** (6 Dray Walk, off Brick Lane, Spitalfields, 7770 6024, www. superdeluxe.net; *see also p165* **Walk on**) are a trainerspotter's heaven; Covent Garden's **Neal Street** has the best chains, including **Size?** (Nos.17-19, 7379 7853) and **Offspring** (No.60 Neal Street, 7497 2463, www.offspring.co.uk).

Kurt Geiger. *See p250.*

Aldo

*3-7 Neal Street, Covent Garden, WC2H 9PU (7836
7692/www.aldoshoes.com). Covent Garden, Holborn
or Leicester Square tube.* **Open** 10am-8pm Mon-Sat;
noon-6pm Sun. **Credit** AmEx, MC, V. **Map** p409 Y2.
For sheer choice at surprisingly cheap prices, it's
hard to beat this vast Canadian shoe emporium,
stocked with a dizzying array of styles for men and
women. Top marks for catwalk styles at lower prices.
Other locations: throughout the city.

Audley

*72 Duke of York Square, King's Road, Chelsea, SW3
4LY (7730 2902/www.audley.com). Sloane Square
tube.* **Open** 10am-6pm Mon, Tue, Thur-Sat; 10am-
7pm Wed; noon-5pm Sun. **Credit** AmEx, MC, V.
Map p399 F11.
Audley started life as a bespoke shoemaker, and it
shows in the artful lines and fine details of these
well-made shoes. Prices are in line with upper-end
high-street chains (around £100 for shoes; £200 for
boots). For an extra £75, you can have a pair made
up in a different colour to match an outfit.

Birkenstock

*70 Neal Street, Covent Garden, WC2H 9PR (7240
2783/www.birkenstock.co.uk). Covent Garden or
Leicester Square tube.* **Open** 10.30am-7pm Mon-
Wed, Fri, Sat; 10.30am-8pm Thur; noon-6pm Sun.
Credit AmEx, MC, V. **Map** p409 Z4.
The only stand-alone Birkenstock store in the UK,
easily identifiable by the queues outside, especially
in summer, offers the ultimate selection of the famous
ergonomic sandals, clogs and shoes, from the best-
selling single-strap Madrid to a funky line styled by
Heidi Klum. Down the road, the Natural Shoe Store
(21 Neal Street, 7836 5254) has a smaller selection.

Kurt Geiger

*65 South Molton Street, Mayfair, W1K 5SU (7758
8020/www.kurtgeiger.com). Bond Street tube.* **Open**
10am-7pm Mon-Wed, Fri, Sat; 10am-8pm Thur; noon-
6pm Sun. **Credit** AmEx, DC, MC, V. **Map** p400 H6.
The ubiquitous department-store label has shaken
off the last vestiges of its staid image with designs
that look like they stepped right off the catwalk – at
surprisingly affordable prices. The younger, edgier
kg range has shoes for around £65. **Photo** *p249*.
Other locations: 30 Hampstead High Street,
Hampstead, NW3 1QA (7794 4290); 133 Kensington
High Street, Kensington, W8 6SU (7937 3716); 33
King's Road, Chelsea, SW3 4LX (7901 9041).

Tracey Neuls

*29 Marylebone Lane, Marylebone, W1U 2NQ (7935
0039/www.tn29.com). Bond Street tube.* **Open** 11am-
6.30pm Mon-Wed, Fri; 11am-8.30pm Thur; noon-5pm
Sat. **Credit** AmEx, MC, V. **Map** p400 H6.
Tracey Neuls is giving footwear clichés a kick in the
kitten heels. After scooping up a string of awards at
Cordwainers, the Canadian designer launched her
TN_29 label and this, her first stand-alone shop.
Neuls' fascination with detail and playful curiosity
are reflected in her eye-catching designs (£120-£300).

Tailors

Since the middle of the 19th century, **Savile
Row**, Mayfair, W1, has been the traditional
home of men's tailoring.

H Huntsman & Sons

*11 Savile Row, Mayfair, W1S 3PF (7734 7441/
www.h-huntsman.com). Piccadilly Circus tube.*
Open 10am-6pm Mon-Fri; 10am-5pm Sat.
Credit AmEx, DC, MC, V. **Map** p408 U3.
H Huntsman & Sons prides itself on creating bespoke
suits that will last a lifetime. Just as well, really, given
the prices – expect to shell out over £3,000 for a suit
handmade on the premises, although ready-to-wear
versions start at £1,000. Huntsman's also produces
its own fabrics, introducing new tweeds each year.

John Pearse

*6 Meard Street, Soho, W1F 0EG (7434 0738/
www.johnpearse.co.uk). Piccadilly Circus tube.*
Open 10am-7pm Mon-Fri; noon-7pm Sat.
Credit AmEx, MC, V. **Map** p408 W3.
Hailed by many as the godfather of new British tailoring, John Pearse combines a playful eccentricity
with rock-solid tailoring credentials. At his laid-back
Soho salon, ready-to-wear suits and coats are displayed in Gothic wardrobes. There's also a selection
of shirts (from £150) and some very naughty hand-
painted silk ties, and an online shirt service is in the
pipeline. Women are also catered for.

Richard James

*29 Savile Row, Mayfair, W1S 2EY (7434 0605/
www.richardjames.co.uk). Green Park or Piccadilly
Circus tube.* **Open** 10am-6pm Mon-Wed, Fri; 10am-
7pm Thur; 11am-6pm Sat. **Credit** AmEx, DC, MC, V.
Map p408 U3.
Credited with pioneering the 'modern classic'
approach for Savile Row, Richard James's premises
exude fashion designer ambiance. The signature
single-breasted suit – heavily weighted with deep
side vents – has attracted a plethora of high profile
customers. Bespoke prices start at £2,290, while off-
the-peg suits range from £575 to £1,150.
Other locations: 12 The Courtyard, Royal
Exchange, The City, EC3V 3PT (7626 4116).

Food & drink

Many department stores (*see p238*) have food
halls. Foodies should also check out **Henrietta
Green's Food Lovers' Market**, in Covent
Garden's Piazza in November (see www.food
loversbritain.com). For food markets, *see p259*.

Bakeries & pâtisseries

In addition to the places listed below there are
other excellent choices in the Restaurants &
Cafés chapter (see *pp194-221*). There are plenty
of great, well-known pâtisseries in Soho (*see
p206*), in particular on Old Compton Street.

Chocs away!

After Tim Burton's *Charlie and the Chocolate Factory* sweetened our cinema screens with mint-sugar grass and chocolate waterfalls, Londoners' tastebuds were left perfectly poised to experience the delights of the city's varied purveyors of the glorious stuff.

First stop, for spectacular – and at times spectacularly weird – ganaches, truffles, mints and candied fruits, is **L'Artisan du Chocolat** (89 Lower Sloane Street, Chelsea, 7824 8365, www.artisanduchocolat.com; *pictured*), London's most experimental independent chocolate shop. Irish-born proprietor Gerard Coleman, the Willy Wonka of home-grown chocolatiers, handmakes his trademark tobacco 'couture chocolate' (smoky, silky and intense) alongside other delicious innovations such as the best-selling liquid salt caramels.

Sublime cocoa creations are also available at chocolatier Chantal Cody's charming **Rococo** (321 King's Road, Chelsea, 7352 5857, and 45 Marylebone High Street, 7935 7780, www.rococochocolates.com). Longer established and less pioneering than L'Artisan, the company still shares a fondness for unusual flavours (cardamom, chilli pepper, or orange and geranium bars, for example), but combines this with some nostalgic English rose and violet creams, plus fresh cream truffles.

Another British business that has long proved that London is up there with Brussels, is **Prestat** (14 Princes Arcade, Mayfair, SW1Y 6DS, 7629 4838, www.prestat.co.uk). Its Appointment to the Queen status is echoed in the glorious packaging – pretty boxes in regal purples and ruby reds, and embellished with gold crowns and script. Filled with the store's forte of rotund, velvety truffles (banoffee, champagne, or orange with lemon, perhaps), they make splendid gifts.

That said, Belgian chocolatiers continue to impress, and while chains such as **Godiva** (17 Russell Street, Covent Garden, 7836 5706, www.godiva.com) and **Leonidas** (37 Victoria Street, Belgravia, 7222 5399, www.leonidasbelgianchocolates.co.uk). beat a box of Thorntons any day, neither approaches the finely honed flavours of independent visionary **Pierre Marcolini** (6 Lancer Square, 7795 6611, www.pierremarcolini.co.uk). He first took Brussels by storm with over 80 varieties of carefully sourced chocolates, focusing on his favourite sweet-tasting Criollo beans. Now, fortunately for us, he also runs a shop-cum-café in Kensington, where there is always an irresistible cake of the day, such as the dark chocolate orange crème brûlée cake.

Similar in style, scope and premium, Robert Linxe's Parisian **Maison du Chocolat** (45-46 Piccadilly, St James's, 7287 8500, www.lamaisonduchocolat.com), is a browser's paradise. Spacious and slick, with giant glass windows, the store is tempting in the extreme and the seasonal individual cakes perhaps a chocolate, mango and ginger Maiko in summer, or a Rigoletto caramel mousse-filled cake in winter – are a huge draw. Indeed, one trip here and the French for 'window shopping' – *lèche-vitrine* (literally meaning 'licking the window glass') immediately becomes appropriate.

& Clarke's

122 Kensington Church Street, Kensington, W8 4BU (7229 2190/www.sallyclarke.com). Notting Hill Gate tube. **Open** 8am-8pm Mon-Fri; 8am-4pm Sat. **Credit** AmEx, MC, V. **Map** p396 B8.

Sally Clarke's bakery sells a vast range of breads, pastries and cakes, many of which are supplied to London's restaurants and delis. Fresh bakes include fig and fennel, and rosemary and raisin breads, jewel-like redcurrant and nectarine tarts, and citrus peel and almond croissants. Also sold are over 40 British and Irish cheeses from Neal's Yard, coffee from Monmouth Coffee House, fresh soups, condiments, olive oils and chocolates, plus seasonal fruit, vegetables and herbs. For the restaurant next door, *see p221*.

Baker & Spice

75 Salusbury Road, Queen's Park, NW6 6NH (7604 3636/www.bakerandspice.com). Queen's Park tube/ rail. **Open** 7am-7pm Mon-Sat; 8.30am-5pm Sun. **Credit** MC, V.

Baker & Spice is a byword for quality in breads, pastries, cakes and tarts. Breads include rye, chollah and San Francisco sourdough, and the soft, crumbly croissants have a loyal local following. Soups and savouries are also available, and you can eat in for a more leisurely experience.

Other locations: 54-56 Elizabeth Street, Belgravia, SW1 9PD (7730 3033); 47 Denyer Street, Chelsea, SW3 2LX (7589 4734).

Jones Dairy

23 Ezra Street, Bethnal Green, E2 7RH (7739 5372/ www.jonesdairy.co.uk). Bus 26, 48, 55. **Open** *Shop* 8am-1pm Fri, Sat; 9am-2pm Sun. *Café* 9am-3pm Fri, Sat; 8am-2pm Sun. **No credit cards.** **Map** p405 S3.
Established in 1902, this shop and café, which also serves up great staples such as bagels and scrambled eggs on toast, is one of the originals in a Welsh chain that was once ubiquitous across London. A huge range of farm cheeses is up for grabs, plus breads, pastries, chutneys, preserves, and fruit and veg.

Delicatessens

For **Flâneur Food Hall**, *see p197.* For **La Fromagerie**, *see p203.* For **Carluccio's Caffè**, *see p200.* For **Villandry**, *see p201.* For **Ottolenghi**, *see p213.*

The Delicatessen Shop

23 South End Road, Hampstead, NW3 2PT (7435 7315). Hampstead tube/Hampstead Heath rail/24 bus. **Open** 9.30am-7pm Mon-Fri; 9am-6pm Sat. **Credit** MC, V.
Popular for its freshly made pesto, roasted coffee and delicious chocolates, this friendly deli also sells an exquisite range of own-made pasta.

The Grocer on Elgin

6 Elgin Crescent, Notting Hill, W11 2HX (7221 3844/www.thegroceron.com). Ladbroke Grove or Notting Hill Gate tube. **Open** 8am-8pm Mon-Fri; 8am-6pm Sat, Sun. **Credit** MC, V.
This spacious, trendy shrine to food is famous for seasonal, handmade ready meals in vacuum-packed pouches. A groovy selection of groceries from around the world is also available.
Other locations: The Grocer on Warwick, 21 Warwick Street, W1R 5RB (7437 7776).

Megan's Delicatessen

571 King's Road, Chelsea, SW6 2EB (7371 7837/ www.megansdeli.com). Parsons Green or Fulham Broadway tube then 11, 14, 22 bus. **Open** 8am-6pm Mon-Fri; 9am-6pm Sat. **Credit** AmEx, DC, MC, V. **Map** p398 C13.
Set over two floors with split-level areas, this attractive deli sells Poilâne bread, cheeses, olives, sauces and own-made jams. All the products are GM- and additive-free, and cakes and muffins are baked on the premises. Home-style hot dishes can be taken away or enjoyed in the 'secret garden' at the back.

Melrose & Morgan

42 Gloucester Avenue, Primrose Hill, NW1 8JD (7722 0011/www.melroseandmorgan.com). Camden Town or Chalk Farm tube. **Open** 9am-8pm Tue-Sat; 10am-6pm Sun. **Credit** AmEx, MC, V.

This beautifully presented deli champions quality produce from small British suppliers and farmers. Standout items include jams and jellies, organic meats, and seasonal fruit and veg. Pâtés, fish pie and even ketchup are made on-site by the house chefs.

Verde & Co

4 Brushfield Street, Spitalfields, E1 6AG (7247 1924). Liverpool Street tube/rail. **Open** 8am-8pm Mon-Fri; 11am-5pm Sat, Sun. **Credit** MC, V. **Map** p405 R5.
This exquisite shop is owned by author Jeanette Winterson and run by ex-chef Harvey Cabannis. Many of the goods are Italian, including fresh pasta flown in twice a week. As well as organic produce, you'll find such delicacies as French white peaches, courgette flowers and Scottish chanterelles.

Wines & spirits

Booze store **Oddbins** (www.oddbins.com for locations around London) is also hard to beat.

The Beer Shop

14 Pitfield Street, Hoxton, N1 6EY (7739 3701/ www.pitfieldbeershop.co.uk). Old Street tube/rail. **Open** 11am-7pm Tue-Fri; 10am-4pm Sat. **Credit** MC, V. **Map** p405 Q3.
A beer lover's mecca, packed with a constantly changing range of around 600 unusual bottled beers from across the globe, with Belgium and Britain making a sizeable contribution. Also on sale are excellent beers brewed at Pitfield's organic brewery next door, including a powerful IPA made to a recipe from 1837.

Berry Bros & Rudd

3 St James's Street, St James's, SW1A 1EG (7396 9600/www.bbr.com). Green Park tube. **Open** 10am-6pm Mon-Fri; 10am-4pm Sat. **Credit** AmEx, DC, MC, V. **Map** p402 J8.
Berry's has been operating in St James's since the mid 17th century, and traditional wine areas rule. Off the georgeously rickety wood-panelled main room are three chambers showing part of the company's vast selection. The fortified range is one of London's best.

Gerry's

74 Old Compton Street, Soho, W1D 4UW (7734 4215). Leicester Square tube. **Open** 9am-6.30pm Mon-Fri; 9am-5.30pm Sat. **No credit cards.** **Map** p408 W3.
There's an incredible variety of spirits at this quirky shop, including a great range of tequilas and rare rums. Lots of miniatures encourage experimentation.

Milroy's of Soho

3 Greek Street, Soho, W1V 6NX (7437 9311/ www.milroys.co.uk). Tottenham Court Road tube. **Open** 10am-8pm Mon-Fri; 10am-7pm Sat. **Credit** AmEx, MC, V. **Map** p408 W2.
London's most famous whisky specialist, founded in 1964, stocks a fine range of over 700 malts and whiskies from around the world, including rare bottles. Also on offer is a full range of wines. Regular tutored tastings are held in the cellar.

Gifts & stationery

Some museum and gallery shops are also great for gifts. Try **Tate Modern** (*see p88*) for stylish gifts, the **British Museum** (*see p109*) for souvenirs and reproductions, and the **Science Museum** (*see p142*) for toys. For the **Design Museum Shop**, *see p257*.

Paperchase

213-215 Tottenham Court Road, Bloomsbury, W1T 7PS (7467 6200/www.paperchase.co.uk). Goodge Street tube. **Open** 9.30am-7pm Mon, Wed, Fri, Sat; 10am-7pm Tue; 9.30am-8pm Thur; noon-6pm Sun. **Credit** AmEx, MC, V. **Map** p401 K5.

The flagship of this stationery superstore is a dream world for office addicts, with its eclectic mix of useful, tasteful and fun items. The ground floor features cards, gift wrap, pens, invitations and coloured notepaper. More upmarket goods are displayed on the first floor, while the second floor is devoted to artists' materials – oil, acrylic, watercolour and fabric paint, plus brushes, pens, pencils and books. Great for cheap gift items, especially at Christmas. **Other locations**: throughout the city.

Smythson

40 New Bond Street, Mayfair, W1S 2DE (7629 8558/www.smythson.com). Bond Street tube. **Open** 9.30am-6pm Mon-Wed, Fri; 10am-6pm Thur, Sat. **Credit** AmEx, DC, MC, V. **Map** p400 H6.

An elegant selection of fine stationery and gifts for those who see the luxuries of creamy paper, bespoke gold stamping and hand-engraving as *de rigueur*. Other classy (and pricey) items include diaries, photo albums, manicure sets and wallets. **Other locations**: 135 Sloane Street, Knightsbridge, SW1X 3XA (7730 5520).

Health & beauty

Department stores (*see p238*) are also a good bet for upmarket make-up brands. Several hotels also have excellent spa facilities open to the public, including the **Sanderson** (*see p51*) and the **Dorchester** (*see p57*).

Aveda Lifestyle Institute

174 High Holborn, St Giles's, WC1V 7AA (7759 7355/www.aveda.com). Holborn tube. **Open** 9.30am-7pm Mon-Fri; 9am-6.30pm Sat. **Credit** AmEx, MC, V. **Map** p409 Z1.

Getting the right treatments

When it comes to pampering oneself, it's only fitting that such a stress-inducing city should be home to the crème de la crème of facials, massages, manicures and other treats. In addition to the spas, and health and beauty shops listed on pp253-256, London has a host of places that are worth seeking out because they excel in (at least) one thing.

For waxing, it has to be **Otylia Adams** (or one of her talented staff) at the Greenhouse salon (142 Wigmore Street, Marylebone, 7486 5537, www.otyliaroberts.co.uk). Otylia has deforested some of the UK's most famous nether regions: stars flock to her as she's one of the fastest waxers in the West. The hot wax method is used (less painful than strip wax), with prices from £45 for a Brazilian.

Set in a converted townhouse, the **Elemis Day Spa** (2-3 Lancashire Court, Mayfair, 7499 4995, www.elemis.com) offers a full programme of treats, but the ones that get the best results are the facials designed to smooth and plump city-worn skin, such as the Visible Brilliance facial (£115 for 75 minutes).

Over in Marylebone (51 Paddington Street, 7224 6088, www.vaishaly.com), **Vaishaly Patel** is a peachy-skinned goddess who tends the faces of many a celeb (Elle Macpherson, Sophie Dahl). Her signature facial (£100 for one hour) includes lymphatic stimulation extraction and microdermabrasion. The results are never less than brilliant.

If money's no object, then we highly recommend the spa at the **Mandarin Oriental** hotel (66 Knightsbridge, 7838 9888, www.madarin oriental.com). Here you pay for a set amount of time – £210 for two hours – and the therapist tailors the massage and facial to your mood. The best in town, without a doubt.

For talons, nail bars may be cheap (*see p40*), but the best manicures, hands down, are by **Leighton Denny**, who has a studio at Urban Retreat (*see p256*); **Bliss London**, a New York-style spa in South Kensington (60 Sloane Avenue, 7584 3888, www.blissworld. com), and dinky salon **Groom** (49 Beauchamp Place, Knightsbridge, 7581 1248, www.groom london.com), where you're pampered by two therapists at a time, from a menu of treats.

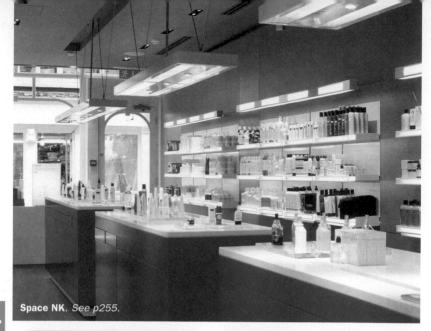

Space NK. *See p255.*

Since 1978 Aveda has flown the flag for environmentally sound beauty products, and it's a boon that most of its goods are a pleasure to use. Haircare products are especially praiseworthy. It's just that bit more expensive, but generally it feels justified. **Other locations**: 28-29 Marylebone High Street, Marylebone, W1U 4PL (7224 3157); 13 Kensington Church Street, Kensington, W8 4LF (7937 6794).

Boots

Sedley Place, 361 Oxford Street, Oxford Circus, W1C 2JL (7229 9266/www.boots.com). Oxford Circus tube. **Open** 8am-8pm Mon-Wed, Fri; 8am-9pm Thur; 9am-8pm Sat; noon-6pm Sun. **Credit** MC, V. **Map** p408 V2.
King of the high-street toiletries market, Boots has just extended its empire with a palatial new four-floor flagship store, selling bathroom staples alongside more exotic fare. Larger stores now stock new lines from the likes of Nails Inc, Naked 97% (natural toiletries), Jemma Kidd (make-up brushes), plus a wide selection of men's ranges.
Other locations: throughout the city.

Calmia

52-54 Marylebone High Street, Marylebone, W1U 5HR (7224 3585/www.calmia.com). Baker Street tube. **Open** *Spa* 9am-9pm Mon-Sat; 10am-7pm Sun. *Store* 10am-7pm Mon-Sat; 10am-6pm Sun. **Credit** AmEx, MC, V. **Map** p400 G5.
On the ground floor of this day spa there's a green tea and 'herbal elixir' bar, plus luxury yoga gear and toiletries. Head to the basement for treatments like the Complete Stress Release or Balinese Blossom Ritual.

Fresh

92 Marylebone High Street, Marylebone, W1U 4RD (7486 4100/www.fresh.com). Baker Street tube. **Open** 10am-7pm Mon-Wed, Fri, Sat; 10am-8pm Thur; noon-5pm Sun. **Credit** AmEx, DC, MC, V. **Map** p400 G5.
These high-end American body- and haircare products aren't just lovely to look at, but with ingredients such as soy, rice and sugar, they smell good enough to eat. Book yourself in for a mini treatment (facials from £65, make-up lesson £85) and you can redeem the cost against products.

HQ hair & beautystore

2 New Burlington Street, Mayfair, W1S 2JE (0871 220 4141/www.hqhair.com). Oxford Circus tube. **Open** 10am-6pm Mon, Sat; 10am-7pm Tue, Fri; 10am-8pm Wed, Thur. **Credit** AmEx, MC, V. **Map** p408 U3.
HQ began life as a humble hair salon on Queensway, before opening this one-stop salon and beauty shop. The huge roster of cult names, from hair- and skincare to make-up, via perfumes, accessories and tools of the trade, includes Mario Badescu and Joey skincare, Comptoir Sud Pacifique and Carthusia perfumes, Joico and Terax hair products, DuWop and Jelly Pong Pong make-up, and accessories such as South Beach Rocks jewellery. The salon offers services such as Dermalogica facials, Aromatherapy Associates massages, waxing, Barielle manicures and pedicures and Fantasy Tans.

Jo Malone

150 Sloane Street, Knightsbridge, SW1X 9BX (7730 2100/www.jomalone.co.uk). Sloane Square tube. **Open** 9.30am-6pm Mon, Tue, Sat; 9.30am-7pm Wed-Fri; noon-5pm Sun. **Credit** AmEx, MC, V. **Map** p399 F10.
In the 11 years since Jo Malone launched her luxurious fragrance brand, the business has been a runaway success, with several London shops, plus stockists around the globe. Her coveted range of scents, candles, skincare and bodycare is sleekly packaged, mainly in glass bottles or jars with simple cream-and-black labels. Pricey but worth it.
Other locations: 24 Royal Exchange, The City, EC3V 3LP (7444 1999); 23 Brook Street, Mayfair, W1K 4HA (7491 9104).

MAC Cosmetics

109 King's Road, Chelsea, SW3 4PA (7349 0022/www.maccosmetics.com). Sloane Square tube. **Open** 10am-6.30pm Mon-Sat; noon-5.30pm Sun. **Credit** AmEx, MC, V. **Map** p399 F11.
This Canadian company is renowned for its bright, long-lasting make-up. It's serious stuff but it has a fun edge – ranges are designed to mix and match and perfect for experimenting with a variety of dramatic looks. Staff are always friendly and full of tips.
Other locations: 28 Foubert's Place, Soho, W1F 7PR (7534 9222); 38 Neal Street, Covent Garden, WC2H 9PS (7379 6820); 28a Kensington Church Street, Kensington, W8 4EP (7937 3738).

Porchester Spa

The Porchester Centre, Queensway, W2 5HS (7792 3980). Bayswater tube. **Open** *Women only* 10am-10pm Tue, Thur, Fri; 10am-4pm Sun. *Men only* 10am-10pm Mon, Wed, Sat. *Mixed couples* 4-10pm Sun. Last entry 2hrs before closing. **Admission** £19.45; £27.50 couples. **Credit** MC, V. **Map** p396 C5.
The Porchester is quite unlike any other spa you'll visit. Forget air-conditioning and tinkly music: this place feels like a municipal swimming pool, just with original art deco architectural touches. The therapies are as good as many of those costing three times as much in more luxurious surroundings.

The Refinery

60 Brook Street, Mayfair, W1K 5DU (7409 2001/www.the-refinery.com). Bond Street tube. **Open** 10am-7pm Mon, Tue; 10am-9pm Wed-Fri; 9am-6pm Sat; 11am-5pm Sun. **Credit** MC, V. **Map** p400 H6.
This spa, within an impressive Mayfair townhouse, is designed entirely for men. The Refinery aims for a 'clubby' feel, and the expert staff cater for the likes of Pierce Brosnan and Rio Ferdinand. Treatments range from facials and massages to LaStone therapy. There's also a concession in Harrods.
Other locations: 38 Bishopsgate, The City, EC2N 4AJ (7588 1006).

Space NK

8 Broadwick Street, Soho, W1F 8HW (7287 2667/www.spacenk.com). Piccadilly Circus or Tottenham Court Road tube. **Open** 10am-7pm Mon-Wed, Fri, Sat; 10am-8pm Thur. **Credit** AmEx, MC, V. **Map** p408 V2.

Eat, Drink, Shop

Harrods' **Urban Retreat** – because you're worth it.

With more than 30 stores in its portfolio, Space NK goes from strength to strength. Of its constantly rotating roster of cult lines, only the best make the grade – Diptyque and L'Artisan Parfumeur candles, Eve Lom, Chantecaille and REN skincare, Nars and Laura Mercier make-up, to name but a few. This branch also has one treatment room; the Westbourne Grove flagship has a full-on spa. **Photo** *p254*.
Other locations: throughout the city.

Urban Retreat

5th Floor, Harrods, Knightsbridge, 87-135 Brompton Road, SW1X 7XL (7893 8333/www.harrods.com). Knightsbridge tube. **Open** 10am-7pm Mon-Sat; noon-6pm Sun. **Credit** AmEx, DC, MC, V. **Map** p399 F9.
While the Urban Retreat's stark design may not be to everyone's taste, there's no denying the pedigree of the treatments available (this is Harrods, after all). Facials and massages are by Crème de la Mer, La Prairie and Thalgo; other services include natural-looking Bali Sun airbrush tans, a Bobbi Brown Make-up Studio, nails by Leighton Denny and eyebrow shaping by Shavata. **Photo** *above*.

Hairdressers

Daniel Hersheson

Harvey Nichols, 109-125 Knightsbridge, SW1X 7RJ (7235 5000/www.danielhersheson.com). Knightsbridge tube. **Open** 10am-8pm Mon-Fri; 10am-7pm Sat; noon-6pm Sun. **Credit** AmEx, MC, V. **Map** p399 F9.
Up on Harvey Nichols' fourth floor is a new pampering experience. Daniel Hersheson and his son Luke (co-owners of the salons) specialise in bang up-

to-date, fashion-led hair styling. Colour is a strong point and, hair aside, there are classy beauty treatment rooms, a nail bar and a food menu.
Other locations: 45 Conduit Street, Mayfair, W1S 2YN (7434 1747).

Geo F Trumper

9 Curzon Street, Mayfair, W1J 5HQ (7499 1850/ www.trumpers.com). Green Park tube. **Open** 9am-5.30pm Mon-Fri; 9am-1pm Sat. **Credit** AmEx, DC, MC, V. **Map** p402 H8.
Every man should have an open-razor shave at least once in his life, and this traditional Mayfair barber's (founded in 1875) is amply qualified to do the honours. With its wood panelling, ancient sinks and leather chairs, it looks every inch the Victorian barber shop, yet does a brisk trade with modern blokes as well as old-school gents.

HOB

60 Baker Street, Marylebone, W1U 7DE (7935 5883/6775). Baker Street tube. **Open** 9am-6pm Mon; 9am-8pm Tue-Fri; 8.30am-6pm Sat; 11am-5pm Sun. **Credit** AmEx, DC, MC, V. **Map** p400 G5.
HOB's new flagship salon boasts plasma screens for when you're *Vogue*-d out and a dedicated area for tans, waxing and face and body treatments. Staff are a talented, award-winning bunch who are strong on both cuts and colour. Prices from £50 for a cut.

Mr Topper's

13A Great Russell Street, Bloomsbury, WC1B 3NH (7631 3233). Tottenham Court Road tube. **Open** 9am-6.30pm Mon-Sat; 11am-5.30pm Sun. **No credit cards**. **Map** p409 X1.

There are no luxury extras in this no-nonsense £6-a-pop establishment. The majority of customers are men, but women are welcome too (for an extra £4). The cutting is competent, the staff are friendly, and for these prices, what more could you ask for? **Other locations**: throughout the city.

Michaeljohn

25 Albemarle Street, Mayfair, W1S 4HU (7629 6969/www.michaeljohn.co.uk). Green Park tube. **Open** 8am-6.30pm Mon, Sat; 8am-8pm Tue-Fri. **Credit** MC, V. **Map** p408 U5.

In spite of its swanky Mayfair location, MJ is a super-friendly but consummately professional salon where you can get a great cut, colour and manicure or pedicure. The client list is full to the brim with stars, politicians and people who simply want good results.

Nyumba/Michael Charalambous

6-7 Mount Street, Mayfair, W1K 3EH (7408 1489/ www.nyumbasalon.com). Bond Street or Green Park tube. **Open** 9am-6pm Tue, Wed, Fri, Sat; 9am-8pm Thur. **Credit** AmEx, MC, V. **Map** p402 H7.

Michael Charalambous is not backwards at coming forwards. He'll tell you straight if your current hair-cut doesn't suit you, but the popularity of his salon speaks for itself. Both cuts and colours are strong points, whether they're by the man himself or one of his team. Additional services include eyebrow threading, waxing, facials, reiki, holistic treatments, reflexology, manicures, pedicures and make-up lessons. Cuts start at £60 (£250 with Michael).

Opticians

David Clulow

185 King's Road, Chelsea, SW3 5EB (7376 5733/ www.davidclulow.com). Sloane Square tube. **Open** 10am-6.30pm Mon-Sat; 11am-5pm Sun. **Credit** AmEx, DC, MC, V. **Map** p399 E12.

This smart optician's is big on lenses, including coloured and hand-painted styles. During the summer, DC slashes the price of its designer frames, including Paul Smith, Prada, Face à Face and Dior. Also concessions in Selfridges and Harrods. **Other locations**: throughout the city.

Kirk Originals

29 Floral Street, Covent Garden, WC2E 9DP (7240 5055/www.kirkoriginals.com). Covent Garden tube. **Open** 11am-7pm Mon-Sat; 1-5pm Sun. **Credit** MC, V. **Map** p409 Y3.

Kirk Originals started life in the early '90s; these days the shop is a byword for cool, with colourful, chunky retro-inspired frames. Also has in-store exhibitions.

Opera Opera

98 Long Acre, Covent Garden, WC2E 9NR (7836 9246). Covent Garden tube. **Open** 10am-6pm Mon-Sat. **Credit** MC, V. **Map** p409 Y2.

The best place to come if you're after something a bit different. As well as providing specs for theatrical productions, the company also makes bespoke glasses for the public, even from a photo.

Homewares

Aria

295-297 Upper Street, Islington, N1 2TU (7704 1999/www.aria-shop.co.uk). Highbury & Islington tube/rail. **Open** 10am-7pm Mon-Fri; 10am-6.30pm Sat; noon-5pm Sun. **Credit** AmEx, MC, V. **Map** p404 O1.

Aria is a good one-stop shop for stylish contemporary home accessories, lighting and furniture. The store brings in big names such as Alessi, Philippe Starck, Jasper Morrison and Ron Arad. Whether you succumb to a dish for £15 or a linear Chair One for £155, you're unlikely to leave empty-handed. The sister store across the road sells smaller items. **Other locations**: 133 Upper Street, Islington, N1 1QP (7226 1021).

Cath Kidston

8 Clarendon Cross, Notting Hill, W11 4AP (7221 4000/www.cathkidston.co.uk). Holland Park tube. **Open** 10am-6pm Mon-Sat; noon-5pm Sun. **Credit** AmEx, MC, V.

Cath Kidston has developed a loyal, mainly female, following over recent years with her adorable polka dots, stripes and floral prints. Bedlinen, cushions, washbags, lamps and numerous other accessories are girlie and cute, with a 1950s feel. **Other locations**: throughout the city.

Conran Shop

Michelin House, 81 Fulham Road, Fulham, SW3 6RD (7589 7401/www.conran.com). South Kensington tube. **Open** 10am-6pm Mon, Tue, Fri; 10am-7pm Wed, Thur; 10am-6.30pm Sat; noon-6pm Sun. **Credit** AmEx, MC, V. **Map** p399 E10.

The Conran Shop was one of the very first retailers to embody the term 'lifestyle' by introducing a set of cosmopolitan shoppers to the notion of buying everything for their home from a single place. Because of the product variation, all budgets are covered. **Other locations**: throughout the city.

Design Museum Shop

Shad Thames, Bermondsey, SE1 2YD (7940 8753/ www.designmuseum.org). Tower Hill tube/London Bridge tube/rail. **Open** 10am-5.15pm daily. **Credit** AmEx, MC, V. **Map** p407 S9.

The Design Museum's shop contains some wonders of its own. Small items prevail, such as the Vitra miniature chair range, vases from Rosenthal, Pigeon lights by Ed Carpenter and various design classics, current and future.

SCP

135-139 Curtain Road, Shoreditch, EC2A 3BX (7739 1869/www.scp.co.uk). Old Street tube/rail. **Open** 9.30am-6pm Mon-Sat; 11am-5pm Sun. **Credit** MC, V. **Map** p405 R4.

SCP has become one of London's leading design stores for expertly sourced contemporary furniture, lighting, ceramics, glass, textiles, and excellent design books. Among the respected designers featured are Jasper Morrison and Michael Sodeau.

Eat, Drink, Shop

Markets

The markets listed below are the most famous in the capital, and not too far away from the centre. There are some fantastic markets in further-flung places. In Battersea, **Northcote Road Market** (9am-5pm Thur-Sat) has lovely food stalls; in Hackney, **Ridley Road Market** (7am-5pm Mon-Sat) is fine for African specialities. Also notable for Afro/Caribbean goodies is **Shepherd's Bush Market**, off Goldhawk Road, W12. To the amazement of Londoners, **Camden Market** (*see p149*) continues to draw the hordes who come looking for cheap designer clothes and crafty things; adjoining **Stables Market** (*see p149*) sell crafts, vintage clothing, antiques and food. **Petticoat Lane Market** (Middlesex Street, Goulston Street, New Goulston Street, Toynbee Street, Wentworth Street, Bell Lane, Cobb Street, Leyden Street, Strype Street, Old Castle Street, Cutler Street, E1, open 10am-2pm Mon-Fri, 9am-2pm Sun) is an East End market of the old school, selling cheap clothes, toys and electronics, as well as beauty, jewellery and kitchen equipment.

General

Brick Lane Market

Brick Lane – north of railway bridge, Cygnet Street, Sclater Street, E1; Bacon Street, Cheshire Street, Chilton Street, E2. Spitalfields. Aldgate East or Shoreditch tube/Liverpool Street tube/rail. **Open** dawn-2pm Sun. **Map** p405 S5.

This positively folkloric East End institution has stalls selling cheap soaps and razors, towels, bric-a-brac, second-hand clothes and old furniture, along with back-of-a-lorry hustlers and East End seafood stalls. The market spreads out along a number of narrow streets lined with trendy clothes shops and expensive home accessories stores alongside Bangladeshi and Pakistani restaurants and sweet-shops. The most browsable bit is Cheshire Street, with retro homewares and fashion. **Photo** *p259*.

Brixton Market

Electric Avenue, Pope's Road, Brixton Station Road, Atlantic Road, Brixton, SW9 8JX. Brixton tube/rail. **Open** 8am-6pm Mon, Tue, Thur-Sat; 8am-3pm Wed. Visiting Brixton's thronging market is like being plunged into another country. Electric Avenue is packed with stalls piled high with exotic fruit and veg – yams, plantains, mangoes, papaya and more – as well as everyday staples. Around Atlantic Road it's more clothes, towels and cheap wallets. 'Brixton Village' (previously Granville Arcade) houses African and Caribbean food stores, household goods, books, crafts and specialist hair and wig shops. Also look out for the compact but well-stocked hip hop specialist HQ (88 Brixton Village, Coldharbour Lane, 7274 4664).

Greenwich Market

(8293 3110/www.greenwichmarket.net). Greenwich rail/DLR/Cutty Sark DLR. **Open** *Antiques & collectibles* 8.30am-5.30pm Thur, Fri. *Village Market* Stockwell Street, 8am-5pm Sat, Sun. *Arts & Crafts* 9.30am-5.30pm Thur-Sun. *Food Court* 9.30am-5.30pm Sat, Sun.

Heading into the town centre from the station, you come first to the antiques market, a collection of bric-a-brac and junk that varies from tat to treasures. Next along is the Village Market, where a second-hand clothes flea market mingles with Chinese silk dresses, cheap trendy clothes, ethnic ornaments, CDs and more. Passing the food court you reach the covered Crafts Market, which is ideal for gift-hunting. The central hub of stalls sells a delicious selection of olives, breads, jam doughnuts and brownies.

Portobello Road Market

Portobello Road, W10, W11; Golborne Road, W10. Ladbroke Grove, Notting Hill Gate or Westbourne Park tube. **Open** *General* 8am-6pm Mon-Wed; 9am-1pm Thur; 7am-7pm Fri, Sat. *Antiques* 4am-6pm Sat. **Map** p396 A6.

Starting at the Notting Hill end are mainly antiques stalls selling toy soldiers, vases, bric-a-brac and general Victoriana. Further up you come to the food stalls, ranging from traditional fruit and veg to tasty cheeses, stuffed olives, organic biscuits and crackers, bratwurst and crêpes. Next up come clothes and jewellery, ranging from cheap trendy club- and casualwear to delightful craft bracelets and earrings. The cafés under the Westway are a good place to rest before plunging into the new designers' clothes and vintage wear along the walkway to Ladbroke Grove.

Spitalfields Market

Commercial Street, between Lamb Street & Brushfield Street, E1 (7247 8556). Liverpool Street tube/rail. **Open** *Antiques* 10.30am-4pm Thur. *General* 10.30am-4pm Mon-Fri, Sun. *Food* 10.30am-4pm Wed. *Fashion* 10.30am-4pm Fri. *Records* 10.30am-4pm 1st & 3rd Wed of mth. **Map** p405 R5.

Surrounded by cool shops selling movie posters, second-hand books and modish vintage furniture, the stalls here offer everything from handmade cards, dyed sheepskin rugs and craft jewellery to aromatherapy products, CDs and quirky fashions. There are cake and bread stalls and a mini food court selling grub from all over the world at bargain prices. A visit to Spitalfields is easily combined with a quick poke around Brick Lane (*see above*).

Flowers

Columbia Road Flower Market

Columbia Road, between Gosset Street & the Royal Oak pub, Bethnal Green, E2 (www.columbia-flower-market.freewebspace.com). Bus 26, 48, 55. **Open** 8am-2pm Sun. **No credit cards. Map** p405 S3.

You know you are nearing this popular street market when you see masses of greenery bobbing down the surrounding streets, held aloft by happy

Brick Lane Market. *See p258.*

gardeners. Alongside the masses of plant stalls there are great cafés and an eclectic range of shops, selling everything from ceramics to hats. Only open on Sundays, the market is immensely popular, so it's worth making the effort to get there before 9am or just before closing time at 2pm to avoid the crush. *See also p160.*

Food

Farmers' markets are the way forward for city folk who want to buy food that has been grown, reared and prepared by the stallholder. The most central ones are in **Marylebone** (Cramer Street car park, 7704 9659, 10am-2pm Sun), **Notting Hill** (the car park behind Waterstone's, access via Kensington Place, at the corner of Kensington Church Street, W8 7PR, 7704 9659, 9am-1pm Sat), **Pimlico** (Orange Square, corner of Pimlico Road and Ebury Street, 7704 9659, 9am-1pm Sat) and **Islington** (behind the town hall, Upper Street, 10am-2pm Sun, 7833 0338). For further information contact the **National Association of Farmers' Markets** (0845 458 8420, www.farmers markets.net).

Berwick Street Market

Berwick Street, Rupert Street, Soho, W1. Piccadilly Circus or Tottenham Court Road tube. **Open** 9am-6pm Mon-Sat. **Map** p408 V2.
A traditional fruit and veg market in the seedy heart of Soho, Berwick Street also has stalls selling flowers, nuts, CDs, sweets, knickers and socks. The fresh produce is delicious, ranging from vine tomatoes, new potatoes and strawberries to mangoes and passion fruit. Like the rest of Soho, the market doesn't get going until a bit later, so there's no need to go early.

Borough Market

8 Southwark Street, SE1 1TL (7407 1002/www. boroughmarket.org.uk). London Bridge tube/rail. **Open** noon-6pm Fri; 9am-4pm Sat. **Map** p407 P8.
Endorsed by many a celebrity chef, Borough Market offers an exciting mix of food from all over the world. Meat encompasses everything from chicken to venison – and on Saturday lunchtime lengthy queues wait for a chorizo sandwich from the Brindisa stall (for Tapas Brindisa restaurant, *see p195*). Add to this fresh fruit and veg of all varieties, organic goods (cakes, breads), exotic teas, flowers, dairy, fish, beers and wines and you've got the makings of a feast. Quality is high and prices match that. **Photo** *p260.*

Borough Market. *See p259.*

Eat, Drink, Shop

Music

Megastores

HMV

150 Oxford Street, Oxford Circus, W1D 1DJ (7631 3423/www.hmv.co.uk). Oxford Circus tube. **Open** 9am-8pm Mon-Wed, Fri, Sat; 9am-9pm Thur; noon-6pm Sun. **Credit** AmEx, DC, MC, V. **Map** p408 U2.
The first and last stop for the record-buying novice in London. With seasonal sales, cut-price box sets and hundreds of rarities and imports, there's little chance you'll leave this behemoth of a store empty-handed. The vast basement houses broad classical and jazz sections, and staff are always on hand to advise. **Other locations**: throughout the city.

Virgin Megastore

14-16 Oxford Street, Fitzrovia, W1D 1AR (7631 1234/www.virgin.com). Tottenham Court Road tube. **Open** 9am-9pm Mon-Sat; noon-6pm Sun. **Credit** AmEx, MC, V. **Map** p408 W1.
The long evolution of Virgin's flagship store has seen renovations aplenty and regular furniture shiftings, but lately it seems to have found its feet. Signings and in-store performances happen almost weekly, and the range of rock, pop and dance is vast. The world, jazz, classical and folk sections are impressive too. It's also big on music merchandise. **Other locations**: throughout the city.

Specialist music shops

Soho's Berwick Street is a CD and LP mecca – **Selectadisc** (No.34) and **Sister Ray** (No.94) are strong on indie and mainstream, while **Reckless** (No.30) is good for mainstream.

Fopp

1 Earlham Street, Covent Garden, WC2H 9LL (7379 0883/www.fopp.co.uk). Covent Garden or Tottenham Court Road tube. **Open** 10am-10pm Mon-Sat; 11am-6pm Sun. **Credit** AmEx, MC, V. **Map** p409 X2.
Boasting a delightfully minimalist aesthetic and low, low prices, this burgeoning national chain is especially brilliant for those looking to replenish their prog back catalogues on the cheap. Also good for picking up a bit of cult fiction and art-house DVDs.

Harold Moores Records

2 Great Marlborough Street, Soho, W1F 7HQ (7437 1576/www.hmrecords.co.uk). Oxford Circus tube. **Open** 10am-6.30pm Mon-Sat; noon-6pm Sun. **Credit** MC, V. **Map** p408 V2.
Famous in classical circles for its marvellous used-LP selection, as well as a treasure trove of rare oddities. Couple this with a large contemporary and avant-garde section, and Harold Moores is most definitely a place for the hardened music collector.

Honest Jon's

278 Portobello Road, Ladbroke Grove, W10 5TE (8969 9822/www.honestjons.com). Ladbroke Grove tube. **Open** 10am-6pm Mon-Sat; 11am-5pm Sun. **Credit** AmEx, DC, MC, V. **Map** p396 A6.
With its own record label and a huge selection of CDs and vinyl, this Damon Albarn-affiliated soul, jazz and hip-hop shop has become something of a London institution. Friendly staff and a laid-back atmosphere complement its enormous spread, which also covers genres from dancehall and ska via dub.

Rough Trade

130 Talbot Road, Ladbroke Grove, W11 1JA (7229 8541/www.roughtrade.com). Ladbroke Grove tube. **Open** 10am-6.30pm Mon-Sat; noon-5pm Sun. **Credit** AmEx, DC, MC, V. **Map** p396 A5.

Arguably London's coolest record shop, Rough Trade stocks some real treasures. Decked with indie-rock obscurities, there are also extensive selections of new hip hop and world music. If there was an award for the friendliest record shop staff in London, Rough Trade would win hands down.
Other locations: 16 Neal's Yard, Covent Garden, WC2H 9DP (7240 0105).

Pharmacies

High-street chemists **Boots** (*see p255*) also has pharmacies in many of its central locations, some of which stay open late.

Bliss Chemist
5-6 Marble Arch, Marylebone, W1H 7EL (7723 6116). Marble Arch tube. **Open** 9am-midnight daily. **Credit** AmEx, MC, V. **Map** p397 F6.
This store has a handy late-night pharmacy.
Other locations: 50-56 Willesden Lane, Willesden, NW6 7SX (7624 8000).

Sport & adventure

Ellis Brigham
Tower House, 3-11 Southampton Street, Covent Garden, WC2E 7HA (7395 1010/www.ellis-brigham.com). Covent Garden tube/Charing Cross tube/rail. **Open** 10am-7pm Mon-Wed, Fri; 10am-7.30pm Thur; 9.30am-6.30pm Sat; 11.30am-5.30pm Sun. **Credit** AmEx, MC, V. **Map** p409 Z4.
Two floors stocked with everything you might need for the outdoors – and decently priced too. There's a lot of camping and trekking equipment, plus a ski and snowboard section that expands during winter. There's even a two-storey ice wall for urban climbers.
Other locations: 178 Kensington High Street, Kensington, W8 7RG (7937 6889).

Lillywhites
24-36 Lower Regent Street, St James's, SW1Y 4QF (0870 333 9600/www.sports-soccer.co.uk). Piccadilly Circus tube. **Open** 10am-9pm Mon-Sat; noon-6pm Sun. **Credit** AmEx, DC, MC, V. **Map** p408 W4.
Since being bought by the Sports Soccer group, Britain's most famous sports store now caters to fewer activities. On the plus side, you can pick up all the gear you need for cricket, golf, football and racket sports at very competitive prices.

Toys & games

Also check out the toy and game sections at the department stores (*see p238*) and some of the children's shops (*see p245*). For computer games, try the music megastores (*see p260*).

Cheeky Monkeys
202 Kensington Park Road, Ladbroke Grove, W11 1NR (7792 9022/www.cheekymonkeys.com). Ladbroke Grove tube. **Open** 9.30am-5.30pm Mon-Fri; 10am-5.30pm Sat. **Credit** MC, V. **Map** p396 A7.

These lovely modern toy shops are strong on presentation and stock unusual, attractive and fun products. An enduring bestseller is the beautiful, shaggy rocking sheep for babies and toddlers to ride. Monkeys also have some of London's best fancy dress (from smart soldiers to tigers and frogs). Pocket-money budgets are also catered to.
Other locations: throughout the city.

Dragons of Walton Street
23 Walton Street, South Kensington, SW3 2HX (7589 3795/www.dragonsofwaltonstreet.com). Knightsbridge or South Kensington tube. **Open** 9.30am-5.30pm Mon-Fri; 10am-5pm Sat. **Credit** AmEx, MC, V. **Map** p399 E10.
Veteran hand-painter of nursery furniture Rosie Fisher opened her first Dragons shop in 1979, and today the name is synonymous with top-quality, exclusive baby rooms. Everything is here, from curtains to cots to chairs. As well as furniture, there are dolls' houses, wooden toys and teddy bears.

Hamleys
188-196 Regent Street, Soho, W1B 5BT (0870 333 2455/www.hamleys.com). Oxford Circus tube. **Open** 10am-8pm Mon-Sat; noon-6pm Sun. **Credit** AmEx, DC, MC, V. **Map** p408 U3.
The largest toy shop in the world (or so they claim) is a loud, frenetic, exciting experience. The ground floor is where the latest fun toys are demonstrated; it also accommodates a mountain of soft toys. The basement is the Cyberzone, full of games consoles and high-tech gadgets. The first floor has items of a scientific bent, and bear depot. The second floor is given over to everything for pre-schoolers. Third is girlie heaven with departments for dressing up, make-up and so on. Fourth has remote-controlled vehicles, plus die-cast models. Fifth houses Lego World, with its own café.

Mystical Fairies
12 Flask Walk, Hampstead, NW3 1HE (7431 1888/ www.mysticalfairies.co.uk). Hampstead tube. **Open** 10am-6pm Mon-Sat; 11am-6pm Sun. **Credit** MC, V.
Mystical Fairies has realised that no corner of the children's market is untouchable by the fairy. There's plenty of fairy bedwear: slippers, dressing gowns, canopies, bed covers and duvet covers, while fairy dresses come from So Fairy Beautiful and Frilly Lilly. The Enchanted Garden in the basement is a splendid space for Mystical Fairies parties; it's also home to Fairy Club and Fairy School.

Traditional Toys
53 Godfrey Street, Chelsea, SW3 3SX (7352 1718/ www.traditionaltoy.com). Sloane Square tube then 11, 19, 22 bus/49 bus. **Open** 10am-5.30pm Mon-Fri; 10am-6pm Sat. **Credit** AmEx, MC, V. **Map** p399 E11.
Every nook and cranny of this terrific little shop is filled with games, books and toys. For pocket-money budgets there are farm animals, stickers, skipping ropes and the like. Pricier offerings include painted ride-on toys for the nursery, a bright-red wooden fire engine. Don't miss the fantastic fancy dresses.

93 FEET EAST

LIVE VENUE - CLUB - COURTYARD - MEMBERS BAR

!!! (CHK CHK CHK) AESOP ROCK ALEX PATTERSON ARCTIC MONKEYS BEANS BETA BAND BLOC PARTY BRITISH SEA POWER COOPER TEMPLE CLAUSE CRAZY P LOMAX LONE PIGEON M83 MAXIMO PARK MEW MODEY LEMON MR SCRUFF NIC ARMSTRONG PEACHES THE YOUNG KNIVES THE ZUTONS TOKYO DRAGONS TOM VEK WE ARE SCIENTISTS ED HARCOURT'S WILD BOAR YEAH YEAH YEAHS YETI YOUNG HEART ATTACK YOUR CODE NAME IS:MILO FORWARD RUSSIA YOUTHMOVIE SOUNDTRACK STRATEGIES DJ FORMAT DO ME BAD THINGS ECHELON EDITORS ERASE ERRATA FOURTET GONZALES GROOVE ARMADA HARD FI RADIO 4 RTX SEAFOOD SOLEDAD BROTHERS THE DIRTBOMBS SOUNDTRACK OF OUR LIVES SOUTH STEPHEN FRETWELL SUNBURNED HAND OF THE MAN T.RAUMSCHMIERE THE BEES HOT CHIP INTERPOL JAMES BLUNT FIGHTSTAR JAMES YORKSTON U72 JETSCREAMER JOHN SPENSER BLUES EXPLOSION THE FOOTLONG HEROES ICE T JON KENNEDY JOSE GONZALES JOSEPH ARTHUR JOY ZIPPER JUNGLE BROTHERS K.T. TUNSTALL KAISER CHIEFS KAITO BATTLES KID 606 KNIFEHANDCHOP KOMAKINO LIARS THE CRIBS THE D4 THE DARKNESS THE DEPARTURE THE DUKE SPIRIT THE EARLIES THE FUTUREHEADS THE KILLS THE LIBERTINES THE NATIONAL THE OTHERS THE PADDINGTONS THE RAKES THE RAPTURE THE RESEARCH THE ROGERS SISTERS THE STANDS THE STILLS THE SUBWAYS THE THRILLS THE WALKMEN THE WHITE STRIPES THE NEW PORNOGRAPHERS CRAZY GIRL ANNIE SKY GUILLEMOTS KINSKI ACID MOTHERS TEMPLE AKRON/FAMILY CENT VINCENT THE VILLAINS CHICKEN LIPS GREG WILSON ROSS ALLEN LADY SOVEREIGN KING BRITT THE BAYS CHAZ JANKEL PUTSCH 79 JEFF AUTOMATIC TOM MIDDLETON WHOMADWHO JAMIE LIDELL SERGE SANTIAGO WILEY MIKE LADD TREVOR JACKSON RIKO GO HOME PRODUCTIONS ANDY SMITH LETHAL B SHAUN KEAVENEY THE BREAKFASTAZ BUGZ IN THE ATTIC THE LOOSE CANNONS TIM 'LOVE' LEE NUPHONIC SECRETSUNDAZE THE CUBAN BROTHERS ESTELLE KITTY YO

93 LIVE
Mon - Thu
Live music events
DJ's in the bar

93 CLUBS
Fri, Sat + Sun
Club nights
& all-day parties

93 MEMBERS
Mon - Sun
93 Members Bar

150 Brick Lane E1
+44 (0)20 7247 3293
info@93feeteast.co.uk

www.93feeteast.com

Arts & Entertainment

Features

Festivals & Events

The fun starts here.

15,000 bras on display at the **Playtex Moonwalk**. *See p266.*

London's full programme of festivals and events reflects and benefits from the city's multicultural status, with every walk of life strutting its stuff. Recent years have seen an increase in outdoor festivals, particularly in summer (*see p271* **Air play**), as well as some imaginative sponsored seasons and one-off events.

We've included as many events as we can here, but also keep an eye out in *Time Out* magazine for events that crop up at short notice. Also note that, if you're going out of your way to attend any festival or event, it's always a good idea to confirm details nearer the time.

All year

Ceremony of the Keys
Tower of London, Tower Hill, The City, EC3N 4AB (08707 515177/www.hrp.org.uk). Tower Hill tube/ Tower Gateway DLR. **Date** *daily. Apr-Oct* max party of 7. *Nov-Mar* max party of 15. **Map** p407 R7.

As part of this 700-year-old ceremony, the Yeoman Warders lock the entrances to the Tower of London at 9.53pm every evening. You assemble at the West Gate at 9pm, and it's all over by 10pm, when the last post sounds. See the website for ticket application – you need to apply three months before your visit.

Changing of the Guard
Buckingham Palace, St James's, SW1A 1AA (7321 2233/www.royal.gov.uk). Green Park or St James's Park tube/Victoria tube/rail. **Ceremonies** *Apr-Aug* 11.30am daily. *Sept-Mar* alternate days (may be cancelled in wet weather). **Map** p402 H9. *Horse Guards & St James's Palace, SW1A 1BQ.* **Ceremonies** 11am Mon-Sat; 10am Sun. **Map** p403 K8.

A regiment of Foot Guards (scarlet coats and bearskin hats) lines up in the forecourt of Wellington Barracks from 10.45am; at 11.27am the soldiers march, accompanied by their regimental band, to Buckingham Palace to relieve the sentries in the forecourt. At Horse Guards in Whitehall, the Household Cavalry mount the guard (10am-4pm daily) then ride to Whitehall via the Mall from Hyde Park for the daily changeover.

Gun Salutes

Green Park, Mayfair & St James's, W1, & Tower of London, The City, EC3. **Dates** 6 Feb (Accession Day); 21 Apr & 17 June (Queen's birthdays); 2 June (Coronation Day); 10 June (Duke of Edinburgh's birthday); 17 June (Trooping the Colour); State Opening of Parliament (*see p270*); 11 Nov (Lord Mayor's Show); 12 Nov (Remembrance Sunday); & state visits. **Map** p402 H8.

The King's Troop Royal Horse Artillery makes a mounted charge through Hyde Park, sets up the guns and fires a 41-gun salute (at noon, except on the occasion of the State Opening of Parliament) opposite the Dorchester Hotel. Not to be outdone, the Honourable Artillery Company fires a 62-gun salute at the Tower of London at 1pm.

January-March 2006

International Mime Festival

Various venues across London (7637 5661/ www.mimefest.co.uk). **Date** 11-29 Jan.

Surely London's quietest festival, the annual LIMF involves companies from the UK and abroad who perform a variety of shows for all ages. There's much more to mime than the white-faced, walled-in stereotype. This year's highlights include France's Compagnie 111, who will perform at the South Bank Centre's Queen Elizabeth Hall, and UK puppeteers Faulty Optic, at the ICA. Free brochures are available via the website or by phoning. **Photo** *p266*.

London Art Fair

Business Design Centre, 52 Upper Street, Islington, N1 0QH (0870 126 1783/www.londonartfair.co.uk). Angel tube. **Date** 18-22 Jan. **Map** p404 N2.

Millions of pounds are spent by art collectors at this large scale sale, on modern British and contemporary works by such artists as Terry Frost, LS Lowry, Ben Nicholson, Bridget Riley and Gavin Turk. More than 100 galleries participate, such as England & Co, Flowers East and Vertigo.

Chinese New Year Festival

Around Gerrard Street, Chinatown, W1, Leicester Square, WC2 & Trafalgar Square, WC2 (7851 6686/ www.chinatownchinese.com). Leicester Square or Piccadilly Circus tube. **Date** 29 Jan. **Map** p408 W3.

A traditional event to welcome in the new year: in 2006 the Year of the Dog will take over from the Year of the Rooster. Celebrations begin at 11am with a children's parade from Leicester Square gardens to Trafalgar Square, where the lion and dragon dance teams perform traditional dances. And there are, of course, firework displays (at lunchtime and at 5pm). About 50,000 people attended the Chinese New Year Celebrations in 2005. This year will also see China in London 2006, an initiative organised by the Royal Academy, the Chinatown Chinese Association and the Mayor of London. The season will celebrate China's cultural history with an interesting programme of performances and film screenings, plus culinary, literary and language events.

Great Spitalfields Pancake Race

Dray Walk, Brick Lane, E1 6QL (7375 0441). Liverpool Street tube/rail. **Date** Shrove Tuesday (28 Feb). **Map** p405 S5.

This traditional tomfoolery starts at 12.30pm, with teams of four tossing pancakes as they run – all for a good cause, of course. Call in advance if you want to take part, or just show up if all you're after is seeing the 'cakes hit the deck.

National Science Week

Various venues across London (www.the-ba.net). **Date** 10-19 Mar.

This annual festival encompasses a wide variety of events from hands-on shows for youngsters to discussions for adults to celebrate all aspects of science, engineering and technology.

St Patrick's Day Parade & Festival

Various venues across London (7983 4100/ www.london.gov.uk). **Date** 12 Mar.

Supported by the Mayor, this popular, thousands-strong parade through central London is followed by a free party. Expect plenty of Irish music and dancing, arts and crafts and activities for all ages.

Don't miss Festivals

Brick Lane Festival

Low-key and loads of fun, the Brick Lane Festival has food, music, dance and more. *See p269.*

Coin Street Festival

This series of themed events, held on the South Bank, is great for all age groups, especially families. *See p266.*

London Film Festival

This world-famous festival attracts equally famous stars, who flock to see the 150 new movies. *See p270.*

Meltdown

Featuring a new guest curator each year, this gigfest attracts the crème de la crème of the music world. *See p267.*

Remembrance Sunday Ceremony

A sombre, moving affair headed by the Queen, dedicated to those who have lost their lives in conflict. *See p270.*

▶ For more festivals, see our specialist Arts & Entertainment chapters. For a list of public holidays, *see p377*.

Arts & Entertainment

International Mime Festival. *See p265.*

April-June 2006

For **Royal Ascot**, *see p329.*

Oxford & Cambridge Boat Race

Thames, from Putney to Mortlake (01225 383483/ www.theboatrace.org). Putney Bridge tube/Putney, Barnes Bridge or Mortlake rail. **Date** 2 Apr.
The 152nd race will take place at 4.35pm. Some 250,000 people are expected to line the Thames from Putney to Mortlake for this annual elitist grudge match, with the riverside pubs in Mortlake and Hammersmith the most popular (read: obscenely crowded and packed with toffs) vantage points. For those who care: Oxford (who won in 2005, with the third fastest time ever) is kitted out in the dark blue, Cambridge is in the light blue.

London Harness Horse Parade

Battersea Park, Albert Bridge Road, Battersea, SW11 4PF (01737 646132). Battersea Park or Queenstown Road rail/97, 137 bus. **Date** 17 Apr. **Map** p399 F13.
An Easter Monday parade of more than 300 working horses, donkeys and mules with their various commercial and private carriages. The horses assemble from 9am; main parade noon-1pm.

London Marathon

Greenwich Park to the Mall via the Isle of Dogs, Victoria Embankment & St James's Park (7902 0200/www.london-marathon.co.uk). Maze Hill rail or Charing Cross tube/rail. **Date** 23 Apr.

As one of the biggest metropolitan marathons in the world, this event attracts 35,000 starters, including a few in outrageous costumes. Would-be runners must apply by the previous October to be entered in the ballot. Spectators are advised to arrive early; the front runners reach the 13-mile mark near the Tower of London at around 10am.

Playtex Moonwalk

Start & finish at Hyde Park, W1 (01483 741 430/ www.walkthewalk.org). **Date** May. **Map** p397 F7.
A charity night walk to raise money for breast cancer research. The 15,000-odd participants – men included – wear specially decorated bras to power walk the 26.2-mile route. **Photo** *p264.*

May Fayre & Puppet Festival

St Paul's Church Garden, Bedford Street, Covent Garden, WC2E 9ED (7375 0441/www.alternative arts.co.uk). Covent Garden tube. **Date** 14 May. **Map** p409 Y4.
Commemorating the first recorded sighting of Mr Punch in England (by diarist Samuel Pepys in Covent Garden, in 1662), this free event offers puppetry galore from 10.30am to 5.30pm.

Chelsea Flower Show

Grounds of Royal Hospital, Royal Hospital Road, Chelsea, SW3 4SR (7649 1885/www.rhs.org.uk). Sloane Square tube. **Date** 23-27 May. **Map** p399 F12.
The hysteria that builds up around this annual flower show has to be seen to be believed. Fight your way past the rich old ladies to see perfect roses bred by experts, or to get ideas for your own humble plot. Tickets go on sale in November and sell out fast; the first two days are reserved for Royal Horticultural Society members. The show closes at 5.30pm on the final day, with display plants sold off from 4.30pm.

Kew Summer Festival

Royal Botanic Gardens, Kew, Richmond, Surrey TW9 3AB (8332 5655/www.kew.org). Kew Gardens tube/rail/Kew Bridge rail. **Date** 27 May-24 Sept.
Each season at the botanical gardens brings its own programme of events, with the summer one lasting the longest. This year's festival is a celebration of Kew's Heritage Year and one of the highlights will be the reopening of Kew Palace, George III's home, following its restoration. There are special activities on bank holidays, such as bluebell walks in May.

Jazz Plus

Victoria Embankment Gardens, Villiers Street, Westminster, WC2R 2PY (7375 0441/www. alternativearts.co.uk). Embankment tube. **Date** June-July. **Map** p409 Y5.
Free lunchtime concerts are performed by a variety of contemporary jazz musicians on Tuesdays and Thursdays.

Coin Street Festival

Bernie Spain Gardens (next to Oxo Tower Wharf), South Bank, SE1 9PH (7401 3610/www.coinstreet. org). Southwark tube/Waterloo tube/rail. **Date** June-Aug. **Map** p406 N8.

A series of eight or so culturally themed weekend and occasional weekday events celebrating different communities in the capital. Events take place on the South Bank and include music, dance and performance events for all ages, (Capital Age, for example, is specifically designed for the more mature dancer) with craft and refreshment stalls and workshops for families at each one. Check the website for details of the festivities nearer the time.

Royal National Theatre Watch This Space Festival

South Bank, SE1 9PX (7452 3400/www.national theatre.org.uk). Waterloo tube/rail. **Date** June-Aug. **Map** p403 M7.

This lively free festival of music, street theatre and films takes place on Theatre Square outside the National Theatre on the South Bank.

Derby Day

Epsom Downs Racecourse, Epsom Downs, Surrey KT18 5LQ (01372 470047/www.epsomderby.co.uk). Epsom rail then shuttle bus. **Date** 3 June.

One of the most important flat races of the season. You'll find a carnival mood, but if you want comfort or a good view, be prepared to pay for it.

Beating Retreat

Horse Guards Parade, Whitehall, Westminster, SW1A 2AX (bookings 7414 2271). Westminster tube/Charing Cross tube/rail. **Date** 7-8 June. **Map** p403 K8.

This ineffably patriotic ceremony begins at 7pm, with the 'Retreat' beaten on drums by the Mounted Bands of the Household Cavalry and the Massed Bands of the Guards Division.

Open Garden Squares Weekend

Various venues across London (myweb.tiscali. co.uk/london.gardens/squares/index.html). **Date** 10-11 June.

Ever wondered what it's like in those enchanting little private parks dotted around the wealthy parts of town? Each year the London Parks and Gardens Trust opens up many of the posh garden squares and roof gardens and allow visitors a peek inside. Maps are available to guide you to the green oases all over town; gardens vary from Japanese-style retreats to secret 'children-only' play areas.

Meltdown

South Bank Centre, Belvedere Road, South Bank, SE1 8XX (08703 800400/www.rfh.org.uk). Embankment tube/Waterloo tube/rail. **Date** Last 2wks in June. **Map** p403 M8.

This enormously successful festival of contemporary culture at the South Bank Centre invites a guest curator each year. A varied selection of bosses in recent years have included Patti Smith, David Bowie and Morrissey. It's perhaps unsurprising, then, that the gigs and special events tend towards the unpredictable (and are occasionally brilliant).

Architecture Week

Various venues across London (www.architecture week.co.uk). **Date** 17-25 June.

Celebrates contemporary architecture with a programme of events, exhibitions, talks and tours, plus an open practice initiative that allows the public into selected architecture practices.

Trooping the Colour

Horse Guards Parade, Whitehall, Westminster, SW1A 2AX (7414 2479). Westminster tube/ Charing Cross tube/rail. **Date** 17 June. **Map** p403 K8.

Though the Queen was born on 21 April, this is her official birthday celebration. At 10.45am she makes the 15-minute journey from Buckingham Palace to Horse Guards Parade, then scurries back home to watch a midday Royal Air Force flypast and receive a formal gun salute from Green Park.

Transe Express at the **Greenwich & Docklands International Festival**. *See p268.*

Fruitstock. *See p269.*

Pride London & EuroPride

Parade from Hyde Park, W1, to Trafalgar Square, WC2 (7494 2225/www.pridelondon.org). Hyde Park Corner or Marble Arch tube/Charing Cross tube/rail. **Date** *Festival* 17 June-1 July. *Parade & rally* 1 July.

In 2006 the annual free bash thrown by London's proud-to-be-gays and lesbians will be even bigger than usual as Pride combines with EuroPride. The Parade, always a colourful affair, will be named Pride Against Prejudice and will head down Oxford Street, Regent Street, Piccadilly and Whitehall, ending up at Victoria Embankment., It will be followed by a rally in Trafalgar Square from 3-9pm. This year Soho will be closed to traffic for the day to make room for dance stages, market stalls and a food festival. Down the road, Leicester Square will be host to cabaret and 'Drag Idol'. The two weeks leading up to the Pride rally are Festival Fortnight, a mix of cultural performances in various venues. Winter Pride (17-25 Feb) is primarily a fundraiser for the main event.

Wimbledon Lawn Tennis Championships

PO Box 98, Church Road, Wimbledon, SW19 5AE (8944 1066/recorded information 8946 2244/ www.wimbledon.org). Southfields tube/Wimbledon tube/rail. **Date** 26 June-9 July.

The world's most prestigious tennis tournament. For more information, including how to get hold of those coveted tickets, *see p330.*

City of London Festival

Various venues across the City, EC2-EC4 (7377 0540/www.colf.org). Bank, Barbican, Moorgate & St Paul's tube/Blackfriars, Cannon Street & Farringdon tube/rail. **Date** 26 June-13 July.

Now in its 44th year, the City of London Festival takes place in some of the finest buildings in the Square Mile, among them the Guildhall and St Paul's Cathedral. The programme comprises traditional classical music, such as concerts from the London Symphony Orchestra, as well as more unusual offerings from the worlds of jazz, dance, visual art, literature and theatre, plus outdoor and free events. This year takes a Japanese theme; in addition to a number of concerts there will be manga film screenings.

Henley Royal Regatta

Henley Reach, Henley-on-Thames, Oxon RG9 2LY (01491 572153/www.hrr.co.uk). Henley-on-Thames rail. **Date** 28 June-2 July.

First held in 1839, Henley is now a five-day affair, and about as posh as it gets, having had royal patronage since 1851. Boat races range from open events for men and women through club and student crews to junior boys.

July-September 2006

Rhythm Sticks

South Bank Centre, Belvedere Road, South Bank, SE1 8XX (08703 800400/www.rfh.org.uk). Embankment tube/Waterloo tube/rail. **Date** July. **Map** p403 M8.

Each year Rhythm Sticks takes a week to celebrate everything that bangs, crashes and, indeed, pings. Performers come from all corners of the world and play in the widest possible range of styles.

Dance Al Fresco

Regent's Park, Marylebone, NW1 (07970 599445/ www.dancealfresco.org). Regent's Park tube. **Date** July-Aug. **Map** p400 G3.

This yearly outdoor social dance event is held over three weekends. Put on your dancing shoes and tango or ballroom dance to your heart's delight from 2pm to 6pm; The usual format is ballroom dancing on Saturdays and tango on Sundays. Dance novices can join the lessons at 1pm. Money raised from the small charge is donated to tree planting in the park.

Greenwich & Docklands International Festival

Various venues in Greenwich & Docklands (8305 1818/www.festival.org). **Date** July.

An exciting mix of free theatrical, musical and site-specific outdoor events is held over several weekends across east London in the vicinity of Canary Wharf, combining community arts with grander projects. There's a strong likelihood that 2006 will see a return of French outfit Compagnie Off, with a new show to follow up the success they had in 2003 with the 'Giraffes' show. **Photo** *p267.*

BBC Sir Henry Wood Promenade Concerts

Royal Albert Hall, Kensington Gore, South Kensington, SW7 2AP (box office 7589 8212/www. bbc.co.uk/proms). Knightsbridge or South Kensington tube/9, 10, 52 bus. **Date** July-Sept. **Map** p399 D9.

This annual event brings together an eclectic range of mostly classical concerts over the course of two months. Most are televised, but there's nothing like attending them in person. *See also p309.*

Great British Beer Festival

Earl's Court, SW5 (01727 867201/www.camra. org.uk). Earl's Court tube. **Date** 1-5 Aug.

During this (not surprisingly) popular event, tens of thousands of visitors get to sample over 500 real ales plus 200 foreign beers and lager, cider and perry. Hiccups, belches and hangovers are guaranteed.

Fruitstock

Regent's Park, Marylebone, NW1 (8600 3939/ www.fruitstock.com). Regent's Park tube. **Date** 1st weekend in Aug.

The Innocent smoothies drink company's free summer bash, established in 2003, has proved extremely popular in past years – 110,000 punters enjoyed the 2005 fest. This year will no doubt build on this success, with plenty of live music, a dance tent, posh food stalls, a farmers' market, activities for children and, pure and simple, the chance to laze on the grass. Good fun, and good for you. **Photo** *p268.*

Notting Hill Carnival

Notting Hill, W10, W11 (www.lnhc.org.uk). Ladbroke Grove, Notting Hill Gate & Westbourne Park tube. **Date** 27-28 Aug.

It calls itself Europe's biggest street party, and that may be true, as hundreds of thousands of revellers show up each year to drink warm beer and wander about in posh Notting Hill. There is occasional live music and unavoidable sound systems loaded on to trucks, followed by unglamorous dancers in T-shirts. There's a costume parade, but all too often you miss it because of the crowds. Sunday is traditionally the kids' day.

Regent Street Festival

Regent Street, Soho/Mayfair, W1B 4JN (7152 5853/www.regent-street.co.uk). Oxford Circus or Piccadilly Circus tube. **Date** 3 Sept. **Map** p408 U2.

An annual celebration of central London in one of the capital's smartest streets, which closes to traffic for the day to make room for fairground rides, theatre, street entertainers, storytelling, a variety of live music and, of course, shopping.

Brick Lane Festival

Brick Lane & Allen Gardens, Spitalfields, E1 (7655 0906/www.bricklanefestival.com). Aldgate East tube/ Liverpool Street tube/rail. **Date** 2nd Sun in Sept. **Map** p405 S4/5.

This colourful annual celebration of Spitalfields' multicultural communities past and present is everything the Notting Hill Carnival (*see above*) isn't. It is a festive, enjoyable event of food, music, dance and performance, rickshaw rides, stilt-walkers, clowns and jugglers. The main stage showcases world music acts, while the children's area has funfair rides, inflatables and workshops.

Great River Race

Thames, from Ham House, Richmond, Surrey, to Island Gardens, Greenwich, E14 (8398 9057/ www.greatriverrace.co.uk). **Date** 16 Sept.

More than 260 'traditional' boats, from Chinese dragon boats to Viking longboats, vie in the UK traditional boat championship over a 22-mile course. The race begins at 9.30am and the winners reaching the finish from around 12.30pm. Best viewing points are Richmond Bridge on the riverside and along the South Bank, Millennium Bridge, Hungerford Bridge and Tower Bridge. Or take a trip on the passenger boat and watch the action up close (£23, £10 concessions, under-6s free).

Mayor's Thames Festival

Between Westminster & Blackfriars Bridges (7983 4100/www.thamesfestival.org). Blackfriars or Waterloo tube/rail. **Date** 16-17 Sept.

Always fun and occasionally spectacular, this waterfest runs from noon to 10pm all weekend and is highlighted by a lantern procession and firework finale on Sunday evening. But before the pyrotechnics kick off, there are food and crafts stalls in a riverside market, environmental activities and creative workshops, and a lively assortment of dance and music performances.

Open House London

Various venues across London (09001 600 061/ www.openhouselondon.org). **Date** 16-17 Sept.

An annual event that allows architecture lovers free access to more than 500 fascinating buildings all over the capital, from palaces to private homes to the latest and greatest office spaces. Apply for a buildings guide from the end of August and plan your route, remembering that you'll need to book ahead for certain buildings.

October-December 2006

Punch & Judy Festival

Covent Garden Piazza, Covent Garden, WC2 (0870 780 5001/www.coventgardenmarket.co.uk). Covent Garden tube. **Date** Oct. **Map** p409 Y3.

This special puppet fest celebrates the shows so beloved of Samuel Pepys. Expect funny-voiced domestic incidents, a crocodile, a policeman, and Mr Punch giving Judy a few slaps (and vice versa). *See also p266* May Fayre & Puppet Festival.

Pearly Kings & Queens Harvest Festival

St Martin-in-the-Fields, Trafalgar Square, Westminster, WC2N 4JJ (7766 1100/www.pearly society.co.uk). Leicester Square tube/Charing Cross tube/rail. **Date** 2 Oct. **Map** p409 X/Y4.

Pearly kings and queens – so-called because of the shiny white buttons sewn in elaborate designs on their dark suits – have their origins in the 'aristocracy' of London's early Victorian costermongers, who elected their own royalty to safeguard their interests. Now charity representatives, today's pearly monarchy gathers for this 3pm thanksgiving service in their traditional 'flash boy' outfits.

London Film Festival

National Film Theatre, South Bank, SE1 8XT (7928 3535/www.lff.org.uk). Embankment tube/Waterloo tube/rail. **Date** 19 Oct-3 Nov. **Map** p403 M8.
Attracting big-name actors and directors from around the world, and offering the public the chance to see around 150 new British and international features, the LFF centres on the NFT (*see p289*) and the Odeon West End (*see p286*).

Diwali

Trafalgar Square, Westminster, WC2 (7983 4100/ www.london.gov.uk). Charing Cross tube/rail. **Date** 19-23 Oct. *Diwali Day* 21 Oct. **Map** p409 X5.
This annual Festival of Light is celebrated in style by the capital's Hindu, Jain and Sikh communities with fireworks and group displays.

London to Brighton Veteran Car Run

From Serpentine Road, Hyde Park, W2 2UH (01280 841062/www.lbvcr.com). Hyde Park Corner tube. **Date** 5 Nov. **Map** p397 E8.
If you're an early riser, you won't mind getting up at the crack of dawn to catch this parade of around 500 vintage motors, none of which exceeds 20mph on the way to Brighton, setting off from the Serpentine in Hyde Park between 7.15am and 9am, aiming to reach Brighton before 4pm. Otherwise, join the crowds lining the rest of the route, which wends down via Westminster Bridge. The vintage vehicles go on display on 4 November along Regent Street from 10am-3pm if you're not a morning person.

Bonfire Night

Date 5 Nov.
This annual pyrotechnic frenzy sees Brits across the country gather – usually in inclement weather – to burn a 'guy' (an effigy of Guy Fawkes, who notoriously failed to blow up James I and his Parliament in the Gunpowder Plot of 1605) on a giant bonfire, and set off loads of fireworks. Most public displays are held on the weekend nearest 5 November; among the best in London are those at Battersea Park, Alexandra Palace and Crystal Palace. Alternatively, try to book a late ride on the London Eye (*see p79*).

Lord Mayor's Show

Various streets in the City (7332 3456/www.lord mayorsshow.org). **Date** 11 Nov.
Today's the day when, under the conditions of the Magna Carta, the newly elected Lord Mayor of London is presented to the monarch or to their justices for approval. Amid a procession of about 140 floats and more than 6,000 people, the Lord Mayor leaves Mansion House at 11am and travels through

the City to the Royal Courts of Justice on the Strand, where he makes some vows before returning to Mansion House by 2.30pm. The procession will take around an hour and a quarter to pass you, wherever you stand. The event is rounded off by a firework display from a barge moored on the Thames between Waterloo and Blackfriars Bridges.

Remembrance Sunday Ceremony

Cenotaph, Whitehall, Westminster, SW1. Charing Cross tube/rail. **Date** 12 Nov. **Map** p403 L8.
In honour of those who lost their lives in World Wars I and II, and subsequent conflicts, the Prime Minister and other dignitaries lay wreaths at the Cenotaph, Britain's memorial to 'the Glorious Dead'. After a minute's silence at 11am, the Bishop of London leads a service of remembrance.

State Opening of Parliament

House of Lords, Palace of Westminster, Westminster, SW1A 0PW (7219 4272/www. parliament.uk). Westminster tube. **Date** Mid-late Nov (call for details). **Map** p403 L9.
In a ceremony that has changed little since the 16th century, the Queen officially reopens Parliament after its summer recess. You can only see what goes on inside on telly, but if you join the throngs on the streets, you can watch Her Maj arrive and depart in her Irish or Australian State Coach, attended by the Household Cavalry.

Christmas Tree & Lights

Covent Garden (0870 780 5001/www.covent gardenmarket.co.uk); Oxford Street (7976 1123/ www.oxfordstreet.co.uk); Regent Street (7152 5853/www.regent-street.co.uk); Bond Street (www.bondstreetassociation.com); Trafalgar Square (7983 4234/www.london.gov.uk). **Date** Nov-Dec.
Though the Christmas lights on London's main shopping streets are an increasingly commercialised affair (they're often sponsored), much of the childhood wonder still remains in the glittering lights on St Christopher's Place, Marylebone High Street, Bond Street and Kensington High Street. The giant fir tree in Trafalgar Square each year is a gift from the Norwegian people, in gratitude for Britain's role in liberating their country from the Nazis. Celebrities of varying fame stature are usually drafted in to flick the switch and turn the lights on.

New Year's Eve Celebrations

Date 31 Dec.
Celebratory events in London tend to be local in nature, though Trafalgar Square has traditionally been an unofficial (and alarmingly crowded) gathering point. No booze is permitted, which may or may not be such a bad thing. For the cash-flash, almost all of the city's nightclubs hold ludicrously expensive New Year parties. If you're feeling up to it the next morning, the extremely raucous New Year's Day Parade starts at Parliament Square at noon, and finishes at Berkeley Square, taking in Whitehall, Trafalgar Square and Piccadilly. One more thing: Happy New Year!

Arts & Entertainment

Air play

In recent years a combination of warm summers, patio heaters and rejuvenated outdoor public spaces has successfully lured the British out of doors in their masses. Suddenly it seems as if the capital has gone all Mediterranean. Plenty of new developments across town are being enjoyed by Londoners and visitors alike. The most high-profile of these has been the pedestrianisation of the north side of Trafalgar Square, transforming it into a pleasant piazza. The annual **Summer in the Square** (7983 4100, www.london.gov.uk) is a popular programme of free cultural events in the square organised by the Mayor of London, which includes live dance and street theatre performances for all ages.

The Serpentine Gallery's **Summer Pavilion** events programme of talks and film screenings is also well attended. Each year the gallery (*see p145*) commissions a world-class architect who has not previously built in the UK to construct a pavilion, which sits on the lawn outside the gallery from July to September. The turnaround is very quick and plans for the structure are not normally confirmed until early in the year.

The South Bank's **National Theatre** (*see p337*) has created a space especially for outdoor events: from June through August, Theatre Square hosts all manner of unstuffy entertainments, from acrobatic 'roadworkers' to outdoor film screenings. Another summer highlight is **Somerset House** (*see p105*), where a welcome oasis of calm can be found in the large fountained courtyard – except

during the weeks in July when it hosts a series of concerts. In previous years Athlete, Starsailor and the Prodigy have played against the neo-classical background.

Londoners love a picnic, more so when combined with a music concert in the setting of a stately home. English Heritage's **Kenwood House** (*see p133*), **Marble Hill House** (*see p183*) and, out near Saffron Walden, **Audley End House** (01799 522399) all host annual open-air concerts throughout July and August that always make a grand day out. Just be prepared: pack a brolly along with your rug. See also www.picnicconcerts.com.

Ironically, recent mild winters have coincided with an increase in outdoor ice rinks in the capital. One old favourite, round the back of Liverpool Street Station, is **Broadgate Circle** (7505 4068, www.broadgateice.co.uk), which has the longest period of operation (from late October to early April). An especially lovely setting for an ice rink is the courtyard of **Somerset House** (late Nov-late Jan; *see p105*). Other venues include **Hampton Court Palace** (Dec-mid Jan; 0870 060 1778, *see p183*), **Duke of York Square**, King's Road, SW3 (early Dec-early Jan; 7730 7978), the **Tower of London** (late Nov-early Jan; 0870 602 1100), the **Old Royal Naval College** in Greenwich (early Dec-mid Jan; 0870 169 0101) and **Kew Gardens** (Dec-early Jan; www.kewgardensicerink.com; *see p180*). In late 2005 the **Natural History Museum** set up a rink for the first time, and hopes to do so in future years too (check www.nhm.ac.uk for details).

Arts & Entertainment

Children

Top tips for tots.

In this chapter we have listed the best of what the capital has to offer families, but check the weekly *Time Out* magazine's Around Town pages for the latest shows and events, and log on to www.london.gov.uk/young-london, the Mayor's website for children, and www.kids lovelondon.com, both of which have useful youth-oriented news and information. In addition, *Time Out London for Children* (£8.99) is a comprehensive, annually updated guide.

The best way of getting around London as a family is by bus. Under-16s go free on buses; we recommend the RV1 (Tower Hill to South Bank), the 12 (Westminster to Notting Hill) and the 52 (Kensington to Knightsbridge).

If you're travelling at the weekend with a family travelcard (*see p361*), the kids go free on all forms of London transport.

Area guide

The South Bank & Bankside pp78-90

The **British Airways London Eye** (*see p79*) is the best thing about the South Bank, say the kids, closely followed by the nearby **London Aquarium** (*see p81*). The **BFI London IMAX Cinema** (*see p289*) usually has a film that will appeal to young tastes. Summertime in this area is lively, thanks to open-air adventures laid on by the **Coin Street Festival** (*see p266*) and the **National Theatre**'s summer fandango, Watch This Space (*see p267*). Visit **Shakespeare's Globe** (*see p87*), then continue east to the **Clink Prison Museum** (*see p85*), then to the **Golden Hinde** (*see p85*), famed for its party and sleepover programme. In nearby Tooley Street, the **London Dungeon** (*see p89*) gives accompanied over-tens (and sometimes their guardians) a bit of a turn. Walk through **Hay's Galleria** (*see p89*) across the street to board warship museum **HMS Belfast** (*see p89*).

The City pp91-102

Wear 'em out with a climb up the 311 steps of the **Monument** (*see p100*), which offers some rewarding views from the top. The best day out in this area is at the **Tower of London** (*see p101*), where Beefeaters provide great entertainment on the regular tours, and the

Gunpowder Plot Exhibition runs until July 2006 The best free day out, meanwhile, is at the **Museum of London** (*see p102*), with its new Medieval London Gallery and demonstrations on London life of yesteryear.

Bloomsbury & Fitzrovia pp108-113

The **British Museum** (*see p109*) is interesting to visitors of all ages, though don't try to see everything, especially with children in tow. See the website for details of sleepovers with the mummies. One of London's best playgrounds is also in this area: **Coram's Fields** (*see p276*), given to London's children in 1936. Over on Brunswick Square is the excellent **Foundling Museum** (*see p111*), while across Tottenham Court Road is the delightful **Pollock's Toy Museum** (*see p113*); what kids love most are the free puppet shows, usually on Saturdays.

Covent Garden pp128-132

London's Transport Museum is closed for refurbishment, and expected to reopen in June 2007. But also in the area is the **Theatre Museum** (*see p129*), which has an excellent programme of children's activities.

Trafalgar Square pp133-134

Overlooking the huge pedestrianised square, the **National Gallery** (*see p133*) has a Micro Gallery, allowing children to create themed tours from computer terminals, plus year-round paper trails and audio tours for children as well as regular kids' workshops. Next door, the **National Portrait Gallery** (*see p134*) provides free family rucksacks filled with activities for three- to 12-year-olds. Nearby, **St Martin-in-the-Fields** (*see p134*) has London's only brass rubbing centre.

South Kensington pp141-145

Young folk zoom in on the dinosaurs at the **Natural History Museum** (*see p141*), but there's more to it than extinct reptiles. Human Biology (Gallery 22) has interactive exhibits; Creepy Crawlies (Gallery 33) has a colony of leafcutter ants; and the Earth Galleries (60-66)

Blue Kangaroo. *See p274*.

have an earthquake simulation. Up the road, the **Science Museum** (see p142) has six play zones for different age ranges. 'Science Night' sleepovers are held once a month. Kids' facilities at the **Victoria & Albert Museum** (see p142) include activity backpacks and an Activity Cart on Sunday mornings.

Greenwich pp168-171

This World Heritage Site is a delight for kids, from the spectacular scenery of hilly **Royal Greewich Park** (see p169), where there are free children's entertainments every summer, to the crumbling romance of the **Cutty Sark** (see p170) and the seafaring adventures of the **National Maritime Museum** (see p170).

Childcare & advice

Parentline Plus (0808 800 2222, www. parentlineplus.org.uk) gives advice to parents; **4Children** (7512 2112/infoline 7512 2100, www.4children.org.uk) has details of useful family services including childcare. **Simply Childcare** (7701 6111, www.simplychildcare. com) provides childcare listings.

Childminders

6 Nottingham Street, Marylebone, W1U 5EJ (7935 3000/www.babysitter.co.uk). Baker Street tube. **Open** 8.45am-5.30pm Mon-Thur; 8.45am-5pm Fri; 9am-4.30pm Sat. **Rates** £5.20-£6.90/hr. **Credit** AmEx, MC, V. **Map** p400 G5.
This agency has more than 1,500 babysitters, mainly London-based nurses, nannies and teachers.

Pippa Pop-ins

430 Fulham Road, Fulham, SW6 1DU (7731 1445/ www.pippapopins.com). Fulham Broadway tube. **Open** 8.15am-6pm Mon-Fri. **Rates** *Sessions* £27-£77. **Credit** MC, V.
A nursery school and kindergarten for one- to five-year-olds, whose staff host parties and activities. **Other locations**: 165 New King's Road, Parsons Green, SW6 4SN (7731 1445).

Eating & drinking

See also **Restaurants & Cafés** (pp194-221) for other child-friendly places, such as **Crumpet**, **Wagamama** and **Carluccio's Caffè**.

Blue Kangaroo

555 King's Road, Fulham, SW6 2EB (7371 7622/ www.thebluekangaroo.co.uk). Fulham Broadway tube/ Sloane Square tube then 11, 19, 22 bus. **Open** 9.30am-7.30pm daily. **Main courses** £7-£16. **Credit** AmEx, MC, V. **Map** p398 C13.
Parents can sit upstairs in the restaurant or eat in the midst of the basement playground. The children's menu has superior versions of kiddy standards such as organic chicken goujons and burgers. **Photo** p273.

Dexter's Grill

20 Bellevue Road, Wandsworth, SW17 7EB (8767 1858). Wandsworth Common rail. **Open** noon-11pm Mon-Fri; 11am-11pm Sat; 11am-10.30pm Sun. **Main courses** £6.50-£12. **Credit** AmEx, MC, V.
A popular diner with a selection of organic specialities for young children. Large, juicy hamburgers and crisp chips are a speciality. There's a separate room with a well-stocked ice-cream bar that is also available to hire for parties.

Giraffe

6-8 Blandford Street, Marylebone, W1H 3AA (7935 2333/www.giraffe.net). Baker Street or Bond Street tube. **Open** 7.45am-11pm Mon-Fri, 9am-11pm Sat, 9am-10.30pm Sun. **Main courses** £7.95-£10.95. **Set meals** (5-7pm) £6.95 2 courses; (7-11pm) £8.95 2 courses. **Credit** AmEx, MC, V. **Map** p400 G5.
An extensive menu for children, including Uncle Jimmy's pomodoro and noodles, is available alongside Giraffe's adult dishes (pancakes, fry-ups, salads, burgers, burritos, steaks and veggie choices). **Other locations**: throughout the city.

Rainforest Café

20 Shaftesbury Avenue, Soho, W1D 7EU (7434 3111/www.therainforestcafe.co.uk). Piccadilly Circus tube. **Open** noon-10pm Mon-Thur; noon-8pm Fri; 11am-8pm Sat; 11.30am-10pm Sun. **Main courses** £11-£16. **Credit** AmEx, MC, V. **Map** p403 K7.
This jungle-themed restaurant with all-too-obvious shopping area is a big hit with kids. Dishes on the children's menu may include fish pie or noodles; older kids will find all they're looking for on the burger-dominated main menu.

Smollensky's on the Strand

105 Strand, Charing Cross, WC2R 0AA (7497 2101/www.smollenskys.co.uk). Embankment tube/ Charing Cross tube/rail. **Open** noon-midnight Mon-Wed; noon-12.30am Thur-Sat; noon-5.30pm, 6.30-10.30pm Sun. **Main courses** £8.85-£19.95. **Set meal** (4.30-7pm, after 10pm Mon-Fri) £9.95 2 courses. **Credit** AmEx, DC, MC, V. **Map** p403 L7.
It's brash, it's touristy, but the food is hard to fault. Steak is the main attraction, with such options as sirloin with béarnaise sauce and ribeye with peppercorn sauce. Over on the children's menu, mini burgers, hot dogs and spaghetti keep little hands occupied, as do the free fun packs.

TGI Friday's

6 Bedford Street, Covent Garden, WC2E 9HZ (7379 0585/www.tgifridays.co.uk). Covent Garden or Embankment tube/Charing Cross tube/rail. **Open** noon-11.30pm Mon-Sat; noon-11pm Sun. **Main courses** £7.45-£17. **Credit** AmEx, MC, V. **Map** p403 L7.
Kids love the perky staff in their badge-festooned uniforms, who proffer balloons and guide them to the free face-painting table at weekends. Children's menus range from the simplest chicken strips and chips selection up to nachos, wings, ribs, seafood and elaborate puddings. Adult portions are huge. **Other locations**: throughout the city.

Entertainment

Little Angel Theatre.

Cinema

The **Clapham Picturehouse** (*see p286*)
runs one of the capital's original Saturday
kids' clubs. It has screenings for parents with
babies under a year old called the Big Scream!
club on Thursday mornings, for a £3 annual
fee, then £6 per screening. At Notting Hill's
Electric Cinema (*see p286*) parents and
their babies can enjoy special Electric Scream
screenings. Movie Magic at the **NFT** (National
Film Theatre, South Bank; *see p289*) is a
programme of films for under-16s. The **Rio
Cinema** in Dalston (*see p288*) has a Saturday
morning kids' club and a parent and baby club.
Brixton's **Ritzy Cinema** (*see p288*) has two
kids' club films showing every Saturday, and
Tuesdays and Thursdays in school holidays.

Puppets

Little Angel Theatre

*14 Dagmar Passage, off Cross Street, Islington,
N1 2DN (7226 1787/www.littleangeltheatre.com).
Angel tube/Highbury & Islington tube/rail.* **Open**
Box office 11am-5pm Mon-Fri; 10am-4.30pm Sat,
Sun. **Tickets** £7.50-£8.50; £5-£6 under-16s.
Some pay-what-you-can performances; phone
for details. **Credit** MC, V.
Established in 1961, the Little Angel is still London's
only permanent puppet theatre. Performances cover
a huge range of styles and just about every kind of
puppet, with an annual calendar peppered with
shows by touring companies. **Photo** *above.*

Puppet Theatre Barge

*Opposite 35 Blomfield Road, Little Venice, W9
2PF (winter 7249 6876/summer 07856 202745/
www.puppetbarge.com). Warwick Avenue tube.* **Open**
Box office 9am-9pm daily. *Children's shows* term-
time Sat, Sun; school hols daily; phone for times.
Tickets £7.50; £7 concessions. **Credit** MC, V.
The Puppet Theatre Barge's high-quality puppet
shows and the loveliness of its location remain
unique. Small and cosy, the 60-seat barge is moored
on the towpath in Little Venice between November
and June, with performances held on Saturday and
Sunday afternoons (3pm) and a more comprehensive
programme during school holidays.

Science & nature

Camley Street Natural Park

*12 Camley Street, King's Cross, NW1 0PW (7833
2311/www.wildlondon.org.uk). King's Cross tube/
rail.* **Open** *May-Sept* 9am-5pm Mon-Thur; 11am-
5pm Sat, Sun. *Oct-Apr* 9am-5pm (or dusk) Mon-
Thur; 10am-4pm Sat, Sun. Closed late Dec-early
Jan. **Admission** free. **Map** p401 L2.

The London Wildlife Trust's flagship reserve may
be set in an unpromising part of town, but it combines woods, ponds, marshes and flower meadows
to lovely effect. The visitors' centre is a rustic cabin
with a wealth of information on urban flora and
fauna. See the website for details and events.

Greenwich Peninsula Ecology Park

*Thames Path, John Harrison Way, Greenwich, SE10
0QZ (8293 1904/www.urbanecology.org.uk). North
Greenwich tube/108, 161, 422, 472, 486 bus.* **Open**
10am-5pm (or dusk) Wed-Sun. **Admission** free.
A pond-dipping, bird-watching haven not far from
the Millennium Dome. Family fun days, like Frog
Day in early March and their annual tree dressing
in December, are increasingly popular events.

London Wildlife Trust Centre for Wildlife Gardening

*28 Marsden Road, East Dulwich, SE15 4EE
(7252 9186/www.wildlondon.org.uk). East
Dulwich rail.* **Open** 10.30am-4.30pm Tue-Thur,
Sun. **Admission** free.
The London Wildlife Trust has been reclaiming
derelict land for nature reserves for more than two
decades, and this is one of its best, with a range of
natural habitats that include a herb garden, a pond
area and a nursery for plants and trees.

Theatre

Half Moon Young People's Theatre

*43 Whitehorse Road, Stepney, E1 0ND (7709 8900/
www.halfmoon.org.uk). Limehouse DLR/rail.* **Open**
Box office 10am-6pm Mon-Fri; 10am-5pm Sat.
Tickets £4. **Credit** MC, V.
The Half Moon is home to two studios, providing a
calendar of performances for kids from six months
old. Children can join one of eight youth theatre
groups, catering for five- to 17-year-olds. The theatre promotes an inclusive policy towards disabled
children and those with sensory impairments.

Polka Theatre

240 The Broadway, Wimbledon, SW19 1SB (8543 4888/www.polkatheatre.com). South Wimbledon tube/Wimbledon tube/rail then 57, 93, 219, 493 bus. **Open** *Phone bookings* 9.30am-4.30pm Mon; 9am-6pm Tue-Fri; 10am-4.30pm Sat. *Personal callers* 9.30am-4.30pm Tue-Fri; 10am-4.30pm Sat. Tickets £5-£10. **Credit** AmEx, MC, V.

This dedicated young persons' theatre has one of the best programmes of children's events in London. Daily shows are staged by touring companies in the main auditorium (10.30am, 2pm), with weekly performances in the Adventure Theatre for under-fours. High-profile supporters include Kenneth Branagh, Sir Alan Ayckbourn and Sophie Dahl.

Theatre Museum

Russell Street, Covent Garden, WC2E 7PR (enquiries 7943 4700/bookings 7943 4750/www. theatre museum.org). Covent Garden tube. **Open** 10am-6pm Tue-Sun. **Admission** *Theatre* free. *Workshops* £5 **Credit** AmEx, MC, V.

Running in conjunction with the Society of London Theatre, the Theatre Museum initiated a programme of 'Kids' West End' workshops in 2005. The workshops, for eight-to-twelve year olds, run every Saturday from 2 to 4pm, and are based on West End musicals. They involve drama games, with the children dressing up and performing for their parents at the end of the session.

Unicorn Theatre

Tooley Street, Bankside, SE1 2HZ (08700 534 534/ 7700 0702/www.unicorntheatre.com). London Bridge tube/rail/Tower Hill tube. **Open** *Box office* 9.30am-6pm Mon-Fri; 10.30am-6pm Sat; noon-5pm Sun. **Credit** MC, V.

Unicorn Theatre, one of the leading producers of professional theatre for children in Britain, moved into its new multi-million pound South Bank home at the end of 2005. There are two auditoria: the Weston Theatre, with 340 seats, for larger-scale work, and a second, smaller space for new work and education called The River Theatre. A production of *Tom's Midnight Garden* was the first play to tread the boards from December 2005 to January 2006, and similar plays will follow hard on its heels. If this all works up an appetite, the foyer also houses a branch of family-friendly café Frizzante (*see p214*).

Spaces to play

Many visitors are under the impression that London is bereft of green spaces, but it doesn't take long to locate one of London's great parks The best include: **Regent's Park** (*see p116*) for boating, sporting activities, open-air theatre and London Zoo (*see p116*); **Hyde Park** and **Kensington Gardens** (*see pp143-145*) for the Diana-inspired memorials; the grounds of **Syon House** (*see p192*) for indoor and outdoor play areas; **Hampstead Heath** (*see p153*) and **Parliament Hill** (*see p153*) for swimming and

kite-flying; **Highbury Fields** (*see p156*) for its playground; **Battersea Park** (*see p179*) for its adventure playground and zoo; **Crystal Palace Park** (*see p174*) for the dinosaurs and maze; **Dulwich Park** (College Road, SE21 7BQ, 8693 5737) for playground, recumbent bikes, and family-friendly café; **Greenwich Park** for trees, views and deer; **Richmond Park** (*see p180*) for the Isabella Plantation, cycling and deer; **Victoria Park** (*see p162*) for a playground, tennis courts and deer; **Mile End Park** (*see p162*) for go-karts, playgrounds and eco-themed holiday activities; **Queen's Park** (Kingsway Avenue, NW6 6SG, 8969 5661) and **West Ham Park** (Upton Lane, E7 9PU, 8472 3584) for sports and summer activities.

Coram's Fields

93 Guilford Place, Bloomsbury, WC1N 1DN (7837 6138/info@coramsfields.org.uk). Russell Square tube. **Open** *Apr-Sept* 9am-7pm daily. *Oct-Mar* 9am-6pm daily. **Admission** free (adults only admitted if accompanied by child under 16). **Map** p401 L4.

This children's park boasts lawns, sandpits, a football pitch, a basketball court and play areas with climbing towers, slides, swings and an assault-course pulley. Other draws include a café and animal enclosures. All kinds of after-school and holiday classes activities are organised for childen.

Diana, Princess of Wales Memorial Playground

Near Black Lion Gate, Broad Walk, Kensington Gardens, W8 2UH (7298 2117/recorded information 7298 2141/www.royalparks.gov.uk). Bayswater or Queensway tube. **Open** *Summer* 10am-7.45pm. *Winter* 10am-4pm (or 1hr before dusk, if earlier) daily. **Admission** free under-12s (adults only admitted if accompanied by a child). **Map** p397 E8.

Inspired by the story of Peter Pan, this commemorative play area is a wonderland for youngsters. There's a pirate ship, a mermaids' fountain and rocky outcrops. Beyond these lie a trio of wigwams and the tree-house encampment. Much of the equipment has been designed for use by children with special needs. Unaccompanied adults can view the gardens from 9.30am to 10am daily.

Discover

1 Bridge Terrace, Stratford, E15 4BG (8536 5555/ www.discover.org.uk). Stratford tube/rail/DLR. **Open** *Term-time* 10am-5pm Tue-Sun. *School hols* 10am-5pm daily. **Admission** *Garden* free. *Story trail* £3.50; £2.50 concessions; free under-2s; half price admission 3-5pm term-time only. **Credit** MC, V.

This interactive play centre takes children aged nought to eight on a storymaking journey. They can fly on a magic carpet, cross a bridge over a sparkly river, and make characters at the well-equipped art tables. The gardens house a space rocket, climbing frames, living willow tunnels for hide and seek, a wet-play area and picnic benches. A variety of weekend drop-in activities include stories and puppet shows.

Indoor playgrounds

When the weather's grim, head to one of these hangar-like spaces with slides, ball ponds and swings. Expect to pay about £4.50 per child.

Bramley's Big Adventure

136 Bramley Road, North Kensington, W10 6TJ (8960 1515/www.bramleysbig.co.uk). Ladbroke Grove tube.

Clown Town

222 Green Lanes, Palmers Green, N13 5UD (8886 7520/www.clowntown.co.uk). Southgate tube/W6, 121, 329 bus.
Other locations: Coppetts Centre, Coppetts Close, Finchley, N12 OAQ (8361 6600).

Discovery Planet

Surrey Quays Shopping Centre, Redriff Road, Rotherhithe, SE16 7LL (7237 2388/www.discovery-planet.co.uk). Canada Water tube.

Eddie Catz

68-70 High Street, Putney, SW15 1SF (0845 201 1268/www.eddiecatz.com). Putney Bridge tube.

It's a Kid's Thing

279 Magdalen Road, Earlsfield, SW18 3NZ (8739 0909/www.itsakidsthing.info). Earlsfield rail.

Kidzmania

28 Powell Road, Clapton, E5 8DJ (8533 5556/www.kidzmania.net). Clapton rail/38, 55, 56, 106, 253 bus.

Tiger's Eye

42 Station Road, Merton, SW19 2LP (8543 1655/www.tigerseye.co.uk). Colliers Wood or South Wimbledon tube.

Theme parks

It's best to call or check the website for details of special events as well as opening times, which vary throughout the year. Also note that height restrictions apply on some rides. As with all theme parks, arriving early in the morning increases your chances of queue-free thrills.

Chessington World of Adventures

Leatherhead Road, Chessington, Surrey KT9 2NE (0870 444 7777/www.chessington.co.uk). **Getting there** *By rail* Chessington South rail then 71 bus or 10-min walk. *By car* J9 off M25. **Open** times vary. Closed Nov-Feb. **Admission** £28 (accompanying under-12 free); £18.50 additional under-12s; £13.50-£18 concessions; £28-£111.50 family; free under-4s. Check website for advance bookings for fast-track entry. **Credit** MC, V.
Chessington's 'families come first' policy means that 90% of the rides and attractions are suitable for the under-12s. Highlights include the Dragon's Fury ride, which curls round the Land of the Dragons, Beanoland, with Dennis the Menace and Gnasher, and Animal Land, with themed enclosures, and huge viewing windows that let you get up close to the animals, including gorillas, big cats. Chessington also runs 'Family Dating' for single parents.

Legoland

Winkfield Road, Windsor, Berks SL4 4AY (0870 504 0404/www.legoland.co.uk). **Getting there** *By rail* Windsor & Eton Riverside or Windsor Central rail then bus. *By car* J3 off M3 or J6 off M4. **Open** times vary. Closed late Nov-mid Mar. **Admission** *1-day ticket* £26; £22 concessions, free under-3s. *2-day ticket* £47; £43 concessions; free under-3s. **Credit** MC, V.

The dinosaur park at **Crystal Palace**.
See p276.

Close encounters of the furred kind

Animal encounters have come a long way since chimps' tea parties and camel rides. The daily Animals in Action show at **London Zoo** (*see p116*) is a case in point. The drama unfolds in a small open-air theatre, where animals appear on cue, flying over the backdrop or dashing in from the wings. As well as the theatricals, children love the regular keeper talks which may involve spider stroking or snake charming.

The zoo's two big successes of 2005 were Meet the Monkeys and African Bird Safari. The first is a walk-through forest which houses a breeding group of black-capped squirrel monkeys. The second is a huge walk-through aviary humming with lilac breasted rollers, Van der Deken's hornbills and other African bird species. For those children longing to get more hands-on, the petting zoo is filled with placid sheep, goats and rabbits.

London Zoo may have all the headline grabbing A-list exotics, but south of the river there's a lower-profile zoo with creatures waiting to make your offspring's acquaintance. At **Battersea Park Children's Zoo** (Battersea Park, SW11 4NJ, 7924 5826) the enclosures for lemurs, otters and meerkats are designed to bring them closer to the children. There are also Shetland ponies, goats and a multi-storey mouse house. Keeper talks and handling sessions take place twice a day.

London is also home to various city farms, with everything from giant Flemish rabbits to llamas to bees. These tend not to have actual petting or handling sessions, instead preferring visitors to admire the animals from a distance (though they'll sometimes make an exception, if you ask nicely). They're dotted around town: in the north you'll find **Freightliners City Farm** (Paradise Park, Sheringham Road, off Liverpool Road, Islington, N7 8PF, 7609 0467, www.freightlinersfarm.org.uk, closed Mon) and **Kentish Town City Farm** (1 Cressfield Close, off Grafton Road, Kentish Town, NW5 4BN, 7916 5421, www.aapi.co.uk/cityfarm), which also offers pony rides at weekend. In the east there are **Mudchute City Farm** (Pier Street, Isle of Dogs, E14 3HP, 7515 5901, www.mudchute.org) and **Surrey Docks Farm** (Rotherhithe Street, Surrey Docks, SE16 5EY, 7231 1010, www.surreydocksfarm.org, closed Mon), while **Vauxhall City Farm** (24 St Oswald's Place, Vauxhall, SE11 5JE, 7582 4204, closed Mon, Tue) is in south London. Contact the British Federation of City Farms (0117 923 1800, www.farmgarden.org.uk) for a complete list of places in and around the capital.

One thing to note: some city farms have rabbits and guinea pigs for sale – only succumb to pet pester power if you're prepared to clean out and feed the lop-eared impulse-buys yourself.

This is a top day out, but be prepared for queues. Visit Miniland, where some 35 million pieces have been used to create scenes from Europe and, since 2005, Cape Canaveral and the John F Kennedy Space Centre (itself comprising 50,000 Lego bricks). The popular Driving School (for six- to 13-year-olds) also has an equivalent for three-to-fives. Don't miss Lego Safari, the Dragon Coaster, Pirate Falls (a soaking is guaranteed) and Jungle Coaster – thrilling stuff! The park closes on selected Tuesdays and Wednesdays throughout their opening period, so check the website in advance.

Thorpe Park

Staines Road, Chertsey, Surrey KT16 8PN (0870 444 4466/www.thorpepark.com). **Getting there** *By rail* Staines rail then 950 bus. *By car* M25 J11 or J13. **Open** times vary. **Admission** £30; £21 concessions; £82 family; free under-4s. Check website or phone for advance bookings. **Credit** MC, V. This place is best suited to thrill-seekers. Slammer provides a free-fall experience; and Colossus, the world's first ten-loop rollercoaster, travels at speeds of up to 40mph. Tamer attractions for littluns include a petting zoo with goats and pigs.

Comedy

Laugh in all the right places.

London is the comedy capital of Europe – but there's much more to the scene than Ricky Gervais DVDs. Comics take to the stage at all kinds of venues, from slick West End theatres to pub backrooms and smoky basements. If you want the big names, though, you're best off at the **Comedy Store**, the **Soho Theatre** or one of the **Jongleurs** venues, as these host the biggest stars – Jimmy Carr, Bill Bailey, Al Murray, Ed Byrne, Phil Jupitus, Paul Merton. But a bill with no familiar monikers can be just as fun, and is usually great value: look out for try-out nights, 'open spots' or new act shows, where you'll see fledgling acts for the entry price of a pint. Few can vouch for quality, but then unpredictability is half the fun. Otherwise, the **Chuckle Club**, **Downstairs at The King's Head** and the **Red Rose** are the places for regular nights that cost less than a tenner.

Note that many clubs, especially the smaller ones, close or run skeleton bills during end of July and August, when most names head up north to milk the Edinburgh festival. However, May and June are awash with preview shows as comics practise material for the festival, while October sees newly polished works return to the London stage. A couple of words of warning to comedy club novices: don't be late to the show (last entry can be up to 45 minutes before the show starts), and don't sit in the front row!

Downstairs At The King's Head. *See p280.*

Major venues

Amused Moose

Camden *The Enterprise, 2 Haverstock Hill, NW3 2BL (8341 1341/www.amusedmoose.com). Chalk Farm tube.* **Shows** 8pm Mon, Fri, Sun. **Admission** £5-£8 (incl membership). **No credit cards.**

Soho *Moonlighting, 17 Greek Street, W1D 4DR (8341 1341/www.amusedmoose.com). Leicester Square, Piccadilly Circus or Tottenham Court Road tube.* **Shows** 8.30pm Sat. **Admission** (incl membership) £12.50. **No credit cards.** **Map** p408 W2.

New talent is big on the agenda at both the older Soho branch of Amused Moose and the newer Camden joint (there's an annual 'Star Search' competition at the Enterprise outlet), though big names such as Ricky Gervais, Bill Bailey and Graham Norton have raised many a chuckle at the original venue. It's a 'first-date' friendly place, so if you're new to comedy, you don't have to worry about sitting in the front row.

Banana Cabaret

The Bedford, 77 Bedford Hill, Balham, SW12 9HD (8673 8904/www.bananacabaret.co.uk). Balham tube/rail. **Shows** 9pm Fri, Sat. **Admission** £4 Tue; £12, £8 concessions Fri; £15, £12 concessions Sat. **No credit cards.**

Four or five stand-ups per show at this Time Out-award-winner. Bills are usually good – Mark Thomas warmed up for his politically charged TV shows here, and Omid Djalili has also graced the stage. On Tuesday nights you can catch new acts for just £4.

Bearcat Club

Turk's Head, 28 Winchester Road, Twickenham, Middx TW1 1LF (8891 1852/www.bearcatcomedy.co.uk). St Margaret's rail. **Shows** 8.45pm Sat. **Admission** £10 non-members; £9 members. **Credit** AmEx, DC, MC, V.

The loveable Bearcat has made its name turning out strong bills of stand-up – usually four names a night – to the well-to-do denizens of Twickenham. The venue is now entirely non-smoking.

Canal Café Theatre

Bridge House, Delamere Terrace, Little Venice, W2 6ND (7289 6054/www.newsrevue.com/ www.canalcafetheatre.com). Warwick Avenue tube. **Shows** *Newsrevue* 9.30pm Thur-Sat; 9pm Sun. Phone box office for details of other shows. **Admission** £9; £7 concessions. **No credit cards.** **Map** p396 C4.

Newsrevue, the Canal Café's topical show of comedy sketches, was awarded a Guinness World Record in 2004 for the longest theatrical run of a comedy show (25 years). Shows are updated every week, so repeat visits are encouraged. The venue also hosts other comedy plays as well as sketch shows and stand-up.

Seriously funny

Can the art of great comedy be taught? We don't know, but there's no denying that a course can help even a natural sharpen up his or her act. Courses can cover everything from gag writing for the stage to writing for TV and radio, and many help with performance, timing and improv. Two of the best in London are run by the **Amused Moose** (www.amusedmoose. co.uk) and the **Mullarkey Workshop** (www.keylark.com). The Moose's popular 11-week Absolute & Almost Beginners courses (in association with StandUp And Deliver) are led by comedian and actor Logan Murray, and feature everything from gag writing to microphone technique. Should all go well, you can even progress to the Taking Your Show to the Fringe seminars. Courses usually end in a showcase to show off new talent – Rhod Gilbert was an early alumnus, and is now managed by the folk at the Comedy Store.

The improv courses at the Mullarkey Workshop, meanwhile, were set up by Neil Mullarkey, one of the founder members of the Comedy Store Players. Aimed at 'bright and ambitious people' – that is, actors and business folk eager to improve their creativity and communication skills – the courses are a more tailor-made affair than those at the Amused Moose, and last from one hour to one day. As Neil himself says, 'This is not conventional training... you are offered the chance to experience a new paradigm.' Which might be a polite way of saying, 'You'll get plenty of laughs... just not in the way you intended.'

Chuckle Club

Three Tuns Bar, London School of Economics, Houghton Street, Holborn, WC2A 2AL (7476 1672/ www.chuckleclub.com). Holborn tube. **Shows** 7.45pm Sat. **Admission** £10; £8 concessions. **No credit cards. Map** p401 M6.

LSE's student union hosts this 20-year-old weekly night, which usually sees resident compere Eugene Cheese introduce three decent comics and three open spots. Stewart Lee, Jack Dee and Mark Lamarr are just three of the comedians who have performed here.

Comedy Café

66-68 Rivington Street, Shoreditch, EC2A 3AY (7739 5706/www.comedycafe.co.uk). Liverpool Street or Old Street tube/rail. **Shows** 7pm Tue; 8.30pm Wed-Sat. **Admission** £15 Sat; £12 Fri; £5 Thur; free Wed. **Credit** MC, V. **Map** p405 R4.

Most nights feature strong bills with three to four stand-ups plying their trade – expect to see the likes of Dan Antopolski, Julia Morris and Rob Rouse. Wednesdays is open mic night, and on occasional Tuesdays a mix of stand-up, sketches, burlesque and cabaret arrives at the Holy City Zoo Cabaret.

Comedy Store

1A Oxendon Street, St James's, SW1Y 4EE (Ticketmaster 08700 602 340/www.thecomedy store.biz). Leicester Square or Piccadilly Circus tube. **Shows** 8pm Tue-Thur, Sun; 8pm, midnight Fri, Sat; occasional Mon. **Admission** £13-£15; £8 concessions. **Credit** AmEx, MC, V. **Map** p408 W4.

The legendary Comedy Store made its name as the home of the alternative comedy scene in the 1980s, and is still the place every comic wants to play, with the best bills on the circuit. The purpose-built venue is designed for the serious punter – a semi-circle of seats surrounding a stage that generally favours trad stand-up, although they do offer a variety of events. Go on Tuesdays for the topical 'Cutting Edge' shows, or on Wednesdays for the highly skilled improv out-fit the Comedy Store Players.

Downstairs At The King's Head

2 Crouch End Hill, Crouch End, N8 8AA (pub 8340 1028/office 01920 823265/www.downstairs atthekingshead.com). Finsbury Park tube then W7 bus. **Shows** 8pm Thur, Sat; 7.45pm Sun. **Admission** £4, £3 concessions Thur; £8, £6 concessions Sat; £7, £5 concessions Sun. **Credit** AmEx, MC, V.

This Crouch Ender started up in 1981, when the alternative comedy scene was just beginning. Nowadays it's a favourite of many a big-name comedian wanting to try out new material. It's also keen on nurturing talent: its long-running weekly 'try out nights' (Thursdays) – where up to 16 new acts can take the mic – have kick-started the careers of Mark Lamarr and Eddie Izzard, among others. **Photo** *p279.*

Ha Bloody Ha

Ealing Studios, Ealing Green, St Mary's Road, Ealing, W5 5EP (8566 4067/www.headliners comedy.biz). Ealing Broadway tube/rail. **Shows** 8.45pm Fri, Sat. **Admission** £8; £5 concessions. **No credit cards.**

Situated in the studios where the famous Ealing Comedies were filmed, this West London institution hosts big names (Bill Bailey, Ed Byrne) every Friday and Saturday night and also produces July's annual Ealing Comedy festival at Ealing's Walpole Park.

Headliners

The George IV, 185 Chiswick High Road, Chiswick, W4 2DR (8566 4067/www.headlinerscomedy.biz). Turnham Green tube. **Shows** 9pm Thur, Fri, Sat. **Admission** £8 Thur, £5 concessions; £10 Fri, Sat, £5 concessions. **No credit cards.**

The younger brother of Ha Bloody Ha (*see above*) was West London's first purpose-built comedy venue when it opened in 2003. Expect stand-ups of big and middle stature in unfussy surroundings.

Hen & Chickens

*109 St Paul's Road, Highbury Corner, Islington,
N1 2NA (7704 2001/www.henandchickens.com).
Highbury & Islington tube/rail.* **Shows** 7.30pm,
9.15pm; days vary. **No credit cards.**
This well-established joint offers similar bills to its
sister venue, Lowdown At The Albany (*see below*),
as they share the same promoters. There's a mix of
big names (like Jimmy Carr) and newcomers, with
lots going on during the Edinburgh preview season.

Jongleurs

Battersea *Bar Risa, 49 Lavender Gardens,
SW11 1DJ. Clapham Junction rail.* **Shows** 8.30pm
Thur; 9pm Fri, Sat. **Admission** £10-£16.
Bow *221 Grove Road, E3 5SN. Mile End tube.*
Shows 8.30pm Fri, Sat. **Admission** £14-£15.
Camden *Middle Yard, Camden Lock, Chalk Farm
Road, NW1 8AB. Chalk Farm tube.* **Shows** 8.30pm
Fri, Sat. **Admission** £15-£16.
All *information 0870 787 0707/box office 7564
2500/www.jongleurs.com.* **Credit** AmEx, MC, V.
Since it opened in 1983, Jongleurs has expanded to
become the biggest comedy franchise in England, and
as such attracts some of the biggest names. This is
corporate do/hen night central, where boozed-up punters eat, drink, dance – and laugh if they're paying
any attention to the poor soul with the mic on stage.

Lee Hurst's Back Yard Comedy Club

*231 Cambridge Heath Road, Bethnal Green, E2 0EL
(7739 3122/www.leehurst.com). Bethnal Green tube/
rail.* **Shows** 8pm Thur; 8.30pm Fri, Sat. **Admission**
£10-£15; £2-£5 discount for members & concessions.
Credit MC, V.
Lee Hurst's purpose-built club features three experienced names each night, with Hurst himself usually
compering. There's also a restaurant, worked to the
bone on Thursdays, which is Curry on Comedy night,
where you get a free curry with every ticket.

Lowdown At The Albany

*240 Great Portland Street, Marylebone, W1W
5QU (7387 5706/www.lowdownatthealbany.com).
Great Portland Street tube.* **Shows** 8pm; days vary.
Credit AmEx, MC, V. **Map** p400 H4.
This rough-around-the-edges basement venue underneath the Albany pub is a simple one-man-and-his
mic set-up (there's not much room for the audience,
even). However, practically everyone who is anyone
does an Edinburgh preview here.

Red Rose

*129 Seven Sisters Road, Finsbury Park, N7 7QG
(7281 3051/www.redrosecomedy.co.uk). Finsbury
Park tube/rail.* **Shows** 9pm Sat. **Admission** £8;
£5 concessions. **Credit** AmEx, MC, V.
This long-standing club was established by out-
spoken comic Ivor Dembina, who dedicated it to
cheap nights and the circuit's biggest names, with
no frills (food and dancing are out). There's no smoking in the backroom where the comedy is performed,
but there is a late bar, where you can smoke.

Up the Creek

*302 Creek Road, Greenwich, SE10 9SW (8858
4581/www.up-the-creek.com). Greenwich DLR/rail.*
Shows 9pm Fri; 8.30pm Sat. **Admission** £10 Fri,
£6 concessions; £14 Sat, £10 concessions. **Credit**
AmEx, MC, V.
The late, great Malcolm Hardee ('To say that he has
no shame is to drastically exaggerate the amount
of shame that he has,' explained one journalist)
established this bearpit of a club in 1990. These days
it primarily concentrates on stand-up and the odd
cabaret set. Hardee passed over the reigns long
before his death in 2005, but his legacy lives on.
Punters here are the rowdiest – and also, some say,
the most discerning – on the circuit.

Other venues

Brixton Comedy Club *The Hobgoblin, 95 Effra
Road, Brixton, SW2 1DF (7633 9539/www.brixton
comedy.co.uk). Brixton tube/rail.* **Shows** 8.30pm Sun.
Comedy Brewhouse *Camden Head, 2 Camden
Walk, Camden Passage, Islington, N1 8DY (7359
0851). Angel tube.* **Shows** 9pm Wed-Sat, fortnightly
Mon; 8.30pm Sun.
Covent Garden Comedy Club *Under the
Arches, Villiers Street, Covent Garden, WC2N
6NG (07960 071340/www.coventgardencomedy.
com). Charing Cross tube/rail.* **Shows** 8pm Fri, Sat.
Map p409 Y5.
Hampstead Comedy Club *The Washington,
50 England's Lane, Hampstead, NW3 4UE (7633
9539/www.hampsteadcomedy.co.uk). Belsize Park
or Chalk Farm tube.* **Shows** 9pm Sat.
Laughing Horse Soho *Coach & Horses, 1 Great
Marlborough Street, Soho, W1F 7HG (bookings
07796 171190/www.laughinghorse.co.uk). Oxford
Circus tube.* **Shows** 8.30pm Tue. **Map** p408 V2.
Laughing Horse Oxford Circus *The Blue Posts,
18 Kingly Street, Soho, W1B 5PX. (bookings 07796
171190/www.laughinghorse.co.uk). Oxford Circus
tube.* **Shows** 8.30pm Tue. **Map** p408 V2.
Also at Camden, Richmond and Wimbledon –
check the website for details.
Mirth Control *West Hampstead Lower Ground
Bar, 269 West End Lane, NW6 1QS (7431
2211/www.mirthcontrol.org.uk). West Hampstead
tube/rail.* **Shows** 9pm Wed.
Monday Club *Tattershall Castle, Victoria
Embankment SW1A 2HR (07932 658895).
Embankment tube.* **Shows** 8.30pm fortnightly
Mon. Closed Aug. **Map** p403 L8.
Oxford Street Comedy Club *The Wheatsheaf,
25 Rathbone Place, Fitzrovia, W1T 1JB (7580
1585). Tottenham Court Road tube.* **Shows** 9pm
Sat, Sun. **Map** p408 W1.
Pear-Shaped in Fitzrovia *Fitzroy Tavern,
16 Charlotte Street, Fitzrovia, W1T 2LY (7580
3714). Goodge Street tube.* **Shows** 8.30pm Wed.
Map p400 J5.
Theatre 503 *The Latchmere, 503 Battersea Park
Road, SW11 3BW(7978 7040/www.theatre503.
com). Clapham Junction rail.* **Shows** 8pm Mon, Sun.

Arts & Entertainment

Dance

All the right moves.

James Thiérrée's *La Veillée des Abysses*, at **Sadler's Wells**. *See p284.*

When you know where to look, London's vital and varied dance scene can prove a box-office bargain. Throughout the year **The Place** presents a diverse programme of rising dance companies from both home and abroad. Performances never cost more than £15, while tickets bought well in advance are only a fiver. The home base for both the Richard Alston Dance Company and the London School of Contemporary Dance, The Place also supports several choreographers-in-residence and fields an associate artists' programme for a rotating selection of emerging dance talents.

Another good deal, this time at Sadler's Wells Theatre, is the **Jerwood Proms**. Appropriately dubbed 'Stand Up for Dance', these performances take place during the annual **Dance Umbrella** (www.dance umbrella.co.uk), recognised as one of the world's finest dance festivals. For two weeks in September/October, seats in the front stalls are replaced by 500 standing places, allowing people to experience up-close some of the top names in international dance and, again, for only £5. Standing places for the **Royal Ballet** at Covent Garden's Royal Opera House are an even more exceptional deal, ranging from £4 to £8 (depending on the ballet), and you'll probably be standing right behind someone who has forked out up to £84 for their seat.

Smaller spaces across London also ensure the artform thrives year-round – and at reasonable prices. What's more, the city is bursting with dance classes: from flamenco, Egyptian, African, street and swing to every variety of Latin dance. Check the Dance listings in the weekly *Time Out* magazine for the most comprehensive, up-to-date information on what to see and where to go. For a run-down of the latest top dance companies in London, *see p283* **Movers and shakers**.

Major venues

Barbican Centre

Silk Street, The City, EC2Y 8DS (0845 120 7553/ www.barbican.org.uk). Barbican, Farringdon or Moorgate tube/rail. **Box office** *In person* 10am-8pm Mon-Sat; noon-8pm Sun daily. *By phone* 9am-8pm daily. **Tickets** £5-£40. **Credit** AmEx, MC, V. **Map** p404 P5.

Now in its ninth year, the Barbican International Theatre Event (BITE) has gradually helped turn this arts centre into a major London player. Dance may be just one component of BITE (for theatrical productions, *see p337*), but it's a crucial one. The Barbican frequently co-commissions works in collaboration with both continental and American theatre and dance companies. Michael Clark, the notorious 'bad boy' of British dance, has recently begun a three-year residency deal with the Barbican as a part of its new Young Genius series.

The Place

17 Duke's Road, Bloomsbury, WC1H 9PY (7387 0031/www.theplace.org.uk). Euston tube/rail. **Box office** noon-6pm Mon-Sat; noon-8pm on performance days. **Tickets** £5-£15. **Credit** MC, V. **Map** p401 K3. This internationally recognised dance venue provides top-notch professional training as well as classes in all genres for all levels. The 300-seat theatre presents innovative contemporary dance from around the globe. Seating isn't numbered; it's a case of first come, first served. As a result, there's sometimes a scrum when the doors are thrown open ten minutes before the show starts.

Royal Opera House

Bow Street, Covent Garden, WC2E 9DD (box office 7304 4000/www.royaloperahouse.org.uk). Covent Garden tube. **Box office** 10am-8pm Mon-Sat. **Tickets** £4-£84. **Credit** AmEx, DC, MC, V. **Map** p409 Y/Z3.
This magnificent theatre's main stage is home to the Royal Ballet, where you can see superstars of the high calibre of Carlos Acosta, Darcey Bussell, Alina Cojocaru and Sylvie Guillem. The Royal Opera House complex also houses the Linbury Studio, a 420-capacity theatre, and the Clore Studio Upstairs, used for rehearsals and workshops as well as experimental performances. Programming responsibility for both spaces, linked together under the name of ROH2, lies with ex-Royal ballerina Deborah Bull. The 'Firsts' programme, now in its fourth year, aims to bring innovative and surprising performances to the stage – in 2005, for example, Wendy's Hesketh's Wired Ariel Theatre impressed audiences with a bungee-assisted ariel dance show.The ROH's main lobby, the Vilar Floral Hall, is one of London's most handsome public spaces. It serves as the venue for afternoon tea dances, usually twice a month. A 90-minute backstage tour is available most days.

Movers and shakers

As you'd expect from a world-class city, London attracts some of the biggest names in dance, as well as being home to plenty of home-based talent. The following are the most exciting names to look out for at the moment.

Wayne McGregor's sharp and edgy **Random Dance** is now the resident company at Sadler's Wells. Matthew Bourne's **New Adventures** (his reformed Adventures in Motion Pictures posse) also now has its London base at the Wells – 2006 opened with his latest work, *Edward Scissorhands*; other Bourne productions will pop up here on a regular basis. The fast-rising **Akram Khan**, hip-hop guru **Jonzi D** and **George Piper Dances** (best known to TV audiences as the Ballet Boyz) are all forward-looking artists who have been invited to form ongoing creative ties with Sadler's Wells. These new partnerships promise to add extra spark to the already bustling London scene. For more information check www.sadlerswells.com.

Rambert (www.rambert.org.uk), the oldest and largest of the country's contemporary operations, is currently soaring under its new artistic director Mark Baldwin. Meanwhile, the highly regarded **Siobhan Davies** (www.sddc. org.uk), has recently, finally, acquired a home of her own – an imaginatively converted Victorian school in south London.

Other choreographers such as **Henri Oguike** (www.henrioguikedance.co.uk) and **Fin Walker** (whose company is Walker Dance Park Music; www.walkerdance.moonfruit.com) are building solid reputations for their vivid takes on contemporary dance. The excellent **Candoco** (www.candoco.co.uk) integrates the work of disabled and non-disabled dancers in often-stunning performances. Still irreverent rebels after 20 years in the game are **DV8 Physical Theatre** (www.dv8.co.uk) and the confusingly named all-female **Cholmondeleys** (pronounced 'Chumlees') and all-male **Featherstonehaughs** ('Fanshaws'; the website for both is www.thecholmondeleys. org). The two latter companies are based on the vision of their iconoclastic director Lea Anderson, a true British eccentric.

On a grander scale are the prestigious **Royal Ballet** (*see p282*), based at the Royal Opera House, and the **English National Ballet** (www.ballet.org.uk). ENB, a touring company, has two annual London seasons: in summer it fills the vast expanses of the Royal Albert Hall (*see p305*); here ballet spectaculars can see cast numbers topping the 150 mark. Over the Christmas holidays – when English National Opera has a break – ENB takes up residence at the London Coliseum (*see p307*).

Sadler's Wells

Rosebery Avenue, Finsbury, EC1R 4TN (box office 0870 737 7737/www.sadlerswells.com). Angel tube. **Box office** *In person* 9am-8.30pm daily. *By phone* 24hrs daily. **Tickets** £10-£40. **Credit** AmEx, MC, V. **Map** p404 N3.

One of the premier dance venues in the world, with the most exciting line-up in town. Top companies from Pina Bausch and William Forsythe to notable British troupes such as Rambert Dance Company and Birmingham Royal Ballet are showcased throughout the year. A major new initiative has brought several important British dancemakers into the theatre; *see p283* **Movers and shakers**. Photo *p282.*

South Bank Centre

Belvedere Road, South Bank, SE1 8XX (box office 0870 380 0400/recorded information 7921 0973/ www.rfh.org.uk). Waterloo tube/rail. **Box office** *In person* 11am-8pm daily. *By phone* 9.30am-8pm daily. **Tickets** £5-£30. **Credit** AmEx, MC, V. **Map** p403 M8.

This multi-building complex usually presents British and international dance companies in three theatres: the huge Royal Festival Hall, the medium-sized Queen Elizabeth Hall and the pocket-sized Purcell Room. However, extensive ongoing renovations in the RFH mean it will be closed until summer 2007. This inconvenience is balanced by the promise of big improvements inside and out, to the stage as well as other facilities. In the meantime, dance and other performances continue in the other buildings.

Other venues

Circus Space

Coronet Street, Hoxton, N1 6HD (7729 9522/ www.thecircusspace.co.uk). Old Street tube/rail. **Open** 9am-10pm Mon-Fri; 10.30am-6pm Sat, Sun. **Classes** phone for details. **Membership** free. **Credit** MC, V. **Map** p405 R3.

Courses and workshops in all types of circus arts, such as trapeze, juggling and live-wire walking. It also presents cabaret-style performances (Medium Rare) in its impressive space (a former power station), though note that there will be fewer of these in 2006 because of renovation work.

Greenwich Dance Agency

Borough Hall, Royal Hill, Greenwich, SE10 8RE (8293 9741/www.greenwichdance.org.uk). Greenwich DLR/rail. **Box office** **Classes** £4-£5.50 **Tickets** £7-£15. **Credit** MC, V.

Several of the country's best young companies and dance artists reside in this large art deco venue, where a variety of classes and workshops are complemented by an inventive programme of shows.

Laban Centre

Creekside, Lewisham, SE8 3TZ (information 8691 8600/tickets from Greenwich Theatre 8858 7755/ www.laban.org). Deptford DLR/Greenwich DLR/rail. **Open** 10am-6pm Mon-Sat; or until start of performance. **Tickets** £1-£15. **Credit** MC, V.

This independent conservatoire for contemporary dance training and research runs undergraduate and postgrad courses. Its stunning, award-winning £22m premises include an intimate 300-seat auditorium for shows by Transitions (Laban's resident company) and visiting companies, plus student showcases.

Dance classes

All-rounders like the Greenwich Dance Agency, The Place and Danceworks are augmented across London by a number of specialists. **Cecil Sharp House** offers fun classes in a wide variety of folk dance styles from around the world, while the **London School of Capoeira** teaches that uniquely energetic Brazilian fusion of dance, gymnastics and martial arts. **Chisenhale Dance Space**, meanwhile, is a seminal research centre for contemporary dance, running a good range of interesting workshops.

Cecil Sharp House English Folk Dance & Song Society

2 Regent's Park Road, Camden, NW1 7AY (7485 2206/www.efdss.org). Camden Town tube. **Phone enquiries** 9.30am-5.30pm Mon-Fri. **Classes** £4.50-£8.50. **Credit** AmEx, MC, V.

Chisenhale Dance Space

64-84 Chisenhale Road, Bow, E3 5QZ (8981 6617/ www.chisenhaledancespace.co.uk). Bethnal Green or Mile End tube. **Phone enquiries** 10am-6pm daily. **Tickets** free-£10. **Credit** MC, V.

Danceworks

16 Balderton Street, Mayfair, W1K 6TN (7629 6183/www.danceworks.net). Bond Street tube. **Open** 9am-10pm Mon-Fri; 9am-6pm Sat, Sun. **Classes** £4-£10. **Membership** £2.50-£4.50/day; £40/mth; £69-£120/yr. *Joining fee* phone for details. **Credit** AmEx, MC, V. **Map** p400 G6.

Drill Hall

16 Chenies Street, Fitzrovia, WC1E 7EX (7307 5060/www.drillhall.co.uk). Goodge Street tube. **Open** 10am-9.30pm Mon-Sat; 10am-6pm Sun. **Classes** £5-£25. **Courses** £30-£125. **Credit** AmEx, MC, V. **Map** p401 K5.

London School of Capoeira

Units 1 & 2, Leeds Place, Tollington Park, Finsbury Park, N4 3RF (7281 2020/www.london schoolofcapoeira.co.uk). Finsbury Park tube/rail. **Classes** phone for details. *Beginners' course* £100; £80 concessions. **No credit cards.**

Pineapple Dance Studio

7 Langley Street, Covent Garden, WC2H 9JA (7836 4004/www.pineapple.uk.com). Covent Garden tube. **Open** 9am-9.30pm Mon-Fri; 9am-7pm Sat; 10am-6pm Sun. **Classes** £5-£10. **Membership** £2/day; £4/evening; £25/mth; £65/quarter; £100 6mths; £140/yr; £70/yr concessions. **Credit** AmEx, MC, V. **Map** p409 Y3.

Film

London's cinephiles are spoilt for choice – unless they happen to live in the suburbs, that is.

Many Londoners still lament the death of the cheap rep houses that served the city's most adventurous film fans until their disappearance in the 1980s. Rising property values and the birth of home cinema has killed off this culture of the fleapit that nurtured some of London's most celebrated recent independent filmmakers, from Derek Jarman to Mike Leigh. Still, the city's film-going scene remains wide and varied, at least partly due to the 50-plus film festivals that are held in the city every year, from specialist events such as the London Czech Film Festival to the all-inclusive annual London Film Festival every autumn. These events offer a pleasing antidote to the shiny, popcorn-pushing multiplexes found in most neighbourhoods (although some London boroughs have fewer cinemas than the national average; Lewisham has none). In the city centre, too, there are also a number of smaller first-run cinemas whose varied programmes stand out from the crowd. The **Curzon Soho** and **Ritzy** lead the pack of new-look arthouse 'miniplexes' offering a mix of new independent releases, classic matinées and special seasons and events. The **ICA** can be relied upon to provide arty, edgy, political and rare fare. The **Riverside** maintains a steady programme of thoughtful repertory double-bills, but the **National Film Theatre** is London's best-appointed showcase for the cinematic treasures of the past. The **Prince Charles** screens recent releases on rotation, offering the chance to see things you missed when all the other cinemas were showing them, for the cheapest prices in town.

Only if you're a Bollywood fan is it worth travelling much out of the centre. The racy potboilers unfold mostly in the suburbs; places like the Grade II-listed **Himalaya Palace** justify a long journey in search of the exotic.

Films released in the UK are classified under the following categories: **U** – suitable for all ages; **PG** – open to all, parental guidance is advised; **12A** – under-12s only admitted with an over-18; **15** – no one under 15 is admitted; **18** – no one under 18 is admitted. Unless noted, all cinemas accept major credit cards.

Programmes change on a Friday in the UK; for the latest film listings, reviews and interviews see *Time Out* magazine each week.

First-run cinemas

The closer to Leicester Square you go, the more you pay. Many cinemas charge less on Mondays or before 5pm from Tuesday to Friday; call or check the weekly *Time Out* for details. Book ahead if you're planning to see a blockbuster on the weekend of its release.

Central London

Apollo West End
19 Lower Regent Street, St James's, SW1Y 4LR (0871 223 3444/www.apollocinemas.co.uk). Piccadilly Circus tube. **Screens** 5. **Tickets** £12.50. **Map** p400 J7.
This refurbished cinema boasts a stylish bar and a modern interior – but tickets are on the pricey side.

Barbican
Silk Street, The City, EC2Y 8DS (information 7382 7000/bookings 7638 8891/www.barbican.org.uk). Barbican tube/Moorgate tube/rail. **Screens** 3. **Tickets** £7.50; £1.50 £6 concessions; £5 Mon. **Map** p404 P5.
The Barbican's cinemas screen new releases with a special focus on world and independent cinema.

Chelsea Cinema
206 King's Road, Chelsea, SW3 5XP (7351 3742/ www.artificial-eye.com). Sloane Square tube then 11, 19, 22, 319 bus. **Screens** 1. **Tickets** £7.50-£8.50. **Map** p399 E12.
Run, like the Renoir (*see p286*), by film distributor Artificial Eye, and specialises in world cinema.

Cineworld
Haymarket *63-65 Haymarket, St James's, SW1Y 4RL (box office 0871 200 2000/0870 777 2775/ www.cineworld.co.uk). Piccadilly Circus tube.* **Screens** 3. **Tickets** £8.70; £5.70 concessions. **Map** p408 W4.
Chelsea *279 King's Road, Chelsea, SW3 5EW (box office 0871 200 2000/7376 4744/www.cineworld. co.uk). Sloane Square tube then 11, 19, 22, 319 bus.* **Screens** 4. **Tickets** £8.50, £6; £5.20 concessions. **Map** p399 E12.
Fulham Road *142 Fulham Road, Chelsea, SW10 9QR (0871 200 2000/www.ugccinemas.co.uk). South Kensington tube.* **Screens** 6. **Tickets** £8.50; £6 concessions. **Map** p399 D11.
Shaftesbury Avenue *7-14 Coventry Street, Soho, W1D 7DH (box office 0871 200 2000/7434 0032/ www.cineworld.co.uk). Piccadilly Circus tube.* **Screens** 7. **Tickets** £8.70; £5.70 concessions. **Map** p408 W4.

Curzon

Mayfair *38 Curzon Street, Mayfair, W1J 7TY (7495 0500/www.curzoncinemas.com). Green Park or Hyde Park Corner tube.* **Screens** 2. **Tickets** £8.50; £5.50 concessions. **Map** p402 H8.
Recently split into a two-screen venue, this cinema sits within the serene pleasant setting of Mayfair.

Soho *99 Shaftesbury Avenue, Soho, W1D 5DY (information 7292 1686/bookings 7734 2255/www. curzoncinemas.com). Leicester Square tube.* **Screens** 3. **Tickets** £8.50; £5.50 concessions. **Map** p409 X3.
Superb programming means shorts, rarities and seasons sit alongside new fare from around the world.

Empire

4-6 Leicester Square, Soho, WC2H 7NA (0871 224 4007/www.uci.co.uk). Leicester Square or Piccadilly Circus tube. **Screens** 3. **Tickets** £8-£10; £5-£5.50 concessions. **Map** p409 X4.
Lowest-common-denominator programming, but the immense main auditorium makes it worthwhile.

ICA Cinema

Nash House, The Mall, St James's, SW1Y 5AH (information 7930 6393/bookings 7930 3647/ www.ica.org.uk). Piccadilly Circus tube/Charing Cross tube/rail. **Screens** 2. **Tickets** £6.50; £5.50 concessions. *Membership £20-£30/yr.* **Map** p403 K8.
The best in town for harder-to-find world cinema.

Odeon

Covent Garden *135 Shaftesbury Avenue, Covent Garden, WC2H 8AH (0871 224 4007/www.odeon. co.uk). Leicester Square or Tottenham Court Road tube.* **Screens** 4. **Tickets** £9; £6 concessions. **Map** p409 X2.

Leicester Square *Leicester Square, Soho, WC2H 7LQ (0871 224 4007/www.odeon.co.uk). Leicester Square tube.* **Screens** 1. **Tickets** £11.50-£17. **Map** p409 X4.

Mezzanine *next to Odeon Leicester Square, Soho, WC2H 7LP (0871 224 4007/www.odeon.co.uk). Leicester Square tube.* **Screens** 5. **Tickets** £8. **Map** p409 X4.

Marble Arch *10 Edgware Road, Marylebone, W2 2EN (0871 224 4007/www.odeon.co.uk). Marble Arch tube.* **Screens** 5. **Tickets** £9.30; £7 concessions. **Map** p397 F6.

Panton Street *11-18 Panton Street, Soho, SW1Y 4DP (0871 224 4007/www.odeon.co.uk). Piccadilly Circus tube.* **Screens** 4. **Tickets** £8.50; £5.50. **Map** p408 W4.

Tottenham Court Road *30 Tottenham Court Road, Fitzrovia, W1T 1BX (0871 224 4007/www. odeon.co.uk). Tottenham Court Road tube.* **Screens** 3. Tickets £9; £7 concessions. **Map** p401 K5.

Wardour Street *10 Wardour Street, Soho, W1D 6QF (0871 224 4007/www.odeon.co.uk). Leicester Square or Piccadilly Circus tube.* **Screens** 4. Tickets £7; £5 concessions. **Map** p408 W4.

West End *40 Leicester Square, Soho, WC2H 7LP (0871 224 4007/www.odeon.co.uk). Leicester Square tube.* **Screens** 2. **Tickets** £11.50; £7 concessions. **Map** p409 X4.

Renoir

Brunswick Square, Bloomsbury, WC1N 1AW (7837 8402/www.artificial-eye.com). Russell Square tube. **Screens** 2. **Tickets** £7.50. **Map** p401 L4.
Buried within a brutalist concrete shopping centre, the Renoir screens top-notch world cinema.

Screen on Baker Street

96-98 Baker Street, Marylebone, W1V 6TJ (box office 7935 2772/7486 0036/www.screencinemas.co.uk). Baker Street tube. **Screens** 2. **Tickets** £8.50. **Map** p400 G5.
Sister to the other Screens (*see p288*), with similar programming.

Vue West End

Leicester Square, Soho, WC2H 7AL (0871 224 0240/ www.myvue.com). Leicester Square tube. **Screens** 9. **Tickets** £11-£12; £7-£8.50 concessions. **Map** p409 X4.

Outer London

Clapham Picturehouse

76 Venn Street, Clapham, SW4 0AT (information 7498 2242/bookings 0870 755 0061/www.picture houses.co.uk). Clapham Common tube. **Screens** 4. **Tickets** £8; £4.50 concessions (Mon-Thur only).
Juggles first-run titles with weekend rep double-bills, kids' clubs and parents-and-babies screenings.

Electric Cinema

191 Portobello Road, Notting Hill, W11 2ED (7908 9696/www.the-electric.co.uk). Ladbroke Grove or Notting Hill Gate tube. **Screens** 1. **Tickets** £10-£12.50; £5-£7.50 Mon. **Photo** *right.*
One of London's oldest cinemas, this is now one of the city's most lavish venues – with two-seater sofas available for the adventurous (and deep-pocketed).

Everyman Cinema

5 Hollybush Vale, Hampstead, NW3 6TX (0870 066 4777/www.everymancinema.com). Hampstead tube. **Screens** 2. **Tickets** £10 (luxury £15); £7.50 concessions.
The revamped Everyman now boasts two-seater 'club suites', complete with foot stools, wine cooler and plush upholstery.

Gate Cinema

87 Notting Hill Gate, Notting Hill, W11 3JZ (7727 4043/Bookings 0870 755 0063/www.gatecinema. co.uk). Notting Hill Gate tube. **Screens** 1. **Tickets** £9; £4.50 concessions. **Map** p396 A7.
Small, unpretentious, with daring programming.

Notting Hill Coronet

103 Notting Hill Gate, W11 3LB (7727 6705/ www.coronet.org). Notting Hill Gate tube. **Screens** 2. **Tickets** £7; £4.50 concessions. **Map** p396 A7.
One of London's most characterful local cinemas.

Odeon

Camden Town *14 Parkway, Camden, NW1 7AA (0871 224 4007/www.odeon.co.uk). Camden Town tube.* **Screens** 5. **Tickets** £8.30.

Arts & Entertainment

Electric Cinema. *See p286*.

Screens on the greens

Despite the unpredictability of the British weather, there's a trend emerging for outdoor film screenings in London during the summer months. Events and locations change year by year, but the **Serpentine Gallery** (*see p145*), **Somerset House** (*see p105*) and the **National Theatre** (*see p133*) have recently emerged as popular venues for moonlit screenings of films such as *Blowup, A Matter of Life and Death* and *Close Encounters of the Third Kind*. If the weather's right, Londoners flock to these events with picnics in tow. One-off special events are becoming popular too: in 2004 the Pet Shop Boys and a full orchestra played a live soundtrack to director Sergei Eisenstein's *Battleship Potemkin* in Trafalgar Square, while in 2005 Kensington Gardens played host to a large screening of *Donnie Darko*. The National Theatre (*see p337*) is especially keen to project silent works such as Fritz Lang's *Metropolis* on to the side of their immense riverside building during the summer months. It's worth checking *Time Out*'s weekly listings for these events between June and September each year.

Kensington *263 Kensington High Street, Kensington, W8 6NA (0871 224 4007/www.odeon. co.uk). Earl's Court/High Street Kensington tube.* **Screens** 6. **Tickets** £9.50; £6 concessions. **Map** p398 A9.

Swiss Cottage *96 Finchley Road, Swiss Cottage, NW3 5EL (0871 224 4007/www.odeon.co.uk). Swiss Cottage tube.* **Screens** 6. **Tickets** £8.30; £5.50-£5.80 concessions.

Phoenix

52 High Road, East Finchley, N2 9PJ (box office 8444 6789/8883 2233/www.phoenixcinema.co.uk). East Finchley tube. **Screens** 1. **Tickets** £4-£7; £4-£5.50 concessions.

One of the country's oldest existing cinemas (1910), this attractive one-screener has good programming.

Rio Cinema

107 Kingsland High Street, Dalston, E8 2PB (7254 6677/www.riocinema.org.uk). Dalston Kingsland rail. **Screens** 1. **Tickets** £7.50; £5.50 concessions.

East London's best independent cinema reflects the diversity in the area, with annual Turkish and Kurdish festivals on top of new releases.

Ritzy

Brixton Oval, Coldharbour Lane, Brixton, SW2 1JG (bookings 0870 755 0062/www.picturehouses.co.uk). Brixton tube/rail. **Screens** 5. **Tickets** £7; £4-£5.50 concessions.

London's biggest independent cinema (370,000 admissions a year). Mix of mainstream and indie.

Screen on the Green

83 Upper Street, Islington, N1 0NP (7226 3520/www.screencinemas.co.uk). Angel tube. **Screens** 1. **Tickets** £7.50; £6 concessions. **Map** p404 O2.

A jewel of a cinema boasting London's best old-style neon billing-board. Mix of indie and mainstream.

Screen on the Hill

203 Haverstock Hill, Belsize Park, NW3 4QG (7435 3366/www.screencinemas.co.uk). Belsize Park tube. **Screens** 1. **Tickets** £8.50; £5.50-£6 concessions. Sister to the other Screens, with similar programming.

Tricycle Cinema

269 Kilburn High Road, Kilburn, NW6 7JR (information 7328 1900/bookings 7328 1000/www.tricycle.co.uk). Kilburn tube. **Screens** 1. **Tickets** £8; £7 concessions (selected times); £5 Mon. Part of an arts complex that includes the politically conscious Tricycle Theatre (*see p342*), this cinema supports small and world releases.

UCI

2nd Floor, Whiteleys Shopping Centre, Queensway, Bayswater, W2 4YL (0870 010 2030/www.uci-cinemas.co.uk). Bayswater or Queensway tube. **Screens** 8. **Tickets** £8.25; £4/£5 concessions. **Map** p396 C6.

Vue

Finchley Road *255 Finchley Road, Swiss Cottage, NW3 6LU (0871 224 0240/www.myvue.com). Finchley Road tube/Finchley Road & Frognal rail.* **Screens** 8. **Tickets** £8.60; £5.70 concessions.

Islington *Parkfield Street, Islington, N1 0PS (0871 224 0240/www.myvue.com). Angel tube.* **Screens** 9. **Tickets** £8.60; £5.60 concessions. **Map** p404 N2.

Shepherd's Bush *West 12 Centre, Shepherd's Bush Green, Shepherd's Bush, W12 8PP (0871 224 0240/www.myvue.com). Shepherd's Bush tube.* **Screens** 12. **Tickets** £7.40; £5.50 concessions.

Repertory cinemas

Several first-run cinemas (*see p285*) also offer a limited selection of rep-style fare. These include the **Barbican, Clapham Picturehouse,** the **Curzons, Electric, Everyman, ICA, Phoenix, Rio, Ritzy** and **Tricycle**.

Ciné Lumière

Institut Français, 17 Queensberry Place, South Kensington, SW7 2DT (7073 1350/www.institut-francais.org.uk). South Kensington tube. **Screens** 1. **Tickets** £7; £3-£5 concessions; £5 members. **Map** p399 D10.

Excellent seasons – with a French focus, of course.

Arts & Entertainment

National Film Theatre (NFT)

South Bank, SE1 8XT (information 7928 3535/ bookings 7928 3232/www.bfi.org.uk/nft). Embankment tube/Waterloo tube/rail. **Screens** 3. **Tickets** £8.20; £6.25 concessions. **Map** p403 M8. London's best cinema, with an unrivalled programme of retrospective seasons and previews.

Prince Charles

7 Leicester Place, Leicester Square, WC2H 7BY (bookings 7494 3654/www.princecharlescinema.com). Leicester Square tube. **Screens** 1. **Tickets** £3-£4; £1-£3 members. **Map** p409 X3. The best value in town for releases ending their first run elsewhere. Tickets start at just £1 for members.

Riverside Studios

Crisp Road, Hammersmith, W6 9RL (8237 1111/ www.riversidestudios.co.uk). Hammersmith tube. **Screens** 1. **Tickets** £6.50; £5.50 concessions. Double-bills, special seasons and festivals.

Watermans Arts Centre

40 High Street, Brentford, Middx TW8 0DS (8232 1010/www.watermans.org.uk). Brentford or Kew Bridge rail. **Screens** 1. **Tickets** £6.50 non-members; £5.85 members; £4.50 concessions. Shows smaller and international titles.

Bollywood cinemas

Belle-Vue Cinema, Willesden

95 High Road, Willesden Green Library, NW10 2ST (8830 0823). Willesden Green tube. **Screens** 1. **Tickets** *Bollywood* £6; £4 all day Wed. *Hollywood* £5; £4 all day Tue.

Boleyn Cinema

7-11 Barking Road, Newham, E6 1PW (8471 4884/ www.boleyncinema.co.uk). Upton Park rail. **Screens** 3. **Tickets** £5, £3.50 Tue. **No credit cards.**

Himalaya Palace

14 South Road, Southall, Middx UB1 1RD (8813 8844/www.himalayapalace.co.uk). Southall rail. **Tickets** £5.95.

Safari Cinema, Harrow

Station Road, Harrow, Middx HA1 2TU (8426 0303/www.safaricinema.com). Harrow & Wealdstone tube/rail. **Tickets** £6; £2-£4 concessions.

Uxbridge Odeon

The Chimes Shopping Centre, Uxbridge, Middx UB8 1GD (0871 224 4007/www.odeon.co.uk). **Screens** 9. **Tickets** £7; £4.80-£5 concessions.

IMAX

BFI London IMAX Cinema

1 Charlie Chaplin Walk, South Bank, SE1 8XR (0870 787 2525/www.bfi.org.uk/imax).Waterloo tube/rail. **Screens** 1. **Tickets** £7.90; £4.95-£6.50 concessions; free under-3s. **Map** p403 M8. The biggest screen in the country for 3-D delight.

Science Museum IMAX Theatre

Exhibition Road, South Kensington, SW7 2DD (0870 870 4868/www.sciencemuseum.org.uk). South Kensington tube. **Screens** 1. **Tickets** £7.50; £6 concessions. **Map** p399 D9. A big noise in a big museum. *See also p142.*

Festivals

For the **London Film Festival**, *see p270.*

Human Rights Watch International Film Festival

Ritzy & various other venues (0870 7550 062/ www.hrw.org/iff). **Date** 16-24 Mar 2006. Fiction, documentary and animated films.

London Lesbian & Gay Film Festival

National Film Theatre, South Bank, SE1 8XT (7928 3232/www.llgff.org.uk). Embankment tube/Waterloo tube/rail. **Date** spring 2006. **Map** p403 M8. Around 190 new and restored films from all corners of the globe.

onedotzero

ICA, Nash House, The Mall, St James's, SW1Y 5AH (7766 1407/box office 7930 3647/www.onedotzero. com). Piccadilly Circus tube/Charing Cross tube/ rail. **Date** May-June 2006. **Map** p403 K8. Showcase of moving-image innovation.

Rushes Soho Shorts Festival

www.sohoshorts.com. **Date** 29 July-4 Aug 2006. Around 60 short films and music videos by new directors are screened for free at venues across Soho.

Portobello Film Festival

Westbourne Studios & other venues (8960 0996/ www.portobellofilmfestival.com). **Date** 3-20 Aug 2006. An open-access neighbourhood film jamboree.

BFM International Film Festival

ICA, Prince Charles & Rio (8531 9199/ www.bfmmedia.com). **Date** Sept 2006. This Black Filmmaker-programmed festival shows works from inside and outside the mainstream.

Resfest

National Film Theatre, South Bank, SE1 8XT (7928 3232/www.resfest.com). Embankment tube/Waterloo tube/rail. **Date** Sept-Oct 2006. **Map** p403 M8. International travelling festival of new wave digitally inflected shorts and more, akin to onedotzero.

Raindance

Shaftesbury Avenue cinemas (7287 3833/www.rain dance.co.uk). Leicester Square tube. **Date** Oct 2006. Britain's largest indie film festival.

Halloween Short Film Festival

ICA, Nash House, The Mall, St James's, SW1Y 5AH (7766 1407/www.shortfilms.org.uk). Piccadilly Circus tube/Charing Cross tube/rail. **Date** 8 Jan 2007. **Map** p403 K8. A shorts showcase with a punk/DIY bent.

Arts & Entertainment

Galleries

Watch these spaces.

In 2003 the inaugural **Frieze Art Fair** (www.friezeartfair.com) cemented the city's reputation as a major player in the international art arena. A success even in its first year, the annual October event attracts 150 of the globe's top contemporary art galleries. Even some of the more established commercial spaces can be found competing for a sought-after spot in the tented venue designed by architect David Adjaye. Frieze's main fringe events also highlight the wealth of mainly London-based, smaller-scale, artist-run and project spaces that continue to emerge. Established in 2004 to showcase galleries less than four years old, the **Zoo Art Fair** (www.zooart fair.com) has had no difficulty finding reputable galleries to promote. Some have even gained entry to the main Frieze Fair the following year.

The two main locations for London's gallery activity continue to be Hoxton, Shoreditch and Hackney in the east and around Cork Street in the West End. The latter may have been superceded long ago in number by galleries with an 'E' postcode, but the attractions of the West End over the more sprawling and edgier east still have an influence, and galleries continue to migrate between the two. Having set up the original **White Cube** in Duke Street, St James's, Jay Jopling chose Hoxton Square for the gallery's current, much more impressive space. However, if plans for a second White Cube go ahead, it is likely to be in Piccadilly. Possibly even more spread out than east London, galleries in the south shouldn't be forgotten either: there are spaces in Deptford, Clapham, Bermondsey and Kennington that are all well worth a visit.

Traditionally, commercial galleries would close in August or present uninspiring group shows during the period. While some still stick to the habit, there are now many more who programme interesting shows throughout the August holiday season. For details of what's on in them all, consult *Time Out* magazine or the comprehensive free pamphlet, *New Exhibitions of Contemporary Art*, available from most galleries and also online at www.newexhibitions.com.

For details of public galleries and exhibition spaces, *see* **Sightseeing**.

Central

Anthony Reynolds Gallery
60 Great Marlborough Street, Soho, W1F 7BG (7439 2201/www.anthonyreynolds.com). Oxford Circus tube. **Open** 10am-6pm Tue-Sat. **No credit cards**. **Map** p408 V2.
Located in a beautifully converted two-floor gallery space, Anthony Reynolds represents a mix of high-profile, established artists such as Mark Wallinger, as well as some lesser-known names. The programme for 2006 features new work from Wallinger and photographer Paul Graham.

Gagosian
6-24 Britannia Street, King's Cross, WC1X 9JD (7841 9960/www.gagosian.com). King's Cross tube/rail. **Open** 10am-6pm Mon-Sat. **No credit cards**. **Map** p401 M3.
US super-dealer Larry Gagosian ('Go-Go' to his friends) opened his first London branch in Heddon Street in 2000, now phased out since the opening of this much more expansive site, converted from a former garage by architects Caruso St John. On the books are a wealth of big names, among them Andy Warhol and Roy Lichtenstein, plus more obscure US and European artists. **Photo** *p291*.

Haunch of Venison
6 Haunch of Venison Yard, between New Bond Street & South Molton Street, Mayfair, W1K 5ES (7495 5050/www.haunchofvenison.com). Bond Street tube. **Open** 10am-6pm Mon-Wed, Fri; 10am-7pm Thur; 10am-5pm Sat. **Credit** AmEx, MC, V. **Map** p400 H6.
This high-ceilinged converted Georgian townhouse, formerly home (at different times) to both Lord Nelson and a car showroom, has lent itself to large-scale installations and exhibitions by major artists such as Turner Prize winners Rachel Whiteread and Keith Tyson, as well as some mid-career and emerging artists. The courtyard, meanwhile, is the perfect setting for private view parties. Highlights for 2006 include a major show of new work by Bill Viola.

Hauser & Wirth
196A Piccadilly, Mayfair, W1J 9DY (7287 2300/ www.hauserwirth.com). Piccadilly Circus tube. **Open** 10am-6pm Tue-Sat. **No credit cards**. **Map** p408 U5.
Founded in 1992 in Zurich, this Swiss-owned gallery opened in London in 2003 in an historic former bank designed by Sir Edwin Luytens, still complete with its basement vaults. Hauser & Wirth represents heavyweight artists including Louise Bourgeois and Paul McCarthy, international names like Anri Sala, and home-grown talents, among them Martin Creed.

Jerwood Space

171 Union Street, Bankside, SE1 0LN (7654 0171/
www.jerwoodspace.co.uk). Borough or Southwark
tube. **Open** 10am-5pm Mon-Sat (during exhibitions;
phone to check). **No credit cards. Map** p406 O8.
Part of a larger set-up of theatre and dance rehearsal
spaces, the soon-to-be-expanded Jerwood Gallery
shows work focused on its numerous prizes and
awards, including the Jerwood Painting Prize,
Jerwood Sculpture Prize and Jerwood Photography
Prize. The Jerwood Artists Platform, supporting
exhibitions by up-and-coming artists, continues in a
different venue, while new initiatives for 2006 include
solo shows by more recent graduates.

Lisson

52-54 Bell Street, Marylebone, NW1 5DA (7724
2739/www.lisson.co.uk). Edgware Road tube.
Open 10am-6pm Mon-Fri; 11am-5pm Sat.
Credit MC, V. **Map** p397 E5.

One of London's more established contemporary
art galleries, on its current site since 1991, the Lisson
is a superb platform for artists including Douglas
Gordon, Tony Oursler, Julian Opie and the 'Lisson
Sculptors': Anish Kapoor, Tony Cragg, Richard
Wentworth and Richard Deacon. A second space
opened in 2002, a stone's throw away at 29 Bell
Street, allowing major exhibitions to be spread across
both sites. Solo shows for 2006 include Anish Kapoor
and Ceal Floyer.

Sadie Coles HQ

35 Heddon Street, Mayfair, W1B 4BP (7434 2227/
www.sadiecoles.com). Oxford Circus or Piccadilly
Circus tube. **Open** 10am-6pm Tue-Sat. **No credit**
cards. Map p408 U3.
Sarah Lucas, Elizabeth Peyton, John Currin, Jim
Lambie... Housed in an upstairs space just off
Regent Street, Sadie Coles presents some of the
hippest artists from both sides of the Atlantic. The

Gagosian. *See p290.*

Arts & Entertainment

HQ continuously scours the globe for new talent: artists for 2006 include Avner Ben Gal, Daniel Singel, and JP Munro.

Sprüth Magers Lee

12 Berkeley Street, Mayfair, W1J 8DT (7491 0100/ www.spruethmagerslee.com). Green Park tube. **Open** 10am-6pm Mon-Fri; 11am-4pm Sat. **No credit cards. Map** p402 H7.

Monika Sprüth, Philomene Magers and Simon Lee are the full names behind this Mayfair gallery, with Magers and Lee also running spaces in Cologne and Munich. Among the major artists they represent are Vito Acconci, Barbara Krueger and Nan Goldin. Solo shows here have included light and text installations by Jenny Holzer and Cindy Sherman's famous clown portraits.

Stephen Friedman

25-28 Old Burlington Street, Mayfair, W1S 3AN (7494 1434/www.stephenfriedman.com). Green Park or Piccadilly Circus tube. **Open** 10am-6pm Tue-Fri; 11am-5pm Sat. **No credit cards. Map** p408 U4.

Stephen Friedman celebrated its tenth anniversary in 2005 with a move into a larger space next door (the old space being retained as offices). To kick off the new premises was a group show featuring Friedman's line-up of international artists, from Yinka Shonibare and Yoshimoto Nara to Thomas Hirschorn and David Shrigley.

Chisenhale Gallery. *See p293.*

Timothy Taylor Gallery

24 Dering Street, Mayfair, W1S 1TT (7409 3344/ www.timothytaylorgallery.com). Bond Street tube. **Open** 10am-6pm Mon-Fri; 11am-1pm Sat. **No credit cards. Map** p400 H6.

Since moving to its current location in 2003, Timothy Taylor has gone some way to filling the gap left by the closure of the Anthony d'Offay Gallery in 2001. Among the high-profile artists shown by the gallery are Lucian Freud, Sean Scully, Richard Patterson and Martin Maloney.

Waddington Galleries

11 Cork Street, Mayfair, W1S 3LT (7437 8611/ www.waddington-galleries.com). Green Park or Piccadilly Circus tube. **Open** 10am-6pm Mon-Fri; 10am-1.30pm Sat. **No credit cards. Map** p408 U4.

If it's a selection of blue-chip stock you're after, this is your place. You're likely to find a smörgåsbord of valuable British and American modernism in the gallery's changing displays, as well as solo shows by UK and US big guns.

East

It's only possible to include a limited selection of East London's myriad galleries, so you may want to do some exploring of your own. Hoxton Square, Cambridge Heath Road, Vyner Street and Broadway Market are all good places to start, but do check details and opening times as many smaller galleries are closed at the beginning of the week.

The Approach

Approach Tavern, 1st Floor, 47 Approach Road, Bethnal Green, E2 9LY (8983 3878/www.the approach.co.uk). Bethnal Green tube. **Open** noon-6pm Wed-Sun; also by appointment. **No credit cards.**

Occupying the converted function room above the Approach Tavern, this gallery, directed by Jake Miller, has a deserved reputation for showing both emerging artists and more established names such as Michael Raedecker and Gary Webb. The location also makes it a great venue for combining an exhibition with a Sunday pub lunch and a pint.

Bloomberg Space

50 Finsbury Square, The City, EC2A 1HD (7330 7959). Moorgate tube/rail. **Open** 11am-6pm Tue-Sat. **No credit cards. Map** p405 Q5.

Instead of simply leasing or buying art for its European HQ, in 2002 the financial news and media providers Bloomberg decided to dedicate a space within their London building and recruited a team of four respected artworld figures to curate an ongoing exhibition programme of contemporary and commissioned art. Any difficulties with the corporate architecture of the space have been overcome by the quality of the exhibitions. Recent highlights have included a major installation by sculptor Phyllida Barlow.

Bright young things

In addition to nurturing the next generation of artists, many of London's art colleges run independent gallery spaces with public exhibition programmes. Opened in March 2005 on its new Millbank campus, Chelsea College of Art & Design's **CHELSEA Space** (www.chelsea.arts.ac.uk; *pictured*) has a far-reaching programme of events that have included an 'in conversation' between artists Vanessa Beecroft and Cornelia Parker and an exhibition re-examining the 1970s New York art magazine *Avalanche*. Chelsea College of Art & Design is one of six London art institutions (including Central Saint Martins and Camberwell) that form the University of the Arts London. Their spacious **Arts Gallery** (7514 8083), centrally located in Davies Street, Mayfair, W1, presents group and solo shows drawn from all the university's alumni; a list of over 200,000 names, among them Patrick Caulfield, Chris Ofili and Mark Wallinger.

Over in South Kensington, next to the Royal Albert Hall on Kensington Gore, is the **Royal College of Art** (7590 4444, www.rca.ac.uk). Alongside its summer postgraduate shows, the gallery hosts external events such as the annual 20/21 British Art Fair and awareness-raising exhibitions including ARTAID, which fundraises for HIV and AIDS. It also holds the annual RCA Secret, where the public can choose from over 1,500 postcard-size artworks, all costing £35, not knowing

whether the artist is David Hockney or a current student until the sale has been made.

University College London, meanwhile, has an art collection founded in 1847, which contains over 10,000 paintings, drawings, prints and sculpture. The Strang Print Room (with works on paper by Dürer, Rembrandt, Turner, Constable) is open 1-5pm Monday to Friday during term time, while the Slade Collection (paintings by Augustus John and Percy Wyndham Lewis) is viewable by appointment (call 7679 2540 for both).

Up in north London, Middlesex University is home to the **Museum of Domestic Architecture and Design** (MoDA). Temporary exhibitions have in the past included displays of outrageous wallpaper designs from MoDA's collections and an investigation into suburbia (Cat Hill, Barnet, Herts, EN4 8HT, 8411 5244, www.moda.mdx.ac.uk, closed Mon).

Chisenhale Gallery

64 Chisenhale Road, Bow, E3 5QZ (8981 4518/ www.chisenhale.org.uk). Bethnal Green or Mile End tube/D6, 8, 277 bus. **Open** 1-6pm Wed-Sun. **No credit cards.**

Accompanied by a strong education programme, Chisenhale commissions up to five shows a year by emerging and early career artists and has a reputation for recognising new talent. Rachel Whiteread's concrete cast of a house *Ghost* and Cornelia Parker's exploded shed were both Chisenhale commissions. **Photo** *p292*.

Counter Gallery

44A Charlotte Road, Shoreditch, EC2A 3PD (7684 8888/www.countergallery.com). Old Street tube/rail. **Open** noon-6pm Thur-Sat. **Credit** MC, V. **Map** p405 R4.

Responsible for such seminal shows as 'Modern Medicine' in 1990, Carl Freedman is an old hand at promoting young British art and, from this smart Shoreditch gallery, continues to focus his attention on emerging artists. Along with the gallery, Freedman co-ordinates Counter Editions, which produces prints and editions by Young British Artists like Jake and Dinos Chapman, Tracey Emin and Gary Hume.

Flowers East

82 Kingsland Road, Hoxton, E2 8DP (7920 7777/ www.flowerseast.com). Old Street tube/rail. **Open** 10am-6pm Tue-Sat; 11am-5pm Sun. **Credit** AmEx, MC, V. **Map** p405 R3.

With a space in the West End in 1970 and the East End in 1988, Angela Flowers is one of the original champions of YBAs. Some, like Patrick Hughes and Derek Hirst, are still with the gallery 35 years on, creating a good age mix. The main gallery in Hoxton also houses Flowers Graphics, while a smaller space, Flowers Central, operates from Cork Street, W1.

Hales Gallery

Tea Building, 7 Bethnal Green Road, Shoreditch, E1 6LA (7033 1938/www.halesgallery.com). Liverpool Street or Old Street tube/rail. **Open** noon-6pm Thur-Sat. **Credit** AmEx, DC, MC, V. **Map** p405 S4.

TATE

A trip to London isn't complete without a visit to **Tate Britain** and **Tate Modern**. See outstanding art, spectacular buildings and amazing exhibitions – all in the heart of London.

Tate Britain
Tate's Collection of British art from 1500 to the present day

BP British Art Displays

supported by BP

Admission free
⊖ Pimlico
⛴ Millbank

Tate Modern
The leading gallery of international modern and contemporary art

Tate Modern Collection Displays in partnership with

❊ **UBS**

Admission free
⊖ Southwark/Blackfriars
⛴ Bankside

To find out more, visit **www.tate.org.uk** and sign up for free monthly email bulletins or call **020 7887 8008**

Having been instrumental in putting Deptford on the contemporary art map, Hales upscaled to impressive, new architect-designed premises. It is now one of several galleries (Rocket and Andrew Mummery among them) that have relocated to the Tea Building, on the corner of Shoreditch High Street and Bethnal Green Road. On the schedule for 2006 are new shows by Tomoko Takahashi and Katy Dove.

Maureen Paley
21 Herald Street, Bethnal Green, E2 6JT (7729 4112/www.interimart.net). Bethnal Green tube. **Open** 11am-6pm Wed-Sun; also by appointment. **No credit cards**.
Maureen Paley's Interim Art is a long-established presence in the area. The gallery represents high-profile artists such as Turner Prize-winners Wolfgang Tillmans and Gillian Wearing along with Beck's Futures 2004 winner Saskia Olde Wolbers plus Paul Noble (who's best known for drawings of the fictitious town, Nobson).

Matt's Gallery
42-44 Copperfield Road, Mile End, E3 4RR (8983 1771/www.mattsgallery.org). Mile End tube. **Open** noon-6pm Wed-Sun; also by appointment. **No credit cards**.
Named after founder and director Robin Klassnik's dog, there are few galleries in town that are as well respected as Matt's. Since 1979 Klassnik has supported artists in their often ambitious ideas for projects. Richard Wilson's sump oil installation *20:50* (now permanently installed in the Saatchi Gallery) and Mike Nelson's *Coral Reef* installation were both Matt's commissions.

Modern Art
10 & 7A Vyner Street, Hackney, E2 9DG (8980 7742/www.modernartinc.com). Bethnal Green tube. **Open** 11am-6pm Thur-Sun; also by appointment. **No credit cards**.
One of the more elite spaces in the East End, Modern Art was opened by Stuart Shave and Detmar Blow in 1998. It's now run by Shave and director Jim Lee on two sites across the street from each other. The space boasts a diverse international stable of artists such as German photographer Juergen Teller, Australian artist Ricky Swallow and Brit duo Tim Noble and Sue Webster.

The Showroom
44 Bonner Road, Bethnal Green, E2 9JS (8983 4115/www.theshowroom.org). Bethnal Green tube. **Open** 1-6pm Wed-Sun. **No credit cards**.
Just around the corner from The Approach (*see p292*), the Showroom has gained a reputation over the years for its commitment to young artists: it often commissions large-scale works at early stages in artists' careers. The triangular space here isn't easy to fill successfully, but it occasionally works perfectly. For 2005 the typically diverse programme included graphic painter Diann Bauer and a performance installation by Aaron Williamson; in 2006 it includes a show by Matti Braun.

Victoria Miro
16 Wharf Road, Islington, N1 7RW (7336 8109/ www.victoria-miro.com). Angel tube/Old Street tube/rail. **Open** 10am-6pm Tue-Sat. **Credit** MC, V. **Map** p404 P3.
A visit to this ex-Victorian furniture factory rarely disappoints; not just because it's a beautifully converted art space but because of the high calibre of its artists whose work is both visually exciting and highly saleable. Included are Chris Ofili, Peter Doig, Chantal Joffe and William Eggleston.

Vilma Gold
25B Vyner Street, Hackney, E2 9DG (8981 3344/www.vilmagold.com). Bethnal Green tube. **Open** noon-6pm Thur-Sun. **No credit cards**.
Under the helm of Rachel Williams and Steven Pippet, Vilma Gold has rapidly gained a reputation as a gallery to watch. The cognoscenti flock here for such fashionable fare as the neo-expressionist paintings of Sophie von Hellermann and the heroic sculptural assemblages of Brian Griffiths.

Wapping Project
Wapping Hydraulic Power Station, Wapping Wall, Wapping, E1W 3ST (7680 2080/ www.thewappingproject.com). Wapping tube. **Open** noon-11pm Mon-Sat; noon-6pm Sun. **Credit** AmEx, DC, MC, V.
Under the direction of Jules Wright the innovative creative programme of this magnificent converted hydraulic power station has included work by artists such as Elina Brotherus and Richard Wilson. Wapping has also filled its cavernous boiler room space with commissions from choreographers and designers. The venue has a popular restaurant too.

White Cube
48 Hoxton Square, Hoxton, N1 6PB (7930 5373/ www.whitecube.com). Old Street tube/rail. **Open** 10am-6pm Tue-Sat. **Credit** AmEx, MC, V. **Map** p405 R3.
White Cube may be the only East End gallery that can attract paparazzi hoping to snap the A-list celebs who turn up in black cabs for its openings. The reason? Its A-list Young British Artists, among them Tracey Emin, Damien Hirst, Jake and Dinos Chapman and Sam Taylor Wood. Having already added a rooftop extension to this gallery, further expansion plans are still in place to open a second space in Piccadilly.

Wilkinson Gallery
242 Cambridge Heath Road, Bethnal Green, E2 9DA (8980 2662/www.wilkinsongallery.com). Bethnal Green tube/rail. **Open** 11am-6pm Thur-Sat; noon-6pm Sun; also by appointment. **No credit cards**.
One of the more established galleries on the Cambridge Heath Road this space run by Anthony and Amanda Wilkinson shows a consistently good range of mainly British and European artists such as George Shaw, AK Dolven, David Batchelor, Tilo Baumgartel and Silke Schatz.

Arts & Entertainment

South-east

Corvi-Mora/Greengrassi

1A Kempsford Road, Kennington, SE11 4NU (Corvi-Mora 7840 9111/www.corvi-mora.com/Greengrassi 7840 9101/www.greengrassi.com). Kennington tube. **Open** 11am-6pm Tue-Sat. **No credit cards.**
These two separate galleries share a building, alternating their shows between a large downstairs space and a much smaller upstairs one. Between them the list of international artists they represent and show includes Pae White, Lari Pittman, Sean Landers, Roger Hiorns and Jim Isermann.

Danielle Arnaud

123 Kennington Road, Lambeth, SE11 6SF (7735 8292/www.daniellearnaud.com). Lambeth North tube. **Open** 2-6pm Fri-Sun. **Credit** AmEx, MC, V.
Established in 1995, Danielle Arnaud works with artists such as Janane Al-Ani, David Cotterell and Helen Maurer. Exhibitions are installed in the Grade II-listed Georgian premises. The gallery also curates exhibitions at venues off-site including the Museum of Garden History (*see p81*).

Gasworks

155 Vauxhall Street, Oval, SE11 5RH (7582 6848/www.gasworks.org.uk). Oval tube. **Open** noon-6pm Wed-Sun. **No credit cards.**
The London base of the Triangle Arts Trust, this space comprises both a gallery and artists' studios, also used for artists taking part in an international residency programme. Refurbished in 2004 the gallery provides a platform for emerging and mid-career artists and has showcased new work by Lali Chetwynd and Beagles & Ramsay.

South London Gallery

65 Peckham Road, Peckham, SE5 8UH (7703 9799/www.southlondongallery.org). Oval tube then 436 bus/Elephant & Castle tube/rail then 12, 171 bus. **Open** noon-6pm Tue-Sun. **No credit cards.**
Present on the site for over a century, the South London Gallery became one of the main showcases for the emerging YBAs in the 1990s, giving solo shows to Tracey Emin, Marc Quinn, and Gavin Turk, among others. Still one of the capital's foremost contemporary art venues, the gallery reopened after an extensive facelift in June 2004. Exhibitions since then include Tom Friedman, Steve McQueen and Saskia Olde Wolbers.

Architecture & design

Architectural Association

36 Bedford Square, Fitzrovia, WC1B 3ES (7887 4000/www.aaschool.ac.uk). Tottenham Court Road tube. **Open** 10am-7pm Mon-Fri; 10am-3pm Sat. **Credit** MC, V. **Map** p401 K5.
Talks, events, discussions and exhibitions: four good reasons for visiting these elegant premises. During the summer, the gallery shows work by graduating students of the AA School.

Crafts Council Gallery

44A Pentonville Road, Islington, N1 9BY (7278 7700/www.craftscouncil.org.uk). Angel tube. **Open** 11am-6pm Tue-Sat; 2-6pm Sun. **No credit cards.** **Map** p404 N2.
Alongside its shop and reference library, the Crafts Council Gallery runs a continuous programme of innovatively designed exhibitions to showcase all forms of contemporary crafts, drawn both from its own collection and further afield. The Gallery also stages the annual Jerwood Applied Art Prize.

Royal Institute of British Architects

66 Portland Place, Marylebone, W1B 1AD (7580 5533/www.architecture.com). Great Portland Street or Regent's Park tube. **Open** 10am-6pm Mon-Fri; 10am-5pm Sat. **Credit** MC, V. **Map** p400 H5.
In 2004 the Royal Institute of British Architects (aka RIBA) opened a new Architecture Gallery at the V&A, featuring models, photographs and artefacts from historical and contemporary architecture. It still runs a programme of temporary exhibitions in its Grade II-listed HQ, which also houses a bookshop, café and the British Architectural Library.

Photography

Michael Hoppen Gallery

3 Jubilee Place, Chelsea, SW3 3TD (7352 4499/www.michaelhoppengallery.com). Sloane Square tube. **Open** noon-6pm Tue-Fri; 10.30am-4pm Sat or by appointment. **Credit** MC, V. **Map** p399 E11.
Shine Gallery was relaunched in 2004 as a three-floor space under the name of Michael Hoppen. It shows a mixture of vintage and contemporary work including Japanese photographer Nobuyoshi Araki.

Photofusion

17A Electric Lane, Brixton, SW9 8LA (7738 5774/www.photofusion.org). Brixton tube/rail. **Open** 9am-10.15pm Tue, Thur; 9am-5.45pm Wed, Fri, Sat. **Credit** MC, V.
Providing darkrooms, studio, picture library and an extensive programme of courses, Photofusion is one of the capital's major photography resources. Highlights of 2005 were Carl De Keyzer's often surprising images of Siberian prison camps and Lydia Goldblatt and Lucy Levene's documentary projects of the Ministry of Sound nightclub.

Photographers' Gallery

5 & 8 Great Newport Street, Covent Garden, WC2H 7HY (7831 1772/www.photonet.org.uk). Leicester Square tube. **Open** 11am-6pm Mon-Sat; noon-6pm Sun. **Membership** £30/yr; £20/yr concessions. **Credit** AmEx, DC, MC, V. **Map** p409 X3.
Home of the annual Deutsche Börse (formerly Citibank) Photography Prize, the Photographers' Gallery also hosts a diverse range of exhibitions. It currently occupies two almost adjacent spaces; plans are under way to relocate by 2008 to prestigious new premises in nearby Ramillies Street.

Gay & Lesbian

What's in for the out.

Heaven. *See p300.*

They used to say that London was a great place to be gay, with plenty of venues to choose from – but only if you happened to be a Muscle Mary who liked house music. Not any more. These days diversity is the name of the game. Muscle Marys are still catered for, of course: in fact, the number of clubs catering to shirtless men with eyes like saucers has grown at such an alarming rate, it could almost be a side effect of all those steroids. Nowhere is this more obvious than in Vauxhall, in the area commonly known as the 'Vauxhall Gay Village', home to a variety of clubs employing many of the same DJs playing the same music. Here you can go out clubbing on Friday and come home on Monday, and have heard the same records over and over.

But look carefully and you'll see people dancing to a different beat. The indie revolution that began a decade ago with **Popstarz** has grown up and produced children of its own. In Vauxhall, the **Duckie** crew provide a happy blend of queer performance art and post-punk pogo-ing. A stone's throw away is **Horse Meat Disco**, where underground disco mixes with '80s electronica and local bears rub shoulders with visiting fashionistas. Meanwhile, up in Soho, the indie kids have taken over the **Ghetto**, producing self-consciously queer club nights like Nag Nag Nag and the Cock.

Soho is also home of the cocktail queen. Such creatures were rumoured to be extinct until a few years ago, when promoter Paul Richardson had the bright idea of taking an old lap-dancing club called the Astral Lounge and turning into a gay members' club. The **Shadow Lounge** proved to be so successful that soon similar venues began springing up all over Soho. Shaun & Joe came and went, while the **Element Bar** is still going strong. As for Richardson, he went on to launch **Too 2 Much** – a glitzy, colourful gay members' club in the former strip joint known as the Raymond Revue Bar.

Surprisingly, it's been left to the lesbians to keep lap-dancing and the spirit of old Soho alive. At **Candy Bar**, punters are invited to ogle erotic dancers on a nightly basis. Attempts to launch similar nights for gay men have failed. The reason seems to be that in London, gay sex is just too easily available, whether it involves a cruise around Hampstead Heath or a visit to one of the city's ever increasing number of saunas. Setting the standard is the **Chariots** chain. With outlets in Waterloo, Shoreditch, Farringdon and Streatham, you're never too far from a steamy encounter. And with online cruising sites such as www.gaydar.com open 24 hours, trade really is booming.

The annual **London Lesbian & Gay Film Festival** (*see p289*) offers a round-up of the latest in lesbian and gay film and video, while the **Soho Theatre** (*see p342*) is the place to catch some of the best queer performance. In June, **Pride** hosts a fortnight of cultural events, culminating in 2006 with EuroPride in Hyde Park (www.PrideLondon.org; *see p268*).

The most celebrated gay shops are the excellent **Gay's the Word** bookshop (66 Marchmont Street, Bloomsbury, 7278 7654), and 'shopping and fucking' emporiums **Clone Zone** (64 Old Compton Street, Soho, 7287 3530) and **Prowler** (3-7 Brewer Street, Soho, 7734 4031). For a fuller take on gay London, pick up Time Out's *Gay & Lesbian London* guide book (£9.99), and for weekly listings of clubs, meetings and groups, check the Gay & Lesbian section of *Time Out* magazine or freesheets *Boyz* and *QX*. In shops, gay lifestyle is covered by *Attitude, AXM, Gay Times* and dyke bible *Diva*.

Note that, with new licensing laws about to come into effect as this guide went to press, clubs may extend their opening times. Again, check *Time Out*, or phone the venue in question.

Cafés & restaurants

Balans

60 Old Compton Street, Soho, W1D 4UG (7439 2183/www.balans.co.uk). Leicester Square or Piccadilly Circus tube. **Open** 8am-5am Mon-Thur; 8am-6am Fri, Sat; 8am-2am Sun. **Admission** £5 after midnight Mon-Thur; £7 Fri, Sat. **Credit** AmEx, MC, V. **Map** p408 W3.

This buzzing brasserie is gay central. Stop in for a steak, omelette or salad – or just eye up the beefcake over a cheesecake. The nearby Balans Café, at No.34, serves up a shorter version of the menu. Both are open almost all night: good for a post-clubbing feast. **Other locations**: 249 Old Brompton Road, Earl's Court, SW5 9HP (7244 8838); 187 Kensington High Street, Kensington, W8 6SH (7376 0115); 214 Chiswick High Road, Chiswick, W4 1BD (8742 1435).

First Out

52 St Giles High Street, St Giles's, WC2H 8LH (7240 8042/www.firstoutcafebar.com). Tottenham Court Road tube. **Open** 10am-11pm Mon-Sat; 11am-10.30pm Sun. **Credit** MC, V. **Map** p409 X1/2.

Opened in 1986, First Out was indeed London's first lesbian and gay café, with an emphasis on the lesbian. It's a right-on place, with a healthy veggie menu; if real men don't eat quiche, real lesbians sure do. Decent prices, friendly vibe and a good basement bar too. **Photo** *p301*.

Steph's

39 Dean Street, Soho, W1D 4PU (7734 5976/www. stephs-restaurant.com). Tottenham Court Road tube. **Open** noon-3pm Mon-Fri; 5.30-11.30pm. Mon-Sat **Credit** AmEx, DC, MC, V. **Map** p408 W3.

This cosy little restaurant has been a firm favourite with gay diners and other theatrical types for nigh on 20 years, and in all that time little has changed. Pink flamingos still adorn the walls, the specials still include Yorkshire puddings with a choice of fillings, the tables are still decked with a variety of board games. And Steph is still there to share a joke with customers and regale you with stories of old Soho.

Clubs

This town moves fast. This is especially true of Vauxhall, where clubs open and close more frequently than the closet door, though surely only an earthquake could stop scene stalwarts **G.A.Y.** or **Heaven**.

Action

The Renaissance Rooms, off Miles Street, Vauxhall, SW8 1SD (07973 233377/www.actionclub.net). Oval tube/Vauxhall tube/rail. **Open** 11pm-6am 1st & 3rd Sat of mth. **Admission** £15; £10 members; £12 before midnight with flyer. **No credit cards.**

A hugely popular dance party for the muscle boy brigade, Action has a massive dance arena, heated outside terrace, cruise maze and chill-out rooms.

Club Kali

The Dome, 1 Dartmouth Park Hill, Dartmouth Park, N19 5QQ (7272 8153). Tufnell Park tube. G Lounge, 18 Kentish Town Road, NW1 9NX (7284 2131). Camden tube. **Open** G Lounge 9pm-2am 1st & 3rd Fri of mth; Dome 10pm-3am 1st & 3rd Fri of mth. **Admission** £8; £5 concessions. **No credit cards.**

The world's largest Asian music lesbian and gay club, Club Kali now divides its time between two venues. The G Lounge hosts dance classes from 9pm, while the Dome simply echoes to the sounds of bhangra, Bollywood and plain old house music.

Club Motherfucker

Upstairs at the Garage, 20-22 Highbury Corner, Highbury, N5 1RD (7607 1818/www.meanfiddler. com). Highbury & Islington tube/rail. **Open** 9pm-3am last Fri of mth; 9pm-3am 2nd Sat of mth. **Admission** £5; £4 concessions. **No credit cards.**

The pleasantly-named Club Motherfucker's polysexual party features DJs Daughters of Kaos, Vic Voltaire and Miss Alabama Cherry. DJs play dirty punk and 'bad-taste' rock. Live bands too.

Crash

66 Albert Embankment, Vauxhall, SE1 7TP (7793 9262). Vauxhall tube/rail. **Open** Club 10.30pm-6am Sat; 10pm-4am Sun. **Admission** Sat £15; £12 with flyer or members. Sun £5, £4 concessions. **Credit** (bar) MC, V.

Crash headlines all-star DJs Steve Pitron, Severino, Paul Heron et al. Under the arches are four bars, two dancefloors, chill-out areas… and lots of muscles. On Sundays Joan Dairyqueen hosts Marvellous, a busy queer alternative night, where DJs play punk, rock, indie and pop.

Discotec

*The End, 18 West Central Street, St Giles's, WC1A
1JJ (7419 9199/www.discotec-club.com). Holborn or
Tottenham Court Road tube.* **Open** 10pm-4am Thur.
Admission £8; £6 before midnight. **Credit** (bar)
MC, V. **Map** p409 Y1.
Fancy a 'midweekend' party spread over two dancefloors? Equipped with air-conditioning and great
sounds, this is one of London's classiest venues, and
it attracts a dressy crowd.

DTPM

*Fabric, 77A Charterhouse Street, Clerkenwell, EC1M
6HJ (7749 1199). Barbican tube/Farringdon tube/
rail.* **Open** 10pm-late Sun. **Admission** £15; £11
members, concessions; £9 before 11pm with flyer.
Credit (bar) MC, V. **Map** p404 O5.
This busy polysexual club night with three dancefloors plays house, R&B, hip hop and disco.

Duckie

*Royal Vauxhall Tavern, 372 Kennington Lane,
Vauxhall, SE11 5HY (7737 4043/www.duckie.
co.uk). Vauxhall tube/rail.* **Open** 9pm-2am Sat.
Admission £5. **No credit cards.**
Expect 'post-gay vaudeville and post-punk pogo-
ing' at this legendary dive. DJs the London Readers
Wifes (sic) play the best retro set in town; Amy
Lamé hosts bizarre cabaret.

Exilio Latino

*LSE, 3 Houghton Street, off Aldwych, Covent
Garden, WC2E 2AS (07956 983230/www.exilio.
co.uk). Holborn tube.* **Open** *Club* 10pm-3am Sat.
Admission £7 before 11pm; £8 after 11pm.
No credit cards. Map p401 M6.
After several changes of venue, this popular les-
bian and gay Latin music club has found its feet at
the LSE and is still going strong.

Fiction

*The Cross, King's Cross Goods Yard, off York Way,
King's Cross, N1 0UZ (7749 1199/www.club-fiction.
net). King's Cross tube/rail.* **Open** 11pm-5am Fri.
Admission £15; £11 concessions; £9 before 11.30pm;
£11 before midnight with flyer. **Credit** (Bar) MC, V.
Map p401 L2.
This polysexual club may be looking a bit straight
these days, but it's still a great night out. Three
dancefloors, five bars and two outside terraces make
it an excellent summer venue. DJs, including Fat
Tony, play house grooves.

G.A.Y.

*Astoria, 157 Charing Cross Road, Soho, WC2H
0EN (7434 9592/www.g-a-y.co.uk). Tottenham
Court Road tube.* **Open** 11pm-4am Mon, Thur, Fri;
10.30pm-4.30am Sat. **Admission** £3-£10; reductions
with flyer. **No credit cards. Map** p409 X2.
London's largest gay venue isn't the swankiest in
town any more, but that doesn't bother the hordes
of disco-bunnies who congregate to dance to poppy
tunes and sing along to Saturday PAs. Friday's
Camp Attack is a must for Kylie fans. Regular short
sets from super pop stars and passing fads.

Trailblazer Trash

When club promoter Simon Hobart
(*pictured*) died suddenly in October
2005, it was a huge blow for the gay indie
scene. Hobart launched London's original
gay indie night **Popstarz** (*see p300*) in
1994. At the time he took swipes at the
mainstream gay scene and its disco diet
of house music and Muscle Marys. Then
Popstarz grew so big it virtually became
part of the mainstream itself, regardless
of whether people shaved their chests and
danced with their shirts off or not. Then
came the **Ghetto** (*see p300*), which took
the Popstarz ethos and developed it into
a series of smaller club nights spread
over seven nights a week.

Hobart's legacy lives on in these clubs,
and also at **Trash Palace** (*see p303*), the
venue he described in his inimitable
fashion as nothing like 'the usual Soho
bollocks'. It's certainly a far cry from the
grungy, underground feel of the Ghetto or
the vastness of Friday night's Popstarz.
Trash Palace is a sparkly, intimate venue
spread over two floors. The upstairs Palace
room is lush and loungey, with cosy seating
and a late-night boudoir feel. Downstairs
things are decidedly more trashy with
punky graphics, plastic-fantastic decor and
painfully trendy people in '80s retro gear.
There's a wonderful artwork of Debbie
Harry in all her punk Monroc glory, and a
general air of wasted youth out for a good
time. A must for surviving New Romantics
and the new generation of club kids.

The in scene for indie queens is at **Popstarz**.

Ghetto

*5-6 Falconberg Court (behind the Astoria), Soho,
W1D 3AB (7287 3726/www.ghetto-london.co.uk).
Tottenham Court Road tube.* **Open** 10.30pm-3am
Mon-Thur; 10.30pm-4am Fri; 10.30pm-5am Sat;
10.30am-3pm Sun. **Admission** £1-£7. **No credit
cards. Map** p408 W1/2.

Heading the backlash against London's snootier
venues, this gritty indie club offers Nag Nag Nag
for electro fans on Wednesday and Mis-Shapes for
cool lesbians on Thursdays, while the Cock puts
the spunk back into Soho on Fridays. Saturdays
is long-running trash night Wig Out; Detox is on
Sunday. *See also p321.*

Heaven

*The Arches, Villiers Street, Covent Garden, WC2N
6NG (7930 2020/www.heaven-london.com).
Embankment tube/Charing Cross tube/rail.* **Open**
10.30pm-3am Mon, Wed; 10.30pm-6am Fri; 10pm-
5am Sat. **Admission** £1-£15. **Credit** (bar) AmEx,
DC, MC, V. **Map** p409 Y5.

London's most famous gay club recently turned 25
and is still a firm favourite. The best nights are
Popcorn (Mondays) and Fruit Machine (Wednesdays)
– both upbeat early-week fun – but Heaven really
comes alive on Saturdays, thanks to a new influx of
DJs who've helped bring the muscle boys back from
the Vauxhall Gay Village. **Photo** *p297.*

Horse Meat Disco

*South Central (formerly Duke's), 349 Kennington
Lane, Vauxhall, SE11 5QY (7793 0903/www.
horsemeatdisco.co.uk). Vauxhall tube/rail.* **Open**
4pm-1am Sun. **Admission** £5. **No credit cards.**

Bears and fashionistas come together at this hip but
unpretentious club night held in a traditional gay
boozer. Excellent DJs spin an eclectic mix, from dance,
disco and soul to new wave and punk. Join the party
4pm, tour Vauxhall, then return for no extra charge.

Orange

*Fire, 39-41 Parry Street, Vauxhall, SW8 1RT
(07905 035 682/www.allthingsorange.com). Vauxhall
tube/rail.* **Open** 11pm Sun-11am Mon. **Admission**
£10; £5 with flyer before 1am. **No credit cards.**

House music, bare torsos and poppers are what to
expect at this quintessential Vauxhall Sunday
night/Monday morning club. Don't you have jobs?

Popstarz

*Scala, 275 Pentonville Road, King's Cross, N1 9NL
(7833 2022/www.popstarz.org). King's Cross tube/
rail.* **Open** 10pm-5am Fri. **Admission** £8; £5
members, concessions. **Credit** (bar) MC, V.
Map p401 L3.

The original indie gay party. The Love Lounge plays
disco and R&B, the Common Room features indie and
dance, with kitsch in the Trash Room. Expect a
mixed, predominantly studenty crowd. **Photo** *above.*

Shinky Shonky

*Polar Bear, 30 Lisle Street, Soho, WC2H 7BA (7479
7981). Leicester Square tube.* **Open** 10.30pm-3am
Sat. **Admission** £6; £5 with flyer. **Credit** AmEx,
MC, V. **Map** p409 X3.

Boogaloo Stu and the gang host a camp party where
it's cool to act the fool. DJs spin pop, rock and disco.
Plus, obnoxious live entertainment from the likes of
Miss High Leg Kick and the Incredible Tall Lady.

Substation South

*9 Brighton Terrace, Brixton, SW9 8DJ (7737
2095/www.substationsouth.co.uk). Brixton tube/rail.*
Open 10.30pm-2.30am Mon, Thur; 10.30pm-3am
Wed; 10.30pm-5am Fri; 10.30pm-6am Sat; 10pm-late
Sun. **Admission** £4-£9. **No credit cards.**

Dark and edgy. Monday is underwear-only night Y-
Front; Wednesday is fetish night Boot Camp; Friday
is new men-only night Sin. On Saturday there's
Queer Nation, a house and garage night, followed
by alternative Free at Last on Sunday.

Pubs & bars

All of the pubs and bars that we list below are open to both gay men and lesbians, unless otherwise indicated.

Admiral Duncan

54 Old Compton Street, Soho, W1U 5UD (7437 5300). Leicester Square tube. **Open** noon-11pm Mon-Sat; noon-10.30pm Sun. **Credit** MC, V. **Map** p409 X2.
This traditional gay bar in the heart of Soho attracts a slightly older, down-to-earth crowd in a darkened setting. Having recovered after a homophobic bombing attack in 1999, this doughty old survivor is still going as strong as ever.

Barcode

3-4 Archer Street, Soho, W1D 7AP (7734 3342/ www.bar-code.co.uk). Leicester Square or Piccadilly Circus tube. **Open** 4pm-1am Mon-Sat; 4pm-10.30pm Sun. **Admission** £3 after 11pm Fri, Sat. **Credit** AmEx, MC, V. **Map** p408 W3.
Just the ticket for those in search of a busy men's cruise bar on two levels, Barcode also has a dance-floor downstairs and a late licence. Tuesday night is Comedy Camp, Simon Happily's popular straight-friendly gay comedy club.

BJ's White Swan

556 Commercial Road, The City, E14 7JD (7780 9870/www.bjswhiteswan.com). Aldgate East tube/ Limehouse DLR. **Open** 9pm-1am Mon; 9pm-2am Tue-Thur; 9pm-3am Fri, Sat; 5.30pm-midnight Sun. **Admission** £4 after 10pm Fri, Sat. **Credit** MC, V. **Map** p407 S6.
This large local attracts a loyal following, who come to savour the amateur male strip and drag shows, and to dance to commercial house music.

Black Cap

171 Camden High Street, Camden, NW1 7JY (7428 2721/www.theblackcap.com). Camden Town tube. **Open** noon-2am Mon-Thur; noon-3am Fri, Sat; noon-1am Sun. **Admission** £2-£4 Mon; £2-£3 Tue, Wed; £3-£4 Thur, Sun; £4-£5 Fri, Sat. **Credit** MC, V.
This famous north London pub/club is renowned for its drag shows, and was once a second home to television's own Lily Savage.

The Box

Seven Dials, 32-34 Monmouth Street, Covent Garden, WC2H 9HA (7240 5828/www.boxbar.com). Leicester Square tube. **Open** 11am-11pm Mon-Sat; noon-10.30pm Sun. **Credit** MC, V. **Map** p409 X/Y2.
By day, a popular café-bar for a mixed crowd, the Box transforms itself into a cruisy Muscle Mary hangout come nightfall.

Bromptons

294 Old Brompton Road, Earl's Court, SW5 9JF (7370 1344/www.bromptons.info). Earl's Court tube. **Open** 9pm-2am Mon-Sat; 7pm-12.30am Sun. **Admission** £1 10-11pm, £3 after 11pm Mon-Thur; £1 10-11pm, £5 after 11pm Fri, Sat; £1 after 10pm, £2 after 10pm Sun. **Credit** MC, V. **Map** p398 B11.

First class, **First Out**. *See p298.*

This busy men's pub-club with cabaret and strippers lures a slightly older crowd with its unpretentious atmosphere.

Candy Bar

4 Carlisle Street, Soho, W1D 3BJ (7494 4041/ www.thecandybar.co.uk). Tottenham Court Road tube. **Open** 5-11.30pm Mon-Thur; 5pm-2am Fri, Sat; 5-10.30pm Sun. **Admission** £6 after 9pm Fri, Sat; £3 after 10pm Thur. **Credit** (bar) MC, V. **Map** p408 W2.
London's best-known lesbian bar attracts a mixed clientele, from students to lipstick lesbians. Drinks aren't exactly the cheapest around, but there's a late licence at weekends, and erotic dancers in the basement bar. **Photo** *p302.*

Compton's of Soho

51-53 Old Compton Street, Soho, W1V 5PN (7479 7961/www.comptons-of-soho.co.uk). Tottenham Court Road tube. **Open** noon-11pm Mon-Sat; noon-10.30pm Sun. **Credit** AmEx, MC, V. **Map** p408 W3.
Popular with blokey gay men in bomber jackets, Compton's cruisy atmosphere extends to both floors.

The Edge

11 Soho Square, Soho, W1D 3QE (7439 1313/ www.edge.uk.com). Tottenham Court Road tube. **Open** noon-1am Mon-Sat; noon-10.30pm Sun. **Credit** MC, V. **Map** p408 W2.
Once at the cutting edge of the gay scene, this busy polysexual bar set out over several floors was looking a bit shabby until its recent refurb. It's great for summer drinking, given the proximity of Soho Square. DJs play most nights, plus there's a piano bar.

Element Bar

4-5 Greek Street, Soho, W1D 4DD (7434 3323/ www.allthingsorange.co.uk). Tottenham Court Road tube. **Open** 5pm-2am Mon-Sat; 5pm-12.30am Sun. **Admission** £5 after 11pm Fri, Sat. **Credit** AmEx, MC, V. **Map** p408 W2.

Candy Bar. *See p301.*

This upmarket venue for the gay cocktail crowd feels almost like a private members' bar. On Fridays and Saturdays there's a lively piano singalong. Downstairs has a bar and dance area.

Escape Bar

10A Brewer Street, Soho, W1F 0SU (7734 2626/ www.kudosgroup.com). Leicester Square tube. **Open** 5pm-3am Mon-Sat. **Admission** £3 after 11pm Tue-Thur; £4 after 10.30pm Fri, Sat. **Credit** AmEx, MC, V. **Map** p408 W3.
This intimate gay dance bar has a large video screen playing music videos to a mixed crowd.

G.A.Y. Bar

30 Old Compton Street, Soho, W1D 4UR (7494 2756/www.g-a-y.co.uk). Leicester Square tube. **Open** noon-midnight daily. **Credit** MC, V.
If you like the Astoria's ever-popular G.A.Y. club (*see p299*), then you'll love this cheesy bar. Girls Go Down is the women's bar in the basement.

Glass Bar

West Lodge, Euston Square Gardens, 190 Euston Road, Bloomsbury, NW1 2EF (7387 6184/www. southopia.com/glassbar). Euston tube/rail. **Open** 10am-11.30pm Mon-Fri; 6pm-3am Sat. **Admission** £1 Mon-Sat. **No credit cards. Map** p401 K3.
This shabby-chic bar is hidden away in the west stone lodge as you enter Euston Station. Rumours that you need to whisper the password 'Martina' have proved false. Strictly women-only.

The Hoist

Railway Arch, 47B&C South Lambeth Road, Vauxhall Cross, Vauxhall, SW8 1RH (7735 9972/ www.thehoist.co.uk). Vauxhall tube/rail. **Open** 8.30pm-midnight 3rd Thur of mth; 10pm-3am Fri; 10pm-4am Sat; 10pm-2am Sun. **Admission** £4 Thur; £5 Fri, Sun; £10 Sat. **No credit cards.**
A popular men's fetish bar in an industrial setting. No surprise, then, that the Hoist's dress code – leather, uniform, rubber, skinhead and boots – is taken rather seriously.

King William IV

77 Hampstead High Street, Hampstead, NW3 1RE (7435 5747/www.kw4.co.uk). Hampstead tube/ Hampstead Heath rail. **Open** 11am-11pm Mon-Sat; noon-10pm Sun. **Credit** MC, V.
Attracting a vaguely affluent crowd and a sprinkling of celebs, this old-fashioned gay local in swanky Hampstead turned gay in the 1930s to cater for Hampstead Heath cruisers. It is notable in the summer months for its busy beer garden.

Kudos

10 Adelaide Street, Covent Garden, WC2 4HZ (7379 4573/www.kudosgroup.com). Charing Cross tube/rail. **Open** noon-11pm Mon-Sat; noon-10.30pm Sun. **Credit** AmEx, MC, V. **Map** p409 Y4.
Close to the Oscar Wilde memorial statue and Charing Cross Station, this busy men's café-bar attracts a mixture of scene queens, tourists and men waiting for the next train back to suburbia.

Oak Bar

79 Green Lanes, Newington Green, N16 9BU (7354 2791/www.oakbar.co.uk). Manor House tube. **Open** 5pm-midnight Mon-Wed; 5pm-1am Thur; 5pm-3am Fri, Sat; 1pm-midnight Sun. **Admission** free-£5. **Credit** AmEx, MC, V.

This unpretentious venue (they run bingo nights on Thursdays) is a mixed gay local by day and a lesbian stronghold by night.

Retro Bar

2 George Court, off Strand, Covent Garden, WC2N 6HH (7321 2811). Charing Cross tube/rail. **Open** noon-11pm Mon-Fri; 5-11pm Sat; 5-10.30pm Sun. **Credit** AmEx, MC, V. **Map** p409 Y4.

True to its name, this mixed gay indie/retro bar plays '70s, '80s, goth and alternative sounds, and has a friendly atmosphere.

Rupert Street

50 Rupert Street, Soho, W1V 6DR (7292 7141). Leicester Square or Piccadilly Circus tube. **Open** noon-11pm Mon-Sat; noon-10.30pm Sun. **Credit** AmEx, MC, V. **Map** p408 W3.

This busy Soho bar has a distinctly '90s feel and attracts a slightly smarter, after-work crowd than many of its near neighbours. Boasts large windows – great for street watching, or checking out the clientele before you enter.

Shadow Lounge

5 Brewer Street, Soho, W1F 0RF (7287 7988/ www.theshadowlounge.co.uk). Piccadilly Circus tube. **Open** 10pm-3am Mon-Wed; 9pm-3am Thur-Sat. **Admission** £2 after 11pm Mon, Tue; £5 Wed, Thur; £10 Fri, Sat. **Credit** AmEx, MC, V. **Map** p408 W3.

Recently refurbished, the original lounge bar and gay members' club is still popular with celebrities and gay wannabes alike. Funky, comfy decor, professional cocktail waiters, friendly door staff and air-conditioning come as standard.

Too 2 Much

11-12 Walker's Court, off Brewer Street, Soho, W1F 0ED (7437 4400/www.too2much.com). Leicester Square or Piccadilly Circus tube. **Open** 5pm-4am Tue-Sat. *Performances* 7pm. **Admission** £10; £5 concessions. **Credit** AmEx, MC, V. **Map** p408 W3.

Following its closure in 2004, glitzy gay venue the Raymond Revuebar rose from its own ashes to become Too 2 Much. Sleaze has been replaced by glamour: the bar has a smart lounge area and there's a snazzy club space.

Trash Palace

11 Wardour Street, Soho, W1D 6PG (7734 0522/ www.trashpalace.co.uk). Piccadilly Circus tube. **Open** 5.30pm-1am Mon-Thur; 5.30pm-3am Fri, Sat; 5.30-10.30pm Sun. **Credit** MC, V. **Map** p408 W4.

The legendary Simon 'Popstarz' Hobart's final venture was this plastic fantastic venue, which is aimed towards the ever-growing indie crowd. Cheap drinks and regular DJs help make this the ideal warm-up spot for a night at the Ghetto (*see p300*). *See also p299* **Trailblazer Trash**.

Two Brewers

114 Clapham High Street, Clapham, SW4 7UJ (7498 4971/www.the2brewers.com). Clapham Common tube. **Open** 5pm-2am Mon-Thur; noon-3am Fri, Sat; noon-12.30am Sun. **Admission** free-£5. **Credit** AmEx, MC, V.

This Clapham gay bar and club is a south London institution. Drag shows are usually the order of the day, and it's always packed at weekends.

Village Soho

81 Wardour Street, Soho, W1V 6QD (7434 2124/ www.village/soho.co.uk). Piccadilly Circus tube. **Open** noon-1am Mon-Sat; 3-11.30pm Sun. **Admission** £3 after 11pm Fri, Sat. **Credit** MC, V. **Map** p408 W3.

A busy boys' café-bar on two floors, Village Soho is popular with a young crowd. Still, it pales in comparison with some of the glitzier venues nearby.

The Yard

57 Rupert Street, Soho, W1V 7BJ (7437 2652/ www.yardbar.co.uk). Piccadilly Circus tube. **Open** *Summer* noon-11pm Mon-Sat; noon-10.30pm Sun. *Winter* 2-11pm Mon-Sat; 2-10.30pm Sun. **Credit** AmEx, MC, V. **Map** p408 W3.

Understandably popular in the summer, this gay men's bar has a coveted courtyard. An upstairs loft bar keeps the smarter, after-work crowd interested during the colder months.

Saunas

Chariots

1 Fairchild Street, Shoreditch, EC2A 3NS (7247 5333/www.gaysauna.co.uk). Shoreditch tube/ Liverpool Street tube/rail. **Open** noon-9am daily. **Admission** £14; £12 concessions. **Credit** AmEx, MC, V. **Map** p405 R4.

Decked out like a Roman bath, Chariots is London's biggest and busiest gay sauna. It comprises a swimming pool, two steam rooms, two saunas, a jacuzzi and a host of private cabins. The Waterloo branch boasts the largest sauna in the UK (with room for 50 guys) and a special baggage check for Eurostar customers – save a bundle on a hotel and get lucky at the same time! The Limehouse site is split into two sections: Heaven is filled with blue walls and soft music, whereas Hell sports sinister black walls and resonates with hard dance music.

Other locations: 57 Cowcross Street, Farringdon, EC1M 6BX (7251 5553); 292 Streatham High Road, Streatham, SW16 6HG (8696 0929); 574 Commercial Road, E14 7JD, Limehouse (7791 2808); 101 Lower Marsh, SE1 7AB, Waterloo (7247 5333).

Sauna Bar

29 Endell Street, Covent Garden, WC2H 9BA (7836 2236). Covent Garden tube. **Open** noon-midnight Mon-Thur; 24hrs from noon Fri-midnight Sun. **Admission** £14; £10 concessions. **Credit** MC, V. **Map** p409 Y2.

A comfy bar, steam room, splash pool, showers and private rooms have all been crammed together in this small men-only sauna.

Music

From punk to the Proms, you heard it here first.

Classical & Opera

The capital's orchestral music scene is undergoing a few changes. Down by the Thames at the **South Bank Centre** (*see p306*), the **Royal Festival Hall** is currently closed for a major refurbishment. The £90m price tag includes £71m for the venue itself, plus £19m for lighting and landscaping in the surrounding area. The RFH is scheduled to re-open in January 2007; until then, its programme of events will be taken up by nearby siblings the **Purcell Room** and, to a lesser extent, the **Queen Elizabeth Hall**, with **Cadogan Hall** in Chelsea providing a temporary home for the Royal Philharmonic Orchestra.

Venerable **Wigmore Hall** is also enduring a period of turmoil, following the shock resignation of artistic director Paul Kildea in May 2005, who replaced much-loved fellow Australian William Lyne and had the tricky task of attracting a fresh audience without alienating the cognoscenti. Executive director John Gilhooly will assume artistic responsibility for the venue until spring 2006, by which time it's hoped a replacement will be found.

Despite all this upheaval, London still has many strings to its bow: the city's tally of five orchestras and two opera houses easily trumps New York (one orchestra), Paris (four orchestras, two opera houses) and Berlin (two orchestras, three opera houses). Moreover, the **Royal Albert Hall**'s annual Proms season has been an international event since the 1950s, and is widely regarded as the best classical music festival on the planet.

Meanwhile, Londoners who once turned their noses up at opera have fallen in love with it. While the English National Opera is going through a testing time, Covent Garden's **Royal Opera House** now ranks alongside La Scala in Milan and the Met in New York as one of the world's top houses.

TICKETS AND INFORMATION

Tickets for most classical and opera events in London are available direct from the venues: book ahead for good seats. Many major venues have online booking systems in addition to the telephone box offices.

A number of venues, such as the Barbican and the South Bank, operate standby schemes,

Cadogan Hall. *See p305.*

in which unsold tickets are sold off at cut-rate prices to students, seniors and others who are eligible for discounted rates hours before the show. Call the establishments for full details.

Classical venues

As well as the following major venues, London's music schools, the **Royal Academy of Music** (7873 7300, www.ram.ac.uk), **Royal College of Music** (7589 3643, www.rcm.ac.uk), **Guildhall School of Music & Drama** (7628 2571, www.gsmd.ac.uk) and **Trinity College of Music** (8305 4444, www.tcm.ac.uk) also hold regular performances during term-time that are worth checking out.

Barbican Centre

Silk Street, The City, EC2Y 8DS (7638 4141/box office 7638 8891/www.barbican.org.uk). Barbican or Moorgate tube/rail. **Box office** 9am-8pm daily. **Tickets** £6.50-£45. **Credit** AmEx, MC, V. **Map** p404 P5.

This arts complex is the home of the London Symphony Orchestra (LSO), widely regarded as the capital's best orchestra. It plays 90 concerts a year here, tours the world and records prolifically. Its rivals include the BBC Symphony Orchestra, which also performs here at subsidised rates. Following a £25-million renovation, the Barbican now enjoys better acoustics, and has managed to attract some of Europe's most prestigious orchestras, among them the Budapest Festival Orchestra, St Petersburg Philharmonic and Vienna Philharmonic. The modern music programming, taking in jazz, rock, world and country, also continues to find ever larger audiences. There is occasional free music in the foyer.

Cadogan Hall

5 Sloane Terrace, Chelsea, SW1X 9DQ (7730 4500/www.cadoganhall.com). Sloane Square tube. **Box office** 10am-7pm Mon-Sat. **Tickets** £10-£65. **Credit** MC, V. **Map** p402 G10.
This 100-year-old building was formerly a Christian Scientist church, but was transformed into a light and airy auditorium with excellent acoustics before reopening in June 2004. It seats around 900 people; the ground floor is raked so that sightlines are excellent and there is an impressive horseshoe balcony that

seems to stretch the entire circumference of the hall. The English Chamber Orchestra plays regularly, and the Royal Philharmonic Orchestra, under Daniele Gatti, has become the resident ensemble while the Royal Festival Hall is renovated. **Photo** *p304.*

Royal Albert Hall

Kensington Gore, South Kensington, SW7 2AP (information 7589 3203/box office 7589 8212/ www.royalalberthall.com). South Kensington tube/9, 10, 52 bus. **Box office** 9am-9pm daily. **Tickets** £4-£150. **Credit** AmEx, MC, V. **Map** p399 D9.
This grand rotunda, which can seat up to 5,200 people, is the home of the Proms (*see p309*), which occupy the building during the summer months each year. Otherwise, the hall, built as a memorial to Queen Victoria's husband, is a venue for all forms of public event including opera, rock, jazz, tennis, boxing, circus, fashion shows, business conventions and awards ceremonies. A refurbishment in 2004 installed soft air-conditioning, modernised the backstage area and moved the main entrance to the south side, right opposite the Royal College of Music.

Classical with a twist

London may have its Royal Albert Hall and its Royal Opera House, but the city is also home to plenty of lesser-known venues hosting classical music of a very high standard. Many are in themselves beautiful places to visit and offer a welcome break from the city centre.

An attractive building in less-than-attractive surroundings, **LSO St Luke's** (161 Old Street, EC1V 9NG, 7490 3939, www.lso.co.uk/ lsostlukes, tickets free-£25) is a more intimate venue at which to view the London Symphony Orchestra. The 18th-century, Grade I-listed ex-church houses the 'Discovery' programme, which aims at making classical music more accessible. This includes open LSO rehearsals, evening concerts and free lunchtime concerts (usually Friday 1-1.45pm).

Situated in the 'village' of Blackheath in south-east London, the atmospheric **Blackheath Halls** (23 Lee Road, SE3 9RQ, 8463 0100, www.blackheathhalls.com, tickets £6-£20) hosts a diverse mixture of concerts, with excellent acoustics. As well as an extensive programme of world music, the building houses a variety of classical concerts, fed largely by talented musicians from the Trinity College of Music.

Overlooking beautiful Waterlow Park, **Lauderdale House** (Highgate Hill, N6 5HG, 8348 8716, www.lauderdalehouse.co.uk, tickets £1-£12) is an easily accessible

escape from central London. Built in 1582, it now functions as an arts and education centre offering a wide programme of musical events. The small, elegant interior is the perfect setting for evening concerts from top-quality soloists and small ensembles. The calendar includes Sunday Morning Concerts, where recent graduates from major music colleges play to a family-friendly audience, and monthly participatory events such as 'Bring a song, Sing a song'.

The open minded **Grosvenor Chapel** (South Audley Street, Mayfair, W1K 2PA, 7499 1684, tickets £5-£15), built in 1730, has recently broadened its repertoire of concerts from organ recitals to include much bigger names. It now boasts the English Sinfonia's programme of 'commuter concerts', refreshing performances from London Pro Arte, and a variety of other concerts.

Opened in late 2004, the **artsdepot** (5 Nether Street, Tally Ho Corner, North Finchley, 8369 5454, www.artsdepot.co.uk, tickets £10-£18) is a multidisciplinary arts centre in the heart of a new development, which has an exciting programme of art, music, theatre and dance. The purpose-built venue has frequent classical concerts from heavyweight performers – names in their first season included Evelyn Glennie, London Jewish Male Choir, Smetana Trio and Guildhall Strings.

Feeling strung out? Unwind at **St Martin-in-the-Fields**.

St James's Piccadilly

*197 Piccadilly, St James's, W1J 9LL (7381 0441/
www.sjpconcerts.org). Green Park or Piccadilly Circus
tube.* **Open** 8am-6.30pm daily. **Admission** free-
£20; tickets available at the door 30mins before
start of performances. **No credit cards**. **Map**
p408 V4.

The only Wren church outside the City, this lovely,
simply designed building holds free lunchtime
recitals (Mon, Wed, Fri at 1.10pm) and a less regular
programme of evening concerts. Performers have
included members of the Beethoven Piano Society.
The church also hosts conventions and lectures by
leading world figures, and has a café and a craft market. It's worth dropping by to pick up a programme
and see what upcoming events are scheduled.

St John's, Smith Square

*Smith Square, Westminster, SW1P 3HA (7222
1061/www.sjss.org.uk). Westminster tube.*
Box office 10am-5pm Mon-Fri, or until start
of performance on concert nights; from 1hr before
start of performance Sat, Sun. **Tickets** £5-£45.
Credit MC, V. **Map** p403 K10.

This elegant 18th-century ex-church hosts a nightly
programme (except during summer) of orchestral
and chamber concerts, with occasional vibrant
recitals on its magnificent Klais organ. There's also
a wonderfully secluded restaurant in the crypt, open
whether or not any musical events are scheduled. In
an interesting historic note, the café is called 'the
Footstool', which has been the building's nickname
ever since Queen Anne was asked how she would
like the new church to look when complete and, kicking hers over, said, 'Like that!'

St Martin-in-the-Fields

*Trafalgar Square, Westminster, WC2N 4JJ (concert
information 7839 8362/www.stmartin-in-the-fields.
org). Charing Cross tube/rail.* **Box office** 10am-5pm
Mon-Sat, or until start of performance. **Admission**
Lunchtime concerts free; donations requested.
Evening concerts £6-£18. **Credit** MC, V.
Map p409 X4.

Overlooking Trafalgar Square, St Martin's hope-
lessly romantic candlelight concerts (7.30-9.30pm
Thur-Sat) are popular with both locals and visitors,
and the free lunchtime recitals (1-2pm Mon, Tue)
are frequently wonderful. Lovely music in lovely
surroundings. **Photo** *above*.

South Bank Centre

*Belvedere Road, South Bank, SE1 8XX (0870 380
0400/www.rfh.org.uk). Embankment tube/Waterloo
tube/rail.* **Box office** *In person* 11am-8pm. *By phone*
9.30am-8pm daily. **Tickets** £5-£75. **Credit** AmEx,
MC, V. **Map** p403 M8.

The South Bank Centre has three concert halls: the
3,000-seat Royal Festival Hall for major orchestral
concerts, the much smaller Queen Elizabeth Hall for
piano recitals and the tiny Purcell Room for chamber
groups and contemporary music concerts. The RFH
is home to six classical music ensembles – including
the Philharmonia and the London Philharmonic
Orchestras, the interesting period instrument
Orchestra of the Age of Enlightenment, the Alban
Berg String Quartet and London Sinfonietta, the
country's leading contemporary music ensemble. The
most advanced concert hall in the world back in the
'50s, the RFH is feeling its age and closed in July 2005
for 18 months of refurbishment.

Arts & Entertainment

Wigmore Hall

36 Wigmore Street, Marylebone, W1U 2BP (7935 2141/www.wigmore-hall.org.uk). Bond Street tube. **Box office** *In person* mid Mar-Nov 10.30am-8pm daily. Nov-Mar 10.30am-8.30pm Mon-Sat; 10.30am-5pm Sun. *By phone* Summer 10am-7pm Mon-Sat; 10am-6.30pm Sun. Winter 10.30am-4.30pm Sun. **Tickets** £8-£60. **Credit** AmEx, DC, MC, V. **Map** p400 G6.

Built in 1901 as the display and recital hall for Bechstein Pianos, this is the jewel of London's music venues. With its perfect acoustics, discreet art nouveau decor and excellent basement restaurant, it remains one of the world's top concert venues for chamber music and song. A £3m refurbishment in 2004 included a new roof and ventilation system, better sightlines, new seats, improved public spaces, and sympathetic lighting. Programming concentrates on the classical and romantic periods, and performers are among the most respected in their fields. The Monday lunchtime BBC concerts are excellent value.

Lunchtime concerts

A great tradition of midday performing mainly by talented music students and burgeoning young professionals has grown up in London's beautiful churches, with admission usually free or by donation. Those listed below are all centrally located in the city but there are many more around town, so consult *Time Out* magazine. Regular organ recitals are held at **Temple Church** (off Fleet Street, The City, EC4 7HL, 7353 8559; *see also p104*), **Grosvenor Chapel** (*see p305* **Classical with a twist**), **St James's** (Clerkenwell Close, EC1R 0EA, 7251 1190) and **Southwark Cathedral** (London Bridge, SE1 9DA; *see also p87*).

St Anne & St Agnes *Gresham Street, The City, EC2V 7BX (7606 4986). St Paul's tube.* **Performances** 1.10pm Mon, Fri. **Map** p406 P6.
St Bride's *Fleet Street, The City, EC4Y 8AU (7427 0133/www.stbrides.com). Blackfriars tube/ rail.* **Performances** 1.15pm Tue, Fri (except Aug, Advent, Lent). **Map** p406 N6.
St John's *Waterloo Road, Waterloo, SE1 8TY (7928 2003/www.stjohnswaterloo.co.uk). Waterloo tube/rail.* **Performances** 1.10pm Wed, call ahead to check. **Map** p406 N8.
St Lawrence Jewry *Guildhall, The City, EC2V 5AA (7600 9478). Mansion House or St Paul's tube/Bank tube/DLR.* **Performances** 1pm Mon, Tue. **Map** p406 P6.
St Margaret Lothbury *Lothbury, The City, EC2R 7HH (7606 8330/www.stml.org.uk). Bank tube/DLR.* **Performances** 1.10pm Thur. **Map** p407 Q6.
St Martin within Ludgate *40 Ludgate Hill, The City, EC4M 7DE (7248 6054). St Paul's tube/Blackfriars tube/rail/City Thameslink rail.* **Performances** 1.15pm Wed. **Map** p406 O6.
St Mary-le-Bow *Cheapside, The City, EC2V 6AU (7248 5139/www.stmarylebow.co.uk). Mansion House tube/Bank tube/DLR.* **Performances** 1.05pm Thur. **Map** p406 P6.

Opera companies

As well as the following, there are also performances at **Sadler's Wells** (*see p284*) and the **Peacock Theatre** (Portugal Street, Covent Garden, 0870 737 0337).

English National Opera

The Coliseum, St Martin's Lane, Covent Garden, WC2N 4BR (box office 7632 8300/fax 7379 1264/ www.eno.org). Leicester Square tube/Charing Cross tube/rail. **Box office** By phone 9.45am-8.30pm Mon-Sat; day tickets can be purchased from 10am on day of performance or by phone from 12.30pm on day of performance. **Tickets** £8-£85. **Credit** AmEx, DC, MC, V. **Map** p409 X4.

Built in 1904 by renowned architect Frank Matcham, the London Coliseum is home to the English National Opera (ENO). This magnificent building reopened in September 2004 following a mammoth £80m restoration. From its marble patterned floor to ornate and colourful foyer, the auditorium has been redecorated in accordance with the original style. The revolving roof-top dome is now complemented by a glass-walled public bar with dramatic views of Trafalgar Square, while the ENO's ambitious performances enjoy much-improved acoustics. The company has been a little beleaguered of late, however, with artistic director Sean Doran struggling to assert his authority.

Royal Opera

Royal Opera House, Covent Garden, WC2E 9DD (7304 4000/www.royaloperahouse.org.uk). Covent Garden tube. **Box office** 10am-8pm Mon-Sat. Tickets £4-£175. **Credit** AmEx, DC, MC, V. **Map** p409 Z3.

Covent Garden is one of the great opera houses of the world, and a hugely expensive refurbishment in 2000 only made it better. The conversion of Floral Hall, the old flower warehouse, into a restaurant and bars is one of London's wonders. The discreetly air-conditioned auditorium and comfy new seating make a night out at the opera a positive prospect, whatever the production. In a nod to the proletariat, a new system allows passers-by in the piazza outside to hear the music.

Festivals

In addition to the annual occasions listed below, the **Barbican Centre** (*see p304*), the **South Bank Centre** (*see p306*) and **Wigmore Hall** (*see above*) all present events throughout the year, while the **Spitalfields Festival** (*see p309*) is held in June and December. There are also open-air festivals of tried-and-tested favourites at Hampstead's **Kenwood House** (*see p153*) and **Marble Hill Park** (*see p183*), in south-west London, in July and August. For more information, call 8233 7435 or visit www.picnicconcerts.com.

Arts & Entertainment

City of London Festival

Venues in & around the City (information 7796 4949/box office 0845 120 7502/www.colf.org). **Date** 26 June-13 July 2006. **Box office** 9am-8pm daily. **Tickets** free-£40. **Credit** AmEx, MC, V.

This rich event continues to expand and become more adventurous, but the core of its annual programme remains chamber music concerts in the beautiful halls of ancient livery companies, such as the Ironmongers' and Goldsmiths', which the public never otherwise see. Concerts, talks and exhibitions also take place in churches as well as venues such as the Barbican and great St Paul's Cathedral itself. Excellent stuff.

Hampton Court Palace Festival

Hampton Court, East Molesey, Surrey (Ticketmaster 0870 534 4444/www.hamptoncourtfestival.com). Hampton Court rail/riverboat from Westminster or Richmond to Hampton Court Pier (Apr-Oct). **Date** mid June 2006. **Tickets** £15-£85. **Credit** AmEx, MC, V.

Cardinal Wolsey built himself this vast luxury home but later gave it to Henry VIII, who frolicked here with Anne Boleyn. The air of idle pleasure persists in the annual summer festival, where overtures and operatic arias have supper intervals during which audiences picnic on the grass or loiter in champagne tents while stilt-walkers and jugglers entertain them.

The great outdoors

Somerset House.

To hear any half-decent live tunes over summer you used to have to pack your tent and head down to Somerset for Glastonbury. But the astonishing recent growth in music festivals nationwide has been mirrored in the capital, with nearly all of London's major parks now hosting concerts over summer. In 2005 the first event of the season was **Park Live**, a new festival held in the second week of June in Brockwell Park, Herne Hill. Each of its three days is devoted to a different type of music – urban, dance and punk. Rather more high profile was the inaugural **Wireless** series (www.wirelessfestival.co.uk), which took place in Hyde Park in late June, just before Live8. Organised by global entertainment giant Clear Channel and sponsored by mobile phone company O$_2$, Wireless features well-known headliners such as New Order and Kasabian. There's no Glastonbury festival in 2006, so expect this corporate newcomer to be heavily promoted.

Over in south-east London, Clapham Common hosts the Latin/funk weekender **B-Live** (www.blivelondon.co.uk) in early July,

while the August bank holiday is given over to house music party **South West Four** and the indie-dance bash **Get Loaded in the Park** (www.getloadedinthepark.com). Also on the bank holiday weekend, the hugely popular **Lovebox on a Summer's Day** (www.lovebox london.com) now takes place in Victoria Park in east London, after moving from Clapham in 2005. The poptastic **Big Gay Out** (www.biggayout.com) remains up north in Finsbury Park, taking place in July.

For left-field sounds in a central location, head to the cobbled courtyard of **Somerset House** on the Strand (www.somerset-house.org.uk). In addition to housing the Courtauld Institute of Art Gallery, this magnificent 18th-century building also stages outdoor summer performances by the likes of Super Furry Animals and the Prodigy. A more genteel experience can be had at the **Kenwood House Picnic Concerts** in Hampstead (www.picnicconcerts.com).

Tickets for the events above range from £12 for the Friday of B-Live to £100 for all four days of Wireless but, happily, the capital also boasts many free outdoor shows. Look out for the **Ealing Jazz Festival** (*see p316*) and the Mayor's anti-racism celebration **Rise** (*see p316*), plus July's eclectic **Croydon World Party** (www.croydon.gov.uk/summerfestival) and Regent Park's laid-back, vitamin-fuelled **Fruitstock** (*see p268*), in August. Finally, the multi-cultural **Diaspora Music Village Festival** (www.culturalco-operation.org) in July is free by downloadable voucher, and takes place in the stunning Royal Botanic Gardens at Kew.

Many of these individual websites have mailing lists that you can join to receive more information; www.efestivals.co.uk is another useful resource.

Arts & Entertainment

Forum. *See p312.*

day for cheap tickets for the seatless promenade area in front of the stage. It's best to buy a festival programme from a bookshop and plan ahead. Tickets for the hilariously over-the-top Last Night, when normally well-behaved grown-ups act like schoolchildren, throwing paper darts and parping klaxons at inappropriate moments, are difficult to get hold of, but a secondary event is staged simultaneously in Hyde Park, featuring the likes of Simply Red and Italian tenor Andrea Bocelli.

Spitalfields Festival

Christ Church Spitalfields, Commercial Street, E1 6QE (7377 1362/www.spitalfieldsfestival.org.uk). Liverpool Street tube/rail. **Dates** 5-23 June; 11-20 December 2006. **Box office** 10am-5.30pm Mon-Fri. **Tickets** free-£30. **Credit** MC, V. **Map** p405 S5.
This enchanting, twice-yearly festival, staged in Hawksmoor's stunning Christ Church (with the odd event elsewhere), features new and old music, works by neglected composers, and walks and talks in and around the Spitalfields area.

Holland Park Theatre

Holland Park, Kensington High Street, Kensington, W8 6LU (0845 230 9769/www.operahollandpark. com). High Street Kensington or Holland Park tube. **Date** June-Aug 2006. **Tickets** £21-£43. **Credit** AmEx, MC, V. **Map** p396 A8.
This open-air, canopied theatre hosts a summer season of opera where the experience can be magical whatever the weather. Although it is harder for the performers in the rain, the audience is correspondingly more appreciative. The cries of unseen peacocks beyond the wall add a surreal touch.

The Proms

Royal Albert Hall, Kensington Gore, South Kensington, SW7 2AP (information 7765 5575/ box office 7589 8212/www.bbc.co.uk/proms). South Kensington tube/9, 10, 52 bus. **Date** 14 July-9 Sept 2006. **Box office** 9am-9pm daily. **Tickets** £4-£35. **Credit** AmEx, MC, V. **Map** p399 D9.
The BBC Sir Henry Wood Promenade Concerts, as they're officially known, comprise what is arguably the world's finest orchestral music festival. Running annually from mid July until mid September, it features around 70 concerts of both staple repertoire and newly commissioned works. The Proms began in 1895 with the aim of occupying idle musicians during the summer holidays and of informally educating those Londoners who could not afford to take holidays. Audiences paid a minimal ticket price provided they were prepared to do without a seat. The tradition continues today, as you can buy reserved seats in advance, but many prefer to queue on the

Rock, Dance, Roots & Jazz

Ludicrous curfews, poor sound and expensive tickets can make gig-going a fraught experience for visitors to the capital. The sale of the Mean Fiddler group in 2005 – which owns the Astoria and Garage, among others – to US corporate behemoth Clear Channel may improve matters, but no one is holding their breath. However, if you're prepared to look beyond the established venues, you'll find that London actually has more to offer than any other city on earth. The garage-rock boom of 2002/3 revitalised the live music scene at a grassroots level, leading to an explosion of local acts and DIY nights across myriad genres, from post-punk to acid folk. What's more, marquee names from the worlds of jazz, reggae, hip hop, metal and country often make this the only UK destination on their European tours, as do top artists from Africa, South America and the Far East. Whether you're a blues boffin or electronica enthusiast, if it's happening, it's happening here.

TICKETS AND INFORMATION

Your first stop should be the weekly *Time Out* magazine, which lists hundreds of gigs all over London. Most venues have websites detailing future shows, and some have online booking. Prices vary wildly: on any given night, you could pay £50 for the privilege of watching Simply Red at Earl's Court, or catch a perfectly serviceable jazz act for nothing in a bar or restaurant. Look out, too, for the regular free signings/early-evening in-store shows

Arts & Entertainment

New faces

Until a few years ago, London was great for seeing bands from other places, but had few major acts of its own. That all changed with the commercial breakthrough of **The Libertines** in 2002: a painfully shambolic, drug-addled punk 'n' roll combo led by unabashed hedonists Pete Doherty and Carl Barat. Doherty's rampant and well-documented substance abuse brought the east Londoners' career to a halt after just two albums (he then went on to form Babyshambles), but their headline-grabbing antics ensured the music industry's spotlight was firmly back on the capital.

Chaotic chancers the Others have emerged from the scene the Libs created around the Rhythm Factory in Whitechapel, the former gaining a degree of notoriety via impromptu 'guerrilla gigs' in tube trains, museum lobbies and so on. Cockney satirists **Art Brut** have put New Cross back on the live music map, while also starting a feud with student disco favourites **Bloc Party**, from Bethnal Green, whose yelping new wave draws heavily on the Cure, Joy Division and Echo & the Bunnymen. The most successful of all these retro indie outfits has been **Razorlight**: a Television- and Patti Smith-influenced vehicle for one-time Libertine and full-time ego Johnny Borrell.

So far, so derivative – but London has much more to offer than skinny boys with guitars. Fuelled by pirate radio and bedroom producers, the inner-city dance genre known as grime continues to mutate into thrilling new forms. Brand leader **Dizzee Rascal** (from Bow) has now been joined in the record racks by near-neighbours **Wiley**, **Kano** and the **Roll Deep Crew**, all oan anthem away from mainstream acclaim. An even better bet for future chart action is cutting-edge rapper Lady Sovereign, aka 19-year-old Neasden resident Louise Harman. Another female MC to look out for is the Sri Lankan-bred **MIA** (real name Maya Arulpragasam; *pictured*), whose pan-global mix of ragga, electro and south London street slang has made her a rising star in America.

If all that sounds too hip, then sing along to Ealing-based **the Magic Numbers**: two sets of brothers and sisters whose harmonious country-pop was just made for lazy summer days. Another bunch doing their own thing are the eclectic synth-funkers **Clor**, who hail from the unfashionable environs of Kennington.

They came to prominence through the monthly Club Clor nights at pub venue the Windmill in Brixton (*see p314*), which has also hosted some of London's loudest ensembles. Camberwell riff lords **Part Chimp** make a sludgy yet melodic din pitched between Black Sabbath and Sonic Youth, while north London's denim demons **Tokyo Dragons** play good-time hard rock that has seen them through two UK tours with Status Quo.

On a more experimental tip, besuited satanists **Akercocke**, also from the north of the capital, create a gothic hybrid of black metal, progressive rock and post-punk. The same part of town gave rise to instrumental quartet **Capricorns**, who release grandiose lyricless excursions through respected underground metal label Rise Above. Somewhat incongruously, Rise Above is also home to one of the capital's weirdest groups. **Circulus** are a seven-piece psychedelic folk troupe who revive the sights and sounds of medieval England, complete with costumes. Based in sleepy south London suburb Plumstead, they're truly olde school.

at **Virgin Megastore**, **HMV**, **Fopp** and **Rough Trade** (for all, *see p260*). You can pay on the night at most roots events, but for everything else it's best to book ahead (for large to mid-sized venues) or get there early (for pub and club gigs). Always check ticket availability before setting off – live music is booming at the moment, with many shows selling out weeks in advance. Likewise, make sure you know when the doors are opening: a 7pm or 8pm start means the headline act should be on around 9pm or 10pm respectively, but timings can vary wildly.

Buy tickets with cash direct from the venue's box office if you want to escape insidious booking fees, which can add as much as 30 per cent to the ticket price. If the venue has sold out, try a ticket agency: the big four are **Ticketmaster** (0870 534 4444, www.ticketmaster.co.uk), **Stargreen** (7734 8932, www.stargreen.com), **Ticketweb** (0870 060 0100, www.ticketweb.co.uk) and **See Tickets** (0870 120 1149, www.seetickets.com). In all cases, avoid the ticket touts outside.

Rock & dance venues

Major venues

In addition to the venues listed below, the **Queen Elizabeth Hall** (*see p305*), **Royal Albert Hall** (*see p305*), **Barbican Centre** (*see p304*) and **Alexandra Palace** (*see p157*) all stage major gigs on a regular basis. There are also occasional shows from acclaimed singer-songwriters and US indie acts at **UCL Bloomsbury Theatre** (15 Gordon Street, Bloomsbury, WC1H 0AH, 7388 8822). Elephant & Castle's **Coronet** (26-28 New Kent Road, Newington, SE1 6TJ, 7701 1500/0870 0601793) is primarily a club and cinema, but also hosts the occasional multi-media gig. Also south of the river, **Blackheath Halls** (*see p305* **Classical with a twist**) presents a variety of different styles, from classical to rock.

Now in its fourth incarnation, the once-legendary **Marquee Club** (1 Leicester Square, Soho, WC2H 7NA) has failed to attract major names, despite its 900-capacity site in the centre of town. During the summer, London's many parks and the cobbled courtyard of **Somerset House** feature a variety of open-air events (*see p308* **The great outdoors**).

Astoria

157 Charing Cross Road, Soho, WC2H 0EL (information 8963 0940/box office 08701 500044/ www.meanfiddler.com). Tottenham Court Road tube. **Box office** *In person* 10am-6pm Mon-Sat. *By phone* 24hrs daily. **Tickets** £10-£20. **Credit** AmEx, MC, V. **Map** p408 W2.

Although a major fixture for alt.rockers old and new (Killing Joke, the Futureheads), this 2,000-capacity sweat box has come to represent the more frustrating aspects of live music in London: poor sound, steep bar prices and a tendency to herd gig-goers out of the building as soon as the headline act has finished.

Carling Academy Brixton

211 Stockwell Road, Brixton, SW9 9SL (information 7771 3000/box office 08707 712 000/www.brixton-academy.co.uk). Brixton tube/rail. **Box office** By phone 24hrs daily. **Tickets** £10-£40. **Credit** MC, V. Excellent sightlines, decent sound and a glorious, cod-Gothic interior ensure that shows at this 4,700-capacity institution are real events. The famous sign on the corner has trumpeted 'Sold Out' notices for everyone from Bob Dylan to Nine Inch Nails, with late-night techno and hip-hop bills (the Chemical Brothers, the Roots) proving especially atmospheric.

Carling Academy Islington

N1 Centre, 16 Parkfield Street, Islington, N1 0PS (information 7288 4400/box office 0870 771 2000/www.islington-academy.co.uk). Angel tube. **Box office** *In person* noon-4pm Mon-Sat. *By phone* 24hrs daily. **Tickets** £3-£20. **Credit** MC, V. **Map** p404 N2.

After a failed attempt by ex-Eurythmic Dave Stewart to relaunch the Marquee Club here, this chrome-plated shopping mall venue is now run by the Academy Music Group. It's still soulless, and blighted by poor design, an expensive cloakroom and a habit of kicking punters out as soon as the show's over. However, the capital's lack of mid-sized spaces means it's become a default haunt for cult international acts, with everyone from Turbonegro to the Drive-By Truckers attempting to inject some life into the place. The adjacent Bar Academy hosts smaller names.

Carling Apollo Hammersmith

Queen Caroline Street, Hammersmith, W6 9QH (information 8748 8660/box office 0870 606 3400/ www.getlive.co.uk). Hammersmith tube. **Box office** By phone 24hrs daily. **Tickets** £10-£40. **Credit** AmEx, MC, V.

The erstwhile Hammersmith Odeon, as popularised by Motörhead, was relaunched in October 2003 by Clear Channel as a 5,000-capacity powerhouse to rival Brixton Academy. AC/DC played a legendary set on its reopening night; recent bookings include Garbage, Feeder, Rufus Wainwright and Joss Stone.

Earl's Court Exhibition Centre

Warwick Road, Earl's Court, SW5 9TA (7385 1200/box office 7370 8078/www.eco.co.uk). Earl's Court tube. **Box office** *In person* 9am-6pm Mon-Fri. *By phone* 24hrs daily. **Tickets** £17-£50. **Credit** MC, V. **Map** p398 A11.

An immense aircraft hangar of a venue (London's largest indoor arena, with a capacity of 20,000), cursed by horrible acoustics and expensive concessions. That doesn't stop the likes of big name acts like Duran Duran and the Foo Fighters from playing here, though it probably should.

Electric Ballroom

184 Camden High Street, Camden, NW1 8QP (7485 9006/www.electricballroom.co.uk). Camden Town tube. **Box office** 9am-5pm Mon-Thur; 10.30am-1am Fri, Sat; 10.30am-5pm Sun. **Tickets** £7-£10. **No credit cards.**

For ages this scuzzy yet spacious hall was threatened with closure by the proposed expansion and redevelopment of Camden Town tube, but now that plan has been shelved the venue's future looks secure for the time being. It continues to feature upcoming alt.rock and punk names on a regular basis. Unfortunately, it can be a bit tricky to see the stage when the place is full.

Forum

9-17 Highgate Road, Kentish Town, NW5 1JY (information 7284 1001/box office 0870 150 0044/ www.meanfiddler.com). Kentish Town tube/rail/N2 bus. **Box office** *In person* from the Astoria or the Jazz Café 10am-5.30pm Mon-Sat. *By phone* 24hrs daily. **Tickets** £10-£20. **Credit** (phone bookings only) MC, V.

This fine old under-used theatre is slightly bigger and infinitely better than the Astoria, with its air of faded grandeur and suitably venerable attractions (Human League, Dinosaur Jr). It's a good idea to buy upstairs tickets: the padded benches are comfortable, there are two bars and the sculpted, chandelier-laden ceiling is worth admiring. **Photo** *p309.*

Koko

1A Camden Road, Camden, NW1 0JH (0870 432 5527/www.koko.uk.com). Mornington Crescent tube. **Box office** phone ahead for details. **Tickets** £3-£15. **Credit** MC, V.

Formerly the Camden Palace, this ornate, multi-level ballroom has been given a lick of paint and a new name. It now hosts the hugely popular Club NME night on Fridays, as well as proving a useful stop-off for respected US indie names such as Mudhoney, Devendra Banhart and Yo La Tengo.

Shepherd's Bush Empire

Shepherd's Bush Green, W12 8TT (8354 3300/box office 0870 771 2000/www.shepherds-bush-empire. co.uk). Shepherd's Bush tube. **Box office** *In person* 4-6pm; 6.30-9.30pm show nights only. *By phone* 24hrs daily. **Tickets** £10-£40. **Credit** MC, V.

This 2,000-capacity former BBC theatre is London's best mid-sized venue. The sound is usually splendid (with the exception of the alcove behind the stalls bar), the atmosphere is warm, and the staff are among London's friendliest. An eclectic booking policy adds to its appeal; last December the venue hosted everyone from New York Antony & the Johnsons to superannuated '80s rocker Shakin' Stevens.

Wembley Arena

Empire Way, Wembley, Middx HA9 0DW (0870 739 0739/www.whatsonwembley.com). Wembley Park tube/Wembley Central tube/rail. **Box office** *In person* 10.30am-4.30pm Mon-Sat. *By phone* 24hrs daily. **Tickets** £5-£100. **Credit**, MC, V.

At the time of writing, this 12,500-capacity hangar of a place was being refurbished. This means that its big name bookings – everything from Alice Cooper to the Backstreet Boys – have to perform at Wembley Pavilion, a temporary marquee that is even worse than the parent venue. The arena itself is due to reopen in spring 2006, with Depeche Mode among the early attractions.

Club venues

As well as the following, the clubs **Cargo** (*see p319*) and **93 Feet East** (*see p322*) feature an interesting mix of shows, with the emphasis on dance music and left-field rock respectively. **The Luminaire** (307-311 Kilburn High Road, Kilburn, NW6 7JR, 7372 8668) and **Pleasure Unit** (359 Bethnal Green Road, Bethnal Green, E2 6LG, 7729 0167) both have an increasing number of decent gig and club nights, as does Soho cabaret fixture **Madame Jo Jo's** (*see p321*). **On the Rocks** (25 Kingsland Road, Shoreditch, E2 8AA, 07753 484 936) has superseded the **Rhythm Factory** (16-18 Whitechapel Road, Whitechapel, E1 1EW, 7375 3774, www.rhythmfactory.co.uk) in the east London hipster stakes. And intimate newbie **Infinity** (10 Old Burlington Street, Mayfair, W1S 3AG, 7287 5255) features a variety of nights of an indie persuasion.

Bush Hall

310 Uxbridge Road, Shepherd's Bush, W12 7LJ (8222 6955/box office 8222 6933/0870 060 0100/ www.bushhallmusic.co.uk). Shepherd's Bush tube. **Box office** 10am-5pm Mon-Fri. **Tickets** £6-£25. **Credit** AmEx, MC, V.

Opened in 1904 as the Carlton Ballroom (the plasterwork is dotted with musical motifs) and then used as a snooker hall, Bush Hall's 21st-century incarnation is as a plush music venue, staging an even spread of chamber music concerts and low-key, often acoustic, rock shows (REM and the Corrs have played here). The interior can make you feel like you're sitting inside an ornate cake – and this is not a bad thing.

Garage

20-22 Highbury Corner, Islington, N5 1RD (information 8963 0940/box office 0870 060 3777/ www.meanfiddler.com). Highbury & Islington tube/ rail. **Box office** 24hrs daily. **Open** *Gigs* 8pm-Mon-Thur, occasional Sun; 8pm-3am Fri, Sat. **Admission** £5-£15. **Credit** MC, V.

A low-ceilinged, black-walled shoebox which every upcoming indie, rock, punk and metal act will play at some point. Positives include a relaxed attitude to closing time – you can usually get a drink after the show. Less welcome is their habit of encouraging customers to hand bags over to the paying cloak-room. Tiny sister venue Upstairs at the Garage (guess where it is) hosts several terrific alternative nights, but gets painfully hot during summer.

Hope of States rock out at the **Buffalo Bar**. *See p315.*

100 Club

*100 Oxford Street, Fitzrovia, W1D 1LL (7636 0933/
www.the100club.co.uk). Oxford Circus or Tottenham
Court Road tube.* **Open** *Gigs* 7.30pm-midnight Mon-
Thur; 8pm-1am Fri; 7.30pm-2am Sat; 7.30-11.30pm
Sun. **Tickets** free-£15. **Credit** AmEx, MC, V.
Map p399 K6.

The 100 Club once numbered Glenn Miller among its
regulars. In the 1950s it became a leading trad-jazz
joint, in the '60s an R&B hangout, and in the '70s it
was the infamous home of punk. These days, the
eccentrically designed, red-walled room hosts a mix
of indie wannabes and jazz/swing acts. Extra points
for real ale at the bar, plus iconic posters and photos.

ICA

*The Mall, Westminster, SW1Y 5AH (box office 7930
3647/www.ica.org.uk). Embankment or Piccadilly
Circus tube/Charing Cross tube/rail.* **Box office**
noon-9.15pm daily. **Tickets** £5-£15. **Credit** AmEx,
DC, MC, V. **Map** p401 K8.

Self-consciously trendy it may be, but the Institute
of Contemporary Arts has a cutting-edge booking
policy and better-than-average sound system.
alt.rock faves such as Sleater-Kinney and dEUS often
showcase new material here before coming back to
play bigger shows.

Lock 17

*11 East Yard, Camden Lock, Chalk Farm Road,
Camden, NW1 8AB (box office 7428 0010/
Ticketmaster 7344 4040/www.dingwalls.com).
Camden Town or Chalk Farm tube.* **Box office** *In
person* tickets from Rhythm Records, 281 Camden
High Street (7267 0123). *By phone* 24hrs daily. **Open**
Gigs 7.30pm-2am; nights vary. **Admission** £5-£15.
Credit AmEx, MC, V.

Formerly Dingwalls, Lock 17 stages some good acts.
However, due to the poor sightlines, it works better
when they put back the tables and it becomes comedy venue Jongleurs (*see p281*) at weekends.

Mean Fiddler

*165 Charing Cross Road, Soho, WC2H 0EL (7434
9592/box office 0870 534 4444/www.meanfiddler.
com). Leicester Square or Tottenham Court Road
tube.* **Box office** *In person* 10am-6pm Mon-Fri;
10am-5pm Sat. *By phone* 24hrs daily. **Tickets**
£10-£25. **Credit** MC, V. **Map** p399 K6.

Little brother to the adjacent Astoria (*see p311*), with
superior sound and sightlines. Expect rock and
metal at this venue, plus Saturday's late-night Frog
club, which has featured many key acts from the
ongoing post-punk/new wave revival. If you think
that the support band's terrible, head to the glassed-
off balcony bar to the left.

Metro

*19-23 Oxford Street, Soho, W1D 2DN (7437 0964/
www.blowupmetro.com). Tottenham Court Road
tube.* **Open** *Office* from 5pm Mon-Fri. *Club* 11pm-
3am Tue-Thur; 11pm-4am Fri, Sat. **Admission**
£5-£10. **No credit cards. Map** p408 W1.

Mushy sound and haphazard layout, but this basement dive earned a reputation as the place to play
during the garage-rock boom of 2002-3. It's not quite
what it was, but it can still get enjoyably messy;
expect to be drenched with both sweat and beer by
the time you leave, whenever that is.

Scala

*275 Pentonville Road, King's Cross, N1 9NL (7833
2022/box office 0870 060 0100/www.scala-london.
co.uk). King's Cross tube/rail.* **Box Office** *24hrs
daily.* **Open** phone for details. **Tickets** £8-£15.
Credit MC, V. **Map** p401 L3.

Iggy and the Stooges played their first (and, until
the recent reunion, last) UK show at this converted
cinema. Expect first-rate names from the worlds of
US indie (Shellac, Mission of Burma) and underground hip hop (Prefuse 73, Saul Williams), in an
attractive venue, itself a landmark at the heart of the
regeneration of King's Cross.

Arts & Entertainment

Spitz

Old Spitalfields Market, 109 Commercial Street,
Spitalfields, E1 6BG (7392 9032/box office 0871
220 0260/www.spitz.co.uk). Liverpool Street tube/
rail. **Open** 11am-midnight Mon-Sat; 10am-10.30pm
Sun. **Box office** 24hrs daily. **Tickets** £4-£12.
Credit MC, V. **Map** p405 R5.
On the edge of Spitalfields, the Spitz tries to be
all things to all people: gallery, restaurant, bar and
(upstairs) live music venue. Expect anything from
avant-garde electronica to gutsy country, via free
jazz, psychedelia and the blues. Hopeless air-conditioning means it's stuffy in summer.

Underworld

174 Camden High Street, Camden, NW1 0NE (7482
1932/0870 060 0100/www.theunderworldcamden.
co.uk). Camden Town tube. **Open** *Gigs* 7-10.30pm;
nights vary. **Admission** £5-£20. **No credit cards**.
A dingy maze of pillars and bars deep in the bowels
of Camden, this subterranean oddity is nevertheless
an essential destination for punk, metal and hardcore fans. Its insalubrious interior is enlivened by
friendly, youthful audiences and a real sense of community. Special daytime events include the monthly all-ages session Subverse and annual grindcore
marathon Deathfest.

University of London

Union (ULU) Malet Street, Bloomsbury, WC1E
7HY (box 7664 2000/www.ulu.lon.ac.uk). Goodge
Street tube. **Box office** 8.30am-11pm Mon-Fri;
9am-11pm Sat, Sun. **Open** *Gigs* 7.30-11pm; nights
vary. **Admission** £8-£15. **No credit cards**.
Map p401 K4.
In 2005 this 800-capacity student hall was redecorated and had a new sound system installed, improving a cosy if anonymous spot. Expect to see indie
and rock acts who've outgrown the Garage but can't
fill the Astoria. (Saying that, the Foo Fighters played
a low-key gig here long after they'd outgrown the
Astoria, so keep your eyes peeled.) There are two
bars, and drinks prices are low.

Pub & bar venues

In addition to the venues listed below, Alan
Tyler's afternoon country-rock session **Come
Down and Meet the Folks**, held on Sundays
at Fiddlers Elbow (1 Malden Road, Kentish
Town, NW5 3HS, 08712 3324495, www.
comedownandmeetthefolks.co.uk), is worth
investigating. More centrally, **Loom** (5-6
Clipstone Street, Fitzrovia, W1W 6BB, 7436
0035) puts on everything from garage-rock
to avant-garde jazz.

Barfly

49 Chalk Farm Road, Chalk Farm, NW1 8AN (7691
4244/box office 0870 907 0999/www.barflyclub.
com). Chalk Farm tube. **Open** 7.30pm-1am Mon-
Thur; 7.30pm-3am Fri, Sat; 7-10.30pm Sun. *Gigs*
7.30pm daily. **Admission** £6-£8. **No credit cards**.

Charlie Brown at the **Windmill**.
See p315.

The nationwide Barfly organisation sure knows
how to churn 'em out. Three acts per night – indie,
rock or metal – play here for a mixture of devotees,
talent scouts and music biz hangers-on. Coldplay,
the Strokes and the Darkness have all clocked in on
their way up. Friday's popular Queens of Noize club
is hectic, bordering on the unbearable.

Betsey Trotwood

56 Farringdon Road, Clerkenwell, EC1R 3BL(7253
4285). Farringdon tube/rail. **Open** noon-11pm Mon-
Fri; 11am-11pm Sat; noon-10.30pm Sun. *Gigs* 8pm
Mon-Sat. **Admission** £4-£5. **Credit** MC, V.
For several years the chaps from Water Rats (*see*
p315) have promoted nights of lo-fi bliss in the 70-
capacity upstairs room at this intimate pub, plus the
odd happening in the tiny basement.

Boston Arms

178 Junction Road, Tufnell Park, N19 5QQ (7272
8153/www.dirtywaterclub.com). Tufnell Park tube.
Open 11am-midnight Mon-Wed, Sun; 11am-1am
Thur-Sat. *Gigs* 10pm, day varies. *Club* 9pm every
other Fri. **Admission** £4-£6. **Credit** MC, V.
This roomy yet welcoming boozer is home to
London's premier garage-rock night the Dirty Water
Club, which takes place most Fridays and was the
White Stripes' hang-out of choice when they first
came to town. A wonderful time is guaranteed –
especially if you're around for Billy Childish & the
Buff Medways' excellent regular shows.

Buffalo Bar
*259 Upper Street, Islington, N1 1RU (7359 6191/
www.thebuffalobar.co.uk). Highbury & Islington
tube/rail.* **Open** 8.30pm-2am Mon-Sat; 7pm-midnight
Sun. **Admission** free-£6. **Credit** MC, V.
Raucous entertainment galore at this cosy basement,
which attracts the hottest underground acts around
and a clued-up crowd. Look out for the Artrocker
nights on Tuesdays, plus the odd event organised by
music magazine *Loose Lips Sink Ships.* **Photo** *p313.*

Dublin Castle
*94 Parkway, Camden, NW1 7AN (7485 1773/www.
bugbearbookings.com). Camden Town tube.* **Open**
noon-1am Mon-Sat; noon-midnight Sun. *Gigs* 8.45pm
Mon-Sat; 8.30pm Sun. **Admission** £4.50-£6. **No
credit cards.**
Though the refurbishment a few years ago
improved it, some think the Dublin Castle still makes
a better pub than music venue. That doesn't stop it
hosting dozens of bands every week – a tiny proportion of whom go on to make it big (Blur, Travis).

Enterprise
*2 Haverstock Hill, Chalk Farm, NW3 2BL (7485
2659). Chalk Farm tube.* **Open** noon-midnight Mon-
Sat; noon-11pm Sun. **Admission** £3-£8. **No credit
cards.**
The snug upstairs room of this book-lovers' pub
hosts acoustic, candlelit sets by pop/rock singer-
songwriters (as opposed to roots troubadours), often
booked by the Barfly (*see p314*) people.

Hope & Anchor
*207 Upper Street, Islington, N1 1RL (7354 1312).
Highbury & Islington tube/rail.* **Open** noon-1am
Mon-Sat; noon-midnight Sun. *Gigs* 8pm daily.
Admission £4-£6. **Credit** MC, V. **Map** p404 O1.
This minuscule cellar was once a rock and punk leg-
end. Today the pub upstairs is smarter and the acts
of little note. Acoustic nights on Monday and
Wednesday; otherwise, indie and punk.

Notting Hill Arts Club
*21 Notting Hill Gate, Notting Hill, W11 3JQ (7460
4459/www.nottinghillartsclub.com). Notting Hill Gate
tube.* **Open** 6pm-1am Mon-Wed; 6pm-2am Thur, Fri;
4pm-2am Sat; 4pm-12.30am Sun. *Gigs* times vary.
Admission free-£8. **Credit** MC, V.
This formerly hip basement has all the charm of root
canal work, and its staff are sometimes easily dis-
tracted. Still, the free Rota session on Saturday afternoons usually throws up some decent live acts, as
does Alan McGee's Wednesday night Death Disco.

Water Rats
*328 Gray's Inn Road, King's Cross, WC1X
8BZ (7837 7269/www.plummusic.com). King's
Cross tube/rail.* **Open** *Gigs* 8.30-11pm Mon-Sat.
Admission £3 £6. **Credit** MC, V. **Map** p401 M3.
Bob Dylan played his first UK gig in the back room
of this King's Cross pub four decades ago, and Oasis
held their first London showcase here in 1994. It's
been redecorated since, but the sounds from the
stage – indie and alt.rock – are still reliably scruffy.

Windmill
*22 Blenheim Gardens, Brixton, SW2 5BZ (8671
0700/www.windmillbrixton.co.uk). Brixton tube/
rail.* **Open** *Gigs* 7-11pm Mon-Sat; 7-10.30pm Sun.
Admission free-£3/£4. **No credit cards.**
At present, the best small venue in London, thanks
to an adventurous bookings policy (anything goes,
from country to techno to punk to folk to metal),
cheap admission, friendly staff, trippy decor and a
relaxed but totally sincere attitude towards entertainment. Pretty much perfect. **Photo** *p314.*

Roots venues

Cecil Sharp House
*2 Regent's Park Road, Camden, NW1 7AY (7485
2206/www.efdss.org). Camden Town tube.* **Open**
Gigs times vary. **Admission** £2.50-£12.50. **Credit**
MC, V.
The home of the English Folk Dance and Song
Society, with barn dances, ceilidhs and folk dance
classes. Sharp's Folk Club on Tuesdays is fun.

Hammersmith & Fulham Irish Centre
*Blacks Road, Hammersmith, W6 9DT (8563 8232/
www.lbhf.gov.uk/irishcentre). Hammersmith tube.*
Open *Gigs* 7.30pm, Fri, Sat. **Admission** £3-£15.
No credit cards.
You'll find all kinds of Irish music events, from free
ceilidhs to biggish-name acts such as the Popes, on
offer at this small, friendly *craic* dealer.

12 Bar Club
*22-23 Denmark Place, St Giles's, WC2H 8NL (office
7240 2120/box office 240 2622/www.12barclub.
com). Tottenham Court Road tube.* **Open** *Café* 9am-
9pm daily. *Gigs* 7.30pm; nights vary. **Admission**
£5-£15. **Credit** MC, V. **Map** p408 W4.
This minuscule hole-in-the-wall books a real grab-
bag of stuff, though its size (the stage is barely big
enough for three people) dictates a predominance of
singer-songwriters. Wonderfully characterful.

Jazz venues

In addition to the venues listed below, the
100 Club (*see p313*) and the **Spitz** (*see
p314*) both stage regular jazz shows, the
former concentrating on trad stuff and the
latter dealing in more modern material. The
Barbican Centre (*see p304*) also offers a
good range of jazz events throughout the year.

Bull's Head
*373 Lonsdale Road, Barnes, SW13 9PY (8876
5241/www.thebullshead.com). Barnes Bridge rail.*
Open 11am 11pm Mon Sat; noon 10.30pm Sun.
Gigs 8.30pm Mon-Sat; 2-4.30pm, 8-10.30pm Sun.
Admission £3-£10. **Credit** AmEx, DC, MC, V.
Saved from possible closure at the 11th hour after
troubles with the local authorities over noise levels,
this delightful riverside pub (and Thai bistro) is

something of a jazz landmark, staging gigs by musicians from both the UK and the States. In true jazz tradition, it also has a well-stocked bar; check out, in particular, the selection of malt whiskies.

Jazz Café

5 Parkway, Camden, NW1 7PG (information 7916 6060/box office 0870 150 0044/www.jazzcafe.co.uk). Camden Town tube. **Open** 7pm-1am Mon-Thur; 7pm-2am Fri, Sat; 7pm-midnight Sun. *Gigs* 9pm daily. **Admission** £8-£25. **Credit** MC, V.

The name doesn't tell the whole story: jazz is only a small piece in the jigsaw of events here, which also takes in funk, hip hop, soul, R&B, singer-songwriters and much more besides. Just pray that the expense-accounters who pack the balcony and eating area don't talk through the entire set.

Pizza Express Jazz Club

10 Dean Street, Soho, W1D 3RW (restaurant 7437 9595/Jazz Club 7439 8722/www.pizzaexpress.co.uk). Tottenham Court Road tube. **Open** *Restaurant* 11.30am-midnight daily. *Jazz Club* 7.45pm-midnight daily. *Gigs* 9pm daily. **Admission** £15-£20. **Credit** AmEx, DC, MC, V. **Map** p408 W2.

The food takes second billing in the basement of this eaterie: this place is all about largely contemporary mainstream jazz. Despite all the pizza, it's a proper venue and audiences are respectful: there's no talking through the sets here.

Ronnie Scott's

47 Frith Street, Soho, W1D 4HT (7439 0747/www. ronniescotts.co.uk). Leicester Square or Tottenham Court Road tube. **Open** 8.30pm-3am Mon-Sat; 7.30-11pm Sun. **Admission** (non-members) £20 Mon-Thur; £25 Fri, Sat; £10 students Mon-Wed; £15 musician union members Mon-Sat. **Credit** AmEx, DC, MC, V. **Map** p408 W2.

Scott died in 1996, but his club, founded in 1959, remains a hugely atmospheric Soho fixture. The roster of acts, which play two sets a night for runs of at least a week, is not as interesting as it was, and the crowds are brasher than ever. That said, the new management team has an evident love for the venue, and there are signs that the emphasis is being shifted back to credible jazz fare. Call to book a table.

606 Club

90 Lots Road, Chelsea, SW10 0QD (7352 5953/ www.606club.co.uk). Earl's Court or Fulham Broadway tube/11, 211 bus. **Open** 7.30pm-1.30am Mon-Wed; 8pm-1.30am Thur; 8pm-2am Fri, Sat; 8pm-midnight Sun. *Gigs* 8pm-1am Mon-Wed; 9.30pm-1.30am Thur-Sat; 9.30pm-midnight Sun. **Admission** *Music charge* (non-members) £7 Mon-Thur; £9 Fri, Sat; £8 Sun. **Credit** AmEx, MC, V. **Map** p398 C13.

A restaurant, late-night club and popular musicians' hangout, this Chelsea joint has the laudable and successful policy of booking British-based jazzers who bring in the crowds. There's no entry fee: instead, the musicians are funded from a music charge that is added to your bill at the end of the night. Note that alcohol is only served with meals.

Vortex Jazz Club

11 Gillet Street, Dalston, N16 8JN (7690 6661/ www.vortexjazz.co.uk). Dalston Kingsland rail. **Open** 8pm-midnight daily. *Gigs* 8.30pm. **Admission** free-£10. **Credit** MC, V.

This longtime Stoke Newington staple looked like it had bitten the dust when it left its former premises in acrimonious circumstances, but secured its future in 2005 by moving to a handsome new site in Dalston. The new room isn't as characterful as the old place, but it's smarter, with improved sightlines and air-conditioning. Expect adventurous home-grown jazz and a convivial atmosphere. Work continues: a café was recently added.

Festivals

For a round-up of the capital's best rockfests, *see p308* **The great outdoors**. If you're looking for information about **Meltdown**, *see p267*, or for **Rhythm Sticks**, *see p268*. You can also catch some sounds at the **Notting Hill Carnival** (*see p269*), **Pride London** (*see p268*) and the **Brick Lane Festival** (*see p269*).

In addition, the **South Bank Centre** (*see p81*) and **Barbican Centre** (*see p304*) put on regular events – such as Only Connect and BITE – that incorporate music with theatre, dance and film. See the weekly *Time Out* magazine for details.

Ealing Jazz Festival

Walpole Park, Matlock Lane, Ealing, W5 (8825 6640/www.ealing.gov.uk/ealingsummer). Acton Town tube. **Date** late July-early Aug 2006.

The largest free jazz event in Europe attracts around 50,000 people to listen to a multitude of top names. Previous performers have included F-ire Collective and Norma Winstone.

Jazz on the Streets

Venues around Soho & Covent Garden (www. jazzonthestreets.co.uk). **Date** July 2006.

A seven-day event drawing talent from all over the world for a series of performances in the West End, at venues including Soho and Trafalgar Squares.

London Jazz Festival

Various venues (7405 9900/www.serious.org.uk). **Date** 10-19 Nov 2006.

This creatively curated festival spans many genres and attracts good artists. It's held at major concert halls and small clubs around London.

Rise

Burgess Park, SE1 (7983 6554/www.london.gov.uk/ rise/index.jsp). **Date** July 2006.

A free music and dance anti-racism festival that is supported by the Mayor's office. Past performers have included Run-DMC and Billy Bragg. 2005's event was renamed London United and celebrated the capital's diversity and defiant spirit it exhibited following the 7 July terrorist attacks.

Nightlife

Raving mad and rocking steady.

London's nightlife reigns supreme, and judging by the number of people who would happily sell their grandmothers to DJ and dance here, the whole world knows it. Forget finding a job and somewhere to stay: if you've just arrived, you're no doubt gagging to get out there and have the time of your life. Places to go, DJs to see...

It's easy to get overwhelmed, though. In London there are more DJs playing more types of music in more quality clubs (not to mention dingy basements and outdoor courtyards) on more days of the week than anywhere else in the world right now. It's no surprise that many people who are new to the capital spend months finding the nightlife utterly impenetrable. To get the most out of London, you just have to get out there. Don't restrict yourself. Sure, it's good to know what gets you on the dancefloor, but you can't beat the thrill of discovering a new DJ, disco space or even entire music genre that you didn't know existed.

There are also decisions to be made as to which night to go out. Friday and Saturday nights are for bridge and tunnellers. The most exciting times tend to be during the week or even during the day, in tiny spaces where the overheads are low enough to allow musical risks to be taken. In the summer, the Secretsundaze parties rock secret East End locations (Google it to find out; *see also p324* **Going underground**) on Sunday afternoons. **Trash** is still one of the most exciting indiepopelectro parties around, and it's on a Monday. No rest for the wicked: while everyone else is getting to bed early on Sunday nights, those in the know head straight for Bones & Ramsey's cult **Machine**.

Not all risks are worth taking, however. If you can't walk home from the club, find out which night bus gets you home and (more importantly) where you get it from before you head out. You'll never regret working out the night bus system, as the tube doesn't start until around 7am on Sundays, and black cabs are expensive and rare. If you must take a minicab, make sure it's an official one (*see p364*).

Note that a recent shake-up in the licensing laws, which took effect just as this guide went to press, means that some of the following clubs may have extended opening hours. For the latest opening times, phone the venue in question. *See also pp222-223.*

Bar Rumba. *See p319.*

FABRIC
+44(0)20 7336 8898
WWW.FABRICLONDON.COM

FABRICLIVE.

Join the club
fabricfirst

Clubs

Aquarium

256 Old Street, Hoxton, EC1V 9DD (7251 6136/ www.clubaquarium.co.uk). Old Street tube/rail. **Open** 10pm-3am Thur; 10pm-4am Fri, Sat; 10am-4am Sun. **Admission** £7-£20. **Map** p405 R4.

The only nightclub in the UK with a swimming pool and a six-person jacuzzi, Aquarium is proud of its aquatic status. And, leaving aside the watersports gags, it certainly ups the fun element no end. Despite being in the ultra-hip Old Street area, nights are strictly tongue-in-cheek affairs, with the '70s funk-fest Carwash still ruling the roost on Saturdays.

Bar Rumba

36 Shaftesbury Avenue, Soho, W1D 7EP (7287 6933/www.barrumba.co.uk). Piccadilly Circus tube. **Open** 9pm-3.30am Mon; 6pm-3am Tue; 7pm-3am Wed; 6pm-3.30am Thur, Fri; 9pm-5am Sat; 8pm-2am Sun. **Admission** £3-£10; free before 9pm Tue; free before 8pm Thur; free before 10pm Fri. **Map** p408 W4.

Just because it's in the West End, don't make the mistake of thinking that this basement club is home to anything other than some of the most respected leftfield nights in town. Drum 'n' bass fans worship at Movement's altar every Thursday and reggaeton fans cram in for Tuesday's essential Barrio Latino. DJ Marky's been a regular fixture here for years, but isn't the only superstar. **Photo** *p317*.

Canvas

King's Cross Goods Yard, off York Way, King's Cross, N1 0UZ (7833 8301/www.canvaslondon.net). King's Cross tube/rail. **Open** 8pm-midnight Thur; 8pm-2am Fri; 10pm-6am Sat. **Admission** £10-£20. **Map** p401 L2.

Part of a cluster of venues in the area that's put King's Cross firmly on the clubbing map, Canvas is a massive warehouse space that takes in three dancefloors and two bars, and a new Ibizan-flavoured terrace. Thursdays and Fridays are disco-tastic, with Roller Disco (best fun on wheels). Keep an eye out for frequent one-off parties, and also the annual TDK Cross Central in August.

Cargo

Kingsland Viaduct, 83 Rivington Street, Shoreditch, EC2A 3AY (7739 3440/www.cargo-london.com). Old Street tube/rail. **Open** 11am-1am Mon-Thur; 11am Fri; 6pm-3am Sat; 1pm-midnight Sun. **Admission** free-£12. **Map** p405 R4.

Shock! Here's an example of the club/bar/restaurant concept that actually works. Down a side street, under some arches, Cargo never deviates from a mantra that's just about quality, quality and more quality. Monthly Saturday bashes include Manchester's legendary hip-hop-fest Friends & Family, and Casual Records Ross Allen's boomer of a night, Destination Out (expect everything electric, from funk to dub to hip hop). If you love music, you should tattoo Cargo's address on your forearm right now.

Cirque

Hippodrome Corner, Leicester Square, WC2H 7JH (7437 4311/www.cirquehippodrome.com). Leicester Square tube. **Open** 9pm-4am Mon, Tue, Fri, Sat. **Admission** £15 Fri; £20 Sat. **Map** p409 X3.

For the more mainstream clubber who doesn't find the West End a nightmare. Famous in its former incarnation as the enormous Hippodrome, it's now become the enormous Cirque instead. Not much else has changed. Every Friday is the hugely successful '80s retrofest, Gold, and there are trapeze artists and plush drinking areas to keep you amused.

The best # Outdoor vibes

While sweaty dark boxes have a lot going for them, sometimes you need to feel the air. OK, London may not be the Caribbean, but there are still plenty of clubs with terraces, gardens and courtyards to groove in.

Cargo

Set under a disused railway arch, Cargo is the place to dance, feast on street food and relax in the enormous, graffiti-sprayed courtyard. *See above.*

EGG

Marooned halfway up York Way, this three-floor venue, with its central, astroturfed terrace, is perfect for finding a vacant sun lounger and pretending that you were anywhere but King's Cross. *See p320.*

Lock 17

Situated right in the middle of Camden, Lock 17 overlooks Regent's Canal. The view might be rustic, but this vibrant bar is anything but. *See p325.*

The Lodge

This gorgeous destination boozer has been a storming success; the 'Balearic Beer Garden' is authentically whitewashed, while the intimate and colourful garden hosts superb parties. *See p325.*

Vibe Bar

This courtyard space has gained itself an enviable reputation thanks to the rammed Sunday sessions, which continue throughout the summer. *See p326.*

As the likes of Thee Unstrung know, Camden Palace is no more – vive **KoKo**! See p321.

The Cross

The Arches, 27-31 King's Cross Goods Yard, off York Way, King's Cross, N1 OUZ (7837 0828/ www.the-cross.co.uk). King's Cross tube/rail. **Open** 10pm-6am Fri, Sat; 11pm-6am Sun. **Admission** £12-£15. **Map** p401 L2.

Three cheers for this stylish brick-and-arches space with a garden full of lush plants and comfy sofas. The wonderful Ibizan spirit flows freely, with a big influx of friendly Italians who help whip up a great atmosphere at the Friday house party, Fiction. Vertigo, the Italo-house bash, is here some bank holidays, while Serious bangs out the house stormers every month on a Saturday.

EGG

200 York Way, King's Cross, N7 9AP (7609 8364/www.egglondon.net). King's Cross tube/rail. **Open** 10pm-6am Fri; 10pm Sat-noon Sun; phone for weekday openings. **Admission** £8-£15. **Map** p401 L2.

Need another reason to head to King's Cross? We give you EGG. With its Mediterranean-style three-floored interior and enormous terrace (complete with a pool), it's big enough to lose yourself in but not so big as to lose the intimate atmosphere. The upstairs bar in red ostrich leather is particularly elegant, while the main dancefloor downstairs achieves a warehouse rave feel. Clubs range from dark electro synth raves to proper house nights; the most famous is Jaded, every Sunday morning.

The End

18 West Central Street, Holborn, WC1A 1JJ (7419 9199/www.the-end.co.uk). Holborn or Tottenham Court Road tube. **Open** 10pm-3am Mon, Wed; phone for details Tue; 10pm-4am Thur; 10pm-5am Fri; 10pm-7am Sat; phone for details Sun. **Admission** £4-£15. **Map** p409 Y1.

The End ticks all the right boxes: from its ultraminimal AKA bar (*see p323*) to the dark and moody lounge and the heady main room with its cheer-from-all-sides island DJ booth. Nights on rotation ooze underground cool: indie Trash, Fabio's Swerve, Bugged Out!, Layo & Bushwacka All Night Long, Derrick Carter's Classic, owner Mr C's tech house session, Superfreq, Darren Emerson's Underwater... All attract an international and super-friendly crowd.

Fabric

77A Charterhouse Street, Clerkenwell, EC1M 3HN (7336 8898/advance tickets for Fri & Sat 0870 902 0001/www.fabriclondon.com). Farringdon tube/rail. **Open** 9.30pm-5am Fri; 10pm-7am Sat; 10pm-5am Sun. **Admission** £12-£15. **Map** p404 O5.

World renowned, thanks to adoring reviews from punters and DJs alike, Fabric is all about the music, usually of the leftfield, extremely underground sort. Its three rooms get pretty packed: the main is home to the stomach wobbling Bodysonic dancefloor; the second's a rave-like warehouse (complete with laser); and the smaller third is where the cool stuff happens. The best club in the world? Definitely a contender.

The Fridge

1 Town Hall Parade, Brixton, SW2 1RJ (7326 5100/www.fridge.co.uk). Brixton tube/rail. **Open** 10pm-6am Fri, Sat. **Admission** £8-£20.

Hailed by many hard house and psy trance heads as their favourite venue in London, the Fridge is Brixton's biggest club, and a south London nightlife landmark. It's nigh on impossible to overstate the importance this place has for the hard dance scene in London and for the profile of the area. Regular and one-off events keep it on the map.

Ghetto

5-6 Falconberg Court (behind the Astoria), Soho, W1D 3AB (7287 3726/www.ghetto-london.co.uk). Tottenham Court Road tube. **Open** 10.30pm-3am Mon-Thur; 10.30pm-4am Fri; 10.30pm-5am Sat; 10.30am-3pm Sun. **Admission** £1-£7. **Map** p399 K6.

Not always easy to find, but always well worth the search, the Ghetto is home to Nag Nag Nag, and you really can't say you've done London until you strut your stuff at this fabulously louche basement venue, which runs very different events every night of the week. Both attract a gay/straight crowd of club characters and disco dollies, who work up a sweat on a dancefloor with minimal air-conditioning. Laudable for their 'squeeze some sense into Soho' drinks price policy – pay no more than £3. *See also p300.*

Herbal

10-14 Kingsland Road, Shoreditch, E2 8DA (7613 4442/www.herbaluk.com). Old Street tube/rail. **Open** 8pm-2am Tue; 9pm-2am Wed, Thur, Sun; 9pm-3am Fri, Sat. **Admission** free-£10. **Map** p405 R3.

If Hoxton and Shoreditch do your head in with pretentious, posing folk, you'll love the two-floored Herbal, where it's all about the music. Grooverider's weekly Grace has settled in a treat, causing roadblocks aplenty on Sunday nights (bank holidays are particularly crazy). Upstairs has an NYC loft feel about it, which only ever adds to the house party vibe. Tuesday is hip hop Spitkingdom, while other nights feature soulful house, eclectic electro sounds, and even party hip hop.

The ICA

The Mall, St James's, SW1Y 5AH (7930 3647/ www.ica.org.uk). Piccadilly Circus tube/Charing Cross tube/rail. **Open** noon-11pm Mon; noon-1am Tue-Sat; noon-10.30pm Sun. **Admission** free-£6. **Map** p403 K8.

A cultural nexus by day, the ICA also has a knack of coming up with some truly great nights out. Their trick is to avoid clichés while spicing things up with VJs and live performances. The monthly Brazilian night, Batmacumba (Saturdays), for example, takes tips from whatever's ripping up dancefloors in São Paolo. Once a month on Thursdays, Blacktronica eschews hiphop and soul in favour of more cutting edge electronic beats; meanwhile downtempo Soultek (once a month on a Friday), hosted by Xfm's Nick Luscombe, is a more subdued but no less enticing affair. *See also p286 and p313.*

Jamm

261 Brixton Road, Brixton, SW9 6LH (7274 5537/ www.brixtonjamm.com) Brixton tube/rail. **Open** 5pm-2am Mon-Thur; 5pm-6am Fri; 11am-6am Sat; 11am-2am Sun. **Admission** £5-£10.

Not the classiest location for a club, but then this place is more about slamming parties than swanky soirées. There's an enormous terrace that's being done up in time for mid 2006, but it overlooks a car park and the busy Brixton Road. Inside, two rooms are on the right side of battered: comfortable sofas, long bars and a straightforward box of a room for dancing. Basement Jaxx throw monthly Inside Out kickers here, plus there are techno, drum 'n' bass and psychedelic parties, and even the odd comedy night.

The Key

King's Cross Freight Depot, King's Cross, N1 0UZ (7837 1027/www.thekeylondon.com). King's Cross tube/rail. **Open** 11pm-5am Fri; 10pm-6am Sat. **Admission** £7-£15. **Map** p401 L2.

This trendy, tiny club is set in an industrial wasteland (it's a glow-stick's throw from the Cross; *see p320*, and in the same building as Canvas; *see p319*): look out for the neon sign jutting from the wall. The Key also has the best dancefloor in London – all glass and flashing lights. Leave any notions of strutting your John Travolta moves at the door, though: it's strictly hedonistic house, deep tech, electro-a-gogo and even party hip hop at nights like All Over My Face, DeepDownandDirty and Issst.

KoKo

1A Camden High Street, Camden, NW1 7JE (0870 432 5527/www.koko.uk.com). Camden Town or Mornington Crescent tube. **Open** 10pm-midnight Mon-Thur; 10pm-3am Fri; 10pm-6am Sat. **Admission** £4 before 11.30pm, £7 (£6 with flyer) after 11pm Fri.

This 19th-century building has worn numerous hats in its time: music hall, BBC radio studio, gig venue and, most recently, nightclub. Under this incarnation it was allowed to fall apart as the Camden Palace. The multi-levelled venue had a makeover a couple of years ago, ditching the run-down '80s look for plush reds and purples reminiscent of its theatrical history. So far, though, it has struggled somewhat to find a niche, with clubs coming and going at a rapid pace. That said, Club NME, with its mix of bands and DJs, appears to be working a treat. **Photo** *p320.*

Madame Jo Jo's

8 Brewer Street, Soho, W1F 0SE (7734 3040/ www.madamejojos.com). Leicester Square or Piccadilly Circus tube. **Open** 10pm-3am Tue-Sat. **Admission** £5-£8. **Map** p408 W3.

A great venue, enhanced by a touch of Soho cabaret sleaze – you'd be forgiven for mistaking the nature of the operation after seeing the name. The big draw remains Keb Darge's Deep Funk on Fridays, where blindingly cool people move furiously to obscure 1960s and '70s cuts, while White Heat (all punk, electro and indie) has recently found a happy home here every Tuesday. **Photo** *p322.*

Madame Jo Jo's. *See p321.*

Ministry of Sound

103 Gaunt Street, off Newington Causeway, Newington, SE1 6DP (0870 060 0010/www.ministry ofsound.com). Elephant & Castle tube/rail. **Open** 10pm-3am Wed (term time only); 10.30pm-5am Fri; 11pm-7am Sat. **Admission** £12-£17. **Map** p406 O10.
With millions of compilations, tours and this famous venue to its name, the Ministry of Sound has to be the world's most recognised clubbing brand. As such, it's sometimes sneered at by more cutting-edge clubbers, but it is nevertheless one of the few UK clubs that can actually afford to put on the likes of NYC house legends Masters at Work all night long. It's no wonder that DJs flock to play here: the sound system is shockingly good.

Neighbourhood

12 Acklam Road, Ladbroke Grove, W10 5QZ (7524 7979/www.neighbourhoodclub.net). Ladbroke Grove or Westbourne Park tube. **Open** 8pm-2am Thur-Sat; call or check website for weeknight times & events. **Admission** £5-£15.
Neighbourhood used to be the sterling Subterrania, and the inside has changed surprisingly little since. The varied repertoire includes live music, one-off week-night events and house music on weekends.

93 Feet East

150 Brick Lane, Spitalfields, E1 6QL (7247 3293/ www.93feeteast.co.uk). Shoreditch or Aldgate East tube or Liverpool Street tube/rail. **Open** 5-11pm Mon-Thur; 5pm-1am Fri; noon-1am Sat; noon-10.30pm Sun. **Admission** free-£5. **Map** p405 S5.
With its huge variety of top-notch live gigs and club nights, 93 Feet East has no problem attracting a trendy, knowledgeable crowd. The three-room venue sports a stylish downstairs bar, kitsch upstairs room and enormous main dancefloor, in addition to

stacks of outdoor space. Hooga, held once a month on a Friday, sees the likes of Tom Vek and the Bays performing and spinning anything from disco to electro, while Wwwhut?! (monthly on a Saturday) pushes the grime, hip hop and MC sounds out. It's a bit of a skinny jeans extravaganza at Sunday's Rock 'n' Roll Cinema, a popular daylong marathon of bands, DJs and screenings.

Notting Hill Arts Club

21 Notting Hill Gate, Notting Hill, W11 3JQ (7460 4459/www.nottinghillartsclub.com). Notting Hill Gate tube. **Open** 6pm-1am Mon-Wed; 4pm-2am Sat; 4pm-1am Sun. **Admission** £5-£8; free before 8pm. **Map** p396 A7.
With much more diversity and creativity than most other clubs combined, the Notting Hill Arts Club is where artists, musos and DJs get together and swap ideas, put on parties and get all arty. It's a sure-fire bet that whatever you like, you'll find it here: Thursday's fierce funk, soul and old school boogiefest at Yo Yo, or the guitar mayhem at Death Disco every Wednesday. *See also p315.*

Pacha London

Terminus Place, Victoria, SW1V 1JR (7833 3139/www.pachalondon.com). Victoria tube/rail. **Open** 10pm-6am Fri, Sat. **Admission** £15-£20. **Map** p402 H10.
This lavish outpost of the global club giant that has dominated Ibiza for years was truly made for lording it. A heady mix of chandeliers, oak panels and a stained-glass ceiling ensure a chic clubbing experience, despite the fact that the club itself is located in a bus depot. The glammed-up clubbers dress as sumptuously as the decor, shaking their booties to the rocking house beats of Hed Kandi (irregular Saturdays), among others.

Plan B

418 Brixton Road, Brixton, SW9 7AY (7733 0926/ www.plan-brixton.co.uk). Brixton tube/rail. **Open** 5pm-2am Wed, Thur; 5pm-4am Fri; 7pm-4am Sat; 7pm-2am Sun. **Admission** free before 9pm; £5 after 9pm; £7 after 11pm Fri, Sat.

This gleaming, spacious club-bar is modern rather than trendy in design. Similarly, it attracts a good-natured local crowd to its weekly hip hop, soul, funk and breaks nights, not least from Mike Skinner's the Beats throwdown once a month on a Thursday. On Saturdays, the ace sound system pumps it out.

Plastic People

147-149 Curtain Road, Shoreditch, EC2A 3QE (7739 6471/www.plasticpeople.co.uk). Old Street tube/rail. **Open** 10pm-2am Mon-Thur; 10pm-3.30am Fri, Sat; 7.30pm-midnight Sun. **Admission** £3-£8. **Map** p405 R4.

This tiny downstairs club is a good place to come for after-hours drinks without breaking the bank, and it's also a music lover's paradise. Sounds range from Afro-jazz and hip hop to Latin, deep house and even grime: watch the little dancefloor get rammed with a chilled but funky crowd. The sound system is bliss.

The Telegraph

228 Brixton Hill, Brixton, SW2 1HE (8678 0777). Brixton tube/rail. **Open** noon-2.30am Mon-Thur; noon-4am Fri; noon-4am Sat; noon-12.30am Sun. **Admission** £5-£10.

Situated at the top of Brixton Hill, further up than some may care to venture, this spacious old pub made its name with the Rooty raves by south London's Basement Jaxx a few years back. You'll still find local DJs and promoters getting the hang of things here, which is the best possible thing: from regular reggae and hip hop parties to big house and electro, the surprisingly big room through the back goes off like few clubs in London. Prepare to sweat.

333

333 Old Street, Hoxton, EC1V 9LE (7739 5949/ www.333mother.com). Old Street tube/rail. **Open** *Bar* 8pm-3am Mon-Wed; 8pm-4am Thur; 8pm-5am Fri, Sat. *Club* 10pm-5am Fri, Sat; 10pm-4am Sun. **Admission** *Club* £5-£10. **Map** p405 Q4.

The dominant landmark on Old Street, this pivotal East End venue houses a no-frills three-storey interior. The lively punters (lots of 'em too: beware the queues) are there for the music, which is always excellent and varied. The basement usually bounces to techno, drum 'n' bass or crazy mash-ups, while the main room heaves to house, electro and even reggae from septuagenarian DJ Derek. The top-floor bar, Mother, is plusher: a great hangout that runs good nights of its own.

Turnmills

63B Clerkenwell Road, Clerkenwell, EC1M 5PT (7250 3409/www.turnmills.com). Farringdon tube/ rail. **Open** 9pm-2am Thur; 10.30pm-7.30am Fri; 10pm-6am Sat; 9pm-3am Sun. **Admission** £8-£15. **Map** p404 N4.

Turnmills' neo-classical, acid-warehouse nooks and crannies are a hedonist's playground; in fact, the whole venue is something of a legend in its own lifetime. While it offers the full musical spectrum, the club's long-running house and trance night, Gallery, on Friday night is particularly well subscribed. Hugely friendly (rather than achingly fashionable), it's one of the most popular venues in town.

DJ bars

Ah, the DJ bar. If there's a pub on the corner, then there's a hopeful little boffin inside trying his or her hand at running a pint-sized night. With licences going later and later in the capital (*see pp222-223*), the line between bar and club is getting ever more blurred.

You'll find that most bars try their hand at being all things to all people – special lunch offers and post-work drinks for the office crowds, up-and-coming DJs and promoters running club-like nights at the weekend, with the odd kooky midweeker thrown in for good measure. While there's a strong argument that the smaller venues are the best ones, we're still not convinced that cranking up endless banging trance in a bar is a surefire way to success. But some owners realise this, and book DJs who have the record collection to soundtrack the wind up and wind down of a night out. On the downside, the last year has seen an increasing number of DJ bars introducing a cover charge.

AKA

18 West Central Street, Holborn, WC1A 1JJ (7836 0110/www.akalondon.com). Holborn or Tottenham Court Road tube. **Open** 10pm-3am Tue; 6pm-3am Thur; 6pm-4am Fri; 7pm-5am Sat; 10pm-4am Sun. **Admission** £3 after 11pm Tue; £5 after 11pm Thur; £7 after 10pm Fri; £10 after 9pm Sat. **Credit** AmEx, MC, V. **Map** p409 Y1.

Joined – physically as well as musically – to the End next door (*see p320*), this popular hangout attracts top international DJs, entertain punters who have been loosened up by good food and cocktails. The venue is incorporated into the End's club nights on Fridays and Saturdays; have patience and be prepared to queue at weekends.

Barfly

49 Chalk Farm Road, Camden, NW1 8AN (7691 4244/www.barflyclub.com). Camden Town or Chalk Farm tube. **Open** 7pm-2am Mon-Thur; 7pm-3am Fri; midday-3am Sat; midday-1am Sun. **Admission** £6-£8. **Credit** MC, V.

This venue is a big part of the reason why indie-guitar-meets-electro parties are doing so well in the capital at the moment. The Barfly might be part of a chain but this is no All Bar One. The intriguingly named night Kill Em All, Let God Sort It Out is every couple of weeks on a Saturday, with bands guaranteed to get the crowd going. *See also p314.*

Big Chill Bar

91-95 Dray Walk, Brick Lane, E1 6QL (7392 9180/ www.bigchill.net). Aldgate East tube or Liverpool Street tube/rail. **Open** noon-midnight Mon-Sat; noon-11.30pm Sun. **Admission** free. **Credit** MC, V.
A big box of a bar with a helpfully long bartop running down the left-hand side, and plenty of comfy sofas, this is the place to head when the famous Big Chill festival seems just too long away. It attracts top DJs, and the atmosphere is just as good as the tunes. It gets super busy at weekends, so expect to spill out on to Dray Walk.

Cherry Jam

58 Porchester Road, Bayswater, W2 6ET (7727 9950/www.cherryjam.net). Royal Oak tube. **Open** 7pm-1.30am Wed-Sat; Sun (phone to check). **Admission** £5-£8 after 10pm, depending on nights; phone for details. **Credit** MC, V. **Map** p396 C5.
You could do far worse in west London than this bar, the hippest for many streets in all directions. There's an elevated area for sitting and supping cocktails (or nursing a beer), and a proper dancefloor that doesn't get as much use as it used to (when Cherry Jam was more of a club).

Dogstar

389 Coldharbour Lane, Brixton, SW9 8LQ (7733 7515/www.thedogstar.com). Brixton tube/rail. **Open** 4pm-2am Mon-Thur; noon-4am Fri, Sat; noon-2am Sun. **Admission** £3 after 10pm Fri, Sat; £5 after 11pm Fri, Sat. **Credit** MC, V.

A Brixton institution, Dogstar is set in a large street-corner pub, and it exudes the urban authenticity loved by clubbers. The atmosphere can be intense, but it is never less than vibrant (it's something of a training ground for the DJ stars of tomorrow, and worth visiting for that reason alone). While the music varies from night to night, the quality always stays high. *See also p233.*

Elbow Room

89-91 Chapel Market, Islington, N1 9EX (7278 3244/www.theelbowroom.co.uk). Angel tube. **Open** 5pm-2am Mon; noon-2am Tue, Wed; noon-3am Thur-Sat; noon-midnight Sun. **Admission** free-£5. **Credit** MC, V. **Map** p404 N2.
The biggest London location of this decidedly upmarket entertainment emporium, Elbow Room follows a well-established, slick, good-time formula that wins it many friends around these parts. A pool room and bar by day, it becomes more clubby at night, and queues can stretch down the street. Its hip hop parties are ones to watch.
Other locations: 103 Westbourne Grove, Notting Hill, W2 4UW (7221 5211); 97-113 Curtain Road, Shoreditch, EC2A 3BF (7613 1316).

Ion

161-165 Ladbroke Grove, W10 6HJ (8960 1702/ www.meanfiddler.com). Ladbroke Grove tube. **Open** 5pm-midnight Mon-Fri, Sun; noon-midnight Sat. **Admission** free; £4 after 9pm Fri, Sat; £5 after 9pm Sun. **Credit** MC, V.

Going underground

You don't have to be a wide-eyed psy-trancer to get the illegal party thrill. Club promoters of all types like to have a bit on the side. In the name of a great time you can find yourself dancing your way through terraces, courtyards, railway arches, warehouses, lofts, shifty watering holes... even an urban 'forest'. It's all very orbital rave, but with a modern twist, so leave your white gloves and whistles at home.

The infamous East End all-day rave Secretsundaze went from underground to overground recently, so expect them to go stratospheric in 2006. Though they don't hide their contact details, not everyone will get that all-important text as to the location. Sign up and cross your fingers when their summer season starts again in May. Druzzi's Baltimore Warehouse Party took over a couple of railway arches in 2005; the door girl initiated a glowstick war after several hundred were chucked into a heaving, jumping crowd. For a short time, simple black Druzzi's posters were plastered over

walls, lamp posts and electricity boxes, and the lucky few who got their tickets early managed to get in. Rumours abound as to upcoming raves, so keep your eyes peeled for the posters. Buttoned Down Disco throws regular parties in a seedy basement in Soho, but it's so small, you have to apply via email to get on the free guest list.

Hoxton Pimps throw an annual three-dayer over the August bank holiday for just a fiver a day, cramming the bill to bursting point with cutting edge leftfield talent that you probably won't have even heard of yet (but soon will). But where to get your paws on a ticket, or even venue location? The cooler record shops are a great bet: **City 16** (47 Charlotte Road, The City, 7729 7839), **Phonica Records** (51 Poland Street, Soho, 7025 6070), and **Eukatech** (33 Rathbone Place, Fitzrovia, 07740 720943) all stock flyers advertising warehouse parties through the summer.

A quick glance around the stacks of flyers and a quiet chat to the staff are a great way to start your search.

The red and brown velvet sofas in this lounge bar make for a particularly relaxing setting. The music is varied and soulful, and the vibe is the purest west London cool. But be prepared to feel like a goldfish in a bowl if you're self-conscious – there's a big glass window in the front.

The Legion
348 Old Street, Shoreditch, EC1V 9NQ (7729 4441/ www.thelegionbar.com). Old Street tube/rail. **Open** 5pm-midnight Mon-Wed; 5pm-2am Thur, Fri; 6pm-2am Sat; 5-10.30pm Sun. **Admission** free. **Credit** AmEx, MC, V. **Map** p404 P4.
A long wood and brick box that has become a must on the DJ bar circuit thanks to its inspired music programming. Everything from High Fidelity (big-name DJs play their all-time fave five records before being quickly kicked off) to live acts, with one of the best jukeboxes in town.

Lock 17
11 East Yard, Camden Lock, Camden, NW1 8AB (7428 0010/www.lock17.com). Camden Town tube. **Open** 11am-11pm Mon-Thur; 11am-midnight Fri, Sat; noon-10.30pm Sun. **Admission** free. **Credit** AmEx, MC, V.
It might be set smack bang in goth and punk territory, but you won't find any lanky-haired folk here. Constant clubbing from Tuesday to Sunday, with a balcony to squeeze on and admire the Camden skyline. During summer, enjoy Sunday alldayers.

Lock Tavern
35 Chalk Farm Road, Chalk Farm, NW1 8AJ (7482 7163). Camden Town or Chalk Farm tube. **Open** noon-11pm Mon-Sat; noon-10.30pm Sun. **Admission** free.
With a beer garden at the back, two floors full of sink-into-and-never-emerge sofas and ample bar space, this is a great place to unwind or play out your recovery session. There are DJs most nights of the week, but Sundays are the musical staples, with DJs stumbling through the doors and splashing their pints over the turntables.

The Lodge
226-228 Harlesden High Street, Harlesden, NW10 4TD (8141 9509/www.thelodgebar.co.uk). Willesden junction tube/rail/Kensal Rise rail. **Open** 5-11pm Tue-Thur; 2pm-3am Fri-Sun. **Admission** free. **Credit** MC, V.
Some say Harlesden doesn't deserve a DJ Bar this good, but that would be mean to NW10 and anyway, that's the point about DJ bars – taking higher standards all over town. House hero Stuart Patterson is the brains behind this successful venture, and it shows. Standards have just been raised with a full revamp of the loos, reception area and bars, and the sound system is as good as it gets in London.

Medicine Bar
89 Great Eastern Street, Shoreditch (7739 5173). Old Street tube/rail. **Open** 5-11pm Mon-Thur; 5pm-2am Fri; 5pm-2am Sat. **Admission** £4-£7 after 9pm. **Credit** AmEx, MC, V. **Map** p405 R4.

The **Social** – come on down! *See p326.*

Stylish but comfortable, this funky and popular Shoreditch hangout fills with pre-clubbers as the post-work City drinkers fade away. The main bar gets pretty busy, so head down to the basement, which doubles as a sweaty party, home to Warm/Sonar Kollectiv's regular house bash. **Other locations**: 181 Upper Street, Islington, N1 1RX (7704 9536).

Meet
85 Charterhouse Street, Clerkenwell, EC1M 6HJ (7490 5790). Farringdon tube/rail. **Open** 11am-midnight Mon-Tue; 11am-1am Wed; 11am-4am Thur, Fri, Sat; 11am-midnight Sun. **Admission** free. **Credit** AmEx, MC, V. **Map** p404 O5.
What used to be the Lifthouse has been given a spanking new overhaul and is now Meet, small but perfectly formed on all three floors. Mixologist Gerry and co shake up fabulous cocktails while you recline on a super-comfy sofa. Up the stairs to the cocktail lounge, ideal for bigger parties, and then the 'club' space on the top floor, lined by sofas and given generous dancefloor space to jive away on. Attracting the cooler end of the post-work crowd before the night owls set in.

The Orwell
382 Essex Road, Islington, N1 3PF (7359 6110). **Open** 5-11pm Mon-Wed; 5pm-midnight Thur; 11am-4am; 5pm-2am Fri; 5pm-2am Sat; 11am-10.30pm Sun. **Admission** free. **Credit** MC, V.
Small but perfectly formed, this is a new and comfy boozer for young people. Which goes some way to explain the vintage children's wallpaper. Maybe not

Arts & Entertainment

All drinkers great and small at the **Vibe Bar**.

that young, then. There's a beer garden, and some of the squishiest sofas we've ever had the pleasure of vegetating on. Best of all, it's got a free jukebox.

Salmon & Compass

58 Penton Street, Islington, N1 9PZ (7837 3891/ www.salmonandcompass.com). Angel tube. **Open** noon-3am Mon-Thur; noon-4am Fri, Sat; noon-2am Sun. **Admission** free; £3 after 9pm Fri; £5 after 9pm Sat. **Credit** MC, V. **Map** p404 N2.
Islington's no-nonsense DJ bar packs in an up-for-it crowd on weekends with a rotating series of theme nights. Early in the week, it's chilled.

The Social

5 Little Portland Street, Marylebone, W1W 7JD (7636 4992/www.thesocial.com). Oxford Circus tube. **Open** noon-midnight; Mon-Fri; 1pm-midnight Sat. **Admission** free; £3 acoustic nights. **Credit** AmEx, MC, V. **Map** p408 U1.
Established by Heavenly Records in 1999, the Social is popular with music industry workers, minor alt-rock celebs and other sassy trendies. **Photo** *p325*. **Other locations**: 33 Linton Street, Islington, N1 7DU (7354 5809).

Vibe Bar

Old Truman Brewery, 91-95 Brick Lane, Shoreditch, E1 6QL (7426 0491/www.vibe-bar.co.uk). Aldgate East tube or Liverpool Street tube/rail. **Open** 11am-11.30pm Mon-Thur, Sun; 11am-1am Fri, Sat. **Admission** £3.50 after 8pm Fri, Sat. **Credit** AmEx, MC, V. **Map** p405 S5.
Rotating DJs and a full book of live acts play diverse styles (reggae to hip hop, proper songs to experimental leftfield). In the summer, folk hang in the fairy-lit courtyard, a convenient stumble across the road from 93 Feet East (*see p322*). **Photo** *above*.

Casinos

Thanks to the betting-friendly Labour government, gambling laws in the UK are currently in the midst of a radical overhaul. And while the newly established Gambling Commission's vow to keep betting fair and to crack down on organised crime means that Britain will have the most heavily regulated gambling industry in the world, changes are already being widely discussed.

Since October 2005, for instance, it is possible to walk into a casino, become a member and then bet straight away (previously you had to apply for membership 24 hours in advance). In addition, the government recently announced plans for a controversial new Las Vegas-style mega casino – tipped to be built in Blackpool – but that is unlikely to be opened before 2009.

Most casinos are open from mid-afternoon through to around 4am every night, and the vast majority are in central London (and as one would expect, many cluster around the traditional rich gent's playground that is Mayfair). A flip through the *Yellow Pages*, a short surf on the internet, or a chat to the concierge of your hotel will help you find a gaming establishment near you.

Check with the casino directly if you're worried about a dress code. As a rule of thumb, while casual attire – though not jeans or trainers – may be acceptable for the afternoons, in the evenings men almost always have to don a jacket and tie.

Sport & Fitness

Keep fit – or just watch and sit.

Westway Sports Centre. *See p331.*

Check the weekly Sport section of *Time Out* magazine for a comprehensive guide to the main action. For a more in-depth approach to keeping fit in the capital, choose the *Time Out Health & Fitness Guide* (£9.99).

For information on the new facilities being built for the Olympics, see www.london2012.org. For sporting events such as the London Marathon, *see pp264-270*.

Major stadiums

Crystal Palace National Sports Centre

Ledrington Road, Crystal Palace, SE19 2BB (8778 0131/www.gll.org). Crystal Palace rail.
This Grade II-listed building is in desperate need of repair. Money from Sport England gave it a stay of execution until 2006, when it will be taken over by the Mayor of London and the London Development Agency. The popular summer Grand Prix athletics event will continue for the time being, although the new Olympic stadium being built in Stratford for the 2012 Games will, when completed, become the main home of British Athletics.

Wembley Arena & Conference Centre/Wembley Stadium

Elvin House, Stadium Way, Wembley, Middx HA9 0DW (8902 8833/box office 0800 600 0870/ www.whatsonwembley.com). Wembley Park tube/ Wembley Stadium rail.

International boxing bouts, snooker and basketball tournaments and showjumping events take place infrequently at the refurbished Wembley Arena. The lavish new Wembley Stadium is due for completion in 2006 (*see p333* **Sporting giant**); for more information, see www.wembleystadium.com.

Spectator sports

Basketball

The **Towers** are in the British Basketball League. For more information, including a list of indoor and outdoor courts, contact the English Basketball Association (0870 7744 225, www.englandbasketball.co.uk).

Norray Properties London Towers

Crystal Palace National Sports Centre, Ledrington Road, Crystal Palace, SE19 2BB (8776 7755/ www.london-towers.co.uk). Crystal Palace rail.
Admission £8; £6 concessions.

Cricket

Test matches are not for those who have busy schedules, so if you're pushed for time, catch a one-day match in the C&G Trophy or Totesport League or, shorter still, the increasingly popular Twenty20 matches (20 overs per side, played in the evening). **Lord's** (home to Middlesex) and the **Brit Oval** (Surrey's home ground) also host

Test matches and one-day internationals. Book ahead, but even then you'll be lucky; your best chance of getting in is on the last day of a Test, for which tickets are not normally sold in advance (play depends on the progress of the match). Interest in the game has revived in recent years as the England team have hauled themselves from the doldrums to win an epic Test victory over the mighty Australians in 2005. The season runs from April to September.

Brit Oval

Kennington Oval, Kennington, SE11 5SS (7582 6660/7764/www.surreycricket.com). Oval tube. **Tickets** *County £10-£15. Test £40-£50.*

Lord's

St John's Wood Road, St John's Wood, NW8 8QN (MCC 7289 1611/tickets 7432 1000/www.lords. org.uk). St John's Wood tube. **Tickets** *County £12-£15. Test £40-£50.*

Football

Tickets for teams in the Barclays Premiership league are all but impossible to get your hands on, especially for glamour sides such as Chelsea and Arsenal, although the latter are moving from their Highbury stadium to a bigger new ground at nearby Ashburton Grove in summer 2006. The two clubs have become the standard-setters in the Premiership in the last two years, with Chelsea securing their first league title for 50 years in 2005. They owe their success in considerable part to the largesse of Russian oil tycoon Roman Abramovich, who has lavished millions on the club since taking over in 2003, and their astute and charismatic Portuguese manager, Jose Mourinho. Arsenal, though they lack the vast resources of their west London rivals, have won the Premiership three times and the FA Cup twice during French manager Arsène Wenger's reign. The capital's other top-flight clubs – Tottenham, West Ham, Charlton and Fulham – can only look on enviously, as the gap between the game's mega-wealthy elite and the rest widens. However, London has at least reasserted its authority over former superstars Manchester United.

There are also London clubs in the Coca-Cola Championship and both divisions of the Coca-Cola Football League, for which tickets are rather cheaper and easier to obtain. For more information, try www.thefa.com. Prices quoted are for adult non-members.

Arsenal

Until May 2006: Arsenal Stadium, Avenell Road, Highbury, N5 1BU (7704 4040/www.arsenal.com). Arsenal tube. **Tickets** *£30-£54.*
From summer 2006: Emirates Stadium, Ashburton Grove, N7. Arsenal tube.

Barnet

Underhill Stadium, Barnet Lane, Barnet. (8441 6932/www.barnetfc.com). High Barnet tube. **Tickets** *Standing £11-£13. Seated £13-£18.*

Brentford

Griffin Park, Braemar Road, Brentford, Middx (08453 456 442/www.brentfordfc.co.uk). South Ealing tube/Brentford rail. **Tickets** *Standing £13; £3-£7 concessions. Seated £17; £3-£12 concessions.*

Charlton Athletic

The Valley, Floyd Road, Charlton, SE7 8BL (8333 4010/www.cafc.co.uk). Charlton rail. **Tickets** *£20-£45.*

Chelsea

Stamford Bridge, Fulham Road, Chelsea, SW6 1HS (0870 300 1212/www.chelseafc.co.uk). Fulham Broadway tube. **Tickets** *£35-£48.* **Map** *p398 B13.*

Crystal Palace

Selhurst Park, Whitehorse Lane, Selhurst, SE25 6PU (0871 200 0071/www.cpfc.co.uk). Selhurst rail/468 bus. **Tickets** *£20-£40.*

Fulham

Craven Cottage, Stevenage Road, Fulham, SW6 6HH (0870 442 1234/www.fulhamfc.com). Putney Bridge tube. **Tickets** *£25-£49.*

Leyton Orient

Matchroom Stadium, Brisbane Road, Leyton, E10 5NF (8926 1111/tickets 8926 1010/www.leyton orient.com). Leyton tube/Leyton Midland Road rail. **Tickets** *£16.*

Millwall

The Den, Zampa Road, Bermondsey, SE16 3LN (7232 1222/tickets 7231 9999/www.millwallfc.co.uk). South Bermondsey rail. **Tickets** *£17-£29.*

Queens Park Rangers

Loftus Road Stadium, South Africa Road, Shepherd's Bush, W12 7PA (0870 112 1967/www.qpr.co.uk). White City tube. **Tickets** *£22-£28.*

Tottenham Hotspur

White Hart Lane Stadium, 748 High Road, Tottenham, N17 0AP (0870 420 5000/www.spurs. co.uk). White Hart Lane rail. **Tickets** *£26-£60.*

West Ham United

Boleyn Ground, Green Street, West Ham, E13 9AZ (0870 112 2700/www.whufc.com). Upton Park tube. **Tickets** *£30-£53.*

Greyhound racing

Watching the dogs is fun and cheap; *see p39.*

Horse racing

The racing year is divided into the flat racing season, which runs from April to September, and the National Hunt season over jumps, going

Taking the lidos

For those who like their swimming a little more bracing, London has a fine array of open-air pools. Though many have closed since the heyday of lidos in the 1920s and '30s, campaigners have been fighting in recent years to reopen some and preserve others that have come under threat of closure. See www.londonpoolscampaign.com for further details.

The following are open daily in summer; there's also one in **London Fields** that is due to reopen in 2006 (call 8356 7605 or go to www.hackney.gov.uk). All have a charge of a few pounds, with reduced fees for children (Hampstead was still free as this guide went to press, but a decision about introducing a fee was pending). The **Oasis Sports Centre** (*see p332*) also has a heated open-air pool.

Hampton Heated Open Air Pool.

Brockwell Lido
Dulwich Road, Herne Hill, SE24 0PA (7274 3088/www.thelido.co.uk). Herne Hill rail.

Charlton Lido
Hornfair Park, Charlton (8856 7180). Charlton rail.

Hampstead Heath Ponds
Hampstead Heath, NW5 1QR (7485 4491). Hampstead tube/Gospel Oak or Hampstead Heath rail/C2, C11, 214 bus.

Hampton Heated Open Air Pool
Old Deer Park, Twickenham Road, Richmond, Surrey TW9 2SF (8940 0561). Richmond tube/rail.

Park Road Pools
Park Road, Hornsey, N8 8JN (8341 3567). Finsbury Park tube/rail/Hornsey rail.

Parliament Hill Lido
Hampstead Heath, Gordon House Road, NW5 1QR (7485 5757). Gospel Oak rail/C11 bus.

Serpentine Lido
Hyde Park, W2 2UH (7706 3422/www. serpentinelido.com). Knightsbridge or South Kensington tube. **Map** p397 E8.

Tooting Bec Lido
Tooting Bec Road, Tooting Bec Common, SW16 1RU (8871 7198). Tooting Bec tube/ Streatham rail.

through the winter from October to April. For more information about the 'sport of kings', visit www.discover-racing.com.

The most famous racecourse of all, **Ascot** (www.ascot.co.uk), will reopen in June 2006 after being closed for a year while undergoing a £185 million redevelopment. The track has been realigned, and new stands and covered areas have been erected.

Epsom
Epsom Downs, Epsom, Surrey KT18 5LQ (01372 726311/www.epsomderby.co.uk). Epsom Downs or Tattenham Corner rail. **Open** *Box office* 9am-5pm Mon-Fri. **Admission** £5-£35.
The annual Derby, held here in June, is one of the great events in Britain's social and sporting calendar, attracting around 15,000 spectators every year. The impressive Queen's Stand and grandstand both offer fine viewing and restaurants.

Kempton Park
Staines Road East, Sunbury-on-Thames, Middx TW16 5AQ (01932 782292/www.kempton.co.uk). Kempton Park rail (race days only). **Open** *Box office* 9am-5pm Mon-Fri. **Admission** £7-£20.
Although it's far from glamorous, this course is the Londoner's local haunt. The year-round meetings are well attended, especially in summer.

Royal Ascot
Ascot Racecourse, Ascot, Berks SL5 7JX (01344 622211/www.ascot.co.uk). Ascot rail. **Open** phone for details.
Royal Ascot will return to its Royal Berks home this year in time for the Royal Meeting, 20-24 June. Get your top hats, posh frocks and credit cards ready for this society bash masquerading as a sporting event. Tickets to the public enclosure are usually available on the day but it's best to ring before making a special journey.

Arts & Entertainment

Sandown Park

Portsmouth Road, Esher, Surrey KT10 9AJ (01372 463072/www.sandown.co.uk). Esher rail. **Open** *Box office* 9am-5pm Mon-Fri. **Admission** £6-£35.
Most famous for hosting the Whitbread Gold Cup in April and the Coral Eclipse Stakes in July, Sandown pushes horses to the limit with a hill finish.

Windsor

Maidenhead Road, Windsor, Berks SL4 5JJ (01753 498400/tickets 0870 220 0024/www.windsor-racecourse.co.uk). Windsor & Eton Riverside rail. **Open** *Box office* 9.30am-5.30pm Mon-Fri. **Admission** £6-£20.
A pleasant Thames-side location in the shadow of Windsor Castle helps to make this a lovely spot for first-timers and families, especially during the three-day festival in May or on one of its summer Monday evening meetings.

Motorsport

Wimbledon Stadium (8946 8000, www.wimbledonstadium.co.uk) is the place to come for pedal-to-the-metal entertainment: speedway motorbike racing takes place on Wednesdays; every other Sunday bangers, hot rods and stock cars come together for family-oriented mayhem.

Rugby league

The heartland of rugby league remains the north of England, where teams such as Leeds, Bradford and Wigan attract large crowds. But the capital's one Super League club, the London Broncos, have remained at the highest level of the domestic game despite leading a somewhat nomadic existence. They will be changing both their name and ground in 2006: so it's bye-bye Broncos, hello **Harlequins Rugby League**. The change is the result of a partnership deal with the rugby union club of the same name, whose ground at the Stoop in **Twickenham** will now be shared with the league club.

Harlequins Rugby League

Stoop Memorial Ground, Langhorn Drive, Twickenham (0871 871 8877). Twickenham rail. **Admission** £12-£15 in advance; £15-£18 on the day.

Rugby union

The popularity of the ruffians' sport is difficult to ignore – particularly after England's historic victory in the 2003 Rugby World Cup. Fans come out in full force to watch the annual **Six Nations Championship** (January to March). Tickets for these games – which take place at Twickenham (Rugby Road, Twickenham, Middx, 8892 2000; *see p183*), the home of English Rugby Union – are virtually impossible to get hold of, but other matches are more

accessible. The **Guinness Premiership** and the three-division **National League** run from August to May; most games are played on Saturday and Sunday afternoons.
Listed below are the Premiership clubs. For a more comprehensive list, contact the Rugby Football Union (8892 2000, www.rfu.com).

London Irish

Madejski Stadium, Shooters Way, Reading, RG2 0SL (0870 999 1871/www.london-irish.com). Reading rail then shuttle bus to ground (£2). **Tickets** £5-£25.

London Wasps

Causeway Stadium, Hillbottom Road, High Wycombe HP12 4HJ (8993 8298/tickets 0870 414 1515/www.wasps.co.uk). High Wycombe rail. **Tickets** £18-£40.

Saracens

Vicarage Road Stadium, Watford, Herts WD18 0EP (01923 475222/www.saracens.com). Watford High Street rail. **Open** *Box office* 9am-5.30pm Mon-Fri. **Tickets** £14-£30.

Tennis

Getting to see the action at the **Wimbledon Championships** at the All England Lawn Tennis Club (26 June-9 July 2006; *see also p182*) requires forethought: seats on Centre and Number One courts are applied for by ballot the previous year, although enthusiasts who queue on the day may gain entry to the outer courts. You can also turn up later in the day and pay a reasonable rate for seats vacated by spectators who have left early. Wimbledon is preceded by the Stella Artois tournament, where stars from the men's circuit can be seen warming up for the main event: the 2006 tournament will be held from 12-18 June at Queen's Club.

All England Lawn Tennis Club

PO Box 98, Church Road, Wimbledon, SW19 5AE (8944 1066/tickets 8971 2700/information 8946 2244/www.wimbledon.org). Southfields tube.

Queen's Club

Palliser Road, West Kensington, W14 9EQ (7385 3421/ticket information 0870 890 0518/www.queens club.co.uk). Barons Court tube.

Participation sports & fitness

Cycling

Speed merchants can pedal round the following bike circuits. For those wanting to hire a bike and zip around town, *see p365*. Current venues include the **Herne Hill Velodrome** (Burbage Road, Herne Hill, SE24 9HE (7737 4647, www.hernehillvelodrome.org.uk), the oldest cycle circuit in the world, and the **Lee Valley Cycle Circuit** (Quartermile Lane, Stratford (8534 6085, www.leevalleypark.org.uk), with facilities for BMX, road-racing, mountain biking, time trials and cyclo-cross. The velopark being built in Stratford for the 2012 Olympics will offer mountain biking and road cycling routes, as well as a BMX circuit, once the Games are over.

Golf

You don't have to be a member to tee off at any of the public courses below – but do book in advance. For a list of clubs in the London area, go to www.englishgolfunion.org.

Dulwich & Sydenham Hill
Grange Lane, College Road, Dulwich, SE21 7LH (8693 8491/www.dulwichgolf.co.uk). Sydenham Hill rail. **Open** 8am-dusk daily. **Green fee** £35; £17.50 members' guests Mon-Fri.
A lovely-looking course with fantastic views. Note that it's members (with guests) only at weekends.

North Middlesex
Manor House, Friern Barnet Lane, Arnos Grove, N20 0NL (8445 3060/www.northmiddlesexgc.co.uk). Arnos Grove or Totteridge & Whetstone tube. **Open** 8am-dusk Mon-Fri; 1pm-dusk Sat, Sun. **Green fee** £15-£27 Mon-Fri; £25-£32 Sat, Sun.
An undulating course set in 74 acres and dating back to 1905. Not one for beginners.

Health clubs & sports centres

Many clubs and centres admit non-members and even allow them to join classes. Some of the main contenders are listed below; for a list of all venues in Camden and Westminster, call 7974 4456 and 7641 1846, respectively. Note that last entry to the following gyms is normally 45-60 minutes before the closing times given. For more independent spirits, Hyde Park, Kensington Gardens and Battersea Park have particularly good jogging trails.

Central YMCA
112 Great Russell Street, Bloomsbury, WC1B 3NQ (7343 1700/www.centralymca.org.uk). Tottenham Court Road tube. **Open** 6.30am-10.30pm Mon-Fri; 10am-8.30pm Sat; 10am-7.30pm Sun. **Map** p401 K5.
Conveniently located and user-friendly, the Y has a good range of cardiovascular and weight-training equipment, a pool, and a squash court, as well as a full timetable of excellently taught classes.

Jubilee Hall Leisure Centre
30 The Piazza, Covent Garden, WC2E 8BE (7836 4835/www.jubileehallclubs.co.uk). Covent Garden tube. **Open** 7am-10pm Mon-Fri; 9am-9pm Sat; 10am-5pm Sun. **Map** p409 Z3.
For cardiovascular workouts in calm surroundings, this central venue is a reliable bet.

Queen Mother Sports Centre
223 Vauxhall Bridge Road, Victoria, SW1V 1EL (7630 5522/www.courtneys.co.uk). Victoria tube/rail. **Open** 6.30am-10pm Mon-Fri; 8am-8pm Sat, Sun. **Map** p402 J10.
A busy venue with a pool, the QM has plenty of decent sweating and lifting facilities.

Seymour Leisure Centre
Seymour Place, Marylebone, W1H 5TJ (7723 8019/ www.courtneys.co.uk). Edgware Road tube. **Open** 6.30am-10pm Mon-Fri; 7am-8pm Sat; 8am-8pm Sun. **Map** p397 F5.
Unglamorous but central, the Seymour has a pool and enough weights to get the job done.

Soho Gym
12 Macklin Street, Holborn, WC2B 5NF (7242 1290/www.sohogyms.com). Holborn tube. **Open** 7am-10pm Mon-Fri; 8am-8pm Sat; noon-6pm Sun. **Map** p409 Y2
Busy and well-equipped, Soho Gym is particularly notable for its gay-friendly atmosphere.

Westway Sports Centre
1 Crowthorne Road, Ladbroke Grove, W10 6RP (8969 0992/www.westway.org). Ladbroke Grove or Latimer Road tube. **Open** 8am-10pm Mon-Fri; 8am-8pm Sat; 10am-10pm Sun.
A smart, diverse activity centre, with all-weather pitches, tennis courts and the largest indoor climbing facility in the country. **Photo** p327.

Ice skating

Broadgate is London's only permanent outdoor rink, but beautiful Somerset House has an outdoor rink over the Christmas period, as does Marble Arch and the spectacular Hampton Court Palace (*see p271* **Air play**).

Alexandra Palace Ice Rink
Alexandra Palace Way, Muswell Hill, N22 7AY (8365 4386/www.alexandrapalace.com). Wood Green tube/W3 bus. **Open** 11am-1.30pm, 2-5.30pm Mon-Fri; 10.30am-12.30pm, 2-4.30pm, 8.30-11pm Sat, Sun. **Admission** £6; £5 concessions.

Riding

There are various riding stables in and around the city; for a list of those approved by the British Horse Society, see www.bhs.org.uk. The following run classes for all ages and abilities.

Hyde Park & Kensington Stables
63 Bathurst Mews, Lancaster Gate, W2 2SB (7723 2813/www.hydeparkstables.com). Lancaster Gate tube. **Open** *Summer* 7.15am-5pm daily. *Winter* 7.15am-3pm daily. **Fees** £45-£85/hr. **Map** p397 D6.

Wimbledon Village Stables
24 High Street, Wimbledon, SW19 5DX (8946 8579/ www.wimbledonvillagestables.co.uk). Wimbledon tube/ rail. **Open** 9am-5pm Tue-Sun. **Fees** £35-£40/hr.

Street sports

Baysixty6 Skate Park under the Westway in Acklam Road, W10, has a large street course and four halfpipes, all wooden and covered (8969 4669, www.baysixty6.com). Though **Stockwell Skate Park** (www.stockwellskate park.com) is the city's most popular outdoor park, it's about to be rivalled by **Cantelowes Gardens** on Camden Road, Camden, due to be finished by the end of 2006 (*see also p83* **Save our South Bank**). Many prefer unofficial street spots such as the South Bank under the **Royal Festival Hall** (banks, steps and blocks, *see p83*). Skaters also collect at the Sprite Urban Games held on Clapham Common every July (see www.spriteurbangames.com).

Inline skaters and BMXers tend to use the same skateparks. Inliners should keep an eye on www.londonskaters.com for a diary of inline events across the city, including free lessons, mass skates, and extreme exhibitions.

Swimming

To find your nearest pool check the *Yellow Pages*. Listed below are three of the best (*see also p331* **Health clubs & sports centres**). For pools particularly well suited to children, check www.britishswimming.co.uk. Or if alfresco swimming is more your thing, *see p329* **Taking the lidos**.

Highbury Pool

Highbury Crescent, Highbury, N5 1RR (7704 2312/ www.aquaterra.org). Highbury & Islington tube/rail. **Open** 6.30am-10pm Mon-Fri; 7.30am-7.30pm Sat; 7.30am-10pm Sun. *Women only* 7.30-10pm Tue. **Admission** £3.20; £1.30-£2.60 concessions; free under-4s.
Hidden away at the bottom of Highbury Fields, this compact pool building is light, airy and has laudably clean facilities. A pleasure to visit.

Ironmonger Row Baths

Ironmonger Row, EC1V 3QF (7253 4011/www.aqua terra.org). Old Street tube/rail. **Open** 6.30am-9pm Mon; 6.30am-8pm Tue-Thur; 6.30am-7pm Fri; 9am-5.30pm Sat; noon-5pm Sun. **Admission** £3.20; £1.50 concessions; free under-3s. **Map** p404 P4.
A 31m pool with excellent lane swimming; the site also features good-value Turkish baths.

Oasis Sports Centre

32 Endell Street, Covent Garden, WC2H 9AG (7831 1804). Holborn tube. **Open** *Indoor pool* 6.30am-6.30pm Mon, Wed; 6.30am-7.15pm Tue, Thur, Fri; 9.30am-9pm Sat, Sun. *Outdoor pool* (lane swimming only) 7.30am-9pm Mon-Wed, Fri; 7.30am-8.30pm Thur; 9.30am-5.30pm Sat, Sun. **Admission** £3.30; £1.30 concessions; free under-5s. **Map** p409 Y2.
A central London gem renowned for its sun terrace and outdoor pool; adjacent is an indoor version.

Tennis

If you're not quite ready to play at Wimbledon (*see p330*), many parks around the city have council-run courts that cost little or nothing to use. For lessons, try the **Regent's Park Golf & Tennis School** (7724 0643, www.rpgts. co.uk). For grass courts, phone the Lawn Tennis Association's Information Department (7381 7000, www.lta.org.uk). The **Westway Sports Centre** in Ladbroke Grove (*see p331*) has both indoor and outdoor courts for hire.

Islington Tennis Centre

Market Road, Islington, N7 9PL (7700 1370/ www.aquaterra.org). Caledonian Road tube/ Caledonian Road & Barnsbury rail. **Open** 7am-10pm Mon-Fri; 7am-9pm Sat, Sun. **Court hire** *Indoor* £17.50; £7.80 concessions. *Outdoor* £7.80; £3.90 concessions. **Credit** MC, V.
Offers both indoor and outdoor courts. Membership card holders qualify for a £1 discount per session, as well as booking privileges. Non-members can only book a maximum of five days in advance.

Ten-pin bowling

A useful first stop when looking for lanes is the **British Ten-pin Bowling Association** (8478 1745, www.btba.org.uk).

Rowans Bowl

10 Stroud Green Road, Finsbury Park, N4 2DF (8800 1950/www.rowans.co.uk). Finsbury Park tube/rail or Crouch Hill rail. **Open** 10.30am-12.30am Mon-Thur, Sun; 10.30am-2.30am Fri, Sat. **Admission** *Per game* £1-£3. **Lanes** 24.

Streatham MegaBowl

142 Streatham Hill, Streatham, SW2 4RU (8678 6007/www.megabowl.co.uk). Streatham Hill rail. **Open** noon-midnight Mon-Tue; noon-1am Wed-Fri; 10am-1am Sat; 10am-midnight Sun. **Admission** *Per game* £5.50; £4.25 concessions. **Lanes** 36.

Yoga & Pilates

For something more than just a quick stretch in your hotel room, check out one of the many special yoga activities and classes (and the fully equipped Pilates studio) at Triyoga. You may want to consult the **British Wheel of Yoga** (www.bwy.org.uk), the excercise's governing body in Britain.

Triyoga

6 Erskine Road, Primrose Hill, NW3 3DJ (7483 3344/www.triyoga.co.uk). Chalk Farm tube. **Open** 6am-10pm Mon-Fri; 8am-8.30pm Sat; 9am-9.30pm Sun. **Cost** *Per session* £6-£13.
Triyoga's large range of yogas includes Ashtanga, Iyengar and Pilates. Massages, facials, homeopathy, acupuncture and other treatments are also offered.

Sporting giant

English football fans remember 7 October 2000 as a day of endings. England lost against Germany in their World Cup qualifying match at Wembley, prompting manager Kevin Keegan's immediate resignation after a forgettable stint at the helm. But Keegan's departure was overshadowed by a second, more heartfelt farewell – to Wembley Stadium itself, whose characteristic twin towers had presided over the home of English football since 1924. In its illustrious lifetime old Wembley saw countless Cup Finals and major internationals; in its latter years it had doubled as a world-famous rock stadium, hosting Live Aid in 1985 and the legendary Queen concert the following summer.

The old stadium was iconic and historic, but the new one is looking firmly to the future by breaking records. When it's completed – and it should be ready in time for the 2006 FA Cup final – Wembley will be the largest football stadium in the world, with room for some 90,000 supporters. Visitors will be able to refuel from one of a reputed 688 food and drink outlets. And 2,618 toilets will also outdo the amenities of any other world stadium (or building, apparently). The iconic twin towers have been replaced by a bigger, bolder feature – an enormous latticed steel arch bestriding the whole stadium, the largest single-span roof structure in the world. At 133 metres tall, it is 100 metres higher than the old towers, and so big that the entire London Eye could be rolled underneath it (if anyone chose to do so).

The arch, which can be seen 13 miles away at Canary Wharf, is prodigious architect Sir Norman Foster's latest stamp on London's skyline, but it's not just a cosmetic addition. It sustains the stadium roof from above, removing the need for supporting pillars inside the stadium – which means that every spectator has an uninterrupted view of the action. But that's not all. The attention to detail in the stadium's planning is frankly phenomenal. Dozens of grass varieties were tested for their suitability on the pitch, and even the stadium's acoustics were calculated meticulously so that the optimum atmosphere could be ensured.

Wembley will begin hosting fixtures again from May 2006. It will remain the national stadium for football – what it's most famous for – but will also be used for rugby, athletics and music concerts. In 2012 it will become a key venue in London's Olympic Games. And by generating thousands of new jobs and many millions of pounds of income for the area, the stadium should accelerate the redevelopment of a decidedly run-down corner of the capital. Brent Council envisages the Wembley of the future as a bustling, cosmopolitan precinct with state-of-the-art living, working and shopping facilities.

Theatre

Tread the boards without breaking a leg.

In London's theatreland, 2005 was a good year for names in neon – Val Kilmer, Brooke Shields, Ewan McGregor, Sienna Miller (admittedly, the latter attracted more attention for her love life than her appearance on stage) – and an even better one for bums on seats. Hollywood film stars increasingly seem to favour a stint on the capital's stage as a means of getting noticed, while audiences lap up the associated glamour (*see p338* **From West Coast to West End**).

Ticket sales are not hitting millions for stardust alone, however. Quality, particularly for musicals, is very high, with the likes of *Billy Elliot* and *Guys and Dolls* deservedly getting top marks from the critics. Crack artistic teams for such big projects are now assembled from the ranks of superior creative venues like the **National Theatre** and **Royal Court**, ensuring a higher class of production.

Of course, there was bad news too in 2005: the clear threat of terrorism created by the bombings of 7 July resulted in the cancellation of all performances, for only the second time since World War II (Princess Diana's funeral also prompted a city-wide shutdown). However, it's clear that a concerted effort by the Mayor's recent tourist drive and the theatres themselves are beginning to woo the luvvie-lovers back in.

But if the cast lists and attendance figures are in good health, the theatres themselves are still a touch on the dusty side. In July 2005 Lord Andrew Lloyd Webber sold four of his 12 West End venues to an American multi-millionaire, saying he plans to use the £10 million raised to improve his remaining dramatic assets. Other West End impresarios, including Sir Cameron Mackintosh, have also promised to put more cash into modernising their theatres, which are often awkwardly designed Edwardian buildings awash with fraying red velvet.

For all the latest developments, reviews and practical information, check the theatre section of the weekly *Time Out* magazine. The Society of London Theatre's website, www.official londontheatre.co.uk, also has some useful links.

WHERE TO GO AND WHAT TO SEE

Although the West End, strictly speaking, is not a geographical term, for most Londoners it is synonymous with the traditional theatre quarter clustered around Shaftesbury Avenue. Venues in this area tend to host transfers of successful smaller-scale productions, plus the usual blockbusting fare. More polished and more innovative venues such as the National Theatre on the South Bank, or the Royal Court in Chelsea, are still considered West End, despite their location.

Off-West End denotes smaller budgets and smaller capacity. These theatres – many of which are sponsored or subsidised – push the creative envelope with new, experimental writing, often brought to life by the cream of acting and directing talent. The **Soho Theatre** and the **Bush** are good for up-and-coming playwrights, while the **Almeida** and **Donmar Warehouse** are safe bets for classy production values, sometimes with big international names. Lurking under the Fringe moniker are dozens of smaller theatres, not always guaranteed to deliver quality, but nevertheless mobbed by hopefuls looking for their London stage debut. The **Menier Chocolate Factory** (51-53 Southwark Street, Bankside, SE1, 7907 7060), which is housed, unsurprisingly, in a former chocolate factory, is an attractive new fringe venue with reliable, mainstream fare and a restaurant attached – great for a glass of wine and pudding post-play. The small but accomplished **Arcola Theatre** (27 Arcola Street, E8, 7503 1646) in Dalston, meanwhile, is worth the trek for fresh writing voices. In Kingston-upon-Thames in Surrey, Sir Peter Hall's pet project, the Elizabethan-style **Rose of Kingston** theatre, is due to open in 2006 (24-26 High Street, 8546 6983).

Last but not least, all-singing, all-dancing Middle Earth adventures are due to arrive in London in autumn 2006, when the musical of the **Lord of the Rings** transfers from its opening run in Toronto. For updates, go to www.lotr.com.

TICKETS AND INFORMATION

The first rule to observe when buying tickets for London performances is to book ahead. The second rule is to bypass agents and go direct to the theatre's box office. Booking agencies such as **Ticketmaster** (7344 4444, www.ticketmaster.co.uk) and **First Call** (7420 0000, www.firstcalltickets.com) sell tickets to many shows, but you'll get hit with booking fees that could top a whopping 20 per cent.

In a late bid to fill their venues, many West End theatres offer reduced-price tickets for shows that have not sold out. These seats,

Arts & Entertainment

available only on the night, are known as 'standby' tickets, and usually sell for about half what a top-priced ticket would normally cost. Always call to check both the availability and the conditions: some standby deals are limited to those with student ID, and some offer reduced sightlines.

Alternatively, try **tkts**, a non-profit-making organisation run from the clocktower building in Leicester Square by the Society of London Theatre. The booths sell tickets for West End shows on a first-come, first-served basis on the day of the performance. For locations of the main central London theatres, see the street maps on pages 408-409.

tkts

Clocktower building, Leicester Square, WC2H 7NA (www.officiallondontheatre.co.uk). Leicester Square tube. **Open** 10am-7pm Mon-Sat; noon-3pm Sun. **Credit** AmEx, DC, MC, V. **Map** p409 X4. **Other locations:** Canary Wharf DLR, Platforms 4/5. **Open** 10am-3.30pm Mon-Sat.

West End

Barbican Centre

Silk Street, City, EC2Y 8DS (0845 120 7550/www. barbican.org.uk). Barbican or Moorgate tube/rail. **Box office** 9am-8pm daily. **Tickets** *Barbican* £7-£50. *Pit* £15. **Credit** AmEx, MC, V. **Map** p404 P5.
The Queen called this concrete behemoth 'one of the wonders of the modern world' when it opened in the 1970s. Most people are not so sure about the architecture, but as an arts centre the Barbican is in good shape. It offers an eclectic mix of touring regional and foreign theatre companies during the BITE season (Barbican International Theatre Events). In addition to the main stage, there is also the more intimate 200-seater Pit theatre.

National Theatre

South Bank, SE1 9PX (information 7452 3400/ box office 7452 3000/www.nationaltheatre.org.uk). Embankment or Southwark tube/Waterloo tube/rail. **Box office** 10am-8pm Mon-Sat. **Tickets** *Olivier & Lyttelton* £10-£36. *Cottesloe* £10-£27.50. *Standby* £18. **Credit** AmEx, DC, MC, V. **Map** p403 M8.
The National continues to be fighting fit under the watch of Nicholas Hytner as artistic director. It can still afford to cherry-pick new writing voices (for example, Rebecca Lenkiewicz with the *Night Season*) and sponsor innovative performing groups such as Shunt, the offbeat, vaudevillesque physical theatre group. Wonderfully crafted takes on classics like *Henry IV* fill its programme out to suit most tastes. The Travelex season, where two-thirds of the seats are offered for £10, has brought new blood to the audiences and is set to continue for at least another year. During the summer the free outdoor performing arts stage is a great way to see booty-shaking Bhangra or fire-swallowing avant-garde dancers by the Thames.

Old Vic

Waterloo Road, Waterloo, SE1 8NB (0870 060 6628/www.oldvictheatre.com). Waterloo tube/ rail. **Box office** 9am-9pm Mon-Sat; 10am-6pm Sun. **Tickets** £10-£40. **Credit** AmEx, MC, V. **Map** p406 N9.
Kevin Spacey's inaugural year as artistic director of this almost 200-year-old theatre was not the firework display that many hoped for. His choices were damned as too safe, but Spacey defended them by saying the more accessible works would tempt otherwise reluctant theatregoers. Box office takings are very much in the pink but the double-Oscar winner will undoubtedly want at least a few crumbs of critical praise. Spacey's biggest coup for the 2006 line-up is set to be Hollywood director Robert Altman staging *Resurrection Blues*, the last play written by Arthur Miller.

Open Air Theatre

Regent's Park, Marylebone, NW1 4NR (7935 5756/box office 0870 060 1811/www.openair theatre.org). Baker Street tube. **Repertory season** June-Sept; phone for details. **Tickets** £10-£32 *Standby* £10 (approx). **Credit** AmEx, DC, MC, V. **Map** p400 G3.
The lovely verdant setting of this alfresco theatre lends itself perfectly to summery Shakespeare romps. Standards are far above village green dramatics, with productions of the Bard particularly imaginative. Book well ahead and take an extra layer for chills in Act 3. Buy good-value, tasty grub on-site, or eat at the funkily refurbed Garden Café.

Royal Court

Sloane Square, Chelsea, SW1W 8AS (7565 5000/ www.royalcourttheatre.com). Sloane Square tube. **Box office** 10am-6pm Mon-Sat. **Tickets** 10p-£27.50; all tickets £7.50 Mon. **Credit** AmEx, MC, V. **Map** p402 G11.
This temple of new writing turns 50 in 2006, and there are lashings of events planned to celebrate. Prestigious British playwrights will premiere new work, including Tom Stoppard with *Rock'n'Roll*, a play about guitars and beliefs set in Prague during the recent revolution. To shine up the theatre's luminous back catalogue, there will also be rehearsed readings of all past Royal Court productions, for which many of the original casts are being reassembled.

Royal Shakespeare Company

Novello Theatre (previously Strand Theatre) Aldwych, WC2B 4CD (0870 950 0940/www. delfontmackintosh.co.uk/www.rsc.org.uk). Holborn tube/Charing Cross tube/rail. **Box office** *In person* 10am-7.30pm Mon-Sat. *By phone* 24hrs daily. **Tickets** £10-£39. **Credit** AmEx, MC, V. **Map** p409 Z3.
Hopping from stage to stage since quitting its Barbican residence in 2002, the RSC can now look forward to a stable London home – it has just signed a deal with Sir Cameron Mackintosh's West End empire to take up a five-year residency at the newly renovated Novello Theatre. The 2006 season is devoted to the Bard's comedies.

Arts & Entertainment

From West Coast to West End

Kevin Spacey in *Richard II*.

Sunset Boulevard must seem a long way away when you're beautifying in a less than palatial West End dressing room. But Hollywood stars these days don't seem to mind. They are flooding on to London stages, red carpet or not. A big starry name almost guarantees fattened ticket sales, but as Val Kilmer discovered recently, when appearing at the Playhouse Theatre in *The Postman Always Rings Twice*, critical praise can't be bought. 'He comes across as a bovine lunk-head,' observed one critic. Leading director Sir Peter Hall last year also attempted a mini backlash against the trend by saying that home-grown talent was being upstaged by West Coast hype. (His stance wobbled slightly when others pointed out that he had directed *Sex and the City*'s Kim Cattrall in *Whose Life Is it Anyway?* at the Comedy Theatre.)

But the line-up of familiar faces who came 'over here' in 2005 suggests that the exchange is still a happy one: audiences get idols in the flesh, and the idols have a chance to get back to their more actorly roots, or to start growing them. Rob Lowe, Matt Damon, David Schwimmer and Christian Slater, all pin-ups of a certain age, declared themselves delighted to be in London and making their

West End debut ('It's an actor's dream,' said Lowe), while Mexican dreamboat Gael García Bernal prompted very un-arthouse ticket queues at the Almeida, the venue for his (so-so) performance in *Blood Wedding*.

Two Tinseltown emissaries involved in the original Atlantic-hopping trend kicked off in the late '90s look set to create headlines again in 2006. Nicole Kidman, whose almost-naked turn in Sam Mendes' 1998 staging of the *Blue Room* at the Donmar Warehouse was famously described as 'theatrical Viagra', is rumoured to coming back to the West End to play the miserable heroine of Ibsen's *Hedda Gabler*. Kevin Spacey, meanwhile, who garnered largely positive reviews for his enigmatic title performance in the 2005 production of *Richard II* at the Old Vic, but criticised for shallowness in his role as artistic director there, has pulled some heavyweight strings for his 2006 season. This time the coup relates to the behind-the-scenes players, with Spacey persuading director Robert Altman to stage *Resurrection Blues*, the last and unfinished play by Arthur Miller. No doubt there will be more than a handful of thesps in Los Angeles ready to fight for a part.

Shakespeare's Globe

21 New Globe Walk, Bankside, SE1 9DT (7401 9919/
www.shakespeares-globe.org). Mansion House tube/
London Bridge tube/rail. **Box office** *Off season*
10am-5pm Mon-Fri. *Theatre* 10am-8pm daily.
Tickets £5-£29. **Credit** AmEx, MC, V. **Map** p406 O7.
Part of a formidable axis of London tourism (as
neighbour to Tate Modern and the Millennium
Bridge), the Globe has sometimes struggled to be
taken seriously as a space for Shakespeare performance. A faithful construction of its Elizabethan
predecessor, and built on the same spot, it trades
well at the box office for the Bard's greatest hits, but
the recently appointed artistic director Dominic
Dromgoole wants to give more muscle to modern
playwrights. Stamina is needed among the foot-
shuffling pit audience, who stand. **Photo** *p342.*

Long-runners & musicals

Billy Elliot the Musical

Victoria Palace Theatre, Victoria Street, Victoria,
SW1E 5EA (0870 895 5577/www.victoriapalace
theatre.co.uk). Victoria tube. **Tickets** £17.50-£55.
Map p402 H10.
Set during the miner's strike of 1984, this lovable
story of a working-class northern boy with balletic
talent burning in his shoes makes an excellent trans-
fer from screen to stage. Scored by Elton John and
directed by Stephen Daldry.

Chicago

Adelphi Theatre, Strand, Covent Garden, WC2E
7NA (Ticketmaster 08704 030303/www.ticket
master.co.uk). Charing Cross tube/rail. **Box office**
In person 10am-8pm Mon-Sat. *By phone* 24hrs daily.
Tickets £12.50-£45. **Credit** AmEx, MC, V.
Map p409 Y4.
The jailbird roles are passed at regular intervals
from one blonde TV star to the next, but this production still razzle dazzles 'em with high spirits.

Guys and Dolls

Piccadilly Theatre, Denman Street, Soho, W1D 7DY
(0870 060 0123/www.guysanddollsthemusical.com).
Piccadilly Circus tube. **Box office** *By phone* 9am-
9pm Mon-Sat; 10am-6pm Sun. 10am-6.30pm Mon-Sat.
Tickets £15-£55. **Map** p408 V4.
The guys shoot craps and the dolls hit the high notes
in Michael Grandage's top-notch take on gamblers,
lovers and losers in 1940s New York.

High Society

Shaftesbury Theatre, Shaftesbury Avenue, Soho,
WC2H 8DP (7379 5399/www.highsocietymusical.
co.uk). Holborn or Tottenham Court Road tube.
Box office *In person* 10am-8pm Mon-Sat. *By phone*
24hrs daily. **Tickets** £17.50-£45. **Credit** AmEx,
MC, V. **Map** p409 Y2.
An heiress has to choose between three suitors in Cole
Porter's classic. No cast will ever match the original
for charisma, but Jerry Hall proved a big attraction
before illness forced her to quit. Hit songs include
'Who Wants to be a Millionaire?'

Les Misérables

Queen's Theatre, Shaftesbury Avenue, Soho, W1D
8AS (7494 5040/www.lesmis.com). Leicester Square
or Piccadilly Circus tube. **Box office** *In person* 10am-
7.30pm Mon-Sat. *Seetickets* 24-hrs daily. **Tickets**
£12.50-£47.50. **Credit** AmEx, MC, V. **Map** p408 W3.
The RSC's version of Boublil and Schönberg's musical continues to idealise the struggles of the poor in
Victor Hugo's revolutionary Paris.

The Lion King

Lyceum Theatre, Wellington Street, Covent Garden,
WC2E 7DA (7420 8112/box office 0870 243 9000/
www.disney.co.uk). Covent Garden tube/Charing
Cross tube/rail. **Box office** 10am-6pm Mon-Sat.
Tickets £14.40-£49.50. **Credit** AmEx, MC, V.
Map p409 Z3.
This Disney extravaganza about an orphaned
young lion cub struggling to grow up and find his
place on the savannah has been widely acclaimed,
particularly by those who have small children.

Mamma Mia!

Prince of Wales Theatre, 31 Coventry Street, Soho,
W1D 6AS (0870 850 0393/www.mamma-mia.com).
Leicester Square tube. **Box office** *In person* 10am-
7.30pm Mon-Thur, Sat; 10am-7.30pm Fri. *By phone*
24-hrs daily. **Tickets** £25-£55. **Credit** AmEx, MC,
V. **Map** p408 W4.
This feel-good musical links Abba's hits into a con-
tinuous but spurious story. Endlessly popular.

Mary Poppins

Prince Edward Theatre, Old Compton Street, Soho,
W1D 4NS (0870 850 9191/www.marypoppinsthe
musical.co.uk). Leicester Square tube. **Box office**
10am-8pm Mon-Sat. **Tickets** £15-£55. **Credit**
AmEx, MC, V. **Map** p408 W2/3.
Chipper chimney sweeps and spoonfuls of magic
in this enchanting take on the children's classic,
directed by Sir Richard Eyre.

The Mousetrap

St Martin's Theatre, West Street, Covent Garden,
WC2H 9NZ (0870 162 8787). Leicester Square tube.
Box office *In person* 10am-8pm Mon-Sat. *By phone*
24hrs. **Tickets** £11.50-£35. **Credit** AmEx, MC, V.
Map p409 X3.
It's looking unlikely the mouse will ever be caught.

The Producers

Theatre Royal Drury Lane, Catherine Street, Covent
Garden, WC2B 5JF (0870 890 1109). Covent
Garden tube. **Box office** *In person* 10am-8pm
Mon-Sat. *By phone* 24 hrs daily. **Tickets** £10-£49.
Credit AmEx, MC, V. **Map** p409 Z3.
Showered with Tony awards on Broadway, this is
Mel Brooks's hilarious story of two producers whose
insurance fraud is bungled when their deliberately
awful show, *Springtime for Hitler*, becomes a hit.

We Will Rock You

Dominion Theatre, Tottenham Court Road, Fitzrovia,
W1P 0AG (7413 1713/ticketmaster 0870 169 0116/
www.londondominion.co.uk). Tottenham Court Road

Arts & Entertainment

tube. **Box office** *In person* 9am-7.45pm Mon-Sat.
By phone 24hrs. **Tickets** £16.50-£49. **Credit**
AmEx, MC, V. **Map** p408 W1.
All your favourite Queen hits, unconvincingly rendered and stitched together by a deeply feeble Ben Elton plot. Freddie would have hated it.

The Woman in White
Palace Theatre, Shaftesbury Avenue, Soho,
W1D 5AY (0870 895 5579/www.womaninwhite
themusical.com). Leicester Square tube. **Box office**
In person 10am-8pm Mon-Sat. *Seetickets* 24hrs
daily. **Tickets** £12.50-£50. **Credit** AmEx, MC, V.
Map p409 X3.
Lloyd Webber's downturned career in musicals gets a jolt with this mostly likeable adaptation of Wilkie Collins's enigmatic Victorian thriller. Woozy stage projections accompany some awkward melodies, refreshed by flashes of wit and a fine cast.

Off-West End

Almeida
Almeida Street, Islington, N1 1TA (7359 4404/
www.almeida.co.uk). Angel tube. **Box office** *In*
person 10am-7.30pm Mon-Sat. *By phone* 24hrs
daily. **Tickets** £6-£29.50. **Credit** AmEx, MC, V.
Map p404 O1.
The well-groomed Almeida turns out thoughtfully crafted theatre for grown-ups. Besides frequent casting coups (most recently, Gael Garcia Bernal in *Blood Wedding*) it also commands loyalty from top directors such as Howard Davies and Sir Richard Eyre. Under artistic director Michael Attenborough, its seasons dust off European plays in translation (recently, Molière's *The Hypochondriac*) and revivals such as Tennessee Williams' *Period of Adjustment*.

BAC (Battersea Arts Centre)
Lavender Hill, Battersea, SW11 5TN (7223 2223/
www.bac.org.uk). Clapham Common tube/Clapham
Junction rail/77, 77A, 345 bus. **Box office** *In*
person 10am-6pm Mon; 10am-9pm Tue-Fri; 4-8pm
Sat, Sun. *By phone* 10am-6pm Mon-Fri; 4.30-7pm
Sat, Sun. **Tickets** £5.50-£12.75; 'pay what you can'
Tue (phone ahead). **Credit** MC, V.
The forward-thinking BAC plays alma mater to new writers and companies. Expect the very latest in quirky, fun and physical theatre, particularly post-Edinburgh festival when BAC scouts return to London with their next big things. Artistic director David Jubb's track record includes starting up the now-infamous Scratch programme, which shows a work in progress to progressively larger audiences until it's finished and polished (this is how *Jerry Springer – The Opera* got started).

The Bush
Shepherd's Bush Green, Shepherd's Bush, W12
8QD (7610 4224/www.bushtheatre.co.uk). Goldhawk
Road or Shepherd's Bush tube. **Box office** *In person*
5-8pm Mon-Sat (performance nights only). *By phone*
10am-7pm Mon-Sat. **Tickets** £8.50-£14. **Credit**
AmEx, MC, V.

Soho Theatre. *See p342.*

A small, cash-poor champion of new writers and performers, the Bush has over 30 years' experience under its belt. Alumni include Stephen Poliakoff, Mike Leigh and Jim Broadbent, so watch that space. The Bush receives – and reads – over 1,500 scripts every year.

Donmar Warehouse
41 Earlham Street, Covent Garden, WC2H 9LX
(0870 060 6624/www.donmarwarehouse.com).
Covent Garden or Leicester Square tube. **Box**
office *In person* 10am-7.30pm Mon-Sat. *By phone*
9am-9pm Mon-Sat; 10am-6pm Sun. *Ticketmaster*
24hrs daily. **Tickets** £15-£29. **Credit** AmEx,
MC, V. **Map** p409 Y2.
Less warehouse, more intimate chamber, the Donmar is another favourite crossover spot for actors more often seen on screen. Artistic director Michael Grandage had an excellent year in 2005 with a praise-showered West End adaptation of *Guys and Dolls* and an adroit, moving take on Schiller's *Mary Stuart*. Top billing for the 2006 season goes to the world premiere of Mark Ravenhill's new play, *The Cut* (23 Feb-1 Apr).

Drill Hall
16 Chenies Street, Fitzrovia, WC1E 7EX (7307 5060/
www.drillhall.co.uk). Goodge Street tube. **Box office**
10am-9.30pm Mon-Sat; 10am-6pm Sun. **Tickets**
£2-£12. **Credit** AmEx, MC, V. **Map** p401 K5.
Polyfunctional (it's a theatre, cabaret, gig venue and photo studio) and polysexual, Drill Hall is London's biggest gay and lesbian theatre, and often premieres exciting new work.

Gate Theatre
Above the Prince Albert pub, 11 Pembridge Road,
Notting Hill, W11 3HQ (7229 0706/www.gate
theatre.co.uk). Notting Hill Gate tube. **Tickets**
£12-£20; £10-15 concessions. **Map** p396 A7.
A doll's house of a theatre, with rickety wooden chairs as seats, the Gate devotes itself entirely to foreign drama, often performed in specially commissioned translations. Rising young star and artistic director Thea Sharrock has kicked off her tenure with some hard-hitting choices.

Arts & Entertainment

Shakespeare's Globe. See p339.

Hampstead Theatre

Eton Avenue, Swiss Cottage, NW3 3EU (7722 9301/ www.hampsteadtheatre.com). Swiss Cottage tube. **Box office** 9am-8pm Mon-Sat. **Tickets** £13-£22; £10-£13 concessions. **Credit** MC, V.
The Hampstead's Portakabin days are officially a distant memory now that it's installed in this gleaming, purpose-built space, the first new London theatre to open since 1976. Its programme of fresh British and international playwrights is astute but accessible. The theatre has recently launched Start Nights, offering nervous fledgling artists 15 minutes each to perform a slice of rehearsed material in its small, 80-seater Michael Frayn Space.

King's Head Theatre

115 Upper Street, Islington, N1 1QN (7226 1916/ www.kingsheadtheatre.org). Angel tube. **Tickets** £12-£19. **Credit** MC, V. **Map** p404 O1.
London's first pub theatre, started in the 1970s with a spectacularly lean budget, is a tiny space at the back of a charming, if ramshackle, Victorian boozer. It has launched a raft of wannabe stars, among them Hugh Grant. As this guide went to press the theatre had just suffered the loss of its founder, Dan Crawford.

Lyric Hammersmith

Lyric Square, King Street, Hammersmith, W6 0QL (0870 050 0511/www.lyric.co.uk). Hammersmith tube. **Box office** 10am-6pm or 8pm (performance nights) Mon-Sat. **Tickets** £9-£25. **Credit** MC, V.
The Lyric has a knack for vibrant, offbeat scheduling, and it also offers good kids' theatre. The frankly hideous façade, built when reinforced concrete was still regarded as an architectural panacea to all building ills, hides a 19th-century gem of an auditorium conceived by the Victorian theatre design supremo Frank Matcham. A smaller space, the Lyric Studio, houses short-run shows. New artistic director David Farr (who joins from the Bristol Old Vic) is thinking big for his first season including a multimedia enactment of the *Odyssey*, the last in a run including *Road to Nowhere*, *Brontë* and the *Magic Carpet*.

Soho Theatre

21 Dean Street, Soho, W1D 3NE (7478 0100/ box office 0870 429 6883/www.sohotheatre.com). Tottenham Court Road tube. **Box office** *In person* 10am-6pm or 7.30pm (performance nights) Mon-Sat. *By phone* 24 hrs daily. **Tickets** £7.50-£15. **Credit** AmEx, V. **Map** p408 W2.
Its cool blue neon lights, front-of-house café and late-night performances of some shows may blend it into the Soho landscape, but since taking up its Lottery-funded residence on Dean Street in 2000, the Soho Theatre has firmly made a name for itself. Sets and costumes are usually frills-free – the priority here is to provide a space for new writing voices. It encourages playwrights to submit their work by offering a free script-reading service, runs numerous workshops and also offers computer facilities to writers looking for some peace and quiet to finish their masterpiece. **Photo** *p341.*

Theatre Royal Stratford East

Gerry Raffles Square, Stratford, E15 1BN (8534 0310/www.stratfordeast.com). Stratford tube/rail/ DLR. **Box office** 10am-7pm Mon-Sat. **Tickets** £8-£20. **Credit** MC, V.
This theatre is an important part of the local community, with a high proportion of shows written, directed and performed by black or Asian artists. Adamantly confronting uncomfortable issues, it regularly turns heads with provocative shows such as *Bashment*. Musicals have been big here – whether they are about hip hop culture or the Windrush generation of immigrants.

Tricycle

269 Kilburn High Road, Kilburn, NW6 7JR (7328 1000/www.tricycle.co.uk). Kilburn tube/Brondesbury rail. **Box office** 10am-9pm Mon-Sat; 2-9pm Sun. **Tickets** £7.50-£22. **Credit** MC, V.
Passionate and political, the Tricycle has been free-wheeling over the past few years with wide acclaim for its 'tribunal' docudramas, which have pursued the dark truths of the Stephen Lawrence case, the Hutton Inquiry, Nuremberg and Guantanamo Bay. Under director Nicolas Kent, it consistently finds original ways into difficult subjects – in *An Arab-Israeli Cookbook*, characters told stories of West Bank traumas while making houmous, meatballs and other dishes live on stage. The centre has a loyal local following and a buzzy interval bar.

Young Vic

From autumn 2006: 66 The Cut, Waterloo, SE1 8LZ (7928 6363/www.youngvic.org). Southwark tube/ Waterloo tube/rail. **Box office** 10am-8pm Mon-Sat. **Tickets** £10-£36. **Credit** MC, V. **Map** p406 N8.
The Young Vic theatre, erected in 1969 as a temporary space, has finally exited, stage left, pursued by memories: it's started to crumble, and will be closed for rebuilding until autumn 2006, when its spanking new premises opens on its previous site at The Cut. It is still short of a few bob to complete the project, which could delay the opening. In the interim, the theatre is going on a 'Walkabout' programme, revisiting some of its greatest production hits from the past few years. Check the website for details.

Trips Out of Town

Cambridge. *See p351.*

Trips Out of Town

Fresh air outside the Big Smoke.

OK, so London's one of the world's greatest city's and you've had a wonderful time. But now you're feeling pastoral pangs and want to escape Smogsford Street. Read on.

A useful first stop for the visitor planning a trip away from London is the **Britain & London Visitor Centre** (*see below*). We've also listed local tourist information centres in each destination, which can provide further information about specific areas. For the main attractions, we've included details of opening times, admission and transport, but be aware that these can change without notice: always phone to check. Major sights are open all through the year, but many of the minor ones close from November to March.

Britain & London Visitor Centre

1 Regent Street (south of Piccadilly Circus), SW1Y 4XT (8846 9000/www.visitbritain.com). Piccadilly Circus tube. **Open** *June-Sept* 9am-6.30pm Mon-Fri; 9am-5pm Sat; 10am-4pm Sun. *Oct-May* 9am-6.30pm Mon-Fri; 10am-4pm Sat, Sun. **Credit** AmEx, MC, V. **Map** p408 W4.

Come in person to pick up free leaflets and advice on destinations in the UK and Ireland. Staff can also help book rail, road or air travel, and reserve tours, theatre tickets and hotels. There's a bureau de change too.

Getting there

By train

For information on train times and ticket prices, call **0845 748 4950**. Ask about the cheapest ticket for the journey you are planning, and be aware that for long journeys, the earlier you book, the cheaper the ticket. If you need extra help, there are rail travel centres in London's main-line stations, as well as in Heathrow and Gatwick airports. These can give you guidance for things like timetables and booking. The journey times we give are the fastest available.

The website **www.virgintrains.co.uk** gives online timetable information for any British train company. You can buy your tickets online for any train operator in the UK via **www.thetrainline.com**.

London main-line rail stations

Charing Cross *Strand, Covent Garden, WC2.* **Map** p401 L7.

For trains to and from south-east England (including Dover, Folkestone and Ramsgate).

Euston *Euston Road, Euston, NW1.* **Map** p401 K3.

For trains to and from north and north-west England and Scotland, and a north London suburban line.

King's Cross *Euston Road, King's Cross, N1.* **Map** p401 L2/3.

For trains to and from north and north-east England and Scotland; lines to north London and Herts.

Liverpool Street *Liverpool Street, the City, EC2.* **Map** p407 R5.

For trains to and from the east coast and Stansted airport; also for trains to East Anglia and suburban services to north and east London.

London Bridge *London Bridge Street, London Bridge, SE1.* **Map** p407 Q8.

For trains to and from south-east England and Kent; also suburban services to south London.

Paddington *Praed Street, Paddington, W2.* **Map** p397 D5/6.

For trains to and from south-west and west England, south Wales and the Midlands.

St Pancras *Pancras Road, King's Cross, N1.* **Map** p401 L3.

For trains to and from the East Midlands, Derby and Sheffield. After redevelopments finish (sometime between 2007 and 2009) this will become the main terminus for Eurostar services.

Victoria *Terminus Place, Victoria, SW1.* **Map** p402 H10.

For fast trains to and from the Channel ports (Dover, Folkestone, Newhaven); also for trains to and from Gatwick, plus services to south London.

Waterloo *York Road, Waterloo, SE1.* **Map** p403 M8/9.

For fast trains to and from the south and south-west of England (Portsmouth, Southampton, Dorset, Devon), the Eurostar to Paris and Brussels, and suburban services to south London.

By coach

National Express (0870 580 8080, www.nationalexpress.com) coaches travel throughout the country and depart from Victoria Coach Station (*see below*), five minutes' walk from Victoria rail and tube stations. Green Line Travel (0870 608 7261) also runs coaches.

Victoria Coach Station

164 Buckingham Palace Road, Victoria, SW1W 9TP (7730 3466). Victoria tube/rail. **Map** p402 H11.

Britain's most comprehensive coach company National Express (*see above*) and Eurolines (01582 404511), which travels to the Continent, are based here, as are many other companies that operate to and from London (some depart from Marble Arch).

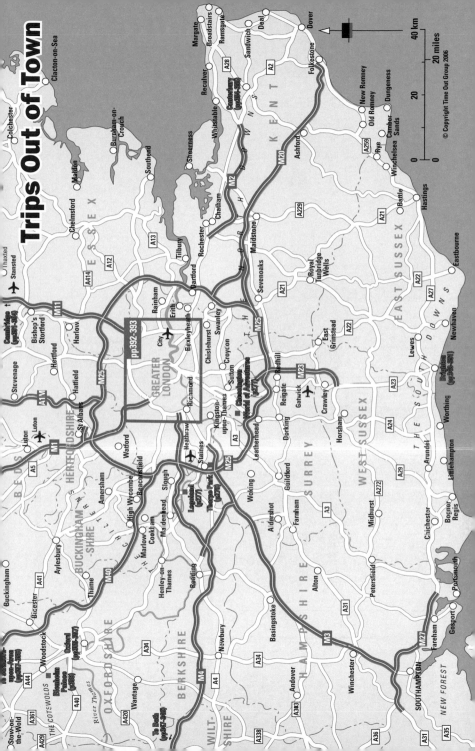

Trips Out of Town

© Copyright Time Out Group 2006

0   20   40 km

0   20 miles

ESSEX

KENT

EAST SUSSEX

WEST SUSSEX

SURREY

HAMPSHIRE

BERKSHIRE

OXFORDSHIRE

BUCKINGHAMSHIRE

HERTFORDSHIRE

BEDS

GREATER LONDON

pp392-393

Clacton-on-Sea
Colchester
Burnham-on-Crouch
Maldon
Southend
Chelmsford
Thaxted
Stansted
Bishop's Stortford
Harlow
Hertford
Stevenage
Hatfield
St Albans
Luton
Aylesbury
Buckingham
Bicester
Woodstock
To Stratford-upon-Avon (pp360-366)
Stow-on-the-Wold
THE COTSWOLDS
Oxford (pp355-357)
Blenheim Palace (p356)
Thame
High Wycombe
Amersham
Beaconsfield
Watford
Maidenhead
Cookham
Marlow
Henley-on-Thames
Reading
Newbury
To Bath (pp367-369)
Vantage
THE CHILTERNS
River Thames
WILTSHIRE
Andover
Basingstoke
Winchester
SOUTHAMPTON
NEW FOREST
Gosport
Portsmouth
Fareham
Chichester
Bognor Regis
Littlehampton
Arundel
Worthing
Brighton (pp349-351)
THE SOUTH DOWNS
Newhaven
Lewes
Eastbourne
Hastings
Battle
Rye
Winchelsea
Camber Sands
Dungeness
Old Romney
New Romney
Folkestone
Dover
Deal
Sandwich
Ramsgate
Broadstairs
Margate
Reculver
Whitstable
Sheerness
Canterbury (pp354-356)
Ashford
Royal Tunbridge Wells
East Grinstead
Crawley
Gatwick
Reigate
Redhill
Dorking
Horsham
Midhurst
Petersfield
Alton
Farnham
Aldershot
Guildford
Leatherhead
Woking
Thorpe Park (p271)
Legoland (p271)
Slough
Staines
Heathrow
Kingston-upon-Thames
Richmond
Sutton
Croydon
Chessington World of Adventures (p271)
Chislehurst
Swanley
Bexleyheath
Erith
Rainham
City
Dartford
Tilbury
Rochester
Chatham
Maidstone
Sevenoaks
Sheerness

M11
M25
M1
A1(M)
M40
M4
M3
M27
M20
M2
M23
M25

A44
A361
A429
A420
A338
A34
A4
A41
A5
A43
A31
A35
A36
A303
A31
A272
A24
A29
A3
A23
A22
A27
A259
A21
A28
A2
A229
A21
A26
A20
A13
A12
A414
A5
A12
A1

THE NORTH DOWNS

THE WEALD

By car

If you're in a group of three or four, it may be cheaper for you to hire a car (*see p365*), especially if you plan to take in several sights within an area. The road directions given in the listings below should be used in conjunction with a comprehensive map.

By bicycle

Capital Sport (01296 631671, www.capital-sport.co.uk) offers gentle cycling tours along the River Thames from London. Leisurely itineraries include plenty of time to explore royal palaces, parks and historic attractions. Or you could try **Country Lanes** (01425 655022, www.countrylanes.co.uk), whose representatives meet you off the train from London and lead you on cycling tours of the New Forest in Hampshire (01590 622627) and the Cotswolds (01608 650065).

Bath

There are two early myths about Bladud, who became ninth king of the Britons in 863BC, which seek to explain the origins of this ancient spa town's healing properties. In one 'the king who learnt to fly' used necromancy to create the hot springs for which the town is famous. In the later, more sophisticated version of the fable, the heir-apparent returned home a leper, after an eleven-year visit to Athens, and was duly confined to prevent the disease spreading. Escaping, he disguised himself as a swineherd. In cold weather, his pigs would wallow in the warm mud, and Bladud noticed how their diseases vanished. Testing the waters himself, he was duly healed, and subsequently inherited the throne.

However, Bath's ability to restore and revive officially dates from Roman times – perhaps appropriately, since both Bath and Rome are surrounded by seven hills. Bath's reputation for healing extended beyond mere livestock until the 18th century, when a housing boom signalled the rise of Georgian Bath. The visionary architect John Wood the Elder (1704-54) was, together with his son, responsible for the extraordinary unity of the architecture, which is elegant English Palladianism.

Bath's heyday lasted almost a century, until Jane Austen's time (she lived here from 1800 to 1805), after which it declined until after World War II, when the current revival began. The city is as beautiful as ever now, although it can be stiflingly crowded in the summer when it often seems as if all of the three million annual visitors have descended at once.

Most head first for the wonderful, steam-enshrouded **Roman Baths** museum. Once a temple to Sulis Minerva, this is now the city's most famous attraction. The hot water bubbles up at a rate of 250,000 gallons (over a million litres) a day, filling a pool surrounded by attractive classical statues. You can taste sulphuric water in the adjoining Pump Room, if you're so inclined. Although its opening is behind schedule, **Thermae Bath Spa** on Hot Bath Street (01225 477051, www.thermae bathspa.com, open daily) is due to welcome its first visitors in April 2006 – the website has regularly updated information.

Adjacent to the Roman baths are the noble towers of **Bath Abbey** (Abbey Churchyard, 01225 422462). It was built on the site of the Saxon church where Edgar, first king of a united England, was crowned back in 973. If the crypt is open, you can trace the building's history back through the centuries in its stones and artefacts.

Bath has close to 20 museums, including the **Building of Bath Museum** (*see p348*) and the **Museum of East Asian Art** (12 Bennett Street, 01225 464640, www.bath.co.uk/museumeastasianart), which contains a fine collection of Chinese jade carvings. Opposite, in the Assembly Rooms (which were the social focus of high society in Georgian times), there's the renowned **Museum of Costume** (*see p348*), where the oldest posh togs displayed date back to the 1660s. On Bridge Street, the **Victoria Art Gallery** (01225 477233) houses a collection of British and European art from the 15th century to the present. The **American Museum in Britain** (*see below*) contains reconstructed US domestic interiors from the 17th, 18th and 19th centuries.

The grandest street in Bath is the much-photographed **Royal Crescent** (*see p348*), a curl of 30 stately white houses designed by John Wood the Younger between 1767 and 1775. The house at **No.1** is furnished in period style with a restored Georgian garden that you can visit (closed Dec-mid Feb). Nearby is the **Circus**, designed by the elder John Wood and completed by his son in 1767.

The **River Avon**, spanned by the Italianate, shop-lined **Pulteney Bridge**, adds to the city's appeal. There are walks beside the river and the Kennet and Avon Canal; in summer boats can be hired from the Victorian **Bath Boating Station** (Forester Road, 01225 312900).

American Museum in Britain

Claverton Manor, BA2 7BD (01225 460503/ www.americanmuseum.org). **Open** *Mid Mar-late Oct, mid Nov-mid Dec* noon-5pm Tue-Sun; also Mon Aug noon-5pm. **Admission** £6.50; £3.50-£6 concessions; free under-5s. **Credit** AmEx, MC, V.

Building of Bath Museum

The Countess of Huntingdon's Chapel, The Vineyards, BA1 5NA (01225 333895/www.bathpreservation-trust.org.uk). **Open** 10.30am-5pm Tue-Sun. Closed Dec-mid Feb. **Admission** £4; £1.50-£3 concessions; free under-5s. **Credit** AmEx, MC, V.

Museum of Costume

The Assembly Rooms, Bennett Street, BA1 2QH (01225 477789/www.museumofcostume.co.uk). **Open** 11am-6pm daily. **Admission** £6.25; £4-£5 concessions; free under-6s. **Credit** MC, V.

No.1 Royal Crescent

1 Royal Crescent, BA1 2LR (01225 428126/www.bath-preservation-trust.org.uk). **Open** *Mid Feb-Oct* 10.30am-5pm Tue-Sun. *Nov* 10.30am-4pm Tue-Sun. *1st 2wks Dec* 10.30am-4pm Sat, Sun. Last entry 30mins before closing. Closed mid Dec-mid Feb. **Admission** £4; £3.50 concessions; £12 family; free under-5s. **Credit** MC, V.

Roman Baths

Abbey Churchyard, BA1 1LZ (01225 477785/www.romanbaths.co.uk). **Open** *Nov-Feb* 9.30am-5.30pm daily. *Mar-June, Sept, Oct* 9am-6pm daily. *July, Aug* 9am-10pm daily. Last entry 1hr before closing. **Admission** £9.50; £5.50-£8.50 concessions; free under-6s. **Credit** MC, V.

Where to eat & drink

Bath has a formidable gourmet reputation. Four of the best restaurants are the classic and Mediterranean **Pimpernel's** (Royal Crescent Hotel, 16 Royal Crescent, 01225 823333, set lunch £18 2 courses, £25 3 courses), classy Modern British **Moody Goose** (7A Kingsmead Square, 01225 466688, main courses £7.50-£14), **Olive Tree** (Queensbury Hotel, Russell Street, 01225 447928, main courses £18-£19.50, set lunch £17.50) and the **Priory** (Bath Priory Hotel, Weston Road, 01225 331922, main courses £26), where you'll find country house dining that dreams are made of.

At **Sally Lunn's Refreshment House & Museum** (4 North Parade Passage, 01225 461634, main courses £8-£9) you can sample the buns made fashionable in the 1680s.

Popular pubs include the **Bell Inn** (01225 460426) in Walcot Street, the **Old Green Tree** (01225 329314) on Green Street, and the 300-year-old **Crystal Palace** (01225 482666) on Abbey Green, with its walled garden.

Where to stay

Harrington's Hotel (8-10 Queen Street, 01225 461728, www.harringtonshotel.co.uk, doubles £88-£114) is the best-value central hotel. **Holly Lodge** (8 Upper Oldfield Park, 01225 424042, doubles £79-£97) is a classy B&B perched high above the city. The **Queensberry Hotel**

(Russell Street, 01225 447928, www.thequeensberry.co.uk, doubles £100-£285) provides Regency elegance in the centre of town. **Royal Crescent** (16 Royal Crescent, 01225 823333, www.royalcrescent.co.uk, doubles £290-£380) is the place to come if money is no object.

Getting there

By train

Trains to Bath Spa leave hourly from Paddington most days (1hr 25mins).

By coach

National Express coaches to Bath leave from Victoria Coach Station (3hrs 20mins).

By car

Take Junction 18 off the M4, then follow the A46 to Bath. Use park & rides to get into the centre.

Tourist information

Tourist Information Centre

Abbey Chambers, Abbey Churchyard, BA1 1LY (0906 711 2000/www.visitbath.co.uk). **Open** *June-Sept* 9.30am-6pm Mon-Sat; 10am-4pm Sun. *Oct-Apr* 9.30am-5pm Mon-Sat; 10am-4pm Sun.

Brighton

Brighton began life as Bristmestune, a small fishing village, and so it remained until 1783, when Prince George (later George IV) rented a farmhouse here. He became the centre of a kind of hip court in waiting, and he kept the architect John Nash busy converting a modest abode into a faux-oriental pleasure palace. That building is now the elaborate-to-the-point-of-gaudy **Royal Pavilion** (*see p350*), where guided tours are full of quirky facts. Next door, the **Brighton Museum & Art Gallery** (Royal Pavilion Gardens, 01273 290900) has entertaining displays and a good permanent art collection.

Only two of Brighton's three Victorian piers are still standing. Lacy, delicate **Brighton Pier** is a clutter of hot-dog stands, karaoke, and fairground rides, filled with customers in the summertime. But sadly, the **West Pier** is now a spooky, twisted ruin. It had been closed since 1975, while the city dithered over what to do about it. Nothing was decided and time did its work, weakening the pier's foundations. Finally, in 2003, a violent storm and fire damage delivered the coup de grâce. The pier's future is undecided, but the West Pier Trust hopes that reconstruction will go ahead.

With seven miles of coastline, Brighton has all the seaside resort trappings, hence the free **Brighton Fishing Museum** (201 King's Road Arches, on the lower prom between the piers,

Brighton's **Royal Pavilion**.
See p350.

01273 723064) and the **Sea-Life Centre** (*see below*), the world's oldest functioning aquarium.

Perhaps reflecting its singular character, the town has a huge number of independent shops, boutiques and art stores. The best shopping for clothes, records and gifts is found in and around **North Laine** and in the charming network of narrow cobbled streets known as the **Lanes**, which contain dozens of jewellers, clothiers and antiques shops.

The town that seems to be on a perpetual holiday received a further boost (to visitor numbers, at least) in spring 2005, when it was announced that Frank Gehry – about to redesign the £250 million King Alfred residential and leisure complex along the town's seafront (officially in Hove, at the western end of the Brighton-Hove sprawl) – would be helped by none other than Brad Pitt, who is charged with designing a restaurant and a penthouse as part of the controversial plan.

The presence of universities and language schools make this one of the youngest and most multicultural cities outside London (which is less than an hour away on train). With more than 60 per cent of the population under the age of 45, the 'vegetarian capital of Europe' also has a large and thriving gay and lesbian scene.

After dark, Brighton rocks. Pick up club flyers on Gardner Street and Kensington Gardens on Saturday afternoons, or check listings mags such as *Latest* or *Brighton Source*.

Royal Pavilion

Brighton, BN1 1EE (01273 292820/www.royal pavilion.org.uk). **Open** *Apr-Sept* 9.30am-5.45pm daily. *Oct-Mar* 10am-5.15pm daily. *Tours* 11.30am, 2.30pm daily. Last entry 45mins before closing. **Admission** £5.95; £3.50-£4.20 concessions. *Tours* £1.50. **Credit** AmEx, MC, V.

Sea-Life Centre

Marine Parade, BN2 1TB (01273 604234). **Open** 10am-5pm daily. **Admission** £9.95; £5.50-£7.50 concessions; free under-2s. **Credit** AmEx, DC, MC, V.

Where to eat & drink

There's a menu of beautifully presented, wholly authentic French fare at **La Fourchette** (105 Western Road, 01273 722556, set lunch £10-£13, set dinner £22-£28).

One of England's most celebrated vegetarian restaurants is also here: **Terre à Terre** (71 East Street, 01273 729051, main courses £10-£13.50) is known for its innovative menu. The newly opened **Real Eating Company** (86-87 Western Road, Hove, 01273 221444, main courses £10-£12) is a great place for lunch, and fantastic food and considerate staff make

Seven Dials (1-3 Buckingham Place, 01273 885555, set lunch £10-£15, set dinner £22.50-£26.50) an excellent choice for dinner.

This city's laid-back attitude makes it ideal for café culture, and the excellent coffeeshops include **Nia Café Bar** (86 Trafalgar Street, 01273 671371) and **Alfresco** (Milkmaid Pavilion, King's Road Arches, 01273 206523).

Of the traditional pubs, the **Cricketers** (15 Black Lion Street, 01273 329472), the **Druid's Head** (9 Brighton Place, 01273 325490) and the **Battle of Trafalgar** (34 Guildford Road, 01273 327996) all have the most charm.

Classic Brighton boozer the **Prince Albert** (48 Trafalgar Street) has theme nights. The **St James** (16 Madeira Place) is a pre-club bar with DJs. **Sidewinder** (65 Upper St James Street) the **Hampton** (57 Upper North Street) and **Riki-Tik** (18A Bond Street) are also reliable bets for a good night out.

Of the gay bars, the most fun is to be had at the **Amsterdam Hotel** (11-12 Marine Parade). **Doctor Brighton's** (16 King's Road), on the seafront, is also worth a punt, with DJs playing house and techno. And for the ladeeez... the **Candy Bar** (129 St James Street) is a strictly women-only lesbian hangout.

Where to stay

Given Brighton's popularity, it's perhaps not surprising that hotel prices can be high. An interesting choice is the **Alias Hotel Seattle** (01273 679799, www.aliasseattle.com, doubles £105-£160), which is situated on the recently developed Brighton Marina and feels much like a state-of-the-art liner. For other good quality stops, try **Hotel du Vin** (2-6 Ship Street, 01273 718588, www.hotelduvin.com, doubles £140-£355), or **Blanch House** (17 Atlingworth Street, 01273 603504, www.blanch house.co.uk, doubles £125-£220), which is unassuming from the outside, but highly chic. **Nineteen** (19 Broad Street, 01273 675529, www.hotelnineteen.co.uk, doubles £90-£140) has just seven rooms in a stylish townhouse. **Hotel Pelirocco** (10 Regency Square, 01273 327055, www.hotelpelirocco.co.uk, doubles £90-£130) is funky, with themed decor in the bedrooms. **Hotel Twenty One** (21 Charlotte Street, 01273 686450, doubles £60-£95) is a well-run B&B a few minutes' walk from the Palace Pier and town centre. **Oriental Hotel** (9 Oriental Place, 01273 205050, doubles Mon-Thur, Sun £60-£100; Fri, Sat £80-£125) is laid-back and centrally located. For a clean, cheap, central but otherwise rather bland chain, you could try **Brighton Premier Lodge** (144 North Street, 0870 990 6340, www.premier lodge.com, doubles £57.95-£64.95).

Getting there

By train

Trains for Brighton leave from Victoria (50mins) or King's Cross (1hr 10mins).

By coach

National Express coaches for Brighton leave from Victoria Coach Station (1hr 50mins).

By car

Take the M23, then the A23 to Brighton.

Tourist information

Tourist Information Centre

10 Bartholomew Square (0906 711 2255/www.visit brighton.com). **Open** *Summer* 10am-5pm Mon-Sat; 10am-4pm Sun. *Winter* 10am-5pm Mon-Sat.

Cambridge

Gorgeous, intimidating Cambridge has the feel of an enclosed city. With its narrow streets and tall old buildings blocking out the sun in the town centre, it has a way of conveying disapproval to visitors architecturally as well as intellectually (before you even reach the 'Keep off the Grass' signs). But once you pluck up the courage to pass through the imposing gates and stone walls, you discover a pretty little town of green parks and streams where time seems to have stopped back in the 18th century.

Cambridge first became an academic centre when a fracas at Oxford – involving a dead woman, an arrow and a scholar holding a bow, apparently – led to some of the learned monks bidding a hasty farewell to Oxford and a hearty how do you do to Cambridge. Once the dust settled, the monks needed somewhere to peddle their knowledge: the first college, **Peterhouse**, was established in 1284. The original hall survives, though most of the present buildings are 19th century. Up the road is **Corpus Christi College**, founded in 1352. Its Old Court dates from that time and is linked by a gallery to its original chapel, the 11th-century **St Bene't's Church** (Bene't Street, 01223 353903), the oldest surviving building in Cambridge.

Down Silver Street is 15th-century **Queens' College**; most of its original buildings remain, including the timbered president's lodge. The inner courts are wonderfully picturesque. Further up on King's Parade, grand **King's College** was founded by Henry VI in 1441 and is renowned for its **chapel** (01223 331155), built between 1446 and 1515. It has a breathtaking interior with the original stained glass. Attend a service in term-time to hear its choirboys.

Further north, pretty **Trinity College** was founded in 1336 by Edward III and then refounded by Henry VIII in 1546. A fine crowd of Tudor buildings surrounds the Great Court where, legend has it, Lord Byron was known to

Traffic jam in **Cambridge.**

Spa treks

London is home to some gorgeous day spas (*see pp253-256*), but sometimes nothing beats escaping to the countryside, where the whiff of petrol can be swapped for the whiff of fresh air. All the following hotels are destinations in their own right, but each of them also has a spa providing much-needed treatments to weary, over-polluted city dwellers. They're not exactly on London's doorstep, but we reckon they're worth going the extra mile for. Besides, that's kind of the point of a country retreat.

Babington House

Babington, nr Frome, Somerset BA11 3RW (01373 812266/www.babingtonhouse. co.uk). **Rates** £215-£315 double (non-members); £180-£275 double (members). **Credit** AmEx, DC, MC, V.
A country outpost of Soho House, the media-oriented members' club in London, Babington House (*pictured above*) believes in showing its guests a good time. An 18th-century manor house at the end of a tree-lined drive, with a charming pepper pot of a chapel and sloping lakeside lawns, it brings a breezy confidence to the sometimes over-

complicated business of hospitality. Young families and sybaritic professionals descend from town and the local area throughout the year to enjoy the Cowshed health club, with its two swimming pools (one in the barn and a wonderful open-air one by the river), grass tennis courts and a wide variety of spa treatments (also available in the Mongolian yurt or Native American tepees, natch). The rooms come complete with massive beds and baths, superb showers, funky furniture and fittings, as well as wide flat-screen TVs with DVD players. The terrace is now fitted with warm-air ducts, making it a pleasant place to enjoy the kitchen's adventurous and accomplished Modern British cuisine year round. During the summer, the lawn by the lake comes into its own for light and reasonably priced lunches.

Calcot Manor Hotel

Junction of A46 & A4153, 3 miles east from Tetbury, Gloucs, GL8 8YJ (01666 890391/ www.calcotmanor.co.uk). **Rates** £185-£335 double; £240-£360 suite. **Credit** DC, MC, V.
Though it started off as a fairly traditional, small country-house hotel in the early 1980s, Calcot Manor has metamorphosed over the years into one of the UK's finest, friendliest, most stylish and most enjoyable places to stay. Its secret seems to lie in its inclusiveness. Calcot is justly famed for family-friendliness – a converted barn houses a series of dedicated family rooms and suites, while another holds the Playzone (open 9am-5.30pm daily), a superbly equipped, supervised crèche and play area catering to a wide age range, from babies to teenagers. For the child-free, one of Calcot's major draws is its impressive spa, which offers a broad spectrum of treatments and features indoor and outdoor pools, a hammam, massage table, dry flotation bed and, best of all, an outdoor hot tub facing a log fire. Only nine of the 30 bedrooms are within the main house, and these have deliberately been given a more traditional (though far from fusty) look than those located in various buildings around the grounds. All display a restrained modernity, muted colours, sleek bathrooms and facilities such as CD systems and swish TVs. For eating and drinking, there are two options: the informal Gumstool Inn and the posher Conservatory.

Charlton House

*Charlton Road, Shepton Mallet, nr Bath,
Somerset BA4 4PR (01749 342008/
www.charltonhouse.com).* **Rates** £165-£325;
£425 1-bedroom suite; £525 2-bedroom
suite. **Credit** AmEx, DC, MC, V.
This 17th-century manor-house hotel (*pictured
above*) has gone from strength to strength
since being bought in 1996 by Roger and
Monty Saul, founder of the Mulberry fashion
label. Famous for its expensive, sophisticated
restaurant, it now also has a wing of luxurious
rooms around a state-of-the-art spa. Bijou,
intimate and beautifully designed, Monty's
Spa features a health-food café, an indoor-
outdoor, ozone treated hydrotherapy pool,
a laconium (steam bath), sauna and steam
room, and light-infused Experience showers.
Two of the bedroooms, called Hayloft and
Chesterblade, have been kitted out to enable
couples to enjoy simultaneous treatments.
This indulgent sanctuary is yet further
inducement to sample the hotel's well-
established atmosphere of courtly nostalgia,
with a comfortable, contemporary twist.

Cowley Manor

*Cowley, Gloucs, GL53 9NL (01242 870900/
www.cowleymanor.com). Five miles south-east
of Cheltenham, off A435.* **Rates** £230-£455
double **Credit** AmEx, DC, MC, V.
Jessica Sainsbury and her husband Peter
Frankopan opened Cowley Manor in 2002,
having transformed the place with the help
of a dedicated roster of designers and
architects. The views of the surrounding

Gloucestershire countryside are lovely; the
manor house is stately on a manageable
scale; the grounds are attractively landscaped
and Grade II-listed; and the C-side spa, is
ultra-modern but blends in beautifully. The
outdoor pool is something special – even
in winter it's possible to swim under the
stars. Treatments range from pedicures
and manicures to facials and aromatherapy
massages. The 30 rooms are excellent:
decorated in strong but appealing splashes
of colour, with striking pieces of furniture.
Bathrooms are tranquil havens, boasting
deep baths and huge showers. Attention
to detail at Cowley is impressive, from the
moment you see the higgledy-piggledy line
of wellies at the entrance, you feel they've
probably thought of everything. You don't
even have to make dinner reservations –
you can just turn up when you want to enjoy
the Modern European food. Or just slob out
in your room with the fab room-service menu.
Contemporary, luxurious and fun too.

Whatley Manor Hotel

*Easton Grey, Malmesbury, Wilts SN16 0RB
(01666 822888/www.whatleymanor.com).*
Rates £250-£450 double; £650-£850 suite.
Credit AmEx, MC, V.
If Calcot Manor prides itself on its inclusivity,
Whatley Manor shamelessly aims for the
reverse. Converted at vast expense and
opened in 2004, Whatley is the 'rarefied
bubble of low-key luxury, peace and total
privacy' that its brochure asserts. This is
the sort of place where, even when all eight
suites and 15 doubles are occupied, guests
rarely glimpse each other. So if you crave
escapism, this is the place for you. Quality
is apparent in everything, from the Cotswold
stone walls lining the hotel drive to the handmade French wallpaper, oak panelling and
Bang & Olufsen TVs in the bedrooms. But one
of Whatley's major draws is its Aquarius Spa,
whose centrepiece is one of the biggest and
best hydrotherapy pools in the country. As well
as a wide range of treatments (by La Prairie,
at extra cost), the spa includes four thermal
cabins, a gym and a 'VIP suite', where couples
can indulge in private pampering. Another
attraction is Martin Burge's superlative
cooking at the hotel's twi restaurants: Le
Mazot and the Dining Room. To burn it all off,
stroll in the terraced gardens, which step down
to a wild-flower meadow that borders the river.

bathe naked in the fountain with his pet bear. Wittgenstein studied and taught here, and the library (designed by Wren) is open to visitors at certain times (noon-2pm Mon-Fri all year, 10.30am-12.30pm Sat term-time, 01223 338400).

Further on, at the corner of Bridge and St John's Streets, is the 12th-century **Round Church** (Church of the Holy Sepulchre, Bridge Street, 01223 311602), the oldest of only four remaining round churches in the country.

Behind the main colleges, the beautiful meadows bordering the willow-shaded River Cam are known as the **Backs**. This is idyllic for summer strolling, or 'punting' (pushing flat boats with long poles). Punts can be hired; **Scudamore's Boatyard** (01223 359750) is the largest operator. If you get handy at the surprisingly difficult skill of punting, you could boat down to the **Orchard Tea Rooms** (Mill Way, Grantchester, 01223 845788) where Rupert Brooke lodged when he was a student. There's a small museum dedicated to the poet (rather prosaically) in the car park outside.

Among Cambridge's relatively few non-collegiate attractions, the **Fitzwilliam Museum** on Trumpington Street (01223 332900) has an outstanding collection of antiquities and Old Masters; **Kettle's Yard** (Castle Street, 01223 352124) has fine displays of 20th-century art; and the **Botanic Gardens** (01223 336265) on Bateman Street offer a relaxing place to watch the grass grow.

Where to eat & drink

Graffiti (Hotel Felix, White House Lane, Huntingdon Road, 01223 277977, main courses £15-£22) has a beautiful terrace for outdoor dining during the summer months, and a fine Mediterranean menu. **Midsummer House** (Midsummer Common, 01223 369299, set lunch £30, set dinner £50) is where chef-patron Daniel Clifford creates posh and inventive French dishes in a bid to earn a second Michelin star. For superlative (but pricey) Chinese food, try **Peking** (21 Burleigh Street, 01223 354755, main courses £7-£14).

Cambridge has many creaky old inns in which to enjoy the city's decent local ales. The **Eagle** on Bene't Street (01223 505020) is the most famous, but there are many, including the **Pickerel Inn** (30 Magdalene Street, 01223 355068), **Fort St George** by the river on Midsummer Common (01223 354327), the **Mill** (14 Mill Lane, 01223 357026) and the **Anchor** (Silver Street, 01223 353554) on the riverbank.

A stroll along the Cam from Midsummer Common will take you to the picturesque **Green Dragon** (5 Water Street, 01223 505035), with its beer garden by the river.

Where to stay

Because of the university, there are plenty of guesthouses in town, and the **Meadowcroft Hotel** (16 Trumpington Road, 01223 346120, www.meadowcrofthotel.co.uk, doubles £120-£140) is one of the best. Also lovely is the **Cambridge Garden House Moat House** (Granta Place, Mill Lane, 01223 259988, www.moathousehotels.com, doubles £100-£220) on the banks of the Cam. A mile out of town, the **Hotel Felix** (Whitehouse Lane, Huntingdon Road, 01223 277977, www.hotelfelix.co.uk, doubles £163-£270) has a great restaurant, landscaped gardens and stylishly elegant rooms. For budget travellers, the simple modern **Sleeperz Hotel** betrays minimalist Scandinavian and Japanese influences (Station Road, 01223 304050, doubles £59).

Getting there

By train
Trains to Cambridge leave from King's Cross (50mins) or Liverpool Street (1hr 15mins).

By coach
National Express coaches to Cambridge leave from Victoria Coach Station (1hr 50mins).

By car
Take Junction 11 or Junction 12 off the M11.

Tourist information

Tourist Information Centre
Old Library, Wheeler Street (0906 586 2526/www. tourismcambridge.com/www.visitcambridge.org). **Open** *Easter-mid Oct* 10am-5.30pm Mon-Fri; 10am-5pm Sat; 11am-4pm Sun. *Mid Oct-Easter* 10am-5.30pm Mon-Fri; 10am-5pm Sat.

Canterbury

The home of the Church of England since St Augustine was based here in 597, the ancient city of Canterbury is rich in atmosphere. Gaze up at its soaring spires, or around you at the enchanting medieval streets, and you'll soon feel blessed, even if you're not an Anglican.

Its busy tourist trade and large university provide a colourful counterweight to the brooding mass of history present in its old buildings and, of course, the glorious **Canterbury Cathedral** (*see p355*). Be prepared to shell out at every step, even to enter the close: this is one of the country's most money-grabbing attactions. However, it is, quite simply, well worth it. The cathedral has superb stained glass, stone vaulting and a vast Norman crypt. A plaque near the altar marks what is believed to be the exact spot where Archbishop Thomas à Becket was murdered. Trinity Chapel contains the site of the original shrine, plus the tombs of Henry IV and the Black Prince.

A pilgrimage to Becket's tomb was the focus of Chaucer's *Canterbury Tales* written in the thirteenth century. At the exhibition named after the book (*see below*), visitors are given a device that they point at tableaux inspired by Chaucer's tales of a knight, a miller and others, enabling them to hear the stories.

Eastbridge Hospital (25 High Street, 01227 471688), founded to provide shelter for pilgrims, retains the smell of ages past. The **Roman Museum** (*see below*) has the remains of a townhouse and mosaic floor among its treasures.

Canterbury Cathedral

The Precincts, CT1 2EH (01227 762862/ www.canterbury-cathedral.org). **Open** *Easter-Sept* 9am-5pm Mon-Sat; 12.30-2.30pm, 4.30-5.30pm Sun. *Oct-Easter* 9am-4.30pm Mon-Sat; 12.30-2.30pm, 4.30-5.30pm Sun. During evensong certain parts of the cathedral are closed. **Admission** £4.50; £3.50 concessions; free under-5s. **Credit** MC, V.

Canterbury Tales

St Margaret's Street, CT1 2TG (01227 454888/ 479227/www.canterburytales.org.uk). **Open** *Mid Feb-June, Sept, Oct* 10am-5pm daily. *July, Aug* 9.30am-5pm daily. *Nov-mid Feb* 10am-4.30pm daily. **Admission** £6.95; £5.25-£5.95 concessions; free under-4s. **Credit** MC, V.

Roman Museum

Butchery Lane, CT1 2JR (01227 785575/www. canterbury-museums.co.uk). **Open** *Nov-May* 10am-5pm Mon-Sat. *June-Oct* 10am-5pm Mon-Sat; 1.30-5pm Sun. Last entry 1hr before closing. **Admission** £2.90; £1.80 concessions; free under-5s. **No credit cards**.

Where to eat & drink

The Goods Shed (Station Road West, 01227 459153, main courses £8-£16) is perfect for a leisurely lunch or dinner, while **Café des Amis du Mexique** (93-95 St Dunstan's Street, 01227 464390, main courses £6.95-£14.95) is upbeat and popular. Stop for a drink in the peaceful **Unicorn** (61 St Dunstan's Street, 01227 463187) with its kitsch garden.

Where to stay

Prices are good at the 19th-century **Acacia Lodge & Tanglewood** B&B (39-40 London Road, 01227 769955, www.acacialodge.com, doubles £48-£60). Mid range is the **Coach House** B&B (34 Watling Steet, 01227 784324, doubles £60-£70). At the other end of the scale, the **Falstaff** is a lovely historic hotel (8-10 St Dunstan's Street, www.corushotels.co.uk, 01227 462138, doubles £115).

Getting there

By train

From Victoria Station to Canterbury East (1hr 20mins), or from Charing Cross to Canterbury West (1hr 30mins).

By coach

National Express from Victoria (1hr 50mins).

By car

Take the A2, the M2. then the A2 again.

Tourist information

Tourist Information Centre

12-13 Sun Street, the Buttermarket, CT1 2HX (01227 378100/www.canterbury.co.uk). **Open** *Easter-Oct* 9.30am-5pm Mon-Sat. *Jan-Easter, Nov-Dec* 10am-4pm Mon-Sat.

Oxford

With its soaring spires, domed library and narrow old streets, Oxford has a noble, ancient beauty. The city's stateliness remains intact, mercifully, despite the packs of continental schoolchildren roaming its streets and giggling while robed students glumly trudge off to take their formal exams. The myriad colleges that make up **Oxford University** have defined this town since the middle of the 12th century. Nearly everything else in town – the galleries and museums, the good restaurants, the expansive green parks – stems from them.

This wasn't always the way. Oxford arose as a Saxon burg built to defend Wessex from the dastardly Danes, who repeatedly attacked the region (the 11th-century **St Michael's Tower** in Cornmarket Street is the only survivor of this period). In the years 1348-50 a great plague hit Oxford. While all the academics moved to safe country retreats, the majority of the population remained, and huge numbers died. Shrewd, if not exactly sympathetic, university magnates promptly bought up residences of the deceased, vastly expanding college property holdings. The dissolution of the monasteries under Henry VIII meant that much of Oxford's land and money passed from the Church to the colleges, setting the town's course.

Most of Oxford's many colleges are open to the public, and the chapel at **Christ Church** also serves as Oxford's cathedral. **Magdalen College** (pronounced 'maudlin') has a lovely meadow and deer park. Nearby **Merton College**, founded in 1264, has a medieval library and garden. Scorch marks can still be discerned on the doors of **Balliol College**, where Bloody Mary burned leading Protestants Latimer and Ridley alive for refusing to recant.

Oxford's Radcliffe Camera. *See p355.*

Other centres of academia include the grand **Bodleian** (*see p357*), the university's huge, reference-only library. It is housed in a spectacular building, with the oldest part dating back to 1488, and contains every book published in the United Kingdom and Ireland.

The **University Botanic Gardens** (Rose Lane, 01865 286690) are the oldest in Great Britain and have occupied this spot by the River Cherwell for more than 375 years.

Oxford's non-university sights include **Carfax Tower** (01865 792653), the only surviving part of the 14th-century church of St Martin, with its two 'quarter-boy' clocks (they chime every quarter-hour). Climb the 99 steps to the top for fantastic views.

A wealth of museums ranges from the quirky (and free) **Pitt Rivers** (Parks Road, 01865 270927), with its voodoo dolls, shrunken heads and other ethnological delights, to the all-embracing **Ashmolean** (Beaumont Street, 01865 278000; also free), the country's oldest museum, which houses the university's collection of art and antiquities. **Modern Art Oxford** (30 Pembroke Street, 01865 722733), has established an international reputation for pioneering exhibitions of contemporary work.

Central Oxford, with its sweet covered market (opened in 1774) linking Market Street to the High Street, its car-unfriendly streets and bicycling youth, is a wonderful place to wander. It can get uncomfortably clogged with tourists, but there are always the neighbourhoods of Jericho, Summertown and Cowley to explore. Beyond Jericho, wild horses roam on the vast expanse of lovely **Port Meadow**.

Eight miles north-west of Oxford, near the pretty town of Woodstock, **Blenheim Palace** (0870 060 2080, www.blenheimpalace.com) is the only non-royal residence in England grand enough to be given the title 'palace'. It was designed by Sir John Banbrugh, and its grounds include a butterfly house, a boating and fishing lake, and a miniature railway.

Bodleian Library

Broad Street, OX1 3BG (01865 277000/Tours 01865 277224/www.bodley.ox.ac.uk). **Open** *Library* term-time 9am-10pm Mon-Fri, 9am-5pm Sat; vacations 9am-7pm Mon-Fri, 9am-1pm Sat. *Shop* 9am-4.45pm Mon-Fri; 9am-1pm Sat. *Tours* Mid Mar-Oct 10.30am, 11.30am, 2pm, 3pm Mon-Fri; 10.30am, 11.30am Sat. Nov-mid Mar 11am, 2pm, 3pm Mon-Fri; 10.30am, 11.30am Sat. **Admission** *Tours* £5-£10. Children under 11 not permitted on tours. **Credit** AmEx, MC, V.

Where to eat & drink

Enjoy excellent lunchtime dim sum at **Liaison** (29 Castle Street, 01865 242944, main courses £6.50-£28). **Branca** (111 Walton Street, 01865 556111, main courses £8.65-£16.95) is perfect for those seeking a zippy atmosphere with their pasta. Popular diner **Joe's** (21 Cowley Road, 01865 201120, main courses £7.95-£11.95) is renowned for its excellent brunches. **Cherwell Boat House** (Bardwell Road, 01865 552746, set lunch £12.50-£21.50, set dinner £24) is a riverside favourite.

Oxford has loads of pubs, but few are cheap or quiet – the 16th-century **King's Arms** in Holywell Street (01865 242369) is studenty with good beer; the **Turf Tavern** (01865 243235) between Hertford and New Colleges is Oxford's oldest inn; and the **Perch** (01865 728891) on Binsey Lane has a garden with play area.

Where to stay

Burlington House (374 Banbury Road, 01865 513513, doubles £80-£95) is an outstanding small hotel with B&B prices, but a little way out of town. The **Old Parsonage** (1 Banbury Road, 01865 310210, doubles £155-£200) is classy and ancient, and the **Old Bank Hotel** (92-94 High Street, 01865 799599, doubles £165-£325) is sleek, modernist and arty. Next to the station is the prosaic **Royal Oxford Hotel** (Park End Street, 01865 248432, doubles £135).

Getting there

By train

There are regular trains from Paddington (1hr); your rail ticket qualifies you for a free ride into the centre on an electric bus (every 10mins).

By coach

There are frequent, cheap, fast services from several London departure points; details from National Express (1hr 40mins), Stagecoach (01865 772250) and Oxford Bus Company (01865 785410).

By car

Take Junction 8 off the M40, and then the A40 into town. Park at the edge and use the park & rides.

Tourist information

Oxford Information Centre

15-16 Broad Street, OX1 3AS (01865 726871/ www.visitoxford.org). **Open** *Easter-Oct* 9.30am-5pm Mon-Sat; 10am-3.30pm Sun. *Nov-Easter* 9.30am-5pm Mon-Sat.

Daily tours of Oxford run from the information centre at 11am and 2pm, with additional departures at busy times, running every day except Christmas Day and Boxing Day. Tickets are sold at the information centre during opening hours, otherwise you can buy them directly from the guide. There's a maximum of 19 people on all tours.

Inspector Morse tours

Depart from information centre. **Time** 1.30pm Sat. Follow the footsteps of the celebrated TV detective.

Ghost tours

Depart from information centre. **Time** *June-late Sept,* 31 Oct 7.45pm Fri, Sat.

Take a walk on the dark side of Oxford's streets and alleyways in search of the city's ghoulish past.

Stratford-upon-Avon

This chocolate-box of a town is England's second biggest tourist draw (after London), and for good reason. Yes, it's the birthplace of the most-marketed author of all time, but it's also charming, historic and filled with interesting little sights. The problem is that unless you visit in the off-season you won't get much chance to appreciate any of that: it gets almost unbearably crowded in the summertime, which can make it hard to enjoy its beauty.

Don't be put off by the aggressive marketing of 'Shakespeare Country' – half-timbered architecture overkill, over-zealous cobbling and teashops everywhere. It can all be forgiven if you're one of Will's fans. There's never a shortage of his works to see, and the **Royal Shakespeare Theatre** is the place to see them. If you can't get a ticket, take a backstage tour and visit the **RSC Collection** museum of props and costumes (for both, *see p.358*).

Stratford has been a market town since 1169 and, in a way, that's still what it does best. See the market on a Friday, when locals flock in from outlying villages to the colourful stalls at the top of Wood Street. In the town centre, with its medieval grid pattern, many fine old buildings survive, among them **Harvard House** (High Street, 01789 204507, open June-Oct), which dates from 1596. It was home to Katharine Rogers, mother of John Harvard, founder of Harvard University, and now houses a pewter collection.

In the town centre are **Shakespeare's Birthplace** (01789 204016) on Henley Street; **Hall's Croft** (01789 292107) on Old Town,

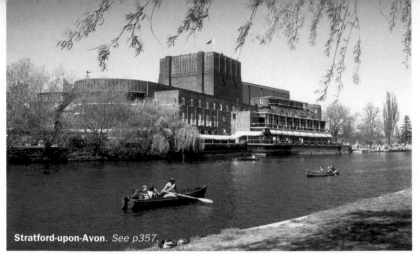

Stratford-upon-Avon. *See p357.*

named after Dr John Hall, who married the Bard's daughter Susanna; and **Nash's House** (01789 292325) on Chapel Street, which once belonged to the first husband of Shakespeare's granddaughter, Elizabeth. In the garden of the latter are the foundations of **New Place**, the writer's last home, demolished in 1759. Shakespeare was educated at **Stratford Grammar School**, on Church Street, and buried in **Holy Trinity** church.

A mile and a half away at **Shottery**, and accessible from Stratford by public footpath, is **Anne Hathaway's Cottage** (01789 292100), where Shakespeare's wife lived before she married him. The girlhood home of his mother, **Mary Arden's House** (01789 293455), is at **Wilmcote**, a pleasant four-mile stroll along the Stratford Canal. Both may also be reached by bus; there are also trains to Wilmcote.

Stratford's charms are enhanced by the **River Avon** and the **Stratford Canal**, and the walks alongside them. Spend some time on the water by hiring a boat at **Stratford Marina**. The long-established **Avon Boating** (01789 267073) has punts and rowing boats for hire.

Royal Shakespeare Company

Waterside, CV37 6BB (box office 0870 609 1110/ tours 01789 403405/www.rsc.org.uk). **Theatre tours** 1.30pm, 5.30pm (11.30am on matinée days) Mon-Fri; 11.30am Sat; noon, 1pm Sun; approx 45min. **Tickets** *Tour* £5; £4 concessions or groups of 10 or more. *Performances* prices vary. **Credit** MC, V.

Where to eat & drink

Callands (First Floor, 13-14 Meer Street, 01789 292282, main courses £5-15) is a wine bar that also offers contemporary English cuisine. For British ingredients with French flair, try **Restaurant Margaux** (6 Union Street, 01789

269106, main courses £8.95-£18), while the **Fox & Goose Inn** (Armscote, off A3400, 01608 682293, main courses £8.95-£14.95) may be off the beaten track but is worth the journey for its boudoir-style dining room and great food. Drink with thesps at the **Dirty Duck** (aka the **Black Swan**, Waterside, 01789 297312).

Where to stay

Caterham House Hotel (58-59 Rother Street, 01789 267309, doubles £80-£85) is close to the Royal Shakespeare Theatre and popular with both audience and actors. The **Falcon Hotel** (Chapel Street, 0870 609 6122, doubles £80-£140) is very olde-worlde: at least 20 of the 84 en suite rooms are in a 16th-century inn. Another good choice, **Victoria Spa Lodge** (Bishopton Lane, 01789 267985, doubles £65) has the feel of a grand country house; Princess Victoria stayed here in 1837.

Tourist information

Tourist Information Centre

Bridgefoot, CV37 6GW (0870 160 7930/www. shakespeare-country.co.uk). **Open** *Early Apr-Sept* 9am-5.30pm Mon-Sat; 10am-4pm Sun. *Oct-early Apr* 9am-5pm Mon-Sat; 10am-3pm Sun.

Getting there

By train

Regular service from Paddington (2hrs 10mins).

By coach

National Express runs regular coaches to Stratford (2hrs 45mins).

By car

Take Junction 15 off the M40, then A46 into town.

Directory

Features

Directory

Getting Around

For London's domestic rail and coach stations, *see p344*.

By air

Gatwick Airport

0870 000 2468/www.baa.co.uk/ gatwick. About 30 miles south of central London, off the M23.
Of the three rail services that link Gatwick to London, the quickest is the **Gatwick Express** (0845 850 1530, www.gatwickexpress.co.uk) to Victoria Station, which takes about 30 minutes and runs from 4.35am to 1.35am daily. Tickets cost £13 for a single, £13.20 for a day return (after 9.30am) and £24 for an open period return (valid for 30 days). Under-16s get half-price tickets; under-5s free.
  Southern (08457 484950, www. southernrailway.com) also runs a rail service between Gatwick and Victoria, with trains every 15-20 minutes (or around hourly 1-4am). It takes about 35 minutes, at £9 for a single, £9.30 for a day return (after 9.30am) and £18 for an open period return (valid for one month). Under-16s get half-price tickets, and under-5s go for free.
  If you're staying in the King's Cross or Bloomsbury area, consider the **Thameslink** service (08457 484950, www.thameslink.co.uk) via London Bridge, Blackfriars, City Thameslink, Farringdon and King's Cross; journey times vary. Tickets to King's Cross cost £10 single (after 9.30am), £10.10 for an off-peak day return and £20.20 for a 3-day open return.
  Hotelink offers a shuttle service (01293 532244, www.hotelink.co.uk) at £22 each way (£20 online). A taxi costs about £100 and takes ages.

Heathrow Airport

0870 000 0123/www.baa.co.uk/ heathrow. About 15 miles west of central London, off the M4.
The **Heathrow Express** (0845 600 1515, www.heathrowexpress.co.uk), runs to Paddington every 15 minutes 5.10am-12.08am daily, and takes 15-20 minutes. The train can be boarded at either of the airport's two tube stations. Tickets cost £14 single or £26 return; under-16s go half-price. Many airlines have check-in desks at Paddington.

A longer but cheaper journey is by tube. Tickets for the 50- to 60-minute **Piccadilly Line** ride into central London cost £3.80 one way (£1.40 under-16s). Trains run every few minutes from about 5am to 11.45pm daily except Sunday, when they run 6am-11pm. Note that the Terminal 4 tube station is closed until summer 2006 while the line is extended to the new Terminal 5 at Heathrow (due for completion in 2008). In the meantime, a shuttle bus service runs from Hatton Cross station to Terminal 4.
  National Express (08705 808080, www.nationalexpress.com) runs daily coach services to London Victoria between 5.35am and 9.35pm daily, leaving Heathrow Central bus terminal around every 30 minutes. For a 90-minute journey to London, you can expect to pay £10 for a single (£5 under-16s) or £15 (£7.50 under-16s) for a return.
  As at Gatwick, **Hotelink** (*see above*) offers an airport-to-hotel shuttle service for £17 per person each way (£16 for online bookings). A taxi into town will cost roughly £100 and take an hour or more, depending on traffic.

London City Airport

7646 0000/www.londoncityairport.com. About 9 miles east of central London.
The Docklands Light Railway (DLR) now includes a stop for London City Airport. The journey into central London takes around 20 minutes, and trains run 5.30am-12.30am Mon-Fri and 7am-11.30pm Sun.
  Most people head to London on the blue **Shuttlebus**, a 25-minute ride to Liverpool Street station via Canary Wharf. It leaves every 15 minutes from 6.30am to 9.30pm, when the terminal closes. Tickets to Liverpool Street station cost £6.50 one-way, or £3.50 to Canary Wharf. Have cash ready to pay the driver. A taxi costs around £20; less to the City.

Luton Airport

01582 405100/www.london-luton. com. About 30 miles north of central London, J10 off the M1.
Luton Airport Parkway Station is close to the airport, but not in it: there's still a short shuttle-bus ride. The **Thameslink** service (*see above*) calls at many stations (King's Cross among them) and has a journey time of 35-45 minutes. Trains leave every

15 minutes or so and cost £10.70 single and £19.70 return, or £10.90 for a cheap day return (after 9.30am Monday to Friday, weekends). The first train from Luton to King's Cross is at 12.06am, the last 2.06am.
  The Luton to Victoria journey takes 60-90 minutes by coach. **Green Line** (0870 608 7261, www.greenline. co.uk) runs a 24-hour service every 30 minutes or so at peak times. A single is £10, £6.50 for under-16s, while returns cost £14 and £11. A taxi costs upwards of £50.

Stansted Airport

0870 000 0303/www.stanstedairport. com. About 35 miles north-east of central London, J8 off the M11.
The quickest way to get to London from Stansted is on the Stansted Express train (08457 484950) to Liverpool Street Station; the journey time is 40-45 minutes. Trains leave every 15-45 minutes depending on the time of day, and tickets cost £14 for a single and £24 for an open period return; under-16s travel half-price, under-5s free.
  The **Airbus** (08705 808080, www. nationalexpress.com) coach service from Stansted to Victoria takes at least an hour and 40 minutes and runs 24 hours. Coaches run roughly every 30 minutes, more frequently at peak times. An adult single costs £10 (£5 for under-16s), a return is £15 (£7.50 for under-16s). A taxi is about £80.

By rail

Eurostar

Waterloo International Terminal, SE1 (08705 186186/www.eurostar.com). Waterloo tube/rail. **Map** p403 M8.
Eurostar trains arrive into the central Waterloo Station (*see p344*).

Information

Details on public transport times and other information can be found online at www.tfl.gov.uk, or by calling 7222 1234. Alternatively see www.journeyplanner.org to help you find the best route.

Travel Information Centres

TfL's Travel Information Centres provide maps and information about the tube, buses and Docklands Light Railway (DLR; *see below*). You can find them in the stations listed below. Call 7222 5600 for more information.

Heathrow Airport Terminals 1, 2 & 3 Underground station 6.30am-10pm daily.
Liverpool Street 7.15am-9pm Mon-Sat; 8.15am-8pm Sun.
Victoria 7.15am-9pm Mon-Sat; 8.15am-8pm Sun.

Travelcards

A flat cash fare of £3 per journey applies across zones 1-6 on the tube; customers save up to £1.50 with Oyster Pre Pay (*see below*). Tube and DLR fares are based on a system of six zones, stretching 12 miles out from the centre of London. Beware of £20 on-the-spot penalty fares, issued to anyone caught without a ticket.

Day Travelcards

If you are only using the Tube, DLR, buses and trams, using Oyster to pay as you go will always be cheaper than a Day Travelcard. If you are also using National Rail services, the Day Travelcard may best meet your needs. Peak Day Travelcards can be used all day Mondays to Fridays (except public holidays). They cost from £6.20 for zones 1-2 (£3.10 child), up to £12.40 for zones 1-6 (£6.20 child). All tickets are valid for journeys started before 4.30am the next day. Most people are happy with the Off-Peak Day Travelcard, which allows you to travel from 9.30am (Mon-Fri) and all day Saturday, Sunday and public holidays. They cost from £4.90 for zones 1-2, rising to £6.30 for zones 1-6.

One-day Family Travelcards

Up to four children travelling with an adult with a valid Travelcard pay £1 for an Off-Peak Day Travelcard. Kids using Oyster to pay-as-they-go pay a maximum of £1 for any Tube/DLR journey within London regardless of time of day or zones travelled.

Three-day Travelcards

If you plan to spend a few days charging around town, you can buy a three-day Travelcard. The peak version can be used all day Monday to Friday on the start date and for any journey that starts before 4.30am on the day following the expiry date, and is available for £15.40 (zones 1-2) or £37.20 (zones 1-6). The off-peak Day Travelcard can be used from 9.30am Monday to Friday and all day on Saturday, Sunday and public

holidays on the start date plus any journey that starts before 4.30am on the day following the expiry date. It is available for £18.90 zones 1-6.

Oyster card

The Oyster card is a travel smart-card, which can be charged with value to pay as you travel and up to three 7-day, monthly or longer period (including annual) travelcards and bus passes at the same time. You can get Oyster cards online from www.tfl.gov.uk/oyster, by calling 0870 849 9999, at tube stations, London travel information centres, some national rail stations and from newsagents. Oyster cards speed up passage through tube station ticket gates as they need only be touched on a special yellow card reader. For most visitors, Oyster is the cheapest way of getting around. Cash single ticket purchases at the time of travel will always cost more than using Oyster to pay-as-you-go.

Any tube journey within Zone 1 using Oyster to pay-as-you-go costs £1.50 (70p for under-16s). A single tube journey within zone 2, 3, 4 5 or 6 costs £1 (50p for under-16s). A single tube journey in zones 1-2 using Oyster to pay-as-you-go costs £2 (7am-7pm Mon-Fri) and £1.50 at other times.

Single tube journeys from zones 1-6 using Oyster to pay-as-you-go is £3.50 (7am-7pm Mon-Fri), £2 at other times and £1 for children.

If you make a number of journeys on the tube, DLR, buses or trams, Oyster fares to pay as you go will always be capped at 50p less than the price of a Day Travelcard, no matter how many journeys in zones 1-6 are made. If you only make one journey using Oyster to pay as you go, you will only be charged a single Oyster fare. You can put up to £90 on to your Oyster card to pay as you go, plus up to three different Travelcards at any one time.

Children

Under-14s can travel free on buses and trams without the need to provide any proof of identity. 14- and 15-year-olds can also travel free but need to get an Under-16 Oyster photocard. For details of how to get this visit www.tfl.gov.uk or call 0845 330 9876.

An Under-16 Oyster photocard is needed by children aged 5-15yrs to pay as they go on the Tube or DLR or to buy 7 Day, monthly or longer period Travelcards and by 11- to 15-year-olds if using the tram to/from Wimbledon (Croydon Tramlink).

Photocards

Photocards are not required for adult rate 7 Day Travelcards, bus passes

or for any adult rate Travelcard or bus pass charged on an Oyster card. Photocards for children can be obtained from any tube or National Rail station, Oyster Ticket stop or London Travel Information Centre. Proof of ID (eg passport) and a photograph are required.

London Underground

Delays are common. Escalators are often out of action. Some lines close at weekends for engineering. It's hot, smelly and crowded in rush hour (8-9.30am and 4.30-7pm Mon-Fri). Nevertheless, the underground rail system – also known as the Tube – is still the quickest way to get around London.

Note that, in addition to the temporary closure of the Heathrow Terminal 4 station on the Piccadilly Line (*see p360*), the whole Waterloo & City Line is closed from 1 April 2006 for five months, and Queensway station is closed until about May 2006.

Using the system

You can get Oyster cards from www.tfl.gov.uk/oyster, by calling 0870 849 9999, at tube stations, London Travel Information Centres, some National Rail stations and newsagents. Single or day tickets can be purchased from a ticket office or from self-service machines. You can buy most tickets and top up Oyster cards at self-service machines. Ticket offices in some stations close early (around 7.30pm), so an Oyster card charged with value is a good way to avoid this.

To enter and exit the Tube using an Oyster card, simply touch it to the yellow reader which will open the gates. Make sure you touch the card when you exit the Tube otherwise you may be charged a higher fare. To enter using a paper ticket, place it in the slot with the black magnetic strip facing down, then pull it out of the top to open the gates. Exiting the system at your destination is done in much the same way, though if you have a single journey ticket, it will be retained by the gate as you leave. There are 12 tube lines, colour-coded on the tube map (*see p416*).

Underground timetable

Underground timetable tube trains run daily from around 5.30am (except Sunday, when they start an hour or

two later, depending on the line). The only exception is Christmas Day, when there is no service. Generally, you won't have to wait more than ten minutes for a train, and during peak times services should run every two or three minutes. Times of last trains vary, though they're usually around 11.30pm-1am daily except Sunday, when they finish 30 minutes to an hour earlier. The only all-night public transport is by night bus (*see below*). There are occasional debates about whether to run the tube an hour later at weekends, but as this would mean starting later it's not a popular idea with early shift workers, who rely on the tube. Watch this space.

Fares

The single fare for adults within Zone 1 is £2 (Pre Pay £1.70). For zones 1-2 it's £2.30 (Pre Pay £2.10 or £2). The zones 1-6 single fare is £3.80 (Pre Pay £3.50 or £2). The single fare for children in Zone 1 is 60p, 80p for zones 1-2, rising to £1.40 for zones 1-6.

Carnet

If you're planning on making a lot of short-hop journeys within Zone 1 over a period of several days, it makes sense to buy a carnet of ten tickets for £15 (£5 for children). Note that if you exit a station outside of Zone 1 and are caught with only a carnet ticket, you'll be liable to a £10 penalty fare.

Docklands Light Railway (DLR)

DLR trains (7363 9700, www.tfl.gov.uk/dlr) run from Bank (Central or Waterloo & City lines) or Tower Gateway, close to Tower Hill tube (Circle and District lines), to Stratford, Beckton and the Isle of Dogs to Island Gardens, then south of the river to Greenwich, Deptford and Lewisham. Trains run from 5.30am to 12.30am Monday to Saturday and 7am to 11.30pm Sunday.

Fares

The adult single fare on DLR, except to/from Bank and Tower Gateway, is £1.50. The adult single fare is £3 for DLR journeys to/from Tower Gateway and Bank.

The DLR also offers one day 'Rail & River Rover' tickets, which combine unlimited DLR travel with a boat trip between Greenwich, Tower and Westminster piers (riverboats run 10am-6pm; call City Cruises on 7740 0400 for round-trip times). Starting at Tower Gateway, trains

leave on the hour (from 10am), with a DLR guide giving a commentary as the train glides along. Tickets cost £9.50 for adults, £4.75 for kids and £25 for a family pass (two adults and up to three kids); under-5s go free.

Note that family tickets can only be bought in person from the piers.

Buses

In the past year, hundreds of new buses have been introduced to London's network, as the famous Routemasters have been phased out. These are all low-floor and more easily accessible to wheelchair-users and passengers with buggies, and run 24 hours. The introduction of 'bendy buses' with multiple-door entry and the 'Pay Before You Board' scheme have also contributed to speeding up boarding times at bus stops. Many buses, particularly in central London, now require you to buy a ticket before boarding. Do so: there are inspectors about, who can fine you £20. You can buy one (or a one-day Bus Pass) from pavement ticket machines, though, frustratingly, they're sometimes out of order. Yellow signs on bus stops show where this is a requirement.

Fares

Using Oyster to pay as you go costs £1 or 80p depending on the time you travel; the most you will pay a day will be £3. Paying by cash at the time of travel costs £1.50 for a single trip. Under-16s travel for free (14- and 15-year-olds need an Under-16 Oyster photocard). A one-day Bus Pass gives unlimited bus and tram travel at £3.50.

Bus Savers

A book of six Saver tickets costs £6 (under-16s travel free) and can be bought at some newsagents and tube station ticket offices.

Night buses

Many buses run 24 hours a day, seven days a week. There are also some special night buses with an 'N' prefix to the route number, which operate from about 11pm to 6am. Most services run every 15 to 30 minutes, but many busier routes have a bus around every ten minutes. Fares for night buses are the same

as for daytime buses. Travelcards and bus passes can be used on night buses at no additional charge – and until 4.30am on the day after they expire. Oyster Pre Pay and bus Saver tickets are also valid on night buses.

Green Line buses

Green Line buses (0870 608 7261, www.greenline.co.uk) serve the suburbs and towns within a 40-mile radius of London. Their main departure point is Eccleston Bridge, SW1 (Colonnades Coach Station, behind Victoria), and they run 24-hour services.

Rail services

Independently run commuter services leave from the city's main rail stations (*see p344*). Travelcards are valid on these services within the right zones. One of the most useful is **Silverlink** (0845 601 4867, www.silverlink-trains.com; or National Rail Enquiries on 08457 484 950), which runs from Richmond in the south-west to North Woolwich in the east, via London City Airport. Trains run about every 20 minutes daily except Sunday, when they run every half-hour.

Tramlink

A tram service runs between Beckenham, Croydon, Addington and Wimbledon in south London. Travelcards that include zones 3, 4, 5 or 6 and all Bus Passes can be used on trams. Single cash tram fares are £1.50 (Oyster fare £1 or 80p; 50p for 16- to 17-year-old photocard holders). A one-day Bus Pass gives unlimited tram and bus travel at £3.50 for adults.

Water transport

The times of London's various river services differ, but most operate every 20 minutes to one hour between 10.30am and 5pm. Services may be more frequent and run later in summer. Call the operators listed below for schedules and fares, or see www.tfl.gov.uk.

Directory

Thames Clippers (www. thamesclippers.com) runs a reliable commuter boat service. Piers to board the Clippers from are: Savoy (near Embankment tube), Blackfriars, Bankside (for the Globe), London Bridge and St Katharine's (Tower Bridge). The names in bold below are the names of piers.

Embankment–Tower 30mins)–
Greenwich (40mins); Catamaran Cruises 7987 1185/www.bateaux london.com.
Greenland Dock–Canary Wharf (8mins)–**St Katharine's** (7mins)–**London Bridge City** (4mins)–**Bankside** (3mins)–**Blackfriars** (3mins)–**Savoy** (4mins); Collins River Enterprises 7252 3018/ www.thamesclippers.com.
Savoy–Cadogan (20mins)–**Chelsea** (2mins); Connoisseur Charters 7376 3344/ www.connoisseur.co.uk.
Westminster–(Thames) Barrier Gardens (1hr 30mins); Thames Cruises 7930 3373/ www.thamescruises.com.
Westminster–Festival (5mins)–**London Bridge City** (20mins)–**St Katharine's** (5mins); Crown River 7936 2033/www.crownriver.com.
Westminster–Greenwich (1hr); Thames River Services 7930 4097/ www.westminsterpier.co.uk.
Westminster–Kew (1hr 30mins)–**Richmond** (30mins)–**Hampton Court** (1hr 30mins); Westminster Passenger Service Association 7930 2062/www.wpsa.co.uk.
Westminster–Tower (40mins); City Cruises 7740 0400/ www.citycruises.com.

Taxis

Black cabs

Licensed London taxis are known as black cabs – even though they come in a variety of colours – and are a feature of London life. Drivers of black cabs must pass a test called 'the Knowledge' to prove they know every street in central London, and the shortest route to it.

If a taxi's orange 'For Hire' sign is switched on, it can be hailed. If a taxi stops, the cabbie must take you to your destination, if it's within seven miles. Expect to pay slightly higher rates after 8pm on weekdays and all weekend. It can be hard to find a free cab, especially just after the pubs close, and the minute it rains.

You can book black cabs in advance. Both **Radio Taxis** (7272 0272; credit cards only) and **Dial-a-Cab** (7253 5000) run 24-hour services (charging a booking fee). Enquiries or complaints about black cabs should be made to the Public Carriage Office. Note the cab's badge number, which should be displayed in the rear of the cab and on its back bumper. For lost property, *see p371*.

Public Carriage Office

15 Penton Street, Islington, N1 9PU (0845 602 7000/www.tfl.gov.uk/pco). **Open** *Phone enquiries* 9am-5pm Mon-Fri. **Map** p404 N2.

Minicabs

Minicabs (saloon cars) are generally cheaper than black cabs, but only use licensed firms (look for the yellow disc in the front and rear windows) and avoid those who tout for business. They'll be unlicensed and uninsured, possibly dangerous, almost certainly won't know how to get around, and will charge huge rates.

There are, happily, plenty of trustworthy and licensed local minicab firms. Londonwide firms include **Lady Cabs** (7272 3300), which employs only women drivers, and **Addison Lee** (7387 8888). In addition, the Mayor recently launched a campaign aimed at reducing the number of assaults on women by unlawful minicab drivers; to find a reputable one in your area, text HOME to 60835. Always ask the price when you book and confirm it with the driver.

Driving

Congestion charge

The Congestion Charging zone operates across eight square miles of central London, bounded by the 'inner ring road' linking Euston Road, Pentonville Road, Tower Bridge, Elephant & Castle, Vauxhall Bridge Road, Park Lane and Marylebone Road. This road provides a route around the charging zone; charges apply only to vehicles inside it, not those travelling on it. In September 2005 plans were announced for the charging zone to be increased westwards, though not until February 2007.

There is an £8 daily charge for driving or parking a vehicle on public roads within this zone between 7am and 6.30pm Monday to Friday. You'll know when you're about to drive into the charging zone from the red 'C' signs painted on the road. There are no tollbooths, barriers or tickets; instead you pay to register your vehicle registration number on a database. Cameras read your number plate as you enter or drive within the zone and check the vehicle registration number has been matched to show that you have paid the charge. Register and pay online (www.cclondon.com) or by calling 0845 900 1234; passes can be bought from newsagents, garages and NCP car parks. You can pay any time during the day of entry, even after your journey, but it's £2 extra between 10pm and midnight on the day of travel. Expect a fine of £100 (£50 if paid within 14 days) if you fail to pay by midnight on the day of travel (rising to £155 if you delay payment). For more details call 0845 900 1234 or go to www.cclondon. com. See also the **Central London by Area** map, *p394*.

Breakdown services

If you're a member of a motoring organisation in another country, check to see if it has a reciprocal agreement with a British organisation.

Both the AA and the RAC offer schemes that cover Europe in addition to the UK.

AA (Automobile Association)
Information 08705 500600/ breakdown 0800 887766/members 0800 444999/www.theaa.com.
Open 24hrs daily. **Credit** MC, V.

ETA (Environmental Transport Association) *68 High Street, Weybridge, Surrey KT13 8RS (01932 828882/www.eta.co.uk).*
Open *Office* 8am-6pm Mon-Fri; 9am-4pm Sat. *Breakdown service* 24hrs daily. **Credit** MC, V.

RAC (Royal Automobile Club)
RAC House, 1 Forest Road, Feltham, Middx TW13 7RR (breakdown 0800 828282/office & membership 0870 572 2722/www.rac.co.uk). **Open** *Office* 8am-Mon-Fri; 8.30am-5pm Sat. *Breakdown service* 24hrs daily. **Credit** AmEx, DC, MC, V.

Parking

Central London is scattered with parking meters, but free ones are rare, they'll cost you up to £1 for every 15 minutes, and you'll be limited to two hours on the meter. Parking on a single or double yellow line, a red line or in residents' parking areas during the day is illegal, and you may end up being fined, clamped or towed.

However, in the evening (from 6pm or 7pm in much of central London) and at various times at weekends, parking on single yellow lines is legal and free. If you find a clear spot on a single yellow line during the evening, look for a sign giving the regulations for that area. Meters also become free at certain times during evenings and weekends. Parking on double yellow lines and red routes is illegal at all times.

NCP 24-hour car parks (0870 606 7050, www.ncp.co.uk) around London are numerous but pricey (£6-£10 for two hours). Central ones include Arlington House, Arlington Street, St James's, W1; Upper Ground, Southwark, SE1; and 4-5 Denman Street, Soho, W1. Many are underground, and a few are frequented by drug users, so be vigilant.

Clamping

The immobilising of illegally parked vehicles with a clamp is commonplace in London. There will be a label on the car telling you which payment centre to phone or visit. You'll have to stump up an £80 release fee and show a valid licence.

The payment centre will de-clamp your car within the next four hours, but they won't say exactly when. If you don't remove your car at once, they might clamp it again, so wait by your vehicle.

Vehicle removal

If your car has disappeared, the chances are, if it was legally parked, that it's been nicked; if not, it's probably been taken to a car pound. A release fee of £150 is levied for removal, plus £25 per day from the first midnight after removal. To add insult to injury, you'll also probably get a parking ticket of £60-£100 when you collect the car (which will be reduced by 50 per cent discount if paid within 14 days). To find out how to retrieve your car, call the Trace Service hotline (7747 4747).

Vehicle hire

To hire a car, you must have at least one year's driving experience with a full current driving licence; in addition, many car hire firms refuse to hire vehicles out to people under 23. If you're an overseas visitor, your driving licence is valid in Britain for a year.

Prices vary wildly; always ring several competitors for a quote. **Easycar's** online-only service, at www.easycar.com, offers competitive rates, just so long as you don't mind driving a branded car around town.

Alamo *0870 400 4508/www.alamo. com.* **Open** 8am-6pm Mon-Fri; 9am-5pm Sat; 10am-3pm Sun. **Credit** AmEx, MC, V.
Avis *08705 900500/www.avis.co.uk.* **Open** 24hrs daily. **Credit** AmEx, DC, MC, V.
Budget *0870 156 5656/www.go budget.com.* **Open** 8am-8pm daily. **Credit** AmEx, DC, MC, V.
Enterprise *0870 607 7757/www. enterprise.com.* **Open** 7am-midnight Mon-Fri; 8am-midnight Sat, Sun. **Credit** AmEx, MC, V.
Europcar *0870 607 5000/www. europcar.co.uk.* **Open** 24hrs daily. **Credit** AmEx, DC, MC, V.
Hertz *0870 599 6699/www.hertz. co.uk.* **Open** 24hrs daily. **Credit** AmEx, MC, V.

Motorbike hire

HGB Motorcycles *69-71 Park Way, Ruislip Manor, Middx HA4 8NS (01895 676451/www.hgbmotor cycles.co.uk). Ruislip Manor tube.*
Open 9am-6pm Mon-Fri. **Credit** MC, V.
Rental prices include 250 miles a day, with excess mileage at 10p a mile, AA cover, insurance and VAT. Bikes can only be hired with a credit card and a deposit (£350-£850). You'll need your own helmet.

Cycling

London isn't the friendliest of towns for cyclists, but the **London Cycle Network** (see www.londoncyclenetwork. org) and **London Cycling Campaign** (7928 7220, www. lcc.org.uk) help make it better. Call **Transport for London** (7222 1234) for cycling maps.

Cycle hire

OY Bike (www.oybike.com) has 28 bike stations in west London where you can rent a bike for a reasonable cost 24/7 by calling in on a mobile phone (the lock is electronically released). You will need to pre-register with £10 credit.

London Bicycle Tour Company
1A Gabriel's Wharf, 56 Upper Ground, South Bank, SE1 9PP (7928 6838/www.londonbicycle.com). Southwark tube, Blackfriars or Waterloo tube/rail. **Open** 10am-6pm daily. **Hire** £3/hr; £16/1st day; £8/day thereafter. **Deposit** £100 cash or £1 by credit card. **Credit** AmEx, DC, MC, V. **Map** p406 N7.
Bikes, tandems and rickshaw hire; bicycle tours Sat, Sun.

Walking

The best way to see London is on foot, but the city is very complicated in its street layout – even locals carry maps around with them. We've included street maps of central London in the back of this book (starting on p392), but, otherwise, the standard Geographers' *A–Z* and Collins' *London Street Atlas* versions are very easy to use.

Directory

Resources A-Z

Addresses

London postcodes are less helpful than they could be for locating addresses. The first element starts with a compass point – out of N, E, SE, SW, W and NW, plus the smaller EC (East Central) and WC (West Central) – which at least gives you a basic idea. However, the number that follows bears no relation to geography (unless it's a 1, which indicates that the address is central), though they apparently follow a rough alphabetical order. So N2, for example, is way out in the boondocks (East Finchley), while W2 includes the very central Bayswater.

Age restrictions

You must be 17 or older to drive in the United Kingdom, and 18 to buy cigarettes or to buy or be served alcohol (to be safe, carry photo ID if you look younger). The age of heterosexual and homosexual consent is 16.

Business

Conventions & conferences

London Tourist Board & Convention Bureau
7234 5800/www.londontown.com. The LTB runs a venue enquiry service for conventions and exhibitions. Call or email for an information pack that lists the facilities offered by various venues.

Queen Elizabeth II Conference Centre
Broad Sanctuary, Westminster, SW1P 3EE (7222 5000/www. qeiicc.co.uk). Westminster tube. **Open** 8am-6pm Mon-Fri. *Conference facilities* 24hrs daily. **Map** p403 K9. This purpose-built centre has some of the best conference facilities in the capital. Rooms have capacities ranging from 40 to 1,100, all with wireless LAN technology installed.

Couriers & shippers

DHL and FedEx offer courier services both locally and internationally; Excess Baggage is the UK's largest shipper of luggage.

DHL *St Alphage House, 2 Fore Street, The City, EC2Y 5DA (7562 3000/www.dhl.co.uk). Moorgate tube/ rail.* **Open** 9am-5.30pm Mon-Fri. **Credit** AmEx, DC, MC, V. **Map** p404 P5.
Excess Baggage *168 Earl's Court Road, Earl's Court, SW5 9QQ (7373 1977/www.excess-baggage.com). Earl's Court tube.* **Open** 8am-6pm Mon-Fri; 9am-1pm Sat. **Credit** AmEx, MC, V. **Map** p398 B10.
FedEx *0800 123800/www.fedex. com.* **Open** 7.30am-7.30pm Mon-Fri. **Credit** AmEx, DC, MC, V.

Office hire & business centres

ABC rents office equipment, while British Monomarks offers communications services.

ABC Business Machines *59 Chiltern Street, Marylebone, W1U 6NF (7486 5634/www.abcbusiness. co.uk). Baker Street tube.* **Open** 9am-5.30pm Mon-Fri; 9.30am-12.30pm Sat. **Credit** MC, V. **Map** p400 G5.
British Monomarks *Monomarks House, 27 Old Gloucester Street, Holborn, WC1N 3XX (7419 5000/ www.britishmonomarks.co.uk). Holborn tube.* **Open** *Mail forwarding* 9.30am-5.30pm Mon-Fri. *Telephone answering* 9am-6pm Mon-Fri. **Credit** AmEx, MC, V. **Map** p401 L5.

Customs

See also www.hmrc.gov.uk.

From inside the EU

You may bring in the following quantities of tax-paid goods, as long as they are for your own consumption (there are some exceptions when coming from Eastern European countries).

● 3,200 cigarettes or 400 cigarillos or 200 cigars or 3kg (6.6lb) tobacco;
● 90 litres wine plus either ten litres of spirits or liqueurs (more than 22% alcohol by volume) or 20 litres of fortified wine (under 22% ABV), sparkling wine or other liqueurs.

From outside the EU

These are total allowances, whether or not the goods were purchased duty-free.

● 200 cigarettes or 100 cigarillos or 50 cigars or 250g of tobacco;
● 2 litres of still table wine plus either 1 litre of spirits or strong liqueurs over 22% volume or two litres of fortified wine, sparkling wine or other liqueurs;
● £145 worth of all other goods including gifts and souvenirs.

Travel advice

For up-to-date information on travelling to a specific country – including the latest news on safety and security, health issues, local laws and customs – contact your home country government's department of foreign affairs. Most have websites packed with useful statistics, advice and background information for would-be travellers.

Australia
www.smartraveller.gov.au

Canada
www.voyage.gc.ca

New Zealand
www.mft.govt.nz/travel

Republic of Ireland
http://foreignaffairs.gov.ie

UK
www.fco.gov.uk/travel

USA
www.state.gov/travel

Directory

Disabled

As a city that evolved long before the needs of disabled people were considered, London is a difficult place for disabled visitors, though legislation is gradually improving access and general facilities. In 2004 anyone who provides a service to the public was required to make 'reasonable adjustments' to their properties, and the capital's bus fleet is now becoming more wheelchair accessible. The tube, however, remains extremely escalator-dependent and can therefore be of only limited use to wheelchair users. The *Tube access guide* booklet is available free of charge from ticket offices, or by calling the Travel and Information line for more information (7222 1234).

Most major visitor attractions and hotels offer good accessibility, though provisions for the hearing- and sight-disabled are patchier. Call businesses in advance to enquire about facilities, and use your judgement in interpreting their response. *Access in London* is an invaluable reference book for disabled travellers, available for a £10 donation (Sterling cheque, cash US dollars or online via PayPal to gordon.couch@virgin.net) from Access Project (www.accessproject-phsp.org), 39 Bradley Gardens, West Ealing, W13 8HE.

Artsline

54 Chalton Street, Somers Town, NW1 1HS (tel/textphone 7388 2227/www.artslineonline.com). Euston tube/rail. **Open** 9.30am-5.30pm Mon-Fri. **Map** p401 K3.
Information on disabled access to arts and entertainment events.

Can Be Done

11 Woodcock Hill, Harrow, Middx HA1 2RZ (8907 2400/www.canbedone.co.uk). Kenton tube/rail. **Open** 9.30am-5pm Mon-Fri.
This company runs disabled-adapted holidays and tours in London and around the UK.

DAIL (Disability Arts in London)

Diorama Arts Centre, 34 Osnaburgh Street, Fitzrovia, NW1 3ND (7916 6351/www.ldaf.org). Great Portland Street tube. **Enquiries** 11am-4pm Mon-Fri. **Map** p400 H4.
DAIL produces a bi-monthly magazine (£9/yr disabled, £15/yr non-disabled, £40 for overseas subscribers). DAIL is part of **LDAF** (London Disability Arts Forum; 7916 5484), which organises events for disabled people in London.

Greater London Action on Disability

1st Floor, Downstream Buildings, 1 London Bridge, SE1 9BG (7022 1890/textphone 7378 1686/www.glad.org.uk). London Bridge tube/rail. **Open** *Phone enquiries* 9am-5pm Mon-Fri. **Map** p407 Q8.
A valuable resource for disabled visitors and residents.

Royal Association for Disability & Rehabilitation

12 City Forum, 250 City Road, Islington, EC1V 2PU (7250 3222/textphone 7250 4119/www.radar.org.uk). Old Street tube/rail. **Open** 9am-5pm Mon-Fri. **Map** p404 P3.
A national organisation for disabled voluntary groups that also publishes books and the bi-monthly magazine *New Bulletin* (£35/yr).

Tourism for All

0845 124 9971/www.tourismforall.org.uk. **Open** *Helpline* 9am-12.30pm Mon-Fri.
Information for older people and people with disabilities in relation to accessible accommodation and other tourism services.

Wheelchair Travel & Access Mini Buses

1 Johnston Green, Guildford, Surrey GU2 9XS (01483 233640/www.wheelchair-travel.co.uk). **Open** 9am-5.30pm Mon-Fri; 9am-noon Sat.
Hires out converted vehicles (driver optional), plus cars with hand controls and 'Chairman' cars.

Electricity

The UK uses the standard European 220-240V, 50-cycle AC voltage. British plugs use three pins, so travellers with two-pin European appliances should bring an adaptor, as should anyone using US appliances, which run off a 110-120V, 60-cycle.

Embassies & consulates

American Embassy *24 Grosvenor Square, Mayfair, W1A 1AE (7499 9000/www.usembassy.org.uk). Bond Street or Marble Arch tube.* **Open** 8.30am-5.30pm Mon-Fri. **Map** p402 G7.
Australian High Commission *Australia House, Strand, Holborn, WC2B 4LA (7379 4334/www.australia.org.uk). Holborn or Temple tube.* **Open** 9.30am-3.30pm Mon-Fri. **Map** p403 M6.
Canadian High Commission *38 Grosvenor Street, Mayfair, W1K 4AA (7258 6600/www.canada.org.uk). Bond Street or Oxford Circus tube.* **Open** 8-11am Mon-Fri. **Map** p402 H7.
Irish Embassy *17 Grosvenor Place, Belgravia, SW1X 7HR (7235 2171/ passports & visas 7225 7700). Hyde Park Corner tube.* **Open** 9.30am-12.30pm, 2.30-5.30pm Mon-Fri. **Map** p402 G9.
New Zealand High Commission *New Zealand House, 80 Haymarket, St James's, SW1Y 4YQ (7930 8422/www.nzembassy.com). Piccadilly Circus tube.* **Open** 9am-5pm Mon-Fri. **Map** p408 W4.
South African High Commission *South Africa House, Trafalgar Square, St James's, WC2N 5DP (7451 7299/www.southafricahouse.com). Charing Cross tube/rail.* **Enquiries** 8.30am-12.45pm Mon-Fri. **Map** p409 X5.

Emergencies

In the event of a serious accident, fire or incident, call **999** – free from any phone, including payphones – and ask for ambulance, fire service or police. For addresses of Accident & Emergency departments, *see p369*; for helplines, *see p370*; and for city police stations, *see p373*.

Gay & lesbian

For a complete gay guide to the capital, purchase the *Time Out Gay & Lesbian London Guide* (£9.99). The phonelines below offer help and information.

London Friend *7837 3337/ www.londonfriend.org.uk.* **Open** 7.30-10pm daily.
London Lesbian & Gay Switchboard *7837 7324/www.queery.org.uk.* **Open** 24hrs daily.

Health

Free emergency medical treatment under the National Health Service (NHS) is available to the following:

● European Union nationals, plus those of Iceland, Norway and Liechtenstein. They may also be entitled to treatment for a non-emergency condition on production of form E112 or E128.
● Nationals of Bulgaria, the Czech and Slovak Republics, Gibraltar, Hungary, Malta, New Zealand, Russia, most former Soviet Union states and the former Yugoslavia.
● Residents, irrespective of nationality, of Anguilla, Australia, Barbados, British Virgin Islands, Channel Islands, Falkland Islands, Iceland, Isle of Man, Montserrat, Poland, Romania, St Helena and Turks & Caicos Islands.
● Anyone who has been in the UK for the previous 12 months.
● Anyone who has come to the UK to take up permanent residence.
● Students and trainees whose courses require more than 12 weeks in employment during the first year.
● Refugees and others who have sought refuge in the UK.
● People with HIV/AIDS at a special clinic for the treatment of STDs. The treatment covered is limited to a diagnostic test and counselling associated with that test.

There are no NHS charges for services including:

● Treatment in Accident & Emergency departments.
● Emergency ambulance transport to a hospital.
● Diagnosis and treatment of certain communicable diseases, including STDs.
● Family planning services.
● Compulsory psychiatric treatment.

Accident & emergency

Below are listed most of the central London hospitals that have 24-hour Accident & Emergency departments.

Charing Cross Hospital *Fulham Palace Road, Hammersmith, W6 8RF (8846 1234). Barons Court or Hammersmith tube.*
Chelsea & Westminster Hospital *369 Fulham Road, Chelsea, SW10 9NH (8746 8000). South Kensington tube.* **Map** p398 C12.
Guy's Hospital *St Thomas Street (entrance Snowsfields), Bankside, SE1 9RT (7188 7188). London Bridge tube/rail.* **Map** p406 P8.

Homerton Hospital *Homerton Row, Homerton, E9 6SR (8510 5555). Homerton rail/bus 242.*
Royal Free Hospital *Pond Street, Hampstead, NW3 2QG (7794 0500). Belsize Park tube/Hampstead Heath rail.*
Royal London Hospital *Whitechapel Road, Whitechapel, E1 1BB (7377 7000). Whitechapel tube.*
St Mary's Hospital *Praed Street, Paddington, W2 1NY (7886 6666). Paddington tube/rail.* **Map** p397 D5.
St Thomas's Hospital *Lambeth Palace Road, Lambeth, SE1 7EH (7188 7188). Westminster tube/ Waterloo tube/rail.* **Map** p403 L9.
University College Hospital *Grafton Way, Fitzrovia, WC1E 3BG (7387 9300). Euston Square or Warren Street tube.* **Map** p400 J4.
Whittington Hospital *Highgate Hill, Archway, N19 5NF (7272 3070). Archway tube.*

Complementary medicine

For a full list of alternative health centres, see the *Time Out Health & Fitness Guide* (£9.99).

British Homeopathic Association

0870 444 3950/www.trust homeopathy.org. **Open** *Phone enquiries* 9am-5pm Mon-Fri.
The BHA will refer you to the nearest homeopathic chemist/doctor.

Contraception & abortion

Family planning advice, contraceptive supplies and abortions are free to British citizens on the NHS; also to EU residents and foreign nationals living in Britain. Phone the Contraception Helpline on 0845 310 1334 or visit www.fpa.org. uk for your local **Family Planning Association**. The 'morning after' pill (around £25), effective up to 72 hours after intercourse, is available over the counter at pharmacies.

British Pregnancy Advisory Service

0845 730 4030/www.bpas.org. Callers are referred to their nearest clinic for treatment. Contraceptives are available, as is pregnancy testing.

Brook Advisory Centre

7284 6040/helpline 0800 018 5023/ www.brook.org.uk). **Open** *Helpline* 9am-5pm Mon-Fri.
Advice and referrals on sexual health, contraception and abortion, plus free pregnancy tests for under-25s. Call for your nearest clinic.

Marie Stopes House

Family Planning Clinic/ Well Woman Centre
108 Whitfield Street, Fitzrovia, W1P 6BE (0845 300 8090/www.marie stopes.org.uk). Warren Street tube. **Open** *Clinic* 8.30am-4.30pm Mon-Fri. *Termination helpline* 7am-10pm Mon-Fri. **Map** p400 J4.
For contraceptive advice, emergency contraception, pregnancy testing, an abortion service, cervical and health screening or gynaecological services. Fees may apply.

Dentists

Dental care is free for resident students, under-18s and people on benefits. All other patients must pay. NHS-eligible patients pay on a subsidised scale. To find an NHS dentist, get in touch with the local Health Authority or a Citizens' Advice Bureau (*see p.370*), or the following:

Dental Emergency Care Service

Guy's Hospital, St Thomas Street, Bankside, SE1 9RT (7188 0511). London Bridge tube/rail. **Open** 9am-5pm Mon-Fri. **Map** p406 Q8.
Queues start forming at 8am; arrive by 10am if you're to be seen at all.

Doctors

If you're a British citizen or working in the United Kingdom, you can go to any general practitioner (GP). If you're not visiting your usual GP, you'll need to give their details so your records can be updated. People ordinarily resident in the UK, including overseas students, are also permitted to register with an NHS doctor. If you fall outside these categories, you can still see a GP but will need to pay. Your hotel concierge should be able to recommend a suitable one.

Directory

Great Chapel Street Medical Centre

13 Great Chapel Street, Soho, W1F 8FL (7437 9360). Leicester Square, Oxford Circus or Tottenham Court Road tube. **Open** *Drop in* 11am-12.30am, 2-4pm Mon, Tue, Thur; 2-4pm Wed, Fri. **Map** p408 W2.
A walk-in NHS surgery for anyone without a doctor. Phone before you go, as it operates different clinics each day.

Hospitals

For a list of hospitals with A&E departments, *see p369*; for other hospitals, see the *Yellow Pages* directory.

Pharmacies

Also called 'chemists' in the UK. Larger supermarkets and all branches of Boots (*see p255*) have a pharmacy, and there are independents on the high street. Staff are qualified to advise on over-the-counter medicines. Most pharmacies keep shop hours (9am-6pm, closed Sun). A few open later; *see p261*.

Prescriptions

A pharmacist will dispense medicines on receipt of a prescription from a GP. NHS prescriptions cost £6.50; under-16s and over-60s are exempt, and contraception is free for all. If you're not eligible to see an NHS doctor, you'll be charged cost price for medicines prescribed by a private doctor.

STDs, HIV & AIDS

NHS Genito-Urinary Clinics (such as the Centre for Sexual Health; *see below*) are affiliated to major hospitals. They provide free, confidential treatment of STDs and other problems, such as thrush and cystitis; offer counselling about HIV and other STDs; and can conduct blood tests.
The 24-hour **Sexual Healthline** (0800 567123, www.playingsafely.co.uk) is free and confidential. Check

their website to find your nearest clinic. For other helplines, *see below*; for abortion and contraception services, *see p369*.

Ambrose King Centre

Royal London Hospital, Whitechapel Road, Whitechapel, E1 1BB (7377 7306/www.bartsandthelondon.nhs. uk). Whitechapel tube. **Open** 9.30am-4pm Mon, Tue; noon-4pm Wed, Thur; 9.30am-noon Fri.
Screening for and treatment of STDs, HIV testing and counselling. Services are provided on a walk-in basis; the average waiting time is 3 hours.

Centre for Sexual Health

Genito-Urinary Clinic, Jefferiss Wing, St Mary's Hospital, Praed Street, Paddington, W2 1NY (7886 1697). Paddington tube/rail. **Open** *Walk-in clinic* 8.45am-6.15pm Mon, Tue, Thur; 11.45am-6.15pm Wed; 8.45am-1.15pm Fri. **Map** p397 D5.
A free and confidential walk-in clinic. New patients must arrive at least 30 minutes before closing.

Mortimer Market Centre for Sexual Health

Mortimer Market Centre, Mortimer Market, off Capper Street, Bloomsbury, WC1E 6JD (appointments 7530 5050). Goodge Street or Warren Street tube. **Open** 9am-6pm Mon, Tue, Thur; 1-5pm Wed; 9am-1pm Fri. **Map** p400 J4.
Axis 22 is a clinic for gay and heterosexual men and women aged 22 and under (3.45pm Mon). Make an appointment if you can.

Terrence Higgins Trust Lighthouse

52-54 Gray's Inn Road, Holborn, WC1X 8JU (office 7831 0330/ helpline 0845 122 1200/www.tht. org.uk). Chancery Lane tube. **Open** *Office* 9.30am-5.30pm Mon-Fri. *Helpline* 10am-10pm Mon-Fri; noon-6pm Sat, Sun. **Map** p401 M5.
This well-known charity advises and counsels those with HIV/AIDS, their relatives, lovers and friends. It also offers free leaflets about AIDS and safer sex.

Helplines

Sexual health helplines can also be found in **STDs, HIV & AIDS** (*see above*).

Alcoholics Anonymous

0845 769 7555/www.alcoholics-anonymous.org.uk.

Citizens' Advice Bureaux

The council-run CABs offer free legal, financial and personal advice. Check the phone book or see www.citizens advice.org.uk for your nearest office.

NHS Direct

0845 4647/www.nhsdirect.nhs.uk. **Open** 24hrs daily.
NHS Direct is a free, first-stop service for medical advice on all subjects.

National Missing Persons Helpline

0500 700 700/www.missing persons.org. **Open** 24hrs daily.
The volunteer-run NMPH publicises information on anyone reported missing, and helps to find missing persons. Its 'Message Home' freephone service (0800 700 740) allows runaways to reassure friends or family of their wellbeing without revealing their whereabouts.

Rape & Sexual Abuse Support Centre

8683 3300/www.rapecrisis.org.uk. **Open** *Helpline* noon-2.30pm, 7-9.30pm Mon-Fri; 2.30-5pm Sat, Sun.
Provides support and information for victims and families.

Samaritans

0845 790 9090/www.samaritans. org.uk. **Open** 24hrs daily.
The Samaritans listen to anyone with emotional problems. It's a busy service, so persevere when phoning.

Victim Support

Head office: Cramner House, 39 Brixton Road, Brixton, SW9 6DZ (0845 303 0900/www.victim support.com). **Open** *Support line* 9am-9pm Mon-Fri; 9am-7pm Sat, Sun.
Volunteer provides emotional and practical support to victims of crime, including information and advice on legal procedures. Interpreters can be arranged where necessary.

Insurance

Insuring personal belongings is highly advisable. It can be difficult to arrange once you've arrived in London, so do so before you leave.
Medical insurance is usually included in travel insurance packages. Unless your country has a reciprocal medical treatment arrangement with Britain (*see p369*), it's very important to check that you do have adequate health cover.

Internet

Most hotels have modem plug-in points (dataports) in each room (increasingly, this is being replaced with broadband or wireless access). Those that don't usually offer some other form of surfing.

There are lots of cybercafés around town, including the **EasyInternetCafé** chain (*see below*), as well as numerous smaller ones. You'll also find terminals in public libraries (*see below*). For more, check www.cybercafes.com. For the 'technology mile' along Upper Street, N1, *see p40*.

Wireless access is just taking off here, slightly more slowly than in the US (perhaps because of higher charges). Some major railway stations, including London Bridge and Charing Cross, parts of the major airports and many Starbucks locations offer it, usually for a fee. For locations, check with your provider or visit www.wi-fihotspotlist.com.

Internet access

easyInternetCafé
160-166 Kensington High Street, W8 7RG (www.easyeverything.com). High Street Kensington tube. **Open** 7am-11pm daily. **Net access** from 50p. **Terminals** 394. **Map** p398 B9. **Other locations**: throughout the city.

Left luggage

Airports

Gatwick Airport *South Terminal 01293 502014/North Terminal 01293 502013.*
Heathrow Airport *Terminal 1 8745 5301/Terminals 2-3 8759 3344/Terminal 4 8897 6874.*
London City Airport *7646 0162.*
Stansted Airport *01279 663213.*

Rail & bus stations

The threat of terrorism has meant that London stations tend to have left-luggage desks rather than lockers; to find out whether a train station offers this facility, call 08457 484950.

Legal help

Those in difficulties can visit a Citizens' Advice Bureau (*see p370*) or contact the groups below. Try the Legal Services Commission (7759 0000, www.legalservices.gov.uk) for information. If you are arrested, your first call should be to your embassy (*see p367*).

Community Legal Services Directory

0845 608 1122/www.clsdirect.org.uk. **Open** 9am-5.30pm daily.
This free telephone service guides those with legal problems to government agencies and law firms.

Joint Council for the Welfare of Immigrants

115 Old Street, Hoxton, EC1V 9RT (7251 8706/www.jcwi.org.uk). **Phone enquiries** 2-5pm Tue, Thur.
JCWI's telephone-only legal advice line offers guidance and referrals.

Law Centres Federation

Duchess House, 18-19 Warren Street, Fitzrovia, W1T 5LR (7387 8570/www.lawcentres.org.uk). Warren Street tube. **Open** *Phone enquiries* 9.30am-5pm Mon-Fri.
Free legal help for people who can't afford a lawyer. Local centres only offer advice to those living or working in their immediate area; this central office connects you with the nearest.

Libraries

Unless you're a London resident, you won't be able to join a lending library. Only the British Library's exhibition areas are open to non-members; other libraries listed can be used for reference.

Barbican Library
Barbican Centre, Silk Street, The City, EC2Y 8DS (7638 0569/www.cityoflondon.gov.uk/barbicanlibrary). Barbican or Moorgate tube/rail. **Open** 9.30am-5.30pm Mon, Wed; 9.30am-7.30pm Tue, Thur; 9.30am-2pm Fri; 9.30am-4pm Sat. **Map** p404 P5.
British Library *96 Euston Road, Somers Town, NW1 2DB (7412 7000/www.bl.uk). King's Cross tube/rail.* **Open** 9.30am-6pm Mon, Wed-Fri; 9.30am-8pm Tue; 9.30am-5pm Sat; 11am-5pm Sun. **Map** p401 L3.

Holborn Library *32-38 Theobald's Road, Bloomsbury, WC1X 8PA (7974 6345). Chancery Lane tube.* **Open** 10am-7pm Mon, Thur; 10am-6pm Tue, Wed, Fri; 10am-5pm Sat. **Map** p401 M5.
Kensington Central Library *12 Philimore Walk, Kensington, W8 7RX (7937 2542/www.rbkc.gov.uk/libraries). High Street Kensington tube.* **Open** 9.30am-8pm Mon, Tue, Thur; 9.30am-5pm Wed, Fri, Sat.
Marylebone Library *109-117 Marylebone Road, Marylebone, NW1 (7641 1041/www.westminster.gov.uk/libraries). Baker Street tube/Marylebone tube/rail.* **Open** 9.30am-8pm Mon, Tue, Thur, Fri; 10am-8pm Wed; 9.30am-5pm Sat; 1.30-5pm Sun. **Map** p397 F4.
Victoria Library *160 Buckingham Palace Road, Belgravia, SW1W 9UD (7641 4287/www.westminster.gov.uk/libraries). Victoria tube/rail.* **Open** 9.30am-7pm Mon, Tue, Thur; 10am-7pm Wed; 9.30am-8pm Fri; 9.30am-5pm Sat. *Music library* 11am-7pm Mon-Fri; 10am-5pm Sat. **Map** p402 H10.
Westminster Reference Library *35 St Martin's Street, Westminster, WC2H 7HP (7641 4636/www.westminster.gov.uk/libraries). Leicester Square tube.* **Open** 10am-8pm Mon-Fri; 10am-5pm Sat. **Map** p409 X4.

Lost property

Always inform the police if you lose anything, if only to validate insurance claims. *See p373* or the *Yellow Pages* for your nearest police station. Only dial 999 if violence has occurred. Report lost passports both to the police and to your embassy (*see p367*).

Airports

For property lost on the plane, contact the relevant airline; for items lost in a particular airport, contact the following:

Gatwick Airport *01293 503162.*
Heathrow Airport *8745 7727.*
London City Airport *7646 0000.*
Luton Airport *01582 395219.*
Stansted Airport *01279 663293.*

Public transport

If you've lost property in an overground station or on a train, call 08700 005151, and give the operator the details.

Transport for London

Lost Property Office, 200 Baker Street, Marylebone, NW1 5RZ (7918 2000/www.tfl.gov.uk). Baker Street tube. **Open** 8.30am-4pm Mon-Fri. **Map** p400 G4.

Allow three working days from the time of loss. If you lose something on a bus, call 7222 1234 and ask for the phone numbers of the depots at either end of the route. If you lose something on a tube, pick up a lost property form from any station.

Taxis

Taxi Lost Property

200 Baker Street, Marylebone, NW1 5RZ (7918 2000/www.tfl.gov.uk). Baker Street tube. **Open** 9am-2pm Mon-Fri. *Phone enquiries* 9am-4pm Mon-Fri. **Map** p400 G4.

This office deals only with property found in registered black cabs. You're advised to allow seven days from the time of loss. For items lost in a minicab, contact the office of the relevant company.

Media

Magazines

Time Out remains London's only quality magazine, widely available every Tuesday in central London, and gives listings for the week from the Wednesday. If you really want to know what's going on and how good it is, this is where you look. An esoteric adjunct is the Talk of the Town section in the *Independent on Sunday*'s *ABC* supplement.

Nationally, *Loaded*, *FHM* and *Maxim* are big men's titles, while women read handbag-sized *Glamour* and new glossy weekly *Grazia* alongside *Vogue*, *Marie Claire* and *Elle*. The appetite for celebrity magazines like *Heat*, *Closer* and *OK* doesn't seem to have abated, while style mags like *i-D* and *Dazed and Confused* have found a profitable niche.

The *Spectator*, *Prospect*, the *Economist* and the *New Statesman* are at the serious end of the market, while the satirical *Private Eye* adds levity. It helps if you buy the *Big Issue*, sold by homeless people.

Newspapers

London's main daily paper is the dull, right-wing *Evening Standard*, which comes out in several editions during the day (Mon-Fri). The free morning paper *Metro* is picked up and discarded at tube stations.

National newspapers include, from right to left, the *Daily Telegraph* and *The Times* (which is best for sport), the *Independent* and the *Guardian* (best for arts). All have bulging Sunday equivalents bar the *Guardian*, which has a sister Sunday paper, the *Observer*. The pink *Financial Times* (daily except Sunday) is the best for business facts and figures. In the middle market, the leader is the right-wing *Daily Mail* (and *Mail on Sunday*); the *Daily Express* (and *Sunday Express*) tries to compete. Tabloids remain strong, with the *Sun* (and Sunday's *News of the World*) the undisputed leader. The *Daily Star* and *Mirror* are the main lowbrow contenders.

Radio

The stations listed below are broadcast on standard wavebands as well as digital, where they are joined by some interesting new channels, particularly from the BBC. The format is not yet widespread, but you might judt be lucky enough to have digital in your hotel room or hire car (it's worth asking about this when you book).

BBC Radio 1 *97-99 FM.* A fairly standard mix of youth-oriented pop, indie, metal and dance.

BBC Radio 2 *88-91 FM.* Still bland during the day, but good after dark.

BBC Radio 3 *90-93 FM.* Classical music dominates, but there's also discussion, world music and arts.

BBC Radio 4 *92-95 FM, 198 LW.* The BBC's main speech station. News agenda-setter *Today* (6-9am Mon-Fri, 7-9am Sat) exudes self-importance.

BBC Radio 5 Live *693, 909 AM.* Rolling news and sport. Avoid the morning phone-ins, but *Up All Night* (1-5am nightly) is terrific.

BBC London *94.9 FM.* A shadow of its former (GLR) self, but Robert Elms (noon-3pm Mon-Fri) is OK.

BBC World Service *648 AM.* A distillation of the best of all the other BBC stations; transmitted worldwide.

Capital FM *95.8 FM.* London's best-known station.

Classic FM *100-102 FM.* Easy-listening classical.

Heart FM *106.2 FM.* Capital for grown-ups.

Jazz FM *102.2 FM.* Smooth jazz (aka elevator music) now dominates.

LBC *97.3 FM.* Phone-ins and features. The cabbies' favourite.

Liberty *963 & 972 AM.* Cheesy hits from the 1970s and '80s.

Resonance *104.4 FM.* Arts radio.

Xfm *104.9 FM.* Alternative rock.

Television

With a multiplicity of formats, there are plenty of pay-TV options. However, the relative quality of free TV (most notably the BBC's new digital channels) keeps subscriptions from attaining US levels.

Network channels

BBC1 The Corporation's mass-market station. Depends perhaps too much on soaps, game shows and reality and lifestyle TV, but has quality offerings, too, particularly in nature, drama and travel. Daytime programming isn't great. As with all BBC radio and TV stations, there are no commercials.

BBC2 A reasonably intelligent cultural cross-section and plenty of documentaries, but upstaged by the BBC's digital arts channel, BBC4, on fresh cultural programming.

ITV1 Carlton provides weekday monotonous, mass-appeal shows, with oft-repeated successes for ITV. LWT (London Weekend Television) takes over at the weekend with more of the same. ITV2 is on digital.

Channel 4 C4's output includes a variety of extremely successful US imports (*Desperate Housewives*, *ER*, *Lost*, *The Sopranos* and so on), but it still comes up with some gems of its own, particularly documentaries.

Five Plenty of sex, US TV movies, a lot of rubbish comedy, US sport and the occasional good documentary.

Selected satellite, digital & cable

BBC3 *EastEnders* reruns and other light fare.

BBC4 Highbrow stuff, including earnest documentaries and dramas.

BBC News 24 The Beeb's rolling news network.

CNN News and current affairs.

Discovery Channel Science and nature documentaries.
FilmFour Channel 4's movie outlet.
ITV4 New channel offering 'challenging' drama, comedy and film.
Sky News Rolling news.
Sky One Sky's version of ITV.
Sky Sports There are also Sky Sports 2 and Sky Sports 3.

Money

Britain's currency is the pound sterling (£). One pound equals 100 pence (p). Coins are copper (1p, 2p), silver (round: 5p, 10p; seven-sided: 20p, 50p), yellowy-gold (£1) or silver in the centre with a yellowy-gold edge (£2). Paper notes are blue (£5), orange (£10), purple (£20) or red (£50). You can exchange foreign currency at banks, bureaux de change and post offices; there's no commission charge at the last of these. Many large stores also accept euros.

Western Union

0800 833833/www.westernunion.com. The old standby for bailing out cash-challenged travellers. Chequepoint (*see below*) also offers this service.

ATMs

As well as inside and outside banks, cash machines can be found in some supermarkets and in larger tube and rail stations. Some commercial premises have 'pay-ATMs', which charge for withdrawals. If you are visiting from outside the UK, your cash card should work via one of the debit networks, but check charges in advance. ATMs also allow you to make withdrawals on your credit card if you know your PIN number; you will be charged interest plus, usually, a currency exchange fee (1% for Visa and Mastercard at press time). Generally, getting cash with a card is the cheapest form of currency exchange but increasingly there are hidden charges, so do your research. Bank of America customers can use Barclays ATMs free.

Gradually, Britain is moving over to the Chip and PIN system, whereby you are required to enter your PIN number rather than sign a credit (and especially) debit card slip. Learn your number. For more information, see www.chipandpin.co.uk.

Banks

No commission is charged for cashing sterling travellers' cheques if you go to one of the banks affiliated with the issuing company. You do have to pay to cash travellers' cheques in foreign currencies, and to change cash. You will always need to produce ID to cash travellers' cheques.

Bureaux de change

You'll be charged for cashing travellers' cheques or buying and selling foreign currency at bureaux de change. Commission varies. Major rail and tube stations have bureaux, and there are many in tourist areas and on major shopping streets. Most open 8am-10pm.
Chequepoint *548-550 Oxford Street, Marylebone, W1C 1LU (7723 1005/0800 699799). Marble Arch tube.* **Open** 8am-11pm Mon-Wed, Sun; 24hrs Fri, Sat. **Map** p400 G6. **Other locations:** throughout the city.
Garden Bureau
30A Jubilee Market Hall, Covent Garden, WC2E 8BE (7240 9921). Covent Garden tube. **Open** 9.30am-6pm daily. **Map** p409 Z3.
Thomas Exchange
13 Maddox Street, Mayfair, W1S 2QG (7493 1300/www.thomas exchange.co.uk). **Open** 8.45am-5.30pm Mon-Fri. **Map** p408 U3.

Credit cards

Credit cards are accepted pretty much ubiquitously in shops (except small corner shops) and restaurants (except caffs), particularly Visa and MasterCard. American Express and Diners Club tend to be accepted at more expensive outlets and multiples.

Report **lost/stolen credit cards** immediately to both the police and the services below.
American Express *01273 696933.*
Diners Club *01252 513500.*
MasterCard/Eurocard *0800 964767.*
Switch *0870 600 0459.*
Visa/Connect *0800 895082.*

Tax

With the exception of food, books, newspapers, children's clothing and a few other items, UK purchases are subject to VAT – Value Added Tax, aka sales tax – of 17.5 per cent. Unlike in the US, this is included in prices quoted in shops. In hotels, always check that the room rate quoted includes tax.

Opening hours

The following are general guidelines. Government offices all close on every bank (public) holiday (*see p377*); shops are increasingly remaining open. Only Christmas Day seems sacrosanct. Most attractions remain open on the other public holidays but always call first.

Banks 9am-4.30pm (some close at 3.30pm, some 5.30pm) Mon-Fri; sometimes also Saturday mornings.
Bars 11am-11pm Mon-Sat; noon-10.30pm Sun.
Businesses 9am-5pm Mon-Fri.
Post offices 9am-5.30pm Mon-Fri; 9am-noon Sat.
Shops 10am-6pm Mon-Sat; some to 8pm. Many are also open on Sunday, usually 11am-5pm or noon-6pm.

Police stations

The police are a good source of information about the area and are used to helping visitors. If you've been robbed, assaulted or involved in an infringement of the law, go to your nearest police station. (We've listed a handful in central London; look under 'Police' in the book or call Directory Enquiries on 118 118/500/888 for more.) If you have a complaint, ensure that you take the offending

Directory

police officer's identifying number (it should be displayed on his or her epaulette). You can then register a complaint with the **Independent Police Complaints Commission** (90 High Holborn, WC1V 6BH, 0845 300 2002).

Belgravia Police Station *202-206 Buckingham Palace Road, Pimlico, SW1W 9SX (7730 1212). Victoria tube/rail.* Map p402 H10.
Camden Police Station *60 Albany Street, NW1 4EE (7404 1212). Camden Town tube* Map p400 H4.
Charing Cross Police Station *Agar Street, Covent Garden, WC2N 4JP (7240 1212). Charing Cross tube/rail.* Map p409 Y4.
Chelsea Police Station *2 Lucan Place, Chelsea, SW3 3PB (7589 1212). Sloane Square tube.* Map p399 E10.
Islington Police Station *2 Tolpuddle Street, Islington, N1 0YY (7704 1212). Angel tube.* Map p404 N2.
Kensington Police Station *72-74 Earl's Court Road, Kensington, W8 6EQ (7376 1212). High Street Kensington tube.* Map p398 B11.
Marylebone Police Station *1-9 Seymour Street, Marylebone, W1H 7BA (7486 1212). Baker Street tube/ Marylebone tube/rail.* Map p397 F6.
Paddington Green Police Station *2-4 Harrow Road, Paddington, W2 1XJ (7402 1212). Edgware Road tube.* Map p397 E5.
West End Central Police Station *27 Savile Row, Mayfair, W1X 2DU (7437 1212). Piccadilly Circus tube.* Map p408 U3.

Postal services

You can buy stamps at all post offices and many newsagents and supermarkets. Current prices are 30p for first-class letters, 21p for second-class letters and 42p for letters to EU countries. Postcards cost 42p to send within Europe and 47p to countries outside Europe. Rates for other letters and parcels vary with weight and destination Ask at any branch for prices.

Post offices

Post offices are usually open 9am to 5.30pm Monday-Friday and 9am to noon Saturday, with the exception of

Trafalgar Square Post Office (24-28 William IV Street, WC2N 4DL, 08457 223344), open 8.30am to 6.30pm Monday to Friday and 9am to 5.30pm on Saturday. It gets very busy from 1pm to 2pm. Listed below are the other main central London offices. For general post office enquiries, call 08457 223344 or consult www.postoffice.co.uk.

43-44 Albemarle Street *Mayfair, W1S 4DS (08456 223344). Green Park tube.* Map p408 U5.
111 Baker Street *Marylebone, W1U 6SG (08456 223344). Baker Street tube.* Map p400 G5.
54-56 Great Portland Street *Fitzrovia, W1W 7NE (08456 223344). Great Portland Street tube.* Map p400 H4.
1-5 Poland Street *Soho, W1F 8AA (08456 223344). Oxford Circus tube.* Map p408 V2.
181 High Holborn *Holborn, WC1V 7RL (08456 223344). Holborn tube.* Map p409 Y1.

Poste restante

If you want to receive mail while you're away, you can have it sent to Trafalgar Square Post Office (*see above*), where it will be kept at the enquiry desk for a month. Your name and 'Poste Restante' must be clearly marked on the letter. You'll need ID to collect it.

Religion

Anglican
St Paul's Cathedral *For listings details, see p94.* **Services** 7.30am, 8am, 12.30pm, 5pm Mon-Fri; 8am, 8.30am, 12.30pm, 5pm Sat; 8am, 10.15am, 11.30am, 3.15pm, 6pm Sun. Map p406 O6.
Times may vary; phone to check.
Westminster Abbey *For listings details, see p138.* **Services** 7.30am, 8am, 12.30pm, 5pm Mon-Fri; 8am, 9am, 12.30pm, 3pm Sat; 8am, 10am, 11.15am, 3pm, 5.45pm Sun. Map p403 K9.
Times may vary; phone to check.

Baptist
Bloomsbury Central Baptist Church *235 Shaftesbury Avenue, Covent Garden, WC2H 8EP (7240 0544/www.bloomsbury.org.uk). Tottenham Court Road tube.* **Open** 10am-4pm Mon-Fri. *Friendship Centre Oct-June* noon-2.30pm Tue.

Services & meetings 11am, 6.30pm Sun. **Classical concerts** 1.10-1.50pm Wed. Map p401 Y1.

Buddhist
Buddhapadipa Thai Temple *14 Calonne Road, Wimbledon, SW19 5HJ (8946 1357/www.buddhapadipa. org). Wimbledon tube/rail, then 93 bus.* **Open** *Temple* 1-6pm Sat, Sun. *Meditation retreat* 7-9pm Tue, Thur; 4-6pm Sat, Sun.

Catholic
Oratory Catholic Church *For listings, see p145.* **Services** 7am, 8am (Latin mass), 10am, 12.30am, 6pm Mon-Fri; 7am, 8.30am, 10am, 6pm Sat; 7am, 8.30am, 10am (tridentine), 11am (sung Latin), 12.30pm, 3.30pm, 4.30pm, 7pm Sun. Map p399 E10.
Westminster Cathedral *For listings, see p140.* **Services** 7am, 8am, 9am, 10.30am, 12.30pm, 5pm Mon-Fri; 8am, 9am, 12.30pm, 6pm Sat; 7am, 8am, 9am, 10.30am, noon, 5.30pm, 7pm Sun. Map p402 J10.

Islamic
London Central Mosque *146 Park Road, St John's Wood, NW8 7RG (7724 3363). Baker Street tube/74 bus.* **Open** dawn-dusk daily. **Services** 5.30am, 1pm, 4.30pm, 8.15pm, 10pm daily.
East London Mosque *82-92 Whitechapel Road, E1 1JQ (7247 1357. Aldgate East or Whitechapel tube.* **Open** 10am-10pm daily. **Services** *Friday prayer* 1.30pm (1.15pm in winter).* Map p407 S6.

Jewish
Liberal Jewish Synagogue *28 St John's Wood Road, St John's Wood, NW8 7HA (7286 5181/www.ljs.org). St John's Wood tube.* **Open** 9am-5pm Mon-Thur; 9am-1pm Fri. **Services** 6.45pm Fri; 11am Sat.
West Central Liberal Synagogue *21 Maple Street, Fitzrovia, W1T 4BE (7636 7627/ www.wcls.org.uk). Warren Street tube.* **Services** 3pm Sat. Map p400 J4.

Methodist
Methodist Central Hall *Central Hall, Storey's Gate, Westminster, SW1H 9NH (7222 8010/www.c-h-w. co.uk). St James's Park tube.* **Open** *Chapel* 8am-6pm daily. **Services** 12.45pm Wed; 11am, 6.30pm Sun. Map p403 K9.

Quaker
Religious Society of Friends (Quakers) *Friends House, 173-177 Euston Road, Bloomsbury, NW1 2BJ (7663 1000/www.quaker.org.uk). Euston tube/rail.* **Open** 8.30am-9.30pm Mon-Fri; 8.30am-4.30pm Sat. **Meetings** 11am Sun. Map p401 K3.

Safety & security

There are no 'no-go' areas as such, but thieves haunt busy shopping areas and transport nodes as they do in all cities. Use common sense and follow these basic rules.

● **Keep** wallets and purses out of sight, and handbags securely closed.
● **Don't** leave briefcases, bags or coats unattended.
● **Don't** leave bags or coats beside, under or on the back of a chair.
● **Don't** put bags on the floor near the door of a public toilet.
● **Don't** take short cuts through dark alleys and car parks.
● **Don't** keep your passport, money, credit cards, etc together.
● **Don't** carry a wallet in your back pocket.
● **Be aware** of your surroundings.

Smoking

Smoking is currently permitted in almost all pubs and bars – though an increasing number have no-smoking areas – and in many restaurants. Specify when you book if you'd like a table in the smoking section. Smoking is forbidden in shops and on public transport, and, from summer 2007, in all workplaces, including bars and restaurants that serve food.

Study

Being a student in London is as expensive as it is exciting; Time Out's *Student Guide*, available from September each year, provides the lowdown on how to enjoy and survive the experience. In this guide, entry prices for students are designated 'concessions'. You'll have to show ID (an NUS or ISIC card) to qualify.

Language classes

Aspect Covent Garden Language Centre
3 4 Southampton Place, Covent Garden, WC1A 2DA (7404 3080/ www.aspectworld.com). Holborn tube. Map p409 Z1.

Central School of English
1 Tottenham Court Road, Bloomsbury, W1T 1BB (7580 2863/
www.centralschool.co.uk). Tottenham Court Road tube. Map p408 W1.

Frances King School of English
77 Gloucester Road, South Kensington, SW7 4SS (7870 6533/ www.francesking.com). Gloucester Road tube. Map p397 F9.

London Study Centre
Munster House, 676 Fulham Road, Fulham, SW6 5SA (7731 3549/ www.londonstudycentre.com). Parsons Green tube.

Sels College *64-65 Long Acre, Covent Garden, WC2E 9SX (7240 2581/www.sels.co.uk). Covent Garden tube.* Map p409 Y3.

Shane Global Language Centre
59 South Molton Street, Mayfair, W1K 5SN (7499 8533/www.shane global.com). Bond Street tube. Map p400 H6.

Students' unions

Many unions will only let in students with ID, so always carry your NUS or ISIC card with you. We've listed those with the best bars, all of which offer a good night out. Call for opening times and specific events, which vary with the academic year.

Imperial College *Beit Quad, Prince Consort Road, South Kensington, SW7 2BB (7594 8060/ www.union.ic.ac.uk). South Kensington tube.* Map p399 D9.

International Students House
229 Great Portland Street, Marylebone, W1W 5PN (7631 8300/ www.ish.org.uk). Great Portland Street tube. Map p400 H4.

King's College *Macadam Building, Surrey Street, Covent Garden, WC2R 2NS (7836 7132/www.kcl.ac.uk). Temple tube.* Map p403 M7.

London Metropolitan University *166-220 Holloway Road, Holloway, N7 8DB (7607 2789/ www.londonmet.ac.uk). Holloway Road tube.*

University of London Union (ULU) *Malet Street, Bloomsbury, WC1E 7HY (7664 2000/www.ulu. co.uk). Goodge Street tube.* Map p401 K4.

Universities

Brunel University *Cleveland Road, Uxbridge, Middx UB8 3PH (01895 274000/students' union 01895 462200/www.brunel.ac.uk). Uxbridge tube.*

City University *Northampton Square, Clerkenwell, EC1V 0HB (7040 5060/students' union 7040 5600/www.city.ac.uk). Angel tube.* Map p404 O3.

London Metropolitan University *166-220 Holloway Road, Holloway, N7 8DB (7607 2789/www.londonmet.ac.uk). Holloway Road tube.*

South Bank University *Borough Road, Borough, SE1 0AA (7928 8989/students' union 7815 6060/ www.lsbu.ac.uk). Elephant & Castle tube/rail.* Map p406 O10.

University of Greenwich *Old Royal Naval College, Park Row, Greenwich, SE10 9LS (8331 8000/ students' union 8331 7629/www. gre.ac.uk). Greenwich DLR/rail.*

University of Middlesex *Trent Park, Bramley Road, Cockfosters, N14 4YZ (8411 5000/students' union 8411 6450/www.mdx.ac.uk). Cockfosters or Oakwood tube.*

University of Westminster *309 Regent Street, Mayfair, W1B 2UW (7911 5000/students' union 7915 5454/www.wmin.ac.uk). Oxford Circus tube.* Map p400 J5.

University of London

The university consists of 34 separate colleges, spread across the city, of which the seven largest are listed below. All except Imperial College are affiliated to the National Union of Students (NUS; 7272 8900, www.nusonline.co.uk).

Goldsmiths' College *Lewisham Way, New Cross, SE14 6NW (7919 7171/students' union 8692 1406/ www.goldsmiths.ac.uk). New Cross tube/rail.*

Imperial College *Exhibition Road, Kensington, SW7 2AZ (7589 5111/ students' union 7594 8060/ www.imperial.ac.uk). South Kensington tube.* Map p399 D9.

King's College *Strand, Covent Garden WC2R 2NS (7836 5454/ students' union 7836 7132/www. kcl.ac.uk). Temple tube.* Map p403 M7.

Kingston University *Penrhyn Road, Kingston, Surrey KT1 2EE (8547 2000/students' union 8547 8868/www.kingston.ac.uk). Kingston rail.*

London School of Economics (LSE) *Houghton Street, Holborn, WC2A 2AE (7405 7686/students' union 7955 7158/www.lse.ac.uk). Holborn tube.* Map p401 M6.

Queen Mary, University of London *327 Mile End Road, Stepney, E1 4NS (7882 5555/ students' union 7882 5390/www. qmul.ac.uk). Mile End or Stepney Green tube.*

University College London (UCL) *Gower Street, Bloomsbury, WC1E 6BT (7679 2000/students' union 7387 3611/www.ucl.ac.uk). Euston Square, Goodge Street or Warren Street tube.* Map p401 K4.

Useful organisations

More useful organisations for students, including BUNAC and the Council on International Educational Exchange, can be found on p378.

National Bureau for Students with Disabilities *Chapter House, 18-20 Crucifix Lane, SE1 3JW (7450 0620/www.skill.org.uk).* **Open** *Phone enquiries* 11.30am-1.30pm Tue; 1.30-3.30pm Thur.

Telephones

London's dialling code is 020; standard landlines have eight digits after that. You don't need to dial the 020 from within the area, so we have not given it in this book. If you're calling from outside the UK, dial your international access code, then the UK code, 44, then the full London number, omitting the first 0 from the code. For example, to make a call to 020 7813 3000 from the US, dial 011 44 20 7813 3000. To dial abroad from the UK, first dial 00, then the relevant country code from the list below. For more international dialling codes, check the phonebook or www.kropla. com/dialcode.htm.

Australia 61; **Canada** 1; **Republic of Ireland** 353; **New Zealand** 64; **South Africa** 27; **USA** 1.

Public phones

Public payphones take coins or credit cards (sometimes both). The minimum cost is 20p, which buys you a 110-second local call. Some payphones, such as the counter-top ones found in many pubs, require more. International calling cards, offering bargain minutes via a freephone number, are widely available.

Operator services

Operator

Call **100** for the operator if you have difficulty in dialling; for an alarm call; to make a credit card call; for information about the cost of a call; and for help with international person-to-person calls. Dial **155** for the international operator if you need to reverse the charges (call collect) or if you can't dial direct, but be warned that this service is very expensive.

Directory enquiries

This service is now provided by various six-digit 118 numbers. They're pretty pricey to call: dial (free) 0800 953 0720 for a rundown of options and prices. The best known is 118 118, which charges 49p per call, then 14p per minute thereafter. 118 888 charges 49p per call, then 9p per minute. 118 180 charges 25p per call, then 30p per minute. Online, use the free www.ukphonebook.co.uk.

Yellow Pages

This 24-hour service lists the numbers of thousands of businesses in the UK. Dial **118 247** (49p/min) and say what type of business you require, and in what area of London.

Telephone directories

There are several telephone directories for London, divided by area, which contain private and commercial numbers. Available at post offices and libraries, these hefty tomes are also issued free to all residents, as is the invaluable *Yellow Pages* directory (also accessible online at www.yell.com), which lists businesses and services.

Mobile phones

Mobile phones in the UK work on either the 900 or 1800 GSM system. If you're a US traveller, your home service provider will use the GSM system, and your phone probably runs on the 800 or 1900 MHz band, so you'll need to acquire a tri- or quad-band handset.

The simplest option may be to buy a 'pay as you go' phone (about £50-£200); there's no monthly fee, you top up talk time using a card. Check before buying whether it can make and receive international calls.

Alternatively, you can rent a mobile phone from the AmEx offices at Terminals 3 and 4 at Heathrow Airport.

Telegrams

To send telegrams abroad, call 0800 190190. This is also the number to call to send an international telemessage: phone in your message and it will be delivered by post the next day.

Time

London operates on Greenwich Mean Time (GMT), which is five hours ahead of the US's Eastern Standard time. In spring (26 March 2006) the UK puts its clocks forward by one hour to British Summer Time. In autumn (29 October 2006) the clocks go back to GMT.

Tipping

In Britain it's accepted that you tip in taxis, minicabs, restaurants (some waiting staff rely heavily on tips), hotels, hairdressers and some bars (not pubs). Ten per cent is normal, with some restaurants adding as much as 15 per cent. Always check if service has been included in your bill: some restaurants include service, then leave the space for a gratuity on your credit card slip blank.

Toilets

Public toilets are few and far between in London, and pubs and restaurants reserve their toilets for customers only. However, all mainline rail stations and a few tube stations – Piccadilly Circus, for one – have public toilets (you may be charged a small fee). Department stores, too, usually have loos that you can use free of charge.

Tourist information

Visit London (7234 5800, www.visitlondon.com) is the city's official tourist information company. There are also tourist offices in Greenwich, Leicester Square and next to St Paul's (www.cityoflondon.gov.uk; *see p93*).

Britain & London Visitor Centre
1 Lower Regent Street, Piccadilly Circus, SW1Y 4XT (8846 9000/ www.visitbritain.com). Piccadilly Circus tube. **Open** *Oct-May* 9.30am-6.30pm Mon; 9am-6.30pm Tue-Fri; 10am-4pm Sat, Sun. *June-Sept* 9.30am-6.30pm Mon; 9am-6.30pm Tue-Fri; 9am-5pm Sat; 10am-4pm Sun. **Map** p408 W4.

London Information Centre
Leicester Square, WC2H 7BP (7292 2333/www.londontown.com). Leicester Square tube. **Open** 8am-11pm Mon-Fri; 10am-6pm Sat, Sun. Info and booking services.

London Visitor Centre *Arrivals Hall, Waterloo International Terminal, SE1 7LT.* **Open** 8.30am-10.30pm Mon-Sat; 9.30am-10.30pm Sun. **Map** p403 M8.

Visas & immigration

EU citizens do not require a visa to visit the UK; citizens of the USA, Canada, Australia, South Africa and New Zealand can also enter with only a passport for tourist visits of up to six months as long as they can show they can support themselves during their visit and plan to return. Use www.ukvisas.gov.uk to check your visa status well before you travel, or contact the British embassy, consulate or high commission in your own country. You can arrange visas online at www.fco.gov.uk. For work permits, *see p378*.

Home Office *Immigration & Nationality Bureau, Lunar House, 40 Wellesley Road, Croydon, Surrey CR9 1AT (0870 606 7766/application forms 0870 241 0645/www.homeoffice.gov.uk).* **Open** *Phone enquiries* 9am-4.45pm Mon-Thur; 9am-4.30pm Fri.

Weights & measures

The United Kingdom is slowly but surely moving towards full metrication. Distances are still measured in miles but all goods are now officially sold in metric quantities, with no legal requirement for the imperial equivalent to be given.

Some useful conversions:

1 centimetre (cm) = 0.39 inches (in)
1 inch (in) = 2.54 centimetres (cm)
1 yard (yd) = 0.91 metres (m)
1 metre (m) = 1.094 yards (yd)
1 mile = 1.6 kilometres (km)
1 kilometre (km) = 0.62 miles
1 ounce (oz) = 28.35 grammes (g)
1 gramme (g) = 0.035 ounces (oz)
1 pound (lb) = 0.45 kilogrammes (kg)
1 kilogramme (kg) = 2.2 pounds (lb)
1 pint (US) = 0.8 pints (UK)
1 pint (UK) = 0.55 litres (l)
1 litre (l) = 1.75 pints (UK)

When to go

Climate

The British climate is famously unpredictable, but Weathercall on 09003 444 900 (60p per min) can offer some guidance. *See also below* **Weather report**. The best websites for weather news and features include www.metoffice.com; www.weather.com; and www.bbc.co.uk/london/weather, which all offer good detailed long-term forecasts and are easily searchable.

Spring extends from March to May, though frosts can last into April. March winds and April showers may be a month early or a month late, but May is often very pleasant.

Summer (June, July and August) can be unpredictable, with searing heat one day followed by sultry greyness and violent thunderstorms the next. There are usually some sunny days, too, though they vary greatly in number from year to year. High temperatures, humidity and pollution can create problems for those with hay fever or breathing difficulties, and temperatures down in the tube can reach horrible levels in rush hour.

Autumn starts in September, although the weather can still have a mild, summery feel. Real autumn comes with October, when the leaves start to fall. When the November cold, grey and wet sets in, you'll be reminded that London is situated on a fairly northerly latitude.

Winter can have some delightful crisp, cold days, but don't bank on them. The usual scenario is for a disappointingly grey, wet Christmas, followed by a cold snap in January and February, when we may even see a sprinkling of snow, and public transport chaos ensues.

Public holidays

On public holidays (bank holidays), many shops remain open, but public transport services generally run to a Sunday timetable. The exception is Christmas Day, when almost everything shuts.

New Year's Day Mon 2 Jan 2006; Mon 1 Jan 2007.
Good Friday Fri 14 April 2006; Fri 6 April 2007.
Easter Monday Mon 17 April 2006; Mon 9 April 2007.

Weather report

Average daytime temperatures, rainfall and hours of sunshine in London

	Temp (°C/°F)	Rainfall (mm/in)	Sunshine (hrs/dy)
Jan	6/43	54/2.1	1.5
Feb	7/44	40/1.6	2.3
Mar	10/50	37/1.5	3.6
Apr	13/55	37/1.5	5.3
May	17/63	46/1.8	6.4
June	20/68	45/1.8	7.1
July	22/72	57/2.2	6.4
Aug	21/70	59/2.3	6.1
Sept	19/66	49/1.9	4.7
Oct	14/57	57/2.2	3.2
Nov	10/50	64/2.5	1.8
Dec	7/44	48/1.9	1.3

Directory

May Day Holiday Mon 1 May 2006; Mon 7 May 2007.
Spring Bank Holiday Mon 29 May 2006; Mon 28 May 2007.
Summer Bank Holiday Mon 28 Aug 2006; Mon 27 Aug 2007.
Christmas Day Mon 25 Dec 2006; Tue 25 Dec 2007.
Boxing Day Tue 26 Dec 2006; Wed 26 Dec 2007.

Women

London is home to dozens of women's groups and networks, from day centres to rights campaigners; www.gn.apc.org and www.wrc.org.uk provide information and many links.

Visiting women are unlikely to be harassed. Bar the very occasional sexually motivated attack, London's streets are no more dangerous for women than for men, if you follow the usual precautions (*see p375*).

The Women's Library

25 Old Castle Street, Whitechapel, E1 7NT (7320 2222/www.thewomens library.ac.uk). Aldgate or Aldgate East tube. **Open** *Reading room* 9.30am-5pm Tue, Wed, Fri; 9.30am-8pm Thur; 10am-4pm Sat.
Europe's largest women's studies archive, with changing exhibitions.

Working in London

Finding temporary work in London can be a full-time job in itself. Those with a reasonable level of English, who are EU citizens or have work permits, should be able to find work in catering, labouring, bars/pubs, coffee bars or shops. Graduates with an English or foreign-language degree could try teaching. Ideas can be found in *Summer Jobs in Britain*, published by Vacation Work, 9 Park End Street, Oxford, OX1 1HJ (£10.99 plus £1.75 p&p).

Good sources of job information are the *Evening Standard*, local/national newspapers and newsagents' windows. Vacancies for temporary and unskilled work are often displayed on Jobcentre noticeboards; your nearest Jobcentre can be found under

'Employment Agencies' in the *Yellow Pages*. If you have good typing (over 40 wpm) or word processing skills, you could sign on with some of the temp agencies. Many have specialist areas beyond the obvious administrative or secretarial roles, such as translation.

For shop, bar and restaurant work, just go in and enquire.

Work permits

With few exceptions, citizens of non-European Economic Area (EEA) countries have to have a work permit before they can legally work in the United Kingdom. Employers who are unable to fill particular vacancies with a resident or EEA national must apply for a permit to the Department for Education and Employment (DfEE; *see below*). Permits are issued only for high-level jobs.

Au Pair Scheme

Citizens aged 17 to 27 from the following non-EEA countries are permitted to make an application to become au pairs (along, of course, with EEA nationals): Andorra, Faroe Islands, Romania, Bosnia-Herzegovina, Greenland, San Marino, Bulgaria, Macedonia, Turkey, Croatia. A visa is sometimes required, so make sure you check. See the appropriate page of www.workingintheuk.gov.uk for details, or contact the **Immigration & Nationality Directorate** (*see below* **Home Office**).

Sandwich students

Approval for course-compulsory sandwich placements at recognised UK colleges must be obtained for potential students by their home country college from the DfEE's **Overseas Labour Service** (*see below* **Work Permits UK**).

Students

Visiting students from the US, Canada, Australia or Jamaica can sign up for the BUNAC programme, which allows them to work in the UK for up to six months. Contact the Work in Britain Department of the **Council on International Educational Exchange** (from the US, call 1-800-40-STUDY, or visit www.ciee.org) or call **BUNAC** direct (*see below*). Students should get an application form OSS1 (BUNAC)

from BUNAC, and submit it to a UK Jobcentre to obtain permission to work. Students may not exceed 20 hours' work during term time.

Working holidaymakers

Citizens of Commonwealth countries aged 17 to 27 are allowed to apply to come to the UK as a working holidaymaker by contacting their nearest British Diplomatic Post in advance. They are then allowed to take part-time work without a DfEE permit. Contact the **Immigration & Nationality Directorate** (*see below* **Home Office**) for more information.

Useful addresses

BUNAC

16 Bowling Green Lane, Clerkenwell, EC1R 0QH (7251 3472/www.bunac. org.uk). Farringdon tube/rail. **Open** 9.30am-5.30pm Mon-Thur; 9.30am-5pm Fri. **Map** p404 N4.

Council on International Educational Exchange

3rd Floor, 7 Custom House Street, Portland, Maine, ME 04101, USA (00 1 207 553 7600/www.ciee.org). **Open** 9am-5pm Mon-Fri.
The Council on International Educational Exchange helps young people to study, work and travel abroad.

Home Office

Immigration & Nationality Directorate, Lunar House, 40 Wellesley Road, Croydon, Surrey CR9 2BY (0870 606 7766/www.ind. homeoffice.gov.uk). **Open** *Phone enquiries* 9am-4.45pm Mon-Thur; 9am-4.30pm Fri.
The Home Office is able to provide advice on whether or not a work permit is required; application forms can be downloaded from the website.

Overseas Visitors Records Office

180 Borough High Street, Borough, SE1 1LH (7230 1208). Borough tube/Elephant & Castle or London Bridge tube/rail. **Open** 9am-4pm Mon-Fri. **Map** p406 P9.
The Overseas Visitors Records Office charges £34 to register a person if they already have a work permit.

Work Permits UK

0114 259 3290/www.workingin theuk.gov.uk. **Open** *Phone enquiries* 9am-5pm Mon-Fri.
Information for UK-based employers about the various routes open to foreign nationals who want to come and work in the UK.

Directory

Further Reference

Books

Fiction

Peter Ackroyd *Hawksmoor; The House of Doctor Dee; Great Fire of London; The Lambs of London* Intricate studies of arcane London.
Monica Ali *Brick Lane* Arranged marriage in Tower Hamlets.
Debi Alper *Nirvana Bites* Peckham-based writer's debut.
Martin Amis *London Fields* Darts and drinking way out east.
Paul Bryers *The Used Women's Book Club* Murder most torrid in contemporary Spitalfields.
Jonathan Coe *The Dwarves of Death* Mystery, music, mirth, male violence and the like.
Norman Collins *London Belongs to Me* A witty saga of '30s Kennington.
Sir Arthur Conan Doyle *The Complete Sherlock Holmes* Reassuring sleuthing shenanigans.
Joseph Conrad *The Secret Agent* Anarchism in seedy Soho.
Charles Dickens *Oliver Twist; David Copperfield; Bleak House; Our Mutual Friend* Four of the master's most London-centric novels.
Maureen Duffy *Capital* The bones beneath us and the stories they tell.
Christopher Fowler *Soho Black* Walking dead in Soho.
Anthony Frewin *London Blues* One-time Kubrick assistant explores '60s porn movie industry.
Neil Gaiman *Neverwhere* A new world above and below the streets by *Sandman* creator.
Graham Greene *The End of the Affair* Adultery and Catholicism.
Alan Hollinghurst *The Swimming Pool Library* Gay life around Russell Square; *The Line of Beauty* Beautiful, ruthless look at metropolitan debauchery. 2004 Booker Prize winner.
Hanif Kureishi *The Buddha of Suburbia* 1970s sexual confusion and identity crisis.
Colin MacInnes *City of Spades; Absolute Beginners* Coffee 'n' jazz, Soho 'n' Notting Hill. Tour of rock history's blue plaque sites.
Derek Marlowe *A Dandy in Aspic* A capital-set Cold War classic.
Michael Moorcock *Mother London* A love letter to London.
Ferdinand Mount *Heads You Win* Tale of East End headhunting scam.
George Orwell *Keep the Aspidistra Flying, Nineteen Eighty-Four* Saga of a struggling writer; bleak vision of totalitarian takeover.
Anthony Powell *A Dance to the Music of Time* Epic novel cycle set during interwar period.

Derek Raymond *I Was Dora Suarez* The blackest London noir.
Nicholas Royle *The Matter of the Heart; The Director's Cut* Abandoned buildings and secrets.
Edward Rutherfurd *London* A city's history given a novel voice.
Will Self *Grey Area* Short stories.
Iain Sinclair *Downriver*, the Thames's *Heart of Darkness; Radon Daughters*, William Hope Hodgson; *White Chappell*, Ripper murders; *Scarlet Tracings*, book dealers.
Evelyn Waugh *Vile Bodies* Shameful antics in 1920s Mayfair.
Virginia Woolf *Mrs Dalloway* A kind of London *Ulysses.*
HG Wells *War of the Worlds; The Time Machine* Early SF classics.

Non-fiction

Peter Ackroyd *London: The Biography* Wilfully obscurantist history of the city.
Marc Atkins & Iain Sinclair *Liquid City* Sinclair haunts photographed.
Nicholas Barton *The Lost Rivers of London* Fascinating studies of old watercourses and their legacy.
James Boswell *Boswell's London Journal 1762-1763* Rich account of ribald literary life.
Anthony Burgess *A Dead Man in Deptford* The life and mysterious murder of Elizabethan playwright Christopher Marlowe.
Daniel Farson *Soho in the Fifties* An affectionate portrait.
Geoffrey Fletcher *The London Nobody Knows* Written by an opinionated expert.
Peter Guillery *The Small House in 18th Century London* Social and architectural history
Derek Hanson *The Dreadful Judgement* The embers of the Great Fire re-raked.
Sarah Hartley *Mrs P's Journey* Biography of Phyllis Pearsall, the woman who created the *A–Z.*
Stephen Inwood *A History of London* A recent, readable history.
Ian Jack (ed) *Granta, London: the Lives of the City* Fiction, reportage and travel writing.
Edward Jones & Christopher Woodward *A Guide to the Architecture of London* What it says. A brilliant work.
Jack London *The People of the Abyss* Poverty in the East End.
Malcolm McLaren *Rock 'n' Roll London* A tour thereof.
Nick Merriman (ed) *The Peopling of London* 2,000 years of settlement.
Tim Moore *Do Not Pass Go* A hilarious Monopoly addict's London.

Gilda O'Neill *Pull No More Bines; My East End* Social histories of the East End of London.
George Orwell *Down and Out in Paris and London* Waitering, begging and starving.
Samuel Pepys *Diaries* Fires, plagues, bordellos and more.
Liza Picard *Dr Johnson's London; Restoration London.* London past, engagingly revisited.
Patricia Pierce *Old London Bridge* The story of the world's longest inhabited bridge.
Roy Porter *London: A Social History* An all-encompassing history.
Jonathan Raban *Soft City* The city as state of mind; a classic.
Iain Sinclair *Lights Out for the Territory; London Orbital.* Time-warp visionary crosses London; and circles it on the M25.
Stephen Smith *Underground London: Travels Beneath the City Streets* Absorbing writing on the subterranean city.
Judith Summers *Soho: A History of London's Most Colourful Neighbourhood.* Great local history.
Richard Tames *Feeding London* Eating history from coffee houses onwards; *East End Past* A close look at the area.
William Taylor *This Bright Field* Spitalfields in enjoyable detail.
Adrian Tinniswood *His Invention So Fertile* Illuminating biography of Sir Christopher Wren.
Richard Trench *London Under London* Beneath the city.
Ben Weinreb & Christopher Hibbert (eds) *The London Encyclopaedia* Fascinating, thorough, indispensable reference guide.
Andrew White (ed) *Time Out Book of London Walks Volumes 1 & 2.* Writers, cartoonists, comedians and historians walk the capital.
Jerry White *London in the 20th Century: A City and Its People.*

Films

Alfie *dir. Lewis Gilbert* (1966) What's it all about, Michael?
Beautiful Thing *dir. Hettie MacDonald* (1996) A tender, amusing coming-of-age flick.
Blow-Up *dir. Michelangelo Antonioni* (1966) Swingin' London captured in unintentionally hysterical fashion.
Bullet Boy *dir. Saul Dibb* (2004) Gritty drama set in Hackney.
A Clockwork Orange *dir. Stanley Kubrick* (1971) Kubrick's vision still has power to shock.
Closer *dir. Mike Nichols* (2004) Infidelity and emotional uncertainty.

In the bloghouse

A weblog gives intimacy through anonymity, bringing a city's thoughts and secrets to your desktop. Check out www.lights.com/weblogs/searching for a list of blog-searching sites, and find your own area of interest.

Belle de Jour
Elegant diary of a London call girl.
www.belledejour-uk.blogspot.com

Blogadoon
Out and about gay life in London.
www.iansie.com/nonsense/blog.html

Hackney Lookout
Keeping tabs on local eccentrics.
www.hackneylookout.blogspot.com

In the Aquarium
Poetic observations and life drawings.
www.intheaquarium.blogspot.com

London geezer
Lists, guides and photos of out-of-the-way London landmarks.
www.lndn.blogspot.com

Londonist
London gossip and goings-on.
www.londonist.com

Londonmark
Off-the-wall take on Camden life.
www.londonmark.blogspot.com

Route 79
A second-generation Indian on London life and aloo gobi.
www.route79.com/journal/

Sashinka
Sharp stories from a Jewish girl-about-town.
www.sashinka.blogspot.com

This isn't London
Delightfully misleading miscellany.
www.thisisntlondon.blogspot.com

Da Vinci Code *dir. Ron Howard* (2006) Film version of Dan Brown's blockbuster novel, partly filmed in London (Inner Temple gets a look-in). **Death Line** *dir. Gary Sherman* (1972) Cannibalism on the tube. Yikes. **Dirty Pretty Things** *dir. Stephen Frears* (2002) Drama centred on immigrant hotel workers. **Jubilee** *dir. Derek Jarman* (1978) A horribly dated but still interesting romp through the punk era. **The Krays** *dir. Peter Medak* (1990) The Kemps as East End gangsters. **Life is Sweet; Naked; Secrets & Lies; Career Girls; All or Nothing; Vera Drake** *dir. Mike Leigh* (1990; 1993; 1996; 1997; 2002; 2004) An affectionate look at Metroland; a character study; familial tensions; old friends meet;

family falls apart; problems of post-war austerity. **Lock, Stock and Two Smoking Barrels; Snatch** *dir. Guy Ritchie* (1998; 2000) Mr Madonna's pair of East End faux-gangster flicks. **London; Robinson in Space** *dir. Patrick Keiller* (1994; 1997) Fiction meets documentary. **The Long Good Friday** *dir. John MacKenzie* (1989) Bob Hoskins stars in the classic London gangster flick. **Mona Lisa; The Crying Game** *dir. Neil Jordan* (1986; 1992) Prostitution, terrorism, transvestism. **Mrs Dalloway** *dir. Marleen Goris* (1997) Vanessa Redgrave stars in this adaptation of the Woolf novel. **Notting Hill** *dir. Roger Michell* (1999) Hugh Grant and Julia Roberts get it on in west London.

Peeping Tom *dir. Michael Powell* (1960) Powell's creepy murder flick: a young man films his dying victims. **Performance** *dir. Nicolas Roeg, Donald Cammell* (1970) The cult movie to end all cult movies made west London cool for life. **28 Days** *dir. Danny Boyle* (2002) Post-apocalyptic London. **Wimbledon** *dir. Richard Loncraine* (2004) Paul Bettany plays up an idyllic, postcard England. **Wonderland** *dir. Michael Winterbottom* (1999) A mix of love, loss and deprivation.

Music

Bad Manners *Vive la Ska Revolution* Jangly ska rampage through '80s London. **Blur** *Modern Life is Rubbish* (1993); *Park Life* (1994) Modern classics by the Essex exiles. **The Clash** *London Calling* (1979) Epoch-making punk classic. **The Jam** *This is the Modern World* (1977) Weller at his splenetic finest. **Madness** *Rise & Fall* (1982) The nutty boys wax lyrical. **Morrissey** *Vauxhall & I* (1994) His finest solo album. **The Rolling Stones** *December's Children (and Everybody's)* (1965) Moodily cool evocation of the city. **Squeeze** *Greatest Hits* (1994) Lovable south London geezer pop.

Websites

BBC London *www.bbc.co.uk/london* Online news, travel, weather, sport etc. **Classic Cafés** *www.classiccafes.co.uk* London's '50s and '60s caffs. **Greater London Authority** *www.london.gov.uk* A wealth of information. **Gumtree** *www.gumtree.com* Online community noticeboard. **Hidden London** *www.hiddenlondon.com* The city's undiscovered gems. **London Active Map** *www.uktravel.com* Click on a tube station and find out which attractions are nearby. **London Footprints** *www.london-footprints.co.uk* Free walks to print out. **Pubs.com** *www.pubs.com* London's traditional boozers. **The River Thames Guide** *www.riverthames.co.uk* Places along the riverbank. **Street Map** *www.streetmap.co.uk* Grid references and postcodes. **This is London** *www.thisislondon.co.uk* The *Evening Standard* online. **Time Out** *www.timeout.com* A vital source. From here you can access our eating and drinking guides.

Index

Advertisers' Index

Please refer to relevant sections for addresses
and /or telephone numbers

Where to Stay

Sightseeing

Eating & Drinking

Shops & Services

Arts & Entertainment

Place of interest and/or entertainment	■
Hospital or college	■
Railway station	■
Parks	■
River	■
Motorway	=
Main road	
Main road tunnel	
Pedestrian road	■
Airport	✈
Church	✚
Synagogues	✡
Congestion charge zone	Ⓒ
Underground station	⊖
Area name	SOHO
Hotels	❶
Restaurants & Cafés.	❶
Pubs & Bars	❶

Maps

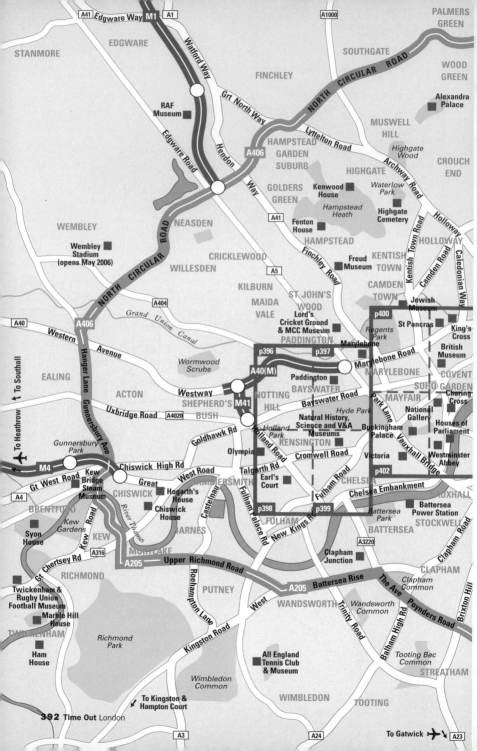

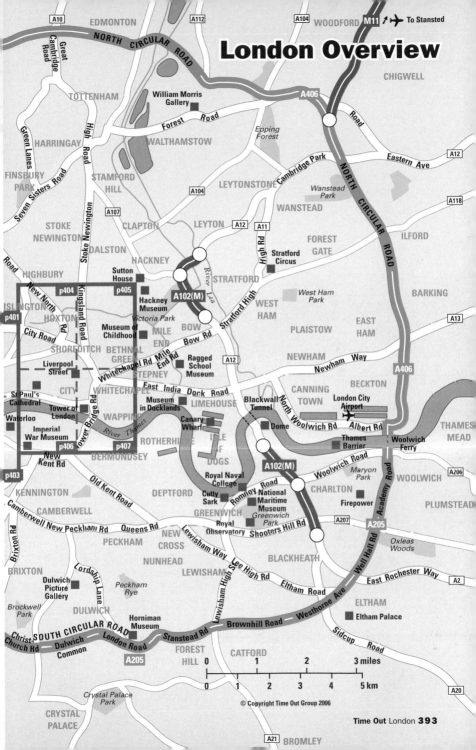

London Overview

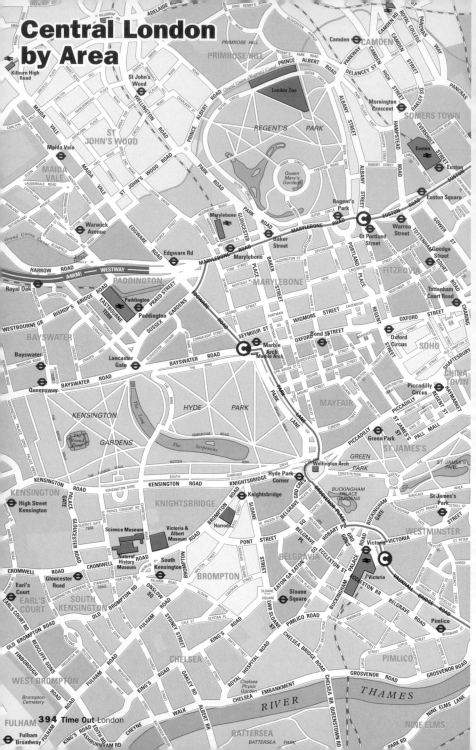

Central London
by Area

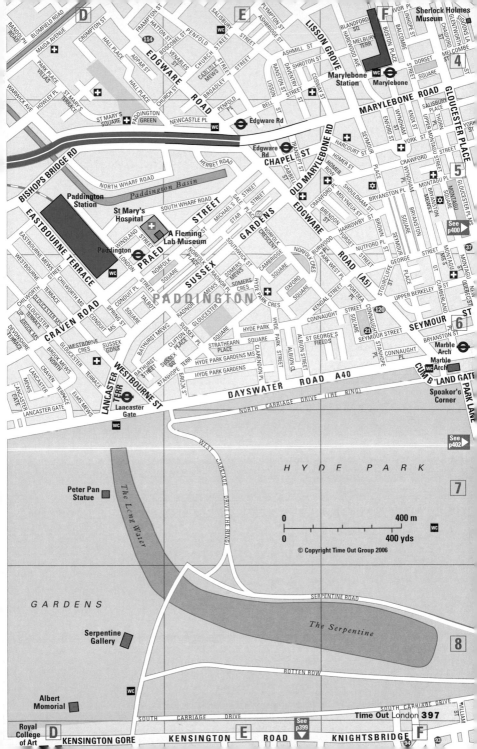

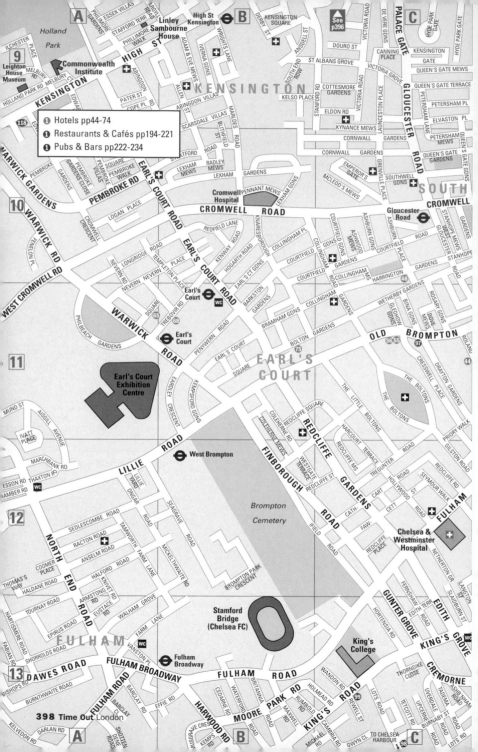

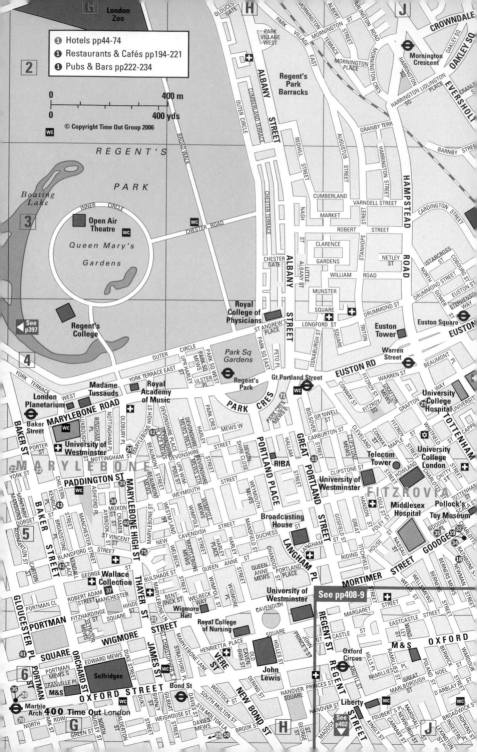

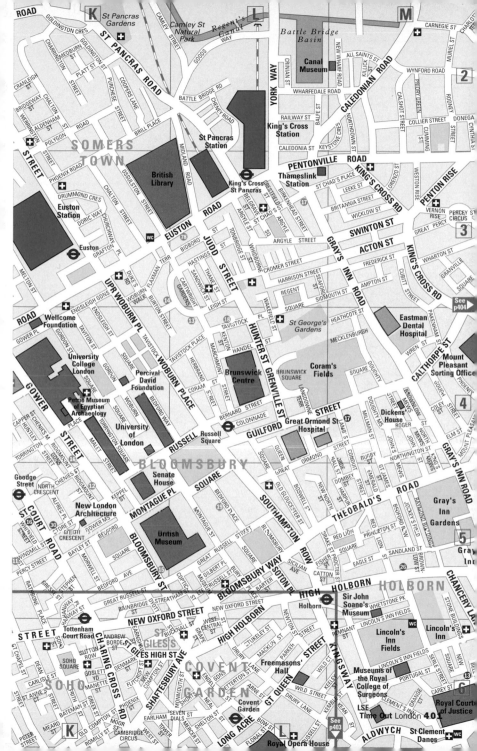

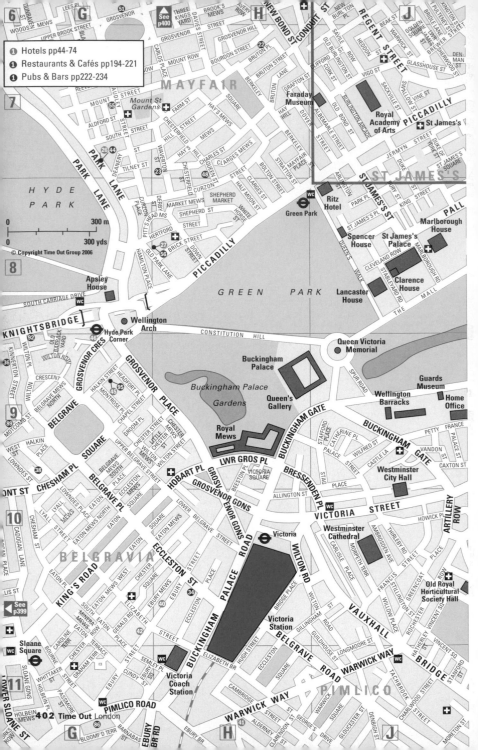

① Hotels pp44-74
① Restaurants & Cafés pp194-221
① Pubs & Bars pp222-234

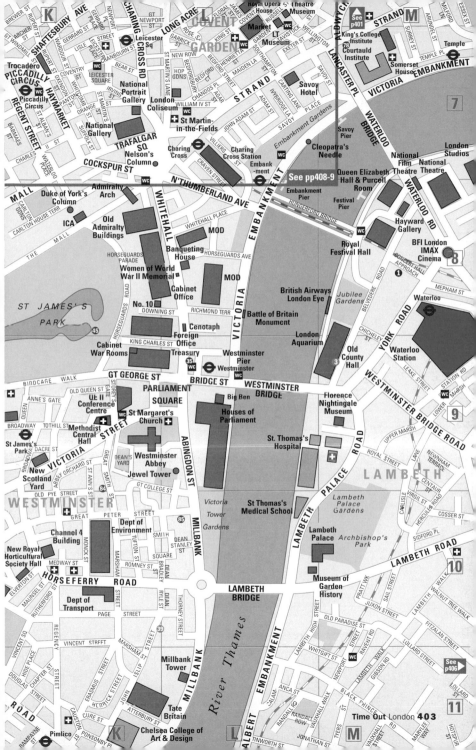

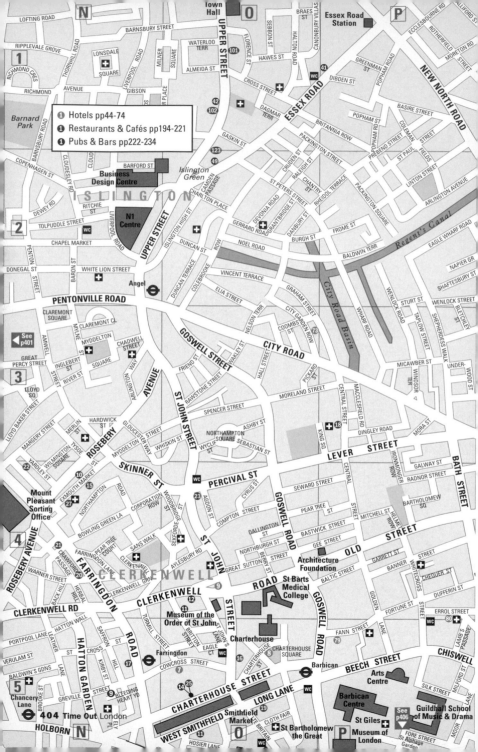

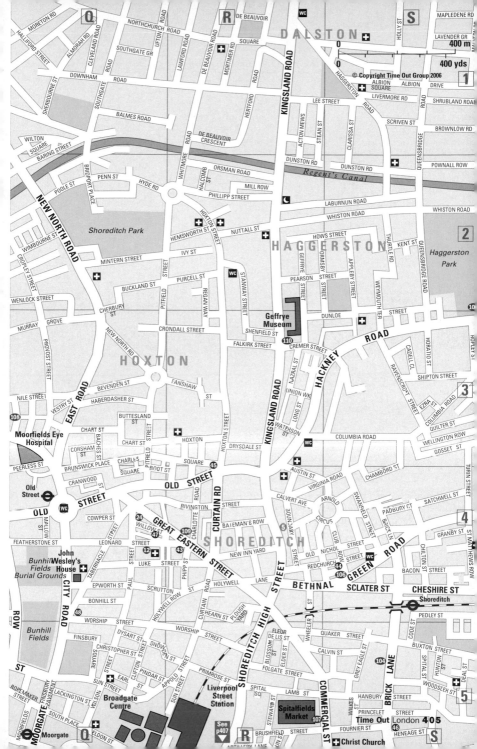

Time Out London **405**

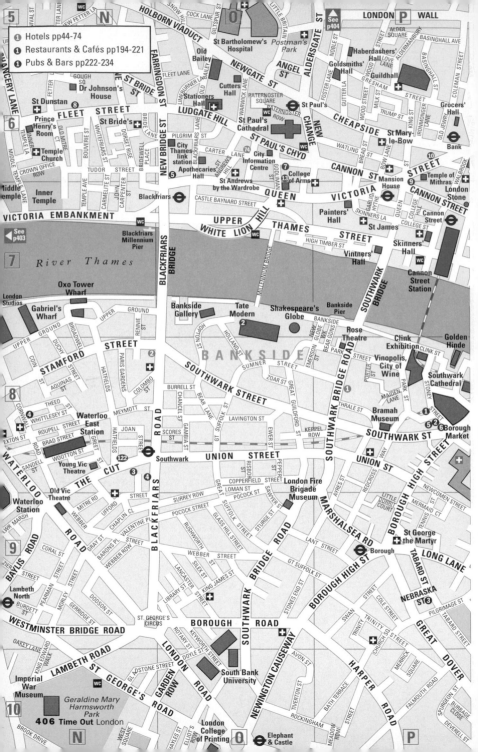

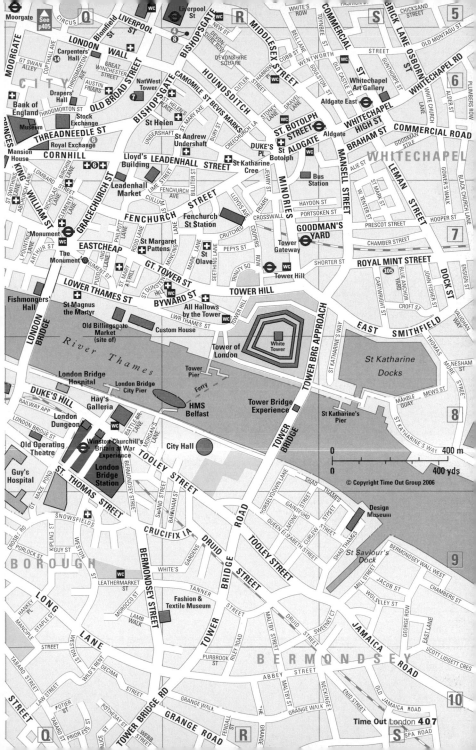

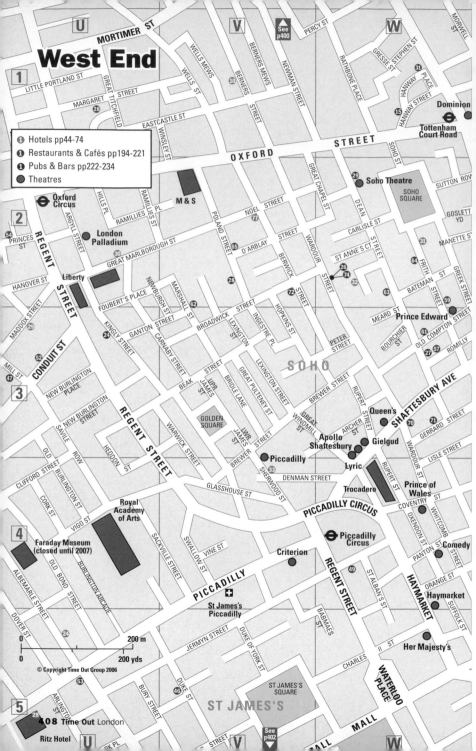

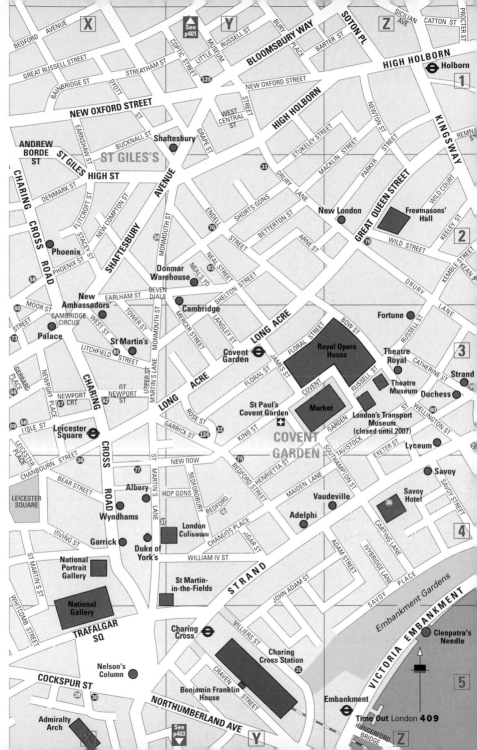

Street Index

Essex Road - 404 O1/P1
Essex Street - 403 M6
Essex Villas - 398 A9
Eustace Road - 398 A13
Euston Road - 400 J4, 401 K3/4/L3/4
Euston Street - 400 J3
Evelyn Gardens - 399 D11
Eversholt Street - 400 J2, 401 K3
Ewer Street - 406 O8
Exeter Street - 403 L7, 409 Z3
Exhibition Road - 399 D9/10
Exmouth Market - 404 N4
Exton Street - 406 N8

Fabian Road - 398 A13
Falkirk Street - 405 R3
Falmouth Road - 406 P10
Fann Street - 404 P5
Fanshaw Street - 405 R3
Farm Lane - 398 A13/B13
Farm Street - 402 H7
Farringdon Lane - 404 N4
Farringdon Road - 404 N4/5
Farringdon Street - 406 N6/O6
Fashion Street - 407 S5
Fawcett Street - 398 C12
Featherstone Street - 405 Q4
Fenchurch Avenue - 407 R7
Fenchurch Street - 407 Q7/R7
Fendall Street - 407 R10
Fenelon Place - 398 A10
Fernshaw Road - 398 C12/13
Fetter Lane - 406 N6
Finborough Road - 398 B12/C12
Finsbury Circus - 405 Q5, 407 Q5
Finsbury Pavement - 405 Q5
Finsbury Square - 405 Q5
First Street - 399 E10
Fisher Street - 401 L5
Fitzalan Street - 403 M10
Fitzhardinge Street - 400 G6
Fitzroy Square - 400 J4
Fitzroy Street - 400 J4
Flaxman Terrace - 401 K3
Fleet Lane - 406 O6
Fleet Street - 406 N6
Fleur de Lis Street - 405 R5
Flitcroft Street - 401 K6, 409 X2
Flood Street - 399 E12/F12
Flood Walk - 399 E12
Floral Street - 401 L6, 403 L6, 409 Y3
Florence Street - 404 O1
Foley Street - 400 J5
Folgate Street - 405 R5
Fore Street - 404 P5
Formosa Street - 394 C4
Forset Street - 397 F5/6
Fortune Street - 404 P4
Foster Lane - 406 P6
Foubert's Place - 400 J6, 408 U2
Foulis Terrace - 399 D11
Fournier Street - 405 S5
Frampton Street - 397 D4
Francis Street - 402 J10
Franklin's Row - 399 F11
Frazier Street - 406 N9
Frederick Street - 401 M3
Friend Street - 404 O3
Frith Street - 401 K6, 408 W2/3
Frome Street - 404 P2
Fulham Broadway - 398 A13/B13
Fulham Road - 398 A13/B13/C12/13/D12, 399 D11/12/E11
Furnival Street - 406 N5

Gainsford Street - 407 R9/S9
Galway Street - 404 P3/4
Gambia Street - 406 O8
Garden Row - 406 O10
Garlicthye - 406 P7
Garrick Street - 403 L7
Garway Road - 394 B6
Gaskin Street - 404 O1
Gate Place - 399 D10
Gaunt Street - 406 O10
Gee Street - 404 O4/4
Geffrye Street - 405 R2
George Row - 407 S9
George Street - 397 F5/6, 400 G5
Gerald Road - 402 G10
Gerrard Road - 404 O2
Gerrard Street - 403 K6/7, 408 W3
Gerridge Street - 406 N9
Gertrude Street - 399 D12
Gibson Road - 403 M11
Gibson Square - 404 N1
Gilbert Place - 401 L5
Gilbert Street - 400 H6
Gillingham Street - 402 H10/J10
Gilston Road - 398 C12
Giltspur Street - 406 O5
Gladstone Street - 406 N10/O10
Glasshill Street - 406 O9
Glasshouse Street - 402 J7, 408 V4
Glebe Place - 399 E12

Gledhow Gardens - 398 C11
Glendower Place - 399 D10
Glentworth Street - 397 F4
Gloucester Gate - 400 H2
Gloucester Mews - 397 D6
Gloucester Place - 397 F5, 400 G5/6
Gloucester Place Mews - 397 F5
Gloucester Road - 398 C9/10
Gloucester Square - 397 E6
Gloucester Street - 402 J11
Gloucester Terrace - 394 C5, 397 D6
Gloucester Walk - 394 B8
Gloucester Way - 404 N3
Godfrey Street - 399 E11
Godliman Street - 406 O6
Golden Lane - 404 P4/5
Golden Square - 402 J7, 408 V3
Goldington Crescent - 401 K2
Goldington Street - 401 K2
Goodge Place - 400 J5
Goodge Street - 400 J5, 401 K5
Goodman's Yard - 407 R7/S7
Goods Way - 401 L2
Gordon Place - 394 B8
Gordon Square - 401 K4
Gordon Street - 401 K4
Gore Street - 399 D9
Gosfield Street - 400 J5
Goslett Yard - 401 K6, 408 W2
Gosset Street - 405 S3
Goswell Road - 404 O3/4/5/P5
Gough Square - 406 N6
Gough Street - 401 M4
Goulston Street - 407 R6/S6
Gower Mews - 401 K5
Gower Place - 401 K4
Gower Street - 401 K4/5
Gower's Walk - 407 S6/7
Gracechurch Street - 407 Q6/7
Grafton Mews - 400 J4
Grafton Place - 401 K3
Grafton Street - 402 H7
Grafton Way - 400 J4
Graham Street - 404 O2/3
Graham Terrace - 402 G11
Granby Street - 405 S4
Granby Terrace - 400 J2
Grange Court - 401 M6
Grange Road - 407 R10
Grange Walk - 407 R10
Grantbridge Street - 404 O2
Granville Place - 400 G6
Granville Square - 401 M3
Gravel Lane - 407 R6
Gray Street - 406 N9
Gray's Inn Road - 401 L3/M3/4/5
Great Castle Street - 400 J6
Great Chapel Street - 401 K6, 408 V2/W2
Great College Street - 403 K9/10
Great Cumberland Place - 397 F6
Great Dover Street - 406 P9/10, 407 Q10
Great Eastern Street - 405 Q4/R4
Great George Street - 403 K9
Great Guildford Street - 406 O8
Great James Street - 401 M5
Great Marlborough Street - 400 J6, 408 U2/V2
Great Maze Pond - 407 Q8/9
Great Newport Street - 403 K6, 409 X3
Great Ormond Street - 401 L5/M4
Great Percy Street - 401 M3, 404 N3
Great Peter Street - 403 K10
Great Portland Street - 400 H5/J5
Great Pulteney Street - 402 J6, 408 V3
Great Queen Street - 401 L6, 409 Z2
Great Russell Street - 401 K5/L5, 409 X1
Great Smith Street - 403 K9/10
Great Suffolk Street - 406 O8/9
Great Sutton Street - 404 O4
Great Titchfield Street - 400 J5/6, 408 U1
Great Tower Street - 407 Q7/R7
Great Western Road - 394 A4/5
Great Winchester Street - 407 Q6
Great Windmill Street - 403 K7, 408 V3
Greek Street - 401 K6, 408 W2
Greencoat Place - 402 J10
Greenman Street - 404 P1
Greenwell Street - 400 H4/J4
Greet Street - 406 N8
Grenville Place - 398 C10
Grenville Street - 401 L4
Gresham Street - 406 P6
Gresse Street - 401 K5, 408 W1
Greville Street - 404 N5
Grey Eagle Street - 405 S5
Greycoat Street - 402 J10, 403 K10
Groom Place - 402 G9
Grosvenor Crescent - 402 G9
Grosvenor Gardens - 402 H9/J10

Grosvenor Hill - 402 H7
Grosvenor Place - 402 G9/H9
Grosvenor Square - 402 G6/7
Grosvenor Street - 402 H6/7
Great Swan Alley - 407 Q6
Guildhouse Street - 402 J10/11
Guilford Street - 401 L4/M4
Gun Street - 405 R5
Gunter Grove - 398 C13
Gunthorpe Street - 407 S6
Gutter Lane - 406 P6
Guy Street - 407 Q9
Gwyn Close - 398 C13

Haberdasher Street - 405 Q3
Hackney Road - 405 R3/S3
Haggerston Road - 405 R1/S1
Haldane Road - 398 A12
Half Moon Street - 402 H8
Halford Road - 398 A12
Halkin Place - 402 G9
Halkin Street - 402 G9
Hall Place - 397 D4/5
Hall Street - 404 O3
Hallam Street - 400 H4/5
Halliford Street - 404 P1, 405 Q1
Halsey Street - 399 F10
Halton Road - 404 O1
Hamilton Park Road - 404 O1
Hamilton Place - 402 G8
Hampstead Road - 400 J3
Hanbury Street - 405 S5
Handel Street - 401 L4
Hankey Place - 407 Q9
Hanover Square - 400 H6
Hanover Street - 400 H6/J6, 408 U2
Hans Crescent - 399 F9
Hans Place - 399 F9
Hans Road - 399 F9
Hans Street - 399 F9
Hanson Street - 400 J5
Hanway Place - 401 K5, 408 W1
Hanway Street - 401 K5, 408 W1
Harbet Road - 397 E5
Harcourt Street - 397 F5
Harcourt Terrace - 398 C11/12
Hardwick Street - 404 N3
Harewood Avenue - 397 F4
Harley Place - 400 H5
Harley Street - 400 H4/5
Harper Road - 406 P10
Harpur Street - 401 M5
Harriet Walk - 399 F9
Harrington Gardens - 398 C10
Harrington Road - 399 D10
Harrington Square - 400 J2
Harrington Street - 400 J2/3
Harrison Street - 401 L3
Harrow Place - 407 R6
Harrow Road - 394 A4/B4/5
Harrowby Street - 397 F5
Hartismere Road - 398 A13
Harwood Road - 398 B13
Hasker Street - 399 F10
Hastings Street - 401 L3
Hatfields - 406 N8
Hatherley Grove - 394 B5/6
Hatherley Street - 402 J10
Hatton Garden - 404 N5
Hatton Street - 397 D4/E4
Hatton Wall - 404 N5
Hawes Street - 404 O1
Hay Hill - 402 H7
Haydon Street - 407 R7/S7
Hayles Street - 406 N10
Haymarket - 403 K7, 408 W4/5
Hay's Mews - 402 H7
Headfort Place - 402 G9
Hearn Street - 405 R4
Heathcote Street - 401 M4
Heddon Street - 402 J7, 408 U3/4
Helmet Row - 404 P4
Hemsworth Street - 405 R2
Heneage Street - 405 S5
Henrietta Place - 400 H6
Henrietta Street - 403 L7, 409 Y4
Herbal Hill - 404 N4
Herbrand Street - 401 L4
Hercules Road - 403 M9/10
Hereford Road - 394 B5/6
Herrick Street - 403 K11
Hertford Road - 405 R1
Hertford Street - 402 H8
Hester Road - 399 E13
Hide Place - 403 K11
High Holborn - 401 L5/6/M5, 409 Y1/Z1
High Timber Street - 406 O7/P7
Hill Street - 402 H7
Hillgate Place - 394 A7
Hillgate Street - 394 A7
Hills Place - 400 J6, 408 U2
Hillsleigh Road - 394 A7
Hobart Place - 402 H9
Hobury Street - 399 D12
Hogarth Road - 398 B10

Holbein Mews - 402 G11
Holbein Place - 402 G11
Holborn - 404 N5
Holborn Viaduct - 406 N5/O5/6
Holland Park Road - 398 A9
Holland Street SE1 - 406 O7/8
Holland Street W8 - 394 B8
Holland Walk - 394 A8
Holles Street - 400 H6
Holly Street - 405 S1
Hollywood Road - 398 C12
Holmead Road - 398 C13
Holywell Lane - 405 R4
Holywell Row - 405 Q4/R4
Homer Row - 397 F5
Homer Street - 397 F5
Hooper Street - 407 S7
Hop Gardens - 403 L7, 409 Y4
Hopkins Street - 400 J6, 408 V3
Hopton Street - 406 O7/8
Horatio Street - 405 S3
Hornton Street - 394 B8
Horseferry Road - 403 K10
Horseguards Avenue - 403 L8
Horseguards Parade - 403 K8
Horseguards Road - 403 K8
Horselydown Lane - 407 R8/9
Hortensia Road - 398 C13
Hosier Lane - 404 O5
Hotspur Street - 403 M11
Houndsditch - 407 R6
Howick Place - 402 J10
Howie Street - 399 E13
Howland Street - 400 J4/5
Howley Place - 397 D4/5
Hows Street - 405 R2/S2
Hoxton Square - 405 R3
Hoxton Street - 405 R2
Hudson's Place - 402 H10
Hugh Street - 402 H10/11
Hungerford Bridge - 403 L8/M8, 409 Z5
Hunter Street - 401 L4
Huntley Street - 401 K4/5
Hunton Street - 405 S5
Hyde Park Crescent - 397 E6
Hyde Park Gardens - 397 E6
Hyde Park Gardens Mews - 397 E6
Hyde Park Gate - 398 C9
Hyde Park Square - 397 E6
Hyde Park Street - 397 E6
Hyde Road - 405 Q2

Ifield Road - 398 B12/C12
Ilchester Gardens - 394 B6
Ilchester Place - 398 A9
Imperial College Road - 399 D9
Ingestre Place - 400 J6, 408 V3
Inglebert Street - 404 N3
Inner Circle - 400 G3
Inner Temple Lane - 406 N6
Inverness Terrace - 394 C6/7
Ironmonger Lane - 406 P6
Ironmonger Row - 404 P3/4
Irving Street - 403 K7, 409 X4
Islington Green - 404 O2
Islington High Street - 404 O2
Istarcross Street - 400 J3
Ivatt Place - 398 A11/12
Iverna Gardens - 398 B9
Ives Street - 399 E10
Ivor Place - 397 F4
Ivy Street - 405 R2
Ivybridge Lane - 403 L7, 409 Z4
Ixworth Place - 399 E11

Jacob Street - 407 S9
Jamaica Road - 407 S9/10
James Street W1 - 400 G6
James Street WC2 - 403 L6, 409 Y3
Jay Mews - 399 D9
Jermyn Street - 402 J7, 408 U5/V4/5
Jewry Street - 407 R6/7
Joan Street - 406 N8
Jockey's Field - 401 M5
John Adam Street - 403 L7, 409 Y4/5
John Carpenter Street - 406 N7
John Fisher Street - 407 S7
John Islip Street - 403 K10/11
John Prince's Street - 400 H6
John Street - 401 M4/5
John's Mews - 401 M4/5
Jonathan Street - 403 L11/M11
Jubilee Place - 399 E11
Judd Street - 401 L3
Juer Street - 399 E13
Juxon Street - 403 M10

Kean Street - 401 M6, 409 Z2
Keeley Street - 401 M6, 409 Z2
Kelso Place - 398 B9
Kelvedon Road - 398 A13
Kemble Street - 401 L6/M6, 409 Z2
Kemps Road - 398 B13
Kempsford Gardens - 398 B11
Kendal Street - 397 E6/F6

Old Park Lane - 402 G8
Old Pye Street - 403 K10
Old Queen Street - 400 G6
Old Queen Street - 403 K9
Old Street - 404 P4, 405 Q4/R4
Oldbury Place - 400 G4
Ongar Road - 398 A12/B12
Onslow Gardens - 399 D11
Onslow Square - 399 D10/11/E10/11
Orange Street - 403 K7, 408 W4
Orchard Street - 400 G6
Orde Hall Street - 401 M5
Orme Court - 394 B7
Orme Lane - 394 B7
Ormonde West Road - 399 F12
Ormsby Street - 405 R2
Orsett Terrace - 394 C5
Osborn Street - 407 S6
Osnaburgh Street - 400 H4
Ossington Street - 394 B7
Ossulston Street - 401 K3
Outer Circle - 400 G4/H2/3/4
Ovington Gardens - 399 E9/10
Ovington Street - 399 F10
Oxendon Street - 403 K7, 408 W4
Oxford Square - 397 E6
Oxford Street - 400 G6/H6/J6, 401 K6

Packington Square - 404 P2
Packington Street - 404 O1/P1
Paddington Green - 397 D5
Paddington Street - 400 G5
Page Street - 403 K10
Pakenham Street - 401 M4
Palace Avenue - 394 B8/C8
Palace Court - 394 B6/7
Palace Garden Mews - 394 B7
Palace Gardens Terrace - 394 B7/8
Palace Gate - 398 C9
Pall Mall - 402 J8, 403 K8, 408 W5
Panton Street - 403 K7, 408 W4
Paradise Walk - 399 F12
Paris Garden - 406 N8
Park Crescent - 400 H4
Park Crescent Mews East - 400 H4
Park Crescent Mews West - 400 H4
Park Lane - 397 F6, 402 G7/8
Park Place - 402 J8, 408 U5
Park Place Villas - 397 D4
Park Square East - 400 H4
Park Square Mews - 400 H4
Park Square West - 400 H4
Park Street SE1 - 406 P8
Park Street W1 - 402 G7
Park Village East - 400 H2
Park Village West - 400 H2
Park Walk - 399 D12
Park West Place - 397 F6
Parker Street - 401 L6, 409 Z1/2
Parkfield Street - 404 N2
Parkgate Road - 399 E13
Parliament Square - 403 K9
Passmore Street - 402 G11
Pater Street - 398 A9
Paternoster Row - 406 O6
Paternoster Square - 406 O6
Paul Street - 405 Q4
Paultons Square - 399 D12
Paultons Street - 399 E12
Pavilion Road - 399 F9/10
Pear Tree Court - 404 N4
Pear Tree Street - 404 O4/4
Pearman Street - 406 N9
Pearson Street - 405 R2
Pedley Street - 405 S4
Peel Street - 394 A7/8
Pelham Crescent - 399 E10
Pelham Place - 399 E10
Pelham Street - 399 E10
Pembridge Crescent - 394 A6
Pembridge Gardens - 394 A7
Pembridge Mews - 394 A6
Pembridge Place - 394 A6
Pembridge Road - 394 A7
Pembridge Square - 394 A5/B6
Pembridge Villas - 394 A6
Pembroke Gardens - 398 A10
Pembroke Gardens Close - 398 A10
Pembroke Road - 398 A10
Pembroke Villas - 398 A10
Pembroke Walk - 398 A10
Penfold Place - 397 E4/5
Penfold Street - 397 E4
Penn Street - 405 Q2
Pennant Mews - 398 B10
Penton Rise - 401 M3
Penton Street - 404 N2
Pentonville Road - 401 L3/M3, 404 N2
Penywern Road - 398 B11
Pepper Street - 406 O8
Pepys Street - 407 R7
Percy Circus - 401 M3
Percival Street - 404 O4
Percy Street - 401 K5, 408 V1/W1

Peter Street - 401 K6, 408 W3
Petersham Lane - 398 C9
Petersham Place - 398 C9
Peto Place - 400 H4
Petty France - 402 J9
Phene Street - 399 E12
Philbeach Gardens - 398 A11
Phillimore Gardens - 394 A8/9, 398 A9
Phillimore Walk - 394 B9, 398 A9
Phillimore Place - 394 A9
Phillip Street - 405 R2
Philpott Lane - 407 Q7
Phoenix Place - 401 M4
Phoenix Road - 401 K2/3
Phoenix Street - 401 K6, 409 X2
Piccadilly - 402 H8/J7, 408 U5/V4
Piccadilly Circus - 403 K7, 408 W4
Pickard Street - 404 O3
Pickering Mews - 394 C5/6
Pilgrim Street - 406 O6
Pilgrimage Street - 406 P9/Q9
Pimlico Road - 402 G11
Pindar Street - 405 Q5
Pinder Street - 405 Q5/R5
Pitfield Street - 405 Q2/3/4/R2
Pitt Street - 394 B8
Platt Street - 401 K2
Plough Yard - 405 R4
Plumbers Row - 407 S6
Plympton Street - 397 E4
Pocock Street - 406 O8/9
Poland Street - 400 J6, 408 V2
Polygon Road - 401 K2
Pond Place - 399 E11
Ponsonby Place - 403 K11
Pont Street - 399 F10, 402 G10
Poole Street - 405 Q2
Popham Road - 404 P1
Popham Street - 404 P1
Poplar Place - 394 B6/C6
Porchester Gardens - 394 B6/C6
Porchester Road - 394 C5
Porchester Square - 394 C5
Porchester Terrace - 394 C6/7
Porchester Terrace North - 394 C5
Porlock Street - 407 Q9
Porter Street SE1 - 406 P8
Porter Street W1 - 400 G4
Portland Place - 400 H4/5
Portman Close - 400 G5
Portman Mews South - 400 G6
Portman Square - 400 G6
Portman Street - 400 G6
Portobello Road - 394 A6
Portpool Lane - 404 N5
Portsea Place - 397 F6
Portsoken Street - 407 R7/S7
Portugal Street - 401 M6
Potier Street - 407 Q10
Powis Gardens - 394 A5
Powis Square - 394 A6
Powis Terrace - 394 A5
Pownall Row - 405 S2
Praed Street - 397 D6/E5
Pratt Walk - 403 M10
Prebend Street - 404 P1/2
Prescot Street - 407 S7
Primrose Street - 405 Q5/R5
Prince Consort Road - 399 D9
Princelet Street - 405 S5
Princes Gardens - 399 D9/E9
Prince's Square - 394 B6
Princes Street EC2 - 406 P6/Q6
Princes Street W1 - 400 H6, 408 U2
Princeton Street - 401 M5
Prioress Street - 407 Q10
Priory Green - 401 M2
Priory Walk - 398 C11
Procter Street - 401 M5, 409 Z1
Provost Street - 405 Q3
Pudding Lane - 407 Q7
Purbrook Street - 407 R10
Purcell Street - 405 R2
Purchese Street - 401 K2

Quaker Street - 405 S5
Queen Anne Mews - 400 H5
Queen Anne Street - 400 H5
Queen Anne's Gate - 403 K9
Queen Elizabeth Street - 407 R9
Queen Square - 401 L4
Queen Street EC4 - 406 P6/7
Queen Street W1 - 402 H7
Queen Victoria Street - 406 O7/P6/7
Queen's Gardens - 394 C6
Queens Gate - 399 D9/10
Queen's Gate Gardens - 398 C10
Queen's Gate Mews - 398 C9
Queen's Gate Place Mews - 399 D10
Queen's Gate Terrace - 398 C9, 399 D9
Queen's Walk - 402 J8
Queensborough Terrace - 394 C6/7
Queensbridge Road - 405 S1/2
Queensbury Place - 399 D10
Queensway - 394 B5/6/C6/7
Quilter Street - 405 S3

Racton Road - 398 A12
Radley Mews - 398 B10
Radnor Mews - 397 E6
Radnor Place - 397 E6
Radnor Street - 404 P4
Radnor Walk - 399 F11/12
Railway Approach - 407 Q8
Railway Street - 401 L2
Raleigh Street - 404 O2
Ramillies Place - 400 J6, 408 U2
Ramillies Street - 400 J6, 408 U2
Rampayne Street - 403 K11
Randall Road - 403 L11
Randall Row - 403 L11
Randolph Road - 394 C4, 397 D4
Ranelagh Grove - 402 G11
Ranston Street - 397 E4
Raphael Street - 399 F9
Rathbone Place - 401 K5, 408 W1
Rathbone Street - 400 J5
Ravenscroft Street - 405 S3
Ravent Road - 403 M10/11
Rawlings Street - 399 F10
Rawstone Street - 404 O3
Raymond Buildings - 401 M5
Red Lion Square - 401 M5
Red Lion Street - 401 M5
Redan Place - 394 B6
Redburn Street - 399 F12
Redchurch Street - 405 R4/S4
Redcliffe Gardens - 398 B11/C12
Redcliffe Mews - 398 C12
Redcliffe Place - 398 C12
Redcliffe Road - 398 C12
Redcliffe Square - 398 B11/C11
Redcliffe Street - 398 C12
Redcross Way - 406 P8/9
Redesdale Street - 399 F12
Redfield Lane - 398 B10
Redhill Street - 400 H2/3
Reece Mews - 399 D10
Reeves Mews - 402 G7
Regan Way - 405 R2/3
Regency Street - 403 K10/11
Regent Square - 401 L3
Regent Street - 400 J6, 402 J6/7, 403 K7, 408 U1/2/3/V4/5
Remnant Street - 401 M6, 409 Z1
Rennie Street - 406 N7
Rewell Street - 398 C13
Rheidol Terrace - 404 P2
Richmond Avenue - 404 N1
Richmond Crescent - 404 N1
Richmond Terrace - 403 L8
Ridgmount Gardens - 401 K4/5
Ridgmount Street - 401 K5
Riding House Street - 400 J5
Riley Road - 407 R9/10
Riley Street - 399 D13
Ripplevale Grove - 404 N1
Risbor Street - 406 O8
Ritchie Street - 404 N2
River Street - 404 N3
Rivington Street - 405 R4
Robert Adam Street - 400 G5
Robert Street - 400 H3/J3
Rochester Row - 402 J10
Rockingham Street - 406 O10/P10
Rodmarton Street - 400 G5
Rodney Street - 401 M2
Roger Street - 401 M4
Roland Gardens - 398 C11, 399 D11
Romilly Street - 401 K6, 408 W3, 409 X3
Romney Street - 403 K10
Rood Lane - 407 Q7
Ropemaker Street - 405 Q5
Ropley Street - 405 S3
Rosary Gardens - 398 C11
Rose Street - 403 L7, 409 Y3
Rosebery Avenue - 404 N3/4
Rosemoor Street - 399 F10
Rotary Street - 406 O9
Rotherfield Street - 404 P1, 405 Q1
Rothesay Street - 407 Q10
Rotten Row - 397 E8/F8
Roupell Street - 406 N8
Royal Avenue - 399 F11
Royal Hospital Road - 399 F11/12
Royal Mint Street - 407 S7
Royal Street - 403 M9
Rugby Street - 401 M4
Rumbold Road - 398 B13
Rupert Street - 403 K6/7, 408 W3/4
Rushworth Street - 406 O9
Russell Square - 401 L4/5
Russell Street - 401 L6, 403 L6, 409 Z3
Russia Row - 406 P6
Rutherford Street - 403 K10
Rutland Gate - 399 E9
Rutland Street - 399 E9

Sackville Street - 402 J7, 408 U4/V4
Saffron Hill - 404 N5
Sail Street - 403 M10

St Alban's Street - 403 K7, 408 W4
St Alphage Gardens - 404 P9
St Andrews Hill - 406 O6
St Andrew's Place - 400 H4
St Anne's Court - 401 K6, 408 W2
St Anne's Street - 403 K9/10
St Botolph Street - 407 R6
St Bride Street - 406 N6
St Chad's Place - 401 L3/M3
St Chad's Street - 401 L3
St Christopher's Place - 400 H6
St Clement's Lane - 401 M6
St Cross Street - 404 N5
St Dunstens Hill - 407 Q7
St George Street - 400 H6, 402 H6
St George's Circus - 406 N9
St George's Drive - 402 H11/J11
St George's Fields - 397 E6/F6
St George's Road - 406 N10/O10
St Giles High Street - 401 K6, 409 X2
St Helen's Place - 407 R6
St James's Place - 402 J8
St James's Square - 402 J7/8, 408 V5
St James's Street - 402 J8
St John Street - 404 O3/4/5
St John's Lane - 404 O4/5
St Katherine's Way - 407 S8
St Leonard's Terrace - 399 F11
St Loo Avenue - 399 F12
St Lukes Road - 394 A5
St Luke's Street - 399 E11
St Mark Street - 407 S7
St Martin's Lane - 403 L7, 409 X4
St Mary At Hill - 407 Q7
St Mary Axe - 407 R6
St Mary's Square - 397 D5
St Mary's Terrace - 397 D4
St Matthews Row - 405 S4
St Michael's Street - 397 E5
St Pancras Road - 401 K2
St Paul Street - 404 P1/2
St Paul's Churchyard - 406 O6
St Peters Street - 404 O2
St Petersburgh Mews - 394 B6/7
St Petersburgh Place - 394 B6/7
St Swithins Lane - 407 Q6/7
St Thomas Street - 407 Q8/9
St Vincent Street - 400 G5
Salamanca Street - 403 L11
Sale Place - 397 E5
Salem Road - 394 B6
Sandell Street - 406 N8
Sandland Street - 401 M5
Sandwich Street - 401 L3
Sans Walk - 404 N4
Savile Row - 402 J7, 408 U3/4
Savoy Place - 403 L7/M7, 409 Z4
Savoy Street - 403 M7, 409 Z4
Sawyer Street - 406 O8/9
Scala Street - 400 J5
Scarsdale Villas - 398 A10/B9
Sclater Street - 405 S4
Scores Street - 406 O8
Scott Lidgett Crescent - 407 S10
Scriven Street - 405 S1
Scrutton Street - 405 Q4/R4
Seacoal Lane - 406 O6
Seaford Street - 401 L3
Seagrave Road - 398 B12
Searles Close - 399 E13
Sebastian Street - 404 O3
Sebbon Street - 404 O1
Sedlescombe Road - 398 A12
Seething Lane - 407 R7
Sekforde Street - 404 O4
Selwood Terrace - 399 D11
Semley Place - 402 G11/H11
Senior Street - 394 B4
Serle Street - 401 M6
Serpentine Road - 397 E8/F8
Seven Dials - 401 L6, 409 X2
Seward Street - 404 O4/4
Seymour Place - 397 F5/6
Seymour Street - 397 F6
Seymour Walk - 398 C12
Shad Thames - 407 R8/S9
Shaftesbury Avenue - 403 K6/7/L6, 408 W3, 409 X2/Y1/2
Shaftesbury Street - 404 P2
Shalcomb Street - 399 D12
Shand Street - 407 Q9/R8
Shawfield Street - 399 E11/F12
Sheffield Terrace - 394 A8/B8
Sheldrake Place - 394 A8
Shelton Street - 401 L6, 409 Y2/3
Shenfield Street - 405 R3
Shepherd Street - 402 H8
Shepherdess Walk - 404 P2/3
Shepherds Market - 402 H8
Shepperton Road - 404 P1, 405 Q1
Sherbourne Street - 405 Q1
Sherwood Street - 402 J7, 408 V4
Shipton Street - 405 S3
Shoe Lane - 406 N5/6
Shoreditch High Street - 405 R4/5
Shorter Street - 407 R7/S7

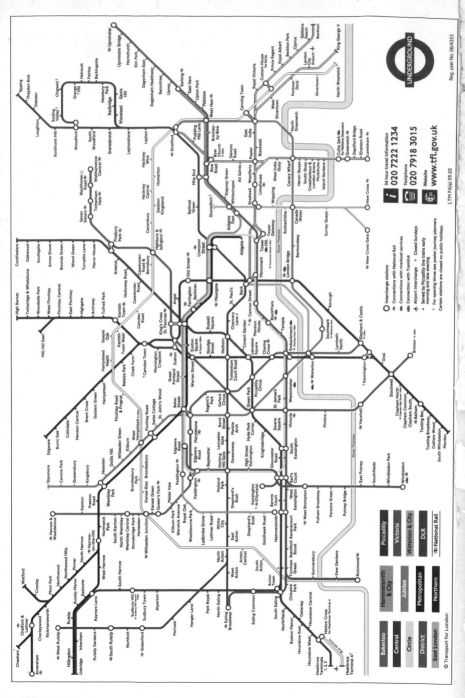